Microsoft® Official Academic Course

Supporting Windows 8.1
Exam 70-688

Richard Watson

Patrick Regan

WILEY

Credits

VP & PUBLISHER	Don Fowley
EXECUTIVE EDITOR	John Kane
EXECUTIVE MARKETING MANAGER	Chris Ruel
MICROSOFT PRODUCT MANAGER	Natasha Chornesky of Microsoft Learning
EDITORIAL PROGRAM ASSISTANT	Jessy Lentz
TECHNICAL EDITOR	Brian Svidergol
ASSISTANT MARKETING MANAGER	Debbie Martin
SENIOR PRODUCTION & MANUFACTURING MANAGER	Janis Soo
PRODUCTION EDITOR	Joyce Poh
CREATIVE DIRECTOR	Harry Nolan
COVER DESIGNER	Georgina Smith
SENIOR PRODUCT DESIGNER	Thomas Kulesa
CONTENT EDITOR	Wendy Ashenberg

This book was set in Garamond by Aptara, Inc. and printed and bound by Bind Rite Graphics. The covers were printed by Bind Rite Graphics.

Microsoft, Active Directory, AppLocker, Bing, BitLocker, DreamSpark, Hyper-V, Internet Explorer, SQL Server, Visual Studio, Win32, Windows Azure, Windows, Windows PowerShell, Windows Server, and Windows Vista are either registered trademarks or trademarks of Microsoft Corporation in the United States and/or other countries. Other product and company names mentioned herein may be the trademarks of their respective owners.

The example companies, organizations, products, domain names, e-mail addresses, logos, people, places, and events depicted herein are fictitious. No association with any real company, organization, product, domain name, e-mail address, logo, person, place, or event is intended or should be inferred.

The book expresses the author's views and opinions. The information contained in this book is provided without any express, statutory, or implied warranties. Neither the authors, John Wiley & Sons, Inc., Microsoft corporation, nor their resellers or distributors will be held liable for any damages caused or alleged to be caused either directly or indirectly by this book.

ISBN 978-1-118-88245-0

Printed in the United States of America

10 9 8 7 6 5 4 3 2 1

Foreword from the Publisher

Wiley's publishing vision for the Microsoft Official Academic Course series is to provide students and instructors with the skills and knowledge they need to use Microsoft technology effectively in all aspects of their personal and professional lives. Quality instruction is required to help both educators and students get the most from Microsoft's software tools and to become more productive. Thus, our mission is to make our instructional programs trusted educational companions for life.

To accomplish this mission, Wiley and Microsoft have partnered to develop the highest-quality educational programs for information workers, IT professionals, and developers. Materials created by this partnership carry the brand name "Microsoft Official Academic Course," assuring instructors and students alike that the content of these textbooks is fully endorsed by Microsoft, and that they provide the highest-quality information and instruction on Microsoft products. The Microsoft Official Academic Course textbooks are "Official" in still one more way—they are the officially sanctioned courseware for Microsoft IT Academy members.

The Microsoft Official Academic Course series focuses on *workforce development*. These programs are aimed at those students seeking to enter the workforce, change jobs, or embark on new careers as information workers, IT professionals, and developers. Microsoft Official Academic Course programs address their needs by emphasizing authentic workplace scenarios with an abundance of projects, exercises, cases, and assessments.

The Microsoft Official Academic Courses are mapped to Microsoft's extensive research and job-task analysis, the same research and analysis used to create the Microsoft Certified Solutions Associate (MCSA) exam. The textbooks focus on real skills for real jobs. As students work through the projects and exercises in the textbooks and labs, they enhance their level of knowledge and their ability to apply the latest Microsoft technology to everyday tasks. These students also gain resume-building credentials that can assist them in finding a job, keeping their current job, or in furthering their education.

The concept of life-long learning is today an utmost necessity. Job roles, and even whole job categories, are changing so quickly that none of us can stay competitive and productive without continuously updating our skills and capabilities. The Microsoft Official Academic Course offerings, and their focus on Microsoft certification exam preparation, provide a means for people to acquire and effectively update their skills and knowledge. Wiley supports students in this endeavor through the development and distribution of these courses as Microsoft's official academic publisher.

Today educational publishing requires attention to providing quality print and robust electronic content. By integrating Microsoft Official Academic Course products, MOAC Labs Online, and Microsoft certifications, we are better able to deliver efficient learning solutions for students and teachers alike.

Joseph Heider

General Manager and Senior Vice President

Welcome to the Microsoft Official Academic Course (MOAC) program for becoming a Microsoft Certified Solutions Associate for Windows 8. MOAC represents the collaboration between Microsoft Learning and John Wiley & Sons, Inc. Microsoft and Wiley teamed up to produce a series of textbooks that deliver compelling and innovative teaching solutions to instructors and superior learning experiences for students. Infused and informed by in-depth knowledge from the creators of Windows 8, and crafted by a publisher known worldwide for the pedagogical quality of its products, these textbooks maximize skills transfer in minimum time. Students are challenged to reach their potential by using their new technical skills as highly productive members of the workforce.

Because this knowledgebase comes directly from Microsoft, architect of Windows 8 and creator of the Microsoft Certified Solutions Associate exams, you are sure to receive the topical coverage that is most relevant to students' personal and professional success. Microsoft's direct participation not only assures you that MOAC textbook content is accurate and current; it also means that students will receive the best instruction possible to enable their success on certification exams and in the workplace.

■ The Microsoft Official Academic Course Program

The Microsoft Official Academic Course series is a complete program for instructors and institutions to prepare and deliver great courses on Microsoft software technologies. With MOAC, we recognize that because of the rapid pace of change in the technology and curriculum developed by Microsoft, there is an ongoing set of needs beyond classroom instruction tools for an instructor to be ready to teach the course. The MOAC program endeavors to provide solutions for all these needs in a systematic manner in order to ensure a successful and rewarding course experience for both instructor and student—including technical and curriculum training for instructor readiness with new software releases; the software itself for student use at home for building hands-on skills, assessment, and validation of skill development; and a great set of tools for delivering instruction in the classroom and lab. All are important to the smooth delivery of an interesting course on Microsoft software, and all are provided with the MOAC program. We think about the model below as a gauge for ensuring that we completely support you in your goal of teaching a great course. As you evaluate your instructional materials options, you may wish to use the model for comparison purposes with available products.

▪ Textbook Organization

This textbook is organized in sixteen lessons, with each lesson corresponding to a particular exam objective for the 70-688 Supporting Windows 8.1 exam. This MOAC textbook covers all the learning objectives for the 70-688 certification exam, which is the second of two exams needed in order to obtain a Microsoft Certified Solutions Associate (MCSA) certification. The exam objectives are highlighted throughout the textbook.

▪ Pedagogical Features

Many pedagogical features have been developed specifically for Microsoft Official Academic Course programs.

Presenting the extensive procedural information and technical concepts woven throughout the textbook raises challenges for the student and instructor alike. The Illustrated Book Tour that follows provides a guide to the rich features contributing to Microsoft Official Academic Course program's pedagogical plan. Following is a list of key features in each lesson designed to prepare students for success on the certification exams and in the workplace:

- Each lesson begins with an overview of the skills covered in the lesson. More than a standard list of learning objectives, the overview correlates skills to the certification exam objective.

- Illustrations: Screen images provide visual feedback as students work through the exercises. The images reinforce key concepts, provide visual clues about the steps, and allow students to check their progress.

- Key Terms: Important technical vocabulary is listed at the beginning of the lesson. When these terms are used later in the lesson, they appear in bold italic type and are defined.

- Engaging point-of-use reader aids, located throughout the lessons, tell students why this topic is relevant (*The Bottom Line*), provide students with helpful hints (*Take Note*), or show cross-references to where content is covered in greater detail (*X Ref*). Reader aids also provide additional relevant or background information that adds value to the lesson.

- Certification Ready features throughout the text signal students where a specific certification objective is covered. They provide students with a chance to check their understanding of that particular exam objective and, if necessary, review the section of the lesson where it is covered.

- Knowledge Assessments provide lesson-ending activities that test students' comprehension and retention of the material taught, presented using some of the question types that they'll see on the certification exam.

- An important supplement to this textbook is the accompanying lab work. Labs are available via a Lab Manual, and also by MOAC Labs Online. MOAC Labs Online provides students with the ability to work on the actual software simply by connecting through their Internet Explorer web browser. Either way, the labs use real-world scenarios to help students learn workplace skills associated with managing and maintaining Windows 8 in an enterprise environment.

■ Lesson Features

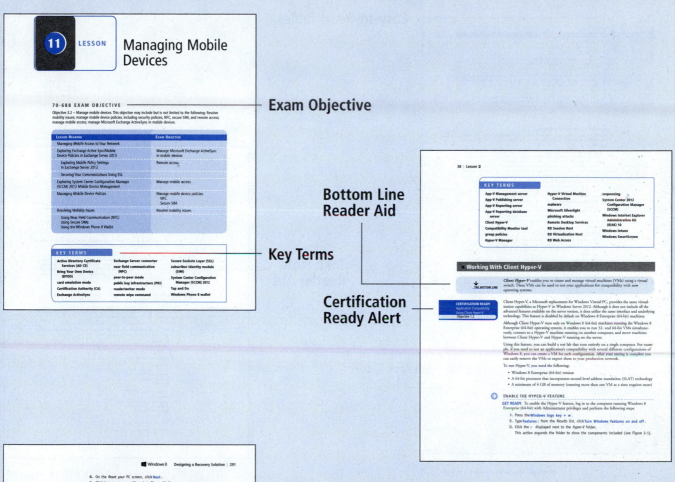

Exam Objective

Bottom Line
Reader Aid

Key Terms

Certification
Ready Alert

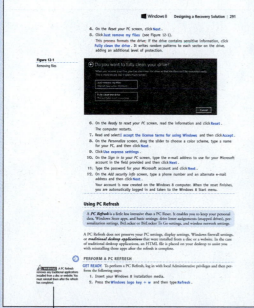

Warning Reader Aid

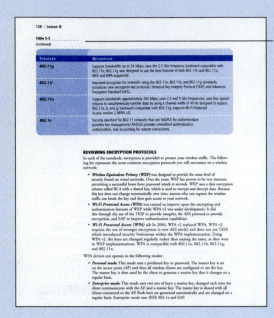

Easy-to-Read Tables

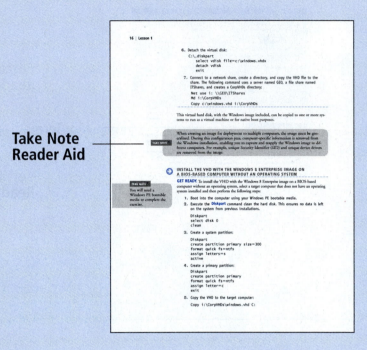

Take Note Reader Aid

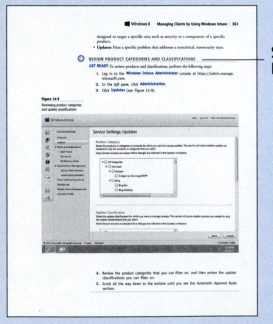

Step-by-step Exercises

Screen Images

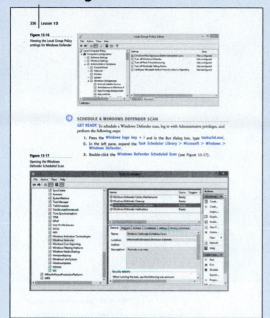

Informative Diagrams

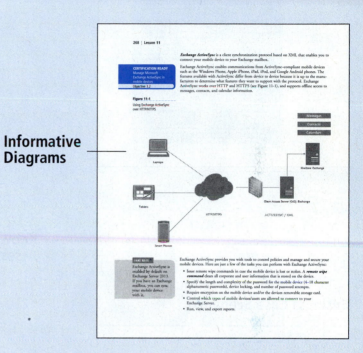

More Information Reader Aid

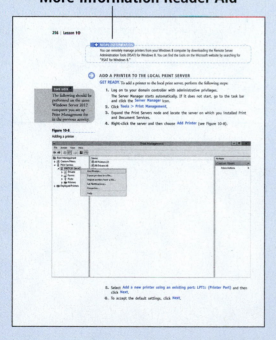

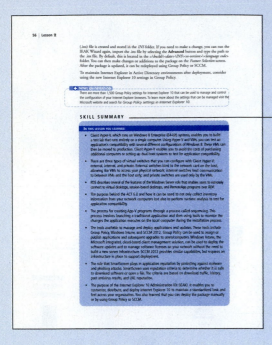

Skill Summary

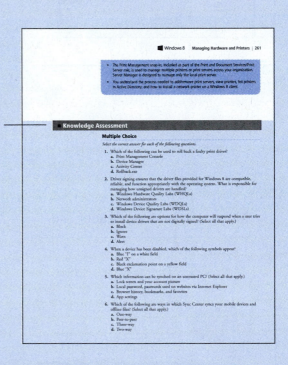

Knowledge Assessment

Business Case Scenarios

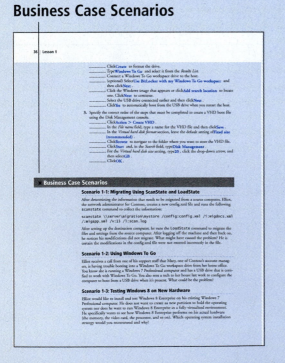

Conventions and Features Used in This Book

This book uses particular fonts, symbols, and heading conventions to highlight important information or to call your attention to special steps. For more information about the features in each lesson, refer to the Illustrated Book Tour section.

CONVENTION	MEANING
↓ **THE BOTTOM LINE**	This feature provides a brief summary of the material to be covered in the section that follows.
CERTIFICATION READY	This feature signals the point in the text where a specific certification objective is covered. It provides you with a chance to check your understanding of that particular exam objective and, if necessary, review the section of the lesson where it is covered.
TAKE NOTE * ✚ **MORE INFORMATION**	Reader aids appear in shaded boxes found in your text. *Take Note and More Information* provide helpful hints related to particular tasks or topics.
⚠ **WARNING**	*Warning* points out instances when error or misuse could cause damage to the computer or network.
X REF	These *X Ref* notes provide pointers to information discussed elsewhere in the textbook or describe interesting features of Windows 8 that are not directly addressed in the current topic or exercise.
A *shared printer* can be used by many individuals on a network.	Key terms appear in bold italic.
cd\windows\system32\ ServerMigrationTools	Commands that are to be typed are shown in a special font.
Click Install Now.	Any button on the screen you are supposed to click on or select will appear in blue.

Instructor Support Program

The Microsoft Official Academic Course programs are accompanied by a rich array of resources that incorporate the extensive textbook visuals to form a pedagogically cohesive package. These resources provide all the materials instructors need to deploy and deliver their courses. Resource information available at www.wiley.com/college/microsoft includes:

- **DreamSpark Premium** is designed to provide the easiest and most inexpensive developer tools, products, and technologies available to faculty and students in labs, classrooms, and on student PCs. A free three-year membership is available to qualified MOAC adopters.

  Note: Windows 8 can be downloaded from DreamSpark Premium for use in this course.

- **Instructor's Guide.** The Instructor's Guide contains solutions to all the textbook exercises as well as chapter summaries and lecture notes. The Instructor's Guide and Syllabi for various term lengths are available from the Instructor's Book Companion site.

- **Test Bank.** The Test Bank contains hundreds of questions organized by lesson in multiple-choice, best answer, build list, and essay formats and is available to download from the Instructor's Book Companion site. A complete answer key is provided.

- **PowerPoint Presentations.** A complete set of PowerPoint presentations is available on the Instructor's Book Companion site to enhance classroom presentations. Tailored to the text's topical coverage, these presentations are designed to convey key Windows 8 concepts addressed in the text.

- **Available Textbook Figures.** All figures from the text are on the Instructor's Book Companion site. By using these visuals in class discussions, you can help focus students' attention on key elements of Windows 8 and help them understand how to use it effectively in the workplace.

- **MOAC Labs Online.** MOAC Labs Online is a cloud-based environment that enables students to conduct exercises using real Microsoft products. These are not simulations but instead are live virtual machines where faculty and students can perform any activities they would on a local virtual machine. MOAC Labs Online relieves the need for local setup, configuration, and most troubleshooting tasks. This represents an opportunity to lower costs, eliminate the hassle of lab setup, and support and improve student access and portability. Contact your Wiley rep about including MOAC Labs Online with your course offering.

- **Lab Answer Keys.** Answer keys for review questions found in the lab manuals and MOAC Labs Online are available on the Instructor's Book Companion site.

- **Lab Worksheets.** The review questions found in the lab manuals and MOAC Labs Online are gathered in Microsoft Word documents for students to use. These are available on the Instructor's Book Companion site.

- **Sharing with Fellow Faculty Members.** When it comes to improving the classroom experience, there is no better source of ideas and inspiration than your colleagues teaching the same material. The Wiley Faculty Network connects teachers with technology, facilitates the exchange of best practices, and helps to enhance instructional efficiency and effectiveness. Faculty Network activities include technology training and tutorials, virtual seminars, peer-to-peer exchanges of experiences and ideas, personal consulting, and sharing of resources. For details visit www.WhereFacultyConnect.com.

Wiley Faculty Network

DREAMSPARK PREMIUM—FREE 3-YEAR MEMBERSHIP AVAILABLE TO QUALIFIED ADOPTERS!

DreamSpark Premium is designed to provide the easiest and most inexpensive way for schools to make the latest Microsoft developer tools, products, and technologies available in labs, classrooms, and on student PCs. DreamSpark Premium is an annual membership program for departments teaching Science, Technology, Engineering, and Mathematics (STEM) courses. The membership provides a complete solution to keep academic labs, faculty, and students on the leading edge of technology.

Software available through the DreamSpark Premium program is provided at no charge to adopting departments through the Wiley and Microsoft publishing partnership.

Contact your Wiley rep for details.

For more information about the DreamSpark Premium program, go to Microsoft's DreamSpark website.

Note: Windows 8 can be downloaded from DreamSpark Premium for use by students in this course.

■ Important Web Addresses and Phone Numbers

To locate the Wiley Higher Education Rep in your area, go to http://www.wiley.com/college and click on the "*Contact Us*" link at the top of the page, or call the MOAC Toll Free Number: 1 + (888) 764-7001 (U.S. & Canada only).

To learn more about becoming a Microsoft Certified Solutions Associate and exam availability, visit Microsoft's Training & Certification website.

Book Companion Web Site (www.wiley.com/college/microsoft)

The students' book companion site for the MOAC series includes any resources, exercise files, and web links that will be used in conjunction with this course.

Wiley E-Text: Powered by VitalSource

Wiley E-Texts: Powered by VitalSource, are innovative, electronic versions of printed textbooks. Students can buy Wiley E-Texts for around 50% off the U.S. price of the printed text and get the added value of permanence and portability. Wiley E-Texts provide students with numerous additional benefits that are not available with other e-text solutions.

Wiley E-Texts are NOT subscriptions; students download the Wiley E-Text to their computer desktops. Students own the content they buy to keep for as long as they want. Once a Wiley E-Text is downloaded to the computer desktop, students have instant access to all of the content without being online. Students can also print the sections they prefer to read in hard copy. Students also have access to fully integrated resources within their Wiley E-Text. From highlighting their e-text to taking and sharing notes, students can easily personalize their Wiley E-Text as they are reading or following along in class.

Microsoft Software

Various Microsoft software is available through a DreamSpark student membership. DreamSpark is a Microsoft program that provides students with free access to Microsoft software for learning, teaching, and research purposes. Students can download full versions of Microsoft software at no cost by visiting Microsoft's DreamSpark website.

▪ Microsoft Certification

Microsoft Certification has many benefits and enables you to keep your skills relevant, applicable, and competitive. In addition, Microsoft Certification is an industry standard that is recognized worldwide—which helps open doors to potential job opportunities. After you earn your Microsoft Certification, you have access to a number of benefits, which can be found on the Microsoft Certified Professional member site.

Microsoft Learning has reinvented the Microsoft Certification Program by building cloud-related skills validation into the industry's most recognized certification program. Microsoft Certified Solutions Expert (MCSE) and Microsoft Certified Solutions Developer (MCSD) are Microsoft's flagship certifications for professionals who want to lead their IT organization's journey to the cloud. These certifications recognize IT professionals with broad and deep skill sets across Microsoft solutions. The Microsoft Certified Solutions Associate (MCSA) is the certification for aspiring IT professionals. These new certifications integrate cloud-related and on-premise skills validation in order to support organizations and recognize individuals who have the skills required to be productive using Microsoft technologies.

On-premise or in the cloud, Microsoft training and certification empowers technology professionals to expand their skills and gain knowledge directly from the source. Securing these essential skills will allow you to grow your career and make yourself indispensable as the industry shifts to the cloud. Cloud computing ultimately enables IT to focus on more mission-critical activities, raising the bar of required expertise for IT professionals and developers. These reinvented certifications test on a deeper set of skills that map to real-world business context. Rather than testing only on a feature of a technology, Microsoft Certifications now validate more advanced skills and a deeper understanding of the platform.

Microsoft Certified Solutions Associate (MCSA)

The Microsoft Certified Solutions Associate (MCSA) certification is for students preparing to get their first jobs in Microsoft technology. Whether in the cloud or on-premise, this certification validates the core platform skills needed in an IT environment. Earning an MCSA: Windows 8 certification will qualify you for a position as a computer support specialist.

The MCSA Windows 8 certification shows that you have the primary set of Windows 8 skills that are relevant across multiple solution areas in a business environment. Candidates for the 70-688 exam will show their knowledge in configuring and supporting Windows 8 computers, devices, users, and associated network and security resources. These networks are configured as a domain-based or peer-to-peer environment with access to the Internet and cloud services. This exam will validate the skills necessary to administer Windows 8-based computers and devices as a portion of broader technical responsibilities.

If you are a student new to IT who may not yet be ready for MCSA, the Microsoft Technology Associate (MTA) certification is an optional starting point that may be available through your school.

You can learn more about the MCSA certification at the Microsoft Training & Certification website.

Preparing to Take an Exam

Unless you are a very experienced user, you will need to use test preparation materials to prepare to complete the test correctly and within the time allowed. The Microsoft Official Academic Course series is designed to prepare you with a strong knowledge of all exam topics, and with some additional review and practice on your own, you should feel confident in your ability to pass the appropriate exam.

After you decide which exam to take, review the list of objectives for the exam. You can easily identify tasks that are included in the objective list by locating the exam objective overview at the start of each lesson and the Certification Ready sidebars in the margin of the lessons in this book.

To register for the 70-688 exam, visit Microsoft Training & Certifications Registration webpage for directions on how to register with Prometric, the company that delivers the MCSA exams. Keep in mind these important items about the testing procedure:

- **What to expect.** Microsoft Certification testing labs typically have multiple workstations, which may or may not be occupied by other candidates. Test center administrators strive to provide a quiet and comfortable environment for all test takers.

- **Plan to arrive early.** It is recommended that you arrive at the test center at least 30 minutes before the test is scheduled to begin.

- **Bring your identification.** To take your exam, you must bring the identification (ID) that was specified when you registered for the exam. If you are unclear about which forms of ID are required, contact the exam sponsor identified in your registration information. Although requirements vary, you typically must show two valid forms of ID, one with a photo, both with your signature.

- **Leave personal items at home.** The only item allowed into the testing area is your identification, so leave any backpacks, laptops, briefcases, and other personal items at home. If you have items that cannot be left behind (such as purses), the testing center might have small lockers available for use.

- **Nondisclosure agreement.** At the testing center, Microsoft requires that you accept the terms of a nondisclosure agreement (NDA) and complete a brief demographic survey before taking your certification exam.

Richard Watson (MCSE, A+, Network+, iNet+) holds an MBA in Information Technology Management and is the Principal/Owner of Bridgehill Learning Solutions, LLC., which provides content conversion, custom course development, strategic planning, technical writing, and learning management system selection services. Previously, Richard was Manager of Instructional Design for the Audigy Group, whereby he was responsible for the identification, creation/modification, and evaluation of both new and existing learning resources to ensure alignment with companies' business objectives; project management of learning initiatives across multiple departments; working with outside vendors to identify, select, and implement learning programs and systems; and assessing the overall effectiveness of programs through report creation/analysis and surveys/interviews with key stakeholders. Richard has authored several MCSE books covering networking, administration, and security for Windows 2000 and 2003 for Prentice Hall.

Patrick Regan has been a PC technician, network administrator/engineer, design architect, and security analyst for the past 23 years. He has taught computer and network classes at Sacramento local colleges (Heald Colleges and MTI Colleges) and participated in and led many projects (Heald Colleges, Intel Corporation, Miles Consulting Corporation, and Pacific Coast Companies). For his teaching accomplishments, he received the Teacher of the Year award from Heald Colleges and he has received several recognition awards from Intel. As a senior system administrator, he supports approximately 120 servers and 1,500 users spread over 5 subsidiaries and 70 sites. He has authored a number of textbooks, including books on SharePoint 2010, Windows 7, and Windows Server 2012 for John Wiley & Sons.

Acknowledgements

We thank the MOAC faculty and instructors who have assisted us in building the Microsoft Official Academic Course courseware. These elite educators have acted as our sounding board on key pedagogical and design decisions leading to the development of the MOAC courseware for future Information Technology workers. They have provided invaluable advice in the service of quality instructional materials, and we truly appreciate their dedication to technology education.

Brian Bridson, Baker College of Flint

David Chaulk, Baker College Online

Ron Handlon, Remington College—Tampa Campus

Katherine James, Seneca College of Applied Arts & Technology

Wen Liu, ITT Educational Services

Zeshan Sattar, Pearson in Practice

Jared Spencer, Westwood College Online

David Vallerga, MTI College

Bonny Willy, Ivy Tech State College

We also thank Microsoft Learning's Tim Sneath, Keith Loeber, Natasha Chornesky, Wendy Johnson, Brian Swan, Briana Roberts, Jim Clark, Anne Hamilton, Shelby Grieve, Erika Cravens, Paul Schmitt, Jim Cochran, Julia Stasio, and Heidi Johnson for their encouragement and support in making the Microsoft Official Academic Course programs the finest academic materials for mastering the newest Microsoft technologies for both students and instructors.

Brief Contents

Contents

Lesson 12: Managing Clients by Using Windows Intune 419

Supporting Operating System Installation

70-688 EXAM OBJECTIVE

Objective 1.1 – Support operating system installation. This objective may include but is not limited to: Support Windows To Go; manage boot settings, including native virtual hard disk (VHD) and multi-boot; manage desktop images; customize a Windows installation by using Windows Preinstallation Environment (PE).

LESSON HEADING	EXAM OBJECTIVE
Using a Troubleshooting Methodology	
Viewing System Information	
Using the Event Viewer	
Supporting Windows To Go	Support Windows To Go
Creating and Deploying a Windows To Go Workspace Drive	
Booting into a Windows To Go Workspace	
Managing Boot Settings	Manage boot settings, including native virtual hard disk (VHD) and multi-boot
Using BCDEdit and BCDBoot	
Configuring a Multi-Boot System	Manage boot settings, including native virtual hard disk (VHD) and multi-boot
Configuring a Native VHD Boot File	Manage boot settings, including native virtual hard disk (VHD) and multi-boot
Understanding VHD Formats	
Installing Windows 8.1 on a VHD with an Operating System Present	
Installing Windows 8.1 on a VHD Without an Operating System Present	
Managing Desktop Images	Manage desktop images
Capturing Images	
Modifying Images using DISM	
Customizing a Windows Installation by Using Windows PE	Customize a Windows installation by using Windows Preinstallation Environment (PE)

KEY TERMS

answer file

Autounattend.xml

Boot Configuration Data (BCD) store

BCDboot (bcdboot.exe)

BCD Editor (bcdedit.exe) or bcdedit

Deployment Image Servicing and Management (DISM)

disk image

Disk Management Console (diskmgmt.msc)

Diskpart

Dynamically Expanding hard disk

file-based disk image

Fixed Size hard disk

Group Policy Object (GPO)

Group Policy Management Console (gpmc.msc)

multi-boot (dual-boot)

native VHD boot

sector-based disk image

System Preparation Utility (sysprep.exe)

System Information (msinfo32. exe)

System Image Manager (SIM)

virtual hard disk (VHD)

VHD format

VHDX format

Windows 8.1 Pre-installation Environment (PE) disk

Windows Deployment Services (WDS)

Windows Image Format (WIM)

Windows PE

Windows To Go workspace

Workspace to Go Creator (pwcreator.exe)

■ Using a Troubleshooting Methodology

THE BOTTOM LINE

Since this course is focuses on supporting Windows 8.1 and resolving issues, you need to understand how to use a troubleshooting methodology. When you encounter computer problems, some problems will have obvious solutions and easy to fix. Many problems will need to be resolved by following a troubleshooting methodology to efficiently troubleshoot a problem. However, before you perform any fix, you need to look at the big picture to determine what the fix will affect. By fixing one problem, you can cause another problem.

The purpose of an effective troubleshooting methodology is to reduce the amount of guess-work and random solutions so that you can troubleshoot and fix the problem in a timely manner. Microsoft Product Support Service engineers use the "detect method," which consists of the following six steps:

1. Discover the problem. Identify and document problem symptoms and search technical information resources, including searching Microsoft Knowledge Base (KB) articles to determine whether the problem is a known condition. In addition, search the organization's knowledge base to determine if your organization has seen the problem before.

2. Gather information. Ask the client or customer and check the system's documentation to determine if any hardware, software, or network changes have been made, including any new additions. Also check any available logs including looking in the Event Viewer. You also need to check the scope of the problem. Does it only affect one computer, does it affect the computers within a specific site or subnet, does it affect the computers within an Active Directory organizational unit, or does it affect the entire organization?

3. Develop an action plan. List or track possible solutions and try to isolate the problem by removing or disabling hardware or software components. You may also consider turning on additional logging or running diagnostic programs to gather more information and test certain components.

4. Execute the action plan. Test potential solutions and have a contingency plan if these solutions do not work or if they have a negative impact on the computer. Of course,

you don't want to make the problem worse, so if possible, back up any critical system or application files.

5. Check results. If the problem is not fixed, go back to develop an action plan.

6. Take a proactive approach. Document any changes that you made along the way while troubleshooting the problem. Also notify the customer or client and document internal systems in case the problem happens again or if those changes that fixed the problem affect other areas.

When troubleshooting problems, several tools can help isolate and fix the problems, including:

- System Information
- Device Manager
- Event Viewer
- Task Manager
- Resource Monitor
- Performance Monitor
- System Configuration
- Memory Diagnostics tool
- Troubleshooting Wizard
- Boot Menu including Safe mode
- Windows Repair

When troubleshooting issues within Windows and related programs, you will eventually deal with problems confound you. In those situations, you will have to ask co-workers and research on the Internet. You will also need to check vendor websites, including Microsoft's website.

Most of the information available from Microsoft to design, plan, implement, manage, and monitor Microsoft products will be found at Microsoft's website, particularly at TechNet. It will include Microsoft Knowledge Base, service packs, security updates, resource kits, technical training, operations and deployment guides, white papers and case studies.

Information used mostly for troubleshooting will be found in Microsoft's Knowledge Base and several online Microsoft forums. These forums provide help for a wide range of problems; you can even leave messages for others to answer. The Microsoft Knowledge Base is a repository of thousands of articles—made available to the public by Microsoft—that contains information on many problems encountered by Microsoft users. Each article bears an ID number and articles are often referred to by their Knowledge Base (KB) ID. The Knowledge Base can be accessed by entering keywords or the ID at Microsoft's support site.

Viewing System Information

When you first begin troubleshooting a computer, you need to know what is in the computer and what is running on the computer. System properties shows you the processor and amount of RAM. Device Manager shows you what hardware is recognized and what drivers are loaded. The System Information program is a useful troubleshooting tool to see what is in a system.

System Information (also known as **msinfo32.exe**) shows details about your computer's hardware configuration, computer components, and software—including drivers. It was originally included with Windows to assist Microsoft support technicians in determining what is in a machine, especially when they were troubleshooting end-users' issues, but System Information can be used by anyone at any time.

System Information lists categories in the left pane and details about each category in the right pane. The categories include:

- System Summary – Displays general information about your computer and the operating system, such as the computer name and manufacturer, the type of basic input/output system (BIOS) your computer uses, and the amount of installed memory.
- Hardware Resources – Displays advanced details about your computer's hardware and is intended for IT professionals.
- Components – Displays information about disk drives, sound devices, modems, and other components installed on your computer.
- Software Environment – Displays information about drivers, network connections, and other program-related details.

To find a specific detail in System Information, type the information you're looking for in the *Find what* box at the bottom of the window and then click Find. For example, to find your computer's Internet protocol (IP) address, type **ip address** in the *Find what* box and then click Find.

Using the Event Viewer

One of the most useful troubleshooting tools is the Event Viewer snap-in, which essentially is a log viewer. Any time you have problems, you should look in the Event Viewer to see any errors or warnings that might reveal the problem.

The ***Event Viewer*** is a Microsoft Management Console (MMC) snap-in that enables you to browse and manage event logs. It is included in Computer Management and is included in Administrative Tools as a stand-alone console. You can also launch it by accessing the eventvwr.msc command.

Event Viewer enables you to perform the following tasks:

- View events from multiple event logs
- Save useful event filters as custom views that can be reused
- Schedule a task to run in response to an event
- Create and manage event subscriptions

The Windows Logs category includes the logs that were available on previous versions of Windows. They include:

- Application log: Contains events logged by applications or programs.
- Security log: Contains events (such as valid and invalid logon attempts) and access to designated objects (such as file and folders), printers, and Active Directory objects. By default, the Security log is empty until you enable auditing.
- Setup log: Contains events related to application setup.
- System log: Contains events logged by Windows system components, including errors displayed by Windows during boot and errors with services.
- ForwardedEvents log: Used to store events collected from remote computers. To collect events from remote computers, you must create an event subscription.

Based on the roles and programs installed on a computer, Windows might have additional logs, such as DHCP, DNS or Active Directory.

Applications and Services logs were first introduced in Windows Vista. These logs store events from a single application or component rather than events that might have system-wide impact:

- Admin: These events are primarily targeted at end users, administrators, and support personnel. The events that are found in the Admin channels indicate a problem and a well-defined solution that an administrator can act on.

- Operational: These events are used for analyzing and diagnosing a problem or occurrence. They can be used to trigger tools or tasks based on the problem or occurrence.

- Analytic: These events are published in high volume. They describe program operations and indicate problems that cannot be handled by user intervention.

- Debug: These events are used by developers troubleshooting issues with their programs.

Table 1-1 shows the common fields displayed in the Event Viewer logs.

Table 1-1

Common fields displayed in the Event Viewer logs

PROPERTY NAME	DESCRIPTION
Source	The software that logged the event, which can be either a program name (such as "SQL Server") or a component of the system or of a large program (such as a driver name).
Event ID	A number identifying the particular event type.
	A classification of the event severity.
	Information: Indicates that a change in an application or component has occurred, such as an operation has successfully completed, a resource has been created, or a service has been started.
	Warning: Indicates that an issue has occurred that can impact service or result in a more serious problem if action is not taken.
Level	Error: Indicates that a problem has occurred, which might impact functionality that is external to the application or component that triggered the event.
	Critical: Indicates that a failure has occurred from which the application or component that triggered the event cannot automatically recover.
	Success Audit: Shown in security logs to indicate that the user right was used
	Failure Audit: Shown in security logs to indicate that the exercise of a user right has failed.

When you open any of these logs—in particular, the Application, Security and System logs—they will show thousands of entries. If you look entry by entry, it could take some time to find what you are looking for. To search more quickly, you can use a filter that reduces the entries shown. To filter a log, open the Action menu and click Filter Current Log.

■ Supporting Windows To Go

 THE BOTTOM LINE
Windows To Go is a feature available with Windows 8/8.1 Enterprise clients that allows you to boot a full version of Windows 8/8.1 Enterprise from an external USB drive on a host computer.

Windows To Go is a feature in Windows 8/8.1 Enterprise edition that allows you to create a *Windows To Go workspace* on an external USB 3.0 drive. This enables your users to boot a full version of Windows 8/8.1 from removable media. The drive uses the same image installed on a corporate desktop and laptop; therefore, you can manage them in the same manner and use the same tools. The drive itself must be connected to a host computer running on a Windows 7 or later certified operating system to function.

CERTIFICATION READY
Support Windows to Go
Objective 1.1

Creating and Deploying a Windows To Go Workspace Drive

You can create a *Windows to Go workspace* drive for employees working from home, contractors on temporary assignment and for employees who travel between sites and need access to corporate resources and applications. This provides them with mobility while also allowing you to manage the devices as part of your corporate policies.

The *Workspace to Go Creator (pwcreator.exe)* is used to create Windows To Go workspaces. You can also use a USB duplicator product but that will require you to duplicate the drive before it is booted and initialized.

To create a Windows To Go workspace, you will need:

- A USB drive that supports Windows To Go (32GB or larger).
- A computer running Windows Windows 8/8.1 Enterprise edition.
- A Windows 8/8.1 Enterprise ISO, Windows 8/8.1 Enterprise installation media, or a corporate Windows image (.wim) created from Windows 8/8.1 Enterprise media.
- Local administrator access on the computer.

To protect the drive in case it is lost or stolen, you have the option to configure *BitLocker To Go* during the setup of the workspace. BitLocker To Go allows you to encrypt a removable drive and restrict access with a password or a smart card.

Once your removable drive is setup, you can deploy the Windows To Go workspace centrally or by allowing individual users to create their own workspaces. Central management and deployment requires System Center Configuration Manager 2012 Service Pack 1.

 CREATE A WINDOWS TO GO WORKSPACE

GET READY. To create a Windows to Go workspace, log on as an administrator to a computer running Windows 8/8.1 Enterprise edition and then perform the following steps:

1. Connect a Windows To Go USB certified device to the host.
2. Press the **Windows logo key + w**.
3. Type **Windows To Go** and then select it from the *Results* list.
4. Select the USB drive you connected earlier and then click **Next**.
5. Click the Windows image that appears or click **Add search location** to locate one. Click **Next** to continue.

6. Click **Create** to format the drive.

7. (Optional) Select the **Use BitLocker with my Windows To Go workspace** checkbox and then type a password. Click **Next**.

 TAKE NOTE* Enabling BitLocker on the Windows To Go workspace will protect the drive if it is lost or stolen. Using this feature will require you to type a password each time you use the workspace.

8. Click **Create** to setup the Windows To Go workspace.

9. Click Yes to automatically boot from the USB drive when you restart the host or click No if you want to change the PC's firmware settings to use the workspace (see Figure 1-1).

Figure 1-1

Selecting the Windows To Go Startup Option

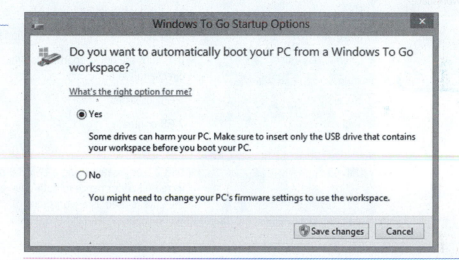

If you click Yes, your computer will automatically boot to the Windows To Go workspace every time a USB drive is detected. If you click No, you will need to change startup options in your computer's firmware. You do this by entering your firmware setup using the appropriate function key for your specific type of BIOS. This is usually the F12 key but you may need to check the manufacturer's website to determine the appropriate key.

If you decide to modify this setting later or want to use the Windows To Go workspace drive on another computer and need to make sure it is configured appropriately, access the Windows To Go control panel using the steps in the following exercise.

 CHANGE WINDOWS TO GO STARTUP OPTIONS

GET READY. To change Windows to Go startup options, perform the following steps:

1. Log in to your Windows 8/8.1 client device with administrative privileges.

2. Press the **Windows log key + r**.

3. In the *Run* dialog box, type **control panel**.

4. Click the **Hardware and Sound** category.

5. In the *Devices and Printers* category, click **Change Windows To Go startup options**.

6. Click **Yes** to automatically boot from an attached USB drive or click **No** to configure the settings manually.

Booting into a Windows To Go Workspace

To take full advantage of the Windows To Go Workspace, you need to have a good understanding of what the requirements for the host computer are and the resources that can and cannot be accessed on the host.

When deciding on the host to use for a Windows To Go workspace drive, you should make sure it has been certified for use with Windows 7 or Windows 8/8.1.

Table 1-2 lists the hardware requirements for Windows To Go workspace hosts.

Table 1-2

Hardware Requirements for Windows To Go Workspace Hosts

HARDWARE	REQUIREMENT
Firmware	Must support booting from USB.
Processor architecture	Must support the image on the Windows To Go drive.
External USB hubs	USB hubs are not supported; you must connect the drive directly to the hos computer.
Processor	1 Ghz or faster.
Memory	2 GB or greater.
Graphics	DirectX 9 graphics device with a WDDM 1.2 or greater driver.
USB ports	USB 2.0 or greater. Using a USB 3.0 port will result in increased performance in both drive provisioning and when the drive is used as a workspace.

In addition to the information listed Table 1-2, the Windows To Go image on the USB drive must be compatible with the processor architecture and the firmware on the host PC.

Table 1-3 lists the processor/firmware types and Windows To Go image requirements for Windows To Go workspace hosts.

Table 1-3

Windows To Go compatibility with Host firmware and processor types

HOST PC FIRMWARE	HOST PROCESSOR	WINDOWS TO GO IMAGE THAT CAN BE USED
32-bit Legacy BIOS 64-bit Legacy BIOS	32-bit 64-bit	32-bit image only
32-bit UEFI BIOS 64-bit UEFI BIOS	32-bit 64-bit	32-bit image only 64-bit image only

Once you have identified a suitable host for your Windows To Go workspace drive, insert the drive and power on the computer. If you configured a BitLocker to Go password, you will need to enter it before you can access the drive. The first time you boot a host from the Windows To Go workspace, it will scan for hardware devices and then install the appropriate drivers. The information it finds is cached; therefore, the next time you boot from the same computer the process will be faster because drivers are loaded automatically. Windows To Go workspace operates just like any other installation of Windows but there are a few differences you will need to be aware of.

Once you log in, you will notice the internal disks on the host system are offline to protect against accidental exposure of data. If you insert the USB drive into a system that is already running, you will also notice that it will not be listed in File Explorer. The Hibernate feature is disabled to prevent data corruption during roaming and the Windows Store is disabled by default. The Windows Store application is disabled because applications licensed through the store are linked to your hardware.

MANAGING WINDOWS TO GO WORKSPACES USING GROUP POLICY

A *Group Policy Object (GPO)* that controls the behavior of Windows To Go workspaces can be created and managed at the enterprise level using the *Group Policy Management Console* (*gpmc.msc*) and Active Directory. A GPO is a collection of settings that determine how the system for a group of users and/or computers will function. The GPO is then associated with Active Directory containers such as sites, domains, or organizational units.

The settings that are applicable to Windows To Go workspace can be found in the following section of a GPO:

Computer Configuration\Policies\Administrative Templates\Windows Components\Portable Operating System

- **Allow hibernate (S4) when starting from a Windows To Go workspace**: Specifies whether the PC can go into hibernation mode when started from a Windows To Go workspace.

- **Windows To Go Default Startup Options**: This policy controls whether the PC will boot to Windows To Go if a USB device containing a Windows To Go workspace is connected and also controls whether users can make changes to the startup options in the Windows To Go Startup Options Control Panel.

- **Disallow standby sleep states (S1-S3) when starting from a Windows To Go workspace**: Determines if the PC can use standby sleep states (S1-S3) when starting from a Windows To Go workspace. S1 through S4 are sleeping states. When your Windows 8/8.1 client computer is in one of these states it is not performing computational tasks and will appear to be off. With each successive sleep state (S1-S4), more of the computer is shut down.

The Windows Store application is disabled by default when booting into a Windows 8/8.1 client computer using a Windows To Go workspace. You should enable this policy setting when the workspace will only be used with a single Windows 8/8.1 computer.

Managing Boot Settings

THE BOTTOM LINE

With Windows NT, Windows 2000, Windows XP, and Windows Server 2003 boot loader used ntldr. Starting with Windows Vista and Windows Server 2008, the Windows boot loader was reduced so it would load Windows quickly and securely; the loader now includes Windows Boot Manager (Bootmgr.exe), Windows operating system loader (Winload.exe), and Windows resume loader (Winresume.exe).

CERTIFICATION READY
Manage boot settings, including native virtual hard disk (VHD) and multi-boot
Objective 1.1

When a system boots, the BIOS looks for an operating system to boot from, finds a Master Boot Record, and then loads Bootmgr.exe. The Bootmgr.exe reads the ***Boot Configuration Data (BCD) store,*** which defines how the boot menu is configured, including which operating system to load and where to find the OS on the boot partition. BootMgr invokes Winload.exe, which loads the Ntoskrnl.exe. Hal.dll then reads the registry files so that it knows which device drivers to load. Ntoskrnl.exe starts the Winlogon.exe program, which displays the Windows login screen.

Using BCDEdit and BCDBoot

`bcdedit` and `bcdboot` are command-line utilities used to control the boot process and manage the boot configuration store.

The Windows startup process is controlled by parameters located in the BCD store. The BCD store contains information about what boot manager to use and the specific boot application/loaders available.

TAKE NOTE＊

The BCD store, which contains the boot configuration parameters and controls how the operating system is started on Windows Vista and later operating systems, replaces the boot.ini text file used in earlier versions of Windows. The location of the store is based on the computer's firmware. On BIOS-based operating systems, you will find it in the \Boot\ Bcd directory of the active partition. On Extensible Firmware Interface (EFI)-based systems, it is stored in the EFI system partition.

When you boot your computer, the Windows boot manager displays a menu of boot loader entries. When you select one of the entries, the Windows boot manager loads the system-specific boot loader for that operating system and passes those parameters for that boot entry to the system-specific boot loader.

You will see one instance of boot loader for each installation of Windows Vista or later operating systems present on the computer. If an earlier Windows operating system is installed, an optional legacy boot loader (ntldr/boot.ini) will be present. You might also see an optional boot application present if you are running applications that perform memory diagnostics. You can use the ***BCD Editor (bcdedit.exe)***, a command-line utility, to view and manage the BCD store. For example, you can use it to set a one-time boot sequence for the boot manager to use, create, import, and export the entire store, create, delete, and modify entries in the store, set the default entry the boot manager will use, list entries in the store, and set the timeout value. Figure 1-2 shows the contents of the BCD store when a system is running Windows 8/8.1 only. Notice, there is only one boot loader listed.

Figure 1-2

Contents of the BCD store on a system running Windows 8/8.1 only

```
C:\>cd \windows\system32

C:\Windows\System32>bcdedit.exe
Windows Boot Manager
--------------------
identifier              {bootmgr}
device                  partition=\Device\HarddiskVolume1
description             Windows Boot Manager
locale                  en-US
inherit                 {globalsettings}
integrityservices       Enable
default                 {current}
resumeobject            {95bc7da5-2d21-11e2-932c-ec4a4369c53a}
displayorder            {current}
toolsdisplayorder       {memdiag}
timeout                 30

Windows Boot Loader
--------------------
identifier              {current}
device                  partition=C:
path                    \Windows\system32\winload.exe
description             Windows 8
locale                  en-US
inherit                 {bootloadersettings}
recoverysequence        {95bc7da7-2d21-11e2-932c-ec4a4369c53a}
integrityservices       Enable
recoveryenabled         Yes
allowedinmemorysettings 0x15000075
osdevice                partition=C:
systemroot              \Windows
resumeobject            {95bc7da5-2d21-11e2-932c-ec4a4369c53a}
nx                      OptIn
bootmenupolicy          Standard

C:\Windows\System32>
```

Figure 1-3 shows the contents of a BCD store on a computer running Windows 7 Professional and Windows 8/8.1 Enterprise. Notice the Windows boot manager displays two boot loaders.

Figure 1-3

Contents of the BCD store on a system running Windows 8/8.1 and Windows 7

```
Windows Boot Loader
--------------------
identifier              {default}
device                  vhd=[C:]\vhdfiles\win8entvhd11142012.vhd
path                    \Windows\system32\winload.exe
description             Windows 8
locale                  en-US
inherit                 {bootloadersettings}
recoverysequence        {849ab75e-2b7d-11e2-9a4d-10bf4879ebe3}
integrityservices       Enable
recoveryenabled         Yes
custom:17000077         352321653
osdevice                vhd=[C:]\vhdfiles\win8entvhd11142012.vhd
systemroot              \Windows
resumeobject            {849ab75c-2b7d-11e2-9a4d-10bf4879ebe3}
nx                      OptIn
custom:250000c2         1

Windows Boot Loader
--------------------
identifier              {current}
device                  partition=C:
path                    \Windows\system32\winload.exe
description             Windows 7
locale                  en-US
inherit                 {bootloadersettings}
recoverysequence        {849ab75a-2b7d-11e2-9a4d-10bf4879ebe3}
recoveryenabled         Yes
osdevice                partition=C:
systemroot              \Windows
resumeobject            {849ab758-2b7d-11e2-9a4d-10bf4879ebe3}
nx                      OptIn
```

CHANGE THE DEFAULT TIMEOUT VALUE USING BCDEDIT

GET READY. To change the default timeout value using `bcdedit`, log on as an administrator to a Windows 8/8.1 Enterprise computer and then perform the following steps:

1. Press the **Windows logo key + r**.
2. In the *Run* dialog box, type **cmd** to open a command console.
3. Type **bcdedit** at the command prompt to view the BCD store.

   Make a note of the current timeout setting under the Windows boot manager section. It should be set to 30 seconds by default.
4. Type the following at the command prompt. (Entering a timeout value of 0 will boot the default operating system automatically.)

   `C:\Users\Administrator>bcdedit /timeout 10`
5. Type **bcdedit** at the command prompt to confirm the timeout setting has been modified.

Table 1-4 shows the bcdedit commands that can be used on the store.

Table 1-4

BCDedit Commands that Operate on the Store

COMMAND	DESCRIPTION
/createstore	Creates a new empty boot configuration store.
/export	Exports the contents of the system store to a file. This file can be used later to restore the state of the system store.
/import	Restores the state of the system store using a backup file created with the /export command.

Table 1-5 shows the bcdedit commands that can be used to modify entries in the BCD store.

Table 1-5

BCDedit Commands that Operate on Entries in the Store

COMMAND	DESCRIPTION
/copy	Makes copies of the entries of the store.
/create	Creates new entries in the store.
/delete	Deletes entries from the store.
/mirror	Creates mirror of entries in the store.

Table 1-6 shows the bcdedit commands that can be used to control the boot manager.

Table 1-6

BCDedit Commands that Control the Boot Manager

COMMAND	DESCRIPTION
/bootsequence	Sets the one-time boot sequence for the boot manager.
/default	Sets the default entry that the boot manager will use.
/displayorder	Sets the order in which the boot manager displays the multi-boot menu
/timeout	Sets the boot manager timeout value.

BCDboot (**bcdboot.exe**) is a command-line utility that allows you to set up a system partition when you deploy a new computer, to set up Windows to boot to a virtual hard disk, and to repair the boot environment if your system partition becomes corrupted.

To initialize a system partition, bcdboot copies a small set of boot environment files from an installed Windows image. For example, if you want to copy boot environment files from the X:\Windows directory, use the following command:

```
X:\Windows\System32\bcdboot X:\Windows
```

To change the default locale from US English to Japanese, use the following command:

```
X:\Windows\System32\bcdboot /l:ja-jp
```

To copy BCD files from the *C:\Windows* directory to a system partition on another drive to be booted from another computer with the system partition volume letter set to V, use the following command:

```
C:\>bcdboot C:\Windows /s V:
```

Table 1-7 lists some of the common bcdboot command switches.

Table 1-7

Common BCDboot Command Switches

Option	Description
<source>	Specifies the location of the Windows directory to use as the source for copying boot environment files.
/l <locale>	Specifies the optional locale parameter to use. The default is US English (en-us).
/s <volume letter>	Specifies the volume letter for the system partition. Use it to specify a system partition when you are configuring a drive that will be booted on another computer (USB flash drive or secondary drive).
/f <firmware type>	Specifies the firmware type. Values can include UEFI, BIOS, and ALL.
/v	Enables verbose mode.
/m [{OS Loader GUID}]	Merges the value from an existing boot entry into a new boot entry.

Configuring a Multi-Boot System

Multi-boot systems provide you with the ability to test a new operating system for hardware and software compatibility prior to deploying it. Each operating system requires its own partition.

A *multi-boot (or dual-boot)* system is a computer that runs multiple operating systems on the same machine. When you boot the system, a boot menu is presented, allowing you to select the operating system you want to work in.

A multi-boot system provides two key benefits:

- It allows you to test a new operating system before fully deploying it to your organization.
- It provides you with the ability to determine how compatible the new operating system will be with your applications and hardware devices.

When you're setting up a multi-boot system, keep the following in mind:

- You should always back up your system before performing a multi-boot setup.
- Each operating system requires its own partition. This differs from the native VHD boot disk previously discussed.
- Programs installed on one operating system are not accessible when booted into the other system; a separate installation is required for each operating system.
- You must reboot the system to switch between operating systems.

You can multi-boot systems running Windows Vista, Windows 7, and Windows 8/8.1. In situations where you want to install multiple operating systems, install Windows 8/8.1 last. Windows 8/8.1 uses a newer boot manager; therefore, installing the older operating last will cause it to be overwritten and disable your ability to boot into Windows 8/8.1.

 CREATE A WINDOWS 7/8/8.1 ENTERPRISE MULTI-BOOT SYSTEM

GET READY. To create a Windows 7/8/8.1 Enterprise multi-boot system, log on as an administrator to a Windows 7 computer and then perform the following steps:

1. Press the **Windows logo key + r**.
2. In the *Run* dialog box, type **diskmgmt.msc** to start the Disk Management Console.
3. Make room for your Windows 8/8.1 installation by right-clicking the **C:** volume and choosing **Shrink**.

TAKE NOTE *

Before you begin, always backup your files to protect against data loss.

TAKE NOTE *

Shrinking a disk decreases the space used by primary partitions and logical drives by shrinking them into adjacent, contiguous space on the same disk. This is necessary if you need an additional partition but do not have additional disks. Any ordinary files are automatically relocated on the disk to create the new unallocated space.

4. In the *Enter the amount of space to shrink in MB* box, type **20480** and then click **Shrink**.
5. Right-click the unallocated partition and then choose **New Simple Volume**.
6. On the *Welcome to the New Simple Volume Wizard* page, click **Next** to start the New Simple Volume Wizard.
7. On the *Specify Volume Size* page, click **Next** to accept the default simple volume size.
8. On the *Assign Drive Letter or Path* page, click **Next** to assign the default drive letter.
9. On the *Format Partition* page, in the *Volume label* field, type **Windows 8.1** and then click **Next** to format the volume with the default settings.
10. On the *Completing the New Simple Volume Wizard* page, click **Finish.**.
11. Insert a bootable Windows 8/8.1 DVD or USB flash drive into your computer and then reboot. Make sure you configure the machine to boot from the device.
12. When prompted, click **Custom: install Windows only (advanced)**.
13. On the *Where do you want to install Windows?* screen, click the new partition you previously created and then click **Next**.

After Windows 8/8.1 has completed the installation process, the boot menu will display, showing both Windows 8/8.1 and Windows 7. By default, the system will boot into Windows 8/8.1 after 30 seconds.

■ Configuring a Native VHD Boot File

THE BOTTOM LINE

A ***virtual hard disk (VHD)*** is single file on your disk that functions like a separate drive. It can host native file systems (NTFS, FAT, exFAT, and UDFS), function as a boot disk, and support standard disk and file operations. This allows virtual disks to run on a computer that doesn't have a VM or hypervisor and also simplifies the image management process.

CERTIFICATION READY
Manage boot settings, including native virtual hard disk (VHD) and multi-boot
Objective 1.1

One benefit provided by VHDs is the ability to run Windows 8.1 on your computer's real hardware (for example, video, memory, network card, or CPU). This allows you to test its performance and compatibility with your computer system. ***Native VHD boot*** means the computer can mount and boot from the operating system contained within the VHD file. Native VHD boot will also work without an operating system present on the host computer.

TAKE NOTE

A virtual hard disk in Windows 8.1 does not require a parent operating system or a virtual machine manager in order to run. A virtual machine manager (hypervisor) is software that manages and monitors virtual machines.

You can also use VHDs to streamline image management in situations where you support an image library holding multiple formats. Instead of using a different process and toolset to manage and deploy each image format, you can standardize on VHDs and use the same image-management tools to create, deploy, and maintain system images installed on hardware or virtual machines.

Understanding VHD Formats

When setting up a VHD, you have to determine the format and hard disk type. Each is designed to meet a specific goal.

There are two VHD formats to choose from when creating a VHD boot file:

- ***VHD format*** supports virtual disks up to 2TB in size.
- ***VHDX format*** supports virtual disks up to 64TB. VHDX is more resilient to power failure but is only supported on Windows 8 systems.

There are two hard disk types available:

- A ***Fixed Size hard disk*** is allocated to its maximum size when the VHD is created. It works well with production servers where user data protection and overall performance is critical.
- A ***Dynamically Expanding hard disk*** will grow to its maximum size as data is written to the virtual hard disk. It should be used in testing and non-production environments. If you are using this disk type, consider storing your critical applications and user data outside the VHD. This reduces the overall file size and makes it easier to recover should the VHD image become corrupted.

To create a VHD file, you can use the *Disk Management Console (diskmgmt.msc)* and/or the Diskpart tool. The Disk Management Console is used to partition, format, delete, shrink and assign and change drive letters for hard disks (internal/external), optical disk drives, and flash drives. Diskpart is a command-line tool that enables you to manage objects (disks, partitions, or volumes) by using scripts or direct input at a command prompt.

In the following example, you will create a VHD Boot file on Windows 7 Professional and then install Windows 8 Enterprise to create a dual-boot system to test Windows 8 performance and compatibility with your existing computer's hardware.

 CREATE A VHD BOOT FILE USING THE DISK MANAGEMENT CONSOLE

GET READY. To create a VHD boot file using the Disk Management Console, log on as an administrator a computer running Windows 7 Professional and then perform the following steps:

1. Click **Start** and in the *Search* box, type **Disk Management**.
2. Click **Action > Create VHD**.
3. Click **Browse** (see Figure 1-4) to navigate to folder where you want to store the VHD file.

Figure 1-4

Navigating to the folder where you will store the VHD

4. In the *File name* field, type a name for the VHD file and then click **Save**.
5. For the *Virtual hard disk size* setting, type **20,** click the drop-down arrow, and then select **GB**.
6. In the *Virtual hard disk format* section, leave the default setting of **Fixed size (Recommended)**.
7. Click **OK**. The VHD file is created.

Installing Windows 8.1 on a VHD with an Operating System Present

After creating a VHD, you install an operating system by booting from a DVD or a bootable USB drive with the appropriate image.

After creating the VHD, your next step is to install the Windows 8 operating system on the VHD. You can perform the installation by booting from a DVD or a bootable USB drive that contains the Windows 8 Enterprise image.

Windows 8 setup will take you through the normal setup screens, prompting you for the language to install, time/currency formats, keyboard or input methods, and licensing terms. When you reach the *Where do you want to install Windows?* screen, you can open a command prompt by pressing **Shift+F10**.

From the command line, you can use ***Diskpart*** to attach the VHD. Attaching the VHD ensures it appears on the host as a drive and not a static file. The following example selects and attaches to the virtual hard disk created earlier:

```
X:\Sources>diskpart
select vdisk file="c:\vhdfiles\win8Ent.vhd"
attach vdisk
exit
```

After attaching the VHD, the *Where do you want to install Windows?* screen displays again and you click Refresh. The VHD will display as an option. Click the VHD disk and continue with the normal Windows installation steps.

On reboot, you have the option to select the instance of the operating system you want to run (see Figure 1-5).

Figure 1-5

The Windows 7/8 boot menu

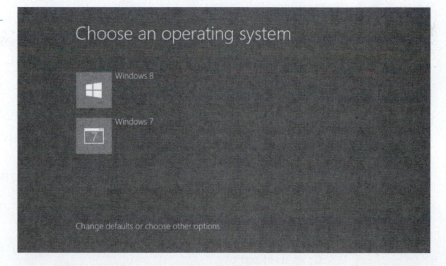

Installing Windows 8.1 on a VHD Without an Operating System Present

You can apply an existing image to a VHD and use a Windows 8 Pre-Installation Environment (PE) Disk to install the operating system on a computer without a current operating system running.

If you are using the ***Deployment Image Servicing and Management (DISM)*** tool—available on the Windows Assessment and Deployment Kit (Windows ADK)—you can apply an existing corporate Windows 8 image (.wim) file to a VHD file. DISM is a command-line tool used to service Windows images offline before they are deployed. It can also be used to install, uninstall, configure, and update Windows packages and drivers. This image can be deployed to computers where an operating system is installed or to computers without an operating system present.

To deploy a Windows 8 Enterprise image/VHD Boot file on a computer without an operating system, you need the following:

- A Windows 7/8/8.1 computer running the Windows ADK tools.
- A Windows 8.1 image (.wim) file.
- A **Windows 8.1 Pre-installation Environment (PE) disk**. This disk is used to boot a computer that has no operating system on it. It can be created on removable media (such as a CD/DVD, USB flash drive, or a USB hard drive).
- A Windows 8.1 computer on which to install the VHD; must have a minimum of 30 GB free disk space.

+ MORE INFORMATION

To learn more about creating a Windows Pre-Installation Environment disk, visit TechNet.

 CREATE A VHD BOOT FILE USING DISKPART AND APPLY AN IMAGE USING DISM

GET READY. To create a VHD boot file using DiskPart and apply an image using DISM, log on as an administrator to a computer running Windows 8 Enterprise. You must have the Windows ADK tools installed, a generalized image named install.wim, and a connection to a server providing a network share. Then perform the following steps:

TAKE NOTE*

The Windows ADK can be downloaded at Microsoft's website.

1. Press the **Windows log key + r**.
2. In the *Run* dialog box, type **cmd** to open a command console.
3. Start the program by typing **diskpart**.
4. Create a fixed disk, attach to it, create a primary partition, and then perform a quick format:
   ```
   C:\>diskpart
   create vdisk file=c:\windows.vhd maximum=25600
   type=fixed
   select vdisk file=c:\windows.vhd
   attach vdisk
   create partition primary
   assign letter=v
   format quick label=vhd
   exit
   ```
5. Use the DISM tool to apply your Windows image file (install.wim) to the primary partition:
   ```
   Dism /apply-image /imagefile: install.wim /index:1 /
   ApplyDir:V:\
   ```
6. Detach the virtual disk:
   ```
   C:\>diskpart
   select vdisk file=c:\windows.vhdx
   detach vdisk
   exit
   ```
7. Connect to a network share, create a directory, and copy the VHD file to the share. The following command uses a server named GEO, a file share named ITShares, and creates a CorpVHDs directory:
   ```
   Net use i: \\GEO\ITShares
   Md i:\CorpVHDs
   Copy c:\windows.vhd i:\CorpVHDs
   ```

This virtual hard disk, with the Windows image included, can be copied to one or more systems to run as a virtual machine or for native boot purposes.

TAKE NOTE

When creating an image for deployment to multiple computers, the image must be generalized. During this configuration pass, computer-specific information is removed from the Windows installation, enabling you to capture and reapply the Windows image to different computers. For example, unique Security Identifier (SID) and unique device drivers are removed from the image.

➔ INSTALL THE VHD WITH THE WINDOWS 8.1 ENTERPRISE IMAGE ON A BIOS-BASED COMPUTER WITHOUT AN OPERATING SYSTEM

TAKE NOTE *

You will need a Windows PE bootable media to complete the exercise.

GET READY. To install the VHD with the Windows 8.1 Enterprise image on a BIOS-based computer without an operating system, select a target computer that does not have an operating system installed and then perform the following steps:

1. Boot into the computer using your Windows PE bootable media.

2. Execute the **Diskpart** command clean the hard disk. This ensures no data is left on the system from previous installations.
   ```
   Diskpart
   select disk 0
   clean
   ```

3. Create a system partition:
   ```
   Diskpart
   create partition primary size=300
   format quick fs=ntfs
   assign letters=s
   active
   ```

4. Create a primary partition:
   ```
   Diskpart
   create partition primary
   format quick fs=ntfs
   assign letter=c
   exit
   ```

5. Copy the VHD to the target computer:
   ```
   Copy i:\CorpVHDs\windows.vhd C:
   ```

6. Attach the VHD file:
   ```
   Diskpart
   select vdisk file=c:\windows.vhd
   attach vdisk
   ```

7. Find the letter associated with the VHD, select the volume, and then assign it the drive letter V:
   ```
   List volume
   select volume <volume_number_of_attached_VHD.
   assign letter=v
   exit
   ```

8. Use **bcdboot** to copy the boot environment files from the \Windows directory (or from the Windows PE media) in the VHD into the system partition. BCDboot creates the BCD configuration to boot from the VHD:
   ```
   cd v:\windows\system32
   bcdboot v:\windows
   ```

9. Detach the disk:
   ```
   Diskpart
   select vdisk file=c:\windows.vhd
   detach vdisk
   exit
   ```

At this point, you can reboot the computer and the Windows 8.1 boot manager will load the Windows 8.1 operating system image contained within the windows.vhd file.

■ Managing Desktop Images

THE BOTTOM LINE

When you manually deploy Windows, you must manually install and configure Windows and then install and configure the applications before the user can use his computer. The manually deploying of Windows is a lengthy process, particularly when you have to do many of these deployments or when you have to perform these deployments often. To simplify and accelerate this deployment process, you can create image files, which are then copied to the individual machines. In addition, by using an image-based installation, deployments are consistent across all client computers. You can also use images to refresh a computer that has been corrupted or badly misconfigured.

CERTIFICATION READY
Manage desktop images
Objective 1.1

A *disk image* is a single file or other storage device that contains the complete contents and structures of a disk. The image has the necessary information to install a copy of Windows onto another machine. Often the images contain additional software packages, drivers, and features, which are also deployed as a single complete package.

The simplest use of an image is as a reference or master computer. On the reference computer, you install Windows and any necessary drivers; you configure Windows; and then you configure additional software. In addition, you update Windows and any applications that run on the computer. When you finish, the reference computer is a pristine computer that is ready to be used by the user. Instead of giving the computer to a user, you take a snapshot of the computer by copying the drive's contents to an image file. The image can be stored and accessed from a central location so that it can be copied to other computers.

Some system image programs use sector-based images and others use file-based images. A *sector-based disk image* copies each sector to a file. One well-known example of a sector-based image is an ISO image, which is an image of a CD or DVD disk. One problem with using sector-based images is that you must take additional steps to remove the computer name and the Security Identifier (SID), which uniquely identifies a computer running Windows on a network. In addition, sector-based images might not work when installed to computers that run on different hardware.

A *file-based disk image* captures images based on files on the disk. The advantage of using a file-based image is that it is hardware-independent, so it can be deployed to computers that are using different hardware. It uses single-instance storage, which keeps a single copy of a file that may be referenced multiple times in a file system tree. When applying a file-based image, the applied image is nondestructive, which means that data files still exist after the image has been applied. Examples of file-based images include virtual hard disk (.vhd) and Windows Imaging Format (WIM).

A *Windows Image Format (WIM)* file is a file-based image format developed by Microsoft that enables a file structure (folders and files) to be stored inside a single WIM database. WIM files have the following features:

- They incorporate compression
- They enable multiple images to be included in a single WIM file

- They use single-instancing of files when multiple WIM files are appended
- Because WIM image format is a file-based image, it can be used on different hardware platforms and various size disks.

WIM file format supports offline servicing, which enables you to open a WIM file in Windows and directly add or remove folders, files, drivers and operating system components.

One common tool used to update or modify a WIM file is DISM, a command-line tool that you can use to service and deploy .wim, VHD, and VHDX files. You also can use DISM to prepare Windows PE images. The DISM command is discussed later in this lesson.

Capturing Images

After you have configured the reference computer and used the **Sysprep** command, which will prepare the computer for capturing and shut down of the computer, you are ready to manually capture the image of a partition.

To manually capture the image using DISM, you need to perform the following steps:

1. Boot the computer using Windows PE.
2. Map a drive to a network share.
3. Use Diskpart to assign a drive letter to any partitions that you need to capture that do not have any driver letters assigned. Unless you customized the system partition, you will not have to create an image of it because it will automatically be re-created.
4. Use DISM to capture the system partition (if the system partition has been customized).
5. Use DISM to capture the primary partitions and any logical partitions.

Before capturing a computer, you need to prepare the reference computer with the Sysprep. exe utility. Microsoft's **System Preparation Utility (sysprep.exe)** prepares a Windows computer for cloning by removing specific computer information such as the computer name and Security Identifier (SID). On Windows 8, Sysprep.exe is located in the C:\Windows\System32\Sysprep folder.

The sysprep.exe command supports the following options:

- /generalize: Instructs Sysprep to remove system-specific data (such as event logs, the computer name, and unique SIDs) from the Windows operating system installation.
- /oobe: Instructs Windows to present the Windows Welcome Wizard when the computer starts next time. The Windows Welcome Wizard enables you to name the computer and generate an SID and any other required unique information.
- /shutdown: Instructs the computer to shut down and not to restart.
- /audit: Instructs the Windows operating system installation to run in audit mode the next time that the computer starts.
- /reboot: Instructs the computer to restart. Use this option if you want to verify that the OOBE phase runs correctly.
- /quiet: Runs Sysprep without displaying onscreen confirmation messages. If you automate Sysprep, use this option with an answer file.
- /unattend:answerfile: Applies settings in an answer file to Sysprep.

The basic command to prepare a computer for imaging is

```
sysprep /generalize /oobe /shutdown
```

To actually capture the images using the DISM command and save the .wim files to the C drive, use the following commands:

```
DISM /Capture-Image /ImageFile:c:\windows-partition.wim /
CaptureDir:C:\ /Name:"Windows partition"
```

```
DISM /Capture-Image /ImageFile:s:\system-partition.wim /CaptureDir:C:\
/Name:"System partition"
```

Note that you can also save the image directly to a network shared folder.

When you use the /Capture-Image option, you can use the following options:

- /ConfigFile: Specifies the location of a configuration file that lists exclusions for image capture and compress commands.
- /Compress: Specifies the type of compression (maximum, fast, and none) used for the initial capture operation.
- /Bootable: Marks a volume image as being a bootable image. This option can be used only with Windows PE images and only one volume image can be marked as bootable in a .wim file.
- /CheckIntegrity: Detects and tracks .wim file corruption when used with capture, unmount, export, and commit operations.
- /Verify: Checks for errors and file duplication.
- /NoRpFix: Disables the reparse point tag fix. A reparse point is a file that contains a link to another file on the file system.

When you capture the image, you need a place to store the image. Therefore, you need to share a folder so that it can be accessed over the network. After you boot the reference computer with Windows PE, you have to execute the following command:

```
Net Use G: \\Server01\Images
```

You are then prompted to enter a username and password. Use the following two commands to copy the image files to the network share.

```
copy C:\windows-partition.wim G:\Images\
```

```
copy c:\system-partition.wim G:\Images\
```

Another tool that can be used to create an image is ***Windows Deployment Services (WDS)***. WDS is a Windows server role used to deploy windows (Windows XP, Windows Vista, Windows 7, Windows 8/8.1, Windows Server 2003, Windows Server 2008, Windows Server 2008 R2, Windows Server 2012, and Windows Server 2012 R2) over the network without little or no user intervention. If the client can perform a PXE boot, you perform an installation over a network with no operating system or local boot device on it. The WDS server can store and help administrators manage the boot and operating system image files used in the network installations.

Besides deploying Windows, WDS can also capture a Windows image using the Windows DS Capture Image program. To capture an image with WDS, you have to do the following:

1. Modify an existing boot image to create a capture image.
2. Boot the reference computer with the modified boot image.
3. Run the Windows Deployment Service Capture Utility.

When you use the Windows Deployment Service Capture Utility, you can use it to capture only volumes that contain operating systems prepared with Sysprep. In addition, the wizard can save an image only to a local drive letter. Although you could use a mapped network drive, it is recommended to use a local location to avoid corruption due to network problems.

Modifying Images Using DISM

> If you are using the **Deployment Image Servicing and Management (DISM)** tool, available on the Windows Assessment and Deployment Kit (Windows ADK), you can apply an existing corporate Windows 8 image (.wim) file to a VHD file. DISM is a command-line tool used to service Windows images offline before they are deployed. It can also be used to install, uninstall, configure, and update Windows packages and drivers. This image can be deployed to computers where an operating system is installed or computers without an operating system present.

DISM has the /Online or /image option. The /Online image specifies that the action is to be taken on the operating system that is currently running. The /image is used to specify an offline Windows image.

To modify an image file, you must mount the Windows image in an NTFS volume using the Mount-Wim option. For example, to mount the D:\Images\install.wim file to the C:\Offline folder, use the following command:

```
Dism /Mount-Wim /WimFile: D:\Images\install.wim /index:1 /MountDir:C:\
Offline
```

After you make changes to the image, you need to commit the changes by using the /Commit-Wim option:

```
Dism /Commit-Wim /MountDir:C:\Offline
```

When using DISM to modify an image, you must first mount the image. When done, you must then commit the changes and dismount the image. To unmount the image, use the /Unmount-Wim option. If you want to commit the changes while you unmount the image, add the /Commit option. To discard the changes, use the /Discard option. For example, to unmount the image mounted to the C:\Offline folder while saving the changes, execute the following command:

```
Dism /Unmount-Wim /MountDir:C:\offline /commit
```

To get information about an image or WIM file, use the /Get-WimInfo option. For example, to get information about the C:\offline\winstall.wim file, execute the following command:

```
Dism /Get-WimInfo /WimFile:C:\offline\install.wim /index:1
```

Microsoft updates, hotfixes, service packs, and language packs are usually downloaded from Microsoft as a Windows Update standalone Installer (.msu) file but sometimes can be downloaded or extracted as a cabinet (.cab) file. The .cab file can be usually extracted from the .msu file using the extract.exe command. To add the software updates hotfix, service pack, and language pack that is in a cabinet (.cab) file or as a Windows Update Stand-alone Installer (.msu) file, you can add the package using the /Add-Package option. For example, to add the C:\Update\Update.cab file, execute the following command:

```
Dism /image:C:\offline /Add-Package /Packagepath:C:\Update\Update.cab
```

To remove a package, use the /Remove-Package option. For example, to remove the update. cab file, execute the following command:

```
Dism /image:C:\offline /Remove-Package /PackagePath:C:\Update\Update.cab
```

You can use the /Add-Driver option to add third-party driver packages that include a valid INF file. For example, to add mydriver to the Windows image, execute the following command:

```
Dism /image:C:\offline /Add-Driver /driver:C:\Drivers\mydriver.INF
```

If you point to a path and use /Recurse, all subfolders will be checked for valid drivers. For example, to add drivers from the C:\Drivers folder, execute the following command:

```
Dism /image:C:\offline /Add-Driver /driver:C:\drivers /recurse
```

To remove a third-party device driver, use the /Remove-Driver option to specify the name of a device driver (such as oem0.inf, oem1.inf, and so on). For example, to remove the second third-party driver (oem1.inf) that has been added to the system, execute the following command:

```
Dism /image:C:\offline /Remove-Driver /driver:oem1.inf
```

To get a list of features that are on an image, execute the following command:

```
Dism /Image:C:\offline /Get-Features |more
```

To enable a specific feature on an image, such as TelnetClient, execute the following command:

```
Dism /image:C:\offline /Enable-Feature /FeatureName:TelnetClient
```

To disable a specific feature on an image, such as TelnetClient, execute the following command:

```
Dism /image:C:\offline /Disable-Feature /FeatureName:TelnetClient
```

If an image is too large for the intended media (such as a CD), you can split the file into multiple parts by using the /Split-Image option. When the /Split-Image option is used, multiple .swm files will be created, starting with filename.swm, filename2.swm, filename3.swm, and so on. For example, to split an image called E:\Images\BasicImage.wim to the E:\Images\SplitBasicImages.swm with a maximum file size of 600 MB, execute the following command:

```
Dism /Split-Image /ImageFile:E:\Images\BasicImage.wim /SWMFile:E:\
imaging\SplitBasicImages.swm /FileSize:600
```

To add an image to an existing .WIM file, you would use the /Append-Image switch instead of the /Capture-Image command:

```
Dism /Append-Image /ImageFile:c:\windows-partition.wim /CaptureDir:C:\
/Name:"Windows partition"
```

■ Customizing a Windows Installation by Using Windows PE

THE BOTTOM LINE

Windows PE is a lightweight and customizable version of Windows that you can start from a CD/DVD, USB drive, or a network drive. It can be used to provide an environment you can then use to install Windows, capture an image, apply an image, or to troubleshoot a Windows installation. If you start a computer using the Windows PE disk, you can run commands to run the built-in tools. In addition, Windows PE can be customized by adding additional components or programs.

CERTIFICATION READY
Customize a Windows installation by using Windows Preinstallation Environment (PE)
Objective 1.1

When Windows PE boots, the winload.exe from the boot.wim file is loaded, which loads the appropriate Hardware Abstraction Layer (HAL), the System registry hive, and necessary boot drivers. Next, Ntoskrrnl.exe is executed, which starts the Session Manager (SMSS), which then loads the registry and configures the environment to run the Win32 subsystem (Win32k.sys) and its various processes. Winlogon.exe runs setup based on the registry value HKLM\SYSTEM\Setup\CmdLine. Winpeshl.exe will launch %SYSTEMDRIVE%\sources\

setup.exe if it exists. If it does not exist, Winlogon.exe looks for an application specified in %SYSTEMROOT%\system32\winpeshl.ini. If no application is specified, Winpeshl.exe will execute cmd /k %SYSTEMROOT%\system32\startnet.cmd.

By default, Windows PE contains a Startnet.cmd file that will launch Wpeinit.exe. Wpeinit. exe loads network resources and coordinates with networking components like DHCP. When Wpeinit.exe completes, the Command Prompt window is displayed. The boot process of Windows PE is complete.

You can add a custom script to an offline image of Windows PE by launching custom scripts using:

- Startnet.cmd
- Winpeshl.ini
- Autounattend.xml

To add a custom script by using Startnet.cmd, perform the following steps:

1. Create a custom Windows PE image.
2. Mount the Windows PE image using the DISM tool.
3. Edit Startnet.cmd to include your customized commands. By default, Windows PE includes a Startnet.cmd script at %SYSTEMROOT%\System32 of in your custom Windows PE image.
4. Commit the changes to the Windows PE image by using the Dism /Commit-Wim command.

To support plug and play or networking, include a call to Wpeinit.exe. Wpeinit.exe specifically installs plug and play devices, processes Autounattend.xml settings, and loads network resources.

The Windows PE default interface is a command-prompt window. Winpeshl.ini controls whether a customized shell is loaded in Windows PE instead of the default Command Prompt window. To load a customized shell, create a file with a text editor named Winpeshl. ini and place it in %SYSTEMROOT%\System32 of your customized Windows PE image.

The winpeshl.ini file will have the following sections (as indicated with brackets [ ]) and entries:

```
[LaunchApp]

AppPath = %SYSTEMDRIVE%\myshell.exe

[LaunchApps]

%SYSTEMDRIVE%\mydir\application1.exe, -option1  -option2

application2.exe, -option1 -option2
```

The AppPath entry specifies the path to the shell application using a fully qualified path or a path with environment variables. For example, by default, %SYSTEMROOT% is the C:\ Windows folder. The [LaunchApps] section is used to run applications with command-line options. The applications are executed in the order listed. When you specify the application options, separate the name of the application from its options with a comma (,). If you create a custom Winpeshl.ini, if you require plug and play or network support, or if you need to process Autounattend.xml settings, you will need to call Wpeinit.exe. When you exit the Command Prompt window or your customized shell application, Windows PE restarts.

You can select a specific answer file during installation by booting to the Windows Preinstallation Environment and using the setup.exe command with the /unattend:filename option.

When you install Windows, you can automate and customize the Windows installation using an *answer file*. For example, the answer file can also be used to partition and format disks, install additional device drivers and specify what Windows features to install, and specify the install language. The answer file is an XML-based file that contains setting definitions and values for using Windows Setup. The answer file for setup is typically called *Autounattend.xml*.

Because an answer file is just a text file based on XML, you create an answer file with a text editor or XML editor. However, Microsoft recommends that you use the *System Image Manager (SIM)*, which is part of the Windows ADK. SIM is a tool used to create and manage unattended Windows setup answer files using a graphical interface and to check answer files.

When you use Windows SIM to create an answer file, you need to create a distribution share and you must open a Windows install WIM file. By defining a Windows image, Windows SIM then knows what options are available for the installation.

CREATE AN ANSWER FILE

GET READY. To create an answer file, log on to the computer where you installed the ADK and then perform the following steps:

1. Click **Start** > **All Apps** > **Windows System Image Manager**. The *Windows System Image Manager* Console opens (see Figure 1-6).

Figure 1-6

Viewing the Windows System Image Manager Console

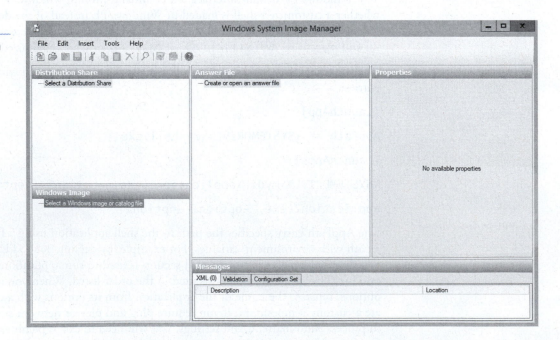

2. Click **Tools > Create Distribution Share**. The *Create Distribution Share* dialog box opens.

3. Browse to the folder where you want to create the distribution share and then click **Open**. The distribution share subfolders display in the *Distribution Share* pane.

4. Insert a Windows 2012 installation disk into the computer's DVD drive.

5. Click **File > Select Windows Image**. The Select a *Windows Image* dialog box opens.

6. Browse to the folder where you are storing an *install.wim* file, select the **install. wim** image file, and then click **Open**. The *Select an Image* dialog box opens.

7. Select the image that you want to use, and then click **OK**.

8. If you are prompted to create a catalog file, click **Yes**.

9. Click **File > New Answer File**. The answer file elements display in the *Answer File* pane.

To add a configuration setting to the answer file, browse through the available settings in the Windows Image pane, right-click the setting you want to add, and then select the configuration pass specifying when you want the setup program to configure the setting. The setting then displays in the Answer File pane and the properties specific to that setting appear in the adjacent Properties pane. After the setting has been added, you modify the values in the properties. If you need clarification on a setting, press F1 while a property or setting is highlighted to open the Unattended Windows Setup Reference Guide.

In the answer file, you can see the seven configuration passes starting with WindowsPE and ending with oobeSystem. To add settings to the configuration pass, go to the Windows Image pane, right-click the component that you want to add, and choose the configuration pass that you want to add the setting to (see Figure 1-7).

Figure 1-7

Using Windows System Image Manager to a configuration pass

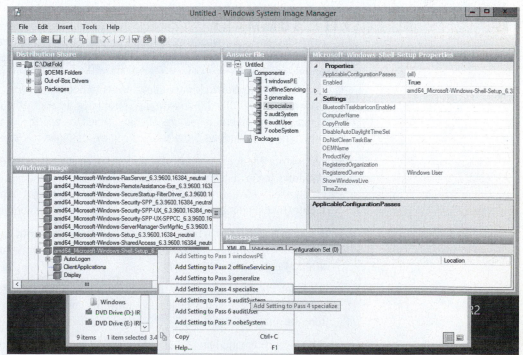

The setting then displays in the Answer File pane and the properties specific to that setting appear in the adjacent Properties pane (see Figure 1-8). After the setting has been added, you modify the values in the properties. If you need clarification on a setting, press F1 while a property or setting is highlighted to open the Unattended Windows Setup Reference Guide.

Figure 1-8

Using Windows System Image Manager to defining settings

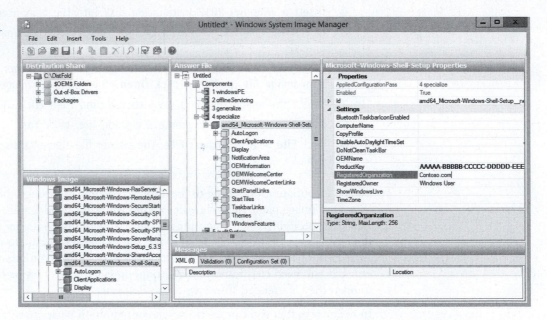

After you configure the answer files, you can validate the answer file by clicking Tools > Validate Answer file. If SIM finds any discrepancies (such as incorrect values or omitted values), SIM will display those discrepancies as errors. It is common for warnings to be displayed the Validation tab. When you finish, click File > Save Answer File.

SKILL SUMMARY

IN THIS LESSON YOU LEARNED:

- The Windows To Go workspace allows users to boot into a full version of Windows 8 from an external USB 3.0 drive. You will not have access to the internal disk on the host computer; the hibernate feature will be disabled, as will the Windows Store application. Hibernate and Windows Store settings can be managed via Group Policy.

- To create a Windows To Go workspace, you need a 32 GB USB drive that supports Windows To Go, a computer running Windows 8 Enterprise edition, a Windows 8 Enterprise ISO, Windows 8 installation media, or a Windows image created from Windows 8 Enterprise media and local administrative access to the computer.

- A disk image is a single file or other storage device that contains the complete contents and structures of a disk. The image has the necessary information to install a copy of Windows onto another machine.

- After you configure the reference computer and you use the Sysprep command to prepare a computer for imaging and shutting down the computer, you are ready to manually capture the image of a partition.

- DISM is a command-line tool used to service Windows images offline before they are deployed. It can also be used to install, uninstall, configure, and update Windows packages and drivers.

- When using DISM to modify an image, you must first mount the image. When completed, you must then commit the changes and dismount the image.

- Windows Preinstallation Environment (Windows PE) is a lightweight and customizable version of Windows that you can start from a CD/DVD, USB drive, or a network drive. It can be used to provide an environment you can then use to install Windows, capture an image, apply an image, or to troubleshoot a Windows installation.

- A virtual hard disk (VHD) is a file that functions much like a separate hard disk. The computer can mount the file and boot from the operating system that it contains. You can also use VHDs to standardize and streamline your image management process.

- There are two VHD formats: VHD (supports up to 2TB) and VHDX (supports up to 64TB). Hard disk types supported include Fixed Size (allocated to its maximum size when created) and Dynamically expanding disk type that will grow as data is written to it.

- The Windows startup process is controlled by parameters in the boot configuration data store. The BCD Editor can be used to modify and configure settings in the BCD store. BCDboot is a command line utility that allows you to setup a system partition when you deploy new computers.

- A multi-boot system (dual-boot) is a computer that runs multiple operating systems. Multi-booting allows you to test a new operating system before fully deploying it and helps you determine if there are any hardware and application compatibility issues. Each operating system requires its own partition, which makes it different from a VHD boot disk. Programs installed on one operating system will not be accessible from the other system.

▣ Knowledge Assessment

Multiple Choice

1. You have just set up a system running Windows 7 Professional and Windows 8.1 Enterprise to test compatibility with your existing hardware. After the installation, the system automatically boots into Windows 8. Which tool and switch should be used to change it so that your computer boots into Windows 7 by default every time?
   a. BCDEdit /default
   b. BCDEdit /displayorder
   c. BCDEdit /bootsequence
   d. BCDEdit /timeout

2. Which of the following commands exports the contents of the system store to a file so that you can use it later to restore the state of the system store?
   a. bcdedit /createstore
   b. bcdboot /export
   c. BCDEdit /createstore
   d. BCDEdit /export

3. Which of the following are requirements of Windows To Go Workspace?
   a. A USB drive that supports Windows To Go Workspace (32GB or larger).
   b. A computer running Windows 8 Professional edition.
   c. A Windows 8 Enterprise image.
   d. A Windows 7- or 8-certified computer.

4. You want to create a new VHD to use on a production server. The VHD file needs to be at least 3040 GB. Which of the following VHD formats and disk types should be used?
   a. VHD, Fixed Size
   b. VHDX, Fixed Size
   c. VHD, Dynamically Expanding
   d. VHDX, Dynamically Expanding

5. What does the Bootmgr.exe use to determine which operating system to load and where the operating system can be located?
   a. BIOS table
   b. NTFS volume store
   c. BitLocker database
   d. Boot Configuration Data store

6. Which of the following are file-based disk images? (Choose all that apply)
   a. ISO
   b. WIM
   c. Ghost
   d. VHD

7. When you are ready to capture an image that will be used with future deployments, which of the following actions must be performed in order to remove the computer name and other specific computer information?
   a. Run the DISM command
   b. Run Startnet.cmd
   c. Run Sysprep
   d. Attach a vdisk.

8. You need to modify a WIM image. Before you can do so, however, which of the following actions must be performed?
   a. Mount the image
   b. Dismount all other WIM images
   c. Commit the changes
   d. Run Sysprep

9. When you modify the changes, which of the following options is used with the dism command to finalize the changes?
   a. /finalize
   b. /commit
   c. /save
   d. /done

10. Which type of file is used to add a Microsoft Windows update to a WIM image using the DISM command? (Choose all that apply)
    a. .exe
    b. .msi
    c. .cab
    d. .msu

Best Answer

Choose the letter that corresponds to the best answer. More than one answer choice may achieve the goal. Select the BEST answer.

1. You are setting up a virtual hard disk on your Windows 8 client computer. The virtual hard disk will be 3 TB in size and may be used on a production server in the near future. Which of the following combinations provide the best solution?
   a. Use the VHD format/Fixed Size hard disk type
   b. Use the VHDX format/Fixed Size hard disk type
   c. Use the VHD format/Dynamically Expanding hard disk type
   d. Use the VHDX format/Dynamically Expanding hard disk type

2. You would like to reduce the amount of time you system waits to load the default operating system. It currently is set to 30 seconds but you would like to change it to 10 seconds. Which of the following commands accomplishes this task?
   a. bcdedit /default /timeout 10
   b. bcdedit /timeout 10
   c. bcdedit /timeout 10 /default
   d. bcdedit /timeout 10 /set

3. You would like to try out Windows 8 on your current computer running Windows 7. You want to simulate as close as possible the impact the new operating system will have on your existing hardware. You do not want to create a new partition for Windows 8. Which option provides the best solution to meet your needs?
   a. Setting up a multi-boot system.
   b. Creating a Windows 7 image, formatting the drive, and installing Windows 8. After testing, restore the Windows 7 image.
   c. Using a Windows To Go workspace disk.
   d. Configuring a VHD on your Windows 7 computer.

4. You want to run a demo of an application that runs on Windows 8.1. However, because the application requires a large, complicated installation, you would like to package Windows and the application into a single package that can then be used to demonstrate the application. Which of the following actions is recommended?
   a. Use a Bootable USB thumb drive
   b. Purchase a mobile server
   c. Create a native VHD boot image stored on a drive on a laptop
   d. Use a bootable ISO

5. Which of the following methods should be used to automatically install Windows using a Windows PE bootable disk?
   a. Use startnet.cmd
   b. Use winpeshl.ini
   c. Use autounattend.xml
   d. Use setup.exe

Matching and Identification

1. Match the tool with the tasks it can perform:
   _____ a) bcdedit.exe
   _____ b) pwcreator.exe
   _____ c) diskpart.exe
   _____ d) gpmc.msc
   _____ e) dism.exe

      1. Attach a VHD so that it appears on the host as a drive and not a static file.

      2. Create a new Windows To Go workspace drive.

      3. Create a Group Policy object to apply to all computers in a domain.

      4. Used to modify a WIM file.

      5. Set the order in which the boot manager displays the multi-boot menu.

2. Write the bcdedit command for the specified function or scenario:

      _____ Create a copy of the entire BCD store.

      _____ Change the order in which the boot manager displays the multi-boot menu.

      _____ Set the boot sequence (one time only) for the boot manager.

      _____ Change the default entry you want boot manager to use

      _____ Remove an entry from the BCD store.

Build a List

1. You want to create a Windows To Go workspace on a Windows 8 Enterprise client computer. Specify the correct order of the steps required to create the Workspace.

      _____ Press the **Windows logo key + w**.

      _____ Click **Create** to set up the Windows To Go workspace.

      _____ Click **Create** to format the drive.

      _____ Type **Windows To Go** and select it from the *Results List*.

      _____ Connect a Windows To Go workspace drive to the host.

      _____ (optional) Select **Use BitLocker with my Windows To Go workspace** and then click **Next**.

      _____ Click the Windows image that appears or click **Add search location** to locate one. Click **Next** to continue.

      _____ Select the USB drive connected earlier and then click **Next**.

      _____ Click **Yes** to automatically boot from the USB drive when you restart the host.

2. Specify the correct order of the steps that must be completed to create a VHD boot file using the Disk Management Console.

      _____ Click **Action > Create VHD**.

      _____ In the *File name* field, type a name for the VHD file and then click **Save**.

      _____ In the *Virtual hard disk format* section, leave the default setting of **Fixed size (recommended)**.

      _____ Click **Browse** to navigate to the folder where you want to store the VHD file.

      _____ Click **Start** and, in the *Search* field, type **Disk Management**.

      _____ For the *Virtual hard disk size* setting, type **20**, click the drop-down arrow, and then select **GB**.

      _____ Click **OK**.

3. Specify the correct order of the steps that must be completed to capture an image using DISM.

      _____ Map a drive to a network share

      _____ Use DISM with the /Capture-Image option to capture each volume

      _____ Assign a drive letter to a partition

      _____ Use Syspep on the reference computer

      _____ Boot the computer using Windows PE

■ Business Case Scenarios

Scenario 1-1: Using Windows To Go

Elliot receives a call from one of his support staff that Mary, one of Contoso's account managers, is having trouble booting into a Windows To Go workspace drive from her home office. You know she is running a Windows 7 Professional computer and has a USB drive that is certified to work with Windows To Go. You also sent a tech to her house last week to configure the computer to boot from a USB drive when it's present. What could be the problem?

Scenario 1-2: Creating Images

You were just hired as a new administrator for the Contoso Corporation, which has hundreds of computers distributed across three buildings. You will be responsible for deploying a standardized version of Windows 8.1 to new computers. Because this effort will consume a lot of your time, you want to identify the best way to simplify this process. Describe the actions you would perform.

2 LESSON

Supporting Desktop Apps

70-688 EXAM OBJECTIVE

Objective 1.2 – Supporting desktop apps. This objective may include but is not limited to: Desktop app compatibility using Application Compatibility Toolkit (ACT), including shims and compatibility database; desktop application co-existence using Hyper-V, RemoteApp, and App-V; installation and configuration of User Experience Virtualization (UE-V); deploy desktop apps by using Windows Intune.

LESSON HEADING	EXAM OBJECTIVE
Dealing with Desktop Application Problems	
Managing Desktop Application Co-Existence	Desktop application co-existence using Hyper-V, RemoteApp, and App-V
Working with Client Hyper-V	
Exploring Remote Desktop Services (RDS)	
Virtualizing Applications Using App-V	
Managing Desktop Application Compatibility Using Application Compatibility Toolkit (ACT)	Desktop app compatibility using Application Compatibility Toolkit (ACT) including shims and compatibility data base
Inventorying Your Computers	
Using Runtime Analysis Packages and Testing Application Compatibility	
Virtualizing the User Experience	Installation and configuration of User Experience Virtualization (UE-V)
Deploying Desktop Applications by Using Windows Intune	Deploy desktop apps by using Windows Intune

KEY TERMS

ACT database

ACT Log Processing Service (LPS)

ACT LPS share

Application Compatibility Toolkit (ACT)

Application Compatibility Manager (ACM)

App-V Management server

App-V Publishing server

App-V Reporting server

App-V Reporting database server

Client Hyper-V

Compatibility Administrator

Compatibility Monitor

Hyper-V Manager

Hyper-V Virtual Machine Connection

inventory-collector package

Microsoft Compatibility Exchange

Microsoft Silverlight

RemoteApp

Remote Desktop Protocol (RDP)

Remote Desktop Services (RDS)

RD Connection Broker

RD Gateway

RD Licensing

RD Session Host

RD Virtualization Host

RD Web Access

runtime-analysis package

sequencing

shims

Standard User Analyzer (SUA)

UE-V Agent

UE-V Generator

User Access Control (UAC)

User Experience Virtualization (UE-V)

Windows Intune

■ Dealing With Desktop Application Problems

THE BOTTOM LINE

While applications are being added to the web every day, you will still not be able to get away from the desktop application that runs directly on the computer. Therefore, as an administrator, you will need to deal with these issues as they arise. Problems with desktop applications can usually be divided into desktop application installation issues or operating the application issues.

If you just have to install a desktop application on one or two computers, it is best to install the application manually. However, if you have multiple computers, it is best to develop a deployment process and technology that will minimize the amount of work required. Most large organizations automate application installation from a central location. Some methods to deploy desktop applications include:

- Group Policy
- Microsoft System Center 2012 R2 Configuration Manager
- Windows Intune

In addition, users can access the desktop applications as a virtualized application.

Some of the common reasons that will cause problems with desktop application deployment are:

- Insufficient permissions.
- Missing dependencies, such as Microsoft .NET Framework, or Java.
- Application is not compliant with User Account Control (UAC).
- Application is prevented by AppLocker or similar technology.
- Compatibility problems such as the wrong version or edition of Windows.

Of course, to avoid these problems, you should always read the documentation for the application, and test the deployment on a standard client computer. Of course, if you do encounter problems, you can check the recheck the documentation, visit the vendor's website, and research any specific errors that appear.

After the application installed, some of the common reasons for desktop application issues are:

- Missing features.
- Incorrect configuration.
- Poor performance.
- Errors.
- Incorrect database connection settings.
- App blocking by AppLocker or similar technology.

Of course, similar to problems with application deployment, you should always check the documentation for the application, visit the vendor's website, and research any specific errors that appear. Some of the fixes may include:

- Install the needed feature.
- Reconfigure the application.
- Repair or reinstall the application.
- Search for and apply updates for Windows or the application.
- Upgrade the application to a newer version.
- Identify performance issues and bottlenecks.
- Reconfigure AppLocker rules or similar technology.

■ Managing Desktop Application Co-Existence

THE BOTTOM LINE

Since Windows 8 follows the same architecture used in with Windows Vista and Windows 7, most applications written for Windows Vista and Windows 7 will run on Windows 8/8.1 The few applications that do not run are usually primarily security-class applications or applications that bypass the Windows application programming interface (API) to communicate with system hardware by performing low-level kernel calls. If an application does not run in Windows 8, even under the application Compatibility Mode, you can try to run the application under a Hyper-V virtual machine, a RemoteApp, or App-V.

CERTIFICATION READY
Desktop Application co-existence using Hyper-V, RemoteApp, and App-V
Objective 1.2

Before you deploy Windows 8.1 in an organization, you must thoroughly test each application to make sure that it runs as expected. If it does not, you will then take additional steps to make the application run on Windows 8.1, or you are going to have to contact the vendor to get an upgraded version of the application.

Of course, as with any problem, when dealing with application compatibility issues, don't forget to follow basic troubleshooting. First record any error messages that are displayed. Then use the Event Viewer to look for additional warnings or errors. If applications seem to be slow, you can use Task Manager and other performance monitoring tools such as Performance Monitor. Lastly, don't be afraid to perform research on the Internet and to check the vendor.

There are several ways in which you can have users run the same application but with different versions. First, you can run Hyper-V on a client machine, so that you create virtual machines that will run other versions of an application. You can also have users connect to remote desktop sessions, which include other versions of the application. You can also access RemoteApps, which are applications hosted on a server running remote desktop service, but appear as an application that is running locally.

Application Virtualization (App-V), which is part of the Microsoft Desktop Optimization Package (MDOP), is used to mitigate application-to-application incompatibilities or conflicts. To run virtual applications, you will use the App-V 5.0 SP2 Sequencer, which converts an application into a virtual package. You then deploy the App-V 5 client, which will run the virtualized application on the computer, and the virtualized application. When you run the virtualized application on a local computer, the virtualized application runs in an isolated environment. Therefore, you could run the different versions of the same application at the same time by using App-V.

Working with Client Hyper-V

Client Hyper-V enables you to create and manage virtual machines (VMs) using a virtual switch. These VMs can be used to test your applications for compatibility with new operating systems.

Client Hyper-V, a Microsoft replacement for Windows Virtual PC, provides the same virtualization capabilities as Hyper-V in Windows Server 2012. Although it does not include all the advanced features available on the server version, it does utilize the same interface and underlying technology. This feature is disabled by default on Windows 8 Enterprise (64-bit) machines.

Although Client Hyper-V runs only on Windows 8 (64-bit) machines running the Windows 8 Enterprise (64-bit) operating system, it enables you to run 32- and 64-bit VMs simultaneously, connect to a Hyper-V machine running on another computer, and move machines between Client Hyper-V and Hyper-V running on the server.

Using this feature, you can build a test lab that runs entirely on a single computer. For example, if you need to test an application's compatibility with several different configurations of Windows 8, you can create a VM for each configuration. After your testing is complete you can easily remove the VMs or export them to your production network.

To run Hyper-V, you need the following:

- Windows 8 Enterprise (64-bit) version
- A 64-bit processor that incorporates second level address translation (SLAT) technology
- A minimum of 4 GB of memory (running more than one VM at a time requires more)

 ENABLE THE HYPER-V FEATURE

GET READY. To enable the Hyper-V feature, log in to the computer running Windows 8 Enterprise (64-bit) with Administrator privileges and perform the following steps:

1. Press the **Windows logo key + w**.
2. Type **Features**; from the *Results* list, click **Turn Windows features on and off**.
3. Click the **+** displayed next to the *Hyper-V* folder.

   This action expands the folder to show the components included (see Figure 2-1).

Figure 2-1

Enabling the Hyper-V feature on Windows 8 Enterprise

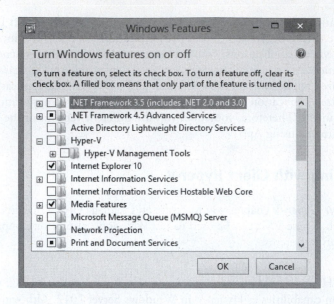

4. Select the check box next to Hyper-V and then click **OK**.

   Windows searches for the required files and then applies the changes to the computer.

5. Click **Close**.

6. Restart your computer to complete the installation.

   A restart starts the Windows hypervisor and the Virtual Machine Management service.

After installing Client Hyper-V, you see two new tiles after logging in with the administrative account

- **Hyper-V Manager** (see Figure 2-2): This is the management console for creating and managing your VMs s and setting up your test network.

- **Hyper-V Virtual Machine Connection:** This is used when working with a single VM that you have already created. It is very similar to the Remote Desktop Connection utility.

Figure 2-2

Reviewing the Hyper-V Manager console

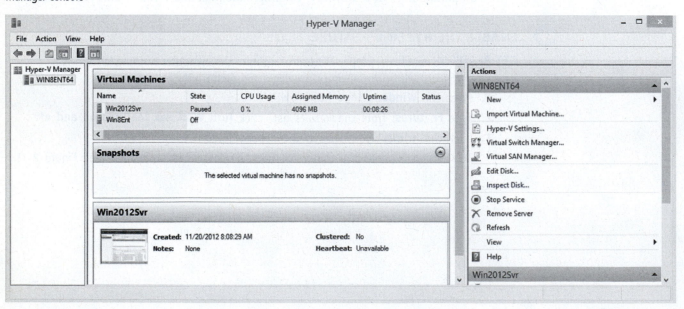

Within the Hyper-V Manager console, you can import VMs (*Action > Import Virtual Machine*) and create virtual hard disks (*Action > New > Virtual Machine*) to be used by VMs or by the host PC. You can also manage a VM's configuration by modifying the startup order of devices (for example, CD, IDE, network adapter, floppy), allocate memory, determine the number of virtual processors to use, and add hard drives/CD drives to an IDE/SCSI controller.

When you are testing an application and want to troubleshoot compatibility issues or test a new application update before rolling it out to production machines, you can use the Hyper-V snapshot feature (right-click the machine and choose *Snapshot*). By taking a snapshot, you can return to a known state on the VM (for example, the state before you installed the application).

To set up a test network that includes multiple systems, you need to configure a virtual switch using the Virtual Switch Manager. This enables your VMs to communicate with each other and access your physical network for Internet access.

Hyper-V includes three types of virtual switches:

- **External:** Creates a virtual switch that binds to the physical network adapter. This enables your VMs to access your physical network.
- **Internal:** Creates a virtual switch that is used only by the VMs that run on the physical computer and between the VMs and the physical computer.
- **Private:** Creates a VM that can only be used by the VMs running on the computer.

To create a virtual switch, under the *Actions* pane, click *Virtual Switch Manager*. From the *Virtual Switch Manager* box, select the type of switch to use and then click *Create Virtual Switch*. If you select the external switch type, you need to specify the physical network adapter (on the host) to connect the switch to.

Exploring Remote Desktop Services (RDS)

Remote Desktop Services (RDS) enable users to connect to virtual desktops and applications providing central management and control of operating systems and applications. This lesson takes a closer look at the components that are necessary to implement RDS.

Remote Desktop Services (called Terminal Services in previous releases of Windows) is a term that describes several features of the Windows server role that enables users to remotely connect to virtual desktops, session-based desktops, and RemoteApp programs over the **Remote Desktop Protocol (RDP)**. RDP is used on the server to render display output, which is then sent in the form of packets to the RDP client. On the client, RDP is used to send mouse and keyboard inputs to the server.

The Windows server running the RDS role includes the following services:

- *RD Virtualization Host:* Integrates with Hyper-V to enable users to connect to a VM on a server hosting Hyper-V.
- *RD Session Host:* Enables a server to host RemoteApp programs or session-based desktops.
- *RD Connection Broker:* Used for session load balancing; enables users to reconnect to a virtual desktop and RemoteApp programs, and provides access to virtual desktops in a virtual desktop collection.
- *RD Web Access:* Enables users to access RemoteApps and desktop connection via the *Start* menu or through a web browser.
- *RD Licensing:* Manages licenses needed to connect to the RD Session Host.
- *RD Gateway:* Enables users to connect to virtual desktops, RemoteApp programs, and session-based desktops from any device connected to the Internet.

An RDS-based Virtual Desktop Infrastructure (VDI) enables you to store, maintain, secure, and manage Windows desktops. When it is configured in combination with Hyper-V, you can assign a unique VM to each user or dynamically assign a machine from a pool of available VMs.

RemoteApp programs stored on a RD Session Host server and virtual desktops hosted on an RD Virtualization Host can be remotely accessed from a client desktop. **RemoteApp** programs, which look and feel like local applications even though they are accessed remotely, can be accessed via a web console, or can be launched from the users' Start menu or when they open a file associated with the application.

In Windows Server 2012 and Windows Server 2012 R2, RemoteApp publishing has been enhanced. To publish and manage RemoteApp programs, you will use the RDMS UI, as shown in Figure 2-3. The RemoteApp Programs will have a link to publish RemoteApp programs or you can publish directly from the Tasks drop-down menu. The Select RemoteApp Programs Wizard presents a listing of all default applications that are available for publishing. Any other applications have to be mapped manually by adding the executable file path for the desired application. When publishing RemoteApp programs in instances where multiple RD Session Host servers are deployed, each RD Session Host server in the collection must have the program installed.

Figure 2-3

Use the RDMS UI to manage
RemoteApps

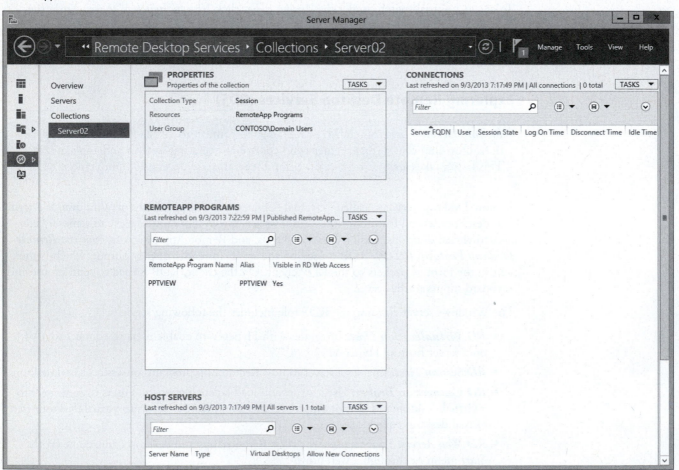

Once published, RemoteApp programs can be configured by editing the application properties. The properties settings allow you to enable or disable a RemoteApp for RD Web Access, create web folders, set command-line parameters, restrict access to users or groups and set file type associations. RemoteApp file type associations apply only to users who connect by using the RemoteApp and Desktop Connection feed. Users who connect by RD Web Access or RDP files will not be able to use file type associations. A user must have access to both the RemoteApp program and the collection it is published to in order to have access to the RemoteApp program. Updating user access at the collection level doesn't change access at the RemoteApp program level. By default, all users that can access the collection have access to the application.

Users can access a secure site, typically at https://*ServerFQDN*/RDWeb, and establish an SSL session between the client and the RD Web Access server. See Figure 2-4. After authenticated, the user sees a list of any applications or desktops that he or she has permission to use.

Figure 2-4

Accessing the RemoteApp
website

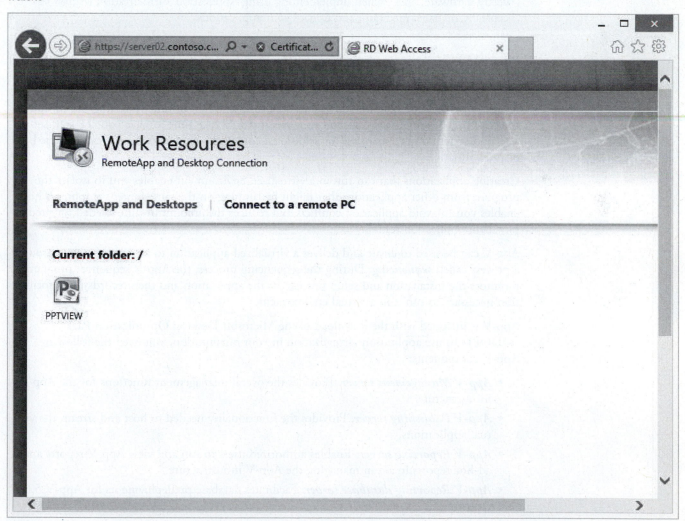

→ CONFIGURE REMOTEAPP

GET READY. To configure a RemoteApp application, perform the following steps:

1. Open Server Manager and click an RDS collection.
2. In the RemoteApp Programs section, click **Publish RemoteApp programs**.
3. On the Select RemoteApp programs page, click the application that you want to make available as a RemoteApp. If the application that you want is not listed, click the Add button to navigate to the executable used to start the program. Click **Next**.
4. On the Confirmation page, click **Publish**.
5. When the application is published, click **Close**.

Virtualizing Applications Using App-V

> Virtualizing applications enables you to test applications side-by-side, avoid purchasing costly hardware, and—when implementing using Application Virtualization (App-V)—centrally manage, maintain, and update your applications.

Prior to App-V, if you wanted to test an older version of an application against a newer release, you had to either create a dual boot system or use two separate computers. The applications could not co-exist on the same computer due to application conflicts. In the first scenario (a dual boot system), you would have to spend a lot of time restarting the computer to access each version. In the second scenario, it would take time to have your IT staff set up a second system, not to mention the additional cost of the hardware. App-V can address both of these situations.

Creating applications that can run in a virtualized environment enables you to isolate the program from other applications that might be running on the same target computer. This enables you to avoid application conflicts and reduces the amount of time needed for predeployment application testing.

App-V can be used to create and deliver a virtualized application to an App-V client through a process called *sequencing*. During the sequencing process, the App-V sequencer program monitors the installation and setup process for the application and then records the information necessary to run it in a virtual environment.

App-V is included with the download of the Microsoft Desktop Optimization Pack (MDOP). To use application virtualization in your organization, you need the following App-V components:

- *App-V Management server:* Provides the overall management functions for the App-V infrastructure.
- *App-V Publishing server:* Provides the functionality needed to host and stream the virtual applications.
- *App-V Reporting server:* Enables authorized users to run and view App-V reports and ad-hoc reports to aid in managing the App-V infrastructure.
- *App-V Reporting database server:* Facilitates database predeployments for App-V 5.0 reporting.

You can deploy App-V in a standalone configuration in which all the server components are installed on a single computer. This works well when you are testing App-V or in smaller organizations. You can also deploy App-V in a distributed environment in which the components are spread across multiple servers to support future scalability. Electronic software distribution solutions are an option as well.

App-V servers deliver virtual applications either by streaming them to App-V clients or by locally caching them. The applications are stored on the App-V server. When a computer with the App-V client installed requests an application from the server, users are presented with a list of the apps they are allowed to use. Policies controlled by the administrator determine who can and cannot use the virtual applications.

The following represent a few characteristics of running virtualized applications:

- No install or configurations requirements on the client machine.
- No changes to the user's computer after opening and closing the application (registry, files, application support files, and so on).
- The applications are isolated from other virtual and local programs running on the computer. This enables the user to run two versions of the same application simultaneously side-by-side if needed.
- The virtual applications are being managed and delivered from a central location, so updating and reconfiguring applications saves time and resources.

To sequence an application, you need the MDOP from Microsoft, which is available for MSDN and TechNet subscribers. After you have MDOP, you must install the App-V 5.0 sequencer on the Windows 8 computer that will be used to create the sequenced applications.

 INSTALL THE APP-V 5.0 SEQUENCER

GET READY. To install the App-V 5.0 sequencer, log in to the computer running Windows 8 Enterprise (64-bit) with Administrator privileges and then perform the following steps:

1. Insert the Microsoft Desktop Optimization Pack (MDOP) disc into your computer.
2. When the *MDOP* menu appears, click **Application Virtualization for Desktops**.
3. Under the *App-V 5.0* category, click **App-V 5.0 Sequencer**.
4. Click **Install**.
5. Review the *Software Licenses Terms* screen, select **I accept the license terms**, and then click **Next**.
6. On the *Customer Experience Improvement Program* screen, click **Install** to accept the default.
7. When the message *Setup completed successfully* appears, click **Close**.
8. Close the *MDOP* menu.

The App-V 5.0 sequencer program is ready for use. After you have installed the program, you are ready to sequence an application. Before starting the sequencing process, you need to obtain the application's installer file from the product's website. When creating sequenced packages, you should also set up a single VM that is used only for this purpose.

 SEQUENCE AN APPLICATION

GET READY. To sequence an application, log in to the computer running Windows 8 Enterprise (64-bit) with Administrator privileges and then perform the following steps:

1. From the Windows 8 *Start* menu, type **sequencer**. In the *Results* list, select **Microsoft Application Virtualization Sequencer**.
2. Click **Create a New Virtual Application Package**.
3. To accept the default setting *Create Package (default)*, click **Next**.
4. On *Prepare the computer for creating a virtual package*, make sure there are no issues listed that need to be resolved and then click **Next**.

Double-click any issues that appear to read how to resolve them and then click **Refresh** after completing the tasks.

5. To accept the default setting, *Standard Application (default)*, click **Next**.

6. On the *Select Installer* screen, click **Browse** to navigate to the folder in which the application to be sequenced is stored. Select the application and then click **Open**.

7. Click **Next** to continue.

8. On the *Package Name* screen, in the *Virtual Application Package Name* field, type the name for the application (for example, **MySequencedApp**).

9. For the *Primary Virtual Application Directory (required)* field, type **c:\program files\<appname>**.

   This is the location where the application would be installed by default. You would need to replace *<appname>* with the actual name of the application you are sequencing and then click **Next**.

10. Install the application to sequence.

    The sequencer program monitors the installation. After your application has completed installing, continue to the next step.

11. On the *You must complete the application installations before you can continue* screen, select **I am finished installing** and then click **Next**.

12. On the *Run each program to manage first use tasks* screen, click **Next**.

13. Review the installation report and then click **Next**.

14. On the *Create a basic package or customize further* screen, select **Customize**.

15. On the *Run each program briefly to optimize the package over slow or unreliable networks* screen, click **Next**.

16. On the *Restrict operating systems for this package* screen, select **Allow this package to run only on the following operating systems**. Select the **Windows 8 32-bit** and **Windows 8 64-bit** options. Click **Next** to continue.

17. Click **Create** to accept the default storage location for the virtualized application.

18. Click **Create**.

    The package is created and placed into a folder with the name you used in Step 8.

19. When the *Package completed* message appears, click **Close**.

20. Close the *Microsoft Application Virtualization Sequencer* window. You have completed the process for virtualizing an application.

You can use the Microsoft installer file you created (*MySequencedApp.msi*) to install the virtual application on a standalone computer, deploy it using Group Policy, or use it with SCCM 2012 to deploy the application to your end users. After the application has been virtualized, you can import it into the Application Management server and manage it via the Application Virtualization Management console. To manage the package, consider using groups to organize the virtual applications (Office Apps, Accounting Apps, and so on.). You can then import the virtual application into the group. After it is in place, you need to determine which group of users will be able to use the application and then assign them to the package.

■ Managing Desktop Application Compatibility Using The Application Compatibility Toolkit (ACT)

Testing an application's compatibility before installing it onto a new operating system is critical. The Application Compatibility Toolkit (ACT) enables you to collect the information you need to determine where to focus your attention.

The *Application Compatibility Toolkit (ACT)* 6.0, included with the Windows Assessment and Deployment Kit (ADK), is used to determine whether or not applications, devices, and computers will work with a new operating system and to gather inventory and assess your current environment in preparation for upgrades and migrations. It can help determine either applications, devices, and computers are compatible with Windows 7 and 8 obtain compatibility information from Microsoft and software vendors, identify compatibility issues, and help analyze and mitigate compatibility issues.

The following components are included with the tool kit:

- *Application Compatibility Manager (ACM):* This is used to create your data-collection package and analyze the collected inventory and compatibility data.
- *Inventory-collector package:* This package is deployed to computers in a test environment to gather inventory data to upload to the ACT database.
- *Runtime-analysis package:* This is a data-collection package that can be deployed to computers in a test environment to test compatibility with the new operating system.
- *ACT Log Processing Service (LPS):* This is a service used to process the ACT log files uploaded from computers where your data-collection packages have been installed. It adds information to the ACT database.
- *ACT LPS share:* This is a file share accessed by the ACT LPS to store the log files. The log files will be processed and added to the ACT database.
- *ACT database:* This is a Microsoft SQL Server database used to store the collected inventory and compatibility data.
- *Microsoft Compatibility Exchange:* This is a web service that broadcasts application-compatibility issues.

Inventorying Your Computers

When using the ACM, you will first collect inventory to identify your applications and devices by creating and deploying an inventory collection package. The package is installed on the computers to gather a list of applications and devices and to send the data back to the ACM.

To determine if your systems are compatible with the Windows 8 operating system, you first need to determine which computers you want to collect information from. If you have a large number of computers on your network and do not have enough resources to manage the information, consider collecting information from a representative subset. For example, if you have a standard build configuration for all laptops on your network and you control the installation of applications, you can inventory a subset of them to get the information you need to determine overall compatibility.

ACT can be installed on Window XP (SP3), Windows Vista (SP2), Windows 7, Windows 8, Windows Server 2008 R2/SP2, Windows Server 2012, and Windows Server 2012 R2. You can deploy inventory-collector packages on the same systems. ACT requires a database component and the .NET Framework 4. The database component can be (Microsoft SQL 2005/2008, Microsoft SQL 2005/2008 Express, Microsoft SQL 2008 R2, Microsoft SQL 2012).

ACT installations can be deployed in the configurations shown in Figure 2-5.

Figure 2-5

Deployment Options for ACT Installations

Distributed ACT Log Processing Service (LPS), ACT Log Processing Service share (LPS share), and ACT database

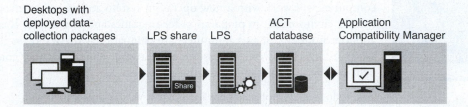

Distributed logging with rollup to a central LPS share

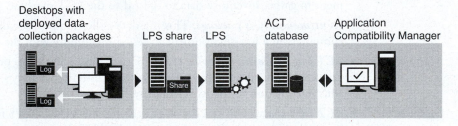

Distributed LPS and ACT database

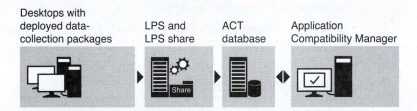

Consolidated server

To collect information on your computers, you need to create an inventory-collector package. These packages collect system information (memory capacity, processor speed, and processor architecture), device information (model and manufacturer), and software information (applications and system technologies).

To create an inventory collector package, you will need to visit Microsoft's website and search for Application Compatibility Toolkit for Windows 8. Download and install the toolkit on your Windows 8 client computer. You will also need to setup a database on your Windows 8 client device.

 CREATE AN INVENTORY COLLECTOR PACKAGE

GET READY. To create an inventory collector package, log on as an administrator to a computer running Windows 7 Professional and then perform the following steps:

1. Start the Application Compatibility Manager (ACM) and then click **Collect**. The *Collect* screen displays.

2. Click **File > New**.

3. Click **Inventory collection package**. The *Set up your inventory package* page displays.

4. Provide the *Name, Output Location*, and the *Label* for the inventory package (see Figure 2-6).

Figure 2-6

Creating an Inventory Package for Sales Desktops

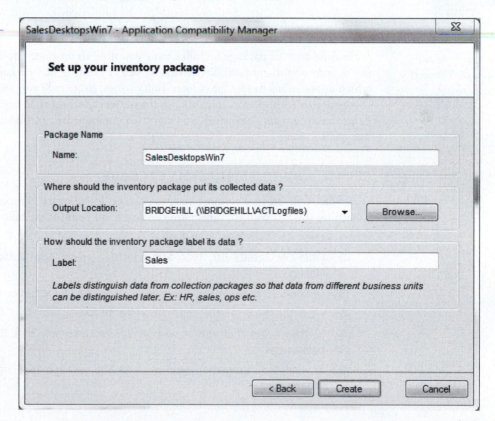

5. Click **Create**.

6. Browse to the location where you want to save the Windows Installer (.msi) file for the package, type a name for the .msi file and then click **Save**.

7. Click **Finish**.

Once your inventory-package has been created, you can choose the following deployment options:

- *Manual distribution*: Stores the package in a shared location on the network; users will need local administrative privileges to install. To deploy, you will need to send an e-mail with a link to the shared folder.
- *Logon script*: Uses the Windows Script Host to create a logon script. Users will need local administrative privileges to install the script.
- *Group Policy Software Installation*: All computers targeted for deployment via Group Policy will need to be part of an Active Directory forest.
- *Microsoft System Center 2012 Configuration Manager*: To deploy the package, you will need to target the package to the appropriate users/devices called a collection. You will also have the option to display the application in the Software Center and allow the user to install or hide the application from the Software center and install it whether or not the user is logged on.

Using Runtime Analysis Packages and Testing Application Compatibility

A runtime analysis package can be used to evaluate whether your existing applications are compatible with a new operating system that you are considering deploying to your organization. This package enables you to identify and address any problems prior to deploying the new operating system to your production environment.

A runtime analysis package includes tools you need to monitor applications for compatibility issues and submit compatibility feedback. Before creating this package, you need to decide which applications to test for compatibility issues, make sure you are working with the latest compatibility information from the Microsoft website, and then organize your applications. After these steps are completed, you can then deploy your runtime-analysis packages to your test environment.

TAKE NOTE*

To deploy the package to off-line computers, burn it to removable media or send it to the user via e-mail. Users can run the package and then return the log file via e-mail or by later connecting to the network and uploading the log file to a shared folder you create.

➔ CREATE A RUNTIME-ANALYSIS PACKAGE

GET READY. To create a runtime analysis package, log in to the computer running Windows 8 Enterprise (64-bit) with Administrator privileges and perform the following steps:

1. Press the **Windows logo key + q**.
2. From the *Results* list, type **acm** and then select **Application Compatibility Manager**.
3. In the left pane of the *Application Compatibility Manager* window, click **Collect**.
4. From the menu at the top, click **File > New**.
5. In the *Choose the type of package to create* screen, click **Runtime analysis package**.
6. Provide the information requested for the package (see Figure 2-7) and then click **Create**.

Figure 2-7

Providing runtime analysis package information

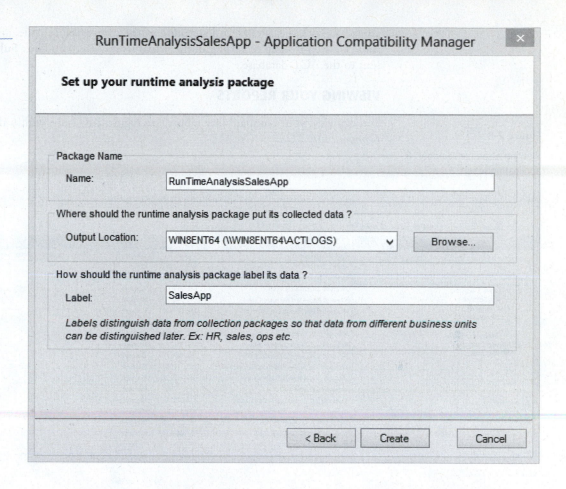

7. Navigate to a folder on your computer where you want to store the Windows installer (.msi) file for the package.

   The .msi file is used to install the runtime analysis package in your test environment.

8. In the *File name* field, type **RunTimeAnalysisSalesApps** and then click **Save**.

9. In the *Next steps for your runtime analysis collection package* screen, review the next steps and then click **Finish**.

You can now deploy the package by using Group Policy, using System Center Configuration Manager (SCCM), via a logon script, storing the file on a network share, or using removable media to distribute it to your Windows 8 test systems.

After it is installed, you can test for application compatibility by using the ***Compatibility Monitor*** tool, which is installed as part of the runtime analysis package. The Compatibility Monitor tool is used to submit compatibility information to the ACT database.

To use it on a Windows 8 target computer, type **monitor** from the Windows 8 *Start* menu. From the list of *Results*, select **Microsoft Compatibility Monitor**. The *Compatibility Monitor* tool appears.

To test for compatibility, click **Start Monitoring** and leave it running while you use the applications to test for compatibility with the new operating system. As compatibility information is detected, the information is sent at regular intervals to the ACT database. When you are done, just click **Stop Monitoring** to complete the data collection.

You can also use the Compatibility Monitor to submit your compatibility rating for the application(s) you are testing. When submitting feedback, you can type a title for the compatibility issue, include a description of the compatibility issue, and then attach a screen-shot or a step-by-step recording of the actual issue. After you click **Submit**, the information is sent to the ACT database.

VIEWING YOUR REPORTS

Figure 2-8

Viewing a sample Windows 8 application report

You can view your compatibility report (see Figure 2-8) from within the *Application Compatibility Manager* (ACM).

Analyze - Microsoft Application Compatibility Manager

File   Go   View   Actions   Filter   Tools   Window   Help

Send and Receive | Toggle Filter

Analyze

Open Reports

Quick Reports

- Windows 8 Reports
  - Applications
  - Computers
  - Devices
  - Internet Explorer Add-ons
  - General Feedback
- Internet Explorer
  - Web Sites

Customize this view...

Analyze

Collect

Windows 8 - Application Report

Application Name	Version	Company	My Assessment	Vendo	Community A	User Assess	Acti	Com	Vers
Intel Processor Graphics	9.17.10.2932	Intel			64 (0	64 (0	0	1	1
Inventory Collection package	6.0	Microsoft			64 (0	64 (0	0	1	1
Microsoft Compatibility Monitor	8.59.25584	Microsoft			64 (0	64 (0	0	1	1
Microsoft Mouse and Keyboard Center	2.1.177.0	Microsoft			64 (0	64 (0	0	1	1
Microsoft Office Professional Plus 2010	14.0.629.1000	Microsoft			64 (0	64 (0	0	1	1
Microsoft Silverlight	5.1.2125.0	Microsoft			64 (0	64 (0	0	1	1
Microsoft SkyDrive	17.0.26.314	Microsoft			64 (0	64 (0	0	1	1
Microsoft SQL Server 2008 (64-bit)		Microsoft			64 (0	64 (0	0	1	1
Microsoft SQL Server 2008 Native Client	10.0.1600.22	Microsoft			64 (0	64 (0	0	1	1
Microsoft SQL Server 2008 Setup Support Files	10.1.2731.0	Microsoft			64 (0	64 (0	0	1	1
Microsoft SQL Server 2008 Setup Support Files (En..	10.0.1600.22	Microsoft			64 (0	64 (0	0	1	1
Microsoft SQL Server 2012		Microsoft			64 (0	64 (0	0	1	1
Microsoft SQL Server 2012 Native Client	11.0.2100.60	Microsoft			64 (0	64 (0	0	1	1
Microsoft SQL Server 2012 Setup (English)	11.0.2100.60	Microsoft			64 (0	64 (0	0	1	1
Microsoft SQL Server 2012 Transact-SQL ScriptDom	11.0.2100.60	Microsoft			64 (0	64 (0	0	1	1
Microsoft Visio Professional 2013	15.0.4420.117	Microsoft			64 (0	64 (0	0	1	1

37 Items | Exchange Status: New Apps Available | Last Updated: Never

The following reports are available within the ACM:

- **Applications:** This report shows information from the applications from which you have collected information (application name, vendor, version, your organization's compatibility rating, compatibility information from the vendor, the number of computers with the application installed, and so on).

- **Computers:** This report provides information collected from your computers (computer name, domain, operating system, number of applications installed on the computer, and any applications or devices that have issues).

- **Devices:** This report provides information on the model and manufacturer of the device, the number of computers that have the device installed, and whether it works on 32- or 64-bit operating systems.

- **Internet Explorer Add-ons:** This report shows the add-ons that are currently installed for the Internet Explorer browser.

- **Internet Explorer\Websites:** This report provides information on the website URL, your organization's compatibility rating for the internet or internal website, and the number of issues/resolved issues for the website.

- **General Feedback:** This report provides general feedback comments submitted by the Compatibility Monitor. These can include step-by-step recordings with attached screen-shots and comments regarding a specific application that was tested.

In addition to these reports, you can also create custom views of each report to filter views. Although these reports are stored in the (.adq) form and can be viewed in ACM, you can also export them to an Excel spreadsheet for further analysis.

IDENTIFYING COMPATIBILITY ISSUES

The *Compatibility Administrator* tool is the component that allows you to resolve many application-compatibility issues for Microsoft and non-Microsoft applications before deploying Windows 7 or 8. It provides individual compatibility fixes (sometimes referred to as *shims*), compatibility modes, and AppHelp messages can be used to resolve specific compatibility issues. It can even help you create your own custom-compatibility fixes and search for installed fixes on local computers. Figure 2-9 shows the Compatibility Administrator.

Figure 2-9

Using Compatibility Administrators to view available compatibility fixes

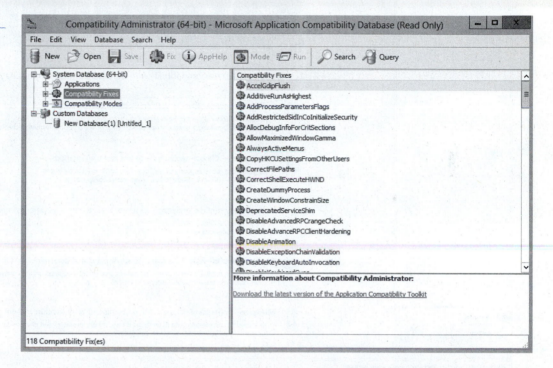

Shims are used to fool Windows when a specific application, without rewriting the code. For example, if an application was written before Windows 8 was created, the application checks to see what version of Windows is running, and the application is written to only work with versions of Windows that applications. The shim can tell Windows to report Windows 7 when the application runs. If an application is looking for a specific file or registry setting that is different from Windows 8 and an older version or Windows, the shim can redirect Windows to the location of the file or registry. You can then use a Group Policy Object (GPO) or System Center 2012 Configuration Manager to install the shim to your clients.

The Application Compatibility Manager (ACM), as shown in Figure 2-10, helps analyze and collection information on running applications, which can be used to test and mitigate your applications. Microsoft also provides an Application Compatibility Toolkit Connector that allows you to integrate ACT with System Center 2012 Configuration Manager.

Figure 2-10

Opening the Application
Compatibility Manager

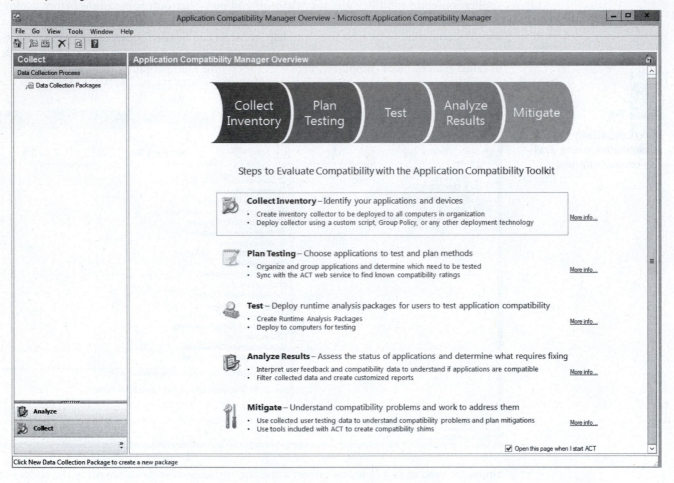

After you have a chance to look at the applications gathered, you will then choose which applications to test. You will then create and deploy a Runtime Analysis Package, which allows you to test an application. As the application runs, the Runtime Analysis Package will monitor the applications for compatibility issues and provide compatibility feedback. You will then use the collected user testing data to create compatibility shims.

The ***User Access Control (UAC)*** is a technology used with Windows Vista, 7 and 8 to enhance system security by detecting and preventing unauthorized changes to the system. Some applications might not run properly using a standard user credential if the application needs to access restricted files or registry location.

The ***Standard User Analyzer (SUA)*** tool allows you to test your application and monitor for Application Program Interface (API) calls to detect issues related to the User Account Control (UAC) feature in Windows. It will monitor and report many issues including issues related to files, registry keys, initialization (.ini) files, tokens, privileges, namespaces, and processes. After you identify potential problems, you can use the Standard User Analyzer to apply the recommended fixes by creating and deploying an .msi file.

■ Virtualizing the User Experience

↓ THE BOTTOM LINE The ability to roam between devices and still maintain the same user experience is important to today's users who work from laptops, desktops, and tablets.

CERTIFICATION READY
Installing and configuring of User Experience Virtualization (UE-V)
Objective 1.2

Roaming user profiles, redirecting folders, and accessing offline folder/files are features that enable you to access your resources while maintaining a consistent look and feel when moving between computers.

Microsoft's *User Experience Virtualization (UE-V)* provides a similar approach across multiple devices (desktop computers, laptops, and Virtual Desktop Infrastructure [VDI] sessions). With UE-V, a user can make changes to his personal settings (operating system or applications) and then log in to a Windows 7 or Windows 8 computer without having to reconfigure them each time. It does this by roaming the operating system settings.

Although the *V* infers virtualization, UE-V does not virtualize system and application settings, but instead monitors those changes using XML templates and then saves them to a file.

Prior to the release of UE-V, you had to create a separate profile for your physical desktop at work and another if you used a session-based desktop to connect when you were away from the office. Using UE-V, you can roam between both while still keeping your application/system settings. For example, using UE-V, you can switch between a laptop running Windows 7/8 and a tablet running Windows 8.

TAKE NOTE*

UE-V is part of the Microsoft Desktop Optimization Pack (MDOP) 2012.

UE-V works on Windows 7, Windows 8 clients and servers, and Remote Desktop Services with App-V.

UE-V templates enable you to control what is stored in your datacenter and differs from a roaming profile that uploads and downloads all the user's desktop/application setting information each time. UE-V includes the following application settings templates, which are monitored by the UE-V agent (installed on each computer). They are applied when you start the computer and are saved when you exit:

- Microsoft Office 2010 and 2013 applications
- Internet Explorer 8, 9, 10, and 11
- Windows accessories (Notepad, Calculator)

UE-V Windows settings templates (monitored by the UE-V agent) are applied when you log on, when you unlock the computer, and when you connect remotely to the computer using Remote Desktop Protocol (RDP):

- Desktop background.
- Ease of use (accessibility and input settings, magnifier, narrator, and the on-screen keyboard).
- Desktop settings

The UE-V components include the following:

- *UE-V Agent:* Watches the applications and operating system processes identified within the templates while you are connected. When you close the application or the operating system is shut down/locked, the information regarding the changes is saved to the settings storage location.
- Settings storage location: A network share folder or the home directory in Active Directory.
- Settings location template: XML files that define what the UE-V Agent captures from and applies to your computers.
- Settings package: This is where the application and operating system settings are stored. It is a collection of the information included in the templates.

- **UE-V Generator:** Used to create your own custom templates. It works by monitoring what the application reads and writes to the registry and what it does with supporting files. After this information is captured, you can use it to create a custom template and deploy it to your computers.

■ Deploying Desktop Applications By Using Windows Intune

 THE BOTTOM LINE
Windows Intune is Microsoft's integrated, cloud-based client management solution for managing computers, tablets, and phones.

CERTIFICATION READY
Deploy desktop applications by using Windows Intune
Objective 1.2

Because Windows Intune is a cloud service, you do not have to set up and maintain a server infrastructure to use it. All you need is a Windows Intune subscription.

Windows Intune is composed of two components:

- Web-based administrative console.
- Windows Intune client software: This is downloaded from the Windows Intune account administration website using the Windows Live ID and password associated with your Windows Intune account.

You can deploy the client software manually and have the target computer navigate to the shared folder and launch the installation, or deploy it using software programs such as Group Policy or SCCM.

After the software is installed on the client, it reports its status to the cloud service from anywhere there is an Internet connection. You can then manage the Intune clients using the web-based administrative console (see Figure 2-11) accessed via a browser that supports Microsoft Silverlight. **Microsoft Silverlight** is a free web-browser plug-in that is designed to provide rich Internet applications and media experiences on the Web.

Figure 2-11

Accessing the Windows Intune administrator dashboard

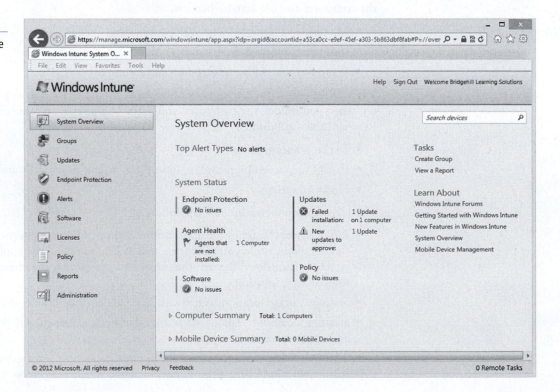

From the console, you can perform the following security and management tasks:

- Protect your computers from malware
- Deploy licensed software (Microsoft Office, third-party applications) to PCs
- Manage the deployment of software updates to Microsoft and most third-party software publishers from a central location
- Receive updates/alerts from the PCs on your network
- Provide remote assistance and perform remote tasks
- Track hardware and software inventory
- Manage software licenses
- Run software update reports, detected software reports, computer inventory reports, and license purchase and installation reports

TAKE NOTE*

Windows Intune can deploy only Windows installer (.msi) or executable (.exe) files that support silent installation.

When deploying software using Windows Intune, you have two installation types:

- A required install automatically installs or pushes the software to the managed computer and requires no user interaction.
- An available install publishes the software to the Windows company portal or on the mobile company portal so your users can choose whether they want to install the software.

The software you upload is stored in the Windows Intune cloud storage that your organization purchased. To deploy software, access the Software workspace (see Figure 2-12).

Figure 2-12

Reviewing the Windows Intune Software workspace

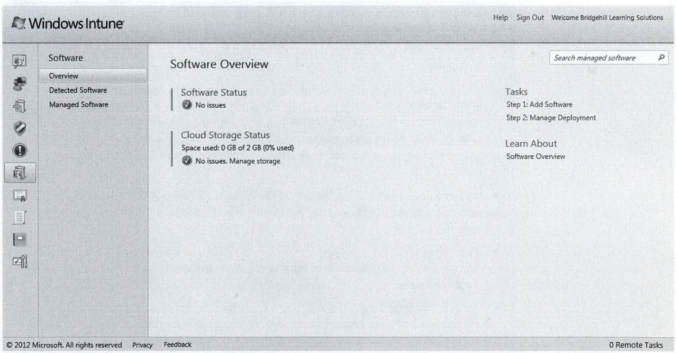

The following steps provide an overview of the process for publishing and updating software:

1. Prepare your software files. The .msi or .exe file must be placed in a single folder along with any supporting files on the administrator's computer.
2. Configure and upload the package. This requires you to type the path to the setup files, the name of the software publisher, the name of the software being deployed, a description,

the required architecture (32- or 64-bit), and which operating systems the package will be installed on.

You also set the detection rule (for example, look for a specific file, registry entry, or MSI product code) to see if the software is already installed when deploying an updated package. After configuration is completed, the file is compressed, encrypted, and uploaded to the Windows Azure storage platform. After it is uploaded, you see the application in the Managed Software workspace.

3. **Deploy the package.** Within the Managed Software workspace, click the package to deploy and select the group to deploy the software package to. The package is now ready for your users.

4. **Client download/installations.** If the client meets all the configuration requirements you set in Step 2, it downloads the package to a temporary folder and begins the silent installation. (The client is configured via a policy to check for new downloads every 8 hours.)

5. **Monitor the deployment status.** To view the progress of installations across your managed computers, you can use the administrative console.

For many applications, the manufacturer includes options to automatically check for updates directly from the client computer. If you want Windows Intune to manage this process, you have to disable the manufacturer's feature on each of the managed computers.

SKILL SUMMARY

IN THIS LESSON YOU LEARNED:

- If an application does not run in Windows 8, even under the application Compatibility Mode, you can try to run the application under a Hyper-V virtual machine, a RemoteApp, or App-V.

- Client Hyper-V, which runs on Windows 8 Enterprise (64-bit) systems, enables you to build a test lab that runs entirely on a single computer. Using Hyper-V and VMs, you can test an application's compatibility with several different configurations of Windows 8. These VMs can then be moved to production. Client Hyper-V enables you to avoid the costs of purchasing additional computers or setting up dual boot systems to test for application compatibility.

- RDS describes several of the features of the Windows Server role that enables users to remotely connect to virtual desktops, session-based desktops, and RemoteApp programs over RDP.

- Creating applications using App-V allow you to run in a virtualized environment, so that you can isolate the program from other applications that might be running on the same target computer.

- The purpose behind the ACT 6.0 and how it can be used to not only collect inventory information from your network computers but also to perform runtime analysis to test for application compatibility.

- The process for creating App-V programs through a process called sequencing. This process involves launching a traditional application and then using tools to monitor the changes the application executes on the local computer during the installation process.

- Microsoft's User Experience Virtualization (UE-V) allows you to have the same application configurations across multiple devices (desktop computers, laptops, and Virtual Desktop Infrastructure [VDI] sessions).

Knowledge Assessment

Multiple Choice

Select the correct answer for each of the following questions.

1. When using Client Hyper-V to set up a test lab, which of the following types of virtual switches would you set up to allow your VMs to access the network through the network adapter on the host machine?
   a. Layer 2 switch
   b. External
   c. Internal
   d. Private

2. After creating a runtime analysis package, which of the following tools can you use to deploy the package on your network? (Choose all that apply)
   a. Group Policy
   b. System Center Configuration Manager
   c. Store the file on a network share
   d. Use removable media to distribute it to your systems

3. Which of the following is not a benefit of running virtual applications?
   a. No install or configuration is needed on the client computer.
   b. No changes to the user's computer are made after opening/closing the application.
   c. Two versions of the application cannot be run on the same computer.
   d. Virtual applications can be managed from a central location.

4. Which of the following represent security and management tasks that can be handled with Windows Intune? (Choose all that apply)
   a. Track hardware and software inventory
   b. Provide remote assistance
   c. Protect computers from malware.
   d. Manage the deployment of software updates.

5. Which of the following reports in the ACM provides you with information on whether your application works on a 32- or 64-bit operating system?
   a. Internet Explorer web site report
   b. Device report
   c. Computer report
   d. Application report

6. Which of the following features provides users with a consistent desktop experience across multiple devices (desktops, laptops, VDI)?
   a. Active Directory Virtualization
   b. App-V
   c. User Experience Virtualization (UE-V)
   d. Roaming User Profiles

7. Which of the following features is *not* a component of UE-V?
   a. UE-V Agent
   b. Settings package
   c. UE-V Generator
   d. GPEditor

8. Which of the following statements is correct? (Choose all that apply)
   a. Client Hyper-V is available on Windows 8 Professional/Enterprise (32-bit) systems.
   b. Client Hyper-V allows you to connect to Hyper-V VMs running on other computers.
   c. Client Hyper-V allows you to create and run virtual machines simultaneously.
   d. Client Hyper-V consists of a Management console and a Virtual Machine Connection component.

9. You have an application that will not run under Windows 8 or Windows 8.1, even after running the Application Compatibility wizard. What can you do so that the users can run the application? (Choose all that apply)
   a. Use RemoteApp
   b. Use UE-V
   c. Use App-V
   d. Use Hyper-V

10. Which tool would you use to overcome problems with User Access Control?
    a. App-V
    b. Standard User Analyzer
    c. Application Compatibility Manager
    d. Hyper-V

Best Answer

Choose the letter that corresponds to the best answer. More than one answer choice may achieve the goal. Select the BEST answer.

1. Which of the following is necessary to setting up a small lab to test applications on Windows 8 using Client Hyper-V?
   a. Windows 8 Enterprise (32-bit) with Hyper-V enabled
   b. Windows 8 Professional (64-bit) with Hyper-V enabled
   c. Windows 8 Enterprise (64-bit) with Hyper-V enabled
   d. Windows 8 Professional (32-bit) with Hyper-V enabled

2. Which of the following types of packages can be created to monitor applications for compatibility prior to migrating to Windows 8?
   a. inventory-collector package
   b. runtime analysis package
   c. migration package
   d. monitor-analysis package

3. Which of the following tools are needed to sequence an existing application and then deploy it to Windows 8 computers?
   a. Application Compatibility Toolkit (ACT)
   b. Microsoft Desktop Optimization Package (MDOP)
   c. System Center 2012 Configuration Manager (SCCM)
   d. Internet Explorer Administration Kit (IEAK) 10

4. What program would you use to manage RemoteApps?
   a. Intune
   b. RemoteApp console
   c. Computer Management
   d. Server Manager

5. You have an application that you have been running for a couple of years. A new version of the software is introduced. Unfortunately, you need to have both versions available on the same computer. Which option should you use to make both versions available even when traveling while keeping the resources used to a minimum?
   a. Hyper-V
   b. RemoteApp
   c. App-V
   d. UE-V

Matching and Identification

1. Match the following terms with the related description or usage.

_____ **a)** Windows Intune
_____ **b)** sequencing
_____ **c)** Client Hyper-V
_____ **d)** Compatibility Monitor
_____ **e)** runtime analysis package
_____ **f)** virtual switch
_____ **g)** RD Session Host
_____ **h)** Application Compatibility Manager

1. A tool installed as part of the runtime analysis package.
2. Used to view general feedback comments submitted by the Compatibility Monitor.
3. Describes the process used to create an application that can run in a virtualized environment.
4. Enables your VMs to access your physical network.
5. A cloud-based management solution for managing your computers, tablets, and phones.
6. Enables a server to host RemoteApp programs or session-based desktops.
7. An .msi package used to monitor applications for compatibility issues and submit compatibility feedback.
8. A Microsoft replacement for Windows Virtual PC.

Build a List

1. Specify the correct order of the steps that must be completed to enable Hyper-V on a Windows 8 Enterprise computer.
   _____ Press the **Windows logo key + w.**
   _____ Click **Close**.
   _____ Select the *Hyper-V* check box and then click **OK**.
   _____ Restart your computer.
   _____ Type **Features**. From the *Results* list, select **Turn Windows features on and off**.

2. Specify the correct order of the steps that must be completed to create a runtime analysis package.
   _____ Press the **Windows logo key + q.**
   _____ Navigate to the folder where you want to store the Windows installer (.msi).
   _____ Click **Finish**.
   _____ From the menu at the top, click **File > New**.
   _____ On the *Choose the type of package to create* screen, click **Runtime analysis package**.
   _____ In the left pane of the *Application Compatibility Manager* window, click **Collect**.
   _____ Type **acm**. From the *Results* list, click **Application Compatibility Manager**.
   _____ Provide the information requested for the package and then click **Create**.
   _____ In the *File name* field, type a name for the package and then click **Save**.

3. Specify the correct order of the steps that must be completed to install the App-V 5.0 sequencer.
   _____ Click **Install**.
   _____ Insert the Microsoft Desktop Optimization Pack (MDOP) disc into your computer.

_____ When the *MDOP* menu appears, click **Application Virtualization for Desktops**.

_____ When the message *Setup completed successfully appears*, click **Close**.

_____ Review the *Software Licenses Terms* screen, select **I accept the license terms**, and then click **Next**.

_____ Under the *App-V 5.0* category, click **App-V 5.0 Sequencer**.

_____ On the *Customer Experience Improvement Program* screen, click **Install** to accept the default.

_____ Close the *MDOP* menu. The App-V 5.0 sequencer program is now ready for use.

Choose an Option

1. Which Windows feature turns your Windows 8 Enterprise computer into a host for VMs?

■ Business Case Scenarios

Scenario 2-1: Testing Line of Business Applications

The Director of IT was reviewing her budget and noticed that three application developers requested additional computers. The developers are currently running Windows 7 computers, but she has already determined they will support Windows 8 Enterprise 64-bit. After talking to one of them, she learned they were requesting additional computers to help test their old line of business application on a 32-bit and a 64-bit Windows 8 operating system computer. What other options would help her reduce costs while providing her application developers with the resources they need?

Scenario 2-2: Testing Compatibility

The Director of IT has contacted you to consult with her on the best way to test the compatibility of applications on computers across her network in preparation for an upgrade to Windows 8. She has approximately 200 systems, all located in the same physical location. Explain how you would advise her to approach the testing.

Scenario 2-3: Managing Application Updates

Over the last few years, Contoso administrators have been managing application updates manually. As they continue to evaluate Windows 8 and as the company continues to grow, they want to find a better solution. The Director of IT asked you to find something that enables administrators to manage the updates from anywhere they have Internet access. She also wants the solution to provide protection against malware, manage deployment of software, provide remote assistance, track applications licenses, perform an inventory of computers, and not require her IT team to have to build an entirely new infrastructure to support it. What should you advise her to consider?

3

LESSON

Supporting Windows Store and Cloud Apps

70-688 EXAM OBJECTIVE

Objective 1.3 – Support Windows Store and cloud apps. This objective may include but is not limited to: Install and manage software by using Office 365 and Windows Store apps; sideload apps by using Windows Intune; sideload apps into online and offline images; deeplink apps by using Windows Intune; integrate Microsoft accounts, including personalization settings and Trusted PC.

LESSON HEADING	EXAM OBJECTIVE
Introducing Public Cloud Services	
Working with Windows Store Applications	Install and manage software by using Office 365 and Windows Store apps
Sideloading Apps into Online and Offline Images	Sideload apps into online and offline images
Sideloading Apps by Using Windows Intune	Sideload apps by using Windows Intune
Deeplinking Apps by Using Windows Intune	Deeplink apps by using Windows Intune
Restricting Access to the Windows Store Using Group Policy	
Restricting Access Using Group Policy	
Assigning Access to a Single Windows Store App	
Using AppLocker to Manage Applications	
Using AppLocker	
Using Microsoft Office 365	
Understanding Microsoft Office 365 Features	
Managing Office 365	Install and manage software by using Office 365 and Windows Store apps
Installing and Managing Software by using Microsoft Office 365	Install and manage software by using Office 365 and Windows Store apps
Integrating Microsoft Accounts	Integrate Microsoft accounts, including personalization settings and Trusted PC

KEY TERMS

Active Directory accounts

AppLocker

Billing Administrator

Bring Your Own Device (BYOD) policies

Certificate Authority (CA)

Charms bar

Deployment Imaging Servicing and Management (DISM)

Domain-based accounts

File hash

Global Administrator

Line of Business (LOB) apps

Local user accounts

Microsoft Office 365

Microsoft user accounts

Password Administrator

Path

provisioned apps

public cloud

Publisher

rule collections

Service Administrator

sideloading

Trusted PC

User Management Administrator

Windows Apps

Windows Store

■ Introducing Public Cloud Services

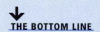

Public cloud services provide a way to access information from anywhere at any time. There are many definitions for the cloud. Microsoft defines a ***public cloud*** as a Web-based service that is hosted outside of your organization. This means the information technology infrastructure (hardware, servers, software, and so on) is located somewhere other than your office and is managed by a third party (such as hosted). If you use mobile banking—accessing web-based e-mail or storing your photos online in one of the many services provided—you are interacting with "the cloud."

Using public cloud services such as OneDrive (formerly known as SkyDrive) and Office 365 enable you to take advantage of hosted solutions. This means users have the ability to access their information from anywhere at any time across multiple devices. By using cloud-based services, your users can collaborate via calendars, e-mail, and through document sharing. From an administrative perspective, it means you gain access to services and programs without the additional overhead of maintenance and software upgrades.

■ Working With Windows Store Applications

Windows Apps are available from the Windows Store. These apps display across multiple devices and are designed to run in a single, full window display.

CERTIFICATION READY
Install and manage software by using Office 365 and Windows Store apps
Objective 1.3

Windows Apps, also called packaged apps, are available from the Windows Store. These applications differ from traditional applications in that they are designed to run in a single, full window display across multiple form factor devices (desktops, laptops, tablets). These devices can be touch-based or use a standard mouse and keyboard. The ***Windows Store*** (see Figure 3-1) provides a central location for you to purchase and download Windows apps that run on Windows 8 and later operating systems. The applications made available through the store must be certified for compatibility and content by Microsoft. When the user installs a Windows App, it shows up as a tile on the Windows 8.1 start page that can be clicked or touched to start the program.

Figure 3-1

Accessing the Windows Store

The Windows Store app comes preinstalled on Windows 8.1 devices. That makes it very easy for your users to connect and access the apps in the Store. When strategizing about how to manage Windows Apps in your organization, you need to consider whether you want to restrict users' access to the Store as a whole or allow access but control which apps the users are allowed to download and install.

Many organizations have policies in place that are designed to standardize the apps being used on company-supplied computers and do not want their users installing any applications they find, even if they are certified to work with Windows 8.1. ***Bring Your Own Device (BYOD) policies*** may also be in place that require you to control access to the Store. A BYOD policy defines the standards, restrictions and procedures for end users who have authorized access to company data from their personal device (tablet, laptop, smartphone). The policy also includes hardware and related software not approved, owned, or supplied by the company. In either case, as the administrator you will need to make sure your strategy for accessing the Windows Store aligns with your company's policies.

In addition to determining your strategy for controlling access to Windows Apps and the Windows Store, you will also need to consider the deployment of ***Line of Business (LOB) apps***. LOB apps include apps that are critical to running the business of the company as well as apps that are unique to the main business of the company. If you want to use the new Windows Apps format for your LOB apps, you can deploy them via the Windows Store or by a process called sideloading. If you choose to deploy your LOB apps via the Windows Store, they must go through a certification process with Microsoft to ensure they are compatible with Windows 8.1 and meet criteria for apps being deployed from the Store. The apps will also be available to the public, which may not be what you want. To bypass the Store requirements and make the apps available to your internal users only, consider sideloading them as part of your overall design strategy.

Sideloading Apps Into Online and Offline Images

Sideloading Windows Apps provides you with a way to enjoy the look/feel of Windows Apps without having to make them available using the Windows Store.

If you have a Windows App that was created in-house and needs to be leveraged across your organization, you have two options:

- You can make it available from the Windows Store, which means the App has to adhere to certification policies and the processes used by all Apps in the Store. This is designed to ensure the App is compatible and meets the criteria of Apps that are allowed to be deployed via the Windows Store.

- If you choose not to take that approach because you don't want the App available to the public but still want to take advantage of the portability and design of Windows Apps, you can use a process called sideloading. **Sideloading** is installing a Windows App without going through the Store by using a tool such as DISM, Windows PowerShell, System Center Configuration Manager (SCCM), or Windows Intune.

To use sideloading, you need to make sure the following are in place with your computers:

- A Windows 8.1 Enterprise/Professional computer joined to an Active Directory domain.
- Group Policy must be set to *Allow all trusted apps to install*
- The App must be signed by a **Certificate Authority (CA)** that is trusted by the targeted PCs on the network. A CA issues digital certificates that certify a person, organization, server or computer is who it claims to be.
- A sideloading product activation key if the Windows 8.1 Enterprise/Windows 8.1 Professional computer is not joined to a domain.

> **TAKE NOTE**
> You can sideload Windows Apps only on Windows Server 2012, Windows Server 2012 R2, Windows 8/8.1 Enterprise, and Windows 8/8.1 Professional devices that are joined to a domain.

The process for sideloading a Windows App is as follows:

1. Create a Windows Store app using Microsoft Visual Studio Express 2012 for Windows 8 or another similar tool. In order to do this, you will need to have a developer's license.

2. Sign the app with a certificate that is chained to a trusted root certificate.

3. Confirm the computers that will be Sideloaded are running Windows 8.1 Enterprise, they are joined to the domain and the *Allow all trusted apps to install* Group Policy setting is enabled. If you need to sideload apps on Windows 8.1 Enterprise/Professional that are not joined to a domain, you will need to install a sideloading product activation key. The key can be obtained from Microsoft's Volume Licensing Service Center (VLSC).

4. Sideload the app using the `add-appxpackage "name of app"` command if you want to make it available for the current user or use the **Deployment Imaging Servicing and Management (DISM)** tool if you want to make it available for multiple users. DISM is a command-line tool used to service an online or offline Windows image. When Windows Apps are installed via a Windows image, they are called **provisioned apps**.

You can set Group Policy for a single Windows 8.1 computer by opening the Local Group Policy Editor and enabling the *Allow all trusted apps to install* setting, which is located in the following location:

Computer Configuration\Administrative Templates\Windows Components\App Package Deployment

If you want to apply the policy to multiple computers, use the Group Policy Management console (GPMC). The *Allow all trusted apps to install* group policy setting is located in the following location:

Computer Configuration\Policies\Administrative Templates\Windows Components\App Package Deployment

It should be noted that the policy created using the Group Policy Management console can also be applied to a single computer. Local Group Policy is most commonly used in work-group settings.

If you receive an activation key from the VLSC, you can add it by using the following commands, from a command prompt window (cmd), while logged on as a local administrator. You will need to run this command from an elevated command prompt.

To add the key:

```
Slmgr /ipk <sideloading product key>
```

To activate the key:

```
Slmgr /ato ec67814b-30e6-4a50-bf7b-d55daf729d1e
```

After the computer is prepared, you can install the package on a per-user basis with the following Windows PowerShell command:

```
Add-appxpackage -Path c:\<directory>\<Winappv1.appx>
```

To update the package at a later date, you can manually update the Windows App with the following command:

```
Add-appxpackage -Path \\<servername>\<share>\<Winappv2.appx>
```

 **MORE INFORMATION**

For more information on how to deploy images with Windows Apps, visit TechNet.

Sideloading Apps by Using Windows Intune

Sideloading is a process for installing Windows Store applications without using the Windows Store. If you have access to the app installation files, you can sideload with Windows Intune. However, the application can only be deployed after the operating system is deployed. When you sideload an application, you can deploy an app to all Windows accounts on a device, or to a specific Windows account on a device.

You can use Windows Intune only or integrate Windows Intune with System Center 2012 R2 Configuration Manager. By manage using System Center 2012 Configuration Manager, you have to install the Windows Intune connector. Before you can deploy or sideload your application to Windows Intune-managed devices, you need to upload the application into Windows Intune.

 SIDELOAD WINDOWS STORE APPS TO WINDOWS INTUNE

GET READY. To upload Windows Store Apps to Windows Intune for Windows 8.1, perform the following steps:

1. Log into the Intune website, click **Admin Console**, and then click the **Software** workspace.
2. Under *Tasks* (see Figure 3-2), click **Step 1: Add Software**. If you are prompted to confirm that you want to run this Windows Intune Software Publisher, click **Run**. If you are asked to sign in, log in with an administrator account for Intune.

Figure 3-2

Managing software with
Windows Intune

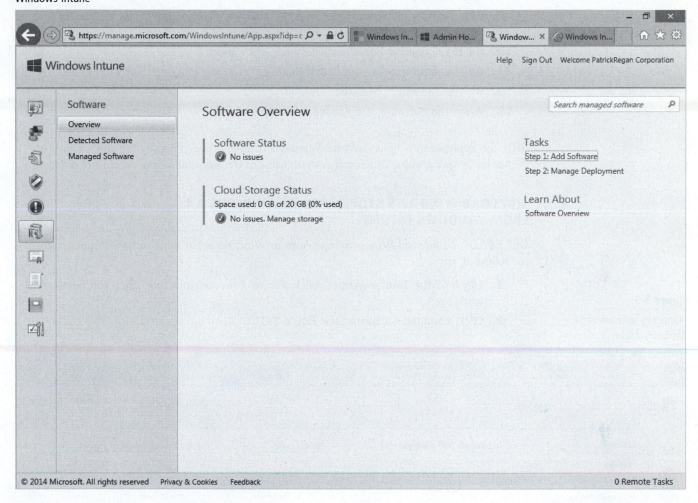

3. In the *Add Software Wizard*, on the *Before you begin* page, click **Next**.

4. On the *Software setup* page, for the *Select the software installer file type* option, select the Windows app package software installer type. Then in the *Specify the location of the software setup files* text box, specify the local or Universal Naming Convention (UNC) path to the application and then click **Next**.

5. On the *Software description* page, in the *Publisher*, *Name* and *Description* text boxes, specify the publisher, user-friendly name, and description of the application.

6. In the *URL for software information* text box, you can specify an URL where more information about the application can be found. Lastly, you can select the category of the software and upload a picture of the software. Click **Next**.

7. On the *Requirements* page, for the *Architecture is* option, specify the architecture (32-bit and/or 64-bit). For the *Operating System* option, select the appropriate operating system. (The default is *Any* for both options.) Click **Next**.

8. On the *Detection Rules* page, specify the rules to detect whether the software is already installed by selecting **Detect whether the software is installed by using the following rules (recommended)**. Click the **Add Rule** option and then select one or more of the following options:

File exists
MSI product code exists
Registry key exists

9. Based on the option selected, specify the file, MSI product code, or the registry key in the appropriate text boxes. Click **Next**.

10. On the *Command line arguments* page, click **Next**.

11. On the *Return codes* page, click **Next**.

12. On the *Summary* page, click **Upload**.

13. When the software is uploaded, click **Close**.

After the application is uploaded into Windows Intune, you can deploy the application to Windows Intune groups, which can contain users or devices that Windows Intune manages.

 SIDELOAD WINDOWS STORE APPS IN WINDOWS 8.1 FROM WINDOWS INTUNE

GET READY. To sideload Windows Store Apps to Windows 8.1 from Windows Intune, perform the following steps:

1. Log into the Intune website, click **Admin Console**, and then click the **Software** workspace.

Figure 3-3

Managing software with Windows Intune

2. Click **Managed Software** (see Figure 3-3).

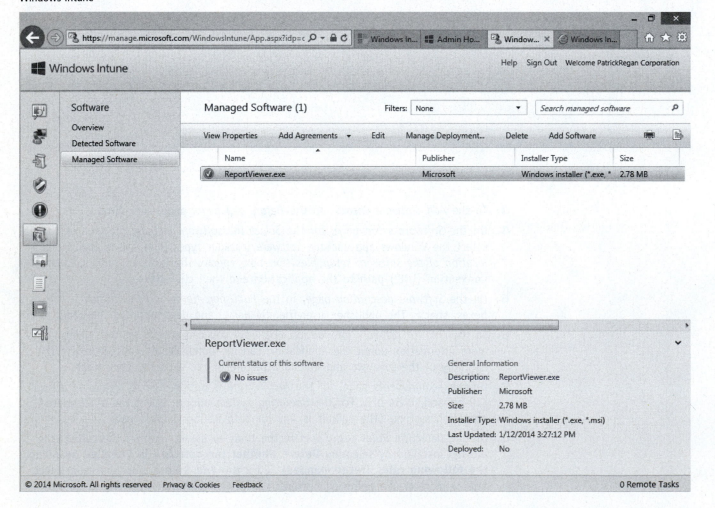

3. Click **Managed Deployment.**

4. In the *Deploy Software Wizard*, on the *Select Groups* page, click the group that you want to deploy to and then click **Add.** Click **Next.**

5. On the *Deployment Action* page, under *Approval*, select **Required Install** from the pull-down menu.

6. Click **Finish.**

Deeplinking Apps by Using Windows Intune

With *deeplinking*, you can identify an application in the Windows store that you want to deploy to Window's 8.1, and a link will be provided to the user that will take them directly to the app in the Windows store. By deeplinking, the user will not have to search for the specific app and potentially load the wrong app.

CERTIFICATION READY
Deeplink apps by using
Windows Intune
Objective 1.3

To deeplink an application, you will need to know the URL of the application. You will run the Add Software Wizard to specify the URL that the users can install the application from. You will then use the Manage Software task to deploy the application to the users.

 DEEPLINK A WINDOWS STORE APP IN WINDOWS 8.1 FROM WINDOWS INTUNE

GET READY. To deeplink a Windows Store App using Windows Intune, perform the following steps:

1. Log into the Intune website, click **Admin Console**, and then click the **Software** workspace.

2. Under *Tasks*, click **Step 1: Add Software**. If you are prompted to confirm that you want to run this Windows Intune Software Publisher, click **Run.** If you are prompted to sign in, log in with an administrator account for Intune.

3. In the *Add Software Wizard*, on the *Before you begin* page, click **Next.**

4. For the *Select how this software is made available to devices* option, select **External link.** In the *Specify the URL* text box, type the URL of the application and then click **Next.**

5. On the *Software description* page, in the *Publisher*, *Name* and *Description* text boxes, specify the publisher, user-friendly name, and description of the application.

6. On the *Summary* page, click **Upload.**

7. When the software is uploaded, click **Close.**

■ Restricting Access to the Windows Store Using Group Policy

THE BOTTOM LINE

Providing users with access to the Windows Store can create problems when you try to standardize applications across your organization. Group Policy can be used to restrict access and maintain your internal policies regarding application usage.

The Windows Store application comes preinstalled on Windows 8.1 devices. That makes it very easy for a user to connect, download and install Windows Apps. Although the Windows Store can provide a wide variety of Apps and tools to enhance Windows 8.1, you might decide to restrict access to it for your users. This restriction might be necessary if you want to make sure your users are working only with authorized applications within your organization. There are two ways to prevent users from installing and using Apps from the Windows Store:

- Use Group Policies
- Configure AppLocker

In this section, we'll take a look at Group Policy.

Restricting Access Using Group Policy

To deny access, you can use the Local Group Policy Editor or the Group Policy Management Console to create a policy that restricts access to the Windows Store for users and computers on your network.

To deny access, you need to set up a policy for a single computer/user or for multiple computers and users. The tool you used depends upon where you want to use the policy. For example, if you want to configure the policy and test it, you can use the Local Group Policy Editor on a Windows 8.1 client machine. If you want to deploy the policy settings across your domain, you need to use the Group Policy Management Console. In either case, the settings are located under the Administrative Templates\Windows Components\Store under the Computer Configuration and User Configuration nodes.

TAKE NOTE* If you create the policy using the Local Group Policy Editor, you can export and import it into a GPO at the domain level. It does not have to be re-created.

When configuring the policy using the Local Group Policy Editor for a user (User Configuration\Administrative Templates\Windows Components\Store), you have one option to set within the policy:

- Turn off the Store application:
  - **Not Configured (default):** If you select this option, access to the Store is allowed.
  - **Enabled:** If you select this option, access to the Store is denied.
  - **Disabled:** If you select this option, access to the Store application is allowed.

If you set the policy for a computer (Computer Configuration\Administrative Templates\Windows Component\Store) you have the following options available:

- Turn off Automatic Download of updates:
  - **Not Configured (default):** Download of updates is allowed.
  - **Enabled:** Automatic downloads are turned off.
  - **Disabled:** Automatic downloads of updates are allowed.
- Allow Store to install apps on Windows To Go workspaces:
  - **Not Configured (default):** Access to the Store is not allowed.
  - **Enabled:** Access to the Store is allowed on the Windows To Go Workspace. Use this option only when the device is used with a single PC.
  - **Disabled:** Access to the Store is denied.
- Turn off the Store application:
  - **Not Configured (default):** If you select this option, access to the Store is allowed.
  - **Enabled:** If you select this option, access to the Store is denied.
  - **Disabled:** If you select this option, access to the Store application is allowed.

→ RESTRICT ACCESS TO THE WINDOWS STORE USING A LOCAL GROUP POLICY

GET READY. Log into a Windows 8.1 computer with administrative credentials. In this activity, you will review the policy settings that control the Windows Store access for both computers and users by performing the following steps:

1. Press the **Windows logo key + r.**

2. In the *Run* box, type **gpedit.msc.** The *Local Group Policy Editor* displays.

3. Expand **Computer Configuration . Administrative Templates . Windows Components** and click the **Store.**

4. Double-click the **Turn off the Store application** setting; the *Turn off the Store application* dialog displays. Click **Enabled.**

5. Attempt to access the Windows Store by clicking on the Store tile located on the Windows 8.1 startup screen. The message *Windows Store isn't available on this PC* displays.

6. Return to the group policy setting you enabled in Step 4 and click **Not Configured** to regain access to the Windows Store.

When working with Group Policy settings, you should be aware of the order in which they are applied to your Windows 8.1 client devices. Having a good understanding of this order will ensure you design them in a way that works for your specific environment. They are processed in the following order:

1. Local Group Policy object.

2. Group Policies linked to the Site container.

3. Group Policies linked to the Domain container.

4. Group Policies linked to the Organizational Unit that is highest in the OU hierarchy are processed first, followed by GPOs linked to the child OU, and so on. If there are multiple GPOs linked to the same OU, they will be processed in the order specified by the administrator.

A shortcut to help you remember the order of precedence is LSDO. This stands for **L**ocal, **S**ite, **D**omain and **O**rganizational Unit.

In the previous example, you can see that local Group Policy settings are processed first. Group Policy settings linked to the OU that contains the user/computer is processed last, which overwrites the earlier GPOs. In situations where you create a GPO and set it to Enforced (No Override) with respect to the site, domain or OU, its setting will not be overwritten by any GPOs that follow it in the order of precedence. If you have two GPOs that are both set to Enforced (No Override), the one that is highest in the Active Directory hierarchy takes precedence.

Assigning Access to a Single Windows Store App

In some situations, you might have a computer that is in a public area (such as a library or kiosk) that needs only to run a single Windows app. In these situations, you can configure Windows 8.1 PC settings to restrict access to a single application.

When you assign access to a single Windows Store App, you are restricting the application to a user account. When the user signs in to the computer, only that user can access the assigned app.

RESTRICT A USER ACCOUNT TO RUN A SINGLE WINDOWS STORE APP

GET READY. To restrict a user account to run a single Windows Store app, perform the following steps:

1. From the *Start* screen, bring up the Charms menu and then click **Settings**.
2. Click **Change PC settings**.
3. Click **Accounts** and then click **Other accounts**.
4. In the right pane, click **Set up an account for assigned access**.
5. Click **Choose an account** and then select the account that you want to restrict.
6. Click **Choose an app** and then select the installed app to which you want to restrict the account.
7. Sign out from the computer to make the changes effective.

To sign in as another user when you are signed in as the restricted user, click the Windows key five times rapidly. Once you are signed in as a non-restricted user, you can disable the setting by configuring the account to *Don't use assigned access.*

■ Using Applocker to Manage Applications

THE BOTTOM LINE

Removing users from the administrative role on computers can reduce the number of applications they can install, but it does not prevent them from loading apps that do not require administrative privilege to run. Using AppLocker, you can fine-tune what programs your users are allowed to run by establishing rules.

AppLocker is a feature found in Windows Server 2012, Windows Server 2012 R2, Windows 7, and Windows 8/8.1 that can be used to control how users access and use programs and files and extends the functionality originally provided by the Software Restriction policy found in earlier versions of Windows operating systems. On Windows 8/8.1, you can find AppLocker in the Local Group Policy Editor.

Using AppLocker

AppLocker uses rules and file properties to determine the programs and files that are allowed to run on the computer.

You can access AppLocker using the Local Group Policy editor (gpedit.msc) by performing the steps in the following exercise.

 ACCESS APPLOCKER

GET READY. To access AppLocker using the Local Group Policy editor (gpedit.msc), perform the following steps:

1. Press the **Windows logo key + r.**
2. In the *Run* box, type **gpedit.msc** and then click **OK.** The *Local Group Policy Editor* displays.
3. Click **Computer Configuration > Windows Settings > Security Settings > Application Control Policies > AppLocker.**

As shown in Figure 3-4, AppLocker includes four *rule collections:*

- Executable Rules
- Windows Installer Rules
- Script Rules
- Packaged app Rules

Figure 3-4

The AppLocker rule collections

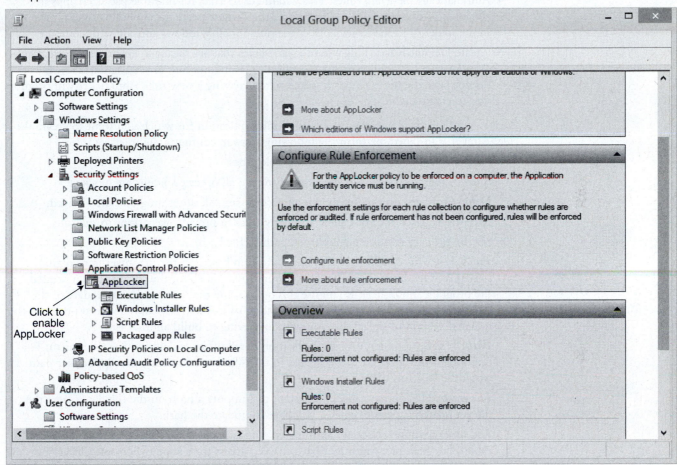

These rule collections allow you to differentiate the rules for different types of applications. AppLocker uses rules and a file's properties to determine whether applications are allowed to run.

A traditional app consists of several components (exe, scripts, and so on). These components may not share the same publisher, product, or product version attribute. In order to manage the traditional app, AppLocker needs to control them using different rule collections. On the other hand, a Windows app (packaged app) shares the same attributes; therefore, you can create a single rule to control the entire application.

Rule collections include:

- Executable files (.exe, .com)
- Scripts (.ps2, .bat, .js, .cmd, vbs)
- Windows Installer files (.msi, .mst, .msp)
- Appx (Packaged apps and Packaged app installers) (.appx) – This includes Windows Apps and side-loaded LOB apps.

By default, there are no rules in any of the rule collections; therefore, AppLocker will allow every file covered in each collection to run.

When creating rules with AppLocker, you have the following options:

- Create New Rule: This wizard walks you through the process of creating one AppLocker rule at a time—setting permissions, publishers, exceptions, and providing a name for the rule.

- Automatically Generate Rules: This wizard creates rules for multiple packaged apps in a single step. You can select a folder and let the Wizard create the applicable rules for the files in the folder or for packaged apps create rules for all Windows apps on your computer.

- Create Default Rules: This wizard creates rules that are meant to ensure that some key Windows paths are allowed for execution (c:\Windows files or c:\Program files). If you do not have the default rules in place, when creating a new rule, AppLocker will prompt you to create them.

Prior to configuring a rule, you must install the application for which you want to create the rule. After it is installed, perform the following steps to configure the rule:

1. Set permissions. AppLocker uses three rule types:

   Allow: Programs on the list are allowed to run; all other programs are blocked.

   Deny: Programs on the list are not allowed to run; all other programs are allowed.

   Exceptions: Used for both allow and deny rules to provide exceptions to the rule.

2. Set the primary condition (publisher, path or file hash):

   Publisher: This option identifies an application based off the manufacturer's digital signature. The digital signature contains information about the company that created the program (publisher). If you use this option, the rule can survive an update of the application as well as a change in the location of its files. This allows you to push out the updated version of the application without having to build another rule.

   Path: This option identifies an application based off its location in the file system. For example, if the application is installed in the Windows directory, the AppLocker path would be %WINDIR%.

   File hash: This option causes the system to compute a hash on the file. Each time the file is updated (upgrade, patch), you have to update the hash.

3. Add an exception (optional). In this step, you can add an exception to the rule (if applicable). For example, you might have enabled access for a suite (Microsoft Office) but you do not want selected users to be able to use Microsoft Access because you have a limited number of licenses.

4. Type a name for the rule. In this step, you give the rule a name and add an optional description.

TAKE NOTE[*] Rules created for a packaged app can use only the Publisher condition. Windows does not support unsigned packaged apps or installers.

 CREATE AND TEST AN APPLOCKER RULE

GET READY. To create and test an AppLocker rule that blocks the use of the Remote Desktop Connection client (mstsc.exe), log into a Windows 8.1 computer as an administrator and then perform the following steps:

1. Press the **Windows logo key + r** and in the *Run* box, type **services.msc** and then click **OK**. The *Services console* displays.

2. Right-click the **Application Identity** service and then choose **Start.** Close the *Services console* after confirming the service is running.

3. Press the **Windows logo key + r** and in the *Run* box, type **gpedit.msc** and then click **OK.** The *Local Group Policy Editor* displays.

4. Click the **Windows Settings > Security Settings > Application Control Policies > AppLocker.**

5. Right-click **Executable Rules** and choose **Create New Rule.**

6. Read the *Before you Begin* screen and then click **Next.**

7. Select **Deny** and then click **Next.**

8. Click **Select** and in the *Enter the object name to select* box, type **Users** and then click **OK.**

9. Click **Next** to continue.

10. Select **Publisher** and then click **Next.**

11. Click **Browse** and then navigate to the *C:\Windows\System32 directory.* Click the **mstsc.exe** file and then click **Open.**

12. Drag the slider to **File name** (see Figure 3-5) and then click **Next.**

    This setting ensures the rule will block all instances of the Remote Desktop Connection client (mstsc.exe) regardless of the version.

Figure 3-5

Viewing the Executable Rules/
Publisher Information for the
AppLocker rule

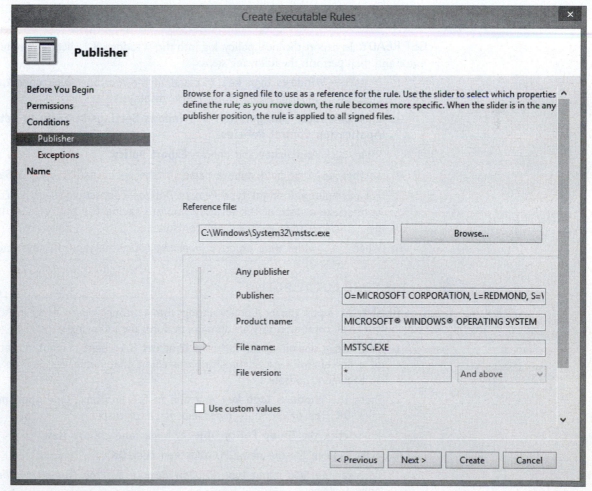

13. Click **Next**. You do not set an exception to this rule.

14. Type a name for the rule and a description (optional). For example, you might type *Disallow Remote Desktop Connection client on Company Systems*.

15. Click **Create**.

16. When prompted to create the default rules, click **Yes**. This ensures important rules are allowed to run.

17. Close the *Local Group Policy Editor*.

18. To force Group Policy to update, press the **Windows logo key + r** and in the *Run* box, type **Gpupdate/force** and then click **OK**.

19. Log on with any nonadministrative account and test the policy

20. Press the **Windows logo key + r** and in the *Run* box, type **mstsc.exe** and then click **OK**. The user will see the *Your system administrator has blocked this program* message.

When you create a policy using the Local Group policy editor, you are applying the policy to the local computer and the users who log into it. If you decide later that you want to use the same policy but apply it to multiple computers across your Active Directory domain, you can simply export the policy and then import it into a Group Policy Object linked to a container in the Active Directory hierarchy (site, domain, or organizational unit). This eliminates the need to recreate the policy settings.

 EXPORT THE LOCAL POLICY

GET READY. To export the local policy, log into the Windows 8.1 client computer as an administrator and then perform the following steps:

1. Press the **Windows logo key + r** and in the *Run* box, type **gpedit.msc** and then click **OK**. The *Local Group Policy Editor* displays.

2. Click **Computer Configuration > Windows Settings > Security Settings > Application Control Policies**.

3. Right-click **AppLocker** and choose **Export Policy**.

4. In the *File name* field, type a name for the policy and then click **Save**.

   For example, you might type *Remote Desktop Connection client on Company Systems*. Make a note of the location you are saving the policy to. This location must be accessible from your domain controller.

5. When the *4 rules were exported from the policy* message displays, click **OK**.

 IMPORT THE LOCAL POLICY

GET READY. To import the local policy settings into a Group Policy Object in Active Directory and apply it to all computers in your domain, perform the following steps:

1. Log into a domain controller or a Windows 8.1 client computer that is a member of a domain with an administrative account that has access to the Group Policy Management console.

2. Press the **Windows logo key + r** and in the *Run* box, type **gpmc.msc** and then click **OK**. The *Group Policy Management Editor* displays.

3. Right-click the **Group Policy Objects** folder and choose **New**.

4. Type a name for the new GPO and then click **OK**.

   For example, you might type *Disallow Remote Desktop Connection client on Company Systems*.

5. Right-click the GPO and choose **Edit**.

6. Click **Computer Configuration** > **Policies** > **Windows Settings** > **Security Settings** > **Application Control Policies**.

7. Right-click **AppLocker** and choose **Import Policy**.

8. Browse to the local policy file you exported earlier, select the policy file, and then click **Open**.

9. When prompted to import the policy now, click **Yes**.

10. When the *4 rules were imported from the policy* message displays, click **OK**.

11. Close the *Group Policy Management Editor*.

12. In the *Group Policy Management* console, right-click the domain name (**contoso**) and choose **Link an Existing GPO**.

13. In the *Group Policy objects* section, click **Disallow Remote Desktop Connection client on Company Systems** and then click **OK**.

   Now, no computer in your domain will be allowed to use the Remote Desktop Connection program.

■ Using Microsft Office 365

THE BOTTOM LINE

Taking advantage of cloud computing services such as Microsoft Office 365 can reduce the workload on your IT staff. It can also improve the collaboration between your team members.

Microsoft Office 365 is a Microsoft subscription–based software service that enables users to access their documents and collaborate with others from anywhere using their computers, the Web, or their smart devices. Microsoft Office takes the traditional Office suite and moves it to the cloud. The service includes Office, Exchange, SharePoint, Lync, and Office Web Apps. By using Office 365, you can offload many of the administrative tasks normally handled by your IT department. These tasks include managing software updates, patches, and service packs; and purchasing additional server hardware to support company growth.

Administration is handled through a Web portal/dashboard in which you can create/manage user accounts and oversee the health of all services. Microsoft also provides tools to migrate from your existing on-premise Exchange Server to Office 365.

The service can be used in combination with the desktop version of Microsoft Office and also works if you don't have Office installed on your computers.

Office 365 is available in a number of different plans designed to meet different segments of the market. Each plan uses a per-user/month charge and provides access to either the entire service or subsets of Office 365.

+ MORE INFORMATION

To compare plans, go to Microsoft's website and search for "Office 365 Plans."

Understanding Microsoft Office 365 Features

Office 365 provides the software and tools you need to manage a fully collaborated workforce while providing a centralized Web portal to oversee and manage the services.

The following are features available with Microsoft Office 365:

- Access e-mail, calendars, and contacts using the Microsoft Exchange service. They can be delivered to Outlook or Outlook Web Access.
- Create, edit, and store documents you create with the Office Web Apps (browser-based versions of the standard Office suite (Word, PowerPoint, Excel). These documents are fully compatible with the desktop version of the programs created in Office.
- Set up and maintain a company website.
- Connect immediately with co-workers via instance messaging using Microsoft Lync.
- Set up and conduct online meetings (audio, video, and web conferencing) with the ability to share desktops, files, and presentations online.
- Share documents inside and outside of your organization and collaborate with your colleagues using Microsoft SharePoint.

From an administrative perspective, Office 365 offers several benefits:

- Maintenance: Microsoft performs the administrative tasks, so you do not have to worry about backups, patches, and software updates.
- Software upgrades: Office 365 includes them with the subscription price.
- Hardware: Because Office 365 runs in the cloud, you don't have to purchase and maintain expensive server hardware. You can migrate Exchange Server over to Office 365 while at the same time increasing the mailbox storage for users.
- Collaboration on projects: Using SharePoint as a document repository and collaboration workspace, you can connect and work with a geographically dispersed workforce. By using team sites, you can share a portfolio of company projects, enable employees to access project information, share documents, and collaborate on project documents.

Managing Office 365

Office 365 is managed by a web console that enables you to set up and manage users and their software regardless of where they connect. The person who signs up your company for Office 365 is the Global Administrator by default. This person can then grant administrator permissions to other users in the organization as needed to distribute the workload.

Office 365 is managed by using the Office 365 admin center (see Figure 3-6). From here, you can create users and groups, manage software licenses, generate reports, and purchase services.

Figure 3-6

Managing Office 365

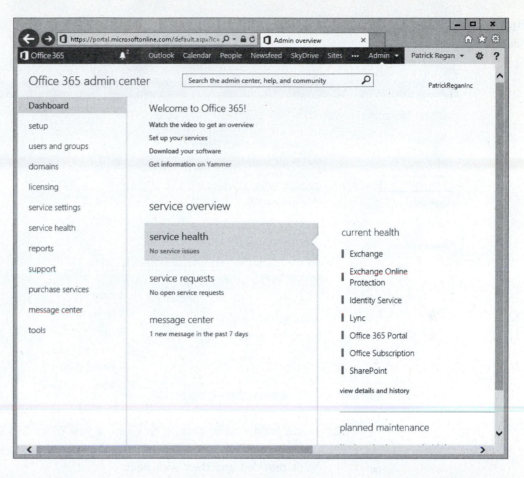

Office 365 provides several administrator roles that can be assigned to help distribute the workload of managing Office 365. The Global Administrator is assigned to the person who sets up Office 365 initially. This is the most powerful account in the organization. The other administrator roles can be assigned to users according to your organization's specific needs.

Five administrator roles are available for Office 365 enterprises:

- *Global Administrator:* Has access to all administrative features. This is the person who signs up for Office 365. Only Global Administrators can assign other administrative roles. Only one person in the company can serve in this role.

- *Billing Administrator:* Manages purchases, support tickets, and subscriptions and monitors the overall health of the services.

- *Password Administrator:* Manages requests for services, resets passwords, and monitors the overall health of the services. Users in this role can reset passwords only for users and other Password Administrators.

- *Service Administrator:* Manages service requests and monitors overall health of services.

- *User Management Administrator:* Manages user accounts and user groups, resets passwords, and manages service requests. User Management Administrators can also monitor the overall health of services. They cannot reset passwords for Billing, Global, or Service Administrators and they cannot delete a Global Administrator or create other administrators.

 ADD A NEW USER TO YOUR OFFICE 365 PORTAL

GET READY. To add a new user in Office 365, log into your Office 365 portal as the Administrator and then perform the following steps:

1. From the menu on the left, click **users and groups** (see Figure 3-7).

Figure 3-7

Adding new users

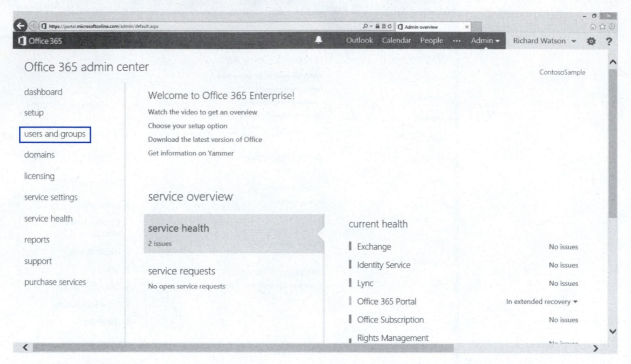

2. In the middle pane, click + to create a new Office 365 user.

3. Under *Details*, type the user's **First name**, **Last name**, and **User name** in the fields provided and then click **next**.

4. Under *Assign role,* select **No** when prompted to assign the user administrative per-missions. Under *Set user location*, choose the user's geographic location and then click **next**.

Figure 3-8

5. Under *Assign licenses,* select the applications (see Figure 3-8), and then click **next**.

Assigning licenses

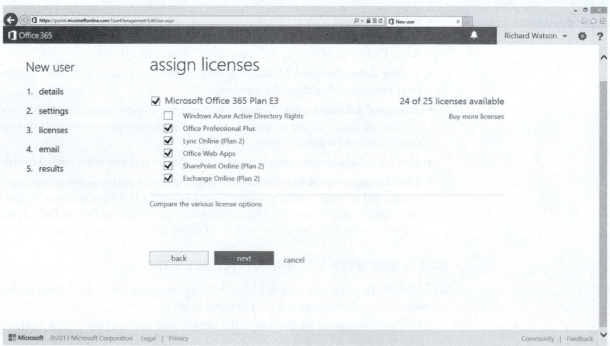

6. Under *send results in e-mail,* select **Send e-mail**, and then click **create**. By default, your e-mail address (the Office 365 Administrator) is entered. To send a copy of the e-mail to the user you are creating the account for, in the field provided, type his e-mail address.

7. Review the *Results* page, and then click **Finish**. You should see the user name you created and the temporary password assigned.

 ASSIGN A USER TO A PASSWORD ADMINISTRATOR ROLE IN OFFICE 365

GET READY. To assign a user to a Password Administrator role in Office 365, log into your Office 365 portal as with the Global Administrator's account and then perform the following steps:

TAKE NOTE* You must log in with an account that has the Global Administrator's role assigned to perform these steps.

1. From the menu on the left, click **users and groups**.

2. Under the *DISPLAY NAME* column, click the user you want to assign the administrative role to

3. From the menu on the left, click **settings**.

4. Under *Assign role,* select **Yes**.

5. Click the down arrow and choose **Password administrator**.

6. Under *Alternate e-mail address,* type an e-mail to use in case you forget your password, and then scroll to the bottom of the page and click **Save**.

7. Click **Save**.

Following are some of the general administrative tasks you will perform in Office 365:

- Reset a user's password.
- Configure a password expiration policy.
- View the overall health of Office 365.
- Personalize the default SharePoint team site.

 RESET A USER'S PASSWORD IN OFFICE 365

GET READY. To reset a user's password in Office 365, log into your Office 365 portal as the Global Administrator, and perform the following steps:

1. From the menu on the left, click **users and groups**.

2. Under the *DISPLAY NAME* column, select the checkbox next to the user you want to reset the password for.

3. In the menu that appears, under *quick steps,* click **Reset passwords**.

4. On the *send results in e-mail* screen, click **reset password**.

5. Click **finish**. The user's temporary password is displayed and mailed to the address you used in the previous step. This information is provided to the user who can now log into their Office 365 account.

CONFIGURE A PASSWORD EXPIRATION POLICY IN OFFICE 365

GET READY. To configure a password expiration policy in Office 365, log into your Office 365 portal as the Global Administrator and then perform the following steps:

1. From the menu on the left, click **service settings**.
2. In the menu at the top, click **passwords**.
3. In the *Days before passwords expire* field (see Figure 3-9), type **100**. The default is set to 90 days.

Figure 3-9

Changing the password expiration policy

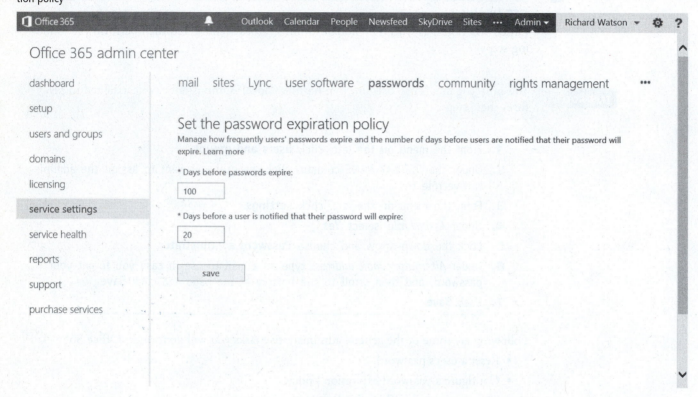

4. In the *Days before a user is notified that their password will expire* field, type **20**. The default is set for 14 days.
5. Click **Save**.

As users start to depend upon Office 365 more and more, you will want to make sure you monitor the health of the services you provide. Office 365 provides an excellent dashboard to monitor the current status of all services and learn about any upcoming planned maintenance.

 VIEW THE OVERALL HEALTH OF OFFICE 365

GET READY. To view the overall health of Office 365, log into your Office 365 portal as the Global Administrator and then perform the following steps:

1. In the menu on the left, click **service health** to view the current status of the services provided by Office 365 (see Figure 3-10).

Figure 3-10

Reviewing the status of Office 365 services

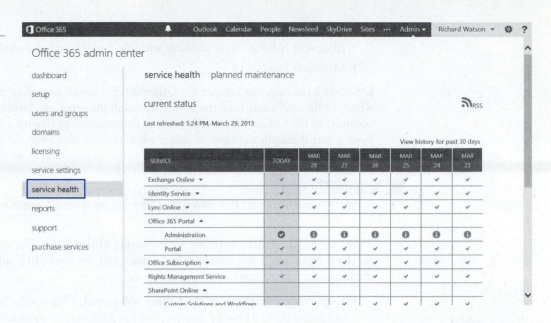

2. In the menu at the top, click **planned maintenance** to determine whether there is an upcoming maintenance planned.

Seven days of health history, including today, are displayed in the service health area of the Office 365 portal. You can also click to view the past 30 days of health history if desired.

When Office 365 is set up, a SharePoint team site is configured for you. This is where you can collaborate on projects and share documents. However, the default site can be personalized.

➕ **MORE INFORMATION**
To learn more about Office 365, visit Microsoft's website and search for "Office 365."

Installing and Managing Software by Using Microsoft Office 365

Microsoft Office 365 is a subscription-based service that offers various services and software that enable you to collaborate and store documents online. When implemented with Office 2013, users can work either online or offline and take advantage of the full features available with the desktop applications in the Office suite.

CERTIFICATION READY
Install and manage software by using Office 365 and Windows Store apps
Objective 1.3

Office 365 offers several different plans designed for small, midsize, and enterprise-level businesses. The Office 365 Small Business Premium (25 users), Office 365 Midsize Business (300 users), and Office 365 Enterprise E3 (unlimited users) plans include a subscription for Office 2013 for up to five PCs/Macs. *Microsoft Office 2013* includes desktop versions of the following applications:

- Microsoft Access 2013
- Microsoft OneNote 2013
- Microsoft Excel 2013
- Microsoft Word 2013
- Microsoft Outlook 2013
- Microsoft PowerPoint 2013
- Microsoft Publisher 2013

- OneDrive Pro 2013
- Microsoft InfoPath (not available with the Small Business Premium plan)
- Microsoft Lync 2013

Office 365 manages the licenses for Office 2013 through an online portal by indicating which Office 365 users have the ability to install the program during the setup of the user's account. In the Office 365 portal, you can delete a user to free up a licenses, remove a license from a user if his job changes, or assign a license for a user after the account is set up. You can also review which licenses are assigned to a user and purchase more if necessary.

+ MORE INFORMATION

To learn more about what is included and pricing for Office 365, visit Microsoft's website and search for "Office 365 plans."

There are several options available for deploying Office 2013. The option you choose depends on the infrastructure you already have in place and the level of IT support available in your organization. The options you can choose are:

- **Deploying directly from the Office 365 portal:** This option is designed for organizations that do not have IT resources; it has a self-service approach. When this option is used, you can download and install only the 32-bit version of Office 2013.
- **Deploying from a network share:** This requires basic IT administration skills and works well in situations where you have a slow network connection. When this option is used, you have the option to deploy both 32-bit and 64-bit versions of Office 2013.
- **Deploying using Group Policy or Microsoft System Center 2012 R2 Configuration Manager:** These two methods are designed to leverage Active Directory and should be used when deploying to large groups of users.

Following is a brief overview of the steps involved to deploy Office 2013 directly from the Office 365 portal. In the exercise that follows, you will learn the following steps in more detail:

1. The administrator signs up for Microsoft Office 365, sets a new domain name, creates user accounts, and assigns licenses to each user.
2. The administrator sends users their temporary passwords by e-mail.
3. Users sign into the Office 365 portal and set up new passwords.
4. Users download and configure their desktops with Office 2013 (32-bit version).

⊙ INSTALL OFFICE PROFESSIONAL 2013 ON WINDOWS 8.1

GET READY. To install Office 2013 and connect it to Office 365, perform the following steps:

1. Reset the Temporary Password.
2. Log into the Windows 8.1 computer where you want to install Office 2013 and open the Internet Explorer browser.
3. In the Internet Explorer *address* field, type **https://portal.microsoftonline.com**.
4. In the *User ID* field, type the user name you assigned to the account and then type the temporary password you received. Click **Sign-in**.
5. Under Welcome to Office 365, click **Download your software**.
6. Accept the default settings for *Language* (English, United States) and *Version* (32-bit recommended), and then click **Install** (see Figure 3-11). The 32-bit version is recommended for most people to protect against compatibility issues with other 32-bit applications being used.

Figure 3-11

Installing Office

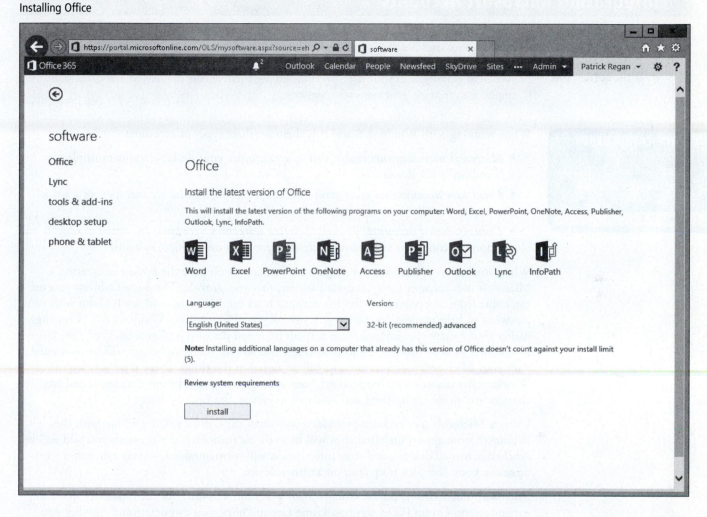

7. In the window that appears at the bottom of the screen, click **Run** to start the installation. If the *User Account Control* box appears, click **Yes** to continue.

8. When the *Welcome to your new Office* message appears, click **Next**.

9. Under *First things first,* select **No thanks** (to *not* send updates to Microsoft) and then click **Accept**.

10. On the *Meet OneDrive* screen, click **Next**.

11. Under *How would you like your office to look?*, click **Next** to accept the default *No Background*.

12. On the *Take a look at what's new* screen, click **No, thanks** and then click **All done!** Minimize your browser window.

    The installation of Office 2013 begins. During this time, you will need to stay connected to the Internet.

13. When the message *You're good to go* appears, click **All done!**

14. Press the **Windows logo key** to toggle to the Windows 8.1 Start menu. A tile is created for each of the Office applications as part of the installation of Office 2013.

■ Integrating Microsoft Accounts

Each type of user account provides a different level of control over the computers in your network. Matching the right type of account to each user will ensure you provide sufficient privileges to your users without giving them access to areas or resources that might compromise your network's security.

When working with Windows 8 and 8.1, there are three types of accounts:

- *Microsoft user accounts* enable you to synchronize your desktop across multiple Windows 8/8.1 devices.
- *Local user accounts* are created on individual computers that are members of a workgroup to provide access to resources on that computer.
- *Domain-based accounts*, also called *Active Directory accounts*, are stored as objects on a domain controller and provide access to resources on multiple systems.

When you set up a Windows 8.1 PC for the first time, you have the option of creating a Microsoft user account using an e-mail address that you provide. The e-mail address you use can come from any provider. After the account is set up, Microsoft will use it along with your password to help manage your settings across all your PCs running Windows 8.1. After organizing your system the way you want it (your preferred desktop background, user tiles, favorite websites in your browser, explorer settings, and so on), the information will be associated with your Microsoft user account and will be stored in the cloud. Every time you log into a Windows 8.1 device using the account, your settings are synched from the cloud, and any changes you make are updated and available to you on the next device.

Using a Microsoft user account provides a consistent experience when working with the Windows Store apps. Purchased apps will be available from each device, feeds you add will be synched across all devices, and state information will be maintained, so you can start a game or read a book and pick it up later on another device.

Microsoft user accounts can be synched with a domain account, but the capability to do so depends upon Group Policy settings. Using Group Policy, you can determine whether you want to allow the synching of the two accounts and what information can be synched.

You create a Microsoft user account during the initial installation of the operating system or after the system is running. The following steps outline the process you can use to create the account after Windows 8.1 is installed using the Charms bar. The *Charms bar* allows you to search, share files and information, gain access to the Windows 8.1 start menu, access devices connected to your computer, and change settings for both your apps and your PC.

 CREATE A MICROSOFT USER ACCOUNT USING THE CHARMS BAR

GET READY. To create the account after Windows 8.1 is installed using the Charms bar, perform the following steps:

1. Log into the Windows 8.1 client computer.
2. Point your cursor to the top- or bottom-right corner of the screen to make the Charms bar appear.
3. Click **Settings** (the gear icon).
4. Click **Change PC Settings**.
5. Click **Accounts** then click **Other accounts**.
6. Click **Add an account** (see Figure 3-12).

Figure 3-12

Adding a user

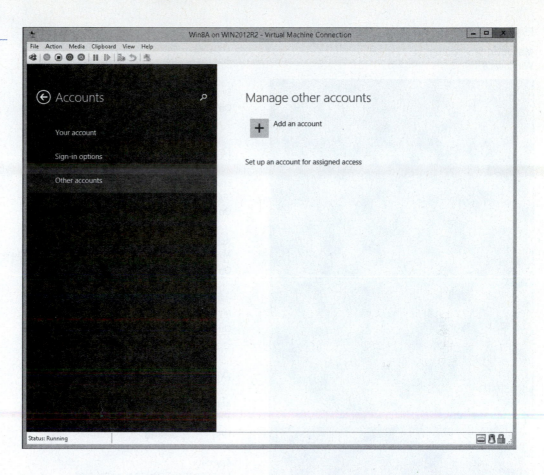

7. In the *Email address* text box, type the e-mail address you want to use and then click **Next**.

8. On the *Create a Microsoft* account page, in the *First name* and *Last name* text boxes, type your first name and last name. In the *Create password* text box and the *Reenter password* text box, type a password. Click **Next**.

9. On the *Add security info* page, in the *Birthday*, *Gender*, *Country code*, and *Phone number* text boxes, specify the birthdate, gender, country code, and phone number. In the *Alternate email address* text box, you can also specify an alternate e-mail address, which can be used to reset passwords.

10. In the *Communication preferences* page, in the *Enter these characters* section, type the code provided and then click **Next**.

11. On the *Add a user* page, Click **Finish**.

When using a connected Microsoft account in Windows 8.1, you can sync your PC settings—even between multiple Windows 8.1 machines—as long as they are connected with the same Microsoft account. Therefore, if you change the wallpaper or add a favorite shortcut in Internet Explorer, those changes will be replicated to the other machines.

The Sync feature (located under OneDrive settings as shown in Figure 3-13) can sync many of your settings between PCs, including the following:

- Personalization settings, such as Start screen colors, background, and lock screen image
- Themes, such as the desktop background and sounds
- Ease of Access settings, such as Speech Recognition, Magnifier, On-screen Keyboard, and Narrator

Figure 3-13

Managing Sync settings in
Windows 8.1

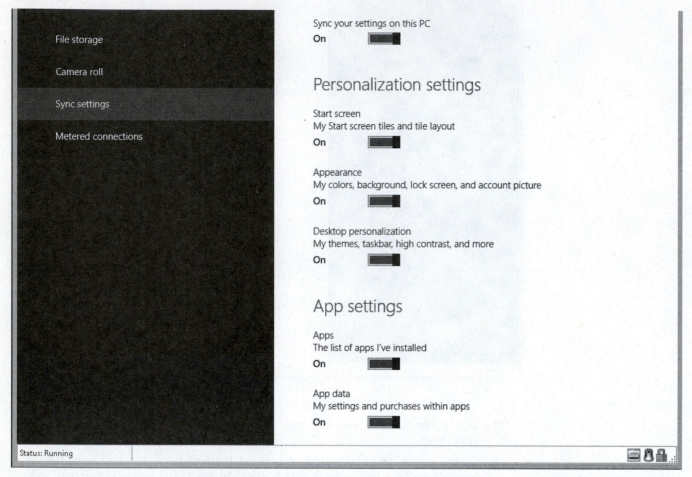

- Language preferences, such as keyboard settings, other input methods, and display language
- Web browser settings, such as history, pinned sites, and favorites for both versions of the browser
- Taskbar settings, such as pinned items and which side of the monitor the taskbar is attached to
- Folder and Search settings for Windows Explorer
- Mouse settings
- Your accounts picture (user tile)
- Per-app notification state
- Settings for Windows Store apps, including third-party apps
- HomeGroup password

You can also sync passwords, including saved network passwords (Credential Vault) and Wi-Fi passwords. However, passwords will only sync when the computer is a Trusted PC. A **Trusted PC** is a personal computer that you have designated as a computer that you use often, which can be uniquely identified, and which can be used as part of an automatic authentication process.

To make a computer a Trusted PC, you need to perform one of the following:

- Under PC Settings, select Sync Your Settings. Under Passwords, click the Trust this PC link.
- From the Desktop, click the Action Center icon and then select Trust this PC.

Internet Explorer will open to the Microsoft Account Settings page. You will then enter a code that Microsoft sends via text to your smartphone or e-mail account. Each Windows 8.1 computer that is trusted will be listed under your trusted devices.

 CONFIGURE THE TRUST YOUR PC OPTION

GET READY. To trust a new PC, log into your Windows 8.1 computer with administrative privileges and perform the following steps:

1. In the Windows 8.1 *Start* menu, press the **Windows logo key + I.**
2. Click **Change PC settings**.
3. Under *PC Settings*, click **Users**.
4. Under *Other users*, click **Add a user**.
5. On the *Add a user* screen, type the e-mail address for your Microsoft user account and click **Next**.
6. Click **Finish**.
7. Press the **Windows logo key** to return to the Windows 8.1 start menu.
8. In the upper right corner, click your user account and then log out.
9. Choose your Microsoft user account, type your password, and then press **Enter**.
10. On the Windows 8.1 Start screen, press the **Windows logo key + I**.
11. Click **Change PC settings**.
12. Under *PC Settings*, click **Users**. Under *Your account*, the message *Your saved passwords for apps, websites, and networks won't sync until you trust this PC* is shown.
13. Click **Trust this PC**. This takes you to the Windows Live website, where you will be prompted to type a code. This code can be sent to you in a variety of ways (via e-mail, text message, or telephone call) depending upon how you set up your initial Windows Live account.
14. On the *Confirm <computername> as a trusted PC* page, type the code provided into the field provided and then click **Submit**.
15. On the *Thanks for confirming <computername>* page, click **OK**.
16. Press the **Windows logo key** to return to the Windows 8.1 Start menu.

The next time you log into the computer, you will have the option to synchronize your password and any other settings on the computer that you choose.

SKILLS SUMMARY

IN THIS LESSON YOU LEARNED:

- The Windows Store app comes preinstalled on Windows 8 devices. That makes it very easy for your users to connect and access the apps in the Store.

- When you sideload an app, the PC must be joined to the domain, Group Policy must be set to allow all trusted apps to install, the Windows App must be signed by a CA that the targeted PC trusts, and you must activate a product key to prepare a system for sideloading.

- Sideloading is defined as the process of installing a Windows App without going through the Store by using a tool such as DISM, Windows PowerShell, System Center Configuration Manager (SCCM), or Windows Intune.

- With deeplinking, you can identify an application in the Windows Store that you want to deploy to Window's 8.1; a link will be provided to the user that will take the user directly to the app in the Windows Store.

- AppLocker can be used to control the way users access and program files. AppLocker can be used to configure rules for executables, Windows installers, scripts, and packaged apps (Windows Apps). There are four steps to setting up a rule: set permissions, set the primary condition, add an exception (optional), and enter a name for the rule.

- Microsoft Office 365 is a subscription-based software service that can be used to access documents and collaborate with others from anywhere. It also allows you to deploy Office 365 to the users.

- When combined with Office 2013, Office 365 allows users to collaborate on documents, work online or offline, and gain access to e-mail, calendars, and documents for their trusted devices.

- There are five administrator roles in Office 365: Global Administrator, Billing Administrator, Password Administrator, Service Administrator, and User Management Administrator.

- Microsoft user accounts enable you to synchronize your desktop across multiple Windows 8 devices.

- A trusted PC is a computer or device that you have added the password reset information for your Microsoft user account. If you forget your password or an unauthorized person gains access to the information, you can reset the password from any trusted PC.

■ Knowledge Assessment

Multiple Choice

1. Which of the following tools can be used to add and activate the sideloading production activation key received from Microsoft's Volume Licensing Service Center?
   - **a.** GPO
   - **b.** Group Policy Editor
   - **c.** Windows PowerShell
   - **d.** cmd

2. Which of the following are requirements of preparing a computer to be sideloaded? (Choose all that apply)
   a. Windows 8/Windows Professional computers must be joined to an Active Directory domain.
   b. Group Policy must be set to *Allow all trusted computers to install.*
   c. A sideloading product key must be activated if the computer is running Windows 7.
   d. The App must be signed by a CA that is trusted by the targeted PCs on the network.

3. When preparing a computer to use a sideloaded app, which of the following commands activates a key?
   a. `Slmgr /ipk <sideloading product key>`
   b. `Slmgr /ato ec67814b-30e6-4a50-bf7b-d55daf729d1e /activate`
   c. `Slmgr /ipk <sideloading product key>`
   d. `Slmgr /ato ec67814b-30e6-4a50-bf7b-d55daf729d1e`

4. Which of the following is a subscription-based software service that enables users to use Office Apps via the Web?
   a. Microsoft Office 365
   b. Skynet
   c. AppLocker
   d. GPOs

5. Which of the following cannot be synched with a Windows 8 PC that is *not* trusted?
   a. Desktop themes
   b. Language preferences
   c. App settings
   d. Passwords

6. The person who signs up for the Office 365 subscription is assigned which of the following roles by default?
   a. Global Administrator
   b. User Management Administrator
   c. Billing Administrator
   d. Service Administrator

7. The default password expiration policy in Office 365 sets passwords to expire after how many days?
   a. 30 days
   b. 60 days
   c. 120 days
   d. 90 days

8. Which Office 365 administrative role can monitor the overall health of Office 365 services? (Choose all that apply)
   a. Password Administrator
   b. Global Administrator
   c. User Management Administrator
   d. Billing Administrator

9. By default, when a new Office 365 user account is created, where is the user name and temporary password e-mailed to?
   a. Global administrator's e-mail address
   b. User's e-mail address
   c. All administrators in Office 365
   d. To both the user and the Global Administrator's e-mail address.

10. Which of the following happens when you add a new user to Office 365? (Choose all that apply)
    a. The user is added to your company's Office 365 subscription.
    b. They are assigned the Global Administrator role.
    c. The user receives a temporary password.
    d. The user is assigned to the Users group in AD Users and Computers.

11. When setting up a rule using AppLocker, which of the following primary conditions should be set if you want to use the same rule again after the manufacture updates the application?
    a. Path
    b. Publisher
    c. File Hash
    d. Execute

12. Which of the following options causes the system to compute a hash on the file when using AppLocker—and each time the app is updated or patched, you will have to update the hash again?
    a. EFS
    b. Path hash
    c. Folder hash
    d. File Hash

13. Which of the following Group Policy settings can be configured for a computer to control how it interacts with the Windows Store? (Choose all that apply)
    a. Turn off Automatic Download of updates.
    b. Allow Store to install apps on Windows To Go Workspaces.
    c. Turn off the Store application.
    d. Turn on Automatic Download of updates.

14. Which of the following rule collections are used in AppLocker? (Choose all that apply)
    a. Executable files
    b. Scripts
    c. Windows Image files
    d. Appx

Best Answer

Choose the letter that corresponds to the best answer. More than one answer choice may achieve the goal. Select the BEST answer.

1. Which of the following options works best when deploying Office 365 in an organization that does not have dedicated IT staff?
    a. Deploy directly from the Office 365 portal
    b. Deploy from a network share
    c. Deploy using Group Policy
    d. Deploy using SCCM

2. If you leave the Office 365 password expiration policy at its default setting, how often must users change their passwords?
    a. Every 90 days.
    b. Set Every 30 days.
    c. Set Every 60 days.
    d. Every 45 days.

3. After setting up a user's account in Office 365, how long does he have to access to the temporary password before it expires?
- **a.** 30 days
- **b.** 90 days
- **c.** 120 days
- **d.** 100 days

4. Which administrator role should you assign to an Office 365 user who needs to manage support tickets for Office 365 only?
- **a.** Service Administrator
- **b.** User Management Administrator
- **c.** Billing Administrator
- **d.** Global Administrator

5. Which version(s) of Office 2013 does Microsoft recommend you install when working with Office 365 to protect against compatibility issues?
- **a.** 16-bit version
- **b.** 32-bit version
- **c.** 64-bit version
- **d.** Both the 32-bit and 64-bit versions

Matching and Identification

1. Match the tool to the correct task:
- _____ **a)** `gpedit.msc`
- _____ **b)** `slmgr`
- _____ **c)** `add-appxpackage`
- _____ **d)** `gpupdate /force`
- _____ **e)** `Windows logo key + r`
  - **1.** Installs a sideloaded package.
  - **2.** Opens the Local Group Policy Editor.
  - **3.** Adds and activates the sideloading product key.
  - **4.** Refreshes local and Active Directory-based Group Policy settings.
  - **5.** Accesses the Run box.

2. Write the command for the specified function or scenario:
- _____ Add a sideloading product key.
- _____ Install a sideloaded package.
- _____ Update a sideloaded package.
- _____ Activate a sideloading product key.

Build a List

1. Specify the correct order of the steps that must be completed to deploy Office 2013 directly from the Office 365 portal:
- _____ Administrator sends users temporary passwords.
- _____ Users download and configure their desktops with Office 2013 (32-bit version).
- _____ Administrator signs up for Office 365, sets new domain name, creates user accounts, and assigns licenses to each user.
- _____ Users sign in to Office 365 portal with temporary password and creates a new password.

2. Specify the correct order of the steps that must be completed to add a new user to your Office 365 portal.

_____ In the menu on the left, click **users and groups**.

_____ Under *details*, type the user's **First name**, **Last name**, and their **User name** in the fields provided and then click **next**.

_____ In the middle pane, click + to create a new Office 365 user.

_____ Under *Assign licenses*, select the applications, and then click **next**.

_____ Under *Assign* role, select **No** when prompted to assign the user administrative permissions. Under *Set user location*, choose the user's geographic location and then click **next**.

_____ Under *send results in e-mail*, select **Send e-mail**, and then click **create**.

_____ Review the Results page and then click **Finish**.

3. Specify the correct order of the steps that must be completed to configure a Trusted PC.

_____ Type the code you receive into the field provided on the Windows Live website to confirm it is trusted.

_____ Log in with your Microsoft user account.

_____ Under *PC settings*, click **Users**.

_____ Press the **Windows logo key + I** and click **Change PC Settings**.

_____ Click the **Trust this PC link**.

Choose an Option

1. Which option should you click in order to configure password expiration policies for your Office 365 users?

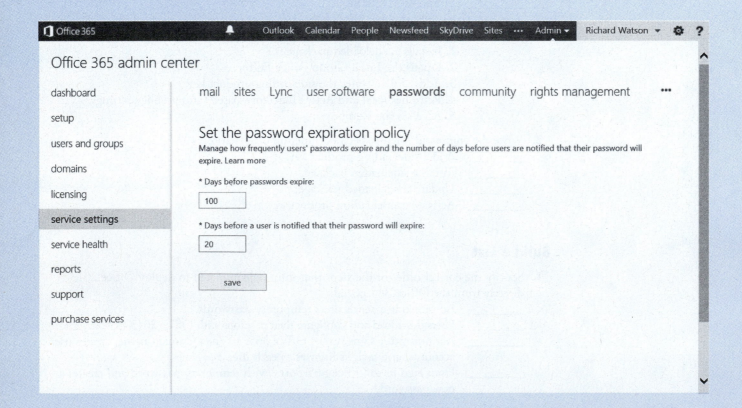

■ Business Case Scenarios

Scenario 3-1: Troubleshooting Sideloaded Apps

Developers at your company created a Windows App that needs to be sideloaded on a Windows 8.1 client computer that is part of your Active Directory domain. They ask you to prepare a computer so the sideloaded app can be installed and tested. After setting up the computer, you attempt to sideload the app but cannot complete the process. After reviewing your notes, you are not sure if you have addressed all of the pre-requisites for sideloading the app. What could you have missed?

Scenario 3-2: Sync Problems

Multiple computers run Windows 8.1 and they are synched across the same Microsoft user account. On one of the devices, you notice that the option to synch passwords is disabled. Why?

4 LESSON

Supporting Network Connectivity

70-688 EXAM OBJECTIVE

Objective 2.1 – Support network connectivity. This objective may include but is not limited to: IPv4 and IPv6 including transition technologies; name resolution, including Peer Name Resolution Protocol (PNRP) and Domain Name System Security Extensions (DNSSECs); wireless networks and connections; network security, including Windows Firewall and IP security

LESSON HEADING	EXAM OBJECTIVE
Supporting Network Connectivity	
Exploring the IPv4 and IPv6 Protocols	IPv4 and IPv6, including transition technologies
Understanding Name Resolution	Name resolution, including Peer Name Resolution Protocol (PNRP) and Domain Name System Security Extensions (DNSSECs)
Exploring Network Settings	
Working with Wireless Networks and Connections	Wireless networks and connections
Implementing Network Security for Windows 8.1	Network security, including Windows Firewall and IP security
Troubleshooting IP Network Problems	
Viewing IP Configuration	
Testing Network Connectivity	
Testing Name Resolution	
Viewing Port Usage	

KEY TERMS

6to4	infrastructure mode	ping command
802.11a	Internet Protocol (IP)	private profile
802.11b	Intra-Site Automatic Tunnel Addressing Protocol (ISATAP)	public profile
802.11g		Remote Authentication Dial-In User Service (RADIUS) server
802.11i	ipconfig command	
802.11n	IP security (IPSec)	resolver
802.1x	key signing key (KSK)	router
ad-hoc	lease period	Service Set Identifier (SSID)
ANDing	Link Local Multicast Name Resolution (LLMNR)	subnetting
connection security rules		telnet
DNS Security Extension (DNSSEC)	name resolution	Teredo
Domain Name System (DNS)	netstat	tracert command
domain profile	network ID	Transmission Protocol/Internet Protocol (TCP/IP)
Dynamic Host Configuration Protocol (DHCP)	network perimeter firewalls	Wi-Fi Protected Access (WPA)
	nslookup.exe	
enterprise mode	outbound rules	Wi-Fi Protected Access (WPA) v2
Extensible Authentication Protocol (EAP)	pathping command	Windows Firewall with Advanced Security (WFAS)
	peer-to-peer (P2P) network	
host ID	Peer Name Resolution Protocol (PNRP)	Windows Internet Name Services (WINS)
host-based firewalls		
inbound rules	personal mode	Wireless Equivalent Privacy (WEP)

■ Supporting Network Connectivity

THE BOTTOM LINE

Designing network connectivity in today's networks requires you to make decisions about using IPv4/IPv6, designing a name resolution strategy, and understanding how to configure your wired and wireless network for security.

When accessing computers on a network, you typically communicate by using their host names. If you are accessing a website, you enter a friendly name such as www.microsoft.com. Every device that connects to your network or the Internet must have an Internet Protocol (IP) address. You also need a way to associate these names to their assigned IP address. This process is called *name resolution*.

Internet Protocol (IP) is the key protocol in the TCP/IP suite. It is responsible for adding addressing information to the packets for the sender and the receiver, as well as adding data to help route and deliver the packet. Windows 8/8.1 uses TCP/IP as its default networking protocol.

Transmission Protocol/Internet Protocol (TCP/IP) is a set of protocols that allows computers to exchange data within a network and between networks. These protocols (or rules) manage the content, format, timing, sequencing, and error control of the messages that are exchanged between the devices. Every device that communicates over TCP/IP must have a unique IP address. Windows 8/8.1 uses a dual-layer architecture that enables it to implement both IPv4 and IPv6 address schemes. Both share the common TCP transport layer protocol.

Before configuring TCP/IP on your network, take time to plan the implementation. For example, how big do you expect your network to be? How will your network be designed from a physical and logical standpoint?

Exploring the IPv4 and IPv6 Protocols

Microsoft, along with other industry leaders, is working hard to make IPv6 the next standard for IP addressing. In the meantime, you have a mixture of IPv4 and IPv6 devices on your network, so you need to understand how these devices are configured and how they interact with each other.

CERTIFICATION READY
IPv4 and IPv6, including transition technologies
Objective 2.1

During the 1960s, several universities and research centers needed a network to share information. To address this need, a U.S. government agency called the Advanced Research Projects Agency (ARPA) developed the ARPANET, which initially used the Network Control Protocol (NCP) to handle file transfers, remote login, and e-mail needs. NCP, the predecessor to TCP/IP, was first used in 1972. By 1973, the protocol no longer met the needs of its users, and research was done to find a better solution. TCP/IPv4 was introduced and standardized in 1981 and is still in use today. Microsoft and other industry leaders have been working for years to roll out a newer version: IPv6.

The goal of IPv6 is to address the exhaustion of the IPv4 address space, which supports about 4 billion addresses. At the time IPv4 was created, no one considered that anything other than computers would be connected. As more computers, smartphones, tablets, and home appliances are being attached to the Internet, the IP4 address space is quickly being exhausted.

TAKE NOTE

IPv6 is not backward-compatible with IPv4. An IPv6-only device cannot talk to an IPv4 device. Your current transition strategy should be to use both in the short term.

Over the years, engineers have found ways to reduce the number of addresses needed through a process called network address translation (NAT). Instead of assigning an IPv4 public address to every device on your network, you can purchase a single IPv4 address and allow all devices behind your router to share the same address. Still, as each year passes and the number of devices connected to the Internet continue to grow exponentially, IPv6 will eventually take over as the main addressing scheme. In the meantime, let's take a closer look at each of the protocols.

UNDERSTANDING IPV4

An IPv4 address is a 32-bit-long number assigned to a host on the network. These addresses are broken into four different sections called octets, which are 8 bits long. For example, the number 192.160.10.2 in binary is 11000000.10100000.00001010.00000010 (see Figure 4-1).

Figure 4-1

Converting binary to decimal

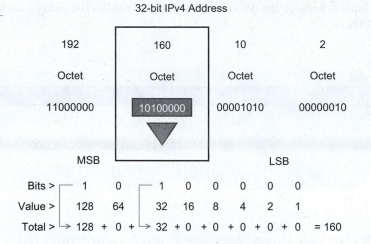

32-bit IPv4 Address

192	160	10	2
Octet	Octet	Octet	Octet
11000000	10100000	00001010	00000010

MSB   LSB

Bits >   1   0   1   0   0   0   0   0

Value >   128   64   32   16   8   4   2   1

Total >   128 + 0 +   32 + 0 + 0 + 0 + 0 + 0 = 160

A portion of the 32 bits is associated with the network on which the computer is physically located. This portion of bits is called the *network ID*. The remaining bits, allocated to the host, are called the *host ID*. All computers on the same local network share the same network ID, but each has its own unique host ID.

A subnet mask, also 32 bits long, is used to determine which of the 32 bits represent the network ID and which represent the host ID (see Table 4-1). The class of IP address you are using determines the default subnet mask. IPv4 addresses are divided into classes based on the number in the first octet of the IP address. These classes were originally designed to support different organizational sizes. However, classful IP addressing is very wasteful and has mostly been discarded.

There are five classes of IP addresses (see Table 4-1).

Table 4-1

TCP/IP v4 Address Classes

CLASS	RANGE	NETWORK ID (OCTET)	HOST ID (OCTET)	NUMBER OF NETWORKS	NUMBER OF HOSTS
A	1–127*	First octet	Second, third, and fourth octet	126	16,777,214
B	128–191	First and second octets	Third and fourth octet	16,384	65,534
C	192–223	First, second, and third octets	Fourth octet	2,097,152	254
D	224–239	N/A	N/A	N/A	N/A
E	240–254	N/A	N/A	N/A	N/A

(*), 0, 127, and 255 are reserved and cannot be used for a specific host. An IP address with all 0s in the host ID describes the network, whereas 127 in the first octet is reserved for loopback testing and handling traffic to the local host. An IP address using 255s in the host ID is a broadcast transmitting to all interfaces on the specified network.

Table 4-2 shows the default subnet masks for each class along with its binary and decimal values.

CLASS	BINARY	DECIMAL
A	11111111.00000000.00000000.00000000	255.0.0.0
B	11111111.11111111.00000000.00000000	255.255.0.0
C	11111111.11111111.11111111.00000000	255.255.255.0

If a host is on the same local network (has the same network ID), it can issue broadcast packets to locate other computers. To communicate with computers on a separate network, the packets have to traverse a router. To determine when a computer is on another network, your computer uses the subnet mask and a process called logical **ANDing**.

Because ANDing is performed using binary, you have to convert the IP address and the subnet mask to binary form. After you complete the conversions, you match up binary 1s (between the IP address and the subnet mask). If there is a 1 in the binary address of the IP and a 1 in the binary address of the subnet mask, set the binary number in the ANDing row to binary 1 (see Figure 4-2). After you complete the process, add up the values, as demonstrated in Figure 4-1. When you are using it for a default subnet mask, it really isn't necessary; but when your network is subnetted, the network ID is a little harder to decipher.

Figure 4-2

Using ANDing to determine network location

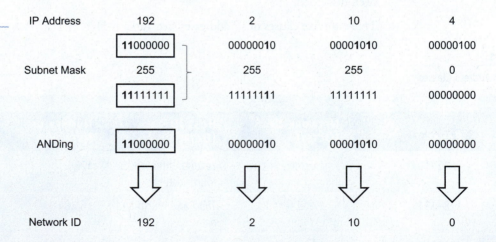

If the computer is determined to be on another network after the ANDing process is completed, the packet is sent to the default gateway configured on the computer (for example, the router's IP address). The router then uses information in its routing tables to locate and transfer your packet to the destination computer.

Subnetting is the process used to break a larger network into smaller segments. For example, a Class B IP address has more than 65,000 host addresses for a single logical segment. Adding that many computers to a single network isn't feasible. If you break the larger network into smaller segments (for example, 254 subnetworks), each can host up to 254 hosts. You accomplish subnetting by stealing bits from the host portion of an address to create a new subnet section.

UNDERSTANDING IPV6

The main advantage that IPv6 has over IPv4 is a much larger address space. An IPv6 address is a 128-bit-long number assigned to a host on the network. These addresses are broken into eight different blocks or groups. Each block is 16 bits long and is represented in hexadecimal, separated by a colon:

Fe80:0:ac4a:aa04:e713A:0:0:CE2B

A standard IPv6 unicast address uses the first 64 bits to represent the network ID and the remaining bits to represent the host's network interface. The host network interface is generated from the interface's Media Access Control (MAC) address. The MAC address is assigned by the manufacturer of the network interface card and is burned into the hardware.

If a block is set to 0 and is followed by another block set to 0, it can be written as ::. Using this notation, the preceding address would be written as Fe80:0:ac4a:aa04:e713A::CE2B.

The transition from IPv4 to IPv6 is expected to take several more years. In the meantime, expect to see a mix of IPv4, IPv4/IPv6 (dual stack), and IPv6-only networks.

TAKE NOTE*

When a network card is configured In Windows 8.1, it automatically has both an IPv4 and IPv6 address by default. This is called a dual stack.

USE CMD AND WINDOWS POWERSHELL TO VIEW IP ADDRESS INFORMATION

GET READY. To use cmd and Windows PowerShell to view your IP address configuration, perform the following steps:

1. Press the **Windows logo key + r.**
2. Type **cmd** and then press **Enter.**
3. Type **ipconfig** and then press **Enter.**
4. Review your settings. You should see both an IPv4 and IPv6 address.
5. Type **exit** and then press **Enter** to close the cmd shell.
6. Press the **Windows logo key + r.**
7. Type **PowerShell.**
8. Type **Resolve-DNSName** <*website address*> (for example, **Resolve-DNSName** www.cnn.com) and then press **Enter.**
9. Review the address records returned.
   Does the site support IPv6?
10. Type **Resolve-DNSName** www.comcast.net and then press **Enter.**
11. Review the address records returned (see Figure 4-3).
    Does the site support IPv6?

Figure 4-3

Analyzing IPv6 records retrieved using resolve-DNSName

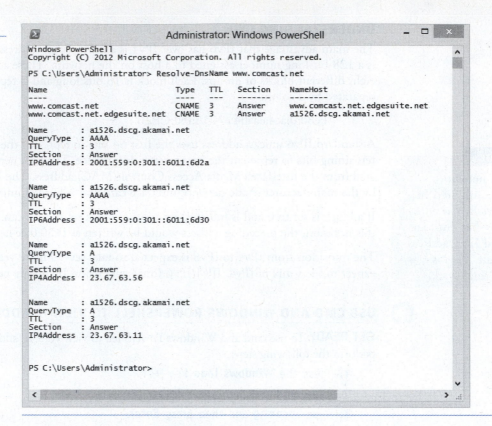

USING TRANSITION TECHNOLOGIES

Most networks are using IPv4. However, because of the impending depletion of public IPv4 addresses, organizations will have to plan for and switch to IPv6. Because the move from IPv4 to IPv6 is not an easy transition, several mechanisms have been developed that allow the creation of tunnels over IPv4. The IPv4 to IPv6 transition technologies that Windows supports are:

- 6to4
- ISATAP
- Teredo

6to4

The *6to4* transition mechanism allows IPv6 packets to be transmitted over an IPv4 network, such as the current Internet. Instead of configuring an explicit tunnel, you define the IPv4 addresses in IPv6 format and then encapsulate IPv6 traffic into IPv4 packets. Since the IPv4 is the underlying technology, you must have a global IPv4 address connected. The sending host and receiving host run both IPv4 and IPv6. The sending host is responsible for encapsulating outgoing IPv6 packets and the receiving host is responsible for encapsulation of incoming 6to4 packets. A router could be configured as the sending or receiving host, which would then forward packets to other clients.

The 6to4 address is formed by combining the prefix 2002::/16 with the 32 bits of a public IPv4 address of the node, forming a 48-bit prefix. Therefore, if you have an IPv4 address (written in decimal format) of 157.54.176.7, when you convert the values to hexadecimal:

157 = 9d

 54 = 36

176 = b0

  7 = 07

You get:

9d36:b007

The last 16-bits of the 64-bit prefix define the subnet and interface behind the same 6to4 router. Since the 6to4 IPv6 address will begin with 2002, the entire 64-bit prefix is:

2002:9d36:b007:*subnetID*:*interfaceID*

Since most IPv6 networks use autoconfiguration, the IPv6 host will have a unique 64-bit portion.

Intra-Site Automatic Tunnel Addressing Protocol (ISATAP)

Intra-Site Automatic Tunnel Addressing Protocol (ISATAP) is an automatic tunneling protocol used by the Windows workstation operating systems allows you use IPv6 applications on an IPv4 network by emulating an IPv6 link using an IPv4 network. The ISATAP address consists of a valid 64-bit unicast address prefix and the interface identifier, such as a link-local address prefix (FE80::/64), site-local prefixes, or global prefixes. The last 64 bits are ISATAP addresses, which are the locally administered interface ID ::0:5EFE:w.x.y.z, where w.x.y.z is any unicast IPv4 address in hexadecimal form.

Therefore, the IPv4 address 157.54.176.7 would have the following as its ISATAP address:

fe80:0000:0000:0000:0000:5efe:9d36:b007

In compressed form, the address appears as follows:

fe80::5efe:9d36:b007

ISATAP hosts perform their own tunneling to other ISATAP hosts by using the Link-local ISATAP addresses if they are on the same logical IPv4 subnet. If you want to communicate with other ISATAP on other subnets, you will communicate using ISATAP-based global addresses through an ISATAP router.

ISATAP does not support multicasting. Therefore, for a ISATAP host to find ISATAP routers, the host will compile a potential routers list (PRL) using DNS queries and send Router Discovery messages to them on a regular basis, using Internet Control Message Protocol version 6 (ICMPv6).

Teredo

Teredo, an IPv4 network address translator (NAT) traversal (NAT-T) for IPv6, is an address assignment and automatic tunneling technology that provides unicast IPv6 connectivity across the IPv4 Internet by encapsulating IPv6 packets within User Datagram Protocol (UDP) datagrams. One advantage of Teredo is that it will function even when the IPv6/Ipv4 hosts are located behind one or multiple IPv4 NATs.

For a Teredo client to function as a tunnel endpoint, it must have access to a Teredo server, which is connected to both the IPv4 and IPv6 networks. The Teredo server will exchange Router Solicitation and Router Advertisement messages to determine whether the client is located behind a NAT router.

Teredo addresses use the following format:

- **Prefix:** A 32-bit field that identifies the system as a Teredo client. Windows clients use the prefix value 2001:0000, or 2001::/32
- **Server IPv4:** A 32-bit field containing the IPv4 address of the Teredo server the client uses
- **Flags:** A 16-bit field, the first bit of which is the Cone flag, set to 1 when the NAT device providing access to the Internet is a cone NAT, which stores the mappings between internal and external addresses and port numbers. The second bit is reserved for

future use. The seventh and eighth bits are the Universal/Local and Individual/Group flags, which are both set to 0. The Teredo standard calls for the remaining 12 bits to be set to 0, but Windows assigns a random number to these bits, to prevent attackers from attempting to discover the Teredo address.

- **Port:** A 16-bit field that specifies the external UDP port that the client uses for all Teredo traffic, in obscured form. The obscuration of the port number (and the following IPv4 address) are to prevent the NAT router from translating the port as it normally would as part of its packet processing. To obscure the port, the system runs an exclusive OR (XOR) with the value ffff.

- **Client IPv4:** A 32-bit field that specifies the external IPv4 address that the client uses for all Teredo traffic, in obscured form. As with the Port field, the obscuration is the result of converting the IPv4 address to hexadecimal and running an XOR with the value ffffffff.

If, for example, the IPv4 address and port of the Teredo client are 192.168.31.243:32000 and the Teredo server uses the address 157.54.176.7, and the client is behind a cone NAT router, the Teredo address, in standard format, would consist of the following elements:

> 2001:0000: Standard Teredo prefix
>
> 9d36:b007: Server IPv4 address (157.54.176.7) converted to hexadecimal
>
> 8000: Flags field with first bit set to 1 and all others 0
>
> 82ff: Client UDP port number (32000), converted to hexadecimal (7d00) and XORed with ffff
>
> 3f57:e00c: Client IPv4 address (192.168.31.243), converted to hexadecimal (C0a8:1ff3) and XORed with ffffffff

Thus, the final Teredo address is as follows:

`2001:0000:9d36:b007:8000:82ff:3f57:e00c`

TAKE NOTE Although the 70-688 exam is not likely to assess your understanding of how to generate a Teredo address, you should be able to recognize one and determine its client IPv4 address and port number. You have access to the Windows Calculator program in Programmer mode during the exam, which you can use to perform the required operations and conversions.

Understanding Name Resolution

Name resolution is the process of converting friendly names to IP addresses. Windows 8.1 uses DNS, WINS, and LLMNR.

CERTIFICATION READY
Name resolution, including Peer Name Resolution Protocol (PNRP) and Domain Name System Security Extensions (DNSSECs)
Objective 2.1

Name resolution is the process of associating host names to IP addresses. The Windows operating system supports three name resolution systems:

- Domain Name System (DNS)
- Windows Internet Name Service (WINS)
- Link Local Multicast Name Resolution (LLMNR)

EXPLORING THE DOMAIN NAME SYSTEM (DNS)

Domain Name System (DNS) servers are used to associate a computer name such as web1.eastcoast.contoso.com to an IP address. It works over TCP/IP and can be integrated with other services such as WINS, DHCP, and Active Directory. To understand DNS, you first need to review its hierarchical structure. This arrangement, which is called the DNS namespace, is shown in Figure 4-4.

Figure 4-4

Exploring the DNS namespace

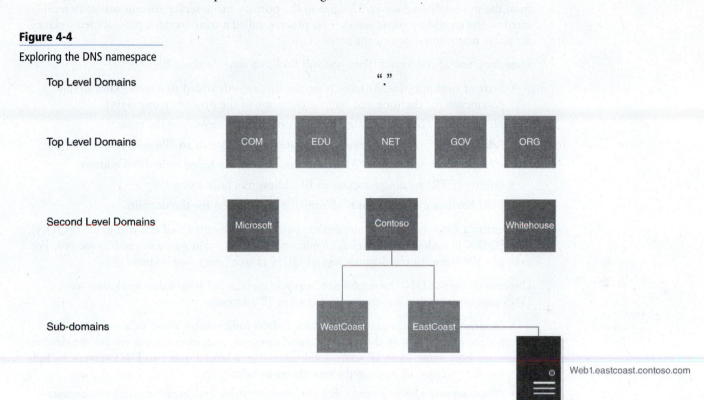

The root domain is managed by the Internet Corporation for Assigned Names and Numbers (ICANN) under the authority of the U.S. Department of Commerce. It is essential for the function of the Internet; without the root domain, services that depend upon DNS (e-mail, browsing the Internet, and so on) would not function. Although the root domain is represented by a single period, it is supported by several hundred root servers spread across the world (to see where they are located, visit the root servers website. The root servers have a file (zone file) that lists the names and IP addresses of the authoritative DNS servers for all top-level domains. Top-level domains define the organization type or geographic location. For example, .com is for commercial organizations, .gov is for government agencies, .org is for nonprofits, and so on.

Second-level domains, also called parent domains, can be divided into subdomains (child domains). When registering a second level domain for an organization, it is common to register multiple second-level domains (microsoft.com, microsoft.org, microsoft.net) to ensure that users can reach them regardless of whether they type .com, .net, or .org at the end of the address.

Active Directory domains utilize DNS when implementing their hierarchy and naming structure. When you install the first domain controller on a network, you are asked to install DNS automatically. When fully integrated with DNS, all domain controllers can access the data, replicate changes throughout the domain, and register clients into their zone. A zone is a scope of names that are served by a specific DNS name server. The part of the namespace that a zone is responsible for is known as the zone of authority. A zone must contain at least one domain, called the root domain of that zone. All the information about each zone is stored in a file called the zone database file. Inside the zone database file are the resource records that DNS uses to resolve host names to IP addresses.

The DNS server that creates and modifies a locally stored zone file is called the primary name server. A secondary name server is often used and holds a copy of the zone file that it gets from the primary name server. Updates to the primary name server are automatically replicated to the secondary name server. This process, called a zone transfer, provides redundancy for name resolution if one of the servers fails.

Here are a few of the record types you will find in a zone database file:

- Start of Authority (SOA) records are the first records added to a zone. They define parameters for the zone and include the name of the primary name server.
- Name Server (NS) records list any additional name servers for the zone.
- Address (host name) (A) records associate a host name to an IP4 address.
- Address (host name) (AAAA) records associate a host name to its IPv6 address.
- Pointer (PTR) records associate an IP address to a host name.
- Mail Exchange (MX) records identify the mail host(s) for the domain.

To identify a DNS host in the namespace, you use its fully qualified domain name (FQDN). The FQDN includes the host name in addition to the domain name where it is located. For example, the server in the diagram has a FQDN of web1.eastcoast.contoso.com.

Understanding the DNS hierarchy can help you understand how name resolution works. DNS uses two components to resolve names to IP addresses:

- **Resolver:** An application that provides address information about other network hosts for the client. During the name resolution process, if a client cannot resolve the destination's host name to an IP address, the resolver will send a query to DNS servers, including root servers, to look up the records on its behalf.
- **Name server:** This is a server that performs recursive and iterative queries to contact other DNS servers in an attempt to resolve a host name to an IP address if the DNS server cannot resolve it using its own records. When a computer uses a recursive query, it is putting the entire responsibility on the other computer to find the IP address. An interactive query is a call to a name server to reply with the requested data or tell it who else to talk to in order to find an answer to its request.

UNDERSTANDING THE DNS NAME RESOLUTION PROCESS

Let's say you have a user located in the microsoft.com domain who wants to access the web1 resource at the eastcoast.contoso.com domain. The DNS server that holds the records for web1 (authoritative server) is located in the eastcoast.contoso.com domain. The process works as shown in Figure 4-5.

Figure 4-5

Tracing DNS name resolution

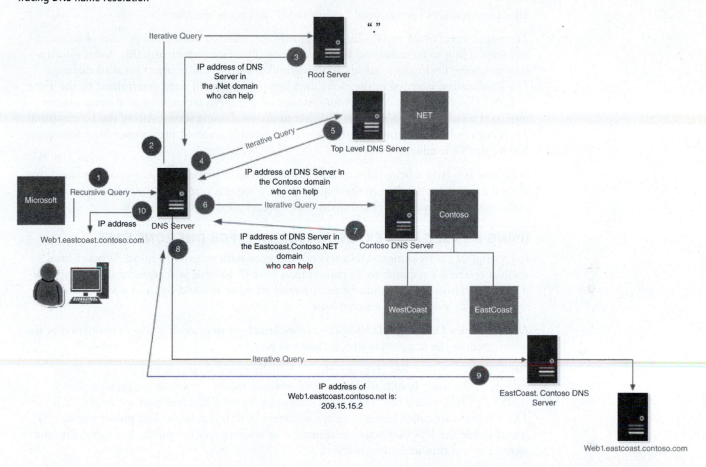

1. The resolver running on the client would send a recursive query to a DNS server located in its local domain, asking it to resolve web1.eastcoast.contoso.com to an IP address. Because this is a recursive query, the client is putting the entire responsibility for finding the answer on its local DNS server.

2. The user's local DNS server would first check its local cache to see whether it has a record on file for web1.eastcoast.contoso.com. Assuming that there was no information available, the DNS server would send an iterative query to a root server.

3. The root server would respond with the IP address of a DNS server located in the top-level domain for .NET.

4. The user's local DNS server would then send an iterative query to the DNS server located in the .NET domain, asking for the IP address to web1.eastcoast.contoso.com.

5. The .NET name server would reply with the IP address of a DNS server located in the contoso domain.

6. The user's local DNS server would then send an iterative query to the DNS server located in the contoso domain.

7. The DNS server located in the contoso domain would then respond with a DNS server located in the eastcoast.contoso domain.

8. The user's local DNS server would send another query to the DNS server located in the eastcoast.contoso.com domain.

9. The DNS server in the eastcoast.contoso.com domain would respond with the IP address for web1.eastcoast.contoso.com.

10. The local DNS server would return the IP address to the client.

The name server's host-to-IP address mappings are collected during the process of receiving and responding to recursive and iterative queries. The name servers use this stored information to resolve host names quickly. This method of storing information is called caching. The information is stored in the cache for a certain amount of time determined by the Time to Live (TTL) setting set by the Administrator on the DNS server located at eastcoast.contoso.com who owns the record. In addition to the local name server storing the information, the client resolver also stores information about recently resolved host names for a time specified by the TTL value.

Now that you have a better idea of how name resolution works, how can you be assured that the name server responding to the request is not a rogue server trying to redirect you to a malicious host or website? That's where DNS Security Extensions comes in.

USING DNS SECURITY EXTENSION (DNSSEC) FOR DNS ZONE FILES

In its original configuration, DNS was not designed with security in mind. When a local resolver received a response to its request for a host IP address, it accepted the first response it received. This response could be from a valid server or it could be from a rogue server attempting to redirect it to another host.

DNS Security Extension (DNSSEC) was implemented to provide a way to confirm that the server sending the response is who it claims to be.

DNSSEC uses public key cryptography to digitally sign a zone that in turn signs all the records in the zone. It adds four new DNS resource records: resource record signature (RRSIG), DNS public key (DNSKey), delegation signer (DS), and next secure (NSEC). These records are called resource record signature (RRSIG) records. The public key is stored inside the DNSKey resource records. The resolver uses the public key to validate the signatures and thus authenticate them.

To sign a DNS zone, right-click the zone and then choose *DNSSEC > Sign the Zone*. As part of the signing process, you choose a key master, which is the DNS server that generates and manages the keys for the DNSSEC-protected zone. Any DNS server that hosts a primary copy of the zone can be the key master. You will also need to configure a *key signing key (KSK)*. The KSK is an authentication key that corresponds to the private key used to sign one or more other signing keys. In most cases, the private key that corresponds to a KSK signs other keys used for signing the zone.

In Windows 8.1 and Windows Server 2012 R2, when the DNS client receives a response to a DNS query, it checks to see whether the response has been validated by a DNS server. When issuing queries, the DNS client relies on its local DNS server to confirm that the validation is successful. In both cases, the DNS client only checks for validation; it does not perform the validation itself.

USING WINDOWS INTERNET NAME SERVICE

Windows Internet Name Services (WINS) is another name resolution service that you find on some networks to help pre–Windows 2000 computers to resolve a computer name to an IP address. These older systems use NetBIOS over TCP/IP, which requires either a static LMHOSTS file (located on each computer) or a WINS server to resolve the names. Without a WINS server, these systems rely on broadcast messages to communicate. This introduces extra traffic on the network and also prevents the computers from accessing systems on other subnets. Since the release of Windows 2000, DNS has been the primary mechanism for name resolution.

USING LINK LOCAL MULTICAST NAME RESOLUTION (LLMNR)

Link Local Multicast Name Resolution (LLMNR), enabled on Windows 7 and later operating systems, is a fallback name resolution technique when DNS or WINS is not available. LLMNR works only on the local subnet, so it does not resolve names for systems that are located on another network. LLMNR can be used on a small home network or an ad-hoc network, or in situations in which the DNS server your client is configured to use is not available.

An LLMNR client tries to reach its primary and secondary DNS servers and fails over to LLMNR only if it cannot locate them. It then uses a multicast message for the name it is trying to resolve. Each computer on the local subnet that supports LLMNR checks its own host name. If it matches, it sends a unicast message along with its IP address to the computer. If it does not match, the packet is discarded.

PEER NAME RESOLUTION PROTOCOL (PNRP)

A *peer-to-peer (P2P) network* is a type of decentralized and distributed network architecture in which nodes or peers provide resources for other peers and use resources from other peers. *Peer Name Resolution Protocol (PNRP)* is a peer-to-peer protocol designed by Microsoft that is used to provide a secure, scalable, and dynamic name resolution for peer communications. One such application that uses the PNRP is Windows Remote Assistance Easy Connect.

The components that make up PNRP are:

- **Peer Name Resolution Protocol (PNRP) protocol:** Determines the interaction of the local computer with the PNRP cloud, which is a grouping of computers that can find each other. The local computer must have a default identity defined and proper permissions assigned in order to interact properly with the cloud.
- **Peer Name Resolution Protocol (PNRP) service:** Provides a secure, scalable, and dynamic name registration and name resolution protocol that relies on Internet Protocol version 6 (IPv6) and enables peer-to-peer functionality for PNRP-enabled applications.

For Windows 8 or 8.1 computer to use the PNRP, the PNRP service has to be started.

Exploring Network Settings

Network settings can be configured either manually or automatically using DHCP. Using manual settings can introduce configuration issues that can affect communications. Using a centralized approach to IP address management requires you to have a solid understanding of DHCP.

Configuring TCP/IP on a Windows 8.1 computer can be done manually or automatically. Setting up TCP/IP manually involves configuring it to use a static IP address. This involves entering an IP address, a subnet mask, and (if you need to access computers outside of the local network segment), a default gateway address. In order to resolve friendly names to IP addresses, you also need to configure at least one IP address for a DNS on your network.

 CREATE A STATIC IP ADDRESS

GET READY. To create a static IP address, perform the following steps:
1. Press the **Windows logo key + r**.
2. Type **cmd** and then press **Enter**.

3. Type **ping** <*ip address*>, where the <*ip address*> is the one you want to manu- ally configure for your computer. If the request times out, the IP address isn't active on the network.

   Write down this IP address.

TAKE NOTE ✱ This IP address must be one that is configured for use on the same network segment as your computer.

4. Type **exit** and then press **Enter** to close the cmd shell.
5. Press the **Windows logo key + i** and then click **Control Panel**.
6. Under *Network and Internet*, click **View network status and tasks**.
7. Click **Change adapter settings**.
8. Right-click your network adapter and then select **Properties**.
9. Click **Internet Protocol Version 4 (TCP/IPv4)** and then click **Properties**.

   Write down your current settings. You will reenter this information after completing the exercise.

10. Select **Use the following IP address** and then type the IP address, subnet mask, and default gateway you want to use.

11. Select **Use the following DNS server addresses** and then type an IP address for a preferred DNS server and an alternate DNS server (see Figure 4-6).

Figure 4-6

Entering a static IP address

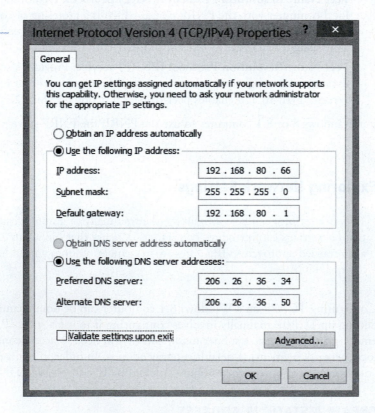

12. Click **OK** to accept your settings and to close the *Internet Protocol Version 4 (TCP/ IPv4) Properties* dialog box.

13. Click **Close** to close the *Ethernet Properties* dialog box.

    Do *not* close the *Network Connections* dialog box.

14. Press the **Windows logo key + r** and then type **cmd** to open a cmd shell.

15. Type **ipconfig/all** and then press **Enter** to confirm that your settings have been changed.

16. Type **exit** and then press **Enter** to close the cmd shell.

17. Return to the *Network Connections* dialog box.

18. Right-click your network adapter and choose **Properties**.

19. Click **Internet Protocol Version 4 (TCP/IPv4)** and then click **Properties**.

20. Reenter the settings that were in place in Step 9 to return your system to its original configuration.

If you selected the *Validate settings upon exit* option, Windows 8.1 performs a network diagnostics test to check your settings for any problems and offers to help to fix them. If you clicked the **Advanced** button, you could make additional configurations to your TCP/IP configuration. For example, in Windows 8.1, you can configure multiple gateways. When you do this, a metric is used to determine which gateway to use. Multiple gateways are used to provide fault tolerance so if one router goes down, the computer defaults to the other gateway.

You can configure additional DNS settings in the *Advanced TCP/IP Settings* dialog box (see Figure 4-7).

Figure 4-7

Reviewing advanced TCP/IP setting options

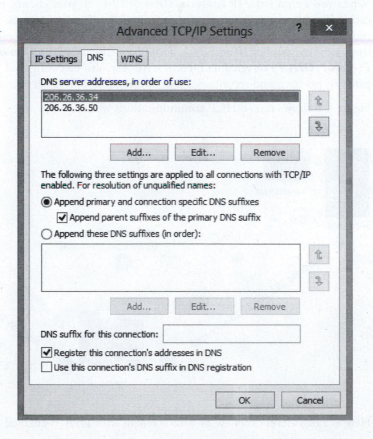

• **DNS server addresses, in order of use:** You can specify multiple DNS servers to use for name resolution. The order listed determines the sequence in which your client will attempt to resolve host names. If the first server does not respond to a name resolution request, the client will contact the next one in the list.

- **Append primary and connection specific DNS suffixes:** This is selected by default. If you attempt to access a computer named FileServer1, and the parent name is contoso. com, the name will resolve to FileServer1.contoso.com. If the FQDN does not exist in the domain, the query will fail. The parent name used (contoso.com) is configured on the *System Properties/Computer Name* tab.

- **Append parent suffixes of the primary DNS suffix:** This is selected by default. It works as follows: If the computer FS2 is in the eastcoast.contoso.com domain, DNS attempts to resolve the name to FS2.eastcoast.contoso.com. If this doesn't work, it tries FS2.contoso.com.

- **Append these DNS suffixes (in order):** Use this option when you want to specify DNS suffixes to use other than resolving names through your parent domain.

- **DNS suffix for this connection:** This setting overrides DNS names that are already configured for this connection. This is typically configured through the *System Properties/Computer Name* tab by clicking the More button.

- **Register this connection's addresses in DNS:** This option, selected by default, will automatically enter the FQDN in DNS records.

- **Use this connection's DNS suffix in DNS registration:** If this option is selected, all IP addresses for this connection will be registered in DNS at the parent domain.

UNDERSTANDING AUTOMATIC IP ADDRESS ASSIGNMENT

When you assign static IP addresses (IPv4 or IPv6) to your clients, you run the risk of duplicating IP addresses on your network or misconfiguring the settings, which can result in communication problems. A better approach is to dynamically assign your TCP/IP configurations from a central pool of IP addresses. This is done by using the ***Dynamic Host Configuration Protocol (DHCP)*** server. The DHCP server can also be configured to provide the default gateway, primary, and secondary DNS information; WINS server; and DNS domain name.

Figure 4-8 shows how DHCP communications work.

Figure 4-8

Understanding DHCP communications

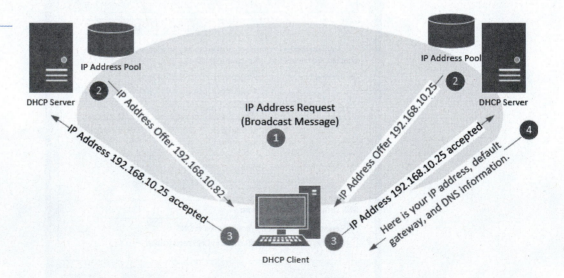

Here is a high-level overview of what happens with DHCP-enabled clients:

1. The DHCP-enabled client starts and broadcasts a request for an IP address over the network.

2. Any DHCP servers that receive the request review their pool of IP addresses (DHCP scope) and select one to offer to the client.

3. The client reviews the offers and broadcasts a message to the servers, letting them know which IP address it has accepted.

4. All DHCP servers see the message. Those whose offers are not accepted place the IP address back into their pool for a future client request. The server the client accepted acknowledges and provides additional information to complete the client configuration (default gateway, DNS information, and so on).

After a client receives an IP address and additional configuration information, it has it for a specific period of time called the *lease period*. When the lease is 50 percent expired, the client will try to renew it with the DHCP server. If the client cannot renew the lease, it will try again before the lease expires. At this point, if it cannot renew the lease, it will try to contact an alternate DHCP server. If all attempts fail, and the client cannot obtain a new IP address, it will autoconfigure with a Microsoft class B subnet (169.254.0.0/255.255.0.0).

Before it chooses an IP address in this network, the client will check to make sure no other client is using the address it wants to assign. After it has an address assigned, it will attempt to make contact with a DHCP server every 5 minutes. Once found, it will be reconfigured to use an address assigned from the DHCP pool.

> **TAKE NOTE***
>
> You can use DHCP to assign IPv6 addresses through either DHCPv6 stateful mode or stateless mode. If DHCPv6 is used, you need to make sure your routers are configured to support it.

USING STATEFUL DHCP AND STATELESS DHCP

There are two ways to configure DHCP when using it for IPv6 implementations: *stateless address configuration* and *stateful address configuration*.

If you are using DHCP to assign IPv6 addresses to stateful mode clients, they work similarly to the IPv4 when obtaining their IP addresses. When a client is configured to use DHCP in stateful mode, it will first use a link local address (IPv6). After it is autoconfigured with the link local address, it will seek out a DHCP server on the network by broadcasting a message every 5 minutes. When the client finally reaches a DHCP server, it will configure itself with the assigned IP parameters.

DHCP servers running in stateful mode will centrally manage the IPv6 addresses and configuration parameters and provide addresses to stateful clients.

> **TAKE NOTE***
>
> Link local addresses are equivalent to Automatic Private IP Addressing (APIPA) IPv4 addresses using the 169.254.0.0/255.255.0.0 prefix. These address always begin with FE80::/64.

Stateless mode clients work a little differently; they assign both a link local address and additional non–link local addresses by exchanging messages with neighboring routers. When a DHCP server is set up to serve stateless clients, the DHCP clients will autoconfigure using router advertisements. These clients do not use the DHCP server to obtain an IP address, but instead use it to only obtain additional configuration information such as DNS recursive name servers and a DNS search list (domains to be searched during name resolution). If a DHCP server has been configured to service stateless clients, it will not respond to clients asking for IP addresses.

IMPLEMENTING FAULT TOLERANCE AND USING DHCP RELAY AGENTS

Most networks implement at least two DHCP servers to provide fault tolerance by sharing a pool of IP addresses. To avoid duplicating IP addresses, the IP address pools on each DHCP are configured to not overlap.

Because clients send their DHCP requests via broadcast messages that do not cross routers, you must also have a way to allow DHCP-enabled clients to reach a DHCP server located on another subnet. This can be done by using **DHCP relay agents**, which convert a client's broadcasts into a unicast message that can then be forwarded directly to a DHCP server running on another subnet (see Figure 4-9).

Figure 4-9

Converting broadcasts into unicast messages using a DHCP relay agent

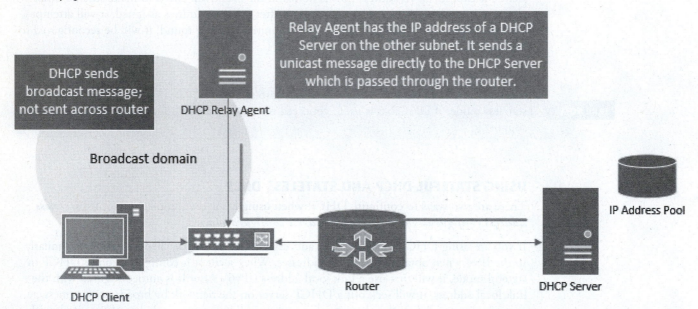

Relay Agent has the IP address of a DHCP Server on the other subnet. It sends a unicast message directly to the DHCP Server which is passed through the router.

DHCP sends broadcast message; not sent across router

DHCP Relay Agent

Broadcast domain

DHCP Client

Router

DHCP Server

IP Address Pool

Working with Wireless Networks and Connections

Introducing wireless networks and devices into your network involves having a strategy for addressing compatibility issues, addressing encryption capabilities for protecting data, and determining when to use ad-hoc versus infrastructure modes.

When designing your wireless network strategy, you must consider compatibility issues between devices, wireless standards, and security.

EXPLORING COMPATIBILITY ISSUES WITH WI-FI DEVICES

When purchasing wireless network equipment, you need to be aware of issues regarding compatibility between devices. You will face an array of different types of wireless equipment, each built against one or more of the Wi-Fi technology standards. Table 4-3 provides a summary for each standard you might encounter, along with a description of each.

Table 4-3

Wi-Fi Technology Standards

STANDARD	DESCRIPTION
802.11b	Supports bandwidth up to 11 Mbps; uses the 2.5 Ghz frequency; susceptible to interference with cordless phones, microwaves operating in same frequency; WEP- and WPA-supported.
802.11a	Supports bandwidth up to 54 Mbps; uses the 5 Ghz frequency; less interference with common household devices; higher frequency means shorter range compared with 802.11b and also less apt to penetrate walls; incompatible with 802.11b because they use different frequencies; WEP- and WPA-supported.
802.11g	Supports bandwidth up to 54 Mbps; uses the 2.5 Ghz frequency; backward-compatible with 802.11b; 802.11g was designed to use the best features of both 802.11b and 802.11a; WEP- and WPA-supported.
802.11i	Improved encryption for networks using the 802.11a, 802.11b, and 802.11g standards; introduces new encryption key protocols: Temporal Key Integrity Protocol (TKIP) and Advanced Encryption Standard (AES).
802.11n	Supports bandwidth approximately 300 Mbps; uses 2.5 and 5 Ghz frequencies; uses four spatial streams to simultaneously transfer data by using a channel width of 40 Hz designed to replace 802.11a, b, and g; backward-compatible with 802.11g; supports Wi-Fi Protected Access version 2 (WPA v2).
802.1x	Security standard for 802.11 networks that use RADIUS for authentication; provides key management; RADIUS provides centralized authentication, authorization, and accounting for remote connections.

REVIEWING ENCRYPTION PROTOCOLS

In each of the standards, encryption is provided to protect your wireless traffic. The following list represents the most common encryption protocols you will encounter on a wireless network:

- *Wireless Equivalent Privacy (WEP)* was designed to provide the same level of security found on wired networks. Over the years, WEP has proven to be very insecure, permitting a successful brute force password attack in seconds. WEP uses a data encryption scheme called RC4 with a shared key, which is used to encrypt and decrypt data. Because this key does not change automatically over time, anyone who can capture the wireless traffic can break the key and then gain access to your network.

- *Wi-Fi Protected Access (WPA)* was created to improve upon the encrypting and authentication features of WEP while WPA v2 was under development. It did this through the use of the TKIP to provide integrity, the AES protocol to provide encryption, and EAP to improve authentication capabilities.

- *Wi-Fi Protected Access (WPA) v2* replaced WPA in 2006. WPA v2 requires the use of stronger encryption (a new AES mode) and does not use TKIP, which introduced security limitations within the WPA implementation. Using WPA v2, the keys are changed regularly rather than staying the same, as they were in WEP implementations. WPA is compatible with 802.11a, 802.11b, 802.11g, and 802.11n.

WPA devices can operate in the following modes:

- *Personal mode* uses a preshared key or password. The master key is set on the access point (AP) and then all wireless clients are configured to use the key. The master key is then used by the client to generate a session key that it changes on a regular basis.

• *Enterprise mode* uses two sets of keys: a session key, changed each time the client communicates with the AP, and a master key. The master key is shared with all clients connected to the AP. Both keys are generated automatically and are changed on a regular basis. Enterprise mode uses IEEE 802.1x and EAP.

TAKE NOTE

The *Extensible Authentication Protocol (EAP)* is used in wireless networks to expand the number of authentication methods available. It supports one-time passwords, certificates, smart cards, and public key encryption. When users connect to an AP using EAP, their authentication request is forwarded to a *Remote Authentication Dial-In User Service (RADIUS) server*. When the RADIUS server receives the request from the AP, it searches its database for the name listed and the password. If the information is correct, the appropriate parameters (IP address, route information, protocol to use) are returned to the AP.

CONNECTING WIRELESS DEVICES

Wireless devices can be connected in two ways (see Figure 4-10):

Figure 4-10

Connecting wireless devices in an ad-hoc network and in infrastructure mode

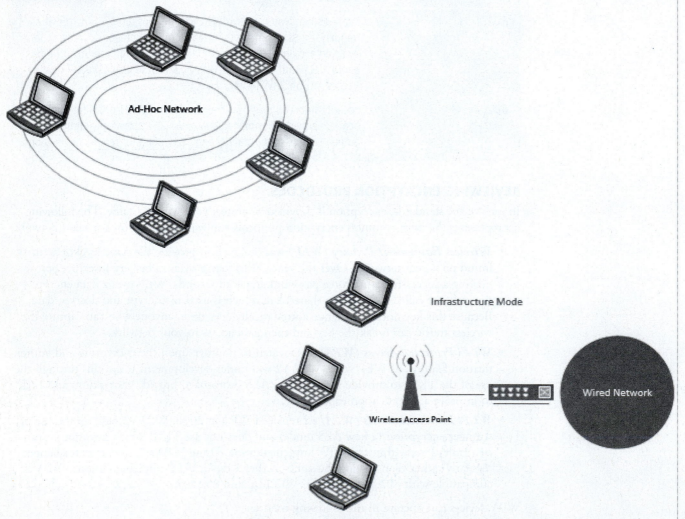

• *Ad-hoc:* Wireless clients connect to each other without the use of a wireless AP.
• *Infrastructure mode:* Wireless clients connect to a wireless AP. The AP does not have to be connected to a wired network.

After determining how you want to structure your wireless network, you need to configure your Windows 8.1 systems to connect to the wireless network.

With Windows 8.1, if you are within the broadcast range of a wireless AP, you do not have to preconfigure the wireless connection; just connect and let Windows determine the appropriate encryption settings.

The available wireless APs are presented, and you can determine which one to connect to. After selecting the AP, you need to enter a key to complete the connection.

CONNECT TO A WIRELESS AP (PRECONFIGURED)

GET READY. To connect to an existing wireless AP, perform the following steps:

1. From the Windows 8.1 start screen, press the **Windows logo key + i** and then click **Internet access**.

2. Choose the wireless network you want to connect to and then click **Connect**.

3. In the *Enter the network security key* field, type your wireless access key and then click **Next**.

4. Click **Yes, turn on sharing and connect to devices (for home or work networks)**.

You are now connected to your wireless network AP.

REVIEW WI-FI PROPERTIES

The Wi-Fi properties (see Figure 4-11) are very similar to the settings for any other network card, but let's take a closer look at what is different. The Wi-Fi properties can be found by pressing the **Windows logo key + i** and then clicking **Control Panel**. Under *Network and Internet*, click **View network status and tasks**. Click **Change adapter settings** and then right-click the wireless adapter and choose **Status**.

Figure 4-11 shows that additional information is provided for a Wi-Fi connection, including the following:

Figure 4-11

Reviewing Wi-Fi status

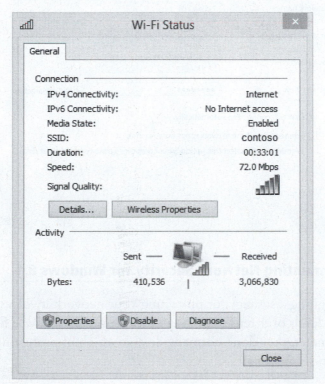

- **SSID:** *Service Set Identifier (SSID)* is the name of the wireless local area network, which consists of a case-sensitive, 32-alphanumeric character string. All wireless clients must use the same SSID to communicate.

- **Signal Quality:** This is the current signal strength between the wireless client and the wireless AP. More bars mean a stronger signal.

- **Details:** Provides network connection details (address, DHCP-enabled, IPv4/IPv6 configuration information).

- **Wireless Properties:** Provides you with the name of the wireless local area network (SSID), network type (ad-hoc vs. AP), and options for connecting to the wireless local area network (WLAN).

- **Security tab:** Provides information regarding the security type used (WPA v2-personal, WPA-enterprise); the encryption type (TKIP, AES); and the network security key, if used.

- **Properties:** Provides access to the connection properties, which are the same types of properties from the earlier discussion on configuring IP manually on a network adapter.

- **Disable:** Disables the wireless adapter and disconnects you from the network.

- **Diagnose:** Launches the Windows diagnostics process that identifies and attempts to correct any problems with connectivity.

If you need to manually connect to a wireless AP, enter information such as the network name, security type, encryption type, and security key. Figure 4-12 provides an example of the settings necessary to make a manual connection.

Figure 4-12

Understanding the wireless AP manual connection requirements

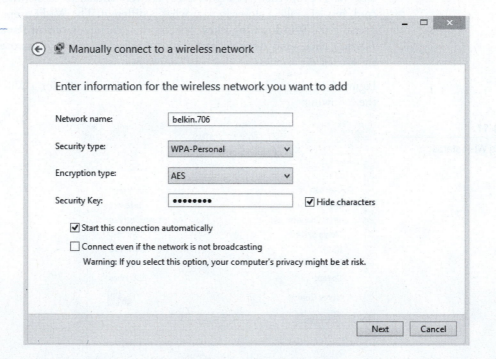

Implementing Network Security for Windows 8.1

Designing a strategy for protecting your network involves implementing multiple levels of defense. Although most companies have a firewall to protect their perimeter, they don't normally do a good job of protecting the individual hosts behind the firewall.

After you determine your IP addressing schemes and how you want to configure your network from a logical/physical layout, it's time to determine how to secure it. This starts with looking at your network perimeter(s), which are the locations in your network in which your trusted network connects to another probably untrusted network. These gateways between networks enable you to implement security, control the types of traffic allowed to enter and exit your network, and reduce your overall network traffic. The most obvious perimeter is where your company's network connects to the Internet, but other perimeters might exist.

It's common for administrators to build network subnets to isolate and control traffic within their own private network so they can restrict traffic to a certain subnet and improve overall performance. It can also help isolate certain areas of the network that contain sensitive information. For example, you might create a subnet that contains just the finance department's systems due to the confidential nature of the information they work with.

The device used to segment a network is a ***router***. Although routers can provide basic traffic management (inbound/outbound), their primary role is to forward traffic between networks. Companies that are serious about their network security will add a commercial-level firewall at the perimeter that leads to the Internet. In most cases, that should be sufficient enough to protect your network, but what happens if something is compromised on that firewall or if misconfiguration allows it to be bypassed? What if mobile users connect behind the firewall and attempt to gain access to a server or computer they are not authorized to use? This is where a host-based firewall can help.

COMPARING NETWORK PERIMETER FIREWALLS TO HOST-BASED FIREWALLS

There are two basic types of firewalls (see Figure 4-13):

Figure 4-13

Reviewing a network firewall and host-based firewall deployment

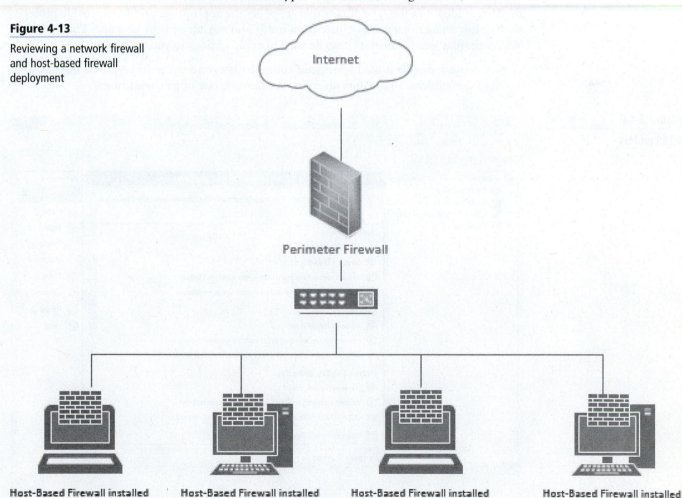

Internet

Perimeter Firewall

Host-Based Firewall installed · Host-Based Firewall installed · Host-Based Firewall installed · Host-Based Firewall installed

- *Network perimeter firewalls:* These firewalls are found on the boundary between an internal and external network. They can be hardware- or software-based, and provide several types of functionality including managing and monitoring traffic through stateful connection analysis, providing Internet Protocol Security (IPsec) authentication and encryption, and providing NAT.
- *Host-based firewalls:* These firewalls run on individual computers (hosts) within the local network. They are designed to provide a second layer of defense, protect the computer from attacks and unauthorized access, and block specific types of traffic.

Because a network perimeter firewall monitors only traffic coming in and out of the network, it represents a single point of failure and does very little to protect against attacks that occur from within the private network. Without an additional layer of defense, using just a network perimeter firewall can put your entire network at risk. To create an additional level of protection, consider using a host-based firewall such as the Windows Firewall with Advanced Security (WFAS).

Windows Firewall with Advanced Security (WFAS) combines a stateful host-based firewall with IPsec. It is designed to protect against attacks that originate from within your network or those that might bypass the network perimeter firewall(s). WFAS inspects both IPv4 and IPv6 packets that enter and leave your computer and then compares them against the criteria contained in the firewall's rules. If the packet matches a rule, the action configured in the rule is applied. If the packet does not match a rule, the firewall will discard it and record an entry in its log files.

EXPLORING THE WFAS PROFILES

WFAS is network location–aware, so it can determine the type of network you are connecting to. After it identifies the type of network, it applies the appropriate profile to provide protection against attacks that can originate from inside and outside of your network. The following WFAS profiles (see Figure 4-14) can be used to apply settings to your computer:

- A *domain profile* is used when your computer is connected to its corporate domain and can authenticate to the domain controller through one of its connections.

Figure 4-14

WFAS profiles

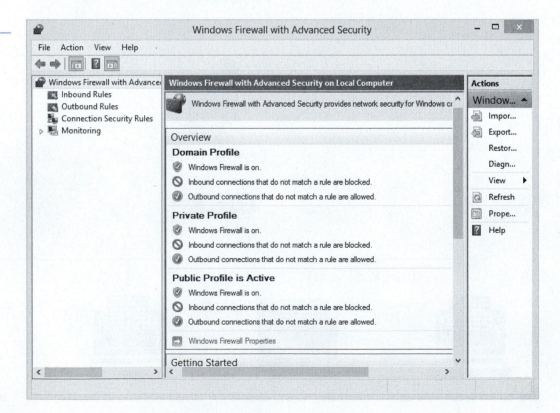

- A *private profile* is used when your computer is connected to a private network location (home or small office network) and is located behind a firewall and/or a device that performs NAT. If you are using this profile with a wireless network, you should implement encryption (WPA v2).
- A *public profile* is used when your computer is connected to a public network (for example, directly connected to the Internet). It is assigned to the computer when it is first connected to a new network; rules associated with this profile are the most restrictive.

You can click the Windows Firewall Properties link to see the range of settings available within each of the three profiles (see Figure 4-15).

Figure 4-15

Understanding WFAS profile property settings

These settings include the following:

- **Firewall state:** Set to On or Off.
- **Inbound connections:** Block, Block all connections, Allow.
- **Outbound connections:** Allow, Block.
- **Protected network connections:** Select the connections/interfaces you want Windows Firewall to help protect.
- **Settings:** Display notifications when a program is blocked from receiving inbound connections; allow unicast response to multicast or broadcast network traffic; rule merging (allow rules created by local administrators to be merged with rules distributed via Group Policy).
- **Logging:** Set the location for storing firewall logs along with the size limit for the log file; log dropped packets; log successful connections.

IPsec settings can be configured to control how keys are exchanged, how your data is protected, and the authentication methods you want to use.

- **IPsec defaults:** These settings determine how your computer will establish a secure connection by identifying how the keys will be exchanged, how data will be protected, and the authentication method to use.
- **IPsec exemptions:** This setting enables you to exempt Internet Control Message Protocol (ICMP) to simplify the troubleshooting process; ICMP is designed to detect and report error conditions.

- **IPsec tunnel authorization:** This setting enables you to specify the users and computers that are authorized to establish IPsec tunnel connections with your computer.

UNDERSTANDING INBOUND RULES, OUTBOUND RULES, AND CONNECTION SECURITY RULES

WFAS enables you to configure three types of firewall rules (inbound, outbound, and connection security) that can be applied to one or more of the profiles (domain, private, public). These rules govern how the computer sends and/or receives traffic from users, computers, applications, and services. When a packet matches the rule's criteria, it will allow the connection, explicitly block the connection, or allow it only if the connection is using IPsec to secure it.

When configuring inbound/outbound rules, you have the option of selecting criteria that include a program name, TCP/UDP port number, system service name, local and remote interfaces, interface types, users/groups, computers/computer groups, and protocols.

- *Inbound rules:* These rules explicitly allow or block inbound traffic that matches the criteria set in the rule. To set up an inbound rule, select the type (program, port, predefined, or custom), select the entity to which the rule applies (for example, program [all or path to specific .exe], port name/number), determine the action (allow, block, or allow if it is secure), select the profile it applies to (domain, private, public), and provide a name for the rule. When your system is set up, it is automatically configured to not allow unsolicited inbound traffic. If you decide to set up a service on your computer (a test website) and want others to connect to it, configure an inbound rule that allows traffic to the web service (typically running on TCP port 80).

- *Outbound rules:* These rules explicitly allow or deny outbound traffic that originates from the computer when it matches the criteria set in the rule. The setup for an outbound rule is identical to the options discussed in the inbound rule. Because outbound traffic is allowed by default, you create an outbound rule to block traffic that you did not want.

- *Connection security rules:* These rules secure the connection with both authentication (Kerberos, digital certificates, preshared keys) and encryption protocols. Connection security rules are used to determine how the traffic between the computer and others is secured. The process for creating a connection security rule involves setting the type of connection security you want to create (isolation, authentication encryption, server-to-server, tunnel), when you want authentication to occur on inbound/outbound connections (request but don't require it, require it for inbound but request for outbound, require for both), select the authentication method to use, which profile to apply the rule to (domain, private, public), and then provide a name for the rule.

TAKE NOTE*

Connection security rules specify how and when authentication occurs, but they do not allow connections. You need to create an inbound or outbound rule to allow the connection.

ADDRESSING CONFLICTS WITH FIREWALL RULES

When firewall rules conflict, they are applied in the following order (as soon as an incoming packet matches a rule, that rule is applied and processing stops):

1. Authenticated bypass rules: These are rules that allow a connection even if the existing firewall rules would block it. For example, you might be blocking a specific type of traffic but then want to allow a certain group of users and computers to bypass the block. These types of rules require that the authenticated computers utilize IPsec to prove their identity.
2. Block connection: Rules block matching inbound traffic.
3. Allow connection: Rules allow matching inbound traffic.
4. Default profile behavior: Block unsolicited inbound traffic; allow all outbound traffic.

CREATE AN OUTBOUND RULE

TAKE NOTE✱

Before performing the
following steps, close
Internet Explorer.

GET READY. To create an outbound rule, perform the following steps.

1. From the Windows 8.1 Start menu, type **Windows Advanced**. From *Results*, choose **Windows Firewall with Advanced Security**.

2. Right-click **Outbound Rules** and then choose **New Rule**.

3. Select **Program** and then click **Next**.

4. Click **Browse** and then navigate to the location of your installation of Internet Explorer. This can usually be found at c:\%ProgramFiles%\Internet Explorer\iexplore.exe.

5. Click **iexplore.exe** and then click **Open**.

6. In the *New Outbound Rule Wizard* dialog box, click **Next**.

7. Select **Block the connection** and then click **Next**.

8. Select **Domain**, **Private**, and **Public**; then click **Next**.

9. For the name of the profile, type **IE Restriction**; for the description, type **Restricts IE from connecting to the Internet**.

10. Click **Finish**.

    Do not close the *Windows Firewall with Advanced Security* dialog box.

11. Attempt to access the Internet using Internet Explorer. You should see the *This page can't be displayed* message.

12. Close the *Internet Explorer* window.

13. In the *Windows Firewall with Advanced Security* window, from the top menu, click **Action** and then choose **Export Policy**.

14. Navigate to a folder that you can access from your Windows Server 2012 R2 domain controller. In the *File name* field, type **IE Restriction** and then click **Save**.

    Make a note of where you stored this policy; you will use it in the next exercise.

15. When *Policy successfully exported* is displayed, click **OK**.

16. Return to the *Windows Firewall with Advanced Security* dialog box and click **Outbound Rules**.

17. Locate the IE restriction rule you created earlier, right-click it, and then choose **Delete**. Click **Yes** to confirm you want to delete the rule.

18. Attempt to access the Internet using Internet Explorer. You should be successful.

19. Close the *Internet Explorer* window and close the *Windows Firewall with Advanced Security* window.

EXPORTING FIREWALL CONFIGURATION RULES

After you export the current firewall configuration from the *Action* menu in the *Windows Firewall with Advanced Security* window, you can then import it on another standalone system or copy it to a folder to use as a backup in case you make changes to the policy and need to return it to a known state. Policy files are exported as (*.wfw) files.

If you want to deploy the firewall configuration to multiple computers in your domain, create a Group Policy Object (GPO) and import the firewall settings into the policy.

→ IMPORT A WINDOW FIREWALL RULE INTO A GROUP POLICY OBJECT

GET READY. To import the firewall policy you created earlier into a GPO and restrict the use of Internet Explorer for your domain, log in with Administrative privileges to your domain controller and then perform the following steps:

1. If Server Manager does not open automatically, click the **Server Manager** icon on the task bar.

2. Click **Tools > Group Policy Management**.

3. Expand the *contoso.com* domain folder, right-click **Group Policy Objects**, and then choose **New**.

4. For the name, type **IE Restriction** and then click **OK**.

5. Double-click the *Group Policy Objects* folder and click **IE Restriction**.

6. Right-click and choose **Edit**.

7. Expand **Computer Configuration > Policies > Windows Settings > Security Settings > Windows Firewall with Advanced Security**.

8. Right-click the **Windows Firewall with Advanced Security** policy and choose **Import Policy**.

9. When asked *Do you want to import a policy now?*, click **Yes**.

10. Browse to the folder where you saved the IE Restriction policy in the previous exercise. Click the **IE Restriction** policy and then click **Open**.

11. When you see *Policy successfully imported*, click **OK**.

12. Click the **Outbound Rules** folder.

    The IE Restriction policy is now listed in the GPO.

13. Close the *Group Policy Management Editor* window.

14. In the *Group Policy Management* console, right-click the **contoso.com** domain and choose **Link an Existing GPO**.

15. Click **IE Restriction** and then click **OK**.

16. Close the *Group Policy Management* console window.

    The GPO is now applied to your domain.

USING IP SECURITY

IP security (IPsec) is a suite of protocols that provides a mechanism for data integrity, authentication, and privacy for the Internet Protocol by providing message authentication and/or encryption. It can be used to protect data sent between hosts on a network by creating a secure electronic tunnel between two hosts. It can also be used for remote access/VPN connections.

To ensure that data cannot be viewed or modified by unauthorized users, the source computer will use IPsec to encrypt the information by encapsulating each data packet in a new packet that contains the information to set up, maintain, and tear down a virtual tunnel. The data is then decrypted at the destination computer.

IPsec includes a couple of modes and a couple of protocols. The two modes include:

- **Transport mode:** Used to secure end-to-end communications such as between a client and a server.

- **Tunnel mode:** Used for server-to-server or server-to-gateway configurations by creating a virtual path that a packet takes from the source computer to the destination computer. When packets are sent along this path, the packets are encrypted.

The two IPsec protocols are:

- **Encapsulating Security Payload (ESP):** Provides confidentiality (encryption), authentication (proves identity), integrity (verifies the packet has not be changed), and anti-replay (prevents packets to be reused to bypass security) for the IP payload only, not the entire packet. ESP operates directly on top of IP, using IP protocol number 50.

- **Authentication Header (AH):** Provides authentication, integrity, and anti-replay for the entire packet (both the IP header and the data payload carried in the packet). Since the payload is not encrypted, it does not provide confidentiality. The data is readable but protected from modification. AH operates directly on top of IP, using IP protocol number 51.

ESP and AH can be combined to provide authentication, integrity, and anti-replay for the entire packet, and confidentiality for the payload.

The AH protocol is not compatible with network address translation (NAT) because NAT devices need to change information in the packet headers. To allow IPsec-based traffic to pass through a NAT device, you must ensure that IPSec NAT-T is supported on your IPsec peer computers.

To configure IPsec between two hosts, you will configure connection security rules using the Windows Firewall with Advanced Security. The rules that you will have create include:

1. Enable the protocol that you want to secure.
2. Create a Connection Security rule on first host.
3. Create a Connection Security rule on second host.
4. Test the rules and monitor the results.

 ENABLE THE ICMP TRAFFIC ON SENDING HOST

GET READY. To enable ICMP traffic on Server01, perform the following steps:

1. Log in to *Server01*.
2. Click **Start**, and in the *Search* box, type **Windows Firewall with Advanced Security** and then press **Enter**.
3. Click **Inbound Rules**, right-click it, and then choose **New Rule**.
4. In the *New Inbound Rule Wizard* dialog box, on the *Rule Type* page (see Figure 4-16), click **Custom** and then click **Next**.

Figure 4-16

Opening the New Inbound Rule
Wizard

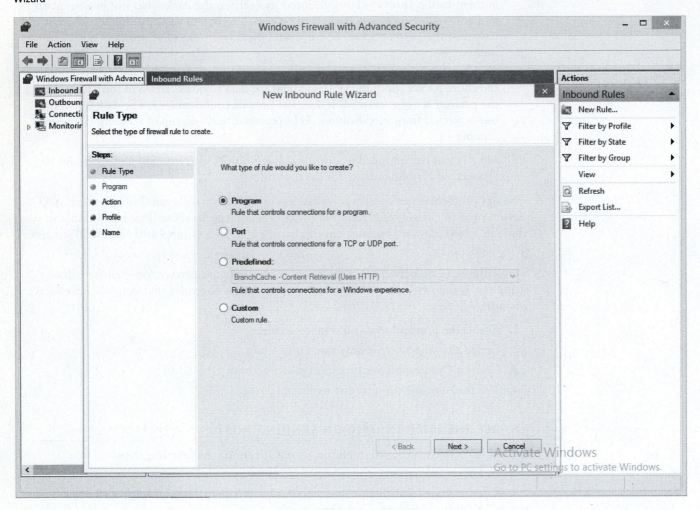

5. On the *Programs* page, click **Next**.

6. On the *Protocols and Ports* page, in the *Protocol type* list, click **ICMPv4** and then click **Next**.

7. On the *Scope* page, click **Next**.

8. On the *Action* page, click **Allow the connection if it is secure** and then click **Next**.

9. On the *Users* page, click **Next**.

10. On the *Computers* page, click **Next**.

11. On the *Profile* page, click **Next**.

12. On the *Name* page, in the *Name* box, type **ICMPv4 Allowed** and then click **Finish**.

CREATE A CONNECTION SECURITY RULE

GET READY. To create the account after Windows 8.1 is installed using the Charms bar, perform the following steps:

1. On *Server01*, in the Windows Firewall with Advanced Security console, click **Connection Security Rules**, right-click it, and then choose **New Rule**.

2. In the *New Connection Security Rule Wizard* (see Figure 4-17), on the *Rule Type* page, click **Server-to-Server** and then click **Next**.

Figure 4-17

Opening the New Connection Security Rule Wizard

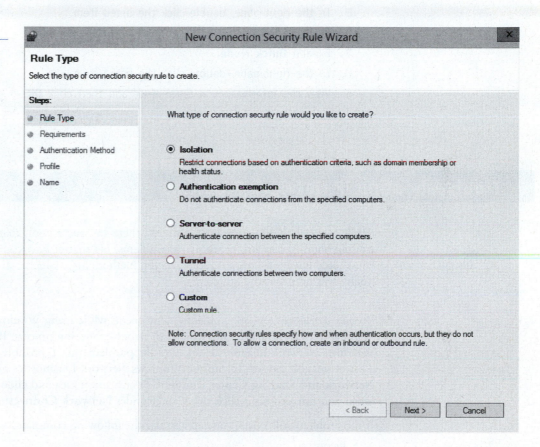

3. On the *Endpoints* page, click **Next**.

4. On the *Requirements* page, click **Require authentication for inbound and outbound connections** and then click **Next**.

5. On the *Authentication Method* page, click **Advanced** and then click **Customize**.

6. In the *Customize Advanced Authentication Methods* dialog box, under *First authentication*, click **Add**.

7. In the *Add First Authentication Method* dialog box, click **Preshared Key**, type **secret**, and then click **OK**.

8. In the *Customize Advanced Authentication Methods* dialog box, click **OK**.

9. On the *Authentication Method* page, click **Next**.

10. On the *Profile* page, click **Next**.

11. On the *Name* page, in the *Name* box, type **Contoso-Server-to-Server** and then click **Finish**.

12. Repeat the steps on Server02.

TEST THE RULES AND MONITOR THE RESULTS

GET READY. To create the account after Windows 8.1 is installed using the Charms bar, perform the following steps:

1. On *Server02*, right-click **Start** and choose **Command Prompt (Admin)**.
2. At the command prompt, type `ping 192.168.1.60` and then press **Enter**.
3. Switch to **Windows Firewall with Advanced Security**.
4. Expand **Monitoring**, expand **Security Associations**, and then click **Main Mode**.
5. In the right-pane, double-click the listed item.
6. View the information in *Main Mode* and then click **OK**.
7. Expand **Quick Mode**.
8. In the right-pane, double-click the listed item.
9. View the information in *Quick Mode* and then click **OK**.

■ Troubleshooting IP Network Problems

↓
THE BOTTOM LINE

While networks can be simple or complex, there are several tools that are invaluable when troubleshooting network connectivity problems. No matter how complex the network is, you should always follow a troubleshooting methodology, which will help you quickly isolate and pinpoint the problem.

If you experience network connectivity problems while using Windows 8.1, you can use Window Network Diagnostics to start the troubleshooting process. If there is a problem, Windows Network Diagnostics analyzes the problem and, if possible, presents a solution or a list of possible causes. To run the Windows Network Diagnostics program, right-click the **Network and Sharing Center** icon in the notification area and choose **Troubleshoot problems**. You can also right-click the adapter under **Network Connections** and click **Diagnose**.

If the problem still exists, you can also use the following command-line tools:

- ipconfig
- ping
- tracert
- pathping
- netstat
- telnet
- nslookup

In addition, you should also look at the logs shown in the Event Viewer. Some error messages might be found in the System and Application logs.

Viewing IP Configuration

When you cannot connect to a website or a server, the first thing you should check is the client IP configuration. This can be done by using Network Connections or the ipconfig command.

To view your network connections, you can open the Network Connections under the Network and Sharing Center and click Status. The General tab will show if the adapter has IPv4 and IPv6 connectivity, if the adapter is enabled, how long the adapter has been running and the speed of the adapter. It will also show you the bytes being sent and received from the adapter. If you click the Details button, you can view the network connection details including IP addresses, subnet mask, gateway, WINS and DNS servers, and physical/MAC address.

The *ipconfig command*—one of the most useful commands when troubleshooting network problems—displays all current TCP/IP network configuration values and refreshes Dynamic Host Configuration Protocol (DHCP) settings. Used without parameters, ipconfig displays the IP address, subnet mask, and default gateway for all adapters. When you execute **ipconfig /all**, it displays the full TCP/IP configuration for all adapters including host name, DNS servers, and the physical/MAC address.

If you are using DHCP servers to assign addresses, ipconfig /renew will renew the DHCP configuration from the DHCP server. This parameter is available only on computers with adapters that are configured to obtain an IP address automatically. You can also use ipconfig / release to release the DHCP address from a network adapter.

If the IP address is invalid, communication might fail. If the subnet mask is incorrect, you might have problems communicating with local or remote hosts. If the default gateway is invalid, you will have problems communicating with remote hosts, but you can still communicate with local hosts. If the DNS server is incorrect or missing, the computer might not be able to resolve names and communication might fail.

If a computer is configured to receive an IP address from a DHCP server and one does not respond, the computer will use the Automatic Private IP addressing, which generates an IP address in the form of 169.254.xxx.xxx and the subnet mask of 255.255.0.0. When you have an Automatic Private IP address, you can only communicate with computers on the same network/subnet that have an Automatic private IP address. Therefore, you will most likely not be able to communicate with any host on the network without the proper IP address and subnet mask.

Testing Network Connectivity

Assuming that you have the correct IP configuration, you need to determine if you can communicate with the destination host. Windows 8.1 provides several tools to determine if you have network connectivity; if you don't have connectivity, Windows 8.1.1 helps you pinpoint where the failure is occurring.

An extremely valuable tool in troubleshooting is the *ping command*. The ping command verifies IP-level connectivity to another TCP/IP computer by sending Internet Control Message Protocol (ICMP) Echo Request messages. The receipt of corresponding Echo Reply messages are displayed along with round-trip times. Ping is the primary TCP/IP command used to troubleshoot connectivity, reachability, and name resolution. Since it gives you the round-trip times, the ping command can also tell you if the link is slow between your host and the destination host.

To ping a host, you would execute ping followed by a host name or IP address. The ping command also supports the following parameters:

- **–t:** Specifies that ping continue sending Echo Request messages to the destination until interrupted. To interrupt and display statistics, press Ctrl+Break. To interrupt and quit ping, press Ctrl+C.
- **–a:** Specifies that reverse name resolution is performed on the destination IP address. If this is successful, ping displays the corresponding host name.
- **–n Count:** Specifies the number of Echo Request messages sent. The default is 4.
- **–l Size:** Specifies the length, in bytes, of the data field in the Echo Request messages sent. The default is 32. The maximum size is 65,527.

A *Request Timed Out* response indicates that there is a known route to the destination computer but one or more computers or routers along the path, including the source and destination, are not configured correctly. *Destination Host Unreachable* indicates that the system cannot find a route to the destination system and therefore does not know where to send the packet on the next hop.

Two other useful commands are the **tracert command** and **pathping command**. The tracert command traces the route that a packet takes to a destination and displays the series of IP routers that are used in delivering packets to the destination. If the packets are unable to be delivered to the destination, the tracert command displays the last router that successfully forwarded the packet. The tracert command also uses the ICMP protocol.

Pathping traces a route through the network in a manner similar to tracert. However, pathping also provides more detailed statistics on the individual hops.

TAKE NOTE *   Since ICMP packets can be used in Denial of Service (DoS) attacks, some routers and firewalls block ICMP packets. Therefore, when you try to ping a host with the ping, tracert, or pathping command, it might not respond even though the host is connected.

To isolate network connectivity problems, use the following troubleshooting process:

1. Verify host IP configuration.
2. Use the ping command to gather more information on the extent of the problem:
   - Ping the destination address.
   - Ping the loopback address (127.0.0.1).
   - Ping a local IP address.
   - Ping a remote gateway.
   - Ping a remote computer.
3. Identify each hop (router) between two systems using the tracert or pathping command.

To determine whether you have a network connectivity problem, you should ping the destination by name or by IP address. If the ping command shows you have network connectivity, your problem is most likely with the host requesting the services; or, the services on the destination could be down. It should be noted that if you ping by name, you should verify that the correct address was used.

If you appear not have network connectivity to a server or service, you will need to isolate where the connectivity problem occurs, starting with the host computer. Therefore, you should ping the loopback address and local IP address to determine whether your TCP/IP components are functioning. Next, if you ping a local IP address, your results will demonstrate whether you can communicate on the local subnet that you are connected to. If you still have not found the problem, you can then ping the remote gateway (most likely your default gateway) to determine if you can communicate with the router. Next, pinging a remote computer determines if you can communicate through your default gateway to a remote subnet. Finally, use the tracert and pathping commands to determine exactly where the problem is.

Testing Name Resolution

Since we often use names instead of addresses, you might need to verify that you have the correct name resolution when specifying a name. In Windows, the most common tool is nslookup.

Nslookup.exe is a command-line administrative tool for testing and troubleshooting DNS name resolution. Entering *hostname* in nslookup will provide a forward lookup of the host name to IP address. Entering *IP_Address* in nslookup will perform a reverse lookup of IP address to host name.

Entering nslookup puts you into an nslookup command environment that allows you to query specific servers using the server command and to query for specific resource records using the set type command.

If you found problems with the DNS, the ipconfig command can be used in certain situations:

- **ipconfig /flushdns:** Flushes and resets the contents of the DNS client resolver cache. During DNS troubleshooting, you can use this procedure to discard negative cache entries from the cache, as well as any other entries that have been added dynamically.

- **ipconfig /displaydns:** Displays the contents of the DNS client resolver cache, which includes both entries preloaded from the local hosts file and any recently obtained resource records for name queries resolved by the computer. The DNS Client service uses this information to resolve frequently queried names quickly, before querying its configured DNS servers.

- **ipconfig /registerdns:** Initiates manual dynamic registration for the DNS names and IP addresses that are configured at a computer. You can use this parameter to trouble-shoot a failed DNS name registration or resolve a dynamic update problem between a client and the DNS server without rebooting the client computer. The DNS settings in the advanced properties of the TCP/IP protocol determine which names are registered in DNS.

If you used the nslookup command to test DNS resolution and found a problem with name resolution, you would fix the problem at the DNS server. Unfortunately, previous DNS results that your system processes, such as when you access a web page using a browser, are cached in your memory. Therefore, if you correct the problem, you might need to flush your DNS cache using the ipconfig /flushdns command so that it can query and obtain the corrected values.

TAKE NOTE * If you use host files or lmhosts files, you should check to see if any entries might be incorrect. NSLookup only tests DNS name resolution and will not check to see if a host file or lmhost file is correct.

Viewing Port Usage

In some situations, you might not be able to test network connectivity with ping or similar utilities because ICMP packets are blocked by a firewall. In addition, even if a computer responds to ICMP packets, it doesn't tell you whether the computer is running the network service that you need to access. Therefore, there are several tools that can be used to look at the client and server network connections and services.

The *netstat* command displays active TCP connections, ports on which the computer is listening, Ethernet statistics, the IP routing table, IPv4 statistics (for the IP, ICMP, TCP, and UDP protocols), and IPv6 statistics (for the IPv6, ICMPv6, TCP over IPv6, and UDP over IPv6 protocols). Used without parameters, netstat displays active TCP connections. See Figure 4-18.

Figure 4-18

Netstat command

Netstat supports the following parameters:

- **–a:** Displays all active TCP connections and the TCP and UDP ports on which the computer is listening.

- **–e:** Displays Ethernet statistics, such as the number of bytes and packets sent and received. This parameter can be combined with –s.

- **–n:** Displays active TCP connections; however, addresses and port numbers are expressed numerically and no attempt is made to determine names.

- **–o:** Displays active TCP connections and includes the process ID (PID) for each connection. You can find the application based on the PID on the Processes tab in Windows Task Manager. This parameter can be combined with –a, –n, and –p.

- **–p Protocol:** Shows connections for the protocol specified by Protocol. In this case, the Protocol can be tcp, udp, tcpv6, or udpv6. If this parameter is used with –s to display statistics by protocol, Protocol can be tcp, udp, icmp, ip, tcpv6, udpv6, icmpv6, or ipv6.

- **–s:** Displays statistics by protocol. By default, statistics are shown for the TCP, UDP, ICMP, and IP protocols. If the IPv6 protocol for Windows XP is installed, statistics are shown for the TCP over IPv6, UDP over IPv6, ICMPv6, and IPv6 protocols. The –p parameter can be used to specify a set of protocols.

- **–r:** Displays the contents of the IP routing table. This is equivalent to the route print command.

- **Interval:** Redisplays the selected information every *x* seconds. Press CTRL+C to stop the redisplay. If this parameter is omitted, netstat prints the selected information only once.

Figure 4-19

Using Networking Monitor to view port usage

If you wish for a graphical tool to view port usage, you can use Resource Monitor's Networking tab, specifically the TCP connections and Listening Ports section. See Figure 4-19.

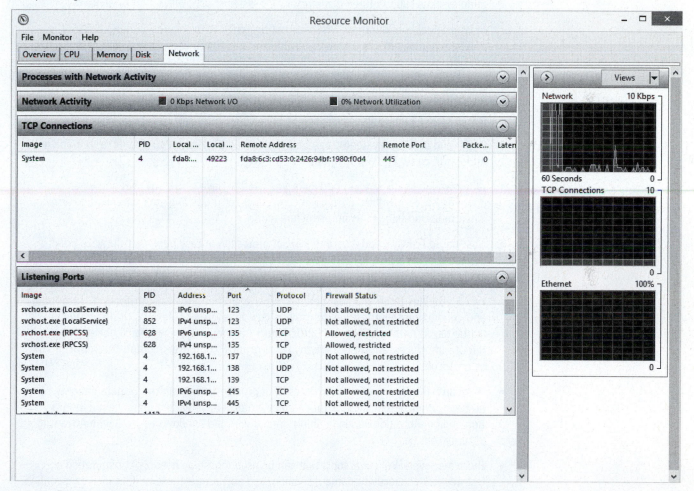

Telnet is a text-based communication program that allows you to connect to a remote server over a network to execute commands at a remote command prompt. Unfortunately, using the telnet command is frowned on in IT because telnet packets are not encrypted. Therefore, it is recommended that you use Secure Shell (SSH). However, you can also use the telnet command to test connectivity to a network service, such as checking a web server (port 80), checking a POP3 mail server (port 110), and checking a SMTP mail server (port 25).

```
telnet hostname port
```

To check the port 25 on a mail server (Server01), you can type:

```
telnet server01 25
```

TAKE NOTE*

Today, client telnet is disabled by default. Therefore, you will have to install or enable the feature before you can use it.

SKILL SUMMARY

- The goal of IPv6 was to address the exhaustion of the IPv4 address space (IPv4 addresses are 32 bits long, and IPv6 addresses are 128 bits long). The transition to IPv6 is expected to take several years; expect to see a mix of IPv4, IPv4/IPv6 (dual stack), and IPv6-only networks.

- To help an organization migrate from IPv4 to IPv6, several transition technologies have been created, including 6to4, ISATAP, and Teredo.

- Name resolution is the process of associating host names to IP addresses. Windows operating systems support three name resolution systems: DNS, WINS, and LLMNR.

- In its original configuration, DNS was not designed with security in mind. DNSSEC was implemented to provide a way to confirm the identity of DNS servers that respond to queries.

- IPv4 and IPv6 addresses can be configured manually or automatically by using DHCP. When configured manually, you introduce the chance for misconfigurations that can affect the computer's ability to communicate.

- DHCP and DHCP relay agents can be used both in IPv4 and IPv6 networks to manage IP address/IP configuration assignments.

- When working with wireless networks, you need to have a strategy that addresses compatibility issues, identifies encryption capabilities for protecting your data, and determines when to use ad-hoc versus infrastructure mode.

- Host-based firewalls add a second level of protection in case perimeter firewalls are bypassed. WFAS combines a stateful host-based firewall with IPsec that can help protect your individual computers.

- WFAS provides three profiles: domain, private, and public. It uses inbound, outbound, and connection security rules to provide custom security solutions that can block traffic based on a program, a TCP/UDP port number, a system service, local and remote interfaces, an interface type, users/groups, computers/computer groups, and/or protocols.

- IP security (IPsec) is a suite of protocols that provides a mechanism for data integrity, authentication, and privacy for the Internet Protocol by providing message authentication and/or encryption. It can be implemented with the Windows Firewall with Advanced Security console.

- There are several Windows tools that can be used to display network configuration and test network connectivity, name resolution, and port usage. These utilities include ipconfig, ping, tracert, nslookup, and netstat.

■ Knowledge Assessment

Multiple Choice

Select the correct answer for each of the following questions.

1. Which of the following are true regarding IPv4?
   a. 32-bit address
   b. 128-bit address
   c. Consists of a network ID and MAC address
   d. Consists of a host ID and MAC address

2. How many bits does a standard IPv6 unicast address use to represent the network ID?
   a. 32
   b. 64
   c. 128
   d. 10

3. Which of the following Windows PowerShell commands performs a DNS name query for www.contoso.com?
   a. `ping www.contoso.com`
   b. `dnsquery www.contoso.com`
   c. `resolve-DNSName -Name www.contoso.com`
   d. `resolve-DNSquery www.comcast.net`

4. Which of the following DNSSEC records stores the information used to validate signatures?
   a. RRSIG
   b. DNSKEY
   c. NSEC
   d. DS

5. Which of the following is a name resolution mechanism supported in Windows? (Choose all that apply)
   a. EFS
   b. WINS
   c. LLMNR
   d. DNS

6. Which of the following converts a DHCP client's broadcast into a unicast message that can be forwarded to a DHCP server located on another subnet?
   a. DHCP forwarder
   b. DNS forwarder
   c. DHCP
   d. DHCP relay agent

7. Which type of wireless network enables clients to connect to a wireless AP?
   a. ad-hoc
   b. WAN
   c. LAN
   d. infrastructure mode

8. Which of the following WFAS profiles is assigned to a computer when it is first connected to a new network?
   a. public profile
   b. domain profile
   c. private profile
   d. WFAS new profile

9. Which of the following rules specifies how and when authentication occurs?
   a. public rule
   b. inbound rule
   c. connection security rule
   d. outbound rule

10. Which of the following is true regarding WFAS rules? (Choose all that apply)
    a. Outbound traffic is allowed by default.
    b. Unsolicited inbound traffic is not allowed.
    c. Solicited inbound traffic is allowed.
    d. Connection security rules require inbound/outbound rules to allow connections.

11. Which IPv6 transition technology starts with the FE80:/64 prefix and includes the IPv4 address in hexadecimal form at the end of the IPv6 address?
    a. 6to4
    b. ISATAP
    c. Teredo
    d. NAT-T

12. Which tool is used to manage secure connections based on IPsec in Windows 8.1?
    a. Windows Firewall
    b. Windows Firewall with Advanced Security
    c. IPsec manager
    d. Server Manager

13. Which command is used to test name resolution problems with DNS?
    a. ipconfig
    b. ping
    c. nslookup
    d. netstat

14. Which command is used test network connectivity between two hosts?
    a. ipconfig
    b. ping
    c. nslookup
    d. netstat

Best Answer

Choose the letter that corresponds to the best answer. More than one answer choice might achieve the goal. Select the BEST answer.

1. Which of the following provides automatic IP addresses for clients located on a subnet without a DHCP server?
   a. DHCP server
   b. static IP address
   c. DHCP relay agent
   d. resolver

2. Which configuration can a DHCPv6 server setup running in stateless mode provide to clients?
   a. IP address
   b. subnet mask
   c. default gateway
   d. DNS recursive name servers

3. Which TCP/IP setting should be configured when you want to specify DNS suffixes to use other than resolving names through your parent domain?
   a. DNS suffix for this connection
   b. Append these DNS suffixes (in order)
   c. Append primary and connection specific DNS suffixes
   d. DNS server address, in order of use

4. When connecting a Windows 8.1 computer to a wireless AP, which of the following Wi-Fi encryption protocols provides the highest level of security?
   a. WPA
   b. WEP
   c. WPA v2
   d. IPsec

5. Which of the following should be used to protect clients from being redirected to a rogue host when using DNS?
   a. IPsec
   b. TLS/EAP
   c. DNSSEC
   d. Cache poisoning

Matching and Identification

1. Match the following terms with the related description or usage.
   _____ a) DNSSEC
   _____ b) AAAA record
   _____ c) DNS server
   _____ d) LLMNR
   _____ e) subnet mask
   _____ f) ANDing
   _____ g) domain profile
   _____ h) WPA enterprise mode
   _____ i) stateful
   _____ j) connection security rule
   1. A feature in WFAS that is used to determine how the traffic between two computers is authenticated and encrypted.
   2. The process a computer uses to determine whether another computer is on the same network.
   3. Used to associate a computer name to an IP address. Stores host to IP address mappings in a zone file.
   4. Used to determine the bits associated with the network ID and host ID.
   5. Uses two sets of keys: a session key that is changed each time the client communicates with an AP and a master key.
   6. An IPv6 address (host name) mapping to its IP address.
   7. A fallback name resolution technique when DNS and WINS are not available.
   8. Used when a computer is connected to its corporate domain and can authenticate to a domain controller.
   9. One of the ways you can configure a DHCP IPv6 server; provides IP address configuration to DHCP clients.
   10. Uses public key cryptography to digitally a zone.

Build a List

1. Specify the correct order of the steps that must be completed for a DHCP-enabled client to obtain IPv4 addressing information. Not all steps will be used.
   _____ Client receives offers of an IP address from a DHCP server.
   _____ DHCP server selects an IP address from the available address pool.

_____ Client broadcasts request for an IP address.

_____ Client sends broadcast message letting other DHCP servers know it has accepted an IP address offer.

_____ Client requests additional IP configuration from a selected DHCP server (DNS, default gateway)

_____ Client sends a recursive query to a DHCP server.

2. Specify the correct order of the steps in which WFAS rules are applied.

_____ Allow connections

_____ Default profile behavior

_____ Block connections

_____ Authenticated bypass rules

3. Specify the correct order of the steps that must be completed to create an outbound rule that blocks a program.

_____ Browse to the program's install location, select the program's executable, and then click **Open**.

_____ Open the *Windows Firewall with Advanced Security* console.

_____ Select the program to block and then click **Next**.

_____ Right-click **Outbound Rules** and then choose **New Rules**.

_____ Select **Block the connection**.

_____ Type a name and description for the rule and then click **Finish**.

_____ Select **Domain, Private, and/or Public profile**.

Choose an Option

1. Identify the option that automatically enters the FQDN of the computer into the DNS records.

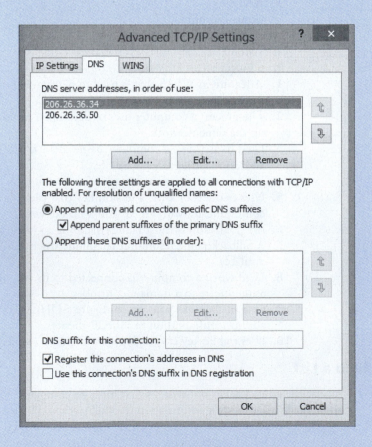

■ Business Case Scenarios

Scenario 4-1: Assigning IP Addresses

You have a network broken into six subnets and have placed a DHCP server on subnets 1, 3, and 5. Computers on subnets 2, 4, and 6 are not receiving IP addresses. How should you address the issue without having to enter static IP addresses on each of those systems?

Scenario 4-2: Configuring WFAS Security Rules

You have Windows 8.1 clients that are configured to use WFAS. You create a new connection security rule and apply it to the computers. What else do you need to do to complete the setup?

Supporting Remote Access

70-688 EXAM OBJECTIVE

Objective 2.2 – Support remote access. This objective may include but is not limited to: Virtual Private Network (VPN), including Connection Manager Administration Kit (CMAK); Remote Desktop Protocol (RDP), including Remote Desktop Services Gateway access; DirectAccess; remote administration; Network Access Protection (NAP)

LESSON HEADING	EXAM OBJECTIVE
Providing Off-Network Use and Management	
Exploring Virtual Private Networks	Virtual Private Network (VPN), including Connection Manager Administration Kit (CMAK)
Understanding PPTP	
Understanding L2TP/IPsec	
Understanding Secure Socket Tunneling Protocol (SSTP)	
Understanding VPN Reconnect (IKEv2)	
Selecting the Appropriate VPN Protocol	
Using Connection Manager and the Connection Manager Administration Kit (CMAK)	Virtual Private Network (VPN), including Connection Manager Administration Kit (CMAK)
Creating a VPN Connection Using the Create a VPN Connection Wizard	
Managing VPN Clients using Windows PowerShell	
Troubleshooting VPN Connections	
Exploring Remote Access using Direct Access and Routing and Remote Access (RRAS)	
Enhancements in DirectAccess with Windows Server 2012 R2	DirectAccess
Understanding How DirectAccess Works	
Planning Your Server Deployment	
Planning Your DirectAccess Client Deployment	
Using the Getting Started Wizard to Set Up a Remote Access Server	
Deploying Remote Access in the Enterprise	Network Access Protection (NAP)

Troubleshooting DirectAccess	
Supporting Remote Desktop Services (RDS)	Remote Desktop Protocol (RDP), including Remote Desktop Services Gateway Access
Supporting Remote Desktop Protocol	
Supporting Remote Desktop Services Gateway Access	Remote Desktop Protocol (RDP), including Remote Desktop Services Gateway Access
Using Remote Assistance	
Performing Remote Administration	
Using Remote Server Administration Tools (RSAT) for Windows 8.1	Remote administration
Using Windows PowerShell Remoting	
Exploring Metered Networks	

KEY TERMS

Connection Manager (CM)

Connection Manager Administration Kit (CMAK)

DirectAccess

L2TP/IPsec

metered internet connections

Network Access Protection (NAP)

Network Location Server (NLS)

Point to Point Tunneling Protocol (PPTP)

Remote Assistance

Remote Desktop Connection (RDC)

Remote Desktop connection authorization policies (RD CAP)

Remote Desktop Connection Broker (RD Connection Broker)

Remote Desktop Gateway (RD Gateway)

Remote Desktop Licensing

Remote Desktop Protocol (RDP)

Remote Desktop resource authorization policies (RD RAP)

Remote Server Administration Tools (RSAT)

Remote Desktop Session Host

Remote Desktop Virtualization Host

Remote Desktop Web Access

Secure Socket Tunneling Protocol (SSTP)

Virtual Private Network (VPN)

VPN Reconnect (IKEv2)

Windows PowerShell Remoting

WMI Filter

■ Providing Off-Network Use and Management

 THE BOTTOM LINE   To manage off-network systems and devices you need to assess their current health, provide remote assistance and apply remediation steps.

To be able to monitor and manage off-network systems effectively, you need to be able assess their current health, provide remote assistance when necessary, and apply the appropriate remediation steps in order to get them back into compliance even when they are outside of your corporate network.

Microsoft offers several ways to manage and protect your off-network computers and devices.

- Windows Intune (discussed in Lesson 12) provides a cloud-based management solution that helps you manage your computers and mobile devices through a Web console. It provides the tools, reports, and licenses to ensure your computers are always current and protected. From a mobile device perspective, it allows you to work through Exchange ActiveSync or directly through Windows Intune to manage your remote workforce. Since Windows Intune is cloud-based, your users will not have to be attached to your corporate network in order to receive updates, patches or receive help removing malware.

- Remote Access Servers with Network Access Protection (discussed later in this lesson) allows you to create and enforce health requirement policies that specify the required software and system configurations the clients must have when connecting to your corporate network. In situations where a remote user has been off-network for a period of time, when they do reconnect, NAP will inspect the system and if not in compliance, redirect it for remediation to an isolated network segment where it can be updated with the latest service packs, updates, and virus definitions before being allowed to reconnect to the rest of the network.

- DirectAccess (discussed later in this lesson) allows users to initiate connections with management servers, which provide services such as Windows Update, Network Access Protection and antivirus support. Management servers can also be setup to communicate with DirectAccess clients to perform software and hardware inventory assessments.

■ Exploring Virtual Private Networks

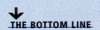 **THE BOTTOM LINE**

A VPN is a private network that uses tunneling, authentication and encryption protocols to allow users to access a private network over the public Internet.

CERTIFICATION READY
Virtual Private Network (VPN), including Connection Manager Administration Kit (CMAK)
Objective 2.2

A *Virtual Private Network (VPN)* is a private network that uses a public network (for example, the Internet) to connect remote sites and users. The VPN makes it appear to computers, on each end of the connection, as if they are actually connected to the same network. This point-to-point connection is emulated by encapsulating the packet in an IP Header. The information in the header is used to route the information between the two VPN endpoints.

Tunneling protocols, authentication protocols and encryption levels applied to the VPN connections determine the level of VPN security you have available. In order for a VPN to work both the client and server will need to utilize the same protocols. Overall, VPNs can provide the following capabilities:

- Data encryption (confidentiality)
- Authentication
- Data Integrity: Ensure the packets are not modified while in transit
- Non-Repudiation: Guarantee the packets came from the source at a specific time

The VPN uses the concept of tunneling (see Figure 5-1) to establish and maintain a logical network connection.

Figure 5-1

VPN tunnel

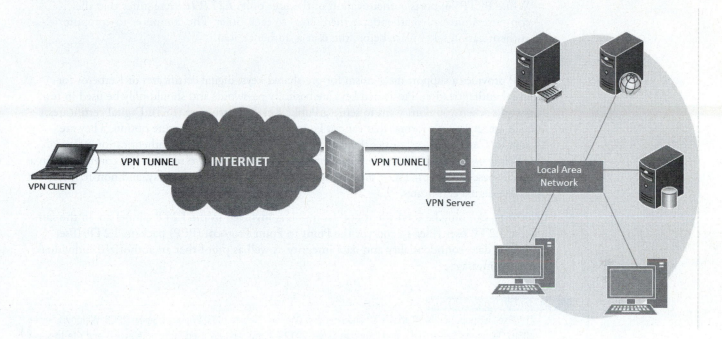

There are four types of VPN Tunneling protocols you will encounter:

- Point to Point Tunneling Protocol (PPTP)
- Layer 2 Tunneling Protocol over IPsec (L2TP/IPsec)
- Secure Socket Tunneling Protocol (SSTP)
- VPN Reconnect (or IKEv2)

Understanding PPTP

> ***Point to Point Tunneling Protocol (PPTP)*** has widespread support with nearly all versions of Windows. It uses the Microsoft Point to Point Encryption (MPPE) protocol with RC4 (128-bit key) to protect data that is in transit.

Although not as secure as L2TP/IPsec (discussed later) it can provide a reasonably secure option for remote access and site-to-site VPNs when used on combination with an authentication protocol such as MS-CHAPv2.

PPTP provides confidentiality meaning that it prevents the data from being viewed but it does not provide data integrity. In other words, it does not protect the packet from being intercepted and modified. PPTP does not implement any mechanisms that ensure the data is actually sent by the authorized person.

➕ **MORE INFORMATION**

You can only encrypt data with PPTP if you use MS-CHAPv2 and EAP-TLS as the authentication protocol. PPTP is supported natively by Windows XP and later client operating systems, Windows Server 2003, 2008, 2008R2, Windows Server 2012, and Windows Server 2012 R2 server operating systems. It is typically used for remote access and site-to-site VPNs; works with IPv4; uses Network Address Translation (NAT), which is supported via PPTP enabled NAT routers. It uses PPP for user authentication and RC4 for data confidentiality.

Understanding L2TP/IPsec

While PPTP supports authentication of the user only, **L2TP/IPsec** requires that the computers mutually authenticate themselves to each other. The computer-to-computer authentication takes place before the user is authenticated.

L2TP provides a support mechanism for pre-shared keys, digital certificates or Kerberos for mutual authentication. Pre-shared keys are basically passwords and should only be used in test networks when you don't want to setup a Public Key Infrastructure (PKI). Digital certificates, which are stored in a format that cannot be modified, offer a more secure option. They are issued by Certificate Authorities that you trust. Kerberos is the native authentication protocol for Windows Server 2003 and later and provides the easiest way to secure VPN connections in a domain-based environment. It provides mutual authentication, anti-replay, and non-repudiation just like digital certificates.

Kerberos can only be used when both computers involved in the L2TP tunnel are in the same forest. L2TP uses IPsec to encrypt the Point to Point Protocol (PPP) packets. L2TP/IPsec provides data confidentiality and data integrity as well as proof that an authorized individual sent the message.

+ MORE INFORMATION

L2TP/IPsec is supported by Windows XP and later and Windows Server 2003, Windows Server 2008, Windows Server 2008R2, Windows Server 2012, and Windows Server 2012 R2. It is typically used for remote access and site-to-site VPNs; works over IPv4 and IPv6; supports Network Address Translation. It uses IPsec with 3DES (168bit key) and uses UDP Ports (500, 1701, 5500). It uses IPsec for machine authentication followed by PPP for user authentication.

Understanding Secure Socket Tunneling Protocol (SSTP)

Secure Socket Tunneling Protocol (SSTP) improved upon the PPTP and L2TP/IPsec VPN tunneling protocols. It works by sending PPP or L2TP traffic through an SSL 3.0 channel.

The SSTP protocol uses SSL and TCP port 443 to relay traffic. By using TCP port 443, it will work in network environments where other VPN protocols might be blocked when traversing firewalls, network address translation (NAT) devices, and web proxies. SSTP uses a 2048bit certificate for authentication and implements stronger encryption, which makes it the most secure VPN protocol.

IKEv2 consists of the following protocols: IPsec Tunnel Mode, IKEv2, Encapsulating Security Payload (ESP), and MOBIKE. IKEv2 is used by IPsec for key negotiations, ESP for securing the packet transmissions, and MOBIKE (Mobility and Multi-homing Protocol) is used for switching tunnel endpoints. MOBIKE ensures that if there is a break in connectivity, the user can continue without restarting the connection.

+ MORE INFORMATION

SSTP is supported by Windows Vista SP1, Windows 7, Windows 8/8.1 client operating systems, Windows Server 2008, Windows Server 2008 R2, Windows Server 2012, and Windows Server 2012 R2 server operating systems. It is designed for remote access VPN and works over IPv4 and IPv6 networks, and traverses NAT, Firewalls and Web proxies. It uses a generic port that is rarely blocked by firewalls. It uses PPP for user authentication and RC4/AES for data confidentiality.

Understanding VPN Reconnect (IKEv2)

> ***VPN Reconnect (IKEv2)*** is a feature introduced with Routing and Remote Access Services (RRAS) in Windows Server 2008 R2 and Windows 7. It is designed to provide users with consistent VPN connectivity and automatically reestablish a VPN when users temporarily lose their Internet connection.

VPN Reconnect was designed for those remote workers who are sitting in the coffee shop, waiting at the airport for their next plane to arrive, trying to submit that last expense report from their hotel room or working anywhere Internet connections are less then optimal.

It differs from other VPN protocols in that it will not drop the VPN tunnel that is associated with the session. Instead, it keeps the connection alive for 30 minutes by default after it's been dropped. This allows you to reconnect automatically without having to go through the process of selecting your VPN connection and re-authenticating yourself all over again.

> ✚ **MORE INFORMATION**
>
> The IKEv2 setting (network outage) can be found in the RRAS console by right-clicking the RRAS server selecting Properties > IKEv2 tab. VPN Reconnect is supported by Windows 7 and Windows 8/8.1 as well as Windows Server 2008 R2, Windows Server 2012, and Windows Server 2012 R2;, it is designed for remote access VPN. It works well over IPv4 and IPv6 networks and traverses NAT. It also supports user or machine authentication via IKEv2 and uses 3DES and AES for data confidentiality.

Selecting the Appropriate VPN Protocol

> When selecting the appropriate VPN protocol to use, you must take into consideration operating systems, authentication requirements, and limitations.

When selecting the appropriate VPN protocol to use, you must take into consideration the following:

- Operating systems you will be using and their ability to traverse firewalls, NAT devices and web proxies.
- Authentication requirements (for computers as well as users).
- Implementations: Site-to-site VPN or a remote access VPN.

In most situations, using VPN Reconnect (IKEv2) will provide you the best option for security and uninterrupted VPN connectivity. You can then use SSTP for your VPN solution as a fall back mechanism.

Using Connection Manager (CM) and the Connection Manager Administration Kit (CMAK)

> ***Connection Manager (CM)*** is a client network connection tool that helps administrators to simply the management of their remote connections.

CM uses profiles that consist of settings that allow connections from the local computer to a remote network.

You use the ***Connection Manager Administration Kit (CMAK)*** to create and customize the profiles for CM and to distribute them to users. The profile, once completed, contains all the settings necessary for the user to connect including the IP address of the VPN server.

CM supports different features in a profile depending upon the operating system that is running on the client computer. You must create a connection profile on a computer that uses the same architecture (32/64-bit) as the clients on which you will install the profile.

When running the CMAK Wizard, you will be asked to specify the operating system on which the Connection Manager profile will be run. Options include:

- Windows Vista or above
- Windows Server 2003, Windows XP, or Windows 2000

 INSTALL CMAK ON WINDOWS SERVER 2012 R2

GET READY. To install CMAK on Windows Server 2012 R2, perform the following steps:

1. Open **Server Manager**.
2. Click **Manage > Add Roles and Features**.
3. Click **Next**.
4. Click **Role-based or feature-based installation**.
5. Select a server from the server pool and then click **Next**.
6. Click **Next** to move past the *Roles* selection.
7. Click **RAS Connection Manager Administration Kit (CMAK)**.
8. Confirm installation selections and then click **Install**.
9. Confirm installation completes and then click **Close**.
10. Select **Tools > Connection Manager Administration Kit**.

 SET UP A SIMPLE VPN ONLY PROFILE USING CMAK

GET READY. To set up a simple VPN only Profile using CMAK, perform the following steps:

TAKE NOTE * This activity is designed to expose the features and options available when creating a Connection Manager profile using CMAK from Windows Server 2012 R2. As you walk through each step, be sure to read the explanation behind it to gain more insight into how CMAK could be used in your specific network environment.

1. Start *Connection Manager* by clicking **Server Manager > Tools > Connection Manager Administration Kit**.
2. After reading the *Welcome* message, click **Next**.
3. On the *Select the Target Operating System* page, click **Windows Vista or above** and then click **Next**.
4. On the *Create or Modify a Connection Manager profile* page, click **New Profile** and then click **Next**.
5. On the *Specify the Server Name and the File Name* page, in the **Service name** text box and the **File name** text box, type **MyVPN** and then click **Next**.
6. On the Specify a *Realm Name*, click **Do not add a realm name to the user name** and then click **Next**.
7. On the *Merge Information from Other Profiles* page, when prompted to merge information with another profile, click **Next**. If you had an additional profile, you could merge phone book information, access numbers and VPN host address information.

8. On the *Add Support for VPN Connections* page, click **Phone book from this profile**. Then in the *Always use the same VPN server* text box, type **RemoteServer.contoso.com** and then click **Next**.

9. On the *Create or Modify a VPN Entry* page, click **Edit** to view the settings that can be configured for this VPN profile (see Figure 5-2).

Figure 5-2

Configuring VPN settings

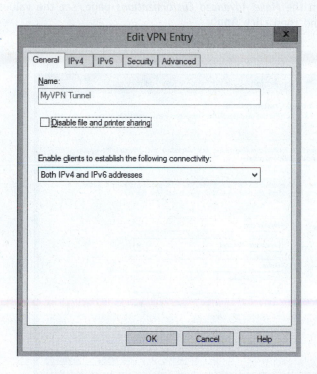

10. Click OK to close the Edit VPN Entry dialog box.

11. Back on the *Create or Modify a VPN entry* page, click Next.

12. On the *Add a Custom Phone Book* page, clear the **Automatically download phone book updates** option and then click **Next**.

13. On the *Configure Dial-up Networking Entries* page, click **Next**.

14. On the *Specify Routing Table Updates* page, make sure the **Do not change the routing tables** option is selected and then click **Next**.

15. On the *Configure Proxy Settings for Internet Explorer* page, make sure **Do not configure proxy setting** is selected and then click **Next**.

16. On the Add Custom Actions page, click **Next** to *not* add any custom actions.

17. On the *Display a Custom Logon Bitmap* page, click **Next** to display a default graphic or select one of your own.

18. On the *Display a Custom Phone Book Bitmap* page, click **Next** to display a default graphic for a custom phone book.

19. On the *Display Custom Icons* page, click **Next** to use a default icon for the Connection Manager user interface.

20. On the *Include a Custom Help File* page, click **Next** to use the default help file.

21. On the *Display Custom Support Information* page, add any text you want to appear in the logon dialog box and then click **Next**. (For example, type **Contact Support at 800-123-1234**.)

22. On the *Display a Custom License Agreement* page, when prompted to display a custom license agreement, click **Next**.

23. On the *Install Additional Files with the Connection Manager profile* page, specify any additional files that the Connection Manager profile will require and then click **Next**.

24. On the *Build the Connection Manager Profile and Its Installation Program* page, select the **Advanced customization** option and then click **Next**.

25. On the *Make Advanced Customizations* page, set the values shown in Figure 5-3 and then click **Apply**.

Figure 5-3

Performing advanced customization of the profile

26. Make a note of the location where the profile will be saved. By default this will be:

c:\Program Files\CMAK\Profiles\Windows Vista and above\MyVPN\MyVPN.exe

27. Click **Finish**.

On the Add Support for VPN Connections page, you can specify the VPN server name or IP address. If you select the Allow the user to choose a VPN server before connecting, you can provide a text file that lists the VPN servers from which the user can choose. The following provides you with an example that can be created and modified within Notepad:

[Settings]

default=Contoso CorpHQ

UpdateURL=http://remoteusers.Contoso.com/MyVPNfile.txt

Message=Select a server that is closest to your location.

[Contoso VPN Servers]

Contoso Computers CorpHQ=remoteusers.contoso.com

Contoso Computers Los Angeles=LA.remoteusers.contoso.com

Contoso Computers Austin=Austin.remoteusers.contoso.com

By using Phone Book Administrator, which is included with Connection Point Services (CPS), you can create a phone book file that contains a list of multiple access numbers that can be used to connect to a remote dial-up network. CPS consists of a Phone Book Service (PBS) and the Phone Book Administrator (PBA). PBS is an extension to Internet Information Services extension. The PBA allows you to create and edit up to 100 unique phone books. Each phone book is a collection of Points of Presence (POPs) or dial up entries. The PBA allows you to associate POPs with the network configurations you define in the Connection Manager profile.

Creating a VPN Connection Using the Create a VPN Connection Wizard

> Windows 8.1 provides a simple Getting Started Wizard—also known as the Get Connected Wizard(GCW)—that helps make the setup and configuration of a VPN connection quick and simple for end users.

To make the process of setting up a VPN profile and connecting to a VPN much simpler in Windows 8.1, you can use the Create a VPN Connection Wizard.

The Getting Started Wizard requires that you enter the server information and then it auto-discovers the authentication methods and tunneling protocols during the initial connection process.

 CREATE A VPN CONNECTION USING THE GETTING STARTED WIZARD

GET READY. To create a VPN using the Getting Started Wizard, perform the following steps:

1. Press the **Windows logo key + q**.
2. Type **VPN** and then set the context to **Settings**.
3. From the *Results* list, click **setup a virtual private network (VPN) connection**.
4. In the *Create a VPN connection* Wizard, on the *Do you want to set up an Internet connection before continuing?* page, click **I'll set up an Internet connection later**.
5. On the *Type the Internet address to connect to* page, in the *Internet address* text box, type the host name or IP address of the Remote Access server. In the *Destination name* text box, type a label that will identify the VPN connection. Click **Create**.

   Authentication and Tunneling protocols will be negotiated and configured during the first successful connection attempt using the user name and password (see Figure 5-4).

Figure 5-4

Creating a VPN Connection

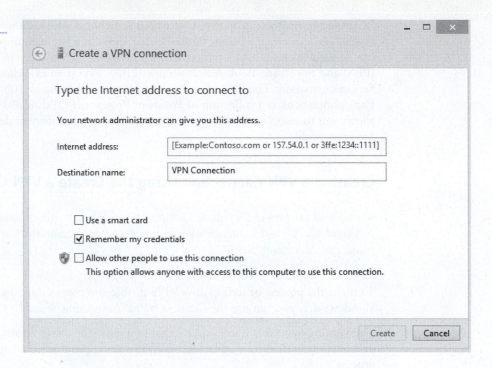

6. Press the **Windows logo key + c** to open the Charms bar.
7. Click **Settings** and then click the Internet access icon.
8. Click the VPN connection you created and then click **Connect**.
9. Type your credentials and then click **OK**.

If you selected *Remember my credentials* after making the initial connection, you can clear them by right-clicking the connection and choosing Clear cached credentials (see Figure 5-5).

Figure 5-5

Viewing the credentials

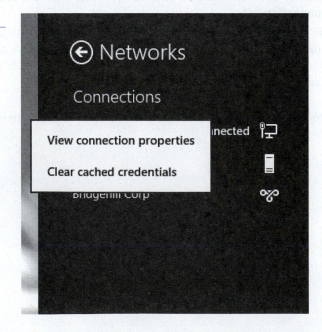

You can also view and edit your connection by clicking the *View connection properties* option (see Figure 5-6).

Figure 5-6

Viewing the VPN connection properties

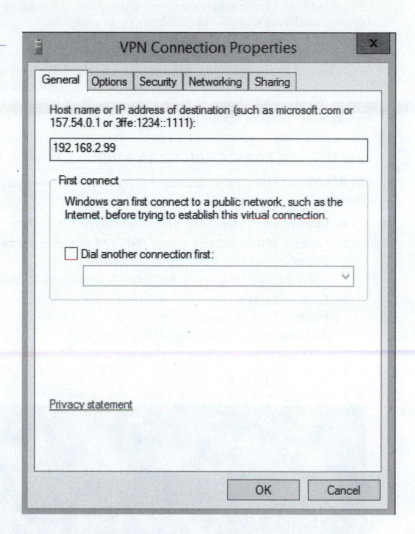

The following provides a brief explanation for each tab:

- **General**: Provides host name and IP address of VPN server.
- **Options**: Enables and disables your credentials, sets idle time before hanging up, and configures PPP settings.
- **Security**: Configures Data encryption settings, authentication, and tunneling protocols.
- **Networking**: Configures transports (IPv6, IPv4, File and Printer Sharing, and Client for Microsoft Networks).
- **Sharing**: Enables settings that allow others to connect through this computer's network connection.

 **MORE INFORMATION**
You can delete the VPN connection at Control Panel > Network and Internet > Network Connections.

Managing VPN Clients Using Windows PowerShell

Windows PowerShell cmdlets allow you to streamline the setup of roles and features during installation and confirm settings on your computer.

As you learned in earlier lessons, Windows PowerShell cmdlets can streamline the setup of VPN connections. You can also use them to view, create, configure and remove VPN connections on Windows 8.1 clients. In this section, you'll learn how to use Windows PowerShell to perform these common administrative tasks.

 CREATE A VPN CONNECTION USING WINDOWS POWERSHELL

GET READY. To create a VPN Connection using Windows PowerShell, perform the following steps:

1. Open Windows PowerShell with Administrator permissions.
2. Create a VPN connection named **MyPSVPN** and then set the server to Remote-Server.Contoso.com by entering the following:

   Add-VpnConnection –Name MyPSVPN –ServerAddress RemoteServer.Contoso.com

3. Confirm the VPN connection was created by executing the following command (see Figure 5-7):

   Get-VpnConnection –Name MyPSVPN

Figure 5-7

Confirming the VPN connection was created

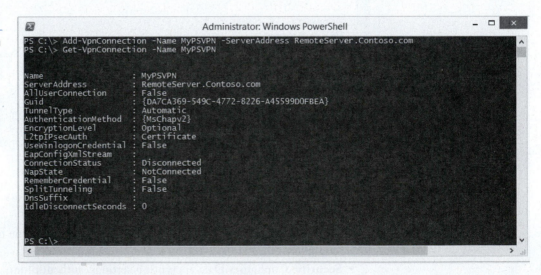

4. Create another VPN connection named VPNInt that uses split tunneling.

   Add-VpnConnection –name VPNInt –ServerAddress RemoteServer.Contoso.com –splittunneling

5. Review the VPN connection currently configured on the client by executing the following command:

   Get-VpnConnection

When viewing the second connection, you see that split-tunneling is enabled. After further research, you learn that split-tunneling allows the remote access VPN client to connect to your corporate network via the VPN link and also connect to the Internet via the interface established by the VPN itself. At this point, the client can connect to the file servers, database servers, mail servers, and other corporate resources using the VPN connection. When the user attempts to connect to an Internet resource (for example, an FTP site or a website) while working on the wireless network provide by her local coffee shop, their connection request does not go through the VPN link but instead goes through the gateway provided by the coffee shop's network. This creates the possibility that someone could use the VPN client's authenticated connection to gain access to the corporate network. You decide this is a security risk, so you delete the setting.

6. Remove split-tunneling from this configuration by entering the following. (Note: Setting-splittunneling to 0 is the equivalent of False, which disables the setting.)

   ```
   Set-VpnConnection -name VPNInt -Server
   RemoteServer.Contoso.com -splittunneling 0
   ```

7. Confirm the split-tunneling setting was changed from True to False by running the following command:

   ```
   Get-VpnConnection
   ```

8. Remove the VPNInt and MyPSVPN connections using the following command. (Note: the -force switch bypasses the need to confirm the deletion.)

   ```
   Remove-VpnConnection -Name MyPSVPN,VPNInt
   -force
   ```

9. Confirm the deletion by executing Get-VpnConnection.

Troubleshooting VPN Connections

As you already know, VPN connections are relatively complicated when compared to connecting to a local area network. Most users don't really care how a VPN works; they care only that their VPN connections work when needed.

When users are having problems with VPN connections, you should check the following:

- Ensure that the user can connect to his or her personal network, and have a connection to the Internet.
- Check to see if the host name used in the VPN connection is resolves properly.
- Verify the credentials of the VPN client, which consist of user name, password, and domain name are correct and that the VPN server can validate them.
- Verify that the user account of the VPN client is not locked out, expired, disabled.
- Verify also that the time the user is attempting the connection is allowed
- Verify that the user is using the correct VPN technology including using the appropriate the correct authentication protocol.
- Verify that the RRAS is running on the VPN server.
- Verify that the VPN server is enabled for remote access from the VPN server Properties dialog box General tab.
- Verify that the WAN miniport PPTP and WAN miniport L2TP devices are enabled for inbound remote access from the properties of the Ports object in the RRAS snap-in.
- Verify that you have free connections available for the remote access connection.

- You need to check the remote access policy that is assigned to the user and ensure that the user is granted access to the remote access connection.
- Check any firewalls to ensure that firewall will allow the necessary connections.
- If you are using L2TP with IPsec, which requires a computer certificate, verify that the proper computer certificate is installed, and that the certificate is not expired or revoked. The certificate should also match the computer name.

Lastly, Table 5-1 shows common VPN connection errors.

Table 5-1

Common VPN connection errors

ERROR MESSAGE	CAUSE	SOLUTION
Error 800: VPN Server is Unreachable	PPTP/L2TP/SSTP packets from the VPN client cannot reach the VPN server.	Ensure the user has Internet access and ensure that the appropriate ports are open on the firewall.
Error 721: Remote Computer is Not Responding	This issue can occur if the network firewall does not permit GRE traffic (IP protocol 47). PPTP uses GRE for tunneled data.	Configure the network firewall between the VPN client and the server to permit GRE. Additionally, ensure that the network firewall permits TCP traffic on port 1723. Both of these conditions must be met to establish VPN connectivity by using PPTP.
Error 741/742: Encryption Mismatch Error	These errors occur if the VPN client requests an invalid encryption level or if the VPN server does not support an encryption type that the client requests.	Check the properties on the Security tab of the VPN connection on the VPN client. If Require data encryption (disconnect if none) is selected, clear the selection and retry the connection. If you are using NPS, check the encryption level in the network policy in the NPS console, or check the policies on other RADIUS servers. Ensure that the encryption level that the VPN client requested is selected on the VPN server.

TAKE NOTE   Many users will try to ping a VPN connection to check their network connectivity. They might not get a successful ping, however, because the packet filter or firewall prevents the delivery of Internet Control Message Protocol (ICMP) messages to and from the VPN server.

Exploring Remote Access Using DirectAccess and Routing and Remote Access (RRAS)

THE BOTTOM LINE

DirectAccess allows your remote users to connect automatically whenever their clients detect an Internet connection. RRAS is used to provide support for legacy VPN clients.

With the release of Windows Server 2012, Direct Access and Routing and Remote Access have now been combined into a single Remote Access role. You can configure both from within a single console that allows you to configure, manage, and monitor the DirectAccess and VPN remote access servers in your organization. Using the built-in dashboard, you can view server and client activity, generate detailed reports and even monitor the resources being accessed by the clients. Windows PowerShell can also be used to create automate scripts for remote access setup, configuration, troubleshooting and management tasks.

Enhancements in DirectAccess with Windows Server 2012 R2

DirectAccess is designed for use by domain-based clients—Windows 7 (Enterprise and Ultimate), Windows 8/8.1 (Enterprise), Windows Server 2008 R2, Windows Server 2012, and Windows Server 2012 R2). Routing and Remote Access Services (RRAS) provides traditional VPN access for legacy clients, non-domain clients, third party VPN clients and site-to-site connections between servers.

In previous releases (Windows Server 2008 R2), you had to deploy Direct Access and RRAS separately. RRAS implements IKEv2 and configures incoming and outgoing packet filters to drop all packets using transition technologies. On the other hand, Direct Access uses IPv6 transition technologies to establish client connections and IPsec Denial of Service Protection (DoSP) to drop all IPv4 traffic and IPv6 traffic not protected with IPsec. In Windows Server 2012 R2, Microsoft resolved these issues by modifying the IKEv2 policies to allow IPv6 transition technology traffic and modified the DoSP to allow VPN traffic.

Windows Server 2012 R2 also removes the need to use Public Key Infrastructure, which was a major obstacle to deploying DirectAccess in Windows Server 2008 R2/Windows 7. It does this by configuring the clients to send authentication requests to a Kerberos proxy service that runs on the Direct Access server. The Kerberos proxy service sends the requests to a domain controller for authentication.

DirectAccess doesn't use a traditional VPN connection. While a traditional VPN required the user to manually initiate and disconnect a VPN connection when they wanted to connect to their corporate office, DirectAccess is designed to establish connectivity whenever an Internet connection is available. This occurs whether the user is logged on or not. From an administrator perspective, this allows you to manage and monitor the remote computer to apply patches and check for compliance enforcement.

Additional Features in Windows Server 2012 and Windows Server 2012 R2 include:

- Force tunneling (sends all traffic through the DirectAccess connection).
- Network Access Protection (NAP) compliance.
- Support for locating the nearest Remote Access server from DirectAccess clients distributed across different geographical locations.
- Deploying DirectAccess for only remote management.

- You can configure the DirectAccess server with two network adapters at the network edge or behind an edge device, or with a single network adapter running behind a firewall or NAT device. By using a single adapter, you remove the requirement of needing dedicated public IPv4 addresses for DirectAccess deployments. Clients connect with the DirectAccess server by using IP-HTTPS.

Understanding How DirectAccess Works

DirectAccess works by establishing two IPsec tunnels from the client to the DirectAccess server. The IPv6 packets, protected using IPsec, are encapsulated inside IPv4 packets to make the transition across the Internet, as shown in Figure 5-8.

Figure 5-8

DirectAccess tunnels

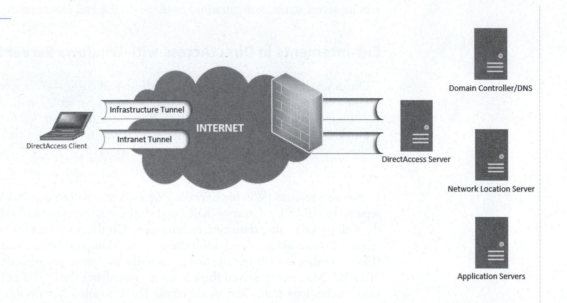

CERTIFICATION READY
DirectAccess
Objective 2.2

The first IPsec tunnel is an infrastructure tunnel that is used to communicate with the DNS server and domain controller to obtain group policy and to request authentication. The second tunnel is used to authenticate the user and provide access to resources inside the network. In the figure below, you will see a *Network Location Server (NLS)*. This can be installed directly on the Remote Access server or on another server in the network. NLS plays a critical role in whether the DirectAccess client components are enabled. In fact, NLS is basically a web server used by the client to determine if it is on the corporate network. If it detects that is it on the corporate network, the DA client components are not enabled. If it cannot connect to the NLS, it assumes it is not on the corporate network and enables DirectAccess. The secret to how this works is a URL written into the client's registry by way of a group policy created during the deployment of the Remote Access Server. The client uses the URL and DNS to attempt to locate the NLS.

The DA clients use IPv6 to connect to resources on the intranet or to other DA clients. In situations where you have servers providing resources running on the intranet that do not support IPv6, or you have disabled IPv6, or you use applications that do not work natively with IPv6, you will need to provide access to these devices for the DirectAccess clients. In Windows Server 2012 R2, this is accomplished through the implementation of a protocol translation and name resolution gateway that supports NAT64 and DNS64.

NAT 64 will receive packets from the DA client and convert them into IPv4 before sending it to the resource on the intranet. It will convert IPv4 packets to IPv6 packets before sending the information back to the DA client. DNS64 handles the client's DNS query by converting the IPv4 answers into an associated IPv6 mapping on NAT64.

Planning Your Server Deployment

When deploying Remote Access on the server, there are several decisions you will need to make.

These decisions include the topology you will use, whether or not you will support Windows 7 and 8/8,1 clients, and if you will implement a VPN for clients that do not support DirectAccess. You will also need to identify your IP addressing requirements; review your firewall settings, certificate requirements, and DNS server information; and you also must address Network Location Service information issues.

- Microsoft's Remote Access supports one and two adapter topologies. When a single adapter is used the server should be installed behind a device such as a firewall or router. If you setup a remote access server with two adapters, one adapter is connected to the internal network and the other to either a perimeter network or directly to the Internet. If two adapters are used, you will need to make sure they are detected appropriately during the setup process. To make this process easier, name one of the internal and the other external prior to starting the installation of Remote Access.

- If you will be supporting Windows 7 and 8/8.1 remote clients, you will need to perform additional advanced configuration steps to enable them to connect via DirectAccess.

- If you will be supporting remote clients that do not support DirectAccess or will be unmanaged, you will need to provide VPN access. Using the Getting Started Wizard configures VPN IP addresses to be distributed by a DHCP Server and also configures the VPN clients to be authenticated using Active Directory.

- Firewall settings will need to be reviewed if you will be placing the RAS on an IPv4 subnet to ensure traffic is allowed to pass through: 6to4 traffic requires IP protocol 41 both inbound and outbound, IP-HTTPS requires TCP destination port 443 and TCP source port 443 outbound; If RAS is deployed with a single adapter and you install the network location service functionality, you will need to exempt TCP port 62000.

- During the setup of Remote Access, you will need to specify and IP address or fully qualified domain. This information, called the ConnectTo address is matched with the self-signed certificate used in IP-HTTPS connections and must be available via the public DNS. It is also used by the remote clients to connect to the server.

- If you configure your remote access server to use SSTP VPN, the wizard will integrate the certificate used by SSTP for IP-HTTPS. If SSTP VPN is not configured, the wizard will check to see if one has been configured for IP-HTTPS. If it can't find one, the wizard will provision a self-singed certificate and automatically enable Kerberos for authentication.

- DNS is used by DirectAccess clients to locate the Network Location Server. If they can reach the NLS, the clients assume they are on the local network and will not use DirectAccess and will rely on the DNS server configured on their local adapter for name resolution. If the client cannot locate the NLS, it will assume it is on the Internet and will use DirectAccess. This means it will consult its name resolution policy table (NRPT) to select a DNS server to use when resolving names. The Network Location Server is basically a website. Using the Getting Started Wizard to setup RAS will result in the NLS being setup on the server itself and a self-signed certificate will be generated.

Planning Your DirectAccess Client Deployment

When planning your client deployment, you will need to make decisions regarding whether you want to make DirectAccess available to mobile computers only or to any computer.

The Getting Started Wizard—which can be run after installing the Remote Server role—will, by default, configure DirectAccess for mobile computers that are members of the Domain Computers security group only. It does this by creating a WMI filter for the DirectAccess Client Settings GPO.

A *WMI filter* is used to control the application of the GPO. The WMI filter is evaluated on the target computer during the processing of the Group Policy. The GPO will only be applied if the WMI filter evaluates as true. In this case, even though there are other computers that are members of the Domain Computers security group, they will not receive the DirectAccess policy because they are not considered to be mobile computers.

Using the Getting Started Wizard to Set Up a Remote Access Server

When setting up the Remote Access Server, you will have the option to use the Getting Started Wizard to complete the post installation setup.

The Getting Started Wizard backs up existing GPOs and then creates two group policy objects (GPOs) that are used by the server and the clients.

- DAServerSettings is filtered to apply to the DirectAccess server computer account only.
- DAClientSettings is filtered to apply to mobile computers in the Domain Computers global security group. If you change this default behavior, you will need to create a new security group for your DirectAccess clients.

These policies are linked to the root of your Active Directory domain automatically if the install is run under the Domain Administrator's account.

The Getting Started Wizard also performs the following tasks:

- Configures the Kerberos proxy, which eliminates the need for you to setup a Public Key Infrastructure. You can also configure DirectAccess to use certificates issued by a PKI Certificate Authority.
- Enables NAT64 and DNS64, which are used for protocol translation in IPv4-only network environments.
- Generates, self-signs and verifies an IP-HTTPS certificate on the DirectAccess Server.
- Identifies the infrastructure servers in the domain
- Registers DNS entries used to check client connectivity.
- Creates client policies
- Applies GPOs to remote access servers

DEPLOY RRAS/DIRECTACCESS USING THE GETTING STARTED WIZARD

GET READY. To set up RRAS/DirectAccess with the Getting Started Wizard, perform the following steps.

This exercise requires a Windows Server 2012 R2 member server, a domain controller, and a DNS server present on the network.

1. Log in with domain administrative credentials to a Windows Server 2012 R2 member server.

2. Open **Server Manager**.

3. Click **Manage > Add Roles and Features**.

4. Click **Next**.

5. Click **Role-based or featured-based installation** and then click **Next**.

6. Select the member server from the Server pool and then click **Next**.

7. Click **Remote Access Role** and then click **Add Features**.

8. Click **Next**.

9. Read the information regarding Remote Access and then click **Next**.

10. Click **DirectAccess and VPN (RAS)** and then click **Next**.

11. Read the Web Server role and then click **Next**.

12. Click **Next**.

13. After confirming your installation selections, click **Install**.

14. After the installation completes, click **Open the Getting Started Wizard** (see Figure 5-9).

Figure 5-9

Opening the Getting Started Wizard

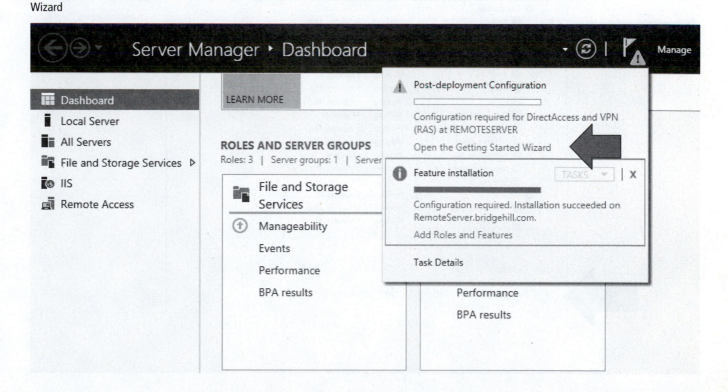

15. Select **Deploy both DirectAccess and VPN (recommended)**.

16. For the *Network Topology*, click **Edge** and then type the public name (FQDN) or IPv4 address used by clients to connect to the Remote Access Server. Click **Next**.

    In this topology, the RAS is deployed at the edge of the internal corporate network and is configured with two network adapters. One connected to the internal network, the other to the Internet.

17. Click **Finish** to apply the settings.

18. Select **More details** to monitor the tasks performed by the Wizard.

19. When the process is completed, click **Close**.

20. Click **Finish**.

21. In the *Remote Access Management Console* (see Figure 5-10), click **Operations Status** to confirm the server is working properly.

Figure 5-10

Confirming the server is working properly

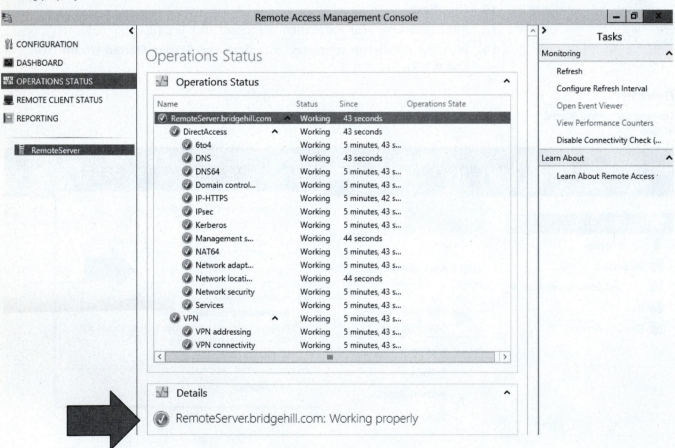

→ **VERIFY YOUR DIRECTACCESS DEPLOYMENT ON A MOBILE COMPUTER**

GET READY. To verify that DirectAccess was deployed to a Windows 8 mobile computer, perform the following steps while connected to the domain.

1. Connect the DirectAccess mobile client to your corporate network and obtain the DAClientSettings GPO.
2. Open Windows PowerShell with administrative privileges.
3. Type **gpresult/r** and press **Enter**.
4. In the *COMPUTER SETTINGS* section of the output, confirm that the DirectAccess Client Settings GPO has been applied.
5. Exit Windows PowerShell.
6. In the notification area, click the **Network connection** icon.
7. Click the **Workplace Connection** option (see Figure 5-11) and you will see you are connected to the network locally.
8. Disconnect the computer and reconnect it to an external network. You should be able to access the DirectAccess server.

Figure 5-11

Workplace Connection

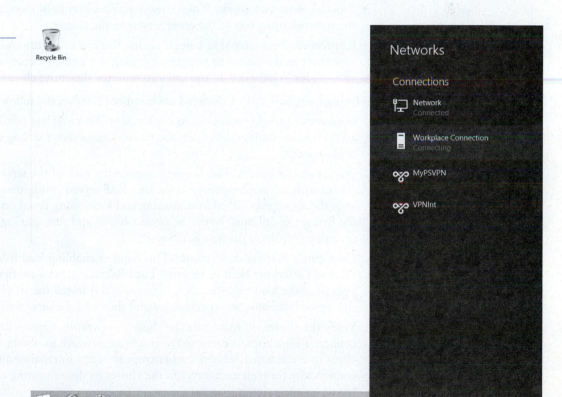

Deploying Remote Access in the Enterprise

Windows Server 2012 R2 Remote Access provides several ways to provide remote access for the organization.

You can deploy Remote Access in larger organizations by using any of the following methods:

- Multi-Site deployment with clustering
- OTP authentication
- Multi-forest
- Network Access Protection

DEPLOYING REMOTE ACCESS SERVERS (MULTI-SITE) WITH CLUSTERING

In some situations, you may want to deploy multiple remote access servers or clusters to provide both redundancy and load balancing. This is especially true in situations where your employees are dispersed across geographical locations. This allows remote users to connect to a remote access server that is closest to their physical location and use it as an entry point into the network. While Windows 8/8.1 computers can automatically identify an entry point or the user can manually select one, Windows 7 requires that you manually enable support for Windows 7 on each entry point.

Cluster Deployments provide the following benefits:

- Grouping two or more remote access servers improves reliability and increases throughput.
- Provides always-on access. If one remote access server fails, users can continue to access the network using one of the other servers in the cluster.
- Clusters can be managed as a single entity. You can configure and manage settings from any server in the cluster or remotely by using the Remote Server Administration Tools (RSAT) for Windows 8.1. You can also monitor the entire cluster from a single console.

Deploying a single RAS in a clustered environment involves the following steps:

1. Implement a single remote access deployment. This involves configuring the remote access infrastructure, configuring the remote access server settings, and verifying the deployment.

2. Prepare cluster servers. This involves configuring each of the servers that will be in the cluster with the same topology as the first RAS server, configuring each of the servers with the appropriate IP address, routing and forwarding based on the configuration of the first server (all must be on the same subnet), and then joining each of the servers to the same domain as the first RAS server.

3. Configure a load-balanced cluster. This requires enabling load balancing, selecting the method (Windows NLB or External Load Balancing), and configuring the virtual IP address of the load-balanced cluster. You will also install the IP-HTTPS certificate and the network location server certificate and then add the servers to the cluster.

4. Verify the cluster. To make sure the cluster is operating appropriately, you will need to connect a DirectAccess client to the corporate network to obtain the policy, connect the client to the external network and attempt to access internal resources. You can then test connectivity through each server in the cluster by disconnecting all but one and then repeat for each cluster member.

DEPLOYING REMOTE ACCESS SERVERS WITH ONE-TIME PASSWORD (OTP) AUTHENTICATION

In addition to configuring Remote Access to authenticate using standard Active Directory credentials, you can also use one-time password (OTP) user authentication. In order to use this option, the Remote Access server must already be deployed. For OTP authentication, you will need a RADIUS-enabled OTP server that supports the password authentication protocol (PAP). This requires that you configure the Remote Access server as a RADIUS agent, synchronize your Active Directory with the RADIUS server, and configure a shared secret and the port number for RADIUS traffic.

To support OTP, you will also need to plan how you will handle certificate authority requirements. DirectAccess clients obtain their OTP certificate by first requesting it from the Remote Access Server (RAS). The RAS server then verifies the credentials to make sure they are valid, signs a signing certificate using the registration authority certificate and then passes the enrollment request back to the DirectAccess client. The client enrolls the OTP certificate from the CA, which also verifies the credentials and the actual request. The CA will only issue the certificate if it has been signed the Remote Access server's registration authority certificate.

➕ **MORE INFORMATION**

The same internal CA that handles your IPsec certificates can be configured to handle DirectAccess OTP certificates

DEPLOYING REMOTE ACCESS SERVERS IN MULTI-FOREST ENVIRONMENTS

To allow remote access between forests, you will need to make sure you configure a two-way transitive trust between the two forests. This will make it possible for administrators to edit the DirectAccess GPOs and use security groups for the other forest when setting up remote access. You will also need to make the Remote Access administrator a local administrator on all Remote Access servers in the new forest. In addition to these changes, you will need to configure at least one security group for the DirectAccess client machines in the new forest. If you have Windows 8/8.1 clients, you will need at least one security group for each forest but best practice dictates having one for each domain that has Windows 8/8.1 clients. You should also have the same setup in place for Windows 7 clients. Client GPOs will need to be created for each additional domain where DirectAccess will be applied.

DEPLOYING REMOTE ACCESS SERVERS WITH NETWORK ACCESS PROTECTION (NAP)

Network Access Protection (NAP) is a feature that combines client and server elements. NAP allows you to create and enforce health requirement polices that specify the required software and system configurations that computers must have to connect to your network. NAP works by inspecting and assessing the health of computers and limiting their access when they are identified as being noncompliant. If a system is identified as non-compliant, NAP can automatically bring the client into compliance through a process called remediation.

Before deploying NAP, you need to determine what constitutes a compliant system and what you consider to be a non-compliant system. For example, you might consider a system to be compliant if it has the firewall running, it has updated antivirus and malware definitions, and it is completely patched. Systems that are assessed as healthy will be allowed to gain access to your entire network while those that are not will be restricted to an area of the network (for example, a subnet) for additional remediation services. This subnet might have basic DNS and IP services as well as the ability to provide Microsoft Updates to bring the system into compliance. Once under compliance, the system will be able to access the rest of the network.

There are five enforcement options you can use for clients running the NAP agent:

➕ **MORE INFORMATION**

NAP client capable systems include Windows XP SP3 and later operating system as well as Windows Server 2008 and later systems. All enforcement methods can be implemented using a minimum of one server running Windows Server 2008, Windows Server 2008 R2, Windows Server 2012, or Windows Server 2012 R2. The additional services you will require are dependent upon the enforcement method you use.

- **NAP with IPsec enforcement:** Requires AD domain controller, Network Policy Server (NPS), Certification Authority (AD or Third Party), and Health Registration Authority role with Internet Information Services. Client must first obtain an IPsec certificate to get access to the network. If the computer is not compliant, it might be allowed to communicate with selected resources on the network (for example, it might communicate with Microsoft Update Server until it gets the certificate).

- **NAP with 802.1x enforcement:** Relies on the routers and switches that support your underlying network. Regardless of how the client connects, it will be checked for compliance against an NPS. If it doesn't meet compliance, it can be restricted to the remediation subnet.

- **NAP with VPN enforcement:** Requires RRAS server, which is running Network Policy Server role or is configured to communicate with an NPS; clients that are healthy are let in; noncompliant systems are restricted to the remediation subnet. This does not protect against clients accessing in some other way.

- **NAP with DHCP enforcement:** Requires MS DHCP server; clients attempt to get IP address and the DHCP server will either have policies or check with a Network Policy Server (NPS). If the client meets those requirements, it gets and IP address otherwise it will be assigned an IP address that lets it gain access to the remediation subnet. This does not protect against a client using a static IP address.

You can implement any of the enforcement methods without restricting the access of computers that are identified as non-compliant. This provides the benefit of automatic remediation and compliance monitoring. You will not have to set up a restricted area to isolate computers that need remediation, but can still generate the same NAP reports.

The option you choose to implement will depend upon what your overall design goal is for your computers, the infrastructure, the cost, the security needs and the overall complexity.

 DEPLOY REMOTE ACCESS IN THE ENTERPRISE FOR DIRECTACCESS CLIENTS ONLY

GET READY. To deploy Remote Access in the Enterprise, perform the following steps on a Windows Server 2012 R2 member server:

1. Install the Remote Access Role by executing the following Windows PowerShell command:

   ```
   Install-WindowsFeature RemoteAccess
   -IncludeManagementTools
   ```

2. In *Server Manager*, Select **Tools > Remote Access Management**.
3. Click the **Run the Remote Access Setup Wizard** link.
4. Click **Deploy DirectAccess only**.
5. Click **Step 1 Remote Clients** and then click **Configure** (see Figure 5-12).

Figure 5-12

Deploying DirectAccess

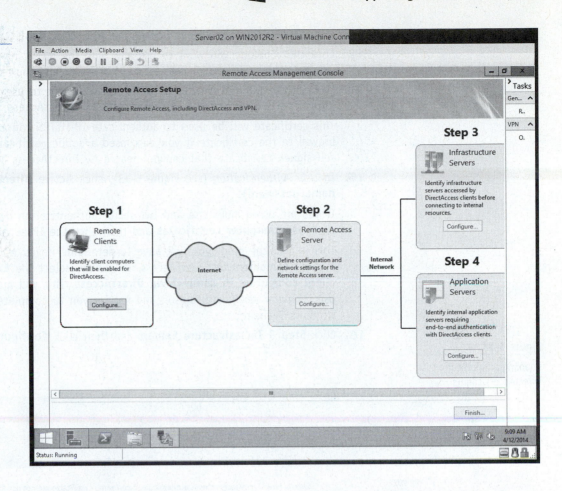

6. Click **Deploy full DirectAccess for client access and remote management** and then click **Next**.

   Using this setting, DirectAccess client computers located on the Internet can connect to the internal network via the Remote Access server. You will also be able to remotely manage the clients.

7. Click **Add** to select one or more security groups that contain the clients that you want to enable DirectAccess for.

   You can select Domain Computers to incorporate all computers in the domain but consider creating a group called DAClients and making only the computers you want to roll out the policy to as members. This can be done via the Active Directory Users and Computers.

8. Deselect the **Enable DirectAccess for mobile computers only** option.

   If this setting is enabled, only mobile computers will be enabled as DirectAccess clients.

9. Deselect **Use force tunneling**.

   If this is enabled, it will not allow split-tunneling for DA client connections, which will force all traffic from the DA client to go over the DA IPsec tunnels. This means traffic going over the intranet and to the Internet.

10. Add a resource that will be used to determine connectivity to the internal network, a help desk e-mail address for users to send information regarding connectivity issues to, and provide a name for the DirectAccess connection. (The default setting is WorkPlace Connection.) Click **Next**.

11. Click **Finish**.

12. Click **Step 2 Remote Access Server** and then click **Configure**.

13. Click the topology you want to use and type the public name or IPv4 address that will be used by clients to connect to this server and then click **Next**.

14. Identify the *Internal network adapter* that you want to use, click **use a self-signed certificate created Automatically by DirectAccess**, and then click **Next**.

    This certificate will be used to authenticate IP-HTTPS connection. You can either browse to the certificate if you purchased a public certificate or you can use a self-signed certificate that can be created by DirectAccess automatically.

15. In *User Authentication* (see Figure 5-13), click **Active Directory credentials (user name/password)**.

    If you are using multi-site and two-factor authentication deployments, you will click **Use computer certificates** and then click the IPsec root certificate.

    This is also the point you will have to determine if you want to support Windows 7 client computers for DirectAccess. If you do, select the **Enable Windows 7 client computers to connect via DirectAccess**. This will automatically enable the *Use computer certificates* option and require you to complete it in order to support Windows 7 clients.

16. Click **Step 3 Infrastructure Servers** and then click **Configure**.

Figure 5-13

Enabling authentication for DirectAccess clients

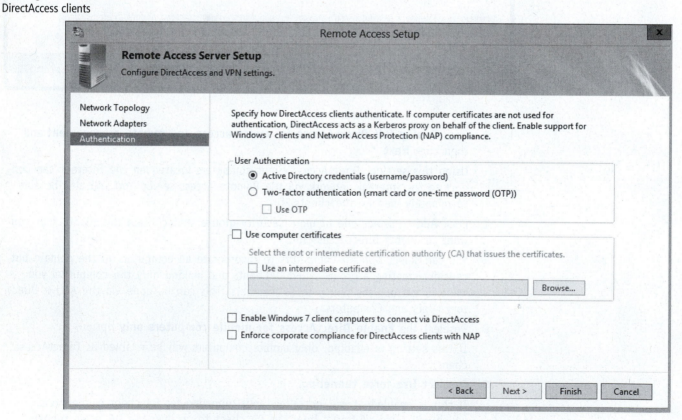

17. Click **The network location server is deployed on the Remote Access server**, click **use a self-signed certificate**, and then click **Next**.

18. After reviewing the DNS Suffix information, click **Next**.

19. Click **Next** to configure the DirectAccess clients with DNS client suffix search list.

20. Click **Finish**.

21. Review the *Configuration Settings* and then click **Apply**.

➕ **MORE INFORMATION**

Configuring application servers is an optional task. This can be done if you require remote access clients to require authentication to selected application servers. This is controlled based on their inclusion into a security group. Traffic to these application servers will also be encrypted by default but you can decide to not encrypt if it makes sense for your environment.

TAKE NOTE ✱

With Windows Server 2012 R2, NAP is deprecated. This means that NAP is available in Windows Server 2012 R2 and the material can be found on the 70-688 exam but it will not be available in future versions of Windows servers.

TROUBLESHOOTING NETWORK ACCESS PROTECTION (NAP)

When you troubleshoot NAP problems, you should first start with the basics. This includes the

- Ensure that you have the correct operating system that supports NAP, which is Windows XP with SP3, Windows Vista, Windows 7, Windows 8/8.1, Windows Serer 2008, Windows Server 2008 R2, Windows Server 2012, and Windows Server 2012 R2.
- Ensure you have the proper IP settings.
- Ensure NAP client settings by using the `netsh nap client show state` command and the `netsh nap client show configure` command.
- Ensure the Network Access Protection Agent service is running.
- Review the Event viewer NAP-related event logs (Applications and Services Logs\Microsoft\Windows\Network Access Protection\Operational).
- Review the NAP-related event logs on the server running NPS or HRA (Custom Views\Server Roles\Network Policy and Access Services).

Table 5-2 shows you the most common problems and how to fix those problems.

Table 5-2

Common NAP problems

ERROR MESSAGE	SOLUTION
NAP client computers are evaluated as non-NAP-capable	A NAP client computer might not be authorized for full networkaccess even though it is compliant with network health requirements because the health state is not being evaluated. The most common causes are: • The NAP Agent service is not running on the client computer. • The NAP enforcement client is not enabled on the client computer. • Health checks are not enabled on the client computer. Health checks only apply to client computers using the 802.1X or VPN enforcement methods.
Client access requests match an incorrect policy	The incorrect connection request policy or network policy being applied because the processing order of policies is not configured correctly. This commonly occurs when a policy that is high in the processing order is configured with less specific requirements than your NAP policies.
The CA type is incorrect	If you select default values during installation of Active Directory Certificate Services (AD CS), your NAP certificate authority (CA) will be installed as an enterprise CA and the Health Registration Authority (HRA) role service uses a standalone CA configuration that is incompatible with an enterprise NAP CA. You will need to change the configuration of HRA or reinstall your NAP CA and choose standalone CA.
The health certificate template is not available	You need to check if the system health authentication template is not available. This is usually caused by the NAP CA is running the Standard edition of the operating system. The NAP CA must be running the Enterprise edition of the operating system.

(continued)

Table 5-2

(continued)

ERROR MESSAGE	SOLUTION
The user attempted to use an authentication method that is not enabled	If you use NAP with 802.1X or VPN enforcement, you must configure settings in the connection request policy to override network policy authentication settings. When the settings are enabled, you will get a *The user attempted to use an authentication method that is not enabled on the matching network policy* message. To fix this issue, configure connection request policy to override network policy authentication settings.
The RADIUS client is not NAP-capable	If you use RADIUS clients with the IPsec enforcement, VPN enforcement, or DHCP enforcement methods, you must enable the RADIUS client as NAP-capable. You can use the NPS console to configure a RADIUS client as NAP-capable.
Access requests are not received by NPS	If you are have RADIUS clients that do not perform local authentication and authorization of network access requests, you must configure these RADIUS clients to forward connection requests. If these RADIUS clients are not configured to forward connection requests, or they are configured to forward requests to the wrong remote RADIUS server group, no events will be generated on the remote server running NPS.

Troubleshooting DirectAccess

DirectAccess is a new technology and it relies on several components, so it can create some problems for you. That said, you should first verify that you have system requirements.

When troubleshooting DirectAccess, you should check the following:

1. The DirectAccess client computer must be running Windows 8/8.1, Windows 7 Ultimate or Windows 7 Enterprise edition.

2. The DirectAccess client computer must be a member of an Active Directory Domain Services (AD DS) domain and its computer account must be a member of one of the security groups configured with the DirectAccess Setup Wizard.

3. The DirectAccess client computer must have received computer configuration Group Policy settings for DirectAccess.

4. The DirectAccess client must have a global IPv6 address, which should begin with a 2 or 3.

5. The DirectAccess client must be able to reach the IPv6 addresses of the DirectAccess server.

6. The DirectAccess client on the Internet must correctly determine that it is not on the intranet. You can type the `netsh dnsclient show state` command to view network location displayed in the Machine Location field (Outside corporate network or Inside corporate network).

7. Use the netsh `namespace show policy` command to show the NRPT rules as configured on the Group Policy.

8. Use the `netsh namespace show effectivepolicy` command to determine the results of network location detection and the IPv6 addresses of the intranet DNS servers.

9. The DirectAccess client must not be assigned the domain firewall profile.

10. The DirectAccess client must be able to reach the organization's intranet DNS servers using IPv6. You can use Ping to attempt to reach the IPv6 addresses of intranet servers.

11. The DirectAccess client must be able to communicate with intranet servers using application layer protocols. If File and Printer Sharing is enabled on the intranet server, test application layer protocol access by typing net view \\IntranetFQDN.

12. Use the DirectAccess Connectivity Assistant on computers running Windows 7 and Network Connectivity Assistant on computers running Windows 8/8.1 to determine the intranet connectivity status and to provide diagnostic information.

■ Supporting Remote Desktop Services (RDS)

THE BOTTOM LINE

Remote Desktop Services (RDS) allows users to access a remote computer just as if they were sitting in front of the computer. Within a Window, the user has a Start button, Desktop, applications, and folders and will even have access to their local resources such as the user's local drive and mapped drives. Based on your needs, users could use the Remote Desktop Services to run an application that they could not run on his or her own machine. You could go one step further to use multiple servers to create an entire RDS infrastructure to provide a robust, resilient service for the users.

Before Windows Server 2008 R2, RDS was known as Terminal Services, which was Microsoft's implementation of thin-client terminal server computing.

Supporting Remote Desktop Protocol

You can connect to a remote session with the *Remote Desktop Protocol (RDP)* using TCP port 3389. Typically, this would be done with *Remote Desktop Connection (RDC)*, which would allow you to connect to a Remote Desktop Session Host or to a Remote Application.

By default, Windows Server 2012 R2 can support up to 2 remote sessions at once, while Windows 8.1 only supports 1 remote connection. For servers, if you need additional users to access the server, you have to install a Remote Desktop Licensing server, and then add licenses based on either the number of devices that can connect to the RDS server or the number of concurrent users.

When planning for remote access, you must deliver a consistent experience to your users whether they connect over the local network or they connect across low-bandwidth networks when working from remote locations. In order for users to be productive while working remotely, they must have access to their remote resources at all times. As part of your remote access design, review your current topology and ensure you have redundancy built in not only to your devices (routers and switches) but to your network links as well.

You will need to ensure that the firewalls do not block access to the remote servers when access is needed. You typically would not make the remote access available through the RDP from the Internet unless the client is connected over a VPN tunnel or is using the Remote Desktop Services Gateway.

Although the RDP uses compression and caching mechanisms to limit the amount of traffic transmitted over network links, consider the different types of traffic that will traverse the network links. For example, if you are using virtualization for your operating systems and applications to support your remote users, expect to see large bursts of data when the operating system and applications are sent to the remote client. Make sure your core infrastructure is capable of providing the bandwidth needed by your users.

If you are concerned about protecting sensitive data sent between remote users and your servers, configure group policies to require the use of a specific security layer to secure communications during RDP connections. RDP connections can be configured to support 128-bit encryption (the maximum level of encryption supported by the client) or 52-bit encryption mechanisms. The option you choose for your design is dependent on the capabilities of your remote clients and the level of encryption needed to meet your specific data protection needs. In general, your design should use the strongest encryption supported by your remote clients.

RDP 8.1 is integrated with Windows 2012 R2 and Windows 8.1. With RDP 8.1, you can deploy remote clients (laptops, desktops, and/or virtual machines hosted in a data center) as part of your remote access strategy. If your remote access needs include supporting Windows 7 Service Pack 1 or Windows Server 2008 R2 Service Pack 1 systems, you should upgrade to RDP 8.1. This enables your older remote clients to gain access to the newer features. These features include an improved video conferencing experience, the ability to run a remote session from within another remote session, improved media streaming over slower public network links, and the ability for the remote client to automatically detect the characteristics of the network connection and optimize the connection accordingly.

Supporting Remote Desktop Services Gateway Access

As previously covered in this lesson, to maintain security, you would not typically want to give access to remote desktop sessions unless you are going through a VPN or through a Remote Desktop Services Gateway. The Remote Desktop Services provides additional security by providing encryption and giving granular control of who can access the services over the network or Internet.

CERTIFICATION READY
Remote Desktop Protocol (RDP), including Remote Desktop Services Gateway Access
Objective 2.2

As the terminal services application matured, Microsoft offered additional RDS roles. Currently, it also has the following:

- *Remote Desktop Session Host:* Enables a server to host session-based desktops or RemoteApp programs.
- *Remote Desktop Gateway (RD Gateway):* Allows a user to tunnel the Remote Desktop Protocol session using HTTPS. By using an RD Gateway, users can connect to a remote session over the Internet, while using the Transport Layer Security (TLS) to maintain security. Alternatively, users can use Internet Explorer as the RDP client. The Remote Desktop Gateway enables authorized users to connect to virtual desktops, session-based desktops, and RemoteApp programs over a private network or the Internet.
- *Remote Desktop Connection Broker (RD Connection Broker):* If you have multiple RDS servers running the Remote Desktop Session Host, the RD Connection Broker will keep track of the current connections and the servers that the sessions reside on. If a user gets disconnected from a running RD session, the RD Connection Broker will allow the user to reconnect to the current session or existing virtual desktop. In addition, the Connection Broker will evenly distribute the load so that one server does not get overloaded. In order to connect to an RD Gateway, a user must match both an RD Connection Authorization Policy (RD CAP) and an RD Resource Authorization Policy (RD RAP). By default both policies are configured to allow Domain Users full network access.
- *Remote Desktop Virtualization Host:* Enables users to connect to virtual desktops by using RemoteApp and Desktop Connection.
- *Remote Desktop Web Access:* Enables users to access Desktop Connection and RemoteApp using a Remote Desktop Connections, or a web browser.
- *Remote Desktop Licensing:* Enables a server to manage Remote Desktop Services client access licenses (RDS CALs) that are required for each device or user to connect to a Remote Desktop Session Host server.

In order to install Remote Desktop Services, any servers that will be part of the deployment must be joined to a Windows domain. There have been several new features added that are enabled when the Remote Desktop Session Host role is deployed. To manage most of RDS, you will use the Server Manager dashboard (see Figure 5-14). RDMS provides a topology overview of the RDS deployment and provides key information on each server.

Figure 5-14

Managing Remote Desktop Services

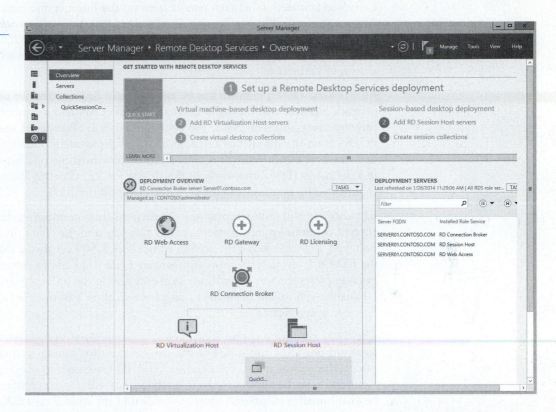

> **USE QUICK START TO INSTALL A REMOTE DESKTOP SESSION-BASED DESKTOP DEPLOYMENT**

GET READY. To install a Remote Desktop Session-based desktop deployment using the Quick Start option, perform the following steps:

1. Open **Server Manager**.

2. Click **Manage > Add Roles and Features**.

3. In the *Add Roles and Features Wizard*, on the *Before You Begin* page, click **Next**.

4. On the *Installation Type* page, select **Remote Desktop services Installation** and then click **Next**.

5. On the *Deployment Type* page, click **Quick Start** and then click **Next**.

6. On the *Select deployment scenario* page, select **Session-based desktop deployment** and then click **Next**.

7. On the *Server Selection* page, click **Next**.

8. On the *Confirmation* page, click to select **Restart the destination server automatically if required** and then click **Install**.

Remote Desktop Gateway (RD Gateway) is a role service in the Remote Desktop Services server role included with Windows Server 2012 R2. RD Gateway enables authorized remote users to connect to resources on an internal corporate or private network, from any Internet-connected device that can run the Remote RDC client. RD Gateway uses RDP over HTTPS to establish a secure, encrypted connection between remote users on the Internet and internal network resources. Network placement of the RD Gateway is one of the biggest considerations when deploying this role service.

The network resources can be RD Session Host Servers, RD Session Host servers running RemoteApp programs, or computers and virtual desktops with Remote Desktop enabled. RD Gateway uses the Remote Desktop Protocol (RDP) over HTTPS to establish a secure, encrypted connection between remote users on the Internet and internal network resources. Access is controlled by configuring **Remote Desktop connection authorization policies (RD CAP)** and **Remote Desktop resource authorization policies (RD RAP)**. An RD CAP specifies who is authorized to make a connection; an RD RAP specifies which resources authorized users may connect to.

An RD Gateway deployment can be as simple as a dedicated server on the LAN with two network interfaces, where one is connected to the LAN and the other is exposed to the Internet using port 443 (SSL). You configure DNS to allow name resolution of servers FQDN from the Internet or LAN. This type of deployment doesn't follow best security practices and isn't recommended. A more secure deployment method is to have the RD Gateway in a perimeter (DMZ) network. In this design the RD Gateway listens on port 443 on the Internet facing interface and on TCP port 3389 on the LAN.

RD Gateway will only accept secure connections from connecting clients. TLS is used to encrypt communications between an RD Gateway and the client. In order for TLS to function, you will need to acquire an SSL compatible X.509 certificate that will be installed on the RD Gateway server. Clients authenticate to an RD Gateway server using SSL, then the gateway passes the server certificate to clients during the SSL handshake process. The RDMS UI enables you to edit deployment properties to allow you to create a new certificate or select an existing certificate.

The create certificate option allows you to generate a self-signed certificate, which can be password protected and stored on the network for distribution to client computers. The certificate name must match the FQDN of the RD Gateway server exactly. Once created the certificate must be applied to the role service that will use the certificate. The certificate must be distributed to clients and must be installed in the trusted root CA certificate store of client computers. The client uses this certificate when connecting for identity authentication. While self-signed certificates are simple to generate and cost nothing to create, the main drawbacks of them are that they are difficult to distribute to clients and the CA isn't trusted.

■ Using Remote Assistance

THE BOTTOM LINE

Most organizations will have a helpdesk support team. Unfortunately, when many problems occur, the helpdesk person needs to see what the user is seeing and needs to interact with the same computer session. Two possible tools are Remote Assistance and Microsoft System Center 2012 Configuration Manager Remote Control.

Remote Assistance is a Windows built-in tool that you can use to control another operating system by connecting to it remotely. While it is similar to Remote Desktop, it allows you to interact with the user's session so that you can see what is on the screen, and control his or her computer just as you were sitting with the user. You can also use the chat feature between you and the user, allowing you to communicate via text messages.

To use remote assistance on a computer, you must first enable Remote Assistance. This can be done using the Control Panel or by using a GPO (Computer Configuration\Policies\Administrative Templates\System\Remote Assistance\Configure Solicited Remote Assistance policy).

ENABLE REMOTE ASSISTANCE

GET READY. To enable Remote Assistance, log on to Windows 8.1 and then perform the following steps:

1. Open **Control Panel** and then click **System and Security > System > Remote settings**.

2. In the *Windows Remote Assistance* window, click to select **Allow Remote Assistance connections to this computer**.

   Note that by clicking **Advanced**, the user can specify whether the expert can take control of the computer or whether the expert can simply view activities on the computer. The user can also specify the amount of time that the invitation for remote assistance remains valid.

3. Click **OK** to close the *System Properties* dialog box.

4. Close the **System** window.

To request a Remote Assistance session, a client must issue an invitation and send it to a particular expert. The client can send the invitation using e-mail, or save it as a file to be sent to the expert in some other manner. To create an invitation, use the following procedure:

 CREATE AN INVITATION

GET READY. To create an invitation, log on to Windows 8.1 and then perform the following steps:

1. Open **Control Panel** and then click **System and Security > Action Center > Troubleshooting > Get help from a friend**.

2. In the *Remote Assistance* window (see Figure 5-15), click **Invite someone to help you**.

Figure 5-15

The *Use Remote Assistance to contact someone you trust for help* page

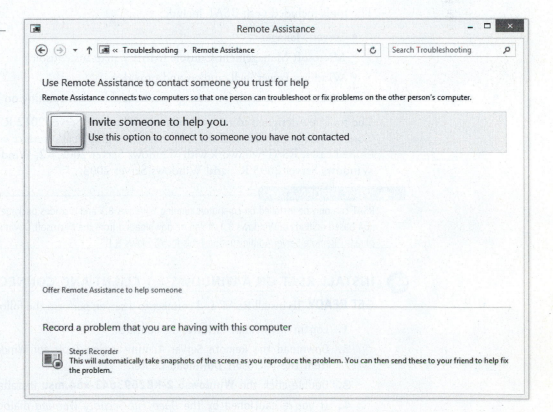

When you are prompted to choose how you want to invite your trusted helper, you can save this invitation as a file, use e-mail to send an invitation, to use Easy Connect.

3. Click **Save this invitation as a file**.

4. In the *Save As* dialog box, type a name for the invitation file and the location of the folder in which the wizard should create the invitation and then click **Save**. The Windows Remote Assistance window appears, displaying the password.

5. The password must be provided to the expert before she can connect to your computer.

■ Performing Remote Administration

↓ THE BOTTOM LINE   Remote administration tools such as RSAT and Windows PowerShell Remoting allow you to manage your clients and servers from anywhere on the network.

At one point in the evolution of servers, it was common to have to walk into the server room to add a user account or perform a specific administrative task. Over the years, that has changed dramatically through the use of remote administration tools. These tools, installed on the client, allow you to perform most high-level administration tasks directly from your desktop. With the release of Windows 8 and Windows Server 2012, you can use Remote Server Administration Tools (RSAT) and Windows PowerShell Remoting to manage your server administration tasks. Let's take a closer look at each of these resources.

Using Remote Server Administration Tools (RSAT) for Windows 8.1

CERTIFICATION READY
Remote administration
Objective 2.2

Remote Server Administration Tools (RSAT) allows you to manage roles and features installed on Windows Server 2012 R2 from a PC running Windows 8.1.

The tools included with RSAT include:

- Server Manager
- Microsoft Management Console (MMC) snap-ins consoles
- Windows PowerShell cmdlets and providers
- Command-line tools for managing roles and features running on Windows Server 2012 R2

The tools are designed to remotely manage Windows Server 2012 R2 running the Server Core installation option and the minimal server graphical interface configuration. In some limited cases, RSAT will work with Windows Server 2008 R2, Windows Server 2008, Windows Server 2003 R2, and Windows Server 2003.

+ MORE INFORMATION

RSAT can only be installed on computers running Windows 8.1 and provides package files that run on both x86 and x64-based editions of Windows 8.1. It can be downloaded from the Microsoft Download Center by searching for the phrase "Remote Server Administration Tools for Windows 8.1."

→ **INSTALL RSAT ON A WINDOWS 8.1 CLIENT AND CONNECT TO A SERVER**

GET READY. To install RSAT and connect to a server, perform the following steps:

1. Log in with Administrative credentials.

2. Download the Remote Server Administration Tools for Windows 8.1 64-bit package from the Microsoft Download Center.

3. Double-click the **Windows6.2-KB2693643-x64.msu** installation file.

4. If you're cautioned by the *Open File-Security Warning* dialog box, click **Open**.

5. When prompted by the *Windows Update Standalone Installer* dialog box to install the update, click **Yes**.

6. Read and the license terms and click **I accept**.

7. Press the **Windows logo key + q** and search for **Administrative Tools** using the Settings context.

8. Click **Administrative Tools**.

9. Click **Server Manager**.

10. Click **Dashboard**.

11. Click **Add other Servers to manage**.

12. Confirm location is set to your domain and then click **Find Now**.

13. Select the server you want to manage and then click the **right arrow**.

14. Click **OK**.

15. Review the roles currently handled by the server you connected to.

In the example shown in Figure 5-16, the server is supporting six roles (AD DS, App Server, DNS, File and Storage Services, IIS, and WSUS). Scrolling down the page, you will be able to see the overall information and health of each service.

Figure 5-16

Viewing Server Roles/Features via Server Manager Console

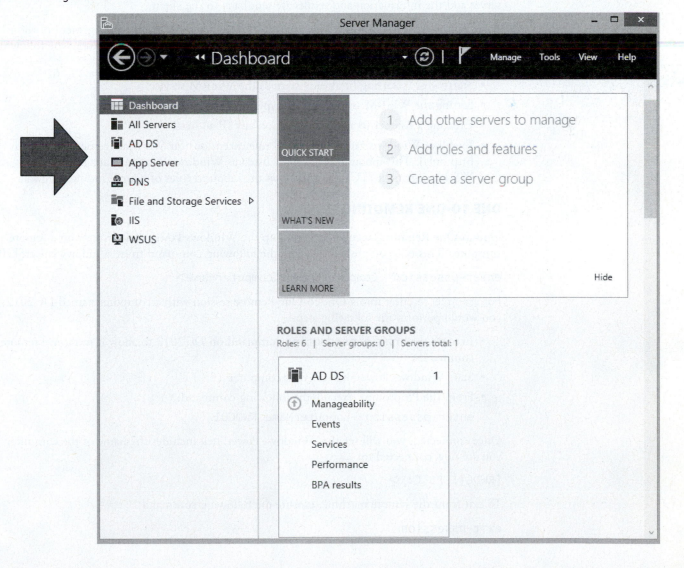

In previous releases of RSAT, you had to access Control Panel > Programs to enable the tools you wanted to use. In Windows 8.1, the tools are enabled by default. You can still turn off tools you don't want to use by going to Control Panel > Programs and Features > Turn Windows features on or off and then selecting the tools that you don't intend to use.

You can also use the Tools menu to access the GUI-based tools from within the Server Manager console.

Using Windows PowerShell Remoting

Windows PowerShell Remoting is a server-client application that allows you to securely connect to a remote Windows PowerShell host and run script interactively.

Windows PowerShell Remoting allows you to run commands on a remote system as though you were sitting physically at its console. Windows PowerShell Remoting is built upon the Web Services for Management protocol and uses Windows Remote Management service to handle the authentication and communication elements.

Windows Remote Management is responsible for routing the packets to the right location while Web Services for Management requires a port to be made accessible via your firewall. The commands that you enter and send to the remote computer are executed on the local server and the information and results are sent back to the client.

You run the `Enable-PSRemoting` command, which enables remote management of the computer by using the Windows Management (WinRM) Service. This includes the following tasks in Enabling Remoting:

- Starting or restarting (if already started) the WinRM service.
- Setting the WinRM service startup type to automatic.
- Creating a listener to accept requests on any IP address.
- Enabling Windows Firewall inbound rule exceptions for WS-Management traffic (for http only). This inbound rule will be listed as Windows Remote Management via WS-Management (TCP port 5985) in the inbound rules of your Windows Firewall.

ONE-TO-ONE REMOTING

One-to-One Remoting involves bringing up the Windows PowerShell prompt on a remote computer. This is accomplished by using the following command from Windows PowerShell:

```
enter-pssession -ComputerName <computername>
```

For example, to enter into a One-to-One Remote session with a computer named DC2012, you would perform the following steps:

- Execute the `enable-psremoting` command on DC2012 to allow it to receive remote commands.
- Start Windows PowerShell on your computer
- From the PS prompt, execute the following command:
  ```
  enter-pssession -ComputerName RWDC01
  ```

Once connected, you will see that Windows PowerShell includes the name of the computer you are now connected to:

```
[RWDC]: PS C:\>
```

To exit from the remote machine, execute the following command:

```
exit-pssession
```

ONE-TO-MANY REMOTING

One-to-Many remoting allows you to send one or more commands to multiple computers. Each of these computers will run the command, produce the results in an XML file and return them to you. This information is then categorized and presented on your client machine.

 CONNECT TO A REMOTE SERVER USING WINDOWS POWERSHELL (ONE-TO-ONE REMOTING)

GET READY. To connect to a remote server using Windows PowerShell, perform the following steps:

1. Open a Windows PowerShell window on your Windows 8.1 computer.
2. Execute the following command to enable remoting on your computer and then select **A** to continue (see Figure 5-17).

    ```
    Enable-PSRemoting
    ```

Figure 5-17

Enabling Windows PowerShell remoting

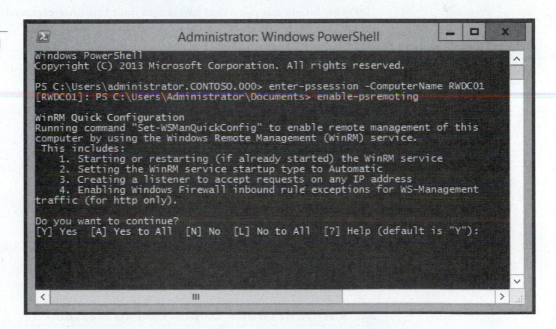

3. Execute the following command to create an interactive remote connection (where *<computername>* is another computer on your network):

    ```
    PS C:\. enter-pssession –ComputerName <computername>
    ```

4. Execute the following command to see a list of all services running on the computer:

    ```
    [RemoteComputerName] PS C:\> Get-Service
    ```

5. Execute the following command to see a list of all processes running on the computer:

    ```
    [RemoteComputerName] PS C:\> Get-Process
    ```

6. Execute the following command to see the access control list applied via NTFS for the c: drive:

    ```
    [RemoteComputerName] PS C:\> Get-acl c:\
    ```

7. Execute the following command to exit from Windows PowerShell:

    [RemoteComputerName] PS C:\> Exit-PSSession

Exploring Metered Networks

THE BOTTOM LINE

Metered connections can result in high costs when it comes to transferring and synching your computers. Windows 8.1 provides a mechanism to help you configure your system to recognize them and reconfigures itself to reduce costs.

The days of unlimited broadband networks are quickly coming to a close as more broadband companies adopt metered plans similar to what they now have in place for your mobile devices. The premise behind metering is that a small percentage of users are consuming the majority of the bandwidth streaming videos, playing online games, or downloading large files from torrents. To protect against exhausting the available bandwidth, Internet Service Providers (ISPs) are rolling out plans that have a data limit that once exceeded, will result in additional billing. These are known as *metered Internet connections*.

Windows 8.1 provides you with a way to reduce the amount of data you send and receive over a metered connection. When a connection is metered, Microsoft indicates you might see the following effects:

- Automatic sync of Offline Files may be disabled
- Updating of the start screen may be stopped
- Windows Store app downloads may be paused
- Only priority updates will be downloaded from Windows Update
- Tile Updates are limited to 50 MB/month

+ MORE INFORMATION

By default, Windows considers Wi-Fi networks to be non-metered while mobile broadband networks and Ethernet network connections are set to metered.

SET A WI-FI NETWORK CONNECTION TO METERED

GET READY. To set a Wi-Fi connection to metered, perform the following steps:

1. Log in to Windows 8 using administrative credentials.
2. Move your mouse to the bottom-right of your screen and, on the Charms bar, click **Settings**.
3. Click the **Internet Access** icon (see Figure 5-18).

TAKE NOTE*

The following exercise requires a Windows 8.1 computer with a Wi-Fi connection.

Figure 5-18

Internet Access icon

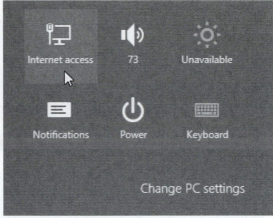

4. Right-click your wireless network connection and choose **Set as metered connection** (see Figure 5-19).

At this point, Windows will keep track of the amount of data you are using.

Figure 5-19

Setting a metered connection

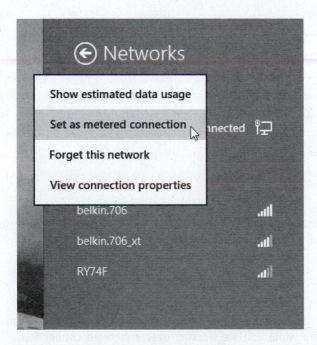

5. To monitor how much data you are using, right-click the wireless network connection and choose **Show estimated data usage**.

TAKE NOTE Clicking Reset will set your data usage counter to zero. This only resets your information. Your ISP will still maintain information regarding your total data usage.

6. Open Task Manager and click the App History tab to view which applications are using the most data over the metered connection (see Figure 5-20).

Figure 5-20

Identifying apps using data over the metered connection

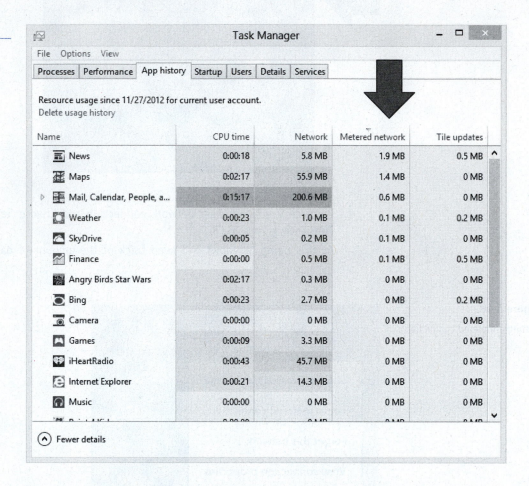

You can lower your data usage costs by performing the following additional tasks on a metered connection:

7. Go to **Settings** and click **Change PC Settings**.

8. Click **PC settings > Devices**.

9. In the *Download over metered connections* section, drag the slider to **Off**.

   This will block the download of device drivers from Windows Update and device info while you are working over a metered connection.

10. Click **PC settings > Sync your settings**.

11. To return your settings to non-metered, drag the *Download over metered connections* slider to **Off** for Sync settings over metered connections.

12. Go to **Settings** and click the **Network Icon**.

13. Right-click your metered connection and choose **Set as non-metered connection**.

SKILL SUMMARY

IN THIS LESSON YOU LEARNED:

- To be able to monitor and manage off-network systems, you need to be able to assess their currently health, provide remote assistance, and apply the appropriate remediation steps to get them back into compliance.

- A VPN is a private network that uses a public network to connect remote users and sites. Tunneling protocols, authentication protocols, and encryption levels are applied to the VPN connection to provide security.

- The four types of VPN tunneling protocols are: PPTP, L2TP/IPsec, SSTP and VPN Reconnect/IKEv2

- In most situations, VPN Reconnect should be your first choice with SSTP as a fall back mechanism.

- DirectAccess and RRAS are now managed from a single console in Windows Server 2012 R2.

- Remote Desktop Services (RDS) allows users to access remote computers just as if they were sitting in front of their computers. To connect to a remote session by using the Remote Desktop Protocol (RDP), you would use TCP port 3389. Typically, this would be done with Remote Desktop Connection (RDC).

- Remote Desktop Gateway (RD Gateway) allows users to tunnel the Remote Desktop Protocol session using HTTPS. By using an RD Gateway, users can connect to a remote session over the Internet while using the Transport Layer Security (TLS) to maintain security.

- DirectAccess clients use two tunnels: Infrastructure and Authentication.

- Network Location Server is really a website used to DirectAccess clients to determine if they are connected directly to the corporate network.

- DirectAccess setup creates two GPOs: The DAServersettings that apply to the DirectAccess server only and the DAClientSettings that apply to mobile clients only if installed via the Getting Started Wizard.

- You can deploy remote access servers in multi-site deployment/clusters, OTP authentication, Multi-forest, and Network Access protection configurations.

- Network Access Protection (NAP) can be used to monitor and assess clients for compliance and provide remediation services for those who fall short.

- Use Connection Manager Administration Kit (CMAK) to create profiles for remote connections.

- Windows 8.1 Create a VPN Connection wizard allows you to enter minimal information when setting up a VPN connection. The authentication and tunneling protocols are managed transparently during the connection process.

- You can manage VPN connections using Windows PowerShell.

- You can perform remote administration using the Remote Server Administration Tools and Windows PowerShell Remoting.

- Windows 8.1 can be configured to recognize and use metered connections more efficiently. When it recognizes a meter connection, it will disable the sync of offline files, pause download of Windows Store Apps, and download only priority updates from Windows Update to reduce costs associated with transferring data across metered connections.

■ Knowledge Assessment

Multiple Choice

Select the correct answer for each of the following questions.

1. Which of the following should you take into consideration when selecting a protocol to use with VPN?
   a. Operating systems
   b. Authentication requirements
   c. Implementation requirements
   d. TPA-chip support on clients

2. When using DirectAccess, how many IPsec tunnels are created?
   a. 1
   b. 2
   c. 3
   d. 4

3. When used for setting up the DAClientSettings GPO, the WMI filter performs which of the following actions?
   a. Allows all computers in the Domain Computers global group to receive the policy settings
   b. Allows all mobile computers in the Domain Computers global group to receive the policy settings
   c. Allows all Individuals, Organizations, Servers, Devices and Administrators to receive the policy settings.
   d. Evaluates as true on the DirectAccess server computer.

4. Which of the following statements are true regarding using the Getting Started Wizard to automate the installation of the DirectAccess server?
   a. The Getting Started Wizard configures the Kerberos proxy and eliminates the need to set up PKI for DirectAccess.
   b. The Getting Started Wizard enables NAT64 and DNS64, which is used by DirectAccess.
   c. The Getting Started Wizard generates and self-signs an IP-HTTPS certificate, which will be used with DirectAccess
   d. The Getting Started Wizard creates two client policies, which will be used to configure the clients to be used by DirectAccess.

5. Which of the following represents a NAP enforcement policy that relies on your routers and switches?
   a. NAP with IPsec enforcement
   b. NAP with VPN enforcement
   c. NAP with Infrastructure enforcement
   d. NAP with 802.1x enforcement

6. Which of the following statements best describe CMAK?
   a. CMAK is used to create and customize profiles for Connection Manager
   b. CMAK requires that you create the connection profile on a computer that uses the same operating system
   c. CMAK requires that you create the connection profile on a computer that uses the same architecture.
   d. CMAK creates a Microsoft installer (.msi) file for distribution.

7. What are the two requirements for setting up a VPN connection using the Getting Started Wizard in Windows 8.1? (Choose two answers)
   a. Address of the remote server
   b. Destination Name
   c. Authentication protocol to use
   d. VPN tunneling protocol to use

8. Which Windows PowerShell command is used to view VPN connections on a client computer?
   a. `Get-VpnConnection`
   b. `Set-VpnConnection`
   c. `View-VpnConnection`
   d. `Add-VpnConnection`

9. Which of the following tools is used to manage roles and features installed on a Windows Server 2012 R2 computer from a Windows 8.1 client?
   a. Server Manager
   b. MMC
   c. RSAT
   d. CMAK

10. When setting up Windows 8.1 for metered connection, which of the following might occur?
    a. Automatic sync of Offline Files may be disabled.
    b. Only Priority updates will be downloaded from Windows Update.
    c. Updating of the start screen will not be disabled.
    d. Windows Store app downloads may be paused.

11. Which of the following Remote Desktop roles is used by users to connect to a remote session over the Internet?
    a. Remote Desktop Web Access
    b. Remote Desktop Web Access
    c. Remote Desktop Connection Broker
    d. Remote Desktop Gateway

12. Which of the following tool policies is used to control access to remote desktop sessions when using the Remote Desktop Gateway? (Choose two answers)
    a. Remote Desktop control list policies
    b. Remote Desktop resource authorization policies
    c. Remote Desktop authorization policies
    d. Remote Desktop connection authorization policies

Best Answer

Choose the letter that corresponds to the best answer. More than one answer choice may achieve the goal. Select the BEST answer.

1. You want to use a VPN tunneling protocol that will provide you with the best option for security and uninterrupted VPN connectivity while at the same time providing you with a fall back mechanism. Which protocol pair will best fit your needs?
   a. VPN Reconnect and PPTP
   b. VPN Reconnect and SSTP
   c. VPN Reconnect and L2TP/IPsec
   d. SSTP and L2TP/IPsec

2. You want to set up a VPN on a Windows 8.1 computer. which of the following tools would require the least amount of effort to complete the job?
   a. Windows PowerShell
   b. Getting Started Wizard in Windows 8.1
   c. CMAK
   d. Manually creating the VPN connection on the client computer

3. You need a tool that allows you to remotely manage Windows Server 2012 R2 running the Server Core installation option from a Windows 8.1 computer. Which of the following would be considered the best to handle the majority of the tasks you will need to perform on a daily basis?
   a. Windows PowerShell Remoting
   b. RRAS console
   c. RSAT
   d. Active Directory Users and Computer snap-in

4. You are running Windows 7 and Windows 8/8.1 clients over a VPN. You need a tunneling protocol that will support both IPv4 and IPv6 protocols. Which of the following is best for that purpose?
   a. SSTP
   b. VPN Reconnect (IKEv2)
   c. L2TP/IPsec
   d. PPTP

5. You are considering setting up DirectAccess in your network, which consists of a Windows Server 2008 R2 and a Windows Server 2012 R2 computer. Your clients are running Windows 7 and Windows 8/8.1. You don't currently have a PKI in place. Which option would provide you with a solution with the least amount of configurations/ infrastructure modifications?
   a. Setting up DirectAccess on the Windows 2008 R2 and create a PKI infrastructure.
   b. Setting up DirectAccess on the Windows Server 2012 R2 and create a PKI infrastructure.
   c. Setting up a DirectAccess on the Windows Server 2012 R2 and use self-signed certificates.
   d. Setting up DirectAccess on the Windows Server 2012 R2 system and the Windows Server 2008R2 system.

Matching and Identification

1. Match the following terms with the related description or usage.
   _____ a) Connection Manager Administration Kit (CMAK)
   _____ b) DirectAccess
   _____ c) L2TP/IPsec
   _____ d) PPTP
   _____ e) Network Access Protection
   _____ f) RSAT
   _____ g) SSTP
   _____ h) VPN Reconnect
   _____ i) WMI Filter
   _____ j) Metered connection

   1. Works by establishing two IPsec tunnels from the client to the server.
   2. Uses the Microsoft Point to Point Encryption (MPPE) protocol with RC4 to protect data.
   3. Designed to provide users with consistent VPN connectivity and re-establish a VPN when users temporarily lose their Internet connections.

4. Allows you to create and enforce health requirement policies that specify the required software and system configurations that computers must have to connect to the network.

5. Can result in high costs when transferring and synching computers over them.

6. Requires computers to mutually authenticate themselves. The computer-to-computer authentication takes place before the user is authenticated.

7. Used to control the application of a GPO; evaluated on the target computer during the processing of the Group Policy.

8. Allows you to manage roles and features on Windows Server 2012 R2 from a PC running Windows 8.1.

9. Approved upon PPTP and L2TP/IPsec; works by sending PPP or L2TP traffic through an SSL 3.0 channel.

10. Used to create and customize profiles that contain settings necessary for a user to connect including the IP address of the VPN server.

Build a List

1. Specify the correct order of the steps required to set a Wi-Fi connection to metered on a Windows 8.1 computer.
   _____ Click the Internet Access icon.
   _____ Log on with administrative credentials.
   _____ Right-click the wireless connection and choose Set as Metered.
   _____ Click Settings from the Charms bar.

2. Specify the correct order of the steps required to use Windows PowerShell Remoting to connect and manage a remote server named Server01.
   _____ Start Windows PowerShell on your computer.
   _____ Perform any remote commands on Server01 to complete the administration task.
   _____ Execute the `enter-pssession –ComputerName Server01` command.
   _____ Execute the `enable-psremoting` command to configure Server01 to receive remote commands.
   _____ Execute the `exit-pssession` command to close the remote session.

3. Specify the correct order of the steps required to validate a DirectAccess deployment on a Windows 8.1 mobile computer.
   _____ Exit Windows PowerShell on the mobile client computer.
   _____ Confirm the DirectAccess Client Settings GPO has been applied under the COMPUTER SETTINGS section of the output on the mobile client.
   _____ Click the Network connection icon in the notification area on the mobile client.
   _____ On the mobile client, click the Workplace Connection option and you will see you are connected to the network locally.
   _____ Disconnect the mobile client computer and reconnect it to an external network. You should be able to access the DirectAccess server.
   _____ Open Windows PowerShell with administrative privileges on the mobile client computer.
   _____ Execute the `gpresult/r` command on the mobile client.
   _____ Connect the DirectAccess mobile client to the corporate network to obtain DAClientSettings GPO.

Choose an Option

1. Which option in the VPN output could potentially introduce a security risk for this VPN client?

Figure 5-21

```
Name                  : MyPSVPN
ServerAddress         : RemoteServer.Bridgehill.com
AllUserConnection     : False
Guid                  : {AC3C7786-4D65-40D4-8274-251DC38E4835}
TunnelType            : Automatic
AuthenticationMethod  : {MsChapv2}
EncryptionLevel       : Required
L2tpIPsecAuth         : Certificate
UseWinlogonCredential : False
EapConfigXmlStream    :
ConnectionStatus      : Disconnected
NapState              : NotConnected
RememberCredential    : False
SplitTunneling        : False

Name                  : VPNInt
ServerAddress         : RemoteServer.Bridgehill.com
AllUserConnection     : False
Guid                  : {2EF4D169-8380-4ECE-A761-A2BCE7646E86}
TunnelType            : Automatic
AuthenticationMethod  : {MsChapv2}
EncryptionLevel       : Required
L2tpIPsecAuth         : Certificate
UseWinlogonCredential : False
EapConfigXmlStream    :
ConnectionStatus      : Disconnected
NapState              : NotConnected
RememberCredential    : False
SplitTunneling        : True
```

■ Business Case Scenarios

Scenario 5-1: DirectAccess

You have set up a Windows Server for DirectAccess using the Getting Started Wizard. You log on to a Windows 8.1 computer in the domain and run the gpresult /r command. After reviewing the output, you notice that the client did not receive the DirectAccess Client GPO. What could be causing the problem?

Scenario 5-2: Network Access Protection

You have configured NAP using the NAP with DHCP enforcement policy yet a user's computer seems to be able to access the network even when it should be directed to remediation. How is this possible?

Supporting Authentication and Authorization

70-688 EXAM OBJECTIVE

Objective 2.3 – Supporting Authentication and Authorization. This objective may include but is not limited to: Multi-factor authentication, including certificates, virtual smart cards, picture passwords, and biometrics; workgroup versus domain, HomeGroup, computer and user authentication, including secure channel, account policies, credential caching, and Credential Manager; local account versus Microsoft account; Workplace Join.

LESSON HEADING	EXAM OBJECTIVE
Supporting Authentication and Authorization	
Using Multi-Factor Authentication	Multi-factor authentication, including certificates, virtual smart cards, picture passwords, and biometrics
Using Local Accounts vs. Microsoft Accounts	Local account versus Microsoft account
Authenticating Computers and Users	Workgroup versus domain, HomeGroup, computer and user authentication, including secure channel, account policies, credential caching, and Credential Manager
Configuring Workplace Join	Workplace Join

KEY TERMS

access token	fine-grained password policies	SSL
authentication	Global Catalog	Server Name Indication (SNI) extensions
authentication factors	HomeGroup	
authorization	integrity	smart cards
biometrics	Kerberos v5	TLS
Bring Your Own Device (BYOD)	Key Distribution Center (KDC)	TLS Handshake protocol
Certificate Authority (CA)	Local Security Authority (LSA)	TLS Record protocol
computer accounts	NTLM	Trusted Platform Module (TPM) chip
confidentiality	nonrepudiation	two-factor authentication
credential caching	Password Settings Object (PSO)	user account
Credential Manager	picture password	virtual smart cards (VSCs)
Device Registration Service (DRS)	public key infrastructure (PKI)	Workplace Join
digital certificate	Security Accounts Manager (SAM)	

■ Supporting Authentication and Authorization

THE BOTTOM LINE

Today's network administrators are faced with securing network resources that are being accessed by employees both inside and outside of the organization. Having a well-designed authentication and authorization strategy is the key to ensuring resource availability and integrity.

Network administrators are often faced with the task of securing network resources that are being accessed by employees from both inside and outside of the company. When designing a strategy to secure these resources, you need to keep in mind these key pillars of information security:

- *Authentication:* Represents the way that security principals (users, computers, and processes) prove their identity before they are allowed to connect to your network. In the past, authentication was handled through the use of passwords. Today, additional authentication tools, including digital certificates, smart cards, picture passwords, and biometrics, are used.

- *Authorization:* After security principals prove their identity, authorization determines what they can do. This is determined through the use of access control lists (ACLs) that are attached to each resource.

- *Confidentiality:* This process is about preventing people from reading information they are not authorized to read. Confidentiality is handled through the use of encryption technologies.

- *Integrity:* This is the ability to guarantee that the information has not been arbitrarily changed from the time it was sent from the original source and received by the other party.

- *Nonrepudiation:* This is a method used to provide proof that a security principal (user, computer, process) is the source of data, an action, or a communication. This is usually provided through the use of public key/private key technologies.

Each of these pillars of security should become part of your overall security design. This lesson focuses on two of them specifically: authentication and authorization.

Using Multi-Factor Authentication

Authentication is the process of verifying you are who you say you are. Two-factor authentication involves proving your identity using at least two authentication factors.

Authentication is the process of verifying that security principals (users, computers, or processes) are who they say they are. To prove their identity, security principals can use one or more authentication factors, which are basically pieces of information.

For example, you could use something you know (a password or PIN); something you have (a smart card); or something that is unique to you (a biometric), such as your fingerprint or an iris scan. These three pieces of information are called *authentication factors* (see Figure 6-1). When only one of these pieces of information is used (e.g., a password), it's called one-factor authentication. *Two-factor authentication* requires the use of two of the three authentication factors. Windows 8.1 supports the following methods of authentication: passwords, picture passwords, digital certificates, smart cards, and biometrics.

Figure 6-1

Authentication factors

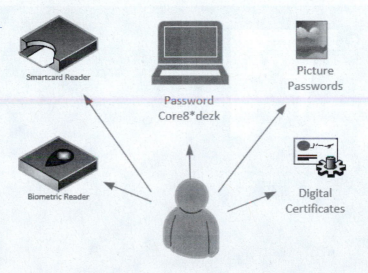

Smartcard Reader

Password
Core8*dezk

Picture
Passwords

Biometric Reader

Digital
Certificates

PASSWORDS

Traditional passwords have been used for years to authenticate users. Although they are the most common method, they are also the weakest. Users will typically choose a very simple password, write it down, and store it in a very insecure place. There are also several different ways for someone to discover your password and assume your identity. Through brute force attacks, social engineering, and eavesdropping, even strong passwords can be compromised.

You can strengthen passwords by instituting the use of strong passwords in your organization and use Group Policy to enforce those policies. A strong password has the following characteristics:

- At least eight characters long
- Uses at least one character from the following: upper- and lowercase letters, punctuation marks, numbers

- Does not include your login name, your real name, or your company name
- Does not include a complete word that can be found in the dictionary
- Should not be the same password that you have used in the past or used on other website accounts

PICTURE PASSWORDS

A *picture password* (see Figure 6-2) consists of two components: a picture and a gesture that you draw on it. You can pick the image from a default set included with the Windows 8.1 installation or select your own. After the picture is selected, you can then place your gestures.

A picture password is limited to three gestures (circles, straight lines, and taps). Because the combination of the three is infinite, a picture password offers more security than a traditional password. When you sign on, the gestures you use are compared with those that you created when the password was set. If they are correct, you are authenticated. If they are wrong (for example, if you used circle instead of a line), authentication fails.

Figure 6-2

Picture passwords

CREATE A PICTURE PASSWORD

GET READY. To create a picture password, perform the following steps:

1. On the *Settings* charm, click **Change PC Settings**.
2. Click **Users**.
3. Click **Create a picture password**.
4. Confirm your password if prompted and then click **OK**.
5. Click **Choose Picture**.

6. Navigate to the picture you want to use.

7. Choose the picture and then click **Open**.

8. Click **Use this Picture**.

9. Draw three gestures on your picture. You can use any combination of circles, straight lines, and taps. Be sure to remember the order in which you use the gestures.

10. Repeat the same three gestures to confirm.

11. Click **Finish**.

12. Sign out with the user account.

13. Choose the user account to log in with.

14. Repeat the gestures you used when setting up the picture password.

DIGITAL CERTIFICATES

A *digital certificate* is a collection of data that binds an identity to a key pair. In addition to authentication, these certificates can be used for authorization, non-repudiation, and other types of security control.

A digital certificate contains a name that indicates who or what owns the certificate, a public key, the name of the *Certificate Authority (CA)* that issued it, and the digital signature of the CA that issued it. A CA is the computer that creates and manages the distribution and revocation of certificates.

SMART CARDS

Smart cards, used with a smart card reader attached to a computer, contain an embedded processor that is used to communicate with the host computer and the card reader. They can be used to authenticate users, ensure data integrity when signing documents, and provide confidentiality when you need encryption. In order to authenticate, users insert their card into a reader connected to their computer and then enter their PIN. The smart card holds the users' logon information, private key, digital certificate, and other private information.

To deploy smart cards, you need a *public key infrastructure (PKI)*, which includes digital certificates, CAs, and other components that are used to create, distribute, validate, and revoke certificates. Smart cards can be credit card–sized devices or a token style (USB device). Information stored on the cards cannot be extracted from the device, all communication with the card is encrypted to protect against malicious software intercepting it, and brute force attempts to hack the PIN will result in the card being blocked until an administrator can unlock it. Because both the smart card and a PIN are required, it is much less likely that someone will be able to steal both.

VIRTUAL SMART CARDS (VSCs)

Windows 8 introduced *virtual smart cards (VSCs)*, which make additional hardware (smart card readers and smart cards) unnecessary. These cards emulate the functionality of regular smart cards but require a *Trusted Platform Module (TPM) chip* to protect the private keys. The TPM is used to encrypt the information, which is then stored on the computer's hard drive. If the user will need to access multiple computers using the VSC, one will have to be created and issued to the user for each system.

It is also possible to have multiple VSCs (one for each user) on multi-use computers. If a computer is lost or stolen, the user can contact an administrator who can revoke the certificate associated with the VSC on the user's computer.

SET UP A VIRTUAL TPM SMART CARD ENVIRONMENT

GET READY. To set up a virtual TPM smart card environment, you must have a computer running Windows 8.1 (TPM supported), you must be connected to a domain, and you must have access to a domain server with a functional CA in place. Then perform the following steps:

1. Create a certificate template (on the domain controller): This is the certificate you request in Step 3 on the client.

2. Create the VSC on the Windows 8.1 client machine using the TPM VSC Manager and then type a PIN.

3. Use the Certificate console on the Windows 8.1 client machine to request a new certificate and then select the one you created in Step 1.

After these steps are complete, you can use the VSC next time you boot your system.

For authentication, virtual smart cards use two-factor authentication. The user must have the computer with the virtual smart card and the user must know the PIN associated with the smart card.

Besides the TPM chip, the computer must be running Windows 8 or 8.1, must be part of the domain, and must have access to the certificate authority (CA). You will then have to:

1. Create the certificate template, which is based on the Smartcard Logon.
2. Create the TPM virtual smart card.
3. Enroll the certificate on the TPM virtual smart card.

 CREATE A CERTIFICATE TEMPLATE

GET READY. To create a certificate template on the Certificate Authority, perform the following steps:

1. Open *Microsoft Management Console (MMC)* by typing **mmc** from the *Start* menu.
2. Click **File > Add/Remove Snap-in**.
3. In the available snap-ins list, double-click **Certificate Templates** and then click **OK**.
4. Double click **Certificate Templates** to view all available certificate templates.
5. Right-click the **Smartcard Logon** template and choose **Duplicate Template**.
6. On the *Compatibility* tab, under *Certification Authority*, click **Windows Server 2003**.
7. On the General tab, specify the following:
   - For the name, type **TPM Virtual Smart Card Logon**.
   - Set the validity period to the desired value.
8. On the **Request Handling** tab, set the *Purpose* to **Signature and smartcard logon**. Then click to select **Prompt the user during enrollment**.
9. On the *Cryptography* tab, set the minimum key size to **2048**. Click to select **Requests must use one of the following providers** and then select **Microsoft Base Smart Card Crypto Provider**.
10. On the *Security* tab, add the security group to which you want to provide enroll access. If you want to give access to all users, select the **Authenticated** users group and then give them **Enroll** permissions.
11. Click **OK** to close the *Properties of New Template* dialog box.
12. Using *Server Manager*, click **Tools > Certificate Authority**.
13. In the left panel of the MMC, expand **Certification Authority (Local)**, and then expand your CA within the Certification Authority list.

14. Right-click **Certificate Templates** and choose **New > Certificate Template to Issue**.
15. From the list, select **TPM Virtual Smart Card Logon** and then click **OK**.

 CREATE A TPM VIRTUAL SMART CARD

GET READY. To create a TPM virtual smart card on a domain-joined computer running Windows 8.1, perform the following steps:

1. Open a command shell with administrative privileges.
2. At the command prompt, execute the following command:

```
tpmvscmgr.exe create /name tpmvsc /pin default /adminkey random /
generate
```

3. When you are prompted for a PIN, type a PIN that is at least 8 characters in length and then confirm it.
4. Wait several seconds for the process to finish.

Upon completion, Tpmvscmgr.exe will notify you of the device instance ID for the TPM VSC. Store this ID for later reference; you will need it to manage or remove the VSC.

 ENROLL FOR THE CERTIFICATE ON THE TPM VIRTUAL SMART CARD

GET READY. To enroll for the certificate on the TPM virtual smart card on the domain-joined computer running Windows 8.1, perform the following steps:

1. Open the *Certificates* console by typing **certmgr.msc** on the *Start* menu.
2. Right-click **Personal** and choose **All Tasks > Request New Certificate**.
3. On the *Before You Begin* page, click **Next**.
4. On the *Select Certificate Enrollment Policy* page, click **Next**.
5. On the *Request Certificates* page, click to select the **TPM Virtual Smart Card Logon** and then click **Enroll**.
6. If you are prompted for a device, select **Microsoft virtual smart card**.
7. Type the PIN for the TPM smart card that you entered when you created the VSC and then click **OK**.
8. Wait for the enrollment to finish and then click **Finish**.

BIOMETRICS

Biometrics takes advantage of the uniqueness of every individual. By using a person's fingerprint, face, voice, or retina, biometrics offers advantages over other methods. For example, the user has to physically be present at the point of identification, does not need to remember passwords or a PIN, and does not have to carry smart cards that can be lost or stolen. Instead of using biometrics to replace other methods, consider using them as an additional layer of security.

In the past, administrators had to struggle with managing third-party software and hardware to support biometrics. With each vendor providing different drivers, software, and management tools, it became very labor-intensive to support. Fortunately, Microsoft introduced native support for biometric technologies through its Windows Biometric Framework (WBF). WBF enables users to manage device settings for biometric devices through the Control Panel, provides support for managing device drivers; and manages Group Policy settings that can be used to enable, disable, or limit use of biometric data for a local computer or domain. A fingerprint reader is the most commonly used biometric device in corporate networks. These devices can be purchased separately or can be built in to new laptops. The reader

CERTIFICATION READY
Multi-factor authentication, including certificates, virtual smart cards, picture passwords, and biometrics
Objective 2.3

captures an image of your fingerprint and then saves it to the computer. The process is called enrolling. When you log on, the reader will scan your fingerprint and compare it with the one on file.

Using Local Accounts vs. Microsoft Accounts

User accounts allow employees to participate on the network and to gain access to the resources that are made available. Understanding which account to use and its limitations in regard to user experience, access to Windows apps, and password management will be important considerations when supporting the users and systems that require authentication.

In Lesson 3, you learned how to set up and configure both local accounts and Microsoft user accounts on your Windows 8.1 computer. In this section, we look at what to consider when determining the type of account to use as part of your authentication strategy.

CERTIFICATION READY
Local account versus
Microsoft account
Objective 2.3

A Microsoft user account is required in order to provide users with the ability to download apps from the Windows Store, synchronize their settings between Windows 8.1 computers and mobile devices, and run Windows 8.1 apps such as Mail, People, OneDrive, and Messaging. Although you can browse the Store with a local user account, you cannot download Windows apps. If your strategy is to continue to use traditional applications (installed from DVDs or websites) and only download Microsoft updates, a local account would suffice.

If your strategy includes setting up multiple Windows 8.1 computers on a network without Active Directory, Microsoft user accounts can reduce the administration overhead that is necessary when implementing local user accounts. Using local user accounts requires that you create the same account on each computer the user needs to access resources. Any changes the user makes to personalize her desktop will not follow her to other Windows 8.1 computers or devices. Using a Microsoft user account allows the user to access any of the Windows 8.1 computers and devices while maintaining a consistent desktop experience across each computer. On each computer or device, she can access her Windows Store apps, browse her favorites, review her history, and use many other settings stored in the cloud.

Implementing Microsoft user accounts can also simplify the process of recovering lost passwords. When you lose the password to a local user account, you must have access to the local administrator account to reset it, you must have created a password-reset disk beforehand or you must use a third-party software program. When you use Microsoft user accounts, you can recover from a lost password by using a previously assigned hint or by resetting you password from Microsoft's website.

If you are considering working with Microsoft accounts in combination with domain-based accounts, there are two options:

- Sign in with your Microsoft user account when you need to run a Windows app.
- Connect your domain account to your Microsoft user account.

If you choose the first option, each time a user logs in with his domain account and then attempts to open a Windows app (Mail, People, OneDrive, or Messaging), he must enter his Microsoft user account credentials. This can become very time consuming because the process is repeated each time he opens another Windows app.

The second option is to connect your Microsoft user accounts to your domain accounts. For enterprise environments, Group Policy can be used to control whether users can link their Microsoft user accounts to their domain accounts as well as what can and cannot be synchronized. If linking your domain credentials to your Microsoft user account fits your authentication strategy, keep in mind that the domain credentials will not be uploaded to the cloud and are never synchronized with other computers.

Authenticating Computers and Users

> When designing an authentication strategy, you can choose between a workgroup and a domain. Workgroups provide a distributed authentication mechanism, whereas domains provide a central authentication mechanism that can support scalability.

A *user account* is used by Windows to determine what changes you can make on the computer, which files and folders you can have access to, and is used to track personal preferences such as your choice of desktop wallpaper, color schemes, drive mappings, and/or screen savers. There are standard accounts used to perform daily tasks on the computer that are limited in what they can do as well as administrative accounts which provide full control over the computer.

Before users can access a network and its available resources, they must be authenticated. This involves entering a user name and password that was configured by the network's administrator as part of the initial setup of their user accounts. Once entered, the computer verifies the credentials against its database and determines whether or not to provide the user with access to its resources. These resources can be located on the local computer, distributed across the network, and/or be located somewhere out on the Internet.

Like user accounts, Windows *computer accounts* provide a means for authenticating and auditing the computer's access to a Windows network and its access to domain resources. Each Windows computer to which you want to grant access to resources must have a unique computer account. It can also be used for auditing purposes specifying what system was used when something was accessed.

Much like user accounts, computer accounts are assigned passwords when the computer is added to the domain and is automatically maintained between the computer and the domain controllers. Unfortunately, from time to time, a computer account can become untrusted where the security identifier (SID) or password is different from those stored in Active Directory. This is done when:

- You deploy a computer from an image of another computer and you do not use the sysprep tool to reset the SID.
- The computer account is corrupted.
- The computer is not connected to the domain network for long periods of time.

Unfortunately, you cannot reset the password. Instead, the best thing to do is to rejoin the computer to the domain. You can also use the `Netdom` command-line tool, which is included with Windows Server 2012 R2.

LOCAL COMPUTER AUTHENTICATION

In Lesson 3, you learned that workgroups are a collection of computers that interact with each other but without any centralized authority. Workgroup computers must be on the same network segment and will maintain their own local security database to store user accounts (see Figure 6-3). This database, also called the *Security Accounts Manager (SAM)*, contains user accounts and their associated passwords. When you enter your user name and password on a Windows computer, a process called the *Local Security Authority (LSA)* queries the SAM database to determine whether an account with the user name and password you

CERTIFICATION READY
Workgroup versus domain, HomeGroup, computer and user authentication, including secure channel, account policies, credential caching, and Credential Manager
Objective 2.3

used exists. If it does, you will be granted access to the system. If the same user needs access to another computer in the workgroup, they must have a separate account stored in that computer's SAM. In addition to verifying users who log on, LSA also handles any password changes and enforces overall security policy on the system.

Figure 6-3

Authenticating in the workgroup model

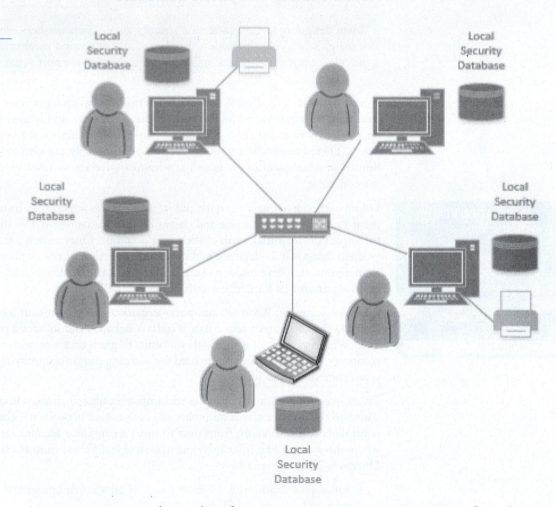

As you can imagine, as the number of computers increases, maintaining accounts for each user on multiple machines can become very labor-intensive. If an account is present on the other computer, users will not have to enter their user name and password again to connect and use the resource; it will be handled automatically in the background. If they attempt to access a resource on another computer and do not have an account, they will be prompted to enter a user name and password before connecting and using the resource. The user name and password must be stored in the computer's local SAM to gain access to its resources. Workgroups are very simple to design and don't require a Windows server to implement. On the other hand, they are designed for small groups of computers and provide very limited scalability.

TAKE NOTE*

It is best practice to have at least two domain controllers on your network at any given time in case one fails or you need to take it down for maintenance.

DOMAINS

When users log on to a computer that is a member of a domain, they are not being authenticated by the computers on which they are working. Instead, their credentials (user name/password) are sent to a special computer that manages Active Directory. Active Directory is a database along with collection of supporting components that are installed on one or more computers in the domain. These computers, called domain controllers, maintain a copy of the Active Directory that stores user accounts in the form of objects. These objects are then replicated between domain controllers. When using a domain model (see Figure 6-4), you have to create only a single user account for each user to provide access to all resources in the domain. When running Windows 8.1, you must have either the Professional or Enterprise edition to join a domain.

Figure 6-4

Authenticating in the domain model

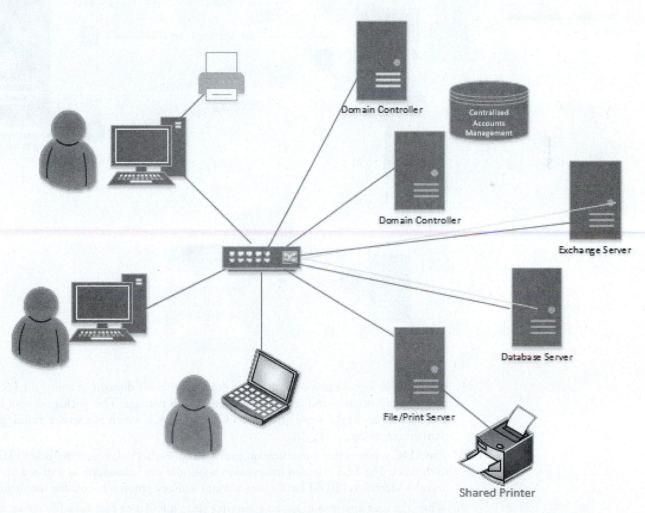

It is possible that a company will have more than one domain as part of its Active Directory implementation. Multiple domains are connected to create trees, and multiple trees can be connected to create a forest. When you implement multiple domains, a feature named the *Global Catalog* is used to find users, computers, and resources throughout the other domains.

KERBEROS AUTHENTICATION

When authenticating and using resources in a domain, you will use **Kerberos v5**. Kerberos v5 is a protocol that defines how clients interact with a network authentication service. Figure 6-5 provides a simplified explanation of what happens between a user/computer, a domain controller (running the **Key Distribution Center**, or **KDC**), and a file server containing the resource the user wants to access. The Key Distribution Center is the network authentication service that supplies ticket-granting tickets (TGTs) used by the Kerberos v5 protocol.

Figure 6-5

The Kerberos authentication process

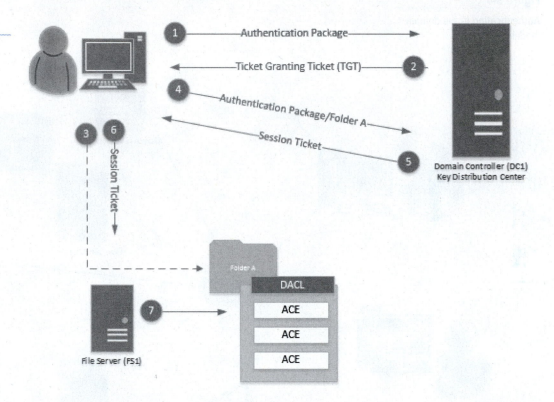

1. When a user logs on to a computer in a domain with the domain account, the LSA takes the information and creates an authentication package. This package is sent by the user's computer to the Key Distribution Center (KDC), which is a service running on a domain controller.

2. The KDC validates the authentication package and sends a ticket-granting ticket (TGT) to the user. The TGT contains information about the user's computer as well as a list of Security Identifiers (SIDS) for the user account and any group accounts the user belongs to.

3. When the user attempts to access a resource (e.g., a folder or file) on a file server named FS1, she will need a session ticket.

4. To get the session ticket, the client will create another authentication package and send it back to the KDC along with a request for that resource.

5. The KDC validates the authentication package and sends the user a session ticket.

6. The session ticket is then used to authenticate to FS1. FS1 will decrypt the ticket and validate it.

7. FS1 will then compare the ticket to a discretionary access control list (DACL) that is attached to the resource. The DACL consists of one or more access control entries (ACEs). Each ACE contains a SID for a user account or group and the permissions applied to it for the resource. If the ACE contains one or more SIDs that matches those in the user's ticket, they are granted the permissions provided for that SID.

WINDOWS NT LAN MANAGER (NTLM) v2

NTLM is a family of authentication protocols first introduced with Windows NT. It is a based on a challenge/response mechanism used to authenticate users and computers. Although Kerberos v5 is the preferred authentication protocol for Active Directory–based environments, NTLM is used for systems running Windows NT 4.0 and earlier and for computers that are a member of a workgroup. It is also used when authenticating to a server that belongs to a different Active Directory forest.

SECURING CHANNELS WITH TRANSPORT LAYER SECURITY (TLS)/SECURE SOCKETS LAYER (SSL)

When communicating across untrusted networks, you need to know that you are connecting to the right servers and that your data is safe during transit. Transport Layer Security (TLS) and Secure Sockets Layer (SSL) are two communication protocols that can securely authenticate servers and clients and protect you from eavesdropping and tampering. Windows implements TLS and SSL through the SChannel security support provider.

TLS is actually based on SSL but uses a different handshake protocol. Although both can protect your systems, they are not interoperable.

TLS uses the TLS Handshake protocol and the TLS Record protocol. Both must be used in combination with a transport protocol, with TCP being the most obvious. TLS allows the client and server to recognize when the message has been interfered with, intercepted, or modified.

- *TLS Handshake protocol:* Establishes the encryption/decryption keys and algorithm, and resumes connections
- *TLS Record protocol:* Uses encryption/decryption keys to secure the data, and validate where it comes from and its overall integrity

Servers that support these protocols must have a digital certificate issued to them by a trusted third party. The role of the certificate is to assure an application or user that it is safe to initiate a connection, and whether encryption is required to determine the shared algorithm to use and provide the necessary encryption/decryption keys. The digital certificates are usually obtained from a well-known CA recognized by the industry as a whole; they are not created and distributed by the organization's own CAs.

TLS uses stronger encryption algorithms and can work across different ports, whereas *SSL,* an encryption protocol that allows you to encrypt communications between users and servers through the use of a digital certificate, uses security features that require a specific port to be secure. TLS is the successor to SSL, and the terms are often used interchangeably.

Windows 8/Windows Server 2012 introduced TLS support for *Server Name Indication (SNI) extensions.* SNI provides enhanced support when a client connects to a server that is virtually hosting multiple domains. If each has its own digital certificate, the server needs to be able to provide the correct certificate to the client computer. SNI allows the client to inform the target domain earlier in the process, enabling it to select the appropriate certificate. By providing this enhancement, you can host multiple SSL websites using a single IP and port combination, allow multiple simultaneous connections to the SSL websites, and help clients determine the appropriate certificate to select during authentication.

ACCOUNT POLICIES

Group Policy is one of the most powerful features of Active Directory that controls the working environment for user accounts and computer accounts. Group Policy provides the centralized management and configuration of operating systems, applications and users' settings in an Active Directory environment. For example, you can use group policies to specify how often a user has to change her password, what the background image is on a person's computer, or you can specify if spell checking is required before sending an e-mail.

CERTIFICATION READY
Workgroup versus domain, HomeGroup, computer and user authentication, including secure channel, account policies, credential caching, and Credential Manager
Objective 2.3

Account policies (see Figure 6-6) are domain-level policies that define the security-related attributes assigned to user objects. Account policies contain three subsets:

- **Password Policy:** Determines settings for passwords, such as enforcement and lifetimes.
- **Account Lockout Policy:** Determines the circumstances and length of time that an account is locked out of the system.
- **Kerberos Policy:** Determines Kerberos-related settings, such as ticket lifetimes and enforcement. Kerberos Policy settings do not exist in local computer policies.

Figure 6-6

Managing Account Policies

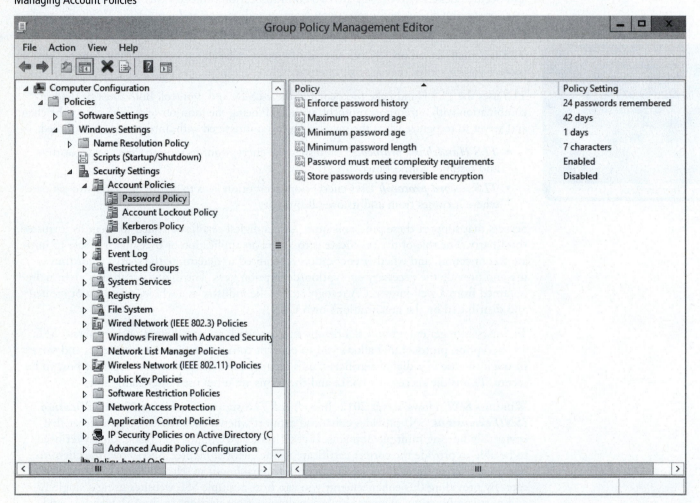

Group Policy can be used to control passwords, including how often a user changes a password, how long the password is, and whether the password is a complex password. To help manage passwords, you can configure settings in the Computer Configuration\Windows Settings\Security Settings\Account Policies\Password Policy node of a group policy. The settings are:

- **Minimum password length:** Determines the minimum number of characters that a user's password must contain. You can set a value between 1 and 14 characters. To specify that no password is required, set the value to 0.

- **Passwords must meet complexity requirements**: If enabled, passwords must be at least six characters long, cannot use parts of the user's name, and must be a combination of at least three of the following four characteristics: upper case, lower case, digits, and non-alphanumeric characters.
- **Maximum Password Age:** The time before a password expires
- **Enforce Password History**: The number of different passwords that users must have before they can reuse a password.
- **Minimum Password Age:** The time before users can change their passwords. This prevents users from changing their passwords numerous times, effectively surpassing the Enforce Password History setting in their efforts to reset their passwords to their original passwords.

If you need to use different password policies for different groups of users, you can use fine-grained password policies, which are applied to user objects or global security groups. *Fine-grained password policies* allow you to specify multiple password policies within a single domain so that you can apply different restrictions for password and account lockout policies to different sets of users in a domain. To use a fine-grained password policy, your domain functional level must be at least Windows Server 2008. To enable fine-grained password policies, you first create a *Password Settings Object (PSO)*. A PSO gives you granular control of password and account settings.

You then configure the same settings that you configure for the password and account lockout policies. You can create and apply PSOs in the Windows Server 2012 R2 environment by using the Active Directory Administrative Center (ADAC) or Windows PowerShell.

 CREATE AND CONFIGURE THE PASSWORD SETTINGS CONTAINER

GET READY. To create and configure the Password Settings Container, perform the following steps:

1. Open **Server Manager**.
2. Click **Tools > Active Directory Administrative Center**. The *ADAC* appears.

3. In the *ADAC* pane, click the arrow next to the domain and then click the **System** folder. Scroll down and double-click **Password Settings Container**. The *Password Settings Container* is shown in Figure 6-7.

Figure 6-7

Opening the Password Settings Container

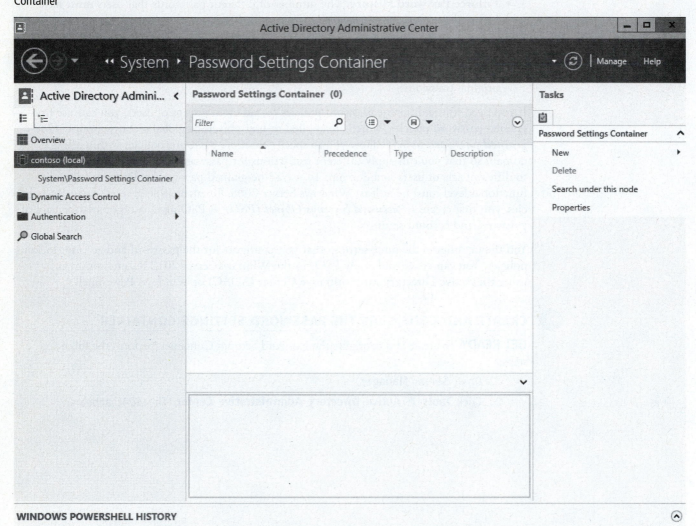

4. In the *Tasks* pane, click **New > Password Settings**. The *Create Password Settings* window appears (see Figure 6-8).

Figure 6-8

Creating a new Password Settings Container

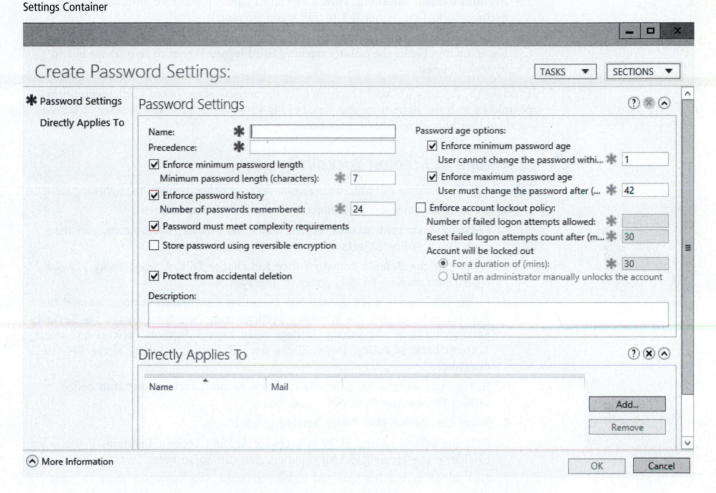

5. In the *Name* text box, type a name of the Password Settings Container.

6. In the *Precedence* text box, type a precedence number.

   Passwords with a lower precedence number overwrite Password Settings Containers that have higher precedence numbers.

7. Complete or edit the appropriate fields for the settings that you want to use.

8. Under *Directly Applies To*, click **Add**. In the *Select Users or Groups* dialog box, specify the name of the user or group that you want the Password Settings Container to affect and then click **OK**.

9. Click **OK** to submit the creation of the PSO.

10. Close the *ADAC*.

An ***Account Lockout Policy*** specifies the number of unsuccessful logon attempts that, if made within a pre-defined amount of time, might indicate that an unauthorized person trying to access a computer or the network. An Account Lockout Policy can be set to lock the account in question after a specified number of invalid attempts. Additionally, the policy specifies the duration that the account remains locked.

The three policy settings used for account lockout are as follows:

- **Account lockout duration:** How long (in minutes) a locked-out account remains locked-out (range is 1 to 99,999 minutes).

- **Account lockout threshold:** How many failed logons it will take until the account becomes locked-out (range is 1 to 999 logon attempts).

- **Reset account lockout counter after:** How long (in minutes) it takes after a failed logon attempt before the counter tracking failed logons is reset to zero (range is 1 to 99,999 minutes).

If you set the Account Lockout Duration to 0, the account stays locked until an administrator unlocks it. If the account lockout threshold is set to 0, the account will never be locked out no matter how many failed logons occur.

 CONFIGURE AN ACCOUNT LOCKOUT POLICY

GET READY. To configure a domain-wide account lockout policy, perform the following steps:

1. Using *Server Manager*, click **Tools > Group Policy Management**.

2. Expand **Forest: contoso.com**, expand **Domains**, expand **contoso.com**, and then click **Group Policy Objects**.

3. Right-click the **Default Domain Policy** and choose **Edit**. A *Group Policy Management Editor* window for this policy is displayed.

4. In the left window pane, expand the **Computer Configuration** node, expand the **Policies** node, expand the **Windows Settings** node, and then expand the **Security Settings** node. In the *Security Settings* node, expand **Account Policies** and select **Account Lockout Policy**. The available settings for this category of the GPO are displayed.

5. In the right window pane, double-click the **Account lockout duration** policy setting to view the *Properties* dialog box.

6. Select the **Define This Policy Setting** check box.

   Note the default setting of 30 minutes for Account Lockout Duration. If you want to change the account lockout duration, you can do so here.

7. Click **OK** to accept the specified lockout duration. The *Suggested Value Changes* dialog box—which indicates other related settings and their defaults—is displayed.

8. Click **OK** to automatically enable these other settings or click **Cancel** to go back to the *Account Lockout Duration Properties* dialog box.

9. Click **OK** to accept the additional setting defaults.

10. Complete any additional changes, as necessary, to the other individual Account Lockout Policy settings.

11. Close the *Group Policy Management Editor* window for this policy.

UNDERSTANDING ACCESS TOKENS

When a user is authenticated, the Local Security Authority (LSA) creates a primary access token for the user. An *access token* contains a security identifier (SID) for the user, all of the SIDs for the groups to which the user belongs, and the user's privileges. As the user access resources, a user does not have to keep entering his password. Instead, Windows will submit the access token on behalf of the user.

If you add a user to a group after the user's access token has been issued, or if you modify privileges assigned to the user account, the user must log off and then log on again in order for the user will get the updated access token.

CREDENTIAL CACHING

Each time a user longs on to Windows, Windows securely caches the user's domain credentials by storing a hash of the password in the system registry (HKEY_LOCAL_MACHINE\ Security\Cache). By caching the user's domain credentials (*credential caching*), the user can log on when the domain controller is not available. When logging on to the domain, the cache credentials only provides the user with access to local resources; the credentials must be checked when accessing remote resources as well as to verify that the user has access.

If you do not want the credentials to be cached, you can disable the credential caching by using a GPO setting (Computer Configuration\Policies\Windows Settings\Security Settings\ Local Policies\Security Options\Interactive logon: number of previous logons to cache (in case domain controller is not available). A value of 0 disables logon caching.

CREDENTIAL MANAGER

Credential Manager allows you to store credentials (such as user names and passwords) that you use to log on to websites or other computers on a network. By storing your credentials, Windows can automatically log you on to websites or other computers. Credentials are saved in special folders on your computer called *vaults*.

Windows and programs (such as web browsers) can securely provide the credentials in the vaults to other computers and websites. Windows automatically adds credentials used to connect to shared folders to the Credential Manager. However, you can manually add a user name and password.

 ADD A WINDOWS CREDENTIAL USING CREDENTIAL MANAGER

GET READY. To add a Windows credential using Windows Manager, perform the following steps:

1. Open the **Control Panel** and click **User Accounts**.
2. Click **Credential Manager > Windows Credentials** (see Figure 6-9).

Figure 6-9

Managing Windows Credentials with Credential Manager

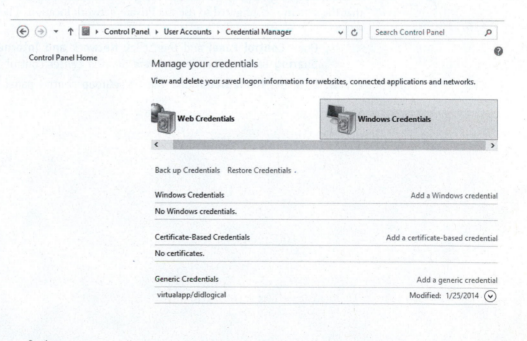

3. Click **Add a Windows credential**.

4. In the *Internet or network address* text box, type the name of the computer on the network that you want to access. This can be the NetBIOS name (for example, **server1**) or the DNS name (for example, **server1.fabrikam.com**).

5. In the *User name* text box and the *Password* text box, type the user name and password that you use for that computer or website and then click **OK**.

You might need to change the Windows credentials or perhaps you no longer wish to store the credentials. In these situations, click the credentials that you want to manage and then click Edit or Remove.

HOMEGROUP

When you are running Windows 8.1 within a domain, Windows servers and clients have several tools and mechanisms to share files and printers. Today, many households have multiple computers. A *HomeGroup* is a group of computers on a home network that can share files and printers. To protect your HomeGroup, you can use a password. Similar to share permissions, other users cannot change the files that you share unless you give them permission to do so. When compared to any folder sharing, HomeGroups are relatively limited, because you can share only the contents of the libraries in the user's profile.

HomeGroup is available with Windows 7, Windows 8 (including Windows 8.1 and Windows RT 8.0/8.1). You can join a HomeGroup on a PC running Windows RT 8.1, but you can't create a HomeGroup or share content with the HomeGroup. In Windows 7 Starter and Windows 7 Home Basic, you can join a HomeGroup, but you can't create one. If the system does not detect a HomeGroup, the Network and Sharing Center control panel contains a link providing access to the Create a HomeGroup Wizard.

CERTIFICATION READY
Workgroup versus domain, HomeGroup, computer and user authentication, including secure channel, account policies, credential caching, and Credential Manager
Objective 2.3

 CREATE A HOMEGROUP

GET READY. Log on to Windows 8.1 using an account with Administrator privileges. Make sure that the system is configured to use the Private network location. Then perform the following steps:

1. Open **Control Panel** and then click **Network and Internet > Network and Sharing Center**. The *Network and Sharing Center* control panel appears.

2. Click the **HomeGroup** link. The HomeGroup control panel appears (see Figure 6-10).

Figure 6-10

Opening the HomeGroup
Control Panel

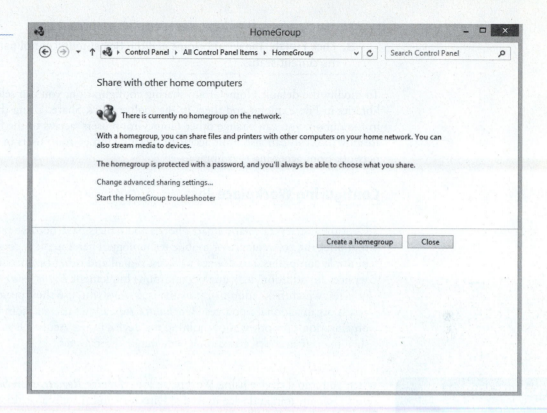

3. Click **Create a HomeGroup**. The *Create a HomeGroup Wizard* appears.

4. Click **Next**. The *Share with other HomeGroup members* page appears.

5. Select the libraries that you want to share and then click **Next**.

   The wizard creates the HomeGroup and assigns it a password. The *Use this password to add other computers to your HomeGroup* page appears.

6. Click **Finish**. The wizard closes and the HomeGroup control panel changes to reflect its current status.

When a Windows 8.1 computer using the Private network location does detect a HomeGroup on the network, the Network and Sharing Center control panel appears with an Available to Join link.

 JOIN A HOMEGROUP

GET READY. Log on to Windows 8.1 using an account with Administrator privileges. Make sure that the system is configured to use the Private network location. Then perform the following steps:

1. Open **Control Panel** and click **Network and Internet > Network and Sharing Center**. The *Network and Sharing Center* Control Panel appears.

2. Click the **HomeGroup** link. The *HomeGroup* control panel appears.

3. Click **Join Now**. The *Join a HomeGroup Wizard* appears.

4. Click **Next**. The *Share with other HomeGroup members* page appears.

5. Select the libraries that you want to share and then click **Next**. The *Type the HomeGroup password* page appears.

6. In the *Type the password* text box, type the password supplied by the *Create a HomeGroup Wizard* and then click **Next**.

7. The *You have joined the HomeGroup* page appears.

8. Click **Finish**. The wizard closes and the HomeGroup control panel changes to reflect its current status.

To modify the default HomeGroup sharing configuration, you can select one of your shared libraries in File Explorer and then, in the toolbar, click Share. Using the controls that appear in the ribbon, you can change other HomeGroup users' access to the library from Read to Read/Write. You can also limit access to specific HomeGroup users or prevent anyone on the network from accessing that library.

Configuring Workplace Join

Over the last several years, smart phones and tablets have become powerful devices that offer the convenience of mobile technology. Therefore, it is common for users use multiple computers and devices to access e-mail and other business-related applications services. In addition, as many organizations implement *Bring Your Own Device (BYOD)* policies, which help administrators manage users who use their personal devices to access organizational resources. *Workplace Join* allows users to join their devices to the organization network without joining the device to the Active Directory domain. You can then manage accessed based on a wide range of attributes.

CERTIFICATION READY
Workplace Join
Objective 2.3

When you join a device using Workplace Join, *Device Registration Service (DRS)* registers a non-Domain Joined device in Active Directory and installs a certificate on the device. By joining the device, Workplace Join provides a secure single sign-on mechanism while controlling which resources can be accessed by the device.

When the user joins the devices using Workplace Join technology, the device becomes a known device. To use Workplace Join, you must have Windows Server 2012 R2 with the AD FS role service installed. In addition, the client must be using the Windows 8.1 client operating system or iOS-based devices (such as an iPad).

The certificate will be used to represent device identity when access organization resources. When accessing resources on the organization, the SSO allows the user to be prompted for their domain credentials only once during the lifetime of the SSO session. However, an administrator can specify resources that enforce a password prompt or reauthentication.

To support Workplace Join, you'll need to install and configure Active Directory Federation Services (AD FS) and the new Device Registration Service. To configure the Device Registration Service, execute the following Windows PowerShell commands:

```
Initialize-ADDeviceRegistration
```

```
Enable-AdfsDeviceRegistration
```

Then open the AD FS Management console, navigate to Authentication Policies, click Edit Global Primary Authentication, click to select the Enable Device Authentication, and then click OK. Lastly, the client must trust the SSL certificate that is used for the federation server and must be able to validate certificate revocation information for the certificate.

 JOIN A DEVICE

GET READY. To join a device, perform the following steps:

1. Log on to the client device with a Microsoft account.

2. On the *Start* screen, open the Charms bar, click the **Settings** charm, and then click **Change PC Settings**.

3. On the *PC Settings* page, click **Network** > **Workplace**.

4. In the *Enter your UserID to get workplace access or turn on device management* dialog box, type the user name (such as **JSmith@contoso.com**) and then click **Join**.

5. When prompted for credentials, type the username and the associated password and then click **OK**. You should now see the message *This device has joined your workplace network*.

SKILL SUMMARY

IN THIS LESSON YOU LEARNED:

- When designing a strategy to secure resources, you need to keep in mind the pillars of security: authentication, authorization, confidentiality, integrity, and non-repudiation.

- Authentication is the process of verifying that users, computers, or processes are who they say they are. This is accomplished through the use of one or more authentication factors: passwords, picture passwords, digital certificates, smart cards, and biometrics. When two are used in combination, it's called two-factor authentication.

- Workgroups provide a decentralized approach to authenticating users in that each computer's SAM database handles its own account management. On the other hand, domains provide a centralized database called Active Directory that enables you to create a single account and access resources throughout the enterprise.

- When authenticating in domains, you use the Kerberos v5 protocol. This protocol uses a KDC, which provides TGTs and session tickets used to validate the user/computer when it attempts to access resources in the domain.

■ Knowledge Assessment

Multiple Choice

Select the correct answer for each of the following questions.

1. Which of the following terms best describes the manner in which security principals prove their identity?
   a. Authorization
   b. Confidentiality
   c. Authentication
   d. Integrity

2. Which of the following are considered authentication factors? (Choose all that apply)
   a. Wi-Fi Protected Access
   b. Biometrics
   c. Picture passwords
   d. Smart cards

3. Which types of gestures are supported by picture passwords support? (Choose all that apply)
   a. Straight lines
   b. Circles
   c. Taps
   d. Angles

4. Which of the following authentication protocols is based on a challenge/response mechanism?
   a. NTLM
   b. Kerberos
   c. TLS/SLS
   d. File Replication Service

5. Which of the following characteristics describe the characteristics of a workgroup? (Choose all that apply)
   a. All computers are located on same network segment.
   b. It centralized management of user accounts.
   c. It is scalable.
   d. It uses the SAM database.

6. Which authentication protocol is used in Windows Active Directory domains?
   a. Kerberos
   b. TGT
   c. KDC
   d. TLS/SSL

7. Which component is used to create virtual smart cards?
   a. SSL certificate
   b. Smartcard reader
   c. Trusted Platform Module
   d. Picture authentication

8. Which type of certificate is used with virtual smart cards?
   a. Smartcard logon
   b. Basic EFS
   c. Workstation authentication
   d. User

9. Which tool is used to remember user names and passwords when accessing a website?
   a. Local security policy
   b. HomeGroup Control Panel
   c. Access token generator
   d. Credential Manager

Best Answer

Choose the letter that corresponds to the best answer. More than one answer choice may achieve the goal. Select the BEST answer.

1. You currently have 10 computers on your network that are configured to share a few printers and a single document folder. Your company is not expected to add more computers or users over the next year. You also don't have an IT staff to support your network. Which of the following models is the best fit for your needs?
   a. Domain model
   b. Workgroup model
   c. Ad-hoc model
   d. Infrastructure model

2. Which of the following authentication factors offers the most security?
   a. Passwords
   b. Picture passwords
   c. Smart cards
   d. Smart cards with a PIN

3. Which of the following authentication types is the least secure?
   a. Passwords (20 characters, mixed with upper- and lowercase, numbers, and symbols)
   b. Smart cards
   c. Smart cards with a PIN
   d. VSCs

4. Which of the following authentication protocols is best designed to support today's Active Directory-based networks?
   a. NTLMv2
   b. NTLMv1
   c. Kerberosv1
   d. Kerberosv5

5. Which of the following is used to verify the trustworthiness of a computer within a domain? (Choose two answers)
   a. Computer SID
   b. Computer certificate
   c. User password
   d. Computer password

Matching and Identification

1. Match the following terms with the related description or usage.

   _____ a) Authentication
   _____ b) SAM
   _____ c) Two-factor authentication
   _____ d) Authorization
   _____ e) Workgroup
   _____ f) Domain
   _____ g) TGT
   _____ h) Digital certificate

   1. Contains user accounts and their associated passwords in a workgroup model.
   2. Determines what a security principal can do after being authenticated.
   3. Requires the use of two of the three authentication factors.
   4. Provides centralized account management.
   5. Is a collection of computers that interact with each other without any centralized authority.
   6. Contains information about the user's computer, a list of SIDs for the user account, and any group account memberships.
   7. Represents the way that security principals prove their identity.
   8. Is a collection of data that binds an identity to a key pair.

Build a List

1. Specify the correct order of the steps that must be completed in order to use Kerberos for authentication.

   _____ An authentication package is created and sent to the KDC.
   _____ The user attempts to access a resource and needs a session ticket.
   _____ The KDC validates the authentication package and sends the user a session ticket
   _____ The KDC validates the authentication package and sends the user a TGT.
   _____ The client creates an authentication package (to get a session ticket) and sends it to the KDC along with a request for the resource.

_____ A session ticket is used to authenticate to the file server that contains the resource the user wants.

_____ The file server compares the ticket to a DACL.

2. Specify the correct order of the steps that must be completed to create a picture password.

_____ Choose **Picture**.

_____ Click **Create a picture password**.

_____ Draw three gestures.

_____ Confirm the gestures.

_____ Log in using the picture password.

■ Business Case Scenarios

Scenario 6-1: Securing Mobile Computers

You are an administrator for Contoso Corporation. You want to enhance the security of mobile computers by using multi-factor authentication without increasing costs. What solution would you suggest? What feature would you need in order to implement your solution?

Scenario 6-2: Securing Smart Phones and Tablets

You are an administrator for Contoso Corporation, which has just implemented a BYOD policy. Your manager has asked you what needs to be done in order to manage those devices by specifying what the device can access or not?

Supporting Data Storage

70-688 EXAM OBJECTIVE

Objective 2.4 – Support data storage. This objective may include but is not limited to: Distributed File System (DFS) client, including caching settings; storage spaces, including capacity and fault tolerance; optimizing data access by using BranchCache; OneDrive

LESSON HEADING	EXAM OBJECTIVE
Resolving Data Storage Issues	
Using Disk Quotas	
Managing Storage Pools and Storage Spaces	Storage spaces, including capacity and fault tolerance
Creating Storage Pools	
Creating Storage Spaces	
Optimizing data access Using BranchCache	Optimizing data access by using BranchCache
BranchCache Benefits	
Understanding Content Servers	
Understanding BranchCache Operating Modes	
Managing Distributed File System (DFS) Client Settings	Distributed File System (DFS) client, including caching settings
Managing DFS Namespaces	
Managing DFS Replication	
Using OneDrive to Manage Files/Folders	OneDrive
Accessing OneDrive from a Browser	
Creating a File Within OneDrive	
Uploading Files to OneDrive	
Sharing a Document in OneDrive	
Accessing OneDrive from the OneDrive Desktop App for Windows	

KEY TERMS

access-based enumeration

BranchCache

BranchCache-enabled server
(content server)

DFS Namespace

DFS Replication

Distributed File System (DFS)

domain-based namespaces

disk quotas

distributed-cache mode

External SATA (eSATA)

fetching

File Server Resource Manager

full mesh topology

hosted-cache mode

hub/spoke topology

OneDrive

OneDrive desktop app for
Windows

referral

replication group

parity

Serial Advanced Technology
Attachment (SATA)

simple (no resiliency)

Small Computer System
Interface (SCSI)

stand-alone DFS

Storage Spaces

storage pools

thin provisioning

three-way mirror

two-way mirror

Universal Serial Bus (USB)

■ Resolving Data Storage Issues

THE BOTTOM LINE

Although the average disk capacity has increased dramatically over the years, there is one thing you can count on: Users will always find a way to store enormous amounts of data on volumes they have access to. Disk quotas, storage spaces and BranchCache are features that can be used to resolve data storage issues within your organization.

User data typically includes multiple versions of their documents, copies of other users' documents, high-definition videos downloaded from the Internet, or just about anything else they're not ready to delete. As users' appetites for more storage continue to increase, administrators find themselves purchasing and using a wide variety of drives with different capacities (100 GB, 500 GB, 10 TB) and different drive interfaces to fit their data storage needs. The type of interface you select depends a lot on the connections available with your motherboard and the performance you need out of the drive. Examples of drive interfaces include:

- *Small Computer System Interface (SCSI)* is a set of standards for interfaces designed to connect and transfer information between high-speed hardware devices and a motherboard. Devices are connected together in a chain. Each device in the chain gets a SCSI ID and the last device in the chain must be terminated. SATA has replaced SCSI on most modern computers.

- *Serial Advanced Technology Attachment (SATA)* is a serial interface that transfers data in bursts instead of parallel. It comes in three varieties: 1.5 Gbps (SATA-1.0), 3 Gbps (SATA-2.0), and 6 Gbps (SATA 3.0). These have maximum throughputs of 150 Mbps, 300 Mbps and 600 Mbps. *External SATA (eSATA)* extends the SATA bus to external devices.

- *Universal Serial Bus (USB)* is a serial interface that is used to connect keyboards, mice, printers, scanners, and removable media drives. Up to 127 peripherals can be connected to a single USB port. USB 2.0 has a maximum transfer rate of 480 Mbps while USB 3.0, released in 2008, claims a theoretical maximum transmission speed of up to 5 Gbps.

In addition to controlling how much data users can store on the network and managing their need for additional storage space, administrators also have to deal with helping users who work in branch offices. These users must traverse slow wide area network (WAN) links to download content from their main office. This is not only frustrating but also affects their overall productivity.

Fortunately, Windows 8.1 provides several options for resolving these types of data storage issues:

- Disk quotas
- Storage spaces
- BranchCache
- Distributed File System
- OneDrive

Using Disk Quotas

Letting users store their files and folders on the network can result in a select few abusing the process. As an administrator, your goal is to provide storage space while at the same time minimizing the costs of adding more storage. **Disk quotas** enable you to maintain a balance between the two by limiting the amount of storage space allocated to your users.

Disk quotas, a feature first introduced in Windows 2000, are available in Windows 8.1 and Windows Server 2012 R2 editions. They enable you to set the amount of storage space available to each user. When enabled, the Disk Quota Manager monitors and tracks the files that are owned by a specific user. It then compares the amount of disk space being consumed by the user to the limit set by the administrator. When users reach their limit, the Disk Quota Manager will notify them and/or restrict them from adding more data to the disk.

Here are a few key things to know about using disk quotas:

- Quotas can be configured only on NTFS volumes.
- Users are charged only for the files they own.
- Quotas must be enabled separately on each volume and are applied on a per-user basis.
- Quotas do not apply to administrators.
- Only domain administrators or local administrators can enable the feature.

Configuring disk quotas involves three steps:

1. Enable quotas on the volume.
2. Configure the quota settings.
3. Create quota entries for specific users.

ENABLING QUOTAS ON INDIVIDUAL COMPUTERS

To enable quota management, you can use Disk Management (diskmgmt.msc) or File Explorer to locate the volume on which you want to enable the feature. Right-click it and choose Properties. Click the Quota tab, which displays the *Enable quota management* option (see Figure 7-1). From the Quota tab, you can also deny disk space to users who exceed their quota limit, set the amount of disk space available to users along with their warning levels, and log events. Logging identifies the user and what triggered the event (for example, a warning or an exceeded quota limit).

Figure 7-1

Reviewing disk quota settings

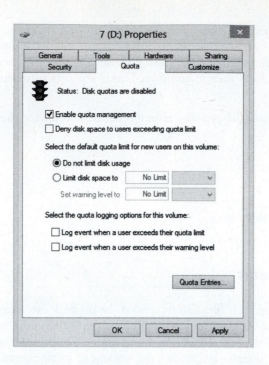

If you enable the *Deny Disk Space to users exceeding quota limit* option, users who reach the limits you set will be denied additional storage space on the volume. Users will receive an "insufficient disk space" error on their screens. If the check box is not selected, users are warned when they reach their limits, but not restricted from adding more data to the volume. By not restricting users initially, you can get a better picture of who is consuming the volume to store data and how much space they are actually using. This information can then be analyzed to determine effective quota policies.

When you configure quotas, you apply a default setting for all users and then click the *Quota Entries* button to configure exceptions for specific users/groups. In other words, when you create a quota entry for a user, the default setting no longer applies to that user. Because quotas are enabled on a per-volume basis, you may decide that you want to configure the exact same quota entries for another volume. You can do this by clicking Quota Entries, choosing the entries you want to use on the other volume, and then clicking Quota > Export. You can then enable quota management on the other volume and import the quota entries.

TAKE NOTE When you enable disk quotas for a volume, they apply only to new users who have yet to place data on the volume. If existing users already have files/folders on the volume, you have to add them as new quota entries.

When planning your quota strategy, consider grouping your users based on the amount of disk space you think they will require. For example, your marketing and graphic design staff typically needs more space than other groups. Set default limits that are not too restrictive for all users' accounts and then modify them for users who need more disk space. Consider growth requirements and increase as needed.

ENABLING QUOTAS USING GROUP POLICY

Group Policy can also be used to manage disk quotas on selected computers at the site, domain, or organizational unit (OU) level. This policy can be found in the Computer Configuration\Administrative Templates\System\Disk Quotas section of a Group Policy. On Windows Server 2012 R2, there are six disk quota settings you can use:

- **Enable disk quotas**: Enabling this setting turns on disk quota management on all NTFS volumes of the computer and users cannot turn it off.

- **Enforce disk quota limit**: Enabling this policy determines whether disk quota limits are enforced and prevents the user from changing the setting.

- **Specify default quota limit and warning level**: This policy setting specifies the default disk quota limit and warning level for all new users as soon as they write to the volume. It does not affect disk-quota limits for current users. The policy settings here determine how much disk space can be used by each user on each of the NTFS file system volumes on a computer. It also specifies a warning level.

- **Log event when quote limit is exceeded**: This setting determines whether the system records an event in the local Application log when users reach their disk quota limit.

- **Log event when quota warning level is exceeded**: This setting determines whether the system records an event in the Application log when users reach their disk quota warning limit.

- **Apply policy to removable media**: This policy extends the disk quota policies in this folder to NTFS file system volumes or other removable media.

 ENABLE DISK QUOTAS ON WINDOWS 8.1

GET READY. To enable a disk quota, perform the following steps:

1. Press the **Windows logo key + r**, type **diskmgmt.msc**, and then click **OK**.

2. Right-click the volume you want to enable quota management on and choose **Properties**.

3. Click the **Quota** tab and then click **Enable Quota management**.

   Do not click the *Deny disk space to users exceeding quota limit* option. By not selecting this option, you will be able to audit how the volume is being consumed without restricting access to users who exceed the quota limit.

4. Select **Limit disk space to** and type **300** in the field provided. Click the arrow to select **MB**.

5. For the *Set warning level to* setting, type **250** in the field provided. Click the arrow to select **MB**.

6. In the *Select the quota logging options for this volume* section, select both **Log event when a user exceeds their quota limit** and **Log event when a user exceeds their warning level**.

7. Click **OK**.

8. After reading the disk quota message, click **OK**.

9. Right-click the volume you enabled quota management on and choose **Properties**.

10. Click the **Quota** tab and then click **Quota Entries** to see whether any user accounts are currently reaching their limits.

11. On the top menu, click **Quota**. (The *Export* option can be used to export your quota settings to another NTFS volume; do *not* export at this time, however.)

12. Click **Quota** > **Close** to exit the *Quota Entries* screen.

13. Remove the check mark next to *Enable quota management* to return your system to its original setting. Click **OK** to close.

14. After reading the message indicating the volume will be rescanned, click **OK**.

The ***File Server Resource Manager***, a feature in Windows Server 2012 R2, provides a more enhanced approach to quota management. This tool enables you to configure disk quotas on a per-volume and per-folder basis and comes with several templates to work from.

These templates are categorized as hard and soft. Hard means the user cannot store files after reaching the defined limit; soft means the user can continue to store files. These templates are entirely separate from the NTFS quota management discussed earlier and in most cases should not be used together with NTFS quota management.

■ Managing Storage Pools and Storage Spaces

THE BOTTOM LINE

Storage Spaces is a feature in Windows 8.1/Windows Server 2012 R2 that allows you to combine multiple disks into a single logical volume that can be mirrored to protect against one or more drive failures.

CERTIFICATION READY
Storage spaces, including capacity and fault tolerance
Objective 2.4

The Storage Spaces feature in Windows 8.1 allows you to combine several physical drives, which the operating system will see as one large drive. The drives can be of any capacity and can consist of a variety of different drive interfaces—Small Computer System Interface (SCSI), Universal Serial Bus (USB), and Serial ATA (SATA).

When the drives are combined, Windows places them into a *storage pool*. These storage pools can then be segmented into multiple storage spaces, which are then formatted with a file system and can be used just like any other regular disk on your computer. New disks (internal/external) can be added to the storage pool as space requirements increase over time.

Although data can be stored on the drives, you cannot use storage spaces to host the Windows operating system files.

TAKE NOTE*

On Windows Server 2012 R2, you can use storage spaces with failover clusters, which are groups of computers connected via physical cables and by clustering software. When one fails, another member of the cluster takes over. To use storage spaces with this type of configuration, you are restricted to using Serial Attached SCSI (SAS) devices. You can manage storage spaces from the Control Panel on Windows 8.1 clients and through the File and Storage Services role in Server Manager. You can also configure it using Windows PowerShell.

Storage spaces offer two key benefits:

- By spreading data across multiple disks you achieve data resiliency (fault tolerance), which can protect your data against hard disk failure.
- Volume sizes can be larger than the actual physical size of your drives in the storage pool (capacity). This is accomplished through a process called thin provisioning.

Creating Storage Pools

Creating a storage pool allows you to combine multiple smaller drives that you might not otherwise be able to use by themselves into a larger single logical volume.

To create a storage pool on a Windows 8.1 client, you access the Manage Storage Spaces tool found in the Control Panel. The Wizard prompts you to select the disks that you want to use and then add them to the storage pool. For example, if you have two physical disks with capacities of 200 GB and 300 GB, it creates a pool that has a total capacity of 500 GB (see Figure 7-2).

Figure 7-2

Creating a storage pool with two disks

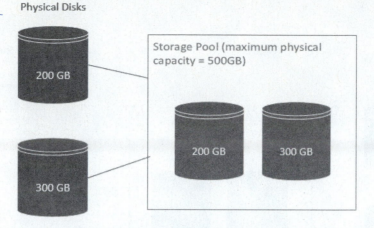

Physical Disks

Storage Pool (maximum physical capacity = 500GB)

200 GB

300 GB

200 GB

300 GB

Creating Storage Spaces

After selecting the drives to include in your storage pool, you will be prompted to create the storage space. This involves entering a name, selecting a drive letter, identifying the type of resiliency you want to configure, and setting the maximum size you want to assign to the storage space.

When creating storage spaces, there are four resiliency types to select from. Only three of them provide real fault-tolerance.

- *Simple (no resiliency):* Writes one copy of your data but doesn't protect against drive failures; requires at least one drive.
- *Two-way mirror:* Writes two copies of your data to protect against a single drive failure; requires at least two drives.
- *Three-way mirror:* Writes three copies of your data to protect against two simultaneous drive failures; requires at least five drives.
- *Parity:* Writes data with parity information to protect against single drive failures; requires at least three drives.

You also need to decide how much of the total storage pool capacity you want to use for your new storage space. In Figure 7-2, you saw the total pool capacity is 500 GB. By using a process called *thin provisioning* (see Figure 7-3), you can create a storage space that is larger than the available capacity of the storage pool. After setting the size, the Wizard will create the storage space based on the parameters you provided.

Figure 7-3

An example of thin provisioning

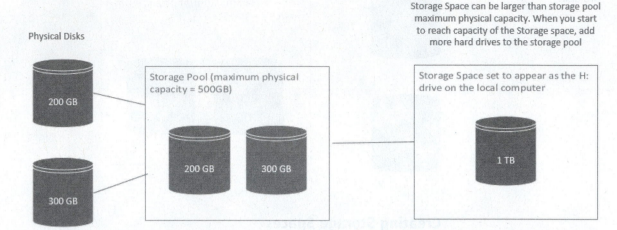

Physical Disks

Storage Space can be larger than storage pool maximum physical capacity. When you start to reach capacity of the Storage space, add more hard drives to the storage pool

Storage Pool (maximum physical capacity = 500GB)

200 GB

300 GB

200 GB

300 GB

Storage Space set to appear as the H: drive on the local computer

1 TB

This will appear in File Explorer with the drive letter you assigned. Just like any other drive.

Thin provisioning reserves the space for future use. For example, in Figure 7-3, you can see there are two physical drives being added to the storage pool to create a total capacity of 500 GB. Even though you have a total capacity of only 500 GB, you can configure the storage space that uses this pool to be 1 TB or greater capacity. When the storage pool approaches capacity, you will receive a warning and need to add more disks to the pool. This approach works well in situations in which you expect your data storage needs will grow, but you don't want to purchase additional disks immediately.

After the storage space is created, it will appear as a drive in File Explorer. The drive can be protected using BitLocker and NTFS permissions, just like any other drive in Windows 8.1.

 CREATE A STORAGE POOL AND A STORAGE SPACE IN WINDOWS 8.1

GET READY. To create a storage pool and storage space, perform the following steps:

1. Log on with administrative credentials.
2. Connect the drives you want to use to your computer.
3. Press the **Windows logo key + w** and then type **Storage Spaces**.
4. From the *Results* list, click **Storage Spaces**.
5. Click **Create a new pool and storage space**.
6. Select the drive(s) you want to include in the new storage pool. (Warning: Any data on these drives will be deleted.)
7. Click **Create pool**.

   Once the pool is created, you will be taken automatically to the *Create a storage space screen* shown in Figure 7-4.

Figure 7-4

Creating a storage space

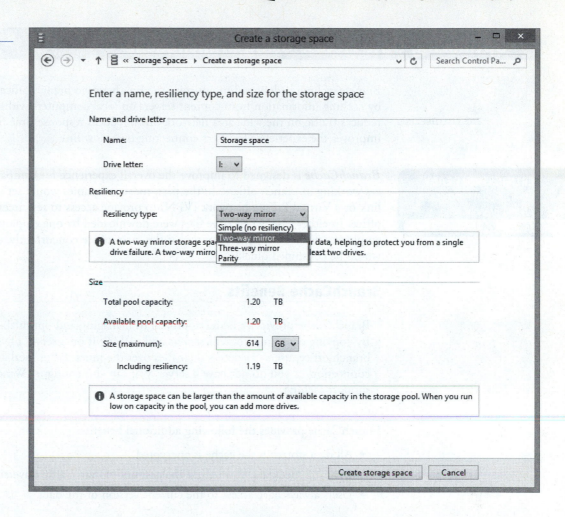

8. In the *Name* field, type a name for your storage space.

9. In the *Drive letter* field, click the down arrow and then choose a driver letter for the storage space.

10. In the *Resiliency type* field, click the down arrow and then choose the resiliency type.

11. In the *Size (maximum)* field, type the maximum size that you want for your storage space.

12. Click **Create storage space**.

13. Open File Explorer and confirm that the new storage space appears under the drive letter you assigned in Step 9.

After completing the setup of your storage space, you can continue to monitor and manage it from the Manage Storage Space tool. You can perform the following tasks:

- View your storage pool(s)
- View the storage spaces in the pools
- View the physical drives included in the pool(s)
- Identify how much pool capacity is currently being used
- Add more drives to the pool
- Rename the pool
- Change the size of storage spaces
- View files stored in storage spaces
- Delete storage spaces

Optimizing Data Access Using BranchCache

THE BOTTOM LINE

BranchCaching is designed to optimize the link between branch offices and main offices by caching information from content servers on local computers within the branch. This reduces traffic on the wide area network links, reduces response time for opening files, and improves the experience for users connecting over slow links.

CERTIFICATION READY
Optimizing data access by using BranchCache
Objective 2.4

BranchCache is designed to improve the overall experience for companies that have employees working in branch offices. In the past, most companies would set up a dedicated WAN link or a Virtual Private Network (VPN) to provide access to resources located at their main office. In either case, when large files were downloaded by one employee or when multiple employees needed access to resources at the main office concurrently, the available bandwidth would be consumed quickly.

BranchCache Benefits

BranchCache provides a better approach to managing and optimizing the WAN link. By copying data from content servers and caching it on a server physically located in the branch office, users can access their files over the much faster local area network (LAN) connection. If you do not have a server, you can also configure Windows 8.1 clients to support caching.

BranchCache provides the following additional benefits:

- All data stored in the cache is encrypted.
- By using metadata, you reduce the amount of data traffic traversing the WAN link.
- Users always have access to the current version of the data.

Understanding Content Servers

Content obtained from a *BranchCache-enabled server*, also called a *content server*, can be cached on the client systems at the branch office or on BranchCache servers at the branch office. Future requests for the same content can be delivered from the client system or the BranchCache server without having to cross the slower WAN link.

The following represent the types of BranchCache enabled servers (content servers) that can be configured. You must deploy at least one or more of these types of servers at your main office:

- **Web servers:** Windows Server 2008 R2/2012 running Internet Information Services (IIS) with BranchCache enabled. These servers use the Hypertext Transfer Protocol (HTTP) and Hypertext Transfer Protocol Secure (HTTPS) protocols.
- **Application (BITS) servers:** Windows Server 2012 R2 running the Background Intelligent Transfer Service (BITS) with BranchCache enabled.
- **File servers:** Windows Server 2008 R2/2012 running the File Service server role and the BranchCache for Network Files role service. These servers use the Server Message Block (SMB) protocol to send content.

Understanding BranchCache Operating Modes

There are two operating modes for BranchCache: hosted-cache mode and distributed-cache mode. You typically use hosted-cache mode when you have more than 50 systems at the branch office. If you have fewer than 50, distributed-cache mode may be a more viable option.

With *hosted-cache mode* (see Figure 7-5), you deploy a computer running Windows Server 2012 R2 at the branch office. The clients are configured with the name of the server and can retrieve content from it. If the content is not available in the cache on the local server, the client will traverse the WAN link, download the data, and then make it available to the hosted cache server for other clients to use. By using the fully qualified domain name (FQDN), the clients can use DNS and thus communicate with the server across subnets.

Figure 7-5

An example of hosted-cache mode

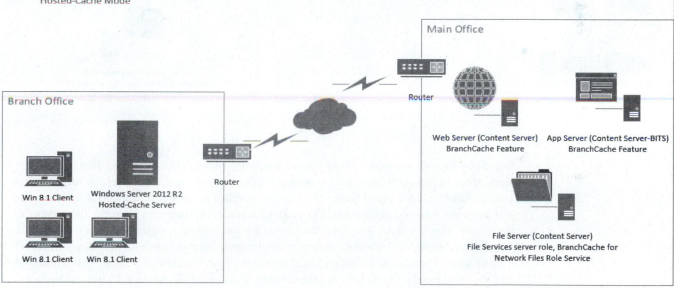

Hosted-Cache Mode

When a Windows 8.1 client connects to a main office File Server and requests a file, the server first authenticates and authorizes the client. If successful, the server returns content metadata (identifiers) to the Windows 8.1 client, which then uses the hash information to search for the file on the hosted-cache server. If this is the first time the file has ever been requested, the Windows 8.1 client will contact the main office file server and retrieve the file. The Windows 8.1 client will then contact the hosted-cache server located at its branch office and offer the content to the server. The hosted-cache server will then retrieve the content and cache it. When another Windows 8.1 client at the branch office requests the same file from the main office file server, the server authenticates and authorizes the client. After the process is complete, the file server returns metadata and the Windows 8.1 client obtains the information from the hosted-cache server at its local branch office.

TAKE NOTE *
Windows Server 2012 R2 can support Windows 7 clients, but it must have a certificate compatible with Transport Layer Security (TLS). To realize the best performance and use the new features in BranchCache, use Windows 8.1 clients.

With ***distributed-cache mode*** (see Figure 7-6), Windows 8.1 client computers request data from the main office and then cache it locally themselves. This content is then made available to other clients on the same branch office network.

Figure 7-6

An example of distributed-cache mode

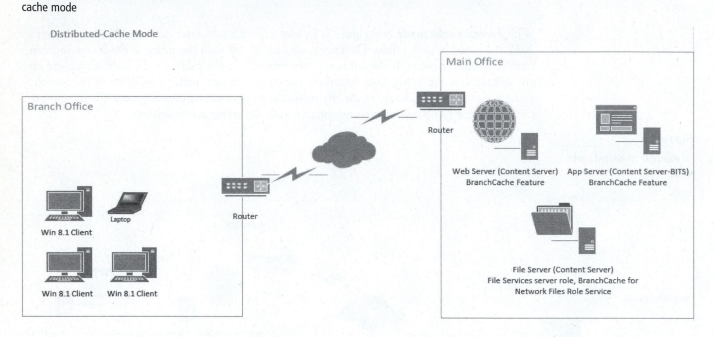

When the first Windows 8.1 client connects and downloads a specific set of files from the main office file server it becomes the source for that content at the local branch office. When another Windows 8.1 client connects to the main office file server to download the same file, it is authenticated and authorized. The content metadata is then sent from the file server to this client. The Windows 8.1 client then sends a request for the segment hashes on the local network to determine if another computer on the same local network has the data cached. This is done using a special multicast packet. Because the first Windows 8.1 client that connected and downloaded the file already has the content, the second Windows 8.1 client retrieves it directly from that computer.

Distributed-cache mode allows you to take advantage of BranchCache with minimal hardware requirements at the branch office. Although this mode works well in small offices with 50 or fewer computers without a server, it can produce situations in which content has to be retrieved from the main office because the computer that has the data is not currently available on the local network.

You can use a combination of these modes across your branch offices. For example, you can have one branch office that uses distributed-cache mode and another that uses the hosted-cache mode.

In both modes, the client will traverse the slower WAN link to communicate with the BranchCache-enabled server located in the main office. After the client is authenticated, content metadata is sent instead of the actual data files. Content metadata is much smaller in size and reduces the bandwidth requirements. It also ensures the clients receive hashes for the most current content. The content itself is broken into blocks (block hashes), each receiving its own hash. The blocks are organized into collections called segments (segment hashes). The content metadata includes both the block and segment hash information. It is the content metadata that the client uses to search for the file in both the hosted and distributed cache modes.

ENABLING BRANCHCACHE ON CONTENT SERVERS

BranchCache is installed and enabled for web servers and application servers by clicking Server Manager > Manage > Add Roles and Features. After selecting the server, you enable the BranchCache feature, confirm the installation, and then click Install. You can also enable BranchCache using the following Windows PowerShell command:

```
Install-WindowsFeature BranchCache
```

To deploy a BranchCache on a Windows Server 2012 R2 file server, you must install the BranchCache for Network Files Role Service and then enable BranchCache on the Shared Folders. The following exercise shows you how to use Windows PowerShell to enable BranchCache on a file server.

 ENABLE BRANCHCACHE ON A FILE SERVER USING WINDOWS POWERSHELL

GET READY. To enable BranchCache on a file server using Windows PowerShell, perform the following steps:

1. Log on with administrative credentials to a Windows Server 2012 R2 File Server.
2. Press the **Windows logo key + r**, type **PowerShell**, and then click **OK**.
3. Execute the following command:

   ```
   Install-WindowsFeature FS-BranchCache - IncludeManagementTools
   ```

   After the install is complete, continue to Step 4. Do not exit Windows PowerShell.
4. Execute the following command:

   ```
   Install-WindowsFeature FS-Data-Deduplication
   -IncludeManagementTools
   ```
5. After the install is complete, close the Windows PowerShell window.

After completing the installation of the BranchCache for Network Files Feature, you must create and share a folder.

 CREATE AND SHARE A FOLDER

GET READY. To create and share a folder, perform the following steps:

1. On the task bar, click the **Server Manager** icon to open the *Server Manager* console.
2. Click **File and Storage Services** > **Shares**.
3. Click **Tasks** > **New Share**.
4. Click **SMB Share-Quick** and then click **Next**.
5. Select the volume that will be used to store your share and then click **Next**.
6. Type a share name (for example, **BranchCacheShare**) and then click **Next**.
7. Select **Enable BranchCache on the file share** (see Figure 7-7) and then click **Next**.

Figure 7-7

Enabling BranchCache on the file share

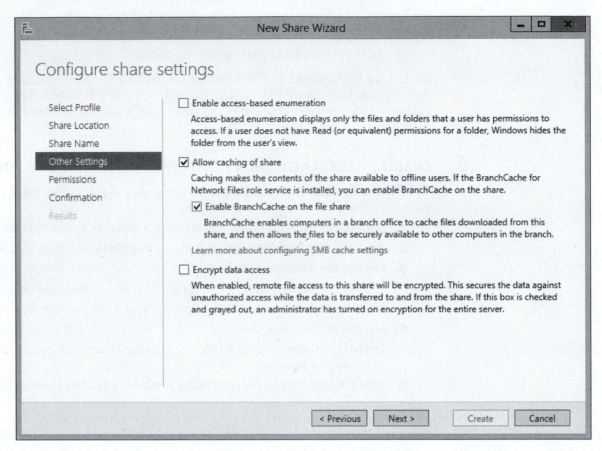

8. Accept the default permissions for the share and then click **Next**.
9. Review your settings and click **Create**.
10. Click **Close** after the share is created.
11. Close **Server Manager**.

 **ENABLE BRANCHCACHE ON A WINDOWS 8.1
CLIENT USING WINDOWS POWERSHELL**

GET READY. To enable BranchCache on a Windows 8.1 client using Windows PowerShell, log on with administrative credentials to a Windows 8.1 client connected to a domain and then perform the following steps:

1. Press the **Windows logo key + r**, type **PowerShell**, and then click **OK**.
2. Execute the following Windows PowerShell command:

   `Enable-BCHostedClient`

3. Type the FQDN of the file server on which you enabled BranchCache earlier and then click **Enter**.
4. Confirm the configuration by typing **Get-BCStatus** and then clicking **Enter**.
5. Review the output to confirm that BranchCacheEnabled is set to True, BranchCacheServiceStatus is set to Running, and BranchCacheServiceStartType is manual.
6. Close the Windows PowerShell window.

■ Managing Distributed File System (DFS) Client Settings

↓ THE BOTTOM LINE   Distributed File System improves on the use of the shared folders by enabling you to organize your shared folders and enabling you to distribute shares on multiple servers.

Distributed File System (DFS) is a set of technologies that enables a Windows server to organize multiple distributed SMB file shares into a distributed file system. Although the shares can be on different servers, the location is transparent to the users. Finally, DFS can provide redundancy to improve data availability while minimizing the amount of traffic passing over the WAN links. The two technologies in DFS include:

- DFS Namespaces
- DFS Replication

Managing DFS Namespaces

If you have a site with many file servers and many shared folders, some users will have difficulty finding the files that they need as they have to remember the server name and shared folder name that make up the Universal Naming Convention (UNC). ***DFS Namespace*** enables you to group shared folders into a single logical structure. In other words, a DFS Namespace is a shared folder of shared folders (which can be on multiple servers).

DFS is a virtual namespace technology that enables you to create a single directory tree that lists other shared folders. Creating a DFS Namespace allows users to locate their files more easily. See Figure 7-8. Users using computers with Windows 8/8.1 access a DFS namespace just like they would any other UNC.

Figure 7-8

Linking to shared folders with
DFS Namespace

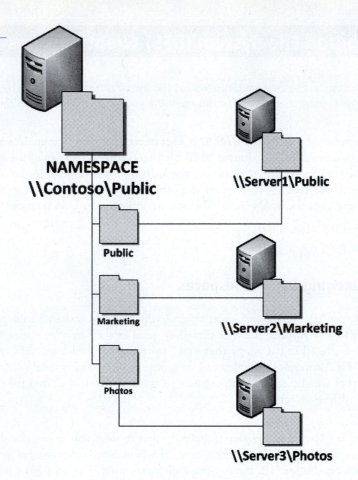

The actual shared folders are referred to as the targets of the virtual folders in the namespace. DFS can be combined with DFS Replication, which increases availability and automatically connects users to shared folders in the same Active Directory site, when available, instead of connecting to another folder connected over a slower WAN link.

Installing DFS Namespace is a simple process of adding the appropriate role using Server Manager. However, you should also install the File Server service so that you can create file shares. The DFS Management Tools installs the DFS Management snap-in, the DFS Namespace module for Windows PowerShell, and command-line tools.

INSTALL DFS NAMESPACE

GET READY. To install DFS Namespace, perform the following steps:

1. On the task bar, click the **Server Manager** button to open *Server Manager*.
2. At the top of *Server Manager*, click **Manage > Add Roles and Features**. The *Add Roles and Feature Wizard* opens.
3. On the *Before you begin* page, click **Next**.
4. Select **Role-based or feature-based installation** and then click **Next**.
5. Click **Select a server from the server pool**, click the name of the server to install DFS to, and then click **Next**.
6. Scroll down and expand **File and Storage Services** and then expand **File and iSCSI Services**. Select **File Server** and **DFS Namespace**.
7. When you are prompted to add features to DFS Namespace, click **Add Features**.

8. On the *Select server roles* page, click **Next**.

9. On the *Select features* page, click **Next**.

10. On the *Confirm installation selections*, click **Install**.

11. When the installation is complete, click the **Close** button.

There are two types of DFS namespaces:

- Domain-based namespace
- Stand-alone namespace

With *domain-based namespaces*, the configuration is stored in Active Directory, which means that you don't have to rely on a single server to provide the namespace information to your clients. By using a domain-based namespace, if you change the name of the server that runs the DFS Namespace service and the name of the server changes, you will not have to change the namespace. The namespace changes only if you rename the domain. With a *stand-alone DFS*, the configuration is stored on the server and the server name becomes part of the main path to the namespace.

When you create a namespace, the Windows Server 2008 mode is selected by default, which supports up to 50,000 folders with targets per namespace and access-based enumeration. Access-based enumeration means that users can see only the folders and files that they have permission to access. If a user does not have permission to the folder or file, the folder or file does not even show in a directory listing. To use Windows Server 2008 mode, Active Directory must use the Windows Server 2008 domain functional level or higher. If you deselect the Windows Server 2008 mode, you will use the Windows 2000 Server mode, which supports only up to 5,000 folders.

 CREATE A DFS NAMESPACE

GET READY. To create a DFS Namespace, perform the following steps:

1. Open **Server Manager**.

2. Click **Tools** > **DFS Management** to open the *DFS Management console* (see Figure 7-9).

Figure 7-9

Using the DFS Management console

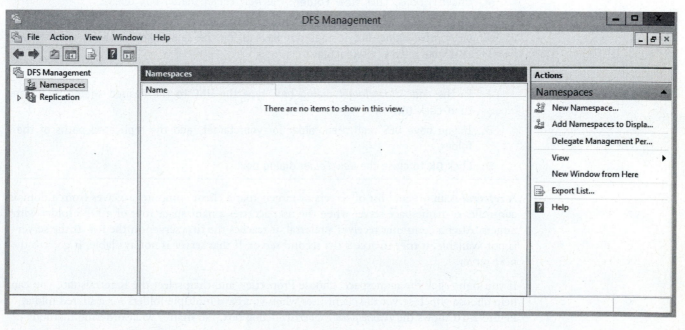

3. In the left-pane, right-click **Namespaces** and choose **New Namespace**. The *New Namespace Wizard* starts.

4. On the *Namespace Server* page, in the *Server* text box, type the name of the server that hosts the DFS Namespace and then click **Next**.

5. On the *Namespace Name and Settings* page, in the *Name* text box, type the name of the namespace. The name appears after the server (stand-alone namespace) or domain name (domain-based namespace). Click **Next**.

6. To change the location of the shared folder on the server and the shared permissions, click **Edit Settings**. The *Edit Settings* dialog box appears.

7. Specify the location of the Shared Folder and specify the Shared folder permissions. Click **OK** to close the *Edit Settings* dialog box.

8. On the *Namespace Name and Settings* page, click **Next**.

9. On the *Namespace Type* page, select either **Domain-based namespace** or **Stand-alone namespace**.

10. Leave the **Enable Windows Server 2008 mode** enabled. Notice the entire path of the domain-based namespace. Click **Next**.

11. On the *Review Settings and Create Namespace* page, click **Create**.

12. When the installation is complete, click the **Close** button.

After you create the namespace, you need to add folders to it that point to the share folders on your network. If you have a DFS replicated folder, you add each replicated folder to the target. By using the DFS replicated folder with the DFS namespace, you provide fault tolerance and better.

 ADD FOLDERS TO THE NAMESPACE

GET READY. To add folders to the namespace, perform the following steps:

1. Open **Server Manager**.

2. Click **Tools > DFS Management**. The *DFS Management* console appears.

3. In the left pane, expand the **Namespaces** folder and select the desired namespace.

4. Under *Actions*, click **New Folder**. The *New Folder* dialog box opens.

5. In the *Name* text box, type the name of the shared folder. The name should be a descriptive name, but it does not have to be the same name as the shared folder that you will be referencing.

6. To choose the shared folder, click **Add**.

7. In the *Add Folder Target* dialog box, type the UNC to the desired shared folder and then click **OK**.

8. If you have DFS replicated folder for your target, add the replicated paths of the folder.

9. Click **OK** to close the *New Folder* dialog box.

A *referral* is an ordered list of servers or targets that a client computer receives from a domain controller or namespace server when the user accesses a namespace root or a DFS folder with targets. After a computer receives a referral, it reaches the first server on the list. If the server is not available, it tries to access the second server. If that server is not available, it goes to the next server.

If you right-click the namespace, choose Properties, and then select the Referrals tab, you can help choose which server the client uses when you have multiple folders for a shared folder. Figure 7-10 shows the *Namespace Properties* dialog box. No matter what ordering method is selected, if a client is on the same site as the target, it always chooses the target. Then, by default, it chooses the closest server (lowest cost). You can also select *Random order*, which performs a load balancing for the targets at the other sites. Lastly, you can select the *Exclude targets outside of the client's side* option, which prevents the clients from accessing targets at other sites.

When a server becomes unavailable, you can have a client fall back to targets that were previously unavailable if the server becomes available again and at a lower cost than the target the client uses. This is done by selecting the *Clients fail back to preferred targets* option.

To control how targets are ordered, you can set priority on individual targets. For example, if you want one server to always be first or always be last, you can use the following procedure.

 SET THE TARGET PRIORITY ON A ROOT TARGET FOR A DOMAIN-BASED NAMESPACE

GET READY. To set the target priority on a root target for a domain-based namespace, perform the following steps:

1. Open **Server Manager**.
2. Click **Tools > DFS Management**. The *DFS Management* console appears.
3. In the left pane, expand the **Namespaces** folder and select the desired namespace.
4. In the center pane, click **Namespace Servers** tab.
5. Right-click the root target with the priority that you want to change and choose **Properties**. The *Properties* dialog box appears.

6. Click the **Advanced** tab (see Figure 7-11).

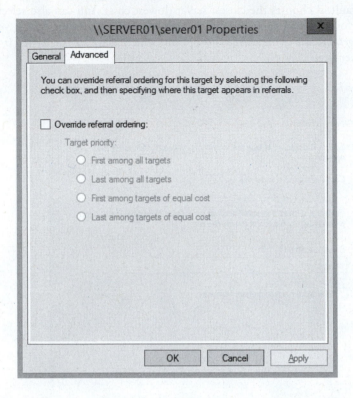

7. Click **Override referral ordering** and then click the priority that you want.

- **First among all targets**: Specifies that users should always be referred to this target if the target is available.
- **Last among all targets**: Specifies that users should never be referred to this target unless all other targets are unavailable.
- **First among targets of equal cost**: Specifies that users should be referred to this target before other targets of equal cost (which usually means other targets in the same site).
- **Last among targets of equal cost**: Specifies that users should never be referred to this target if there are other targets of equal cost available (which usually means other targets in the same site).

8. Click **OK** to close the *Properties* dialog box.

9. Close the **DFS Management** console.

To change the amount of time that clients cache namespace root referrals, you open the namespace properties, and click the Referrals tab. The default setting is 300 seconds. To change the amount of time that the clients cache folder referrals, open the namespace folder properties and click the Referrals tab. The default setting is 1800 seconds.

Because DFS Namespace is a specialized shared folder of shared folders, you still secure these folders with share permissions and NTFS permissions. It is recommended that you first configure the share and NTFS permissions on folders that host namespace roots and folder targets before configuring DFS. If you have multiple namespace root servers or folder target servers will be utilized, you need to manually synchronize permissions between the servers to avoid access problems.

Access-based enumeration hides files and folders that users do not have permission to access. To control access-based enumeration of files and folders in folder targets, you must enable access-based enumeration on each shared folder by using the following procedure.

ENABLE ACCESS-BASED ENUMERATION FOR A NAMESPACE

GET READY. To enable access-based enumeration for a namespace, perform the following steps:

1. Open **Server Manager**.
2. Click **Tools** > **DFS Management**. The *DFS Management* console appears.
3. In the left pane, right-click the namespace and choose **Properties**.
4. Click the **Advanced** tab.
5. Select the **Enable access-based enumeration for this namespace**.
6. Click **OK** to close the *Properties* dialog box.
7. Close the *DFS Management* console.

Managing DFS Replication

> The other part of DFS is DFS Replication. ***DFS Replication*** enables you to replicate folders between multiple servers. To allow efficient use of the network, it propagates only the changes, uses compression, and uses scheduling to replicate the data between the servers.

To enable replication between multiple targets, you first create a replication group. The ***replication group*** is a collection of servers, known as servers, each of which holds a target of a DFS folder. You need a minimum of two targets to perform DFS Replication.

When you create a DFS replication group, you designate one server as the primary member of the replication group. Files then copy from the primary member to the other target servers. If any of the files in the target folders are different, DFS Replication overwrites the other files.

The best method to recover from a disaster is to use backups. DFS Replication can also be used in conjunction with backups to provide a WAN backup solution. For example, if you have multiple sites, it becomes more difficult to perform backups, particular over the slower WAN links. One solution for this is to set up DFS Replication between the site servers to a central server or servers at the corporate office. Replication occurs when the WAN links are utilized the least such as in the evenings and during the weekends. You then back up the central computers located at the corporate office.

When you replicate folders using DFS, you are replicating local folders on a server to another local folder on another server. The folder is most likely shared so that users can access the folder, but this is not necessary.

By default, replication groups use a ***full mesh topology***, which means that all members replicate to all other members. If you have a simple DFS implementation consisting of two servers, there is some replication traffic between the two servers. However, by adding multiple servers to a replication group, replication traffic increases even more. Therefore, instead of using a full mesh topology, you can use a ***hub/spoke topology***, where one server is used to replicate to the other members, limiting the replication traffic to specific pairs of members.

When you configure DFS Replication, you can configure the following settings:

- Bidirectional or unidirectional
- Percentage of available bandwidth
- Schedule when replication will occur

By default, DFS replication between two members is bidirectional. Bidirectional connections occur in both directions and include two one-way connections. If you desire only a one-way connection, you can disable one of the connections or use share permissions to prevent the replication process from updating files on certain member servers.

Because DFS Replication often occurs over a WAN link, you have to be aware of how much traffic DFS uses and how you can configure it when replication occurs to best utilize the WAN links. Therefore, you can schedule replication to occur only during the night when the WAN links are not used as much or you can specify the bandwidth used by DFS Replication.

To make shared files fault tolerant, you need to use both DFS Namespace and DFS Replication. Each technology used in DFS has some impressive capabilities. DFS Namespace offers ease of use when trying to locate a shared folder and DFS Replication replicates files from one server to another. However, when they are combined, they can offer fault tolerance on the network.

1. Create the same folder on multiple servers. Although the folders don't have to have the same name, it simplifies management minimizes confusion.

2. Share the folders.

3. Configure DFS Replication between the folders on the various servers.

4. Create a DFS Namespace that includes targets of all target folders for a replication group.

DFS Replication ensures the files are replicated between the servers, providing multiple copies of the files. The DFS namespace makes the access of the replicated folders transparent to users when accessing the replicated folder. Users access the DFS namespace/shared folder and then they go to one of the replicated folders. If one of the replicated folders is not available, it is rerouted to another replicated folder.

Using Onedrive to Manage Files/Folders

THE BOTTOM LINE

OneDrive, formerly named SkyDrive, is a file hosting service that allows you to store and create files and folders and share them with other users and groups.

CERTIFICATION READY
OneDrive
Objective 2.4

OneDrive is a free, secure file-hosting service that enables your users to store, synch, and share files across devices using the cloud. It integrates with your Microsoft account, offering 7 GB of free space. You can purchase additional storage space as you need it. Using OneDrive, you can create folders, create or upload files, and share your documents with others. You can also use it to synchronize files and folders that you select across multiple devices. If you forget to include a file within your synch folder, you can use OneDrive to connect to your remote computer, locate the file, and then upload it to your OneDrive space. This process is called *fetching*.

Accessing OneDrive from a Browser

You can access OneDrive from a browser using your Microsoft User Account from anywhere you have an Internet connection.

OneDrive can be accessed from a browser at http://onedrive.live.com. After reaching the site, you are prompted to log on using your Microsoft User Account. After you are logged in, you see your OneDrive Dashboard (see Figure 7-12), in which you can upload, download, create, and share folders and files. If your computer is configured to support fetching, you can also connect to it remotely from the OneDrive Dashboard.

The following provides an overview of each of the options available with the OneDrive Dashboard:

- **Files:** Includes folders created on the OneDrive account. You can also see the number of files each folder contains by looking at the number located in the lower-right corner of each folder. Selecting any of these folders opens and displays its content.

Figure 7-12

The OneDrive Dashboard

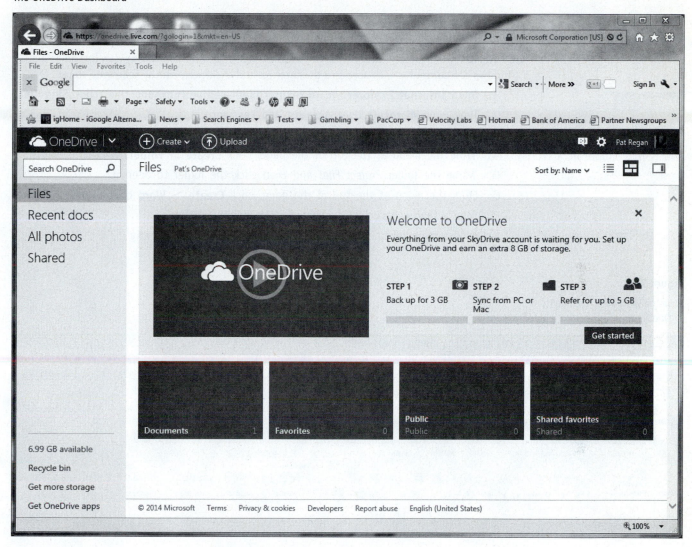

- **Recent docs:** Includes a list of documents that have been recently created on the OneDrive account.

- **Shared**: Provides a list of documents or folders that have been shared with you.

- **Groups**: Displays a list of groups that includes users with whom you frequently communicate and share documents. When you create a group, users receive e-mails asking them to join. After clicking the link, they are taken to the Groups page, in which they can communicate with other members via e-mail and also view any files that have been shared to the group.

- **PCs**: Provides access through fetching. Use this option if you forget to place a file on your OneDrive folder but still need to gain access to it on your PC back in the office. This process requires the OneDrive for Windows app be installed on the target computer.

Creating a File Within OneDrive

OneDrive allows you to collaborate with others users on documents (provided those users have Microsoft accounts.) Because documents are stored on the cloud, you can access these documents anytime you are connected to the Internet.

OneDrive includes a light version of Microsoft Office apps (Word, Excel, PowerPoint, OneNote). This allows you to create and edit documents directly from your browser.

 CREATE A WORD DOCUMENT WITHIN ONEDRIVE USING A WEB BROWSER

GET READY. To create a Word document within OneDrive using a web browser, log on to a Windows 8.1 computer with access to the Internet and then perform the following steps:

1. Open **Internet Explorer**, go to **http://onedrive.live.com,** and then click **Sign In**.
2. Type your **Microsoft User Account** and **Password**.
3. Click the **Documents** folder.
4. From the menu at the top of the page, click **Create > Folder**.
5. Name the folder *Project Files* and then click the folder to open it.
6. From the menu at the top of the page, click **Create > Word document**.
7. Type a few words in the document (see Figure 7-13).

   As you type text, The Word document will be saved frequently.

Figure 7-13

Saving a Word Web document in OneDrive

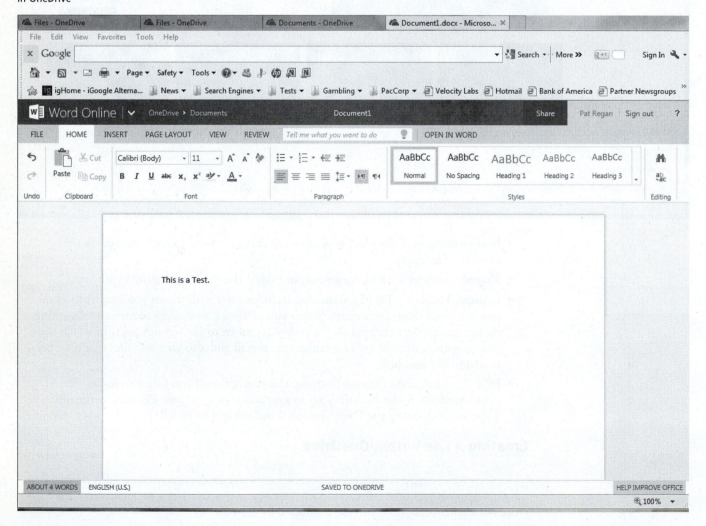

8. To specify a file name, click **Document1** at the top of the window and then replace that name by typing **Project Scope**.

9. Click the **OneDrive** link (located at the upper-left corner, next to *Word Online*) to return to the main screen.

Uploading Files to OneDrive

In the previous activity, you learned how to create a file directly on OneDrive using the Word Web App. You can also upload files directly to OneDrive.

If you have existing files on your computer that you want to upload to OneDrive, you can use either of the following two options:

- From the OneDrive Dashboard, navigate to the folder in which you want to store the file. On the menu, click Upload, browse to the file you want from your computer, and then click Open.

- From the OneDrive app installed on your local computer, you can drag and drop the files you want to upload into the OneDrive folder. This automatically syncs with OneDrive. You can also configure OneDrive for the desktop to allow you to fetch files on your PC from other devices.

Sharing a Document in OneDrive

You can also share a document with others by sending it via e-mail, posting it, or sending others a link to it.

When sharing documents, you have the following options:

- **Send e-mail:** This option should be used if you want to give individual users or groups permission to a file or folder. You can then remove permissions for a specific group or individual if necessary. When users receive the link via e-mail and visit OneDrive, the file or folder will appear in their list of shared files. You do not have to know their Microsoft user account address. If they do not have one, they can create one for free after clicking on the link.

- **Post to:** This option allows you to share the link on Facebook, LinkedIn, or Twitter. Anyone who views the post on your network can forward the link. If you selected the option to allow recipients to edit the document, anyone the link is forwarded to can view and edit the file or folder.

- **Get a link:** This option should be used if you want to share the file with a larger number of recipients. For example, you could post the link on your blog or your website. You can also include this link in an e-mail or via an instant message. When using this option, you can choose from the following types of links:

  - **View only:** Anyone who receives this link can see the files you share.

  - **View and edit:** Anyone with this link can see and edit the files you share.

  - **Public**: Anyone can search for and view your public files, even if you don't share a link if you decide to make it public.

SHARE A DOCUMENT VIA E-MAIL

GET READY. To share the Word document you created in the previous exercise with others via e-mail, perform the following steps:

1. From the main screen of OneDrive, click **Files > Documents > Project Files**.

2. Right-click the Word document you saved in the previous exercise (**Project Scope. docx**) and choose **Share**.

3. Type the e-mail address of the person you want to share it with and, if necessary, type a message.

4. If you want the recipient to be able to edit the document, click the **Recipients can edit** option.

5. Click **Share** to send the e-mail message.

6. Click **Close**.

Accessing OneDrive from the OneDrive Desktop App for Windows

With the *OneDrive desktop app for Windows* installed on your local computer, you can automatically sync files and folders with the OneDrive cloud. You can then access your resources across multiple devices, such as computers and smartphones.

The OneDrive desktop app for Windows 7 or 8 can be downloaded directly from your OneDrive account. The OneDrive app is already built into Windows 8.1. When you install the app, a folder will be created on your desktop automatically. Anything that you place into this folder is synched with OneDrive.com as well as with your other computers. You can access the folder from within File Explorer, drag new files into the folder, and choose the folders you want to sync on your computer.

 INSTALL THE ONEDRIVE DESKTOP APP FOR WINDOWS

GET READY. To install the OneDrive desktop app for Windows, log on to a Windows 8.1 computer with administrative credentials and access OneDrive.

1. Open **Internet Explorer**, go to **http://onedrive.live.com**, and then click **Sign In**.

2. Type your *Microsoft User Account* and *Password*.

3. In the left pane, scroll down and click the **Download OneDrive for Windows** link.

4. When prompted with the *Do you want to run or save OneDriveSetup.exe?* message, click **Run**.

5. After the OneDrive installation is completed and the *Introducing your OneDrive folder* dialog box appears, click **Get started**.

6. In the *Microsoft OneDrive* window, provide the Microsoft Account and password. Click **Sign In**.

7. By default, the OneDrive folder will be stored in the *c:\users\%username%\OneDrive* folder. On the *Introducing your OneDrive folder* page, click **Next**.

8. On the *Sync only what you want* page, *All files and folders on my OneDrive* is already selected. To choose a different folder, click **Choose folders to sync**. Click **Next**.

9. On the *Fetch your files from anywhere* page, *Let me use OneDrive to fetch any of my files on this PC* is already selected. Click **Done**.

   This setting will download everything but the files that are shared with you from your OneDrive.

10. Click **Done**.

As part of the setup of OneDrive, the *Let me use OneDrive to fetch any of my files on this PC* option is enabled, allowing you to use OneDrive to fetch files from this PC. This process works well a file is in a folder outside the OneDrive folder on your PC or is a file that you did not configure to synch with OneDrive when you initially set it up. When a PC has been configured to allow fetching, you see it in your OneDrive Dashboard, under PCs, when you log on to http://onedrive.live.com.

 FETCH A FILE USING ONEDRIVE

GET READY. To fetch a file using OneDrive, log on to a Windows 8.1 computer with access to the Internet and then perform the following steps:

1. Open **Internet Explorer**, go to **http://onedrive.live.com,** and then click **Sign In**.

2. Type your *Microsoft User Account* and *Password*.

3. In the left pane, click the remote PC from which you want to fetch files. Remote PCs will appear under the *PCs* section of the left pane.

4. If this is the first time you have attempted to connect to the PC, you will be presented with a security page when you first attempt to connect to it. When the page appears, click **Sign in with a security code**.

   This option automatically sends a seven-digit code to the device you configured when setting up your Microsoft account. This could be your cell phone number or an e-mail address you provided.

5. After you receive the code, type it into the field provided. The folders on your remote PC will appear in OneDrive.

6. Navigate to any folder and select a file that you want to upload. Notice that you have access to your entire PC. This includes all partitions as well as the DVD drive and any externally attached drives on the computer.

7. Right-click the file and choose **Upload to OneDrive**.

8. When *The selected item will be uploaded to:* dialog box appears, double-click **Documents**, choose **ProjectFiles**, and then click **Upload**.

9. From the main screen of OneDrive, click **Files > Documents > Project Files** and then confirm the file you uploaded appears in the folder.

SKILL SUMMARY

IN THIS LESSON, YOU LEARNED:

- Using the disk quota management enables you to set the amount of storage space available to users. It is set up on NTFS volumes, charges users only for the files they own, and can be enabled separately on each volume.

- Disk quotas can be configured on individual computers by using Disk Management (diskmgmt.msc) or Group Policy.

- Storage spaces can be used to combine multiple drives with different interfaces/capacities into single or multiple storage pools. Storage spaces can be configured using one of four resiliency settings: Simple, two-way mirror, three-way mirror, and Parity.

- Thin provisioning enables you to configure your storage space with a size that exceeds the actual size of your current storage pool. You can reserve space for the future; when you start to reach the capacity, you will be prompted to add more disks to the storage pool.

- BranchCache is a feature designed to improve the overall experience for companies that have employees working in branch offices. BranchCache uses BranchCache enabled servers (also called content servers) that are located in the main office to provide resources to client comptuers: Examples of content severs include web servers, application servers, and file servers.

- Hosted-cache mode is implemented by adding a server at the branch office that is used by the client computers to retrieve content instead of downloading it from the main office.

- Distributed-cache mode is used when a server is not available at a branch office, but instead you want to use the clients to cache data and provide it to other computers on the local network.

- In hosted-cache and distributed-cache modes, the clients will still traverse the WAN link to communicate with a BranchCache-enabled server. Instead of transferring over the entire file, content metadata is used to reduce the bandwidth requirements and optimize use of the link. The content metadata is used by the client to search for the actual data file, which can be on a local server or on another client on their local network segment.

- Distributed File System (DFS) is a set of technologies that enables a Windows server to organize multiple distributed SMB file shares into a distributed file system.

- OneDrive—formerly named SkyDrive—is a file hosting service that allows you to store and create files and folders and share them with other users and groups.

■ Knowledge Assessment

Multiple Choice

Select the correct answer for each of the following questions.

1. Which of the following are true characteristics of disk quotas? (Choose all that apply)
   a. They can be configured only on NTFS volumes.
   b. They do not apply to administrators.
   c. Users are charged for files they own.
   d. They cannot be implemented on Windows 7/8 computers.

2. Which of the following tools is used to enable Disk Quotas on a FAT 32 volume?
   a. diskmgmt.msc
   b. discmgmt.msc
   c. Disk Quota Manager
   d. None of the above

3. Which of the following drives can be added to a storage pool? (Choose all that apply)
   a. SATA
   b. eSATA
   c. USB
   d. SCSI

4. Which of the following resiliency settings requires at least five drives?
   a. Parity
   b. Three-way mirror
   c. Two-way mirror
   d. Simple

5. Which of the following content servers can be used with BranchCache? (Choose all that apply)
   a. Web servers
   b. File servers
   c. Application (BITS) servers
   d. RADIUS servers

6. Which of the following commands can be used to enable BranchCache on a File server using Windows PowerShell?
   a. `Install-Windows Feature FS_Branch Cache`
   b. `Install-WindowsFeature FS-BranchCache -IncludeManagementTools`
   c. `Install-WindowsFeature -Branch Cache`
   d. `Install-WindowsFeature BranchCache`

7. Which BranchCache mode enables clients to cache information and share it with each other?
   a. Client-cache mode
   b. Hosted-cache mode
   c. Distributed-cache mode
   d. Client distribution mode

8. Which of the following terms best describes the information returned by content servers when requests are made by clients?
   a. Hashes
   b. Content metadata
   c. Streamed content
   d. Replicated metadata

9. Which process reserves space for future use when working with storage spaces/storage pools?
   a. Partitions
   b. Thin provisioning
   c. SMB blocks
   d. Provisioned storage blocks

10. How many disks are needed when setting up parity for your resiliency settings in a storage pool?
    a. 2
    b. 3
    c. 5
    d. 4

11. What are the two types of DFS Namespace? (Choose two answers)
    a. Domain-based namespace
    b. Replicated named space
    c. Stand-alone namespace
    d. Server-based namespace

12. Which of the following terms best describes an ordered list of servers and targets that a client computer receives from a domain controller or namespace server when a user accesses a namespace root or a DFS folder with targets?
    a. Replication list
    b. Referrals
    c. Target priority list
    d. SID control list

13. You have an Active Directory domain named contoso.com and you have two servers—server1 and server2—which are namespace servers for the \\contoso\.com\DFS1 namespace. Which of the following actions should you perform in order to configure the \\contoso.com\DFS1 namespace so that you connect only to Server2 when Server1 is unavailable?

    a. On the \\contoso.com\DFS1 namespace, modify the referrals settings.

    b. On the \\contosol.com\DFS1 namespace, modify the advanced settings.

    c. From the properties of the \\Server1\DFS1 namespace servers entry, modify the advanced settings.

    d. From the properties of the \\Server2\DFS1 namespace servers entry, modify the advanced settings.

14. You have a domain-based namespace named DFS that is running Windows Server 2008 Server mode. How do you ensure that users see only the files and folders for which the users have permission to access?

    a. Modify the discretionary access control list.

    b. Enable access-based enumeration.

    c. Modify the view permissions.

    d. Disable referrals.

Best Answer

Choose the letter that corresponds to the best answer. More than one answer choice may achieve the goal. Select the BEST answer.

1. Which type of resiliency works best for protecting yourself from two drives failing simultaneously while setting up your storage space?

    a. Three-way mirror

    b. Two-way mirror

    c. Parity

    d. Simple

2. Which of the following solutions enables you to reduce the traffic load originating from your branch office for files and folders at the main office while still not requiring you to add any servers at your branch office location?

    a. Setting up an existing Windows 8.1 computer to run in hosted-cache mode.

    b. Setting up an existing server to use hosted-cache mode.

    c. Setting up Windows 8.1 computers to use distributed-cache mode.

    d. Increasing the bandwidth available over the WAN link.

3. Which of the following solutions is best for applying disk quotas on a volume in which existing users have files/folders already in place?

    a. Moving the user's data to another volume and then copying it back after setting the new quota.

    b. Requesting that users move their data.

    c. Adding them as new quota entries.

    d. Excluding the users from disk quotas.

4. Which of the following approaches is best when you would like to reserve at least 500 GB of space for a new storage space yet you have only 100 GB of actual physical disk space?

    a. Wait until you have enough physical disk capacity to create the 500 GB storage space.

    b. Purchase new drives before creating the space.

    c. Use thin provisioning and go ahead and create the space. You can purchase drives later when you need them.

    d. Configure one pool now and another when you have the drives.

5. Which of the following tools is the best solution for adding more drives to your storage pool and also renaming the pool?
   a. Windows PowerShell
   b. Disk Manager
   c. Manage Storage Space
   d. You cannot add additional drives to the pool without re-creating it

Matching and Identification

1. Match the following terms with the related description or usage.
   _____ a) BranchCache
   _____ b) Hosted-cache mode
   _____ c) Disk quota
   _____ d) Storage space
   _____ e) Storage pool
   _____ f) Thin provisioning
   _____ g) Content server
   _____ h) three-way mirror
   _____ i) Parity
   _____ j) two-way mirror
   1. Clients are configured with the name of a server from which they retrieve content.
   2. Enables you to set the amount of storage space available for each user.
   3. Writes three copies of your data to protect against the simultaneous failure of two drives; requires at least five drives to implement.
   4. Writes data with parity information to protect against single drive failures; requires at least three drives.
   5. Contains source content downloaded by the branch office computers.
   6. A feature designed to improve the overall experience for branch office employees connecting over slow WAN links.
   7. A collection of disks that are combined to create one or more storage spaces.
   8. Enables you to create a storage space that is larger than the available capacity of the storage pool.
   9. Writes two copies of your data to protect against a single drive failure; requires at least two drives.
   10. Enables you to take multiple drives and combine them into a storage pool.

Build a List

1. Specify the correct order of the steps that must be completed to create a storage pool.
   _____ Click **Create pool**.
   _____ Log on with administrative credentials.
   _____ Select the drive(s) you want to include in the new storage pool.
   _____ Click **Create a new pool and storage space**.
   _____ Connect the drives to your computer.
   _____ Press the **Windows logo key > r, type Storage Spaces**, and then select it from the *Results* list.
   _____ From the *Results* list, click **Storage Spaces**.

2. Specify the correct order of the steps that must be completed to create a storage space.
   _____ Choose a drive letter.
   _____ Type a name for the storage space.
   _____ Choose the resiliency type.
   _____ Click **Create storage space**.
   _____ Type the maximum size for your storage space.

3. Specify the correct order of the steps required to share a document using OneDrive:
   _____ Click **Done**.
   _____ Click **Share** to send the e-mail message.
   _____ Type the e-mail address.
   _____ Right-click the document and choose **Sharing**.
   _____ Click **Files > Documents > Project Files**.
   _____ Type your *Microsoft User account* and *Password*.
   _____ Log on to a Windows 8.1 client computer and open your browser to http://onedrive.live.com.

4. Specify the correct order of the steps required to install the OneDrive App on your desktop computer:
   _____ Click the **Download now** link.
   _____ Click **Next** to leave the default setting *All files and folders on my OneDrive*.
   _____ In the *Introducing your OneDrive folder* dialog box, click **Next**.
   _____ Log on to a Windows 8.1 client computer and open your browser to http://onedrive.live.com
   _____ Click the **Get OneDrive apps** link.
   _____ When prompted with *Do you want to run or save OneDriveSetup.exe?* click **Run**.
   _____ Click the **Windows Desktop**.
   _____ Type your *Microsoft User Account* and *Password*.
   _____ Click **Done**.

Choose an Option

1. Identify the setting that restricts a user's access to the volume if they exceed their quota limit.

Business Case Scenarios

Scenario 7-1: Configuring BranchCache

You have 10 computers running Windows 8.1 at a branch office. After setting up BranchCache in distributed mode, you notice they are still using the slow WAN link to attempt to access files/folders. Is that a normal operation? If not, what could be causing it?

Scenario 7-2: Configuring Storage Space/Storage Pools

You create a new storage pool for the following disks on your Windows 8.1 computer:

- SATA: 1 TB
- SAS: 1 TB

What is the maximum size you can allocate for your new storage space?

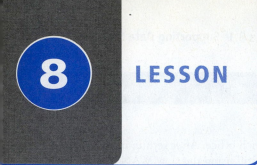

8 LESSON

Supporting Data Security

70-688 EXAM OBJECTIVE

Objective 2.5 – Support data security. This objective may include but is not limited to the following: Permissions, including share, NTFS, and Dynamic Access Control (DAC); Encrypting File System (EFS), including Data Recovery Agent; access to removable media; BitLocker and BitLocker To Go, including Data Recovery Agent and Microsoft BitLocker Administration and Monitoring (MBAM).

LESSON HEADING	EXAM OBJECTIVE
Managing Share Permissions and NTFS Permissions	
Configuring Share Permissions	Permissions, including share, NTFS, and Dynamic Access Control (DAC)
Configuring NTFS Permissions	Permissions, including share, NTFS, and Dynamic Access Control (DAC)
Combining NTFS and Share Permissions	
Using Dynamic Access Control (DAC)	Permissions, including share, NTFS, and Dynamic Access Control (DAC)
Configuring User and Device Claim Types	
Configuring File Classification	
Configuring the Encrypting File System (EFS)	Encrypting File System (EFS), including Data Recovery Agent
Using Data Recovery Agent (DRA)	Encrypting File System (EFS), including Data Recovery Agent
Configuring Security for Removable Media	Access to removable media
Managing BitLocker and BitLocker To Go	BitLocker and BitLocker To Go, including Data Recovery Agent and Microsoft BitLocker Administration and Monitoring (MBAM)
Using BitLocker Drive Encryption on Operating System Drives	
Using BitLocker To Go on Workspace Drives	
Using BitLocker To Go on Removable Media	
Managing BitLocker To Go	
Using Microsoft BitLocker Administration and Monitoring (MBAM)	BitLocker and BitLocker To Go, including Data Recovery Agent and Microsoft BitLocker Administration and Monitoring (MBAM)

■ Managing Share Permissions and NTFS Permissions

↓ **THE BOTTOM LINE**   Share permissions and NTFS permissions are used to control access to resources located in your storage space.

As you learned in Lesson 8, storage spaces appear just like any other drive in File Explorer, so you can apply permissions to the files and folders it contains.

The format of your disk (FAT16, FAT32, exFAT, NTFS) determines the type of security available to you. Windows 8.1 and Windows Server 2012 R2 still rely on the basic approach to securing resources used by previous versions, but they do introduce new features. Before we review those changes, let's take a quick look at share and NTFS permissions and how they work.

Configuring Share Permissions

Share permissions are the permissions you set for folders when you share them either on a workgroup or domain-based network. The permissions you set determine the type of access users have to the folder and its contents.

CERTIFICATION READY
Permissions, including share, NTFS, and Dynamic Access Control (DAC)
Objective 2.5

Share permissions are set for folders when they are shared in workgroups and domain-based networks and are only associated with the folder. They determine the type of access that others will have to the folder when they connect to it over the network.

If they log on locally where the share is located, these permissions will not apply. Share permissions are not granular; therefore, the permission you assign to the share will automatically apply to the files and subfolders within the share itself.

For drives formatted with the FAT/FAT32 file system, share permissions are the only option available, as shown by the Sharing tab shown in Figure 8-1. Table 9-1 provides more information on share level permissions that are available.

For drives formatted with the FAT/FAT32 file system, share permissions are the only option available, as shown by the Sharing tab in Figure 8-1. Table 8-1 provides more information on share level permissions that are available.

Figure 8-1

Reviewing the Sharing tab on a FAT32 volume

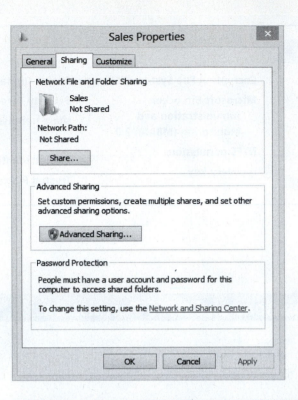

Table 8-1

Understanding Share Permissions

PERMISSION	DESCRIPTION
Read	Enables user/group to view file and subfolder names, view data in files, and run programs
Change	Enables user/group to add files and subfolders to the shared folder, change data in files, delete subfolders and files, and change any permission associated with Read
Full Control	Enables user/group to change file permissions (NTFS only), take ownership of files (NTFS only), and perform tasks associated with Change/Read

Configuring NTFS Permissions

NTFS file permissions is a powerful tool that enables you to control access to your files and folders whether they are accessed across the network or by someone logging on to the computer locally.

CERTIFICATION READY
Permissions, including share, NTFS, and Dynamic Access Control (DAC)
Objective 2.5

In addition to the permissions you set when sharing a folder, Windows offers a more comprehensive set of permissions called *NTFS permissions*. These permissions are available on volumes formatted with the NTFS file system.

NTFS permissions differ from share permissions in two ways.

- They apply to files and folders on NTFS volumes.
- They apply whether the user attempts to access them over the network or locally.

In Figure 8-2, an additional Security tab is present because the folder is located on an NTFS volume. As you can see, there are a number of different permissions available for selected users and groups (see Table 8-2).

Figure 8-2

Reviewing the Security tab on
an NTFS volume

Table 8-2

NTFS Permissions

PERMISSION	DESCRIPTION
Read	Folder: Enables user/group to read the contents of the folder.
	File: Enables user/group to read the contents of the file.
Read & Execute	Folder: Enables user/group to read the contents of the folder and execute programs in the folder.
	File: Enables user/group to read the contents of the file and execute the program.
Write	Folder: Enables user/group to create files and folders.
	File: Enables user/group to create a file.
Modify	Folder: Enables user/group to read and write permissions. User can delete files within the folder and view the contents of subfolders.
	File: Enables user/group to read and write permissions. User can modify the contents of the file.
List Folder Contents	Folder: Enables user/group to view a list of files in the selected folder; user is not allowed to read the contents of a file or execute a file.
	File: There is no equivalent permission for files.
Full Control	Folder: Enables user/group to add, change, move, and delete items. User can also add and remove permissions on the folder and its subfolders.
	File: Enables user/group to change, move, delete, and manage permissions. User can also add, change, and remove permissions on the file.

In Windows 8.1 and Windows Server 2012 R2, the Share tab can be found by clicking the Advanced button. This tab provides information about security settings on a remote file share.

NTFS permissions are cumulative. For example, if you give a user in the sales group Read permissions to a folder and its contents, and the user is also a member of the marketing group, which has been given the Write permission to the same folder, the user will have Read + Write permissions. In this type of situation, if you do not want the user to be able to write to the folder, you can use the Deny permission and select the specific user account. The Deny permission always overrides the Allow permission.

Combining NTFS and Share Permissions

It is very common to combine share and NTFS permissions when providing access to resources on NTFS volumes. When this happens, you must have a good understanding of the cumulative effects to ensure that your resources remain protected. Now that you have a better understanding of NTFS permissions and share permissions, you need to understand what happens when you combine the two on the same resource.

For example, let's say you create and share a folder with the following settings:

- Share permission (Share tab)—Sales group: Read
- NTFS permission (Security tab)—Sales group: Full Control

When users connect to the share over the network, both the share and NTFS permissions combine, and the most restrictive set is applied. In the preceding example, the share permission of Read is more restrictive then the NTFS permission, so users could read the folder and its contents. If the same users were to log on locally to the computer in which this share is located, they would bypass the share permissions, and their level of access would be based on the NTFS permission. In this example, they would have Full Control.

VIEWING EFFECTIVE PERMISSIONS ON A RESOURCE

In Windows 8.1, the Effective Access tab has been added to enable you to view the effective permissions for a user, group, or device account on a resource. You can access this tab by right-clicking the file or folder, choosing Properties, clicking the Security tab, and then clicking Advanced.

For example, let's say you create a folder called *MyPubFiles* and then share the folder, allowing the *Sales* group *Full Control*. You also configure the NTFS permissions for Matthew, a member of the group, with the following settings: *Read & Execute*, *List Folder Contents*, and *Read*. What would Matthew's effective permission be?

To determine Matthew's effective permissions, you would right-click the *MyPubFiles* folder and choose *Properties*. You can then click the *Security* tab and then click *Advanced*. Once you are in the Advanced Security Settings for *MyPubFiles* dialog box, click *Select a user* and then search for Matthew's account. Once it's located, click *View effective access* to see what permissions he has for the folder.

As shown in Figure 8-3, even though Matthew has *Full Control* to the share due to his membership in the *Sales* group, NTFS permissions are restricting him to only reading, listing folder contents, and executing files within the folder. He cannot create files, folders, or make any changes to the documents.

Figure 8-3

Viewing a user's effective permissions

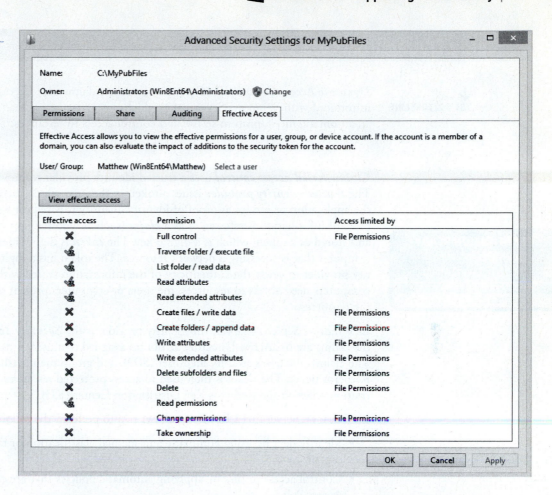

REVIEW PERMISSIONS USING THE EFFECTIVE ACCESS TAB

GET READY. To view the effective permissions for the local Administrator account, log on to your computer with Administrative credentials and then perform the following steps:

1. Press the **Windows logo key + q** and then type **File Explorer**.
2. Click **Local Disk (C:)** and browse to the *C:\Windows* folder.
3. Right-click the **Windows** folder and choose **Properties**.
4. Click the **Security** tab and then click **Advanced**.
5. Click the **Effective Access** tab.
6. Click **Select a user**.
7. In the *Enter the object name to select* field, type **Administrator** and then click **OK**.
8. Click **View effective access**.
9. Review the current permissions for the local Administrator account on *C:\Windows* and then click **OK**.
10. Click **OK** to accept your changes and to close the *Windows Properties* dialog box.

When planning your NTFS/Share permissions on storage spaces or any volumes in which files/folders are shared, the best approach is to set the Share permissions to provide Full Control to the appropriate user group and then use NTFS permissions to further lock down access to the resource. This process ensures that resources are secured regardless of how they are accessed (remotely or locally).

■ Using Dynamic Access Control

THE BOTTOM LINE

Dynamic Access Control (DAC), originally called claims-based access control, was introduced with Windows Sever 2012, which is used for access management. It provides an automatic mechanism to secure and control access to resources.

CERTIFICATION READY
Permissions, including share, NTFS, and Dynamic Access Control (DAC)
Objective 2.5

Claims-based access control uses a trusted identity provider to provide authentication. The *trusted identity provider* issues a token to the user, which the user then presents to the application or service as proof of identity. Identity is based on a set of information. Each piece of information is referred to as a *claim* (such as who the user or computer claims to be), and stored as a token, which is a digital key. The *token* is digital identification for the user or computer that is accessing a network resource. The token has a digital signature of the identity provider to verify the authenticity of the information stored within the token. As users or computers need access to resources, the users or computers present the tokens to get access to the resources.

In Windows Server 2012 R2, the identity provider is the *Security Token Service (STS)* and the claims are the Active Directory attributes assigned to a user or device (such as a computer). The claims, the user's security identifier (SID), and group membership are stored inside the Kerberos ticket. The ticket is then used to access protected resources. Of course, claims authorization relies on the Kerberos Key Distribution Center (KDC).

In Windows Server 2012 R2, DAC allows you to perform the following:

- Identify data by using automatic and manual classification or tagging files in an organization.
- Control access to files by applying automatic policies that are controlled by Central Access Policies.
- Audit access by using a Central Audit Policy to ensure compliance and to be used in forensic analysis.
- Use Active Directory Rights Management Service (RMS) to encrypt sensitive documents.
- Offer Access-Denied Assistance, which provides a method for users to request access from the owner of data when he or she is denied access.

To use claims-based authorization, you need the following:

- Windows Server 2012 or Windows Server 2012 R2 must be installed on the file server that hosts the resources that DAC protects.
- At least one Windows Server 2012 or Windows Server 2012 R2 domain controller must be accessible by the requesting client.
- If you use claims across a forest, you must have a Windows Server 2012 or Windows Server 2012 R2 domain controller in each domain.
- If you use device claims, clients must run at least Windows 8/8.1.

When you enable DAC, you have the option to support claims, compound authentication, and Kerberos armoring. Compound authentication is an extension to Flexible Authentication Secure Tunneling (FAST), which allows Kerberos to create service tickets to devices. The Kerberos armoring fully encrypts Kerberos messages and signs Kerberos errors. Although Kerberos armoring enhances security, it also increases processing time.

→ **ENABLE DAC FOR ACTIVE DIRECTORY DOMAIN SERVICES (AD DS)**

GET READY. To enable DAC for Active Directory Domain Services (AD DS), perform the following steps:

1. Create a new Group Policy Object (GPO) and link the GPO to the *Domain Controllers* organizational unit (OU) or edit the *Default Domain Controllers Policy* GPO. Open **Server Manager** and then open **Group Policy Management**.

2. In the *Group Policy Management* console, double-click the GPO assigned to the Domain Controllers OU that you want to use to enable DAC.

3. In the *Group Policy Management Editor* console, navigate to **Computer Configuration\Policies\Administrative Templates\System\KDC** and double-click **KDC support for claims, compound authentication and Kerberos armoring**.

4. Click **Enabled**.

5. Under *Options*, **Supported** is already selected.

6. Click **OK** to close the *KDC support for claims, compound authentication and Kerberos armoring* dialog box.

7. Close the **Group Policy Management Editor**.

Configuring User and Device Claim Types

After you enable support for DAC in AD DS, you must create and configure claims and resource property objects. To create and configure claims, you primarily use the Active Directory Administrative Center.

The most common types of claims are attribute-based claims, which are usually configured with Active Directory Administrative Center, specifically using the Dynamic Access Control node (see Figure 8-4). All claims are stored in the configuration partition in AD DS, which is a forest-wide partition. As a result, all domains in the forest share the claim dictionary.

Figure 8-4

Managing DAC using Active
Directory Administrative Center

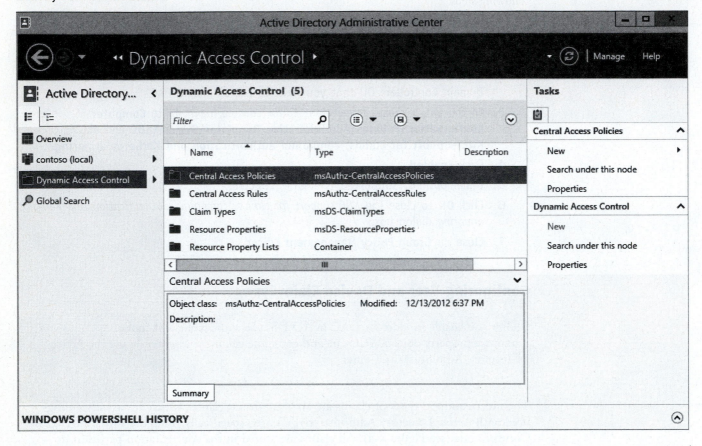

To create a claim type, specify a specific attribute from Active Directory. Of course, for DAC to be effective, Active Directory must contain accurate information. By default, the claim name is the name of the selected attribute name. However, you can modify this to give a more meaningful name. Lastly, you have the option to provide suggested values for the claim.

 CREATE A CLAIM TYPE

GET READY. To create a claim type, perform the following steps:

1. Open **Server Manager**.
2. Click **Tools > Active Directory Administrative Center**. The *Active Directory Administrative Center* appears.
3. Navigate to the **Dynamic Access Control** node and then click the **Claim Types** container.
4. In the *Tasks* pane, under *Claim Types*, click **New > Claim Type**. The *Create Claim Type* dialog box appears.
5. With *User* already selected on the right side of the dialog box, under *Source Attribute*, scroll down and click **department**.
6. For the display name, to provide a more meaningful name, type **Company Department** and then click **OK**. An entry for *Company Department* is listed under *Claim types*.

7. In the *Tasks* pane, under *Claim Types*, click **New > Claim Type**.

8. Click **OK** to close the *Create Claim Type* dialog box. The *description* claim type appears.

After you create the claim types, you must configure the resource property objects such as a folder or a file using the Active Directory Administrative Center. You can create your own resource property, or you can use preconfigured properties, such as Project, Department, or Folder Usage. If you choose to use a preconfigured property, they are disabled by default. Therefore, you have to enable the preconfigure property.

 ENABLE A RESOURCE PROPERTY

GET READY. To enable a resource property, perform the following steps:

1. In *Active Directory Administrative Center*, navigate to and click the **Dynamic Access Control** node. Then double-click **Resource Properties**.

2. To enable the *Department* resource property, under *Resource Property*, right-click **Department** and choose **Enable**.

3. To enable the *Confidentiality* resource property, under *Resource Property*, right-click **Confidentiality** and choose **Enable**.

4. To view the *Confidentiality* settings, double-click **Confidentiality**. The *Confidentiality* dialog box appears.

5. Click **Cancel** to close the *Confidentiality* dialog box.

6. Close *Active Directory Administrative Center*.

Configuring File Classification

When planning DAC implementation, you should include file classification. Although file classification is not mandatory for DAC, it can enhance the automation of access control because it can be used to identify documents that you need to protect and classify them appropriately.

Classification management tasks and file management tasks enable administrators to manage groups of files based on various file and folder attributes. After folders and files are classified, you can automate file and folder maintenance tasks, such as cleaning up stale data or protecting sensitive information. Although classification management can be done manually, you can automate this process with the File Server Resource Manager console.

Classification rules can be created and then scheduled to be applied on a regular basis so that files are automatically scanned and classified based on the content of the file. When you want to perform file classification, you need to determine the following:

- Classifications that you want to apply to documents
- The method that you will use to identify documents for classification
- The schedule for automatic classifications

Of course, to determine the success of the classification, you have to establish periodic reviews.

To manually configure a folder with a classification, right-click the folder and click *Properties*. When the Properties dialog box appears, choose the name of the classification and select the appropriate value. For example, you can select *Department* and then click *Human Resources*. Then all documents within the folder will automatically be classified as the department of Human Resources.

After DAC is configured, you can use it to apply permissions based on a condition. For example, if the user's department is set to Human Resources, you can grant specific permissions (as shown in the next exercise).

 IMPLEMENT CONDITIONAL ACCESS ON A FOLDER'S ACL

GET READY. To implement conditional access on a folder's ACL, perform the following steps:

1. Using *Windows Explorer*, right-click a folder and choose **Properties**. The *Properties* dialog box appears.

2. Click the **Security** tab.

3. Click the **Advanced** button. The *Advanced Security Settings* dialog box appears.

4. Click **Add**. The *Permission Entry for Data* dialog box appears.

5. Click **Select a principal**. In the *Select User, Computer, Service Account, or Group* dialog box, type the name of the user or group and then click **OK**.

6. Specify the *Basic permissions* as necessary.

7. At the bottom of the dialog box, click **Add a condition**.

8. For the condition, you can then configure the following:

Figure 8-5

Configuring a condition for an ACL

Resource > Department > Equals > Value > Human Resources (see Figure 8-5). Click **OK**.

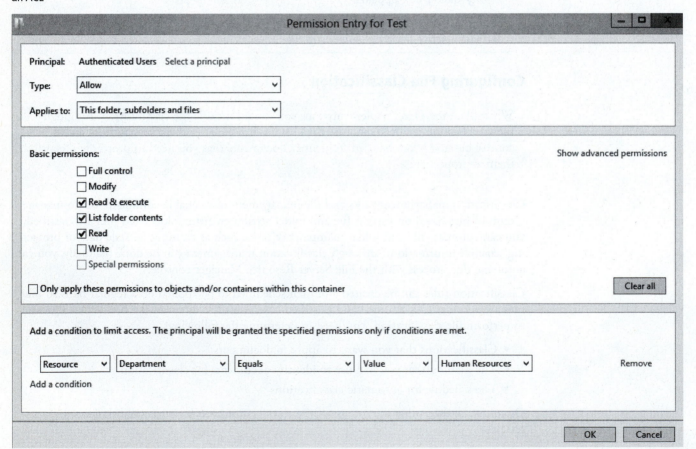

9. Back on the *Advanced Security Settings* dialog box, you see the condition. Click **OK** to close the *Advanced Security Settings for Data* dialog box.

10. Click **OK** to close the *Properties* dialog box.

■ Configuring The Encrypting File System (EFS)

Encrypting File System (EFS) is an encryption service built into Windows 8.1 that has been around since the release of Windows XP. EFS is designed to provide file level encryption to protect your confidential files when others have physical access to your computer.

Using EFS, users can encrypt and decrypt their files/folders to protect sensitive data on their computer in case it's lost or stolen. The encryption key is associated with the user's logon account and is stored as part of the user profile.

CERTIFICATION READY
Encrypting File System (EFS), including Data Recovery Agent
Objective 2.5

To use EFS, you must store your files on an NTFS volume. If you are using Windows compression on the file/folder, you have to uncompress it before you can encrypt it.

Encrypting a folder or file is as simple as right-clicking the object, choosing Properties, clicking the General tab, and then clicking Advanced. The Advanced Attributes dialog box appears (see Figure 8-6). To enable encryption, select the *Encrypt contents to secure data* option. If the folder contains files and subfolders, you will be prompted to apply encryption to just the folder or to apply changes to the folder, subfolder, and files.

Figure 8-6

Enabling encryption

The first time you encrypt a file or folder in Windows 8.1, you will be prompted to backup your file encryption certificate and key. Doing so will launch the Certificate Export Wizard, in which you can apply a password to the exported file, provide a name, and then determine a location to store the file. You should always make a backup of the key to make sure you can recover your encrypted information if you lose the key. Consider placing it somewhere other than your computer, such as in a shared folder on the network or on a USB flash drive.

Files and folders that you encrypt will display ingreen color in File Explorer.

Encrypted files/folders can be moved and copied, but you should keep the following in mind:

- Moving an encrypted file from an NTFS volume to a FAT/FAT32 volume will decrypt it. FAT/FAT32 does not support encryption. It will also remove any NTFS permissions configured on the file.
- Moving an encrypted file between NTFS volumes on the same computer will maintain the encryption. NTFS permissions will also be maintained when the file is moved.

If you want to use your encrypted files on another computer, you need to export the EFS certificate and key from your computer and then import it at the other computer. If you want to share your encrypted files with another user, the other person has to export the EFS certificate and then import it on your computer. After it is imported, you will add the certificate to the file you want to share through the file's property settings. Exporting and importing are done via the Certification snap-in (certmgr.msc).

 ENCRYPT FILES AND FOLDERS USING EFS

GET READY. To encrypt files using EFS, perform the following steps:

1. Press the **Windows logo key + q** and then type **File Explorer**.
2. Choose **File Explorer** from the *Results* list.
3. Right-click the Local Disk (C:) and choose **New > Folder**.
4. Right-click the new folder and choose **Rename**. Type **MyEncryptedFiles** and then press **Enter**.
5. Double-click the **MyEncryptedFiles** folder to open it.
6. In the MyEncryptedFiles folder, right-click and choose **New > Folder**. Type **Marketing** and then press **Enter**.
7. Right-click and choose **New > Folder**. Type **Sales** and then press **Enter**.
8. Right click and choose **New > Text Document**. Type **Agenda12162012** and then press Enter.
9. Press the **Backspace** key to navigate back to the Local Disk (C:). Right-click the **MyEncryptedFiles** folder and choose **Properties**.
10. Click **Advanced**.
11. Select the **Encrypt contents to secure data** check box and then click **OK**.
12. When the *MyEncryptedFiles* dialog box appears, click **OK** to close it.
13. Click **Apply changes to this folder, subfolders, and files** and then click **OK**. The *MyEncryptedFiles* folder will appear as green to indicate it has been encrypted.
14. Double-click the **MyEncryptedFiles** folder and review the files and subfolders to confirm that they are also encrypted (they appear in green). Minimize the **MyEncryptedFiles** window to return to your desktop.
15. Right-click anywhere on your desktop and choose **New > Text Document**. Type **SalesFigures** and then press **Enter**.
16. Right-click the **SalesFigures.txt** document and choose **Copy**.
17. Maximize the *MyEncryptedFiles* window and double-click the **Sales** folder to open it. Right-click and choose **Paste** to copy the *SalesFigure.txt* document into the *Sales* folder. The file will be encrypted (turn green) automatically.
18. Right-click the **SalesFigures.txt** file that is now encrypted and choose **Copy**.
19. Minimize the *MyEncryptedFiles* window.
20. Right-click anywhere on your desktop and choose **New > Folder**. Type **Transfer** and then press **Enter**.
21. Double-click the **Transfer** folder to open it.

22. Right-click and choose **Paste** to copy the *SalesFigures.txt* file into the *Transfer* folder. The file will remain encrypted (green).

23. (Optional) If you have a USB drive formatted with FAT32, drag the file to the USB drive. (You will receive a message that indicates the file is being copied to a destination that does not support encryption. Click **Yes** to continue.)

24. Open the USB drive and confirm the file is not decrypted.

Using Data Recovery Agent

> If an employee leaves the company or a loses the original key and the encrypted files cannot be read, you can set up a *Data Recovery Agent (DRA)* that can recover EFS encrypted files for a domain. This must be set up before the documents are encrypted.

CERTIFICATION READY
Encrypting File System (EFS), including Data Recovery Agent
Objective 2.5

To define DRAs, you can use Active Directory Group Policy to configure one or more user accounts as DRAs for your entire organization. However, to accomplish this, you need to have an enterprise CA.

ADD DATA RECOVERY AGENTS FOR EFS

GET READY. To add new users as recovery agents, assign the EFS recovery certificates issued by the enterprise CA to the user account and then perform the following steps:

1. Log in as the DRA account.

2. Open the **Group Policy Management console**.

3. Expand **Forest**, expand **Domains**, and then click the **name of your domain**.

4. Right-click the **Default Domain Policy** and choose **Edit**.

5. Expand **Computer Configuration\Policies\Windows Settings\Security Settings\ Public Key Policies**.

6. Right-click **Encrypting File System** and choose **Create Data Recovery Agent**. Alternately, you can select **Add Data Recovery Agent** to run the *Add Recovery Agent Wizard*.

7. Click **Encrypting File System** and notice the certificates that are displayed (see Figure 8-7).

Figure 8-7

Viewing the Encrypting File
System certificates

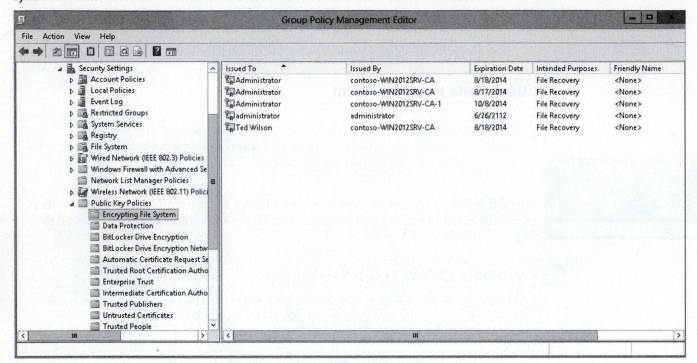

8. Close the **Group Policy Editor**.

9. Close the **Group Policy Management console**.

To recover the file, log on under the DRA account, locate the file and then take ownership of it. After you have ownership of the file, view its property settings and deselect *Encrypt contents to secure data.*

Configuring Security for Removable Media

THE BOTTOM LINE

In today's networks, the biggest concern of administrators has been the arrival of removable storage devices. With Windows 8.1 and Windows Server 2012 R2, you fortunately have several options for monitoring and securing these types of devices. Controlling the use of removable media is critical to the overall security of your network.

CERTIFICATION READY
Access to removable media
Objective 2.5

Monitoring and securing removable media include using Group Policy to control whether users are allowed to use removable media on your network or on specific computers; and whether they can deploy BitLocker/BitLocker To Go to encrypt and protect removable media that is lost or stolen.

You can configure GPOs to monitor the use of removable storage devices on your network. The setting can be found in the following location using the GPMC:

- **Computer Configuration\Policies\Windows Settings\Security Settings\Advanced Audit Policy Configuration\Audit Policies**. The Audit Removable Storage setting enables you to audit user attempts to access file system objects on a removable storage device. If you enable this policy, a security audit event is generated each time an account accesses the removable storage device.

You can also configure GPOs to prevent the use of removable media on your network for computers and/or users.

The settings can be found in both Computer and User locations in the GPMC:

- **Computer Configuration\Policies\Administrative Templates\System\Removable Storage Access**. These settings will be applied to the computer and every user who logs on to it.
- **User Configuration\Policies\Administrative Templates\System\Removable Storage Access**. These settings will be applied only to users/groups that are included in an Active Directory container to which you link the GPO.

On Windows 8.1 clients, you can configure similar settings using the Local Group Policy Editor (LGPE)—gpedit.msc. When enabled and applied, the *Prevent installation of removable devices* setting (see Figure 8-8) prevents Windows from installing removable devices. A device is considered removable when the driver for the device to which it is connected indicates the device is removable. For example, a USB device is reported removable by the drivers for the USB hub to which it is connected.

Figure 8-8

Preventing the installation of removable devices using a local GPO

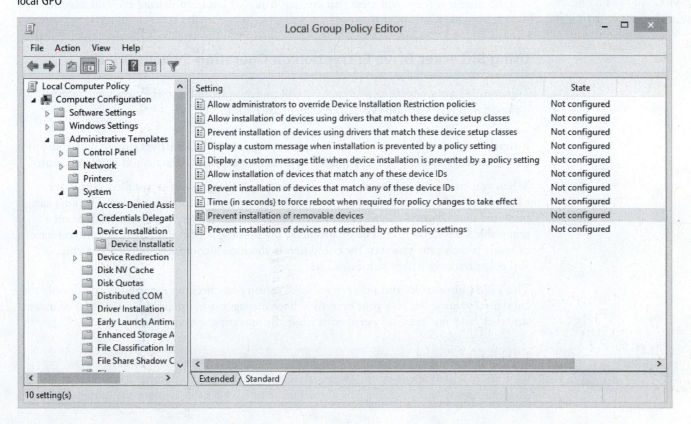

■ Managing BitLocker and BitLocker To Go

THE BOTTOM LINE

BitLocker Drive Encryption and BitLocker To Go are designed to protect sensitive data stored on fixed and removable drives even in situations where they are lost, stolen or moved to another computer.

BitLocker Drive Encryption is designed to protect against brute force attacks to gain access to your fixed drive or situations in which someone tries to install and access your fixed drive from another computer. It provides full disk encryption capabilities for fixed drives (including storage pools) and operating system drives. You can further enhance security by checking the integrity of boot files if a *Trusted Platform Module (TPM)* chip is available on your computer. The TPM is a dedicated cryptographic processor chip that the computer uses to store the BitLocker encryption keys.

BitLocker To Go is BitLocker Drive Encryption on removable media drives. This includes *Secure Digital (SD) cards*, USB flash drives, and external hard disk drives. SD cards are non-volatile memory cards used in mobile phones, digital cameras, and tablet computers.

BitLocker Drive Encryption and BitLocker To Go are available in Windows 8.1 Professional/Enterprise operating systems and Windows Server 2012R2. They are not designed to replace EFS or NTFS permissions. Instead, they are designed to add an additional layer of security and protection.

When encrypting affixed disk, storage pool, or removable media, there are two options:

- **Encrypt used disk space only:** This option encrypts only the part of the drive that currently has data stored on it.
- **Encrypt entire drive:** This option encrypts the full volume and offers more security because it will encrypt areas that contain data that has been deleted but still may be retrievable from the drive.

CERTIFICATION READY
BitLocker and BitLocker To Go, including Data Recovery Agent and Microsoft BitLocker Administration and Monitoring (MBAM)
Objective 2.5

TAKE NOTE *

In order to encrypt a drive, the drive must be formatted using FAT, FAT32, or NTFS and must have at least 64MB of space available.

Using BitLocker Drive Encryption on Operating System Drives

Encrypting your operating system drive will protect it from being tampered with even if the drive is taken offline and placed into another computer.

BitLocker was designed with the goal of protecting the fixed data drives (internal hard disks) on computers that are physically located in areas where sensitive data could be compromised.

When you encrypt the drive where the Windows operating system is installed, BitLocker must store the keys it uses to encrypt/decrypt on a separate piece of hardware. The keys can be stored on a *Trusted Platform Module (TPM)* version 1.2 (or later) microchip or on a removable USB flash drive. The disadvantage of choosing a USB flash drive is that you have to insert it each time you start the computer. If you have a computer with a TPM chip, BitLocker retrieves its key automatically.

The TPM chip enables BitLocker to enhance security by checking the validity of not only the encrypted volume but also your boot files, boot manager, and operating system files to make sure they have not been tampered with while the operating system was offline.

TAKE NOTE *

You can determine if you have a TPM chip by pressing the Windows logo key + r and typing tpm.msc. This opens the TPM console on a Windows 8.1 computer. If the TPM chip does not appear in the console, you should make sure it is enabled via the computer's BIOS.

To support BitLocker Drive Encryption on the drive that contains your operating system, you need the following:

- **Two partitions:** BitLocker will hold files needed to start your computer on one partition. This is called the system partition and needs to be a minimum of 100 MB in size. This partition is not encrypted. The second partition, encrypted by BitLocker, will hold the operating system. This allows BitLocker to protect the operating system and the information in the encrypted drive and to perform its pre-startup authentication steps and verify system integrity.
- **NTFS file system:** The partitions have to be formatted using the NTFS file system.
- **TPM-compatible BIOS:** Your basic input/output system (BIOS)must be compatible with TPM version 1.2 or 2.0; otherwise, the BIOS firmware must be able to read from a USB drive that contains the startup key on boot to enable BitLocker on an operating system drive. BitLocker needs the startup key from either the TPM or the USB flash drive before it can unlock the protected drive. If a USB drive is used on a non-TPM system, BitLocker cannot verify the integrity of the system.

UNDERSTANDING TPM MODES

When using TPM with BitLocker, you can select from the following modes; each provides a different level of security:

- **TPM-Only mode:** Validates boot files, operating system files, and any BitLocker-encrypted volumes. The user doesn't have to enter a key when the computer boots into Windows. Using this mode enables someone to hard-boot your system and gain access to the system if the hardware has not been tampered with.
- **TPM-PIN mode:** Validates boot files, operating system files, and any BitLocker-encrypted volumes. The user must enter a PIN before the computer can boot into Windows. A GPO can be configured to require a more stringent password instead of using simple numbers for the PIN.
- **TPM-Startup Key mode:** Validates boot files, operating system files, and any BitLocker-encrypted volumes. The user must use a USB flash drive with the keys before the computer can boot into Windows.
- **TPM-SmartCard mode:** Validates boot files, operating system files, and any BitLocker-encrypted volumes. The users must insert a smartcard that includes a valid certificate before the computer can boot into Windows.
- **No TPM mode:** Validates BitLocker-encrypted volumes, but does not protect the boot environment. Used in computers without a TPM v1.2 or later chip. The user requires a USB flash drive, used during boot, to read the keys when the computer starts.

In each case, if the TPM is missing or the integrity of the files is in question, BitLocker will go into Recover mode, which requires you to enter a key or password to regain access. If you can't remember the password, you can use a recovery key. If the recovery key is stored on a USB flash drive, you can insert the USB when prompted and press Enter. You do not have to enter a recovery key; the computer will reboot and unlock automatically. However, if the key was saved to another computer or in another location, you need to retrieve the recovery key and enter it to continue.

TAKE NOTE ✱ If the computer halts earlier in the process due to a problem with TPM or boot data corruption, you do not have access to enter the information from the keyboard. Instead, use the F1–F9 function keys that represent the digits 1–9. F10 represents 0.

Here are a few scenarios that cause BitLocker to go into recovery mode:

- Changing the boot order to another fixed drive in an attempt to access the lost/stolen hard drive protected by BitLocker
- Setting the CD/DVD drive before the hard drive in the boot order and then inserting or removing a CD/DVD
- Entering a PIN too many times
- Adding or removing hardware (PCMCIA wireless cards, video cards, network cards)
- Moving the BitLocker-protected drive to another computer
- Using a BIOS hot key during the boot process to change the boot order to another drive
- Pressing the F8 or F10 key during the boot process

When using BitLocker on domain-based computers that use the TPM-PIN mode, the system volume will automatically unlock without needing the user to enter a PIN if the following conditions are met:

- TPM is enabled.
- The computer is a member of the domain and is currently connected to it over a wired connection.
- A Network Unlock server (used to distribute the Network Unlock certificates to clients, which then use them to create the network unlock keys) is installed on a Windows Deployment Services server.

If the computer is a member of a domain but does not meet these conditions, the users have to enter their PIN during the boot process.

If you attempt to enable BitLocker using the BitLocker Drive Encryption Control Panel for your operating system drive and you do not have a compatible TPM, the warning message shown in Figure 8-9 is displayed.

Figure 8-9

Viewing the TPM warning message

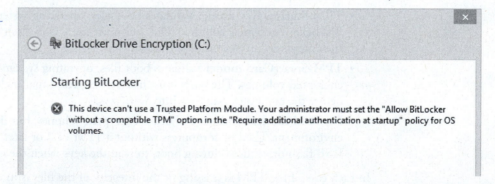

If this happens, you need to make the changes to Group Policy, as indicated in the message, and set your system to boot from a USB drive. These settings can be found in the LGPE if you want to configure the policy on a computer that is not a member of a domain. If you want to configure and apply the policy to multiple computers across your domain, use the GPMC. These settings can be found in the following locations:

- **Local Group Policy Editor:** The settings are located in *Computer Configuration\ Administrative Templates\Windows Components\BitLocker Drive Encryption\Operating System Drives*. Select *Require additional authentication at startup*. Under the *Options* section, make sure *Allow BitLocker without a compatible TPM (requires a password or a startup key on a USB flash drive)* is checked.
- **Group Policy Management Console:** The settings are located in *Computer Configuration\Policies\Administrative Templates\Windows Components\BitLocker Drive*

Encryption\Operating System Drives. Select *Require additional authentication at startup*. Under the *Options* section, make sure *Allow BitLocker without a compatible TPM (requires a password or a startup key on a USB flash drive)* is checked.

After configuring the appropriate policy settings, you can go back to the hard drive and turn on BitLocker. After BitLocker has prepared the drive, you will be asked to restart the system. After the computer boots, you will be prompted to set your BitLocker startup preferences. Your options include the following:

- Use BitLocker without additional keys
- Require a PIN at every startup
- Require a Startup key at every startup

After selecting *Require a Startup key at every startup*, you will be asked to save your Startup key. Insert the USB drive and the keys will be copied to the device. From this point on, each time you boot the system, you will need to use the USB drive to provide the BitLocker keys.

Using BitLocker To Go on Workspace Drives

Enabling BitLocker To Go on a Windows To Go workspace drive ensures that the data is protected and unauthorized users cannot access your data or use the workspace drive if it is lost or stolen.

In Lesson 1, you learned that you can configure encryption on Windows To Go workspace drives during the initial setup of the workspace. These types of drives are designed for roaming (using multiple computers); therefore, the TPM chip cannot be used by BitLocker to protect the drive. Instead, you provide a recovery password to unlock the drive and boot into the workspace. By default, the password must be at least eight characters long unless you have configured stronger password policies on your network using Group Policy.

The recovery password is saved in the documents library of the computer used to create the workspace.

If the computer was a member of an Active Directory domain, and you are using Active Directory Domain Services (AD DS) to store recovery passwords, it may also be saved under the computer account of the computer used to create the workspace. You can use this recovery password if the password you created earlier is lost or stolen.

Using BitLocker To Go on Removable Media

In addition to using BitLocker to protect a Windows To Go Workspace drive, you can also use it to protect removable media containing your data files.

Using BitLocker To Go on removable media involves the following steps:

1. Connecting the drive.
2. Enabling BitLocker To Go Encryption.
3. Setting a password or using a smart card for authentication.
4. Backing up the recovery key.
5. Encrypting the drive (entire drive or used space only).

A *recovery key* is a string of 48 random numbers (for example, 031449-152141-040282-547360-281974-173019-554092-404162) that enables you to access the encrypted drive if you forget the password. If you are using a removable data drive, the key cannot be stored on the removable media you are encrypting. You can back up the recovery key to your Microsoft user account, save it to a file, or print the recovery key.

When saving the key initially, you will be prompted to store the key in more than one place. If you select Yes, you will be asked to select a second location for the keys. Although not required, it is best practice to have the recovery key stored in more than one place to provide a second level of back up.

⊕ ENABLE ENCRYPTION ON A REMOVABLE DATA DRIVE

GET READY. To enable encryption on a removable drive, log on to a Windows 8.1 computer as an administrator and then perform the following steps:

1. Insert a USB drive into a USB port on your computer.
2. Press the **Windows logo key + w** and then type **BitLocker**.
3. From the *Results* list, click **Manage BitLocker**.
4. Under *Removable data drives – BitLocker to Go,* click **Turn on BitLocker**.
5. Select **Use a password to unlock the drive**.
6. In the *Enter your password* field and *Reenter your password* field, type the same password and then click **Next**.
7. In the *How do you want to back up your recovery key* dialog box, click **Save to a file**.
8. In the *Save BitLocker recovery key as* dialog box, choose **Desktop** and then click in the *File name* field and type **MyBitLockerRecoveryKey**.
9. Click **Save** and then click **Next** to continue.
10. Select **Encrypt entire drive (slower but best for PCs and drives already in use)** and then click **Next**.
11. Click **Start encrypting**.
12. Click **Manage BitLocker**.

    During the encryption process, *BitLocker Encrypting* will be shown next to the removable drive. After encryption has completed, this will change to *BitLocker on*.
13. Close the *BitLocker Drive Encryption* Control Panel.
14. Eject the USB drive, wait for a few seconds, and then insert the drive back into the system.
15. Open File Explorer and then locate the USB drive that is being protected by BitLocker To Go (see Figure 8-10).

Figure 8-10

The padlock icon indicates BitLocker is protecting the removable disk

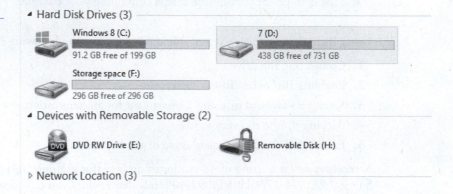

◢ Hard Disk Drives (3)

Windows 8 (C:)
91.2 GB free of 199 GB

7 (D:)
438 GB free of 731 GB

Storage space (F:)
296 GB free of 296 GB

◢ Devices with Removable Storage (2)

DVD RW Drive (E:)

Removable Disk (H:)

▷ Network Location (3)

16. Double-click **Removable Disk**.

17. In the *Enter password to unlock this drive* field, type your BitLocker password to access the disk and then click **Unlock**.

18. Browse the files on the removable disk to confirm you can now access the data.

19. After you have confirmed access, close the dialog box.

Managing BitLocker To Go

After BitLocker To Go is configured on your removable media drives, there are several administrative tasks that can be performed from the BitLocker Drive Encryption Control Panel. For example, you may need to change your password if it is compromised, create an additional backup of your recovery key, or turn off encryption on the drive so you can install additional applications.

After completing the encryption of the USB drive, any new files added to it will automatically be encrypted. If you copy these files to another drive or to a different PC, they will be decrypted. If you share the files with others over a network, they will be encrypted as long as they are on the drive.

You can perform the following tasks from the Manage BitLocker tool on this encrypted USB data drive:

- **Back up recovery key:** This option enables you to back up the recovery key by saving it to your Microsoft user account, saving it to a file, or printing the recovery key.
- **Change password:** This option enables you to change the password. You have to enter the old password and then input and confirm a new password.
- **Remove password:** This option enables you to remove the current password, but requires that you add another unlocking method before removing it.
- **Add smart card:** This option prompts you to insert a smart card to use.
- **Turn on auto-unlock:** This option (available for data drives) can be set to automatically unlock when you sign in to the PC.
- **Turn off BitLocker:** This option enables you to turn off BitLocker temporarily to install an application or decrypt the drive.

Using Microsoft BitLocker Administration and Monitoring (MBAM)

As the number of computers using BitLocker on your network increases, you will find that tasks such as recovering lost PINs, making sure critical systems have BitLocker enabled, and controlling what can be encrypted (used disk space, entire drive) can become very labor-intensive. Microsoft BitLocker Administration and Monitoring (MBAM)—which is part of the Microsoft Desktop Optimization Pack (MDOP) 2012—can help.

Microsoft BitLocker Administration and Monitoring (MBAM) 2.0 is a simple administrative interface for setting encryption policies, monitoring computers against those policies, and reporting the encryption status across your organization. It can also be used to access recovery information when users forget their passwords, lose their PINs, or when a computer enters into recovery mode when its BIOS or boot record is changed. MBAM is part of the Microsoft Desktop Optimization Pack (MDOP), which is available as part of the Microsoft Software Assurance or via Microsoft Volume Licensing.

CERTIFICATION READY
BitLocker and BitLocker
To Go, including Data
Recovery Agent and
Microsoft BitLocker
Administration and
Monitoring (MBAM)
Objective 2.5

MBAM is composed of the following components:

- **Administration and Monitoring server:** Hosts the management console and monitors web services. It is used to review audit activities, compliance, and status; manage hardware capability; and access BitLocker recovery keys.
- **Compliance and audit database:** Holds compliance information for MBAM clients; used for reporting functions.
- **Recovery and hardware database:** Stores recovery information and hardware information that is obtained from the MBAM clients.
- **Compliance and audit reports:** Provides MBAM reports that can be viewed from the Management console or from SQL Server Services (SSRS).
- **Policy template:** Specifies MBAM settings for BitLocker drive encryption.
- **MBAM client agent:** Uses Group Policy to enforce encryption settings; collects recovery keys, recovery, and hardware information from MBAM clients and compliance data that is passed to the reporting system. The client software can be installed on Windows 7 (Enterprise/Ultimate Editions) and Windows 8/8.1 (Professional/Enterprise Editions). The clients must be TPM v 1.2–capable, and the chip must be enabled in the BIOS.

When integrated with System Center Configuration Manager (SCCM), you can see BitLocker reports and hardware management integrated within SCCM while recovery keys can be handled via the Recovery console or through a self-service portal that allows users to look up their own keys.

SKILL SUMMARY

IN THIS LESSON YOU LEARNED:

- Share permissions are applied only when accessing a folder over the network. NTFS permissions are applied to files and folders, and are enforced both locally and remotely.

- When you combine share and NTFS permissions, the more restrictive of the two wins. Use the Effective Access tab to see the permissions (share and NTFS) applied to a specific resource.

- Dynamic Access Control (DAC), originally called claims-based access control, was introduced with Windows Sever 2012 and is used for access management. It provides an automatic mechanism to secure and control access to resources.

- The Encrypting File System (EFS) can be used to protect sensitive data from others who may use your system, or to offer protection in the case of loss or theft. To encrypt a file/folder, it must be on an NTFS volume and not be compressed. Encrypted files/folders appear green in File Explorer.

- If an employee leaves the company or loses the original key and the encrypted files cannot be read, you can set up a Data Recovery Agent (DRA) that can recover EFS encrypted files for a domain.

- Moving an encrypted file/folder from an NTFS volume to a FAT/FAT32 volume will decrypt it; moving it between NTFS volumes will maintain encryption.

- Using the GPMC and the LGPE enables you to create policies to restrict users' access to removable media.

- BitLocker Drive Encryption and BitLocker To Go provide encryption for hard drives. Neither is a replacement for EFS; they are additional layers of defense you can add to protect your computer.

- You can encrypt the entire hard drive or used space only. Encrypting the entire hard drive ensures that "deleted" areas on the disk are also encrypted.

- Trusted Platform Module (TPM) v 1.2 or later chips are required to provide enhanced security by checking the validity of not only the encrypted volume but also your boot files, boot manager, and operating system files.

- Recovery keys are used to gain access to encrypted drives. They can be backed up to a USB drive, saved to a file, or printed out. They can also be saved to Active Directory.

- MBAM provides a simple administrative interface for setting encrypting policies, monitoring computers against those policies, and reporting the encryption status across you organization.

- Microsoft Diagnostics and Recovery kit is used to diagnose and recover Windows systems that will not boot.

■ Knowledge Assessment

Multiple Choice

Select the correct answer for each of the following questions.

1. Which of the following share permissions on a FAT32 volume enable you to add files and folders to a shared folder? (Choose all that apply)
   a. Read
   b. Write
   c. Change
   d. Full Control

2. Which of the following actions decrypts a file that has been encrypted using EFS? (Choose all that apply)
   a. Using ERA
   b. Moving it to another NTFS volume
   c. Moving it to a FAT32 volume
   d. Moving it to another NTFS volume on another computer

3. Which of the following tools prevents the installation of removable devices on a standalone Windows 8.1 computer?
   a. GPMC
   b. LGPE
   c. BitLocker Group Policy
   d. BitLocker To Go Group Policy

4. Which of the following statements best describes a characteristic of a folder that is encrypted with EFS? (Choose all that apply)
   a. The color of the folder appears as green in File Explorer.
   b. The color of the folder appears as blue in File Explorer.
   c. The *Encrypt contents to secure data* attribute is checked in the folder's Advanced attributes dialog box.
   d. The folder appears in italic font.

5. Which of the following statements is true of BitLocker Drive Encryption? (Choose all that apply)
   a. BitLocker encrypts used disk space only.
   b. BitLocker encrypts files only.
   c. BitLocker encrypts folders only.
   d. BitLocker encrypts the entire drive.

6. Which of the following versions of TPM is required in order to enhance security by checking the validity of not only the encrypted volume but also boot files, boot manager, and operating system files?
   a. TPM v1
   b. TPM v1.2
   c. TPM v1.1
   d. TPM

7. Which of the following scenarios could cause BitLocker to go into recovery mode? (Choose all that apply)
   a. Adding a video card
   b. Changing the boot order to another drive
   c. Moving the BitLocker drive to another computer
   d. Entering your PIN too many times

8. A recovery key is a string of how many random numbers?
   a. 128
   b. 64
   c. 48
   d. 6

9. Which of the following are options for backing up a BitLocker recovery key when encrypting your removable media? (Choose all that apply)
   a. Print it.
   b. Save it to a file.
   c. Store it on the removable media you are encrypting.
   d. Back it up to your Microsoft user account.

10. To encrypt a drive, what is the minimal amount of space that must be available?
    a. 60 MB
    b. 1 GB
    c. 64MB
    d. 50MB

11. You have several files and more will be added in the future. You want to define the NTFS permissions for these files that contain the word "legal" for users who are part of the Legal department. What should you do?
    a. Enable and configure EFS.
    b. Enable and configure DAC.
    c. Enable and configure BitLocker.
    d. Enable and configure DRA.

12. How do you assign a recovery agent for EFS?
    a. Configure a DRA in a GPO.
    b. Add an entry in the RecoveryAgent file in the %NETLOGON% folder.
    c. Select the Recovery Agent option using Active Directory Users and Computers.
    d. Select the Recovery Agent option using Active Directory Administrative Center.

Best Answer

Choose the letter that corresponds to the best answer. Select the BEST answer. You might need to choose more than one answer choice to achieve the goal.

1. Which of the following is the best solution to protecting files and folders on your hard drive when multiple users are provided access to the same computer?
   a. BitLocker Drive Encryption
   b. EFS
   c. BitLocker To Go
   d. NTFS

2. Which of the following methods is the fastest way to decrypt a file stored on a computer that has both NTFS and FAT32 volumes?
   a. Use EFS Recovery agent.
   b. Move it to a FAT32 volume.
   c. Move it to another NTFS volume.
   d. Move it to another NTFS volume on another computer.

3. Which of the following methods is most effective for disabling the use of removable media across your entire network?
   a. Use LGPE on each computer.
   b. Use GPMC to create a GPO and apply it across your domain.
   c. Develop a written policy and distribute it to all employees.
   d. Disable the USB ports on each computer using Device manager.

4. Which of the following methods is most effective for confirming that you have a TPM chip in your computer?
   a. Press theWindows logo key + q and then type tpm.msc.
   b. Consult the manual that came with your motherboard.
   c. Research the manufacturer's website.
   d. Open the computer and locate the TPM chip.

5. Which of the following TPM modes provides the strongest protection?
   a. TPM-Smart Card mode
   b. TPM-Only mode
   c. TPM-Startup key
   d. No TPM

Matching and Identification

1. Match the following terms with the related description or usage.
   _____ **a)** EFS
   _____ **b)** MBAM
   _____ **c)** NTFS permissions
   _____ **d)** Recovery key
   _____ **e)** ERA
   _____ **f)** TPM-Startup key
   _____ **g)** Share permission
   _____ **h)** Recover mode
   _____ **i)** TPM v1.2 chip
   _____ **j)** Effective Access tab
   1. Apply whether a resource is accessed locally or across the network.
   2. A system response to BitLocker, detecting that the boot files have been tampered with.
   3. Encrypts files and folders to protect sensitive data.
   4. Provides 48 random numbers that enable you to access a BitLocker-encrypted drive.
   5. Permissions set for folders when you share them in workgroups and domains.
   6. Simple administrative interface for setting encryption policies across your organization.
   7. A microchip in which BitLocker stores its keys.
   8. Additional tab added in Windows 8.1 to enable you to view the effective permissions on a resource.
   9. Validates boot files, operating system files, and any BitLocker-encrypted volumes; user must have a USB flash drive before the computer can boot into Windows.
   10. Automatically created by EFS. You can recover files/folders when people lose their keys or leave the company.

Build a List

1. Specify the correct order of the steps that must be completed to use BitLocker To Go on removable media.

   _____ Backup your recovery key.

   _____ Connect the drive.

   _____ Encrypt the drive.

   _____ Set a password for authentication.

   _____ Enable BitLocker To Go encryption.

2. Specify the correct order of the steps that must be completed to use EFS to encrypt a compressed folder with its subfolders and files.

   _____ Check **Encrypt contents to secure data** and then click **OK**.

   _____ Right-click the folder, choose **Properties**, and then click **Advanced**.

   _____ Deselect **Compress contents to save disk space**.

   _____ Click **Apply changes to this folder, subfolders, and files**.

3. Specify the correct order of the steps that must be completed to access a BitLocker drive that has gone into Recover mode. You have multiple recovery keys printed out in a document you carry with you.

   _____ Turn on your computer.

   _____ Type the recovery key and press **Enter**.

   _____ Computer boots into Recover mode.

   _____ Compare the printed password file with the password ID on the Recovery console display.

   _____ Computer boots into the system.

Choose an Option

1. Identify the option that, when enabled, prevents you from encrypting the folder.

■ Business Case Scenarios

Scenario 8-1: Configuring Permissions

You have setup a shared folder on a FAT32 volume that is set with the following permissions:
Share name: **MyDocs**
Share Permission: **Read**
Group: **Everyone**

After configuring the share, you notice that multiple people have added files to it. What is the problem and how should you address it?

Scenario 8-2: Encrypting Files

You have a computer that is shared by multiple users. You want to make sure the files you have on the system are protected from prying eyes. You are considering using BitLocker Drive Encryption. Is that a viable solution? Explain your answer.

9 LESSON

Supporting Operating System and Hardware

70-688 EXAM OBJECTIVE

Objective 3.1 – Support operating system and hardware. This objective may include but is not limited to: Resolve hardware and device issues, including STOP errors and Reliability Monitor; optimize performance by using Windows Performance Toolkit (WPT), including Xperf.exe, Xbootmgr.exe, XperfView.exe, and Windows Performance Recorder (WPR); monitor performance by using Data Collector Sets, Task Manager, and Resource Monitor; monitor and manage printers, including NFC Tap-to-Pair and printer sharing; remediate startup issues by using the Diagnostics and Recovery Toolkit (DaRT)

LESSON HEADING	EXAM OBJECTIVE
Resolving Hardware and Device Issues	Resolve hardware and device issues, including STOP errors and Reliability Monitor
Using Device Manager	
Exploring Driver Signing	
Performing Driver Roll Backs	
Identifying Problem Devices	
Troubleshooting Problem Devices	
Refreshing or Resetting Your PC	
Creating a Windows 8.1 File Recovery Drive	
Using Reliability Monitor	Resolve hardware and device issues, including STOP errors and Reliability Monitor
Performing a System Restore	
Resolving STOP Errors	Resolve hardware and device issues, including STOP errors and Reliability Monitor
Optimizing Performance by using Windows Performance Toolkit	Optimize performance by using Windows Performance Toolkit (WPT), including Xperf.exe, Xbootmgr.exe, XperfView.exe, and Windows Performance Recorder (WPR)
Monitoring Performance	
Using Task Manager	Monitor performance by using Data Collector Sets, Task Manager, and Resource Monitor

Using Resource Monitor	Monitor performance by using Data Collector Sets, Task Manager, and Resource Monitor
Using Performance Monitor	
Using Common Performance Counters	
Configuring Data Collector Sets (DCS)	Monitor performance by using Data Collector Sets, Task Manager, and Resource Monitor
Monitoring and Managing Printers	Monitor and manage printers, including NFC Tap-to-Pair and printer sharing
Exploring the v4 Print Driver Model	
Managing Printers	
Supporting Printer Sharing	Monitor and manage printers, including NFC Tap-to-Pair and printer sharing
Supporting NFC Tap-to-Pair	Monitor and manage printers, including NFC Tap-to-Pair and printer sharing
Remediating Startup Issues by Using DaRT 8.1	Remediate startup issues by using the Diagnostics and Recovery Toolkit (DaRT)
Understanding the DaRT 8.1 Recovery Image Tool	
Reviewing the Tools Included with DaRT	

KEY TERMS

Action Center
Data Collector Sets (DCS)
Device Manager
distributed scan server
Driver Roll Back
driver signing
Internet printing
Line Printer Daemon (LPD) service
Microsoft Desktop Optimization Pack (MDOP)
Microsoft Diagnostics and Recovery Toolset (DaRT)
near field communication (NFC)
performance
Performance Monitor

print device
print driver
printer
Print and Document services role
Print Management snap-in
print queue
print server
Print Spooler service
process
Reliability Monitor
Resource Monitor
restore point
Roll Back Driver
Server Manager

spooling
STOP error
Tap and Do
Task Manager
Windows 8.1 File Recovery drive
Windows 8.1 System Restore
Windows Hardware Quality Labs (WHQL)
Windows Performance Analyzer (WPA)
Windows Performance Recorder (WPR)
Windows Performance Toolkit (WPT)

◼ Resolving Hardware and Device Issues

↓ THE BOTTOM LINE   In combination with Windows Server 2012 R2, Windows 8.1 provides several tools you can use to manage hardware and printers on your network.

On a Windows 8.1 computer, you use Device Manager to identify and resolve hardware and device issues. You can use the ***Roll Back Driver*** recovery feature to reinstall device drivers after a newer driver fails.

Using Device Manager

Device Manager enables you to install and update drivers for your hardware devices, make changes to the hardware settings on a device, and troubleshoot hardware configuration problems.

CERTIFICATION READY
Resolve hardware and device issues, including STOP errors and Reliability Monitor
Objective 3.1

Device Manager can be found in the Control Panel in Windows 8.1. The easiest way to access the tool is to press the *Windows logo key + w*, type *Device Manager*, and then select it from *Results*.

After you open the tool, drill down to Device Manager, which provides you with a detailed listing of all devices installed on the computer.

➕ MORE INFORMATION
When you install a device, Windows Update checks for the latest drivers if you have Automatic Updates enabled. You will learn more about Windows Update in Lesson 11.

By default, devices are listed alphabetically by device type, but you can adjust them (select View from the menu) to Device by type or connection, and Resource by type or connection.

To update a driver for a device, scan for hardware changes, view the device's properties, or disable or uninstall a device, right-click and select the option from the menu (see Figure 9-1). To view a device's properties, double-click the device.

Figure 9-1

Reviewing options for
configuring devices

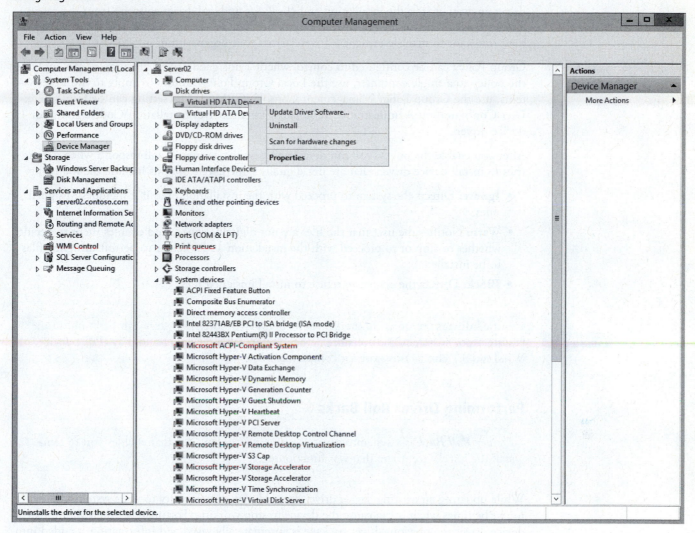

Exploring Driver Signing

> **Driver signing** ensures the device drivers used by Windows include a digital signature.
> This digital signature indicates who the publisher of the software is and can alert you if
> the driver has been altered form its original contents.

For each piece of hardware in your computer, there is a device driver. Windows 8.1 interacts
with the device driver rather than the device itself by calling functions in the drivers that carry
out the actions on the device. The driver files provided with Windows 8.1 have been digitally signed. This means they have been tested and verified for compatibility, reliability, and
functionality with Windows 8.1. These tests, conducted by the **Windows Hardware Quality
Labs (WHQL)**, are designed to ensure that your system maintains stability. The signature is
also designed to ensure that the file has not been overwritten by another program as part of
its installation process or has been altered from its original package contents.

When you install a driver, Windows checks the driver's digital signature. When the driver is not signed by Microsoft, a message displays alerting you to the fact that *Windows cannot verify the digital signature for the drivers required for this device . . .* You can then choose to install the driver anyway or stop the installation and check for updated driver software from the manufacturer's website. Although this is the default behavior, you can use Group Policy to control how you want to manage unsigned drivers across your organization.

Group Policy can be configured to control whether unsigned drivers are allowed. To apply the policy to a single computer, use the Local Group Policy Editor. To apply to multiple systems, use the Group Policy Management Console (GPMC). The setting can be found here: User Configuration\Administrative Templates\System\Driver Installation\Code signing for device drivers.

After you enable the policy, you can determine how the computer will respond when a user tries to install device drivers that are not digitally signed. The options include the following:

- **Ignore:** Directs the system to proceed with the installation even if it includes unsigned files.
- **Warn:** Notifies the user that the files are not digitally signed, and enables them to decide whether to stop or to proceed with the installation and whether to permit unsigned files to be installed.
- **Block:** Directs the system to refuse to install unsigned files.

TAKE NOTE* Certified drivers are stored in the Windows 8.1 driver store. This store can be found in the %systemroot%\system23\driverstore. When you install a new plug-and-play (PnP) device, Windows 8.1 checks this store for compatible drivers.

Performing Driver Roll Backs

Driver Roll Back is a system recovery feature in Windows 8.1 that enables you to reinstall the last device driver that was functioning.

While updating an existing device driver can add new functionality to your system, there might be times when it can cause the device to stop working. Fortunately, when you update a device driver the previous driver package is automatically saved and information is added into the registry. This allows you to roll back one prior driver version.

If the current driver is the only one that was ever installed, the Roll Back feature is not available. Roll Back is not available if you have not updated the driver in the past.

 ROLL BACK A DEVICE DRIVER

GET READY. To roll back a device driver, log in with local Administrative privileges and then perform the following steps:

1. Press the **Windows logo key + w** and then type **Device Manager**.
2. Choose **Device Manager** from the *Results*.
3. Expand **Network Adapters**.
4. Right-click the adapter and choose **Update Driver Software**.
5. Click **Browse my computer for driver software**.
6. Click **Let me pick from a list of device drivers on my computer**.
7. Deselect **Show compatible hardware**.

8. Click **Marvel** for the manufacturer and click **Marvel 3COM 3C2000-T Gigabit Adapter** for the network adapter and then click **Next**.

9. When the *Update Driver Warning* message appears, click **Yes**.

10. When the *Windows has successfully updated your driver software* message appears, click **Close**.

11. Click **Yes** to restart the computer and then log back in.

12. Press the **Windows logo key + w**, type **Device Manager**, and then choose it from *Results*.

13. Expand **Network Adapters** and then locate the network adapter you updated the driver for.

14. Right-click the adapter and choose **Properties**.

15. Click the **Driver** tab and then click **Roll Back Driver**.

16. When prompted to roll back the driver, click **Yes**.

17. Click **Close** to exit out of the *Adapter Properties* dialog box and then close the *Device Manager* window.

Identifying Problem Devices

Device Manager also displays all of the devices installed on your computer. When a device is experiencing problems, Device Manager uses symbols to provide information about the particular error condition.

When there is an issue with a device, you will see one of the following symbols (each symbol represents a specific type of problem):

- Blue question mark inside white circle: Driver installed; may not provide full functionality.
- Red "X": Disabled device: device is installed in computer and is consuming resources; protected mode driver not loaded; device installed improperly.
- Black exclamation point on yellow field: Device in problem state; the device might be functioning; problem code will be displayed with device.
- Blue "I" on white field: Use automatic settings not selected for device; resource was manually selected; does not indicate a problem or disabled state.
- Problem code: Code explaining the problem with the device.
- White circle with down arrow: Device was disabled by an administrator or user.
- Yellow warning symbol with exclamation point: There is a problem with the device.

Troubleshooting Problem Devices

TAKE NOTE *

To disable a problem device in Device Manager, right-click it and choose Disable.

The *Action Center* shows important notifications related to the security and maintenance of your computer. When problems occur, you will be alerted to investigate them further.

Windows 8.1 uses built-in hardware diagnostics to detect hardware problems on your computer. When problems are identified, a message appears that lets you know about the problem. If you select the message, you will be taken to the Action Center, which provides a central location to view any problems with your hardware or software.

When there is a problem, you will see two types of messages in the notification area (bottom-right corner of your desktop):

- Red items (white flag, red circle with white x): These are important messages that indicate a significant problem that needs to be addressed. For example, your firewall is turned off, or spyware or antivirus applications need to be updated.

- Yellow items: These are messages that suggest tasks that can make your computer run better. For example, updating an application or configuring Windows Update to automatically download and install updates rather than checking with you beforehand.

How you troubleshoot a device depends upon the type of problem you encounter. For example, let's say you notice a USB printer device under Other Devices that has a white circle with a blue question mark. Windows places devices that don't have a device driver available under this folder. If you double-click the device and navigate to the Driver tab, you can gain more information about the problem with the device.

Figure 9-2 shows that the driver provider is unknown and there is no information on a driver at all. If you click the Driver Details button, you will receive a message indicating there are no driver files loaded for the device.

Figure 9-2

Troubleshooting a USB device

At this point, you can click Update Driver and allow Windows 8.1 to search automatically for an updated driver, or browse your computer for the device driver. If you allow Windows 8.1 to search automatically, and it does not locate a device, you will be prompted to visit the manufacturer's website to check for updated drivers.

In this situation, the USB device is an HP LaserJet 1018 printer that is not supported on Windows 8.1.

Refreshing or Resetting Your PC

Sometimes you might want to refresh, reset, or restore a PC to clean up the PC or to put the PC back to a new state. Refreshing your PC reinstalls Windows and keeps your personal files and settings. It also keeps the apps that came with your PC and the apps you installed from the Windows Store. Resetting your PC reinstalls Windows but deletes your files, settings, and apps, except for the apps that came with your PC. Restoring your PC is a way to undo recent system changes you've made.

In most cases, when you start to refresh or reset your PC, it will finish on its own. However, if Windows needs missing files, you'll be asked to insert recovery media, which is typically on a DVD disc or thumb drive.

 REFRESH YOUR PC

GET READY. To perform a PC Refresh or PC Reset on a computer running Windows 8.1, log in with local Administrative privileges and then perform the following steps:

1. Insert your Windows 8.1 installation media.
2. Swipe in from the right edge of the screen, tap **Settings**, and then tap **Change PC settings**. Alternatively, you can point to the upper-right corner of the screen, move the mouse pointer down, click **Settings**, and then click **Change PC settings**.
3. Tap or click **Update and recovery**, and then tap or click **Recovery**.

   Figure 9-3 shows the Recovery options.

Figure 9-3

Refreshing your PC

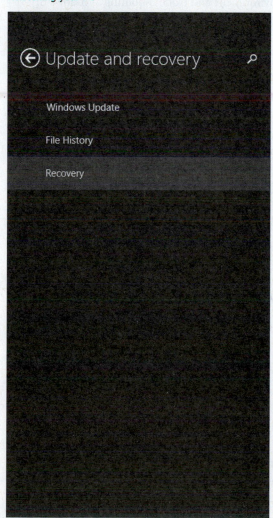

Refresh your PC without affecting your files

If your PC isn't running well, you can refresh it without losing your photos, music, videos, and other personal files.

Get started

Remove everything and reinstall Windows

If you want to recycle your PC or start over completely, you can reset it to its factory settings.

Get started

Advanced startup

Start up from a device or disc (such as a USB drive or DVD), change Windows startup settings, or restore Windows from a system image. This will restart your PC.

Restart now

4. Under *Refresh your PC without affecting your files*, tap or click **Get started**. If you want to perform a PC Reset, then under the *Remove everything and reinstall Windows* section, click **Get started**.

5. On the *Refresh your PC* page, click **Next**.

6. On the *Ready to refresh your PC* page, click **Refresh**. The computer restarts.

7. On the *Windows 8.1 lock* screen, press the **space bar** and then type your password to log in.

If your Windows 8.1 computer has traditional applications that were installed from a disc or from other websites, they are removed from your computer during a PC Refresh. Windows puts a link to a list of the removed applications on your desktop. If you click the link, you see a list of the applications removed. Clicking the application's name directs you to the manufacturer's website from which you can download and reinstall it.

Creating a Windows 8.1 File Recovery Drive

If your system fails to boot and you do not have access to the installation media, you can create a recovery drive that includes a boot environment and troubleshooting Windows 8.1 tools to regain access to your computer.

With improvements in operating system design, system crashes have been reduced over the years. The keyword in that last sentence is *reduced*, not eliminated; therefore, it's important to have the right tools in place to recover from a system failure even when you can't start your Windows 8.1 system.

A **Windows 8.1 File Recovery drive** can help by providing enough of a boot environment to get you back into the system so you can begin the troubleshooting process It can be used to refresh or reset your computer, restore your computer to a previously created system restore point, recover your Windows installation from a specific system image file, automatically fix startup problems, and perform advanced troubleshooting from the command prompt.

If you create a Windows 8.1 File Recovery drive on a Windows 8.1 32-bit system, you cannot use it to repair a 64-bit system, and vice versa.

After creating the recovery drive, you need to enable your system to boot from a USB device in the basic input/output system (BIOS). When booting into the drive, you see the Windows logo displayed on a black screen and then you are prompted to choose your keyboard layout. This takes you to the *Choose an option* screen, on which you can access the troubleshooting tools and start troubleshooting your computer.

 CREATE A WINDOWS 8.1 RECOVERY DRIVE

GET READY. To create a recovery drive, log in with local Administrative privileges and then perform the following steps:

1. Connect a USB drive to your computer. The drive must hold at least 256 MB and all data on the drive deleted.

2. Press the **Windows logo key + w** and then type **Create recovery drive**.

3. From *Results*, click **Create a Recovery Drive**.

4. If you're prompted to *Allow the Recovery Media Center to make changes to the computer*, click **Yes**.

5. Click **Next**. Windows 8.1 searches and displays the available drives.

6. Click **Next** to use the drive you inserted.

7. After reviewing the *Everything on the drive will be deleted* message, click **Create**.

8. Click **Finish**.

Using Reliability Monitor

> *Reliability Monitor* is a Control Panel/Action Panel tool that measures hardware and software problems and other changes to your computer that could affect the reliability of the computer.

CERTIFICATION READY
Resolve hardware and device issues, including STOP errors and Reliability Monitor
Objective 3.1

The Reliability Monitor provides a stability index that ranges from 1 (the least stable) to 10 (the most stable). You can use the index to help evaluate the reliability of your computer. Any change you make to your computer or problem that occurs on your computer affects the stability index.

To open the Reliability Monitor, execute the following command at a command prompt:

```
perfmon /rel
```

Or you can open it from Performance Monitor.

In the Reliability Monitor (see Figure 9-4), you can:

Figure 9-4

Viewing the Reliability Monitor information

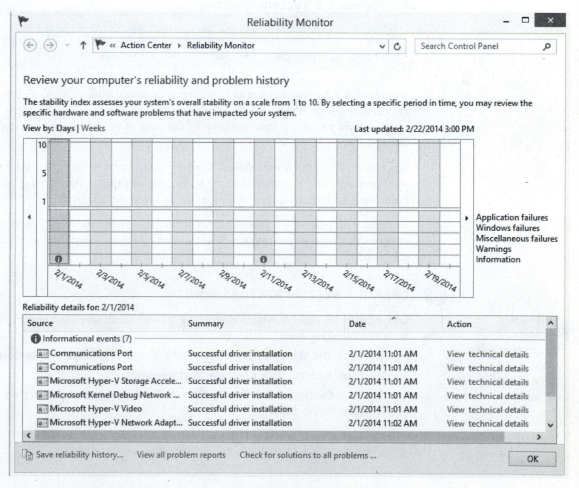

- Click any event on the graph to view its details.
- Click *Days* or *Weeks* to view the stability index over a specific period of time.
- Click items in the *Action* column to view more information about each event.
- At the bottom of the page, click *View all problem reports* to view only the problems that have occurred on your computer. This view doesn't include the other computer events that show up in Reliability Monitor, such as events about software installation.

If the Reliability Monitor is blank, you need to enable Reliability Monitor.

 ENABLE RELIABILITY MONITOR

GET READY. To enable Reliability Monitor, perform the following steps:

1. Open **Task Scheduler** and navigate to **\Microsoft\Windows\RAC\RacTask**.
2. Right-click **RacTask** and choose **Enable**.
3. Right-click **RacTask** and choose **Run**.
4. Use the **Registry Editor** to change the **HKEY_LOCAL_MACHINE\SOFTWARE\ Microsoft\Reliability Analysis\WMI\WMIEnable** value to **1**.
5. Reboot the computer.

After you reboot the computer, it might take several hours for it to compile the data that will be displayed in the Reliability Monitor.

Performing a System Restore

> Windows 8.1 System Restore is another recovery option for your computer; it backs up your settings and registry, but does not back up your personal data.

Windows 8.1 System Restore saves information about your drivers, registry settings, programs, and system files in the form of restore points for drives with system protection turned on. A *restore point* is a representation of the state of your computer's system files and settings.

You can then use the restore points to return these items to an earlier state without affecting your personal files. You should create restore points prior to performing any major system event such as the installation of a program or a new device driver.

By default, Windows 8.1 automatically creates restore points every 7 days if you have not created one during that time period. You can also create restore points manually any time you want.

 CREATE A SYSTEM RESTORE POINT

GET READY. To create a System Restore, log in with local Administrative privileges and then perform the following steps:

1. Press the **Windows logo key + w** and then type **System Restore**.
2. From *Results*, click **Create a Restore point**.
3. Click **Configure** and then make sure **Turn on system protection** is selected (see Figure 9-5).

Figure 9-5

Confirming system protection
is enabled

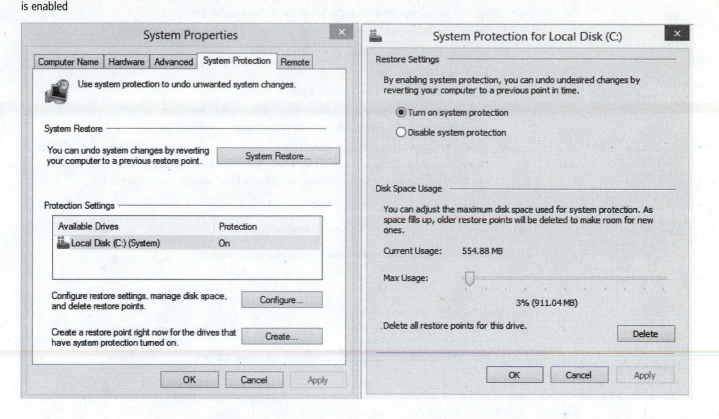

4. Drag the *Max Usage* slider to **10%**.

   This adjusts the disk space for system protection. When the space fills up, older restore points are deleted to make room for new ones.

5. Click **Apply** and then click **OK**.

6. Click **Create** to create a new restore point.

7. In the *Description* text box, type a description that describes the application or device driver that you are installing or the change that you are making.

8. Click **Create**.

9. When notified that the restore point was created successfully, click **Close**.

10. Click **OK** to accept your settings and to close the *System Properties* dialog box.

In most cases, you want to restore the most recent restore point, but you can choose from a list of restore points if you have more than one. The best approach is to use the restore point that was created just before you starting experiencing problems with your computer.

In the exercise that follows, assume that the installation of the application was completed, and your system is not functioning normally. To return your computer to a functioning state, use the restore point you just created.

PERFORM A SYSTEM RESTORE USING A RESTORE POINT

GET READY. To perform a System Restore using a restore point, log in with local Administrative privileges and then perform the following steps:

1. Press the **Windows logo key + w** and then type **System restore**.

2. From *Results*, click **Create a Restore point**.

3. Click **System Restore**.

4. Click **Next** to start the *System Restore Wizard*.

   A system restore does not affect your documents, pictures, or other personal data. Recently installed programs and drivers may be uninstalled.

5. Select the desired restore point (see Figure 9-6) and then click **Scan for affected programs**. After the scan is completed, you see any programs and drivers that will be deleted, as well as programs and drivers that might be restored.

Figure 9-6

Selecting a restore point

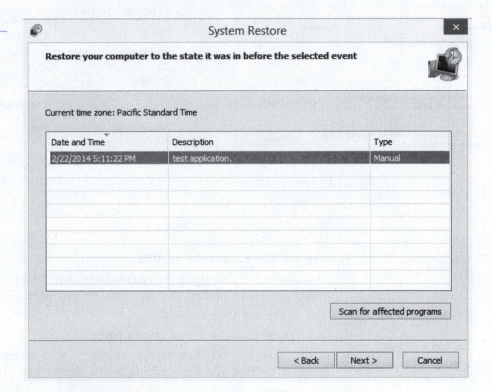

6. Click **Close** and then click **Next**.

7. Click **Finish**.

8. If you changed your Windows password, you should also create a password reset disk by pressing the **Windows logo key + w** and then searching for **Create a password reset disk**.

9. Click **Yes** to begin the system restore process.

   Windows restarts the computer, restores your files and settings, restores the registry, and removes temp files as part of the restore process.

10. When the restore process is completed, log back in to your system.

Resolving STOP Errors

A ***STOP error***—also referred to as the bluescreen, the Blue Screen of Death, or BSoD—is an error screen displayed when the kernel or a driver running in kernel mode encounters an unrecoverable error. With Windows 8.1, the STOP error has a blue screen with a ASCII frown face and the statement "Your PC ran into a problem and needs to restart" followed by the error message. Figure 9-7 shows a STOP error with the message *HAL_INITIALIZATION_FAILED*.

Figure 9-7

Viewing a Windows 8.1 STOP error

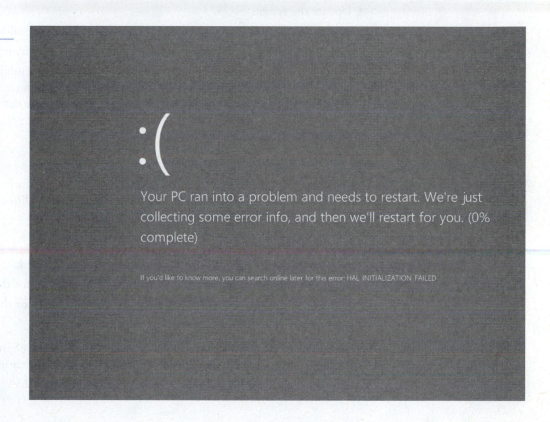

:(

Your PC ran into a problem and needs to restart. We're just collecting some error info, and then we'll restart for you. (0% complete)

If you'd like to know more, you can search online later for this error: HAL_INITIALIZATION_FAILED

CERTIFICATION READY
Resolve hardware and device issues, including STOP errors and Reliability Monitor
Objective 3.1

When a STOP error occurs, you must first consider the task you were performing at the time that the STOP error occurred and then research the error message that appears on the screen. Windows 8.1 STOP errors are collected in the Action Center and in Event Viewer System logs.

You can also check the Event Viewer System and Application logs for errors or warnings that might provide some clues for the BSOD.

If you were installing a new program, installing hardware, updating a driver, or installing an update when the STOP error occurred, this action likely caused the STOP error. To undo the action, you can try one of the following:

- Start up the computer using Last Known Good Configuration.
- Use System Restore to undo recent system changes.
- Roll back the device driver to the prior version.

In all cases, you should check the following:

- Verify that you have sufficient free disk space in the Windows partition.
- Check for viruses and other forms of malware.
- Apply all available Windows service packs and other updates.
- Update drivers for your hardware.
- Return hardware settings to their default settings in Device Manager.
- Return BIOS settings to their default levels.
- Update the system BIOS.
- Make sure all cables, memory components, and cards are installed and seated properly.
- Perform diagnostic tests on all hardware, including system memory and hard disk drives.
- Start your computer in Safe mode, which will load only essential hardware and software components, helping you isolate the problem. If your computer starts successfully, it proves that one of the removed hardware devices or software components was the cause of the STOP message.
- Perform a PC reset.
- Check for faulty hardware devices.

If your computer crashes and you still cannot figure out why it crashes, you might need to look at a memory dump. The memory dump file contains the following information:

- The Stop message, its parameters, and other data.
- A list of loaded drivers.
- The processor context (PRCB) for the processor that stopped.
- The process information and kernel context (EPROCESS) for the process that stopped.
- The process information and kernel context (ETHREAD) for the thread that stopped.
- The Kernel-mode call stack for the thread that stopped.

Windows keeps a list of all the small memory dump files in the %SystemRoot%\MEMORY. DMP folder. While this contains valuable information, the information might only be useful for Microsoft or other support personnel. The Complete memory dump will write everything that is memory.

 SPECIFY THE TYPE OF MEMORY DUMP

GET READY. To specify the type of memory dump, perform the following steps:

1. Right-click the **Start** menu and choose **System**.
2. When the System window opens, click **Advanced system settings**.
3. In the *System Properties* dialog box, under *Startup and Recovery*, click **Settings**.
4. In the *Startup and Recovery* dialog box (see Figure 9-8), under the *Write debugging information* section, select the type of memory dump. The default is **Automatic memory dump**.

Figure 9-8

Selecting the type of memory dump

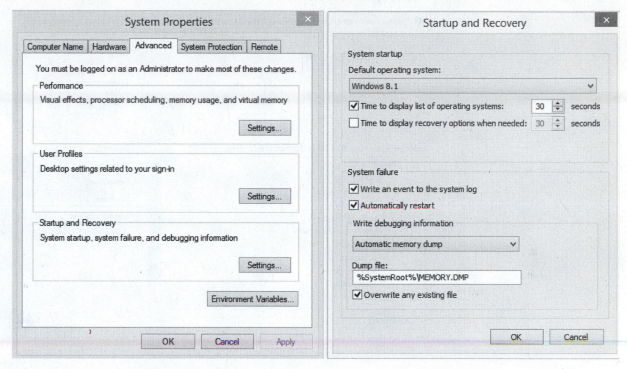

5. Click **OK** to close the *Startup and Recovery* dialog box and then click **OK** to close the *System Properties* dialog box.

■ Optimizing Performance by using Windows Performance Toolkit (WPT)

THE BOTTOM LINE

The ***Windows Performance Toolkit (WPT)***, which is part of the Windows Assessment and Deployment Kit (ADK) and the windows Software Developer Kit (SDK), contains the ***Windows Performance Recorder (WPR)*** and ***Windows Performance Analyzer (WPA)***. WPR is a recording tool that creates Event Tracing for Windows (EDW recordings), which can be analyzed when performing certain activities. WPA is a graphical analysis tool with graphic capabilities and data tables with full text search capabilities that can help explore the root cause of performance problems.

CERTIFICATION READY
Optimize performance by using Windows Performance Toolkit (WPT), including Xperf.exe, Xbootmgr.exe, XperfView.exe, and Windows Performance Recorder (WPR)
Objective 3.1

In Windows Performance Recorder, to start Recording events, click the Start button; WPR will record using the default settings from the General profile. WPR recording profiles contain all the information that is necessary to enable performance recording for a specific scenario. If you click *More options*, you can select additional profiles to record, such as CPU usage and Disk I/O activity (see Figure 9-9). You can include multiple profiles in a single recording. You can also author and add custom profiles (.wprp files) to record sets of events.

Figure 9-9

Using Windows Performance Recorder

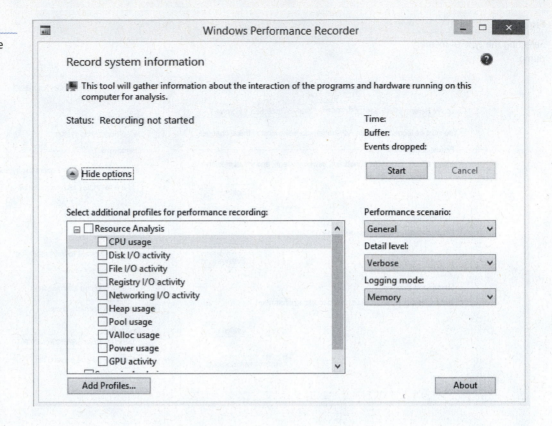

You can select a detail level (Light or Verbose) for each recording. The Light detail level is used primarily for timing recordings. The Verbose detail level provides the detailed information that you need for analysis.

WPR can log events either to a sequential file or to circular buffers in memory. Logging to a file is used for short traces, when you know when to expect the events that you want to trace. Logging to memory is used for continuous tracing, when you want to log events that can occur at any time. In some scenarios, you might want to run both types of logging. When you are done recording, you then click Save.

After you have saved the recording, you will then analyze the recording with WPA. WPA consists of a collection of docked windows that surround a central workspace. When you open a recording in WPA, thumbnails of all the graphs that apply to that recording appear in the Graph Explorer window.

To expand/analyze a graph, click the small triangle next to the graph name and drag the graph to the Analysis tab (see Figure 9-10). You can use the right drop-down arrow on the graph title bar to change from a line graph to a stacked-line graph or to a stacked-bar graph. You can use the left drop-down arrow on the graph title bar to select different parameters for the graph (if more parameters are available). For example, you can view CPU usage by process, by CPU, or by process and thread.

Figure 9-10

Using Windows Performance
Analyzer

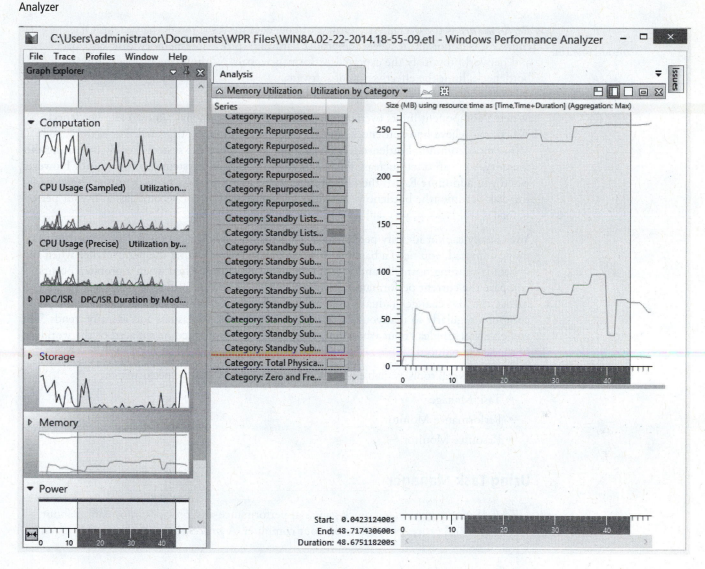

If there are any issues identified by WPA, those issues will be shown in the Details window.
When you click an issue in this window, details for that issue appear in the Details window.

The executables/commands for the Windows Performance Toolkit are:

- xperf.exe: Windows Performer Recorder Captures
- xperfview.exe: Windows Performance Analyzer
- xbootmgr.exe: Automates on/off state transitions and captures traces during these
  transitions

■ Monitoring Performance

Performance is the overall effectiveness of how data moves through the system. Of course, it is important to select the proper hardware (processor, memory, disk system, and network) to satisfy the expected performance goals. Without the proper hardware, bottlenecks limit the effectiveness of software.

When a component limits overall performance, that component is known as a bottleneck. When you relieve one bottleneck, another bottleneck might be triggered. For example, one of the most common bottlenecks is the amount of memory the system has. By increasing the memory, you can often increase the overall performance of a system (up to a point). However, when you add more RAM, then RAM needs to be fed more data from the disk. Therefore, the disk becomes the bottleneck. So, although the system might become faster, if your performance is still lacking, you will have to look for new bottlenecks.

You usually cannot identify performance problems just by taking a quick look at performance. Instead, you need a baseline. You can get one by analyzing the performance when the system is running normally and within design specifications. Then when a problem occurs, compare the current performance to your baseline to see what is different. Because performance can also change gradually over time, it is highly recommended that you baseline your computer regularly so that you can chart your performance measures and identify trends. This will give you an idea about when the server needs to be upgraded or replaced or the workload of the server reduced.

There are several tools available with Windows for you to analyze performance:

- Task Manager
- Performance Monitor
- Resource Monitor

Using Task Manager

Task Manager gives you a quick glance at performance and provides information about programs and processes running on your computer. A **process** is an instance of a program that is being executed.

Task Manager is one of the handiest programs you can use to take a quick glance at performance to see which programs are using the most system resources on your computer. You can see the status of running programs and programs that have stopped responding, and you can stop a program running in memory.

To start Task Manager, right-click the empty space on the taskbar and choose *Task Manager* (or you can open the Security menu by pressing the *Ctrl+Alt+Del* keys and choosing *Start Task Manager*). When Task Manager starts, it displays only the running applications.

Click the *More Details* down-arrow to show the available tabs (see Figure 9-11). When you first start the Performance Monitor on a computer running Windows 8.1, five tabs are opened for Task Manager:

- Processes
- Performance
- App history
- Startup

CERTIFICATION READY
Monitor performance by using Data Collector Sets, Task Manager, and Resource Monitor
Objective 3.1

- Users
- Details
- Services

Figure 9-11

Viewing the Task Manager tabs

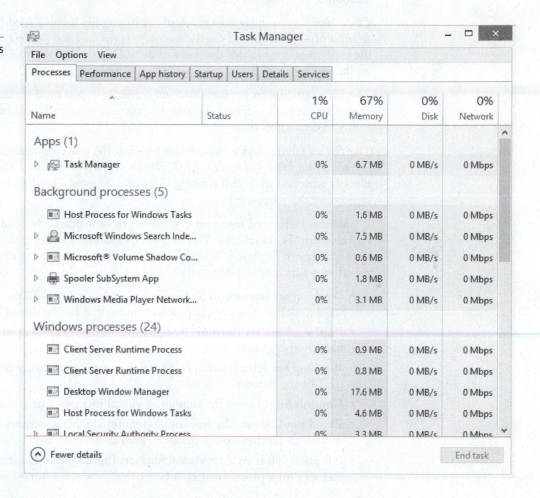

The Processes tab shows all processes running in memory and how much processing and memory each process uses. The processes will display applications (as designated by apps), background processes, and Windows Processes. On the Processes tab, you can perform the following tasks:

- To see the processes that use the most CPU utilization and memory, click the *CPU* column header.
- To stop a process, right-click the process and choose *End task*.
- To jump to the *Details* tab for a particular process, right-click the process and choose *Go to details*.
- If you want to see the executable that is running the processes, right-click the process and choose *Open file location*.

The *Performance* tab displays the amount of *CPU* usage, physical *Memory* usage, and *Ethernet* throughput. For CPU usage, a high percentage indicates the programs or processes are requiring a lot of CPU resources, which can slow your computer. If the percentage seems frozen at or near 100%, then a program might not be responding.

The *App history* tab shows the usage of applications by CPU time. It also displays the amount of network and metered network that each application transfers in megabytes.

The *Startup* tab shows the programs that are configured to automatically start when you start Windows. You can disable the startup programs by right-clicking an item and clicking disable. You can also access the properties of the program file for the application, and the location of the program file.

Click *Memory* to display how much of the paging file is being used (*In use* and *Available*), the amount of *Committed* and *Cached* memory, *Paged pool* and *Non-paged pool*. It also shows you the total amount of RAM, the *Speed* of the RAM, and the number of *Slots used* for memory on the motherboard.

The *Users* tab displays the users who are currently logged in, the amount of CPU and memory usage that the each user is using, and the processes the user is running. It also gives you the ability to disconnect them.

The *Details* tab displays a more detailed look at the processes running on the computer, including the *Process Identification (PID)*. The PID is comprised of unique numbers that identify a process while it is running. Similarly, you can stop the process and you can increase or decrease the process priority.

If you are an advanced user, you might want to view other advanced memory values on the Processes tab. To do so, click View > Select Columns and then select or deselect values to be displayed or not displayed. While there are nearly 40 columns to display, some of the more useful values include the following:

- **Working set (memory):** Shows the amount of memory in the private working set plus the amount of memory the process is using that can be shared by other processes.
- **Peak working set (memory):** Shows the maximum amount of working set memory used by the process.
- **Working set delta (memory):** Shows the amount of change in working set memory used by the process.
- **Commit Size:** Shows the amount of virtual memory that is reserved for use by a process.
- **Paged pool:** Shows the amount of committed virtual memory for a process that can be written to another storage medium, such as the hard disk.
- **NP pool:** NP is an abbreviation for Non-Paged. Shows the amount of committed virtual memory for a process that can't be written to another storage medium.

The *Services* tab displays all services on the computer that are running and not running. Similar to the Services console, you can start, stop, or restart services.

Using Resource Monitor

Resource Monitor is a system tool that allows you to view information about the use of hardware (CPU, memory, disk, and network) and software resources (file handlers and modules) in real time. You can filter the results according to specific processes or services that you want to monitor. In addition, you can use Resource Monitor to start, stop, suspend, and resume processes and services, and to troubleshoot when an application does not respond as expected.

CERTIFICATION READY
Monitor performance by using Data Collector Sets, Task Manager, and Resource Monitor
Objective 3.1

Resource Monitor (see Figure 9-12) is a powerful tool for understanding how your system resources are used by processes and services. In addition to monitoring resource usage in real time, Resource Monitor can help you analyze unresponsive processes, identify which applications are using files, and control processes and services. To start Resource Monitor, start Server Manager and click *Tools > Resource Monitor*. Or you can use Windows PowerShell and execute the `resmon.exe` command.

Figure 9-12

Viewing Resource Monitor

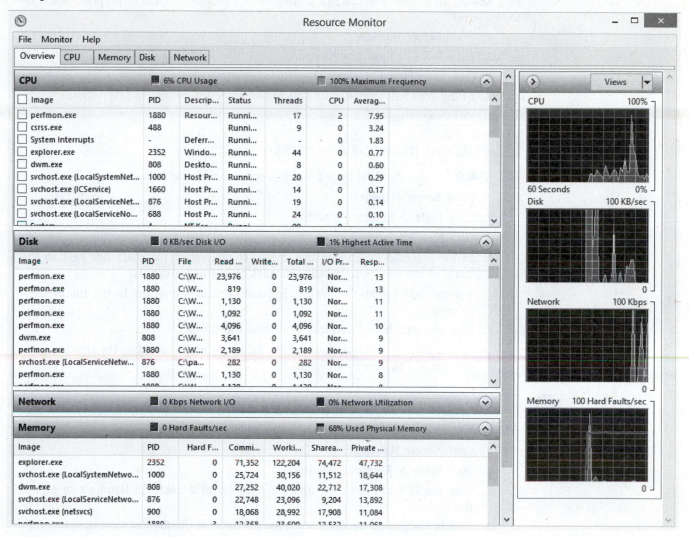

Resource Monitor includes five tabs:

- Overview
- CPU
- Memory
- Disk
- Network

The *Overview* tab displays basic system resource usage information; the other tabs display information about each specific resource. Each tab in Resource Monitor includes multiple tables that display detailed information about the resource featured on that respective tab.

The next four exercises cover common tasks for which to use the resource monitor. For example, if you want to find determine the program (process) that is hogging the processor resources, you can use *Identify the highest current CPU usage*. If a file is locked and you cannot delete it because it is in use, you can use the *Identify the process that is using a file exercise* to see which process has the file open.

IDENTIFY THE HIGHEST CURRENT CPU USAGE

GET READY. To identify a process that is using the highest current CPU usage, perform the following steps:

1. Open **Server Manager**.
2. Click **Tools > Resource Monitor**.
3. Click the **CPU** tab.
4. In the *Processes* section, click **CPU** to sort processes by current CPU resource consumption.

 VIEW THE CPU USAGE OF A PROCESS

GET READY. To view the CPU usage for each process, perform the following steps:

1. Open **Server Manager**.
2. Click **Tools > Resource Monitor**.
3. Click the **CPU** tab.
4. In the *Processes* section, in the *Image* column, select the check box next to the name of the service for which you want to see usage details.

   You can select multiple services. Selected services are moved to the top of the column.
5. Click the title bar of **Services** to expand the table.

   Review the data in Services to see the list of processes hosted by the selected services and to view their CPU usage.

 IDENTIFY THE PROCESS THAT IS USING A FILE

GET READY. To identify the process that is using a file, perform the following steps:

1. Open **Server Manager**.
2. Click **Tools > Resource Monitor**.
3. Click the **CPU** tab and then click the title bar of **Associated Handlers** to expand the table.
4. Click in the **Search Handlers** box, type the name of the file you want to search for, and then click **Search**.

 IDENTIFY THE NETWORK ADDRESS TO WHICH A PROCESS IS CONNECTED

GET READY. To identify the network address that a process is connected to, perform the following steps:

1. Open **Server Manager**.
2. Click **Tools > Resource Monitor**.
3. Click the **Network** tab and then click the title bar of **TCP Connections** to expand the table.
4. Locate the process whose network connection you want to identify. If there are a large number of entries in the table, click **Image** to sort by executable filename.
5. Review the *Remote Address* column and the *Remote Port* column to see which network address and port the process is connected to.

Using Performance Monitor

Performance Monitor is an Microsoft Management Console snap-in that provides tools for analyzing system performance. It is included in the Computer Management and it can be opened as a stand-alone console from Administrative Tools. It can also be started by executing the `perfmon` command. From a single console, you can monitor application and hardware performance in real time, specify which data you want to collect in logs, define thresholds for alerts and automatic actions, generate reports, and view past performance data in a variety of ways.

Performance Monitor (see Figure 9-13) provides a visual display of built-in Windows performance counters, either in real time or as a way to review historical data.

Figure 9-13

Viewing Performance Monitor

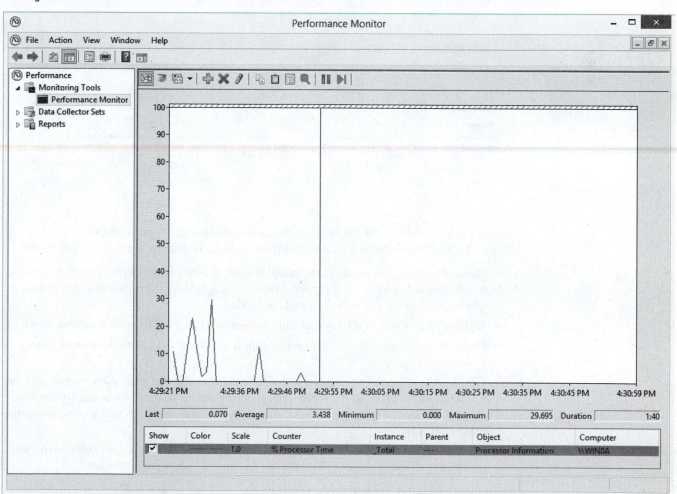

You can add performance counters to Performance Monitor by right-clicking the main pane and choosing Add Counters. Another way to add performance counters is to create and use custom Data Collector Sets. (Data Collector Sets will be explained later in this lesson.) Figure 9-14 shows the Add Counters dialog box. You can create custom views that can be exported as Data Collector Sets for use with performance and logging features.

Figure 9-14

Adding counters to
Performance Monitor

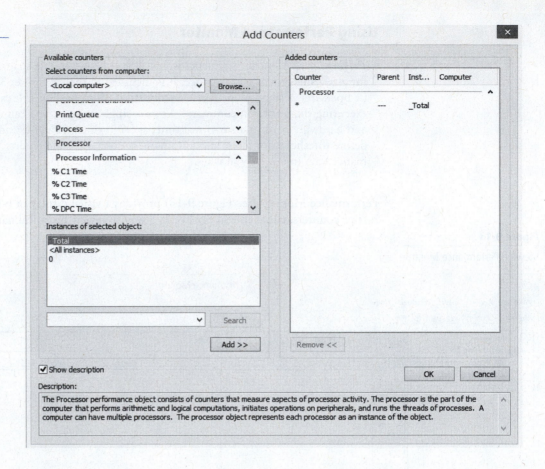

To control how and what is displayed, right-click Performance Monitor and choose
Properties. The Performance Monitor Properties dialog box displays the following five tabs:

- **General:** Allows you to adjust the samples, such as how often samples are taken and how
  much data is displayed on the graph before the graph is redrawn. You can also choose to
  display the legend, the value bar, and the toolbar.

- **Source:** Allows you to display real-time data or to open a log file that you have saved.

- **Data:** Allows you to choose counters to appear as well as the color and scale of those
  counters.

- **Graph:** Allows you to configure the available views and if the view starts over or you can
  scroll to look at previous displayed data. It allows you to display or not display the vertical grid, horizontal grid, vertical scale numbers, time axis labels, as well as determine the
  maximum scale.

- **Appearance:** Allows you to display the color and fonts used by various components so
  that you can distinguish one Performance Monitor window from another.

Performance Monitor has multiple graph types that enable you to visually review performance
log data. They include:

- **Line:** The default graph type; connects points of data with lines.

- **Histogram Bar:** A bar graph showing data.

- **Report:** Values are displayed as text.

Performance programs and performance information is not available to everyone. Therefore, if a user needs to use Performance Monitor to view performance information, the user can be added to one of the following groups:

- Administrators can access all of the performance tools and data.
- Performance Monitor Users can view both real-time and historical data within the Performance Monitor console and can use the Reliability Monitor. However, they cannot create or modify Data Collector Sets or use the Resource View.
- Performance Log Users group can view both real-time data and historical data within the Performance Monitor console. However, these users can create or modify Data Collector Sets if the user has *Log on as a batch user* rights on the server.

Using Common Performance Counters

As previously mentioned, there are hundreds of counters available in Performance Monitor and as you add other services or applications (such as Microsoft Exchange or Microsoft SQL Server), other counters are made available that will allow you to monitor the performance of those applications. Although using all of these counters might take some heavy research, you should always start with some basic performance counters to get a glimpse on how your system is running.

A computer is comprised of four primary systems: a processor, memory, disk, and a network. For the processor, memory, and disk performance, you should always start with these counters:

- Processor: % Processor Time measures how busy the processor is. Although the processor might jump to 100 percent processor usage, the processor should not be working at 80 percent capacity most of the time. If it is, you should upgrade the processor (using a faster processor or add additional processors) or move some of the services to other systems.
- A page fault occurs when a process attempts to access a virtual memory page that is not available in its working set in RAM. If the pages/sec is 1,000 or higher, you should increase the memory.
- Paging File: % Usage shows how much of the paging file is actually being used. If the paging file % usage is above 75%, you might need to increase memory or reduce the server's memory usage.
- Physical Disk: % Disk Time indicates how busy a disk is as measured by the percentage of time that disk was busy. If a disk is consistently approaching 100%, the disk is being over utilized.
- Physical Disk: % Avg. Disk Queue Length is the average number of read requests or write requests queued for the disk in question. A sustained average higher than two times the number of spindles (physical hard drives) indicates that the disk is being over utilized.

Configuring Data Collector Sets (DCS)

Rather than add individual performance counters each time you want to view the performance of a system, you can create **Data Collector Sets (DCS)** that allow you to organize a set of performance counts, event traces, and system configuration data into a single object that can be reused as needed.

Windows Performance Monitor uses performance counters, event trace data, and configuration information, which can be combined into Data Collector Sets as follows:

- Performance counters are measurements of system state or activity. They can be included in the operating system or can be part of individual applications. Windows Performance Monitor requests the current value of performance counters at specified time intervals.

- Event trace data is collected from trace providers, which are components of the operating system or of individual applications that report actions or events. Output from multiple trace providers can be combined into a trace session.

- Configuration information is collected from key values in the Windows registry.

Windows Performance Monitor can record the value of a registry key at a specified time or interval as part of a file.

 CREATE A DATA COLLECTOR SET (DCS)

GET READY. To create a DCS, perform the following steps:

1. Open **Server Manager**.
2. Click **Tools > Performance Monitor**.
3. In the left pane, expand **Data Collector Sets**.
4. Right-click the **User Defined** folder and choose **New > Data Collector Set**.
5. On the *Create new Data Collector Set* page, when you are prompted to create a new data collector set, type a name in the **Name** text box. Ensure that the **Create from a template (Recommended)** option is selected and then click **Next**.
6. When you are prompted to choose a template, click **System Performance** and then click **Next**.
7. When you are prompted to choose where you would like the data to be saved, click **Next**. If you run Performance Monitor to collect data over an extended period, you should change the location to a nonsystem data drive.
8. When you are prompted to create the data collector set, with the **Save and close** option selected, click **Finish**.
9. To start the Data Collector Set, right-click the DCS and choose **Start**.
10. Close **Performance Monitor**.

■ Monitoring and Managing Printers

THE BOTTOM LINE

Windows Server 2012 R2 provides the Server Manager and the Print Management snap-in to manage printers and print servers in your organization. Windows 8.1 and Windows Server 2012 R2 have also introduced new features that will make the process of monitoring and managing print servers much easier.

Before we review these new features, let's cover a few terms that you need to be familiar with:

- *Print device:* The actual physical hardware that prints the data.
- *Printer:* The software interface that is used by your operating system to deliver requests to the physical print device.
- *Print server:* A computer that is connected to and shares one or more print devices.

- ***Print driver:*** The software used by the operating system to convert your print commands into a printer language (Printer Control Language (PCL)/PostScript). It also tells the operating system about the attributes or capabilities of the printer.

- ***Spooling:*** The process of caching your print request to a hard disk. By spooling the print job, the operating system sends the print job to the background, enabling the application to resume rather than waiting for the job to finish.

- ***Print queue:*** A representation of a print device (physical printer) in Windows. Opening a print queue displays active print jobs and their status.

- ***Print Spooler service:*** A service that manages all the print jobs and print queues on a server.

Exploring the v4 Print Driver Model

The v4 print driver model includes changes to printer sharing known as enhanced Point and Print which eliminates the need to install cross platform drivers and removes the need to use the Print Server as a single distribution point for print drivers.

For Windows 8.1/Windows Server 2012 R2, Microsoft redesigned the print driver architecture used in previous releases of its operating systems. This new version (v4) offers several advantages over the previous release (v3). With v3 (available from Windows 2000 through Windows 7), you had to install specific drivers provided by the original equipment manufacturers (OEMs) for each printer, make sure the client and server used the same driver, and install separate drivers based on the client's architecture (32 vs. 64-bit). In v3, the print server also provided a central software distribution point to distribute printer drivers to clients who wanted to print to its shared printers.

As you can imagine, this accounted for a large number of drivers required to manage printers on the average network. It also forced Microsoft to include multiple printer drivers in the Windows installation media to ensure that users always had the appropriate drivers for any printer they were using. Thousands of other printer drivers were accessible via Windows Update.

TAKE NOTE Prior to Windows 8.1 and Windows Server 2012 R2, a large percentage of the Windows installation files consisted of driver files for printers that would never be used by the client. Windows 7 currently allocates about 450 MB of space for print drivers. Windows 8.1 uses about 185 MB.

To address these issues, Microsoft worked with OEMs to develop a new printer driver model (v4) that provides the following benefits:

- Separate drivers for client architecture (32/64-bit) are no longer required.

- Drivers are isolated to eliminate conflicts. These drivers are isolated from the print spooler process and loaded into a shared area with other isolated drivers. This keeps drivers that have a problem from affecting the print spooler process and other printers and drivers that are loaded. An administrator can also configure the drivers to run in a process that is separate from the spooler process and not shared with other printer drivers.

- Print class drivers that support a wide set of devices that use the same printer description language (PCL, PS, XPS) result in fewer drivers along with smaller drivers' files.

- The print server no longer serves as a software distribution point. Instead, the printer configuration and its capabilities are sent to the client who uses them without needing a specific printer driver.

Windows 8.1 and Windows Server 2012 R2 also use the new enhanced Point and Print feature. This feature allows users to connect to a shared printer without having to install the printer driver software. When the user connects to a print queue using a v4 driver from a client computer, the user's computer installs the print queue using the enhanced Point and Print process.

If the computer is running Windows 8.1, the driver will be downloaded from the local driver store, Windows Update, or Windows Server Update Services (WSUS). Users will not be prompted to provide credentials to install the driver but will see a printer installation indicator in their status bar. After the install is completed, the printer is ready to use.

> **TAKE NOTE***
>
> Systems prior to Windows 8 do not support the v4 print model, but can print to a v4 queue shared from a Windows Server 2012 R2 print server by using the enhanced Point and Print compatibility driver found on any print server running Windows Server 2012 R2.

Managing Printers

The ***Print and Document services role*** in Windows Server 2012 R2 allows you to centralize Print Server and network printer tasks. You can use it to monitor print queues and receive notifications when print jobs stop processing. You can also use it to migrate Print Servers and deploy printer connections using Group Policy.

In Windows Server 2012 R2, you can manage printers using one of the following:

- ***Server Manager:*** Displays print-related events from Event Viewer and includes an instance of the Print Management snap-in, but can only manage the local server.
- ***Print Management snap-in*** (included as part of the Print and Document Services/Print Server role): Manages multiple printers and print servers across your organization and migrates printers to and from other Windows print servers. This tool provides a single interface, enabling you to manage printers and printer servers running on Windows 2000, Windows XP, Windows Server 2003, Windows Server 2008, and Windows Server 2012 R2.

 INSTALL THE PRINT AND DOCUMENT SERVICES ROLE ON A DOMAIN CONTROLLER

GET READY. To set up the Print Management snap-in, perform the following steps:

> **TAKE NOTE***
>
> The following exercise requires a Windows Server 2012 R2 computer that is part of an Active Directory domain.

1. Log on to your domain controller with administrative privileges. The Server Manager will start automatically. If it does not start, select the Server Manager icon from the task bar.
2. Click **Manage > Add Roles and Features**.
3. On the *Before you begin* screen, click **Next**.
4. Click **Next** to accept the default setting *Role-based or feature-based installation*.
5. Choose your domain controller form the Server Pool and click **Next**.
6. On the *Select server roles* screen, select **Print and Document Services**.
7. In the *Add Roles and Features Wizard* dialog box, click **Add Features** and then click **Next**.
8. On the *Select server roles* screen, click **Next**.
9. On the *Select features* screen, click **Next**.
10. On the *Print and Document Services* screen, click **Next**.
11. Select **Print Server** and then click **Next**.

12. Select **Restart the destination server automatically if required** and then, when you're prompted to allow automatic restarts, click **Yes**.

13. Click **Install**.

14. When the installation is completed, click **Close**.

During the installation, you selected Print Server as the role service. This adds the Print Management console (see Figure 9-15), which is used to manage multiple printers/print servers and can be used to move printers to and from other Windows print servers.

Figure 9-15

The Print Management console

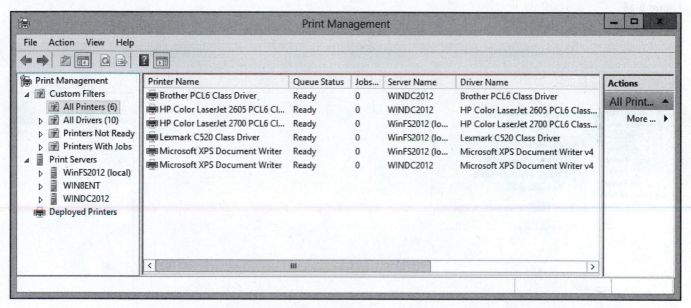

There are other role services included in Print and Document Services.

Here is a brief overview of what each service provides:

- *Distributed scan server:* Provides a service that receives scanned documents from network scanners and routes them to the correct destinations. It also includes the Scan Management snap-in that you can use to manage network scanners and configure scan processes.

- *Internet printing:* Creates a website in which users can manage print jobs on the server. Also enables users to use a web browser to connect and print to shared printers on the server using the Internet Printing Protocol.

- *Line Printer Daemon (LPD) service:* Enables UNIX-based computers using the Line Printer Remote (LPR) service to print to shared printers available on this server.

> **+ MORE INFORMATION**
>
> You can remotely manage printers from your Windows 8.1 computer by downloading the Remote Server Administration Tools (RSAT) for Windows 8.1. You can find the tools on the Microsoft website by searching for "RSAT for Windows 8.1."

 ADD A PRINTER TO THE LOCAL PRINT SERVER

GET READY. To add a printer to the local print server, perform the following steps:

1. Log on to your domain controller with administrative privileges.

TAKE NOTE*

The following should be performed on the same Windows Server 2012 R2 computer you set up Print Management for in the previous activity.

The Server Manager starts automatically. If it does not start, go to the task bar and click the **Server Manager** icon.

2. Click **Tools** > **Print Management**.

3. Expand the **Print Servers** node and locate the server on which you installed Print and Document Services.

4. Right-click the server and then choose **Add Printer** (see Figure 9-16).

5. Select **Add a new printer using an existing port: LPT1: (Printer Port)** and then click **Next**.

6. To accept the default settings, click **Next**.

Figure 9-16

Adding a printer

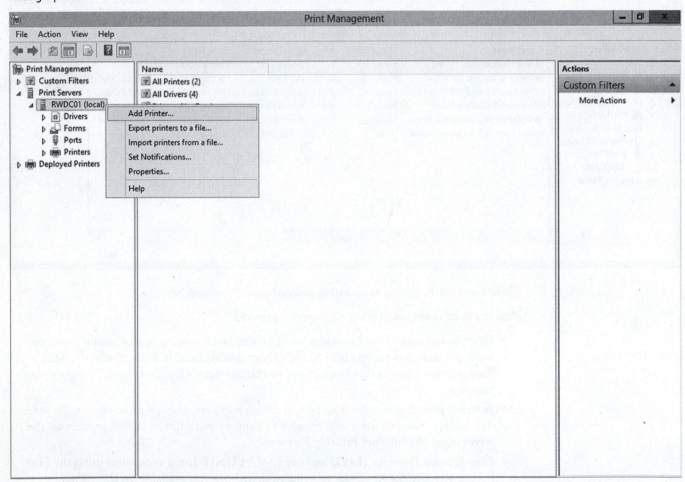

7. Click **Windows Update**.

This allows Windows to update the list of printers.

8. Select **HP** as the manufacturer and select the model **HP Color LaserJet 2550 PS**. Click **Next**.

9. To accept the default settings for the printer name and share name, click **Next**.

10. Review your settings and then click **Next**.

11. After the driver installs successfully, click **Finish**.

12. Click the **All Printers folder** and then confirm the new printer appears under the *Printer name* column.

13. Right-click the printer and choose **List in Directory** (see Figure 9-17).

Listing printers in Active Directory helps users to locate and install them more efficiently.

Figure 9-17

Listing a printer in the directory

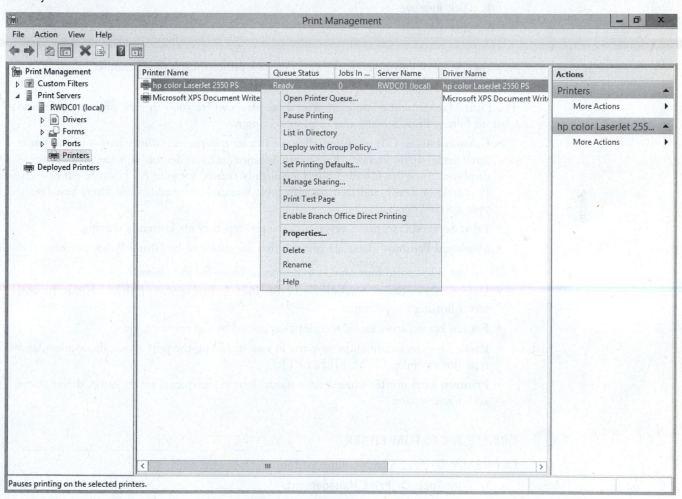

Your printer is now available for users to select as a resource.

14. Close the **Print Management console**.

The following exercises show you how to do a few others things with Print Manager.

 ADD A PRINT SERVER

GET READY. To add a print server, perform the following steps:

1. Click **Tools > Printer Management**.
2. Right-click the **Print Servers** node and choose **Add/Remove Servers**.
3. Type the name of the print server or click **Browse** to locate the server you want to add.
4. Click **Add to List**.
5. Click **OK**.

REMOVE A PRINT SERVER

GET READY. To remove a print server, perform the following steps:

1. Click **Tools > Printer Management**.
2. Right-click **Print Servers** node and choose **Add/Remove Servers**.
3. Under *Print servers*, choose the print server you want to remove.
4. Click **Remove**.
5. Click **OK**.

As shown in the following exercises, you can view printers using the Customer Filters, Print Servers, and Deployed Printers nodes.

The Print Management console provides three places where you can view printer information: Custom Filters, Print Servers, and Deployed Printers.

- **Custom Filters:** Custom filters allow you to set criteria (ex: printer name, queue status, serer name, driver version, share name, location, etc.) to determine what printers are displayed. Four pre-installed filters are already created for you: All Printers, All Drivers, Printers Not Ready, and Printers with Jobs. You can create additional filters based on your specific needs.

- **Print Servers:** Lists print servers and the printers they are currently sharing.

- **Deployed Printers:** These are printers that are managed by Group Policy objects.

Each printer is linked to four objects that serve as filters for the object:

- **Drivers:** Drive Name, Environment (x86/x64), Driver version, Drive isolation, Provider, server hosting the printer.

- **Forms:** Form names and dimensions supported by the printer.

- **Ports:** Provides information on ports in use, including the port name, description, and type (for example, COM, FILE, LPT).

- **Printers:** Lists printer name, queue status, jobs in the queue, server name, driver name, and driver version.

 CREATE A CUSTOM FILTER

GET READY. To create a custom filter, perform the following steps:

1. Click **Tools > Print Management**.
2. Right-click **Custom Filters** and choose **Add New Printer Filter**.
3. In the *Name* field, type **HP Printers** and then click **Next**.
4. On the *Define a filter* page (see Figure 9-18), click the arrow under the *Field* column and choose **Printer Name**. Under the *Condition* column, choose **contains**. In the *Value* field, type **HP**.

Figure 9-18

Creating a custom filter

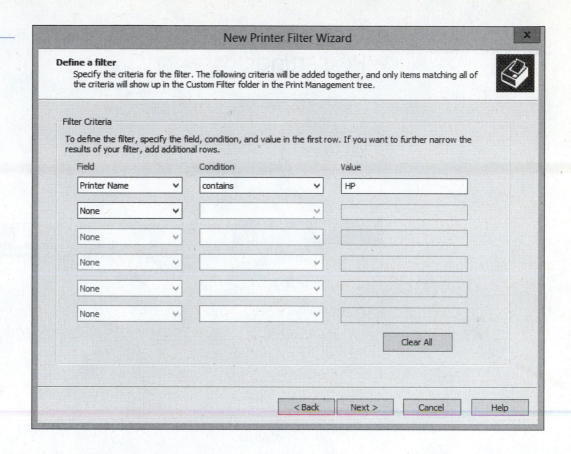

5. Click **Next** to continue.

6. On the *Set Notifications (Optional)* page, click **Finish**.

7. Under *Custom Filters*, click **HP Printers** (the custom filter you just created).

   You will see the HP Color LasetJet 2550 PS printer that you installed earlier. It is the only HP printer currently in operation.

Now that you have a better understanding of how to perform basic printer administrative tasks using the Print Management console, you can now turn your attention to installing a printer on a Windows 8.1 client computer.

 INSTALL A PRINTER FOR A WINDOWS 8.1 CLIENT

GET READY. To install a printer on a Windows 8.1 client, perform the following steps:

1. Log on to the Windows 8.1 client computer with a domain user account.

2. Press the **Windows logo key + c** to activate the Charms bar.

3. Click **Settings > Change PC Settings.**

4. Under *PC settings*, click **Devices** (see Figure 9-19).

TAKE NOTE

The Windows 8.1 client should be connected to the same domain as the print server.

Figure 9-19

Adding a device in Windows 8.1

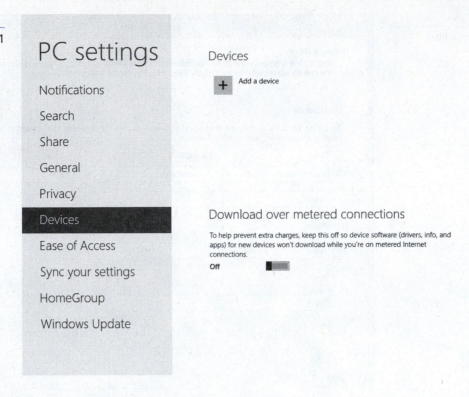

5. Click *Add a device*.

   Windows scans the network for devices. Because the printer was published to Active Directory earlier, it should show up at the top of the list.

6. Click **HP Color Laserjet 2550 PS**.

   Once the installation completes, the printer will appear under *Devices*.

7. Press the **Windows logo key** to return to the Windows 8.1 start menu.

8. Type **Notepad** and then select it from *Results*.

9. Type a few characters into the Notepad application and then click **File > Print**.

10. Choose the **HP Color Laserjet 2550 PS** printer and then click **Print**.

11. Close the Notepad document. You do not have to save the file.

Supporting Printer Sharing

> While users can connect to any network printer (a printer connected directly to the network or a printer that is shared by a server or other workstation), you can also make any local printer available to other users by sharing the printer.

CERTIFICATION READY

Monitor and manage printers, including NFC Tap-to-Pair and printer sharing

Objective 3.1

After sharing the printer, any user can connect to a shared printer by using the Uniform Naming Convention (UNC), which will be \\computername\sharename or \\ipaddress\sharename. To prevent users from access the shared printer, you can use printer permissions.

➜ SHARE A PRINTER

GET READY. To share a printer on Windows 8.1, perform the following steps:

1. Swipe in from the right edge of the screen and then tap **Search**.
2. In the search box, type **Devices and Printers** and then tap or click **Devices and Printers**.
3. Under *Printers*, press and hold (or right-click the mouse button) the printer you want to share and then choose **Printer properties**. If you don't see the printer you want to share, you'll need to add it.
4. Tap or click the **Sharing** tab (see Figure 9-20).

Figure 9-20

Sharing a printer

5. If you see a button that reads *Change Sharing Options*, tap or click it. If administrator permission is required, you might be asked for an admin password or to confirm your choice.
6. Select **Share this printer**.
7. To modify the printer permissions, click the **Security** tab. To add a user or group, click **Add**, type the name of the user or group, and then click **OK**. Then select the **Allow Print** permission.
8. Tap or click **OK**.

Supporting NFC Tap-to-Pair

Near field communication (NFC) is a short-range wireless communication system supported natively in Windows 8.1. It enables NFC-capable devices that are in close proximity to each other (within 4 centimeters) to exchange information. It uses technology similar to radio frequency identification (RFID) tags and operates at 13.56 MHz, supporting data rates of 106 kbps, 212 kbps, and 424 kbps.

NFC-enabled devices can operate in the modes shown in Figure 9-21.

Figure 9-21

Exploring the NFC operating modes

- **Peer-to-Peer mode** enables two devices to share data. For example, you can share your Wi-Fi settings or exchange your contact information.
- **Reader/Writer mode** enables your NFC-enabled device to read NFC tags embedded in magazines, posters, and so on. An NFC tag is a passive element that stores data that can be read by the NFS-enabled device.
- **Card Emulation mode** allows for contactless payments and ticketing. For example, proof of registration needed to receive a travel discount can be stored on the phone; also, tickets can also be purchased, downloaded, and accessed on the phone.

Sounds interesting, but what are the practical uses for NFC? Imagine being able to share URLs, documents, pictures, or contact information with a friend by simply touching your phones together. What about touching your device to an NFC tag that provides information about a product you are considering purchasing, using your device to purchase tickets to a movie, or using it to buy groceries at your local neighborhood store? These are just a few examples of how Microsoft envisions the integration of NFC with Windows 8.1.

Microsoft's implementation of NFC has been coined **Tap and Do**, which is described as a gesture that represents an interaction between two people that triggers an exchange of information between their devices (phones, tablets, laptops). The *Windows 8 Near Field Proximity Implementation Specification* whitepaper, located at www.microsoft.com, provides an excellent review of their use cases:

- Tap and Setup: Set up peripheral wireless devices.
- Tap and Reconnect: Reconnect with previous paired devices.
- Tap and Use: Connect an app running on your phone with an app running on the other person's phone.
- Tap and Launch: Invite another person to start an app that you are running.
- Tap and Acquire: Invite other users to obtain an app that you are running.
- Tap and Send: Send content on your device to the other person's device.
- Tap and Receive: Receive content from another device or poster.

➕ MORE INFORMATION

For a more detailed look at Microsoft's implementation of NFC, go to www.microsoft.com and search for the whitepaper entitled, "Windows 8 Near Field Proximity Implementation Specification."

For a printer to support NFS, you will have to retrofit an existing printer with an NFS tab or deploy a printer that natively supports NFC. Windows 8.1 supports the following types of connections supported by NFS printer installation:

- **Universal Naming Convention** (UNC - \\servername\sharename): Requires a user to be already connected to the same network as the print server.
- **Web Services on Devices (WSD) configured on a WSD port** (such as http:// PrintDeviceIP): Requires the user to be already connected to the same network as the physical print device.
- **Wi-Fi Direct:** Printer discovery is accomplished using the Add Device Wizard or requires proprietary software to configure the built-in NFC implementation.

■ Remediating Startup Issues Using DaRT 8.1

↓
THE BOTTOM LINE

The Microsoft Diagnostics and Recovery Took Kit (DaRT) 8 provides the tools needed to diagnose and recover Windows systems when they do not boot.

CERTIFICATION READY
Remediate startup issues using Diagnostics and Recovery Toolkit (DaRT)
Objective 3.1

The *Microsoft Diagnostics and Recovery Toolset (DaRT)* 8.1 is part of the *Microsoft Desktop Optimization Pack (MDOP)*. DaRT provides you with a set of tools that diagnose and recover your Windows systems when they are offline.

Following are some of the administrative tasks you can do with DaRT 8.1:

- Review the computer's event logs.
- Determine the cause of a computer crash.
- Recover boot volumes and restore the master boot record.
- Restore files that are accidentally deleted.
- Reset or change a local administrator's password.
- Uninstall hot fixes and service packs.
- Detect and remove malware and root kits.

 INSTALL THE MICROSOFT DIAGNOSTICS AND RECOVERY TOOLSET (DART) 8

GET READY. To install the Microsoft Diagnostic and Recovery Toolset (DaRT) 8.1, log in to your Windows 8.1 computer with administrative privileges and then perform the following steps:

TAKE NOTE*

Before starting this activity, install the Windows Assessment and Deployment Kit (Windows ADK) if it is not already installed on your Windows 8.1 computer. Visit Microsoft's website and search for *ADK for Windows 8.1.*

1. Insert the **Microsoft Desktop Optimization Pack 2013 R2 DVD**; if the DVD does not automatically open, right-click the DVD drive and choose **Auto-Play**. In the menu, click **Run launcher.hta**.
2. In the *MDOP* menu, click **Microsoft Diagnostics and Recovery Toolset** (see Figure 9-22).

Figure 9-22

Selecting DaRT 8 from the
MDOP menu

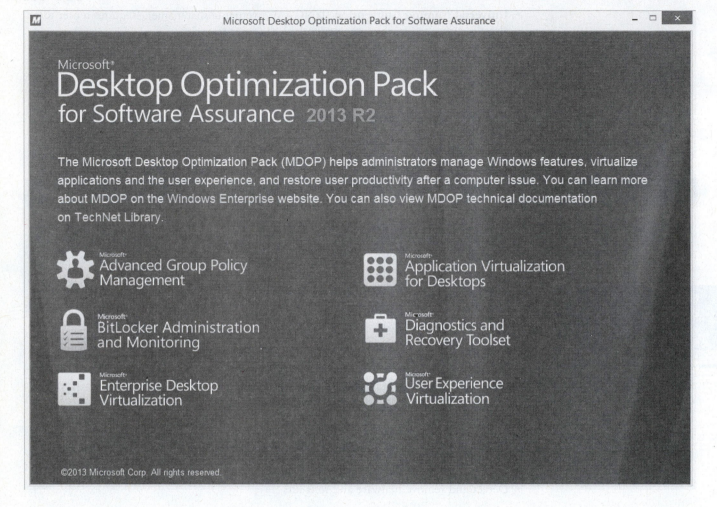

3. Under the *DaRT 8 for Windows 8.1 and Windows Server 2012 R2* menu, click **DaRT 8.1: 64-bit**.

4. On the Microsoft *DaRT 8.0 Setup Wizard* screen, click **Next**.

5. On the *End-User License Agreement* screen, click **I Agree**.

6. Select **Use Microsoft Update when I check for updates (recommended)** and then click **Next**. This ensures you have the latest updates for the DaRT 8.1 toolset.

7. On the *Select Installation Folder* screen, click **Next**.

   The default installation folder is *c:\Program Files\Microsoft DaRT 8*.

> **+ MORE INFORMATION**
>
> You can click Disk Space to determine available space on other drives along with the amount of space required for DaRT 8.1 prior to selecting the folder.

8. On the *Setup Options* screen, click **Next**.

9. Click **Install**.

10. Click **Finish**.

11. Close the **Microsoft Diagnostics and Recovery Toolset** box.

➕ MORE INFORMATION

You should install the Windows 8.1 debugging tools after you complete the installation of the DaRT kit. The Crash Analysis tool uses these tools to debug drivers, applications, and services. They can be found on Microsoft's website by searching for "Download and Install Debugging Tools for Windows."

Understanding the DaRT 8.1 Recovery Image Tool

The DaRT 8.1 Recovery Image tool creates a bootable image that contains the DaRT. When creating the recovery image, you need to decide which tools to include on the image. If you are an administrator, you probably want to include all of the tools on the media that you will use to troubleshoot your user's computers. When troubleshooting computers remotely, you might want to disable tools such as Disk Wipe and Registry Editor.

Using the DaRT Recovery Image tool, you can create a 32-bit and 64-bit DaRT recovery image from the same computer; however, you cannot create one image that works for both architectures on the same media. To run DaRT on a Windows 8.1 x64 PC, you need at least 2.5 GB of memory; on a Windows 8.1 x32 PC, you need at least 1.5GB of memory; and on Windows Server, you need a minimum of 1GB of memory.

TAKE NOTE*

Using the wizard, you can create International Organization for Standardization (IOS) files and Windows Image Format (WIM) images. You can also use Windows PowerShell to create a script that captures the options you select while running the wizard. To rebuild recovery images, use the same settings in the future.

➕ MORE INFORMATION

If you want to bypass the wizard and create a recovery image by using Windows PowerShell, you can learn more by visiting Microsoft's website and searching for "How to Use a Windows PowerShell Script to Create the Recovery Image."

Following is an overview of the steps for creating a DaRT Recovery Image:

1. Start the DaRT Recovery Image Wizard (DaRTImage.exe).

2. Choose the type of DaRT Recovery image you want to create.

3. Provide the path to the matching Windows 8.1 media files.

4. Select the tools you want to include with the image.

5. On the Crash Analyzer Tab/Advanced options page, include the Windows 8.1 Debugging Tools.

6. Download the latest malware definitions for Windows Defender.

7. Set the default path and name for the recovery image.

8. Select *Create to generate the image files (ISO, WIM)*.

9. Burn the image to bootable media (CD, DVD, and USB Flash Drive).

CREATE A DART RECOVERY IMAGE

GET READY. To create a DaRT 8.1 recovery image and burn it to a DVD, log in to your Windows 8.1 computer with administrative privileges and then perform the following steps:

1. On the Windows 8.1 *Start* menu, click the **DaRT Recovery Image** tile.

2. Read the information about the wizard and then click **Next**.

3. On the *Windows 8 Media* screen, select **Create 64-bit DaRT image** and specify the root path to your Windows 8.1 installation media. Click **Next** to continue.

4. On the *Tools* screen, click **Next** to install all of the tools available (see Figure 9-23).

Figure 9-23

Selecting DaRT 8 tools

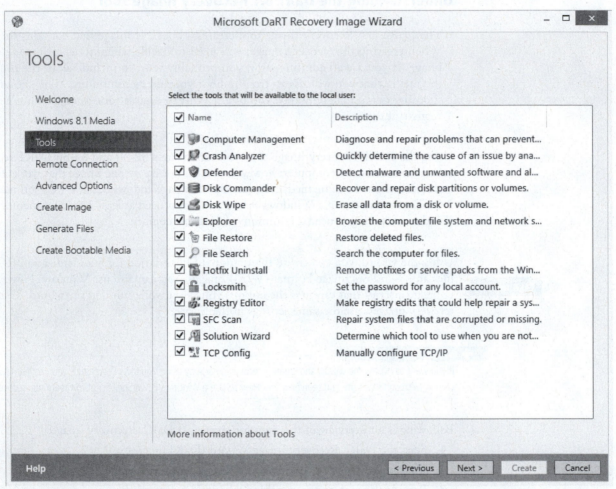

5. On the *Remote Connection* screen, read the information about the *Remove Connection* tool and then click **Next**.

 **MORE INFORMATION**

Selecting *All Remote Connections* allows the Helpdesk administrator connect to the DaRT tools remotely and use all of the tools on the end user's computer even if they are disabled for a local user. The end user would need to first boot his computer using the DaRT recovery image from either the recovery partition on the local computer or boot into DaRT from a remote partition on the network.

6. On the *Advanced Options* screen, click each tab and then read the explanation that follows for each of the advanced options:

- **Drivers:** You can add additional device drivers needed to repair the computer. These include storage or network adapter drivers not included with Windows 8.1. Note that drivers for wireless connectivity are not supported in DaRT.

- **WinPE:** You can add additional WinPE packages to the image if you choose. By default, any required packages are added automatically based on the tools you selected earlier.

- **Crash Analyzer:** If you download and install the Windows 8.1 debugging tools on your computer, the Wizard includes them. You can also click the *Download the Debugging Tools* link or use the *Debugging Tools from the computer that is being debugged*.

- **Defender:** Options on this tab allow you to download and install the latest definitions, or, you can choose to download them later. If you select *Download the latest definitions (Recommended)*, the definitions are added to the DaRT recovery image. If you select to download later, they are not included in the image.

7. On the *Crash Analyzer* tab, be sure the option **Use the Debugging Tools from the computer that is being debugged is** selected. On the *Defender* tab, be sure **Download the latest definitions** is selected. Then click **Next**.

8. On the *Create Image* screen, review the defaults for the *Output folder* and *Image* name. Make sure *Create WIM (Windows Imaging Format)*, *Create ISO*, and *Create PowerShell script* options are selected (see Figure 9-24). Click **Create** to generate the DaRT image.

Figure 9-24

Creating the DaRT 8.1 image

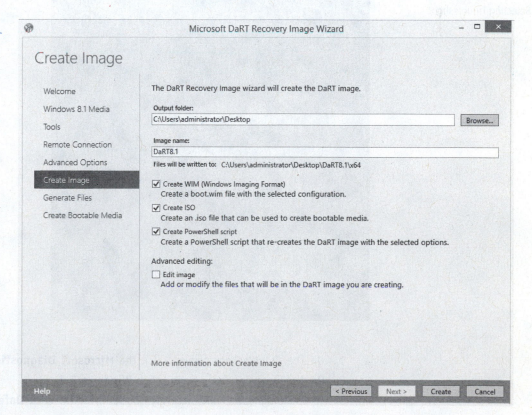

9. When the message *The DaRT image was successfully created* appears, click **Next**.

10. On the *Create Bootable Media* screen, click **Open Folder** to view the files created. You should see the Windows Image file (boot.wim), the Disc Image file (DaRT8. iso), and the Windows PowerShell script (DaRT8.ps1).

11. Close the folder and return to the DaRT Recovery Image Wizard.

12. Insert a blank recordable DVD.

13. Click **Create Bootable Media**.

14. When the message *Bootable media successfully created* appears, click **Close**.

You can now use the DaRT recovery disk to boot and repair Windows 8.1.

BOOT INTO A RECOVERY ENVIRONMENT USING DART AND EXPLORE AVAILABLE TOOLS

GET READY. To boot into a recovery environment using DaRT and run a virus scan, perform the following steps.

1. Insert your DaRT recovery disk into the DVD drive on your Windows 8.1 computer.

2. Restart the computer.

3. If prompted, choose DVD as the **boot device**.

4. When the message *Would you like to initialize network connectivity in the background?* appears, click **Yes**.

5. On the *Choose your keyboard layout* screen, click **US**.

6. On the *Choose an option* screen, click **Troubleshoot** (see Figure 9-25).

Figure 9-25

Selecting Troubleshoot

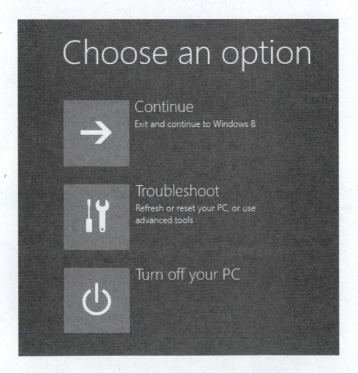

7. On the *Troubleshoot* screen, click the **Microsoft Diagnostics and Recovery Toolset**.

8. On the *Recovery Tool* screen, click **Windows 8.1**.

9. In the *Diagnostics and Recovery Toolset* window, click **Defender** (see Figure 9-26).

Figure 9-26

Selecting available tools

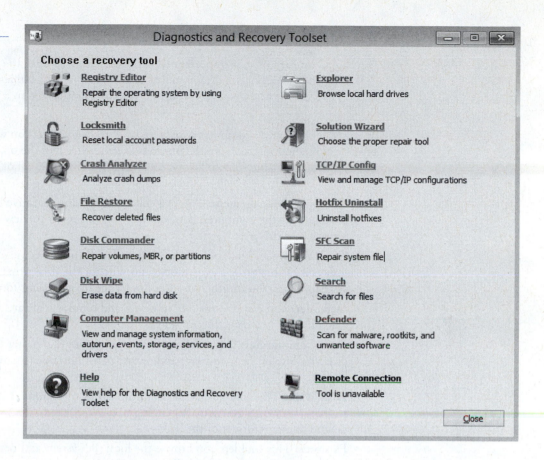

10. After the virus scan has completed, close the **Windows Defender** program.

11. Click **Explorer** and then confirm you can browse through the directories on the computer's hard drive. Close the **Explorer** box when you are done.

12. Click **Computer Management**. In the *Computer Management* console, you can expand the Event Viewer to search your Windows logs for errors. From *Services and Drivers*, you can view and disable services that might cause problems or use Disk Management to view the health of your partitions and volumes. Close the **Computer Management** console.

13. From the *Diagnostics and Recovery Toolset* window, click **Close**.

14. Remove the DaRT recovery disk from the computer's DVD drive.

15. On the *Choose an option* screen, click **Continue** to exit and continue to Windows 8.1.

If you use a Windows 8.1 (64-bit) DaRT recovery disk to boot into a computer running a Windows 8.1 (32-bit) operating system, you can run some of the tools, but others will not be available.

TAKE NOTE*

You can use the DaRT Recovery Image tool to create both 32/64-bit DaRT recovery images from the same computer, but you cannot create one image that works for both architectures on the same media.

Reviewing the Tools Included with DaRT

As an administrator, it is important to familiarize yourself with the tools available in DaRT. Understanding what each tool is used for can make troubleshooting more efficient and less stressful when you are faced with a recovery situation on a production computer.

When you boot into a computer with the DaRT recovery disk, you will have access to a variety of troubleshooting tools. In the previous exercise, you had the opportunity to explore just a few of those available. The following provides a closer look at all of the tools on the recovery disk:

- **Computer Management:** This is a collection of administrative tools that can be used to troubleshoot the computer. For example, you can use it to view event logs and manage services and drivers.

- **Crash Analyzer:** This tool can be used to determine the cause of a computer failure. It does this by analyzing the memory dump file for the driver that caused the operating system to fail. You can then use the Computer Management tool to disable the driver.

- **Defender:** You can use this tool to detect and remove malware. It works especially well when it comes to detecting rootkits.

- **Disk Commander:** Using this tool, you can restore the master boot record, recover one or more lost volumes, and save and restore partition tables to and from Disk Command backups.

- **Disk Wipe:** This tool deletes all data from a disk or volume. You can use either a single-pass or a four-pass overwrite depending upon your needs. This wipes data that is left behind after a reformat of the disk.

- **Explorer:** This tool lets you browse the local file system and network shares. Using this tool, you can locate and copy files to another location before attempting to repair or reimage a computer.

- **File Restore:** This tool lets you restore files that were accidentally deleted or were too big to fit into the recycle bin. It works on regular disk volumes, lost volumes and volumes encrypted by BitLocker.

- **File Search:** This tool allows you to search and find files that need to be recovered.

- **Hotfix Uninstall:** This tool allows you to remove a hotfix or service pack. Although you can uninstall multiple hotfixes at one time, best practice will be to uninstall the one at a time.

- **Locksmith:** This tool allows you to set or change a password for any local account on the system without having to know the current password. Although it can be used to set or change a password for the local administrator account, it does not allow you to set passwords for domain accounts.

- **Registry Editor:** This tool is used to gain access to the registry. Using this tool, you can add, remove, edit keys and values, and import registry files.

- **SFC Scan:** This tool is the System File Repair Wizard, which is used to repair system files that prevent the operating system from starting. It automatically repairs missing or corrupt files but can be configured to prompt you before performing a repair.

- **Solution Wizard:** This wizard presents a series of questions to determine the best tool to use for a given situation.

- **TCP/IP Config:** A system booted with a DaRT disk automatically obtains its TCP/IP information from a DHCP sever. If a DHCP server cannot be bound, you can use TCP/IP Config to manually configure the TCP/IP settings by first selecting a network adapter and then configuring the IP address and DNS Server for the selected adapter.

+ MORE INFORMATION

To learn more about how to use each of these recovering tools, visit Microsoft's website and search for "DaRT 8 Overview."

SKILL SUMMARY

IN THIS LESSON, YOU LEARNED:

- You can use the Device Manager to resolve hardware and device issues by updating drivers, scanning for hardware changes, viewing device properties, and disabling or uninstalling a device.

- The driver files provided with Windows 8.1 have been digitally signed and tested for compatibility, reliability, and functionality with Windows 8.1.

- You can control how Windows 8.1 handles unsigned device drivers by using the Local Group Policy Editor or the GPMC. Options include ignore, warn, and block.

- Driver Roll Back is a system recovery feature in Windows 8.1 that enables you to reinstall the last device driver that was functioning.

- Windows 8.1 uses built-in hardware diagnostics to detect hardware problems on your computer. If problems are detected, Action Center displays messages to alert you to the problem.

- Windows 2012 Server R2 and Windows 8.1 have been designed to use new print driver architecture (v4), which reduced the number of separate drivers that have to be installed and removed the need for a central distribution point for printer drivers required in previous releases.

- The Print Management snap-in, included as part of the Print and Document Services/Print Server role, is used to manage multiple printers or print servers across your organization. Server Manager is designed to manage only the local print server.

- You understand the process needed to add/remove print servers, view printers, list printers in Active Directory; and install a network printer on a Windows 8.1 client.

- A STOP error—also referred to as the bluescreen, the Blue Screen of Death, or BSoD—is an error screen displayed when the kernel or a driver running in kernel mode encounters an unrecoverable error.

- The Windows Performance Toolkit contains the Windows Performance Recorder (WPR) and Windows Performance Analyzer (WPA), which can be used to record and analyze Event Tracing.

- Performance is the overall effectiveness of how data moves through the system. Of course, it is important to select the proper hardware (processor, memory, disk system, and network) to satisfy the expected performance goals. Without the proper hardware, bottlenecks limit the effectiveness of software.

- Task Manager, Performance Monitor, and Resource Monitor help you analyze performance.

- The Microsoft Diagnostics and Recovery Toolset (DaRT) 8.1 provides you with a set of tools that diagnose and recover your Windows systems when they are offline.

■ Knowledge Assessment

Multiple Choice

Select the correct answer for each of the following questions.

1. Which of the following can be used to roll back a faulty print driver?
   a. Print Management Console
   b. Device Manager
   c. Activity Center
   d. Rollback.exe

2. Driver signing ensures that the driver files provided for Windows 8.1 are compatible, reliable, and function appropriately with the operating system. What is responsible for managing how unsigned drivers are handled?
   a. Windows Hardware Quality Labs (WHQLs)
   b. Network administrators
   c. Windows Device Quality Labs (WDQLs)
   d. Windows Device Signature Labs (WDSLs)

3. Which of the following indicate how the computer will respond when a user tries to install device drivers that are not digitally signed? (Choose all that apply)
   a. Block
   b. Ignore
   c. Warn
   d. Alert

4. When a device has been disabled, which of the following symbols appear?
   a. Blue "I" on a white field
   b. Red "X"
   c. Black exclamation point on a yellow field
   d. Blue "X"

5. Which term best describes the actual physical hardware that prints data?
   a. Print server
   b. Printer
   c. Print device
   d. Print spooler

6. Which of the following tools can be used to manage a local print server? (Choose all that apply)
   a. Server Manager
   b. Print Management snap-in
   c. Device Manager
   d. Action Center

7. Which of the following programs allows you to stop a running process?
   a. Performance Monitor
   b. Reliability Monitor
   c. Task Manager
   d. Event Viewer

8. Which of the following programs is used to determine what process is using a file?
   a. Performance Monitor
   b. Reliability Monitor
   c. Task Manager
   d. Resource Monitor

9. Which of the following is used to group multiple performance counters so that they can be used over and over in Performance Monitor?
   a. Replay Monitor
   b. Event Viewer
   c. Data Collector Sets
   d. Task Manager

10. Which of the following is a prerequisite before installing the DaRT Kit on Windows 8.1?
    a. SCCM
    b. Service Pack 2
    c. Windows Assessment and Deployment Kit (Windows ADK)
    d. RSAT

11. Which DaRT tool can be used to change the password for any local account on the system without having to know the password for the account?
    a. File Restore
    b. Locksmith
    c. DaRT Password Recovery
    d. User Account Reset

12. Members of which of the following groups have full access to all BitLocker Administration and Monitoring features in the MBAM Administration website?
    a. MBAM Helpdesk users group
    b. MBAM Advanced Helpdesk users group
    c. MBAM Report users group
    d. MBAM System Administrators group

Best Answer

Choose the letter that corresponds to the best answer. More than one answer choice may achieve the goal. Select the BEST answer.

1. When setting up a policy that determines how to best manage device drivers that are not digitally signed in your organization, which of the following options provide the best stability for your Windows 8.1 systems?
   a. Ignore
   b. Warn
   c. Block
   d. Alert

2. Which of the following tools provides a central location from which the print services can be managed for the entire network?
   a. Event Viewer
   b. Server Manager
   c. Print Management snap-in
   d. Computer Management

3. You currently cannot print to a USB print device after updating its driver files. Which of the following tasks is the quickest way to return your print device back to normal operation?
   a. Reinstalling the driver
   b. Rolling back the driver
   c. Researching the manufacturer's website for current driver information
   d. Installing a generic driver

4. While running Windows 8.1 and connecting to a shared print queue using a v4 driver, which of the following locations is the *least* likely location from which the driver will be downloaded?
   a. WSUS server
   b. Windows Update
   c. Windows 8.1 local driver store
   d. From the print server itself

5. Which of the following tools provides you with the best information about why a computer has crashed when using DaRT?
   a. Computer Management
   b. Crash Analyzer
   c. SFC Scan
   d. Registry Editor

6. Which of the following actions is most effective when deploying MBAM clients to 100 Windows 8.1 computers when your administrators are inexperienced with SCCM?
   a. Perform a manual installation.
   b. Use System Center 2012 Configuration Manager.
   c. Use Group Policy.
   d. Set up a share and asking users to connect and install.

Matching and Identification

1. Match the following terms with the related description or usage.

   _____ a) Action Center
   _____ b) Device Manager
   _____ c) Driver Roll Back
   _____ d) Printer
   _____ e) Print server
   _____ f) Print device
   _____ g) WHQL
   _____ h) PC settings

   1. Provides a detailed listing of all devices on your computer
   2. Provides a central location to view any problems with hardware or software
   3. A system recovery feature in Windows 8.1 that enables you to reinstall the last device driver that was functioning
   4. Responsible for driver signing
   5. The software interface that is used by your operating system to deliver request to the physical print device
   6. Used with your Microsoft user account to sync PC settings across multiple Windows 8.1 devices
   7. A computer that is connected to and sharing one or more print devices
   8. The actual physical hardware that prints the data

Build a List

1. Specify the correct order of the steps that must be completed to remove a print server.
   _____ Choose **Tools > Print Management**.
   _____ Choose the print server you want to remove.
   _____ Click **OK**.
   _____ Right-click the **Print Servers** node and choose **Add/Remove Servers**.
   _____ Click **Remove**.

2. Specify the correct order of the steps that must be completed to roll back a device driver.

_____ Click **Roll Back Driver**.

_____ Open **Device Manager**.

_____ Right-click the device and select **Properties**.

_____ When prompted to roll back the driver, click **Yes**.

_____ Click the **Driver** tab.

3. Identify the maximum value of the following performance counters.

_____ % Processor Time

_____ Pages/sec

_____ Paging File: % Usage

_____ % Avg. Disk Queue Length

4. Specify the correct order of the steps that must be completed to create a DaRT Recovery Image.

_____ Select Create to generate the image files (ISO and WIM).

_____ On the Crash Analyzer tab/Advanced options page, include the Windows 8.1 Debugging tools.

_____ Choose the type of DaRT Recovery image you want to create.

_____ Select the tools you want to include in the image.

_____ Burn the image to bootable media.

_____ Provide the path to the matching Windows 8.1 media files.

_____ Download the latest malware definitions for Windows Defender.

_____ Set the default path and name for the recovery image.

_____ Start the DaRT Recovery Image Wizard.

5. Specify the correct order of the steps that must be completed to boot into a recovery environment using DaRT:

_____ Select the tool you want to use from the DaRT tool kit.

_____ Select the target operating system Windows 8.1.

_____ Select Microsoft Diagnostics and Recovery Toolset.

_____ Select Troubleshoot.

_____ Choose your keyboard layout.

_____ Select Yes if you are asked to initialize network connectivity in the background.

_____ Select the boot device if prompted.

_____ Restart the computer.

_____ Ensure your computer is configured to boot from a DVD drive or USB bootable device.

Choose an Option

1. Which option helps users find their printers in Active Directory?

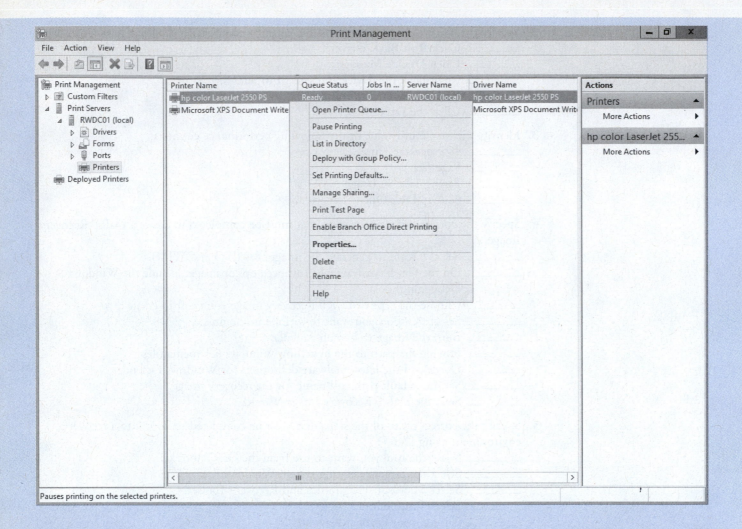

■ Business Case Scenarios

Scenario 9-1: Troubleshooting Print Devices

A user has contacted you because he cannot print documents to a device that is directly connected to a USB port. After talking to him, you discover that he updated the driver before
leaving the office yesterday. What is the problem and how should you address it?

Scenario 9-2: Controlling Driver Signing

You are concerned that users will install device drivers in your organization that are not tested
with Windows 8.1. You currently have 200 Windows 8.1 computers in an Active Directory–
based network and have only 2 people working on your help desk. What is the best way to
maintain the stability of your Windows 8.1 systems?

Supporting Mobile Devices

70-688 EXAM OBJECTIVE

Objective 3.2 – Support mobile devices. This objective may include but is not limited to: Support mobile device policies, including security policies, remote access, and remote wipe; support mobile access and data synchronization, including Work Folders and Sync Center; support broadband connectivity, including broadband tethering and metered networks; support Mobile Device Management by using Windows Intune, including Windows RT, Windows Phone 8, iOS, and Android.

LESSON HEADING	EXAM OBJECTIVE
Supporting Mobile Access and Data Synchronization	Support mobile access and data synchronization, including Work Folders and Sync Center
Synchronizing Your PC Settings and Files	
Using Work Folders	
Exploring Exchange Active Sync/Mobile Device Policies in Exchange Server 2013	Support mobile device policies, including security policies, remote access, and remote wipe
Exploring Mobile Policy Settings in Exchange Server 2013	
Securing Your Communications Using SSL	
Supporting Broadband Connectivity	Support broadband connectivity, including broadband tethering and metered networks
Supporting Mobile Device Management by Using Windows Intune	Support Mobile Device Management by using Windows Intune, including Windows RT, Windows Phone 8, iOS, and Android
Resolving Mobility Issues	

KEY TERMS

Active Directory Certificate
   Services (AD CS)

Bring Your Own Device (BYOD)

Certificate Authority (CA)

Exchange ActiveSync

Exchange Server connector

Internet Sharing

metered Internet
   connections

one-way sync

public key infrastructure (PKI)

remote wipe command

Secure Sockets Layer (SSL)

Sync Center

sync conflict

sync share

tethering

tethering access
   point

two-way sync

Work Folders

Supporting Mobile Access and Data Synchronization

THE BOTTOM LINE

Employees who bring their own smartphones, laptops, and tablets to work are quickly becoming the norm in most businesses. In fact, the term *Bring Your Own Device (BYOD)* has already been coined to identify this group. Today's employees expect to be able to use their mobile devices at work, making security a major concern for IT staff.

CERTIFICATION READY
Support mobile access
and data synchronization,
including Work Folders
and Sync Center
Objective 3.2

Preparing a BYOD policy is critical to protecting your network from users who want to connect their personal devices to your network. This means you need to develop an acceptable use policy, gain management support, and then communicate the policy to your end users. The policy has to describe the expectations and consequences of mobile devices usage across your organization. After you have a policy in place, you can select the appropriate software and infrastructure to design and implement.

When creating a BYOD policy, your questions usually revolve around how the mobile devices are protected, what users can and cannot access, and what happens when they leave the company. Here are a few questions to ask when developing your own BYOD acceptable use policy:

- How can you identify the BYOD devices used on your network?
- Who are the owners of the devices that are being used?
- Should you require that the entire device be encrypted?
- What type of password requirements should employees use?
- What activity will you allow with the devices?
- What happens in case the devices are lost or stolen?
- What services can employees use with the mobile device?
- Will employees only be able to use e-mail? Should e-mail access be limited to corporate e-mail accounts?
- How frequently should you audit employees' devices against your corporate policy?

A failure to establish a BYOD policy means that you allow employees to access your corporate network, with or without your knowledge. If not done securely, this access can affect your company's reputation and bottom line in case of a security breach.

Microsoft offers several methods for protecting your mobile devices. We look at the following two options in this lesson:

- **Exchange ActiveSync:** Exchange Server 2013 enables you to manage which mobile devices are allowed to connect to your network; and to control encryption, password and access requirements. You can also remotely wipe a device if it is lost or stolen.

- **System Center Configuration Manager (SCCM) 2012:** SCCM 2012 comes with an *Exchange Server connector* that enables you to manage your mobile devices that are synced with your Exchange Server. You can collect inventory information, perform a remote wipe of devices, quarantine or block the device, and change and manage Exchange ActiveSync mailbox policies.

Synchronizing your PC Settings and Files

Users who work across multiple devices want to be able to keep their address books, music, and document files in sync and accessible, regardless of the device they are using at the time. Windows 8.1 provides several ways to ensure that the user has a consistent experience.

You can use your Microsoft account, PC settings, and Sync Center to ensure a consistent experience for users who move between devices. Solutions include synchronizing your PC settings across your desktop, laptop, and smartphone using your Microsoft account; and configuring Sync Center to maintain access to files and folders stored on a network file share when you are offline.

SYNCHRONIZING YOUR PC SETTINGS

When you sign into the Windows 8.1 computer with your Microsoft account, the system will automatically sync most of the settings for you. Only passwords, which require the PC to be trusted, are not synchronized automatically.

Information that can be synchronized includes the following:

- General (colors, background, lock screen, and your account picture)
- Desktop personalization (themes, taskbar)
- Passwords (local password, passwords used on websites via Internet Explorer, network passwords)
- Ease of access (customizations made to magnifier, narrator, and the onscreen keyboard)
- Language preferences
- App settings (app settings, app purchases made)
- Browser (history, bookmarks, and favorites)
- Other Windows settings (File Explorer, mouse)

 SYNC YOUR PC SETTINGS

GET READY. To sync your PC Settings, log into a Windows 8.1 computer using your Microsoft account and then perform the following steps:

1. Press the **Windows logo key + i**.
2. Click **Change PC settings**.
3. Under *PC settings,* click **Sync your settings** and then confirm that **Sync settings on this PC** is set to **On** (see Figure 10-1).

Figure 10-1

Synchronizing via PC Settings

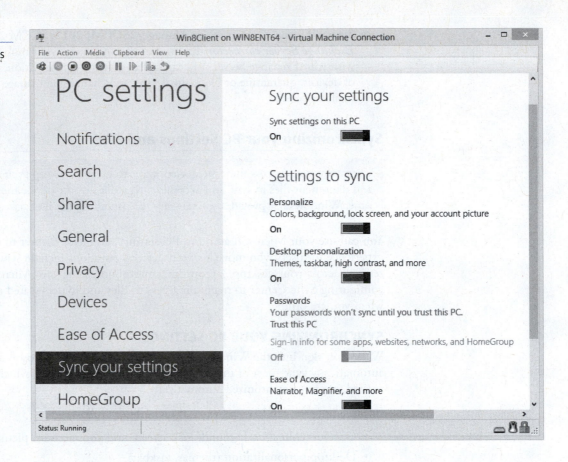

4. Under *Settings to Sync*, drag the slider bar all the way to the left to turn off sync for each item that you do not want to synchronize between your devices.

5. After configuring your sync settings, press the **Windows logo key** to return to the Windows 8.1 start screen.

To sync passwords, you will need to trust the PC. You can do this by clicking the *Trust this PC* link, which takes you to Microsoft's Account settings web page. From there, you will login with your Microsoft account and select how you want to receive the security code (e-mail, phone, or text message). Once you have the security code, you can type it to complete the trust process. After the PC has been trusted, you will be able to sync your password settings.

You can also determine if you want to sync over metered connections. Metered connections are those where the provider charges a certain fee based on the data sent and received from your computer. In most cases, you will turn off sync when working over metered connections and wait until you are on a non-metered connection to enable it.

USING SYNC CENTER

Sync Center enables you to sync certain mobile devices as well as files stored in folders on network servers (offline files). Sync Center offers two ways to sync your data:

- *One-way sync:* Data kept in a primary location is synchronized with data in another location. For example, if you have a portable mp3 device, you can configure a one-way sync so that you maintain the music files on your computer and the mp3 player holds only a copy of the files. When it comes time to sync, only data on the computer will be transferred to the mp3 player, not vice versa.

- *Two-way sync:* Data is transferred in both directions. This works well when you want to make sure key files you work with on the network and on your device are always in sync (offline files).

When working with mobile devices, Microsoft recommends using the software that comes with your device (mobile phone, music device, and so on) to perform synchronization. If your device is compatible with Sync Center, you can perform the next exercise to sync your device.

 SYNCH A DEVICE

GET READY. If your device is compatible with Sync Center, sync your device by performing the following steps:

1. Turn on the device and then connect it to your PC.
2. Open **Sync Center** and then click **Set up new sync partnerships**.
3. Click **Set Up**.
4. Configure the settings and schedule for how and when you want to sync with the device.

MANAGING OFFLINE FILES

Sync Center's primary purpose is to synchronize files available on your network. When you set up an offline files sync partnership with a folder, any time you disconnect from the network, you can continue to work on the files.

Changes you make to the files while offline will be made to the files in the network folder when you reconnect. Sync Center tracks the version number for a file. If the file has changed, it copies the updated version to the other location to keep both locations in sync. In case of conflicts, Sync Center will notify you and you can choose to address the conflict.

When you click the *Manage offline files* link within Sync Center, the Offline Files dialog box opens (see Figure 10-2), displaying the following tabs:

Figure 10-2

Reviewing Offline Files
property settings

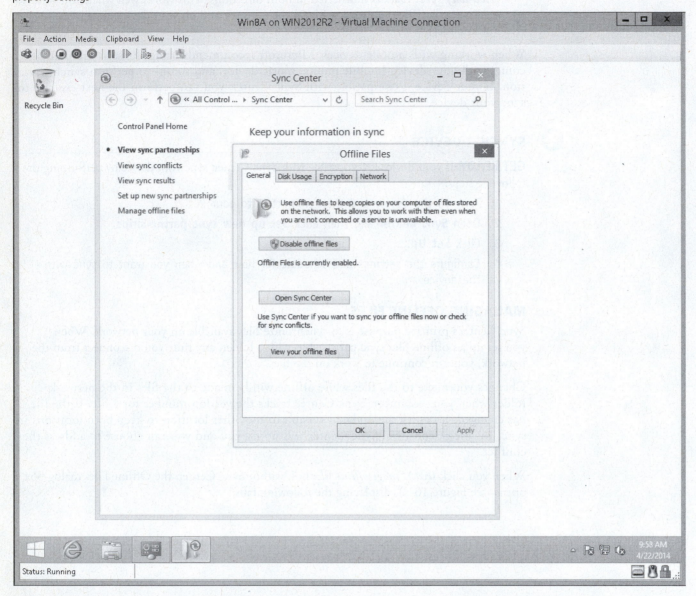

- **General:** Configures how offline files are used and synced.
  - **Disable Offline Files:** Enables and disables the Offline Files feature.
  - **Open Sync Center:** Opens Sync Center and checks for conflicts.
  - **View Your Offline File:** Provides access to your offline files.
- **Disk Usage:** Provides information on how much disk space is currently used and is available for storing offline files; enables you to change the maximum amount of space offline files and temporary files can use on your computer.
- **Encryption:** Enables you to encrypt and unencrypt your offline files.
- **Network:** Settings here determine how often the computer will check for a slow connection. By default, it is set to 5 minutes.

SCHEDULING FOR OFFLINE FILES

To set a schedule for the items you want to synchronize along with the date/time or the event that triggers the synchronization, simply right-click the Offline Files icon and choose Schedule for Offline Files. The options are as follows:

- **At a scheduled time:** Enables you to set a start date and time, and determine the frequency you want to repeat the schedule (minutes, hours, days, weeks, or months).
- **When an event occurs:** Configures synchronization to occur when one of the following events occurs:
  - You log on to your computer.
  - Your computer is idle for *x* minutes/hours.
  - You lock Windows.
  - You unlock Windows.

Additional start-and-stop scheduling options include the following:

- Start sync only if the computer is awake, has been idle for *x* minutes, and/or the computer is running on external power.
- Stop sync if the computer wakes up from being idle or the computer is no longer running on external power.

RESOLVING SYNC CONFLICTS

Although synchronizing can help keep your files in a consistent state, there will be times that you will experience a conflict that must be resolved to ensure you have the right file in the right place. Understanding what causes conflicts and your options to resolve them will help you protect your files.

A *sync conflict* occurs when you have two copies of a file stored in different locations (e.g., locally and in a network folder) that have both changed since the last sync. A conflict can also occur if someone deletes a file (located in a shared folder) while another person makes a change to the same file while they are offline. In either case, Sync Center will ask you how you want to address the conflict. You typically will overwrite the older file, but if you choose to keep both, Sync Center will rename one version and make a copy of both files in both locations. At this point, the files are no longer synchronized.

SET UP OFFLINE FILES AND RESOLVE A CONFLICT

GET READY. To set up offline files and resolve conflicts, perform the following steps:

> **TAKE NOTE** * The following activity requires a domain controller and a Windows 8.1 client computer connected to the domain.

First, from your Windows Server 2012 R2 domain controller, create a folder, share it, and then create a file called *MyFile.txt* in the folder.

1. Log on to your domain controller with administrative credentials.
2. Press the **Windows logo key + e**.
3. Double click the **C: drive** on your computer to open it.
4. Right-click and choose **New > Folder** and then type **Harmony**.
5. After the folder is created, right click and choose **Share with > Specific people**.
6. In the *File Sharing* dialog box, type **Everyone** and then click **Add**.
7. Under the Permission Level column, click the **Read** permission for **Everyone** and then change it to **Read/Write**.

8. Click **Share** and then click **Done** to complete the setup of the shared folder.

9. Double-click the **Harmony** folder to open it.

10. Right-click and choose **New > Text Document**.

11. Type **MyFile** for the name and then press **Enter**.

   Now, from a Windows 8.1 client computer, connect to the shared folder on the domain controller.

12. Log on to the Windows 8.1 client computer with a regular domain user account.

13. Press the **Windows logo key + r**, type *servername*\harmony, and then press **Enter**. (Replace *servername* with the name of your domain controller.)

14. Double-click **Myfile.txt** to open it and then type **Connected over network** into the file.

15. Click **File > Save**.

16. Right-click the file and choose **Always available offline**.

17. Close the dialog box and then close the Harmony dialog box.

18. Press the **Windows logo key + w**, type **View network connections**, and then choose it from *Results*.

19. Right-click your Ethernet adapter and choose **Disable**.

20. When the User Account Control dialog box appears, type **Administrator** for the user name, type its associated password, and then click **Next**.

   Your Ethernet adapter is now disabled which simulates an offline environment for this computer.

21. From the Windows domain controller, delete the file while the Windows 8.1 client computer is disconnected from the network.

   This creates a conflict that you will need to resolve later.

22. Log on to your domain controller with administrative credentials.

23. Press the **Windows logo key + e**.

24. Double-click the **C: drive** on your computer to open it.

25. Double-click the **Harmony** folder on your computer to open it.

26. Right-click **Myfile** and choose **Delete**.

   From the Windows 8.1 client computer, make a change to the file while you are still offline.

27. Press the **Windows logo key + r**, type *servername*\harmony, and then press **Enter**. (Replace *servername* with the name of your domain controller.)

28. Double-click **Myfile.txt** to open it and then type **Changes made while offline** into the file.

29. Click **File > Save**.

30. Close the *Myfile.txt* dialog box.

   From the Windows 8.1 client computer, enable your Ethernet adapter and reconnect to the network.

31. Press the **Windows logo key + w**, type **View network connections**, and then choose it from *Results*.

32. Right-click your Ethernet adapter and choose **Enable**.

33. When the User Account Control dialog box appears, type **Administrator** for the user name, type its associated password, and then click **Next**.

34. Once your Ethernet adapter has reconnected to the network, close the Network Connections dialog box.

35. Right-click **Myfile.txt** and choose **Sync > Sync selected offline files**.

36. When the *Resolve Conflict* dialog box appears, select **Keep this version and copy it to the other location**.

37. Close the dialog box.

The file has now been restored on the domain controller.

Using Work Folders

Work Folders allow users to store and access work files on a *sync share* from multiple devices including personal computers and devices (including bring-your-own devices). Work Folders are for only individual data and do not support sharing files between users. However, while these files can be accessed from anywhere, the organization maintains control over corporate files by storing the files on centrally managed file servers. To maximize accessibility, you can provide file share-based access to the files stored in a Work Folder, use Work Folders with Folder Redirection and Offline Files. In addition, since the files are stored centrally, you can back up the data on a regular basis.

Work Folders use the https protocol to transport data between devices and the Work Folders server. When you configure Work Folder for a user, you configure sync access to a specific sync share. The folder for the user is created in this sync share. When you assign a group with sync access, each user in the group is given a folder on that server. Since Work Folders client synchronizes only with a single server, you should not assign a user sync access on multiple servers.

When Work Folders is configured on a device, you have the option to wipe the Work Folders data from the device, which will remove the Work Folders data only. When the user leaves your organization, it is simple to remove the Work Folders data from all of their devices.

CREATING A WORK FOLDER

To use Work Folders, Windows Server 2012 R2 uses the HTTPS protocol for performing Work Folders communication. Therefore, the Work Folder server will need to have a certificate, that must be must be trusted by the Work Folders devices. In most cases, you should obtain a certificate from an external third-party CA so that it will be automatically trusted.

To create a Work Folder, you will need to:

1. Install the Work Folders role.

2. Create a Sync Share.

 INSTALL THE WORK FOLDERS ROLE

GET READY. To install the Work Folders role, perform the following steps:

1. Using *Server Manager*, click **Manage > Add Roles and Features**.

2. When the *Add Role and Features Wizard* starts, on the *Before you begin* page, click **Next**.

3. On the *Select installation type* page, click **Next**.

4. On the *Select destination server* page, click **Next**.

5. On the *Select server roles* page, select **File and Storage Services\File and iSCSI Services\Work Folders**.

6. When you are prompted to install additional features, click **Add Features**.
7. Back on the *Select server roles* page, click **Next**.
8. On the *Select features* page, click **Next**.
9. On the *Confirm installation selections* page, click **Install**.
10. When the installation completes, click **Close**.

When you create the Sync Share, you have the following available policies:

- **Encrypt Work Folders:** The data on the devices is encrypted, but the data on the file server is not encrypted, which will mitigates the risk of data being accessed if a device is lost or stolen.

- **Automatically lock screen, and require a password:** When selected, devices using Work Folders lock the screen after 15 minutes and require a password of at least six characters to unlock. Additionally, if there are 10 unsuccessful sign in attempts, the device is locked out.

 CREATE A SYNC SHARE

GET READY. To create a Sync Share, perform the following steps:

1. Using *Server Manager*, click **File and Storage Services** > **Work Folders**. Figure 10-3 shows the Work Folders page.

Figure 10-3

Opening the Work Folders page

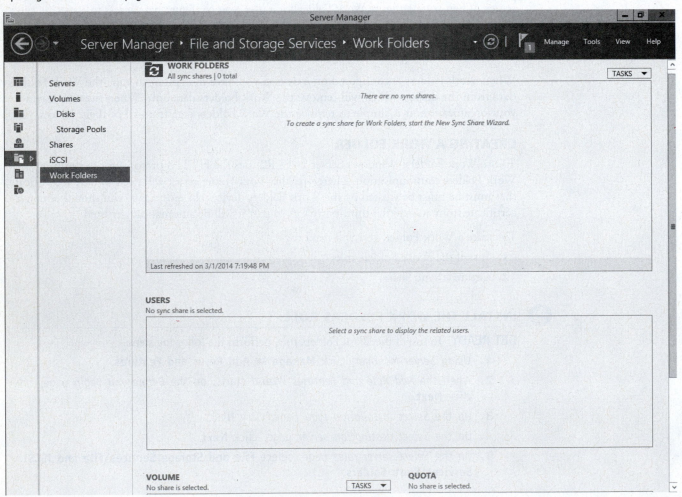

2. Click the **To create a sync share for Work Folders, start the New Sync Share Wizard** link. Alternatively, you can click **Tasks > New Sync Share**.

3. On the *Before you begin* page, click **Next**.

4. On the *Select the server and path* page, you can select a folder that is already shared or you can specify a local path (such as **D:\Folder1**). Click **Next**.

5. On the *Specify the structure for user folders* page, select either **User alias (default)** or **User alias@domain**. The user alias is compatible with other technologies, such as folder redirection or home folders. The alias@domain option allows you to use folder names for users across domains. Click **Next**.

6. On the *Enter the sync share name* page, in the *Name* and *Description* text boxes, type a sync share name and description. Click **Next**.

7. On the *Grant sync access to groups* page, click **Add**. In the *Select User or Group* dialog box, in the *Enter the object name to select* text box, type a username or group name and then click **OK**. Back on the *Grant sync access to groups* page, click **Next**.

8. On the *Specify device policies* page, you can select the following options:

   • **Encrypt Work Folders**

   • **Automatically lock screen, and require a password**

9. On the *Confirm selections* page, click **Create**.

10. When the sync share is created, click **Close**.

CONNECTING TO A WORK FOLDER

To connect to a Work Folder, the computer or device would use one of the following methods:

- Auto Discovery
- URL Entry
- Group Policy

When you use Auto Discovery, you are prompted for an e-mail address. The domain name that is derived from the e-mail address is prepended with Work Folders to create an URL. Therefore, if the e-mail address is JJackson@contoso.com, the resulting URL would be https://workfolders.contoso.com. If the URL does not resolve to the server with Work Folders installed, then the Auto Discovery fails.

If you have multiple Work Folders servers, you can still use Auto Discovery by modifying the msDS-SyncServerUrl attribute on the user object using ADSIEdit. You can also modify this attribute to direct users to a new Work Folders server if you move Work Folders for a specific set of users.

If Auto Discovery fails during device configuration, you can use URL Entry, which will prompt for a URL where Work Folders are installed. This can be useful if you have multiple Work Folders servers and do not have the msDS-SyncServerUrl attribute configured on the user object. This can also be useful if you have not configured a DNS host record for Work Folders in your domain.

Another way to configure devices with the URL of a Work Folders server is to use Group Policy. You can force automatic setup for Work Folders by using a computer policy or a user policy. A user policy takes effect for specified users on all devices that they access. A computer policy takes effect for all users on that device.

The user setting is stored in Users\Policies\Administrative Templates\Windows Components\Work Folders\Specify Work Folders. After you enable the GPO setting, you will type in the

Work Folder URL (such as *https://workfolders.contoso.com/sync/1.0*). If you then want the policy to automatically configure with the Work Folders client, check the *Force automatic setup* option. You can use Windows Intune to deliver Group Policy Objects (GPOs) for Work Folders to devices that are not domain members.

When you use Group Policy to configure Work Folders, you have the option to force automatic setup. If you force automatic setup, users are not given the option to select where Work Folders data will be stored on the local device. Work Folders data will be stored in the default location of %USERPROFILE%\WorkFolders.

CONNECT TO A WORK FOLDER

GET READY. To connect to a Work Folder, perform the following steps:

1. On a computer running Windows 8.1, open **Control Panel** and click **System and Security > Work Folders**.

2. On the *Manage Work Folders* page, click **Set up Work Folders**.

3. On the *Enter your work email address* page, in the *Work email address* text box, type the user's e-mail address. Alternatively, you can click **Enter a Work Folders URL** and, in the *Work Folders URL* text box, type the Work Folders URL. Click **Next**.

4. On the *Introducing Work Folders* page, click **Next**.

5. On the *Security policies* page, select **I accept these policies on my PC** and then click **Set up Work Folders**.

6. Click **Close**. Figure 10-4 shows the user's Work Folder.

Figure 10-4

Managing your Work Folders

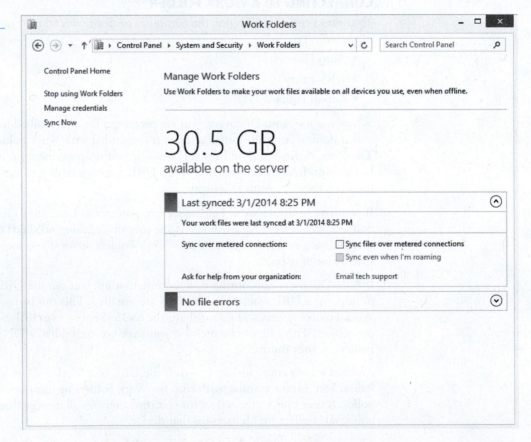

Work Folders uses the https protocol to transport data between devices and the Work Folders server. By using a reverse proxy server, Work Folders can be securely used over the Internet. In addition, you can use Web Application Proxy to enhance the security of Web Folders by integrating Web Folders authentication with AD FS, which will allow you to implement multi-factor authentication and restrict connectivity to Work Folders to authorized devices.

If you integrate Windows Azure Multi-Factor Authentication with AD FS, you can implement the following methods for additional authentication:

- **Phone calls:** You receive a call on your phone to confirm your authentication and you press the # (pound) symbol to confirm after receiving the call.
- **Text messages:** You receive a text message with a passcode. You respond to the text message and include the passcode.
- **Mobile App:** An authentication prompt appears in the mobile app that you must acknowledge.

When Work Folders is configured on a device, you can wipe the Work Folders data from the device, which will remove the Work Folders data only. When the user leaves your organization, it is simple to remove the Work Folders data from all of the user's devices.

Since Work Folders data is stored on a file server, you can perform all of the typical file management functions using File Server Resource Manager and Rights Management Services, including quotas, file screening, classification, and Rights Management.

When you modify a file, the file is replicated very quickly. However, while it is unlikely that a user will change a file on two separate devices before replication occurs, it can happen if one of the devices is offline for an extended period. In addition, if synchronization does not occur, you should check the following:

- Work Folders does not synchronize individual files larger than 10 GB.
- Ensure that there is at least 5 GB of free space on the volume with the Work Folders.
- Ensure that Quotas is not restricting access to a Work Folder.

■ Exploring Exchange Active Sync/Mobile Device Policies In Exchange Server 2013

↓ THE BOTTOM LINE   Exchange ActiveSync enables you to create mobile device policies that can increase security for your corporate network.

CERTIFICATION READY
Support mobile device policies, including security policies, remote access, and remote wipe
Objective 3.2

Exchange ActiveSync is a client synchronization protocol based on XML that enables you to connect your mobile device to your Exchange mailbox.

Exchange ActiveSync enables communications from ActiveSync–compliant mobile devices such as the Windows Phone, Apple iPhone, iPad, iPod, and Google Android phones. The features available with ActiveSync differ from device to device because it is up to the manufacturers to determine what features they want to support with the protocol. Exchange

TAKE NOTE✱   Exchange ActiveSync is enabled by default on Exchange Server 2013. If you have an Exchange mailbox, you can sync your mobile device with it.

ActiveSync works over HTTP and HTTPS (see Figure 10-5), and supports offline access to messages, contacts, and calendar information.

Figure 10-5

Using Exchange ActiveSync over HTTP/HTTPS

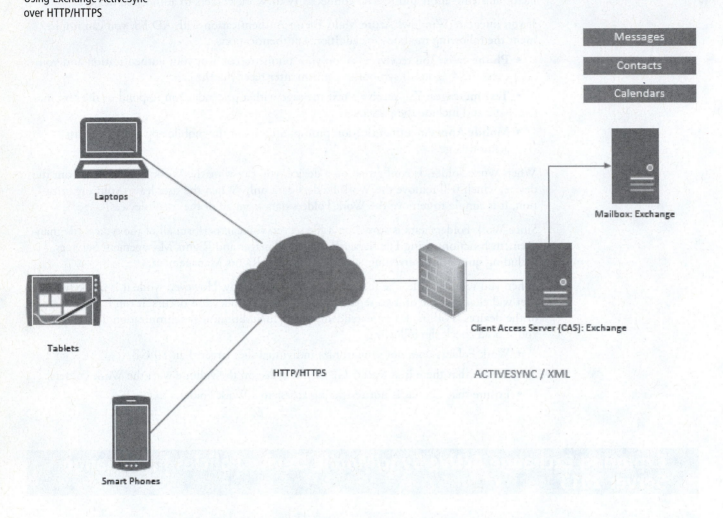

Exchange ActiveSync provides you with tools to control policies and manage and secure your mobile devices. Here are just a few of the tasks you can perform with Exchange ActiveSync:

- Issue remote wipe commands in case the mobile device is lost or stolen. A ***remote wipe command*** clears all corporate and user information that is stored on the device.
- Specify the length and complexity of the password for the mobile device (4–18 character alphanumeric passwords), device locking, and number of password attempts.
- Require encryption on the mobile device and/or the devices removable storage card.
- Control which types of mobile devices/users are allowed to connect to your Exchange Server.
- Run, view, and export reports.

Exploring Mobile Policy Settings in Exchange Server 2013

Some of the built-in security features in mobile devices can be controlled from Exchange Server, so you can create security policies that are automatically sent to each device the next time the mobile device starts synchronizing. These settings can harden security on the devices by requiring stronger passwords, enabling encryption, and controlling which older devices are allowed to connect to your network.

You create Exchange ActiveSync mailbox policies to make management of mobile devices easier. These policies, which can be applied to each of your Exchange ActiveSync users, enable you to apply settings to a user's mobile device.

A new mobile device mailbox policy includes the following settings:

- **Name:** Displays the name of the mobile policy.
- **This is the default policy:** Sets the policy as the default.
- **Allow mobile devices that do not fully support these policies to synchronize:** Enables you to decide whether to allow mobile devices that do not support some or all of the selected policies.

Policies for Exchange ActiveSync:

- **Require a password:** This option enables you to configure additional password requirements, as follows:

  o **Allow simple passwords:** Enables mobile devices to use simple passwords (for example, 1234).

  o **Require an alphanumeric password:** Requires lower- and uppercase letters, numbers, and symbols.

  o **Password must include this many character sets:** Options include 1, 2, 3, or 4. Selecting 2 means you need to use at least 2 of the character sets (for example, letters and numbers).

- **Require encryption on device:** Enables encryption on the mobile device.
- **Minimum password length:** Sets minimum length for password; specify the number in the space provided.
- **Number of sign-in failures before device is wiped:** If a user fails to sign in after the specified number of attempts, the device is wiped.
- **Require sign-in after the device has been inactive for (minutes):** Locks devices after they are idle for the number of minutes you specify, requiring users to sign in again.
- **Enforce password lifetime (days):** Specifies the number of days before the password must be changed. If you enable this feature, users are prompted to reset their password after the number of days you specify.
- **Password recycle count:** Enables you to determine the number of different passwords a user must use before they can reuse a password. You can specify from 0–50.

 CREATE A MOBILE DEVICE MAILBOX POLICY

GET READY. To create a mobile device mailbox policy, perform the following steps.

TAKE NOTE The following exercise requires a Microsoft Exchange 2013 Server running the Mailbox and Client Access Server (CAS) roles.

1. Log in with local Administrative privileges to your computer.

2. In the Internet Explorer browser address field, type **https://\<exchangeserver\>/ ecp** and press Enter to open the Exchange administrator center (EAC). Replace *\<exchangeserver\>* with the actual name of your Exchange server.

3. In the *Domain\user name* and *Password* fields, type your administrative credentials and then click **OK** to access the EAC.

4. From the menu on the left, click **mobile** and then, from the center pane, choose **mobile device mailbox policies**.

5. In the center pane, click the **+** symbol to create a new mobile device mailbox policy.

6. In the *Name* field, type a name for the policy (for example, **My Mobile Policy**).

7. Select **This is the default policy**.

8. Select **Require a password**.

9. Select **Require an alphanumeric password**.

10. Under the *Password must include this many character sets* section, click the drop-down box and then select **3**.

11. Select **Minimum password length** and, in the field that appears, type **6** (see Figure 10-6).

Figure 10-6

Configuring a mobile device policy

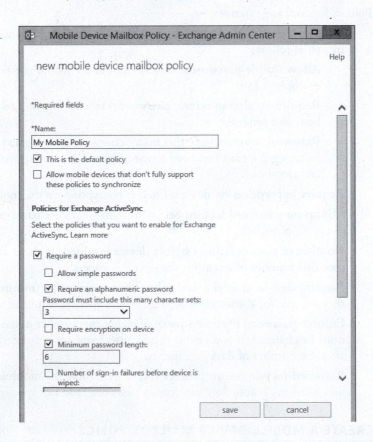

12. Select **Enforce password lifetime (days)** and, in the field that appears, type **60**.

13. Under *Password recycle count*, type **5**.

14. Click **Save**.

The new policy appears in the middle pane.

15. Close the Exchange admin center browser window.

Having a strong mobile policy in place goes a long way toward protecting your user's mobile device, but when one of your users loses a phone or it is stolen, you need to rely on something more than just your mobile policy. In those situations, the best approach is to remotely wipe the device.

PERFORM A MOBILE DEVICE REMOTE WIPE

GET READY. To wipe a mobile device, perform the following steps:

1. In the Internet Explorer browser address field, type your Outlook Web Access (OWA) web address (**https://<exchangeserver>/OWA**) and then press Enter.

2. In the *Domain\user name* field and *Password* field, type your login information and then click **Sign-in**.

3. From the menu at the top, click **Exchange** and then choose **Options** (see Figure 10-7).

TAKE NOTE

The following exercise requires a Microsoft Exchange 2013 Server running the Mailbox and CAS roles.

Figure 10-7

Selecting Options

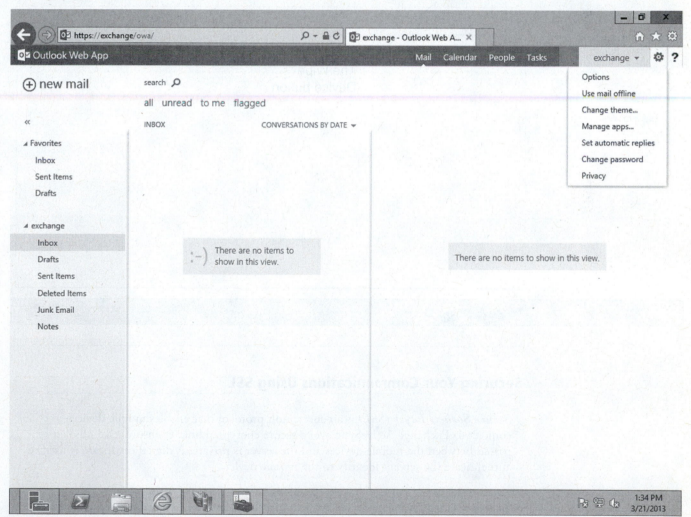

4. From the options menu on the left, click **Phone**.

5. In the middle pane, click the **Wipe Device** button (see Figure 10-8).

   If the device is lost, the user can also remove it from the list by clicking the Delete (trashcan) icon.

Figure 10-8

Wiping a mobile device

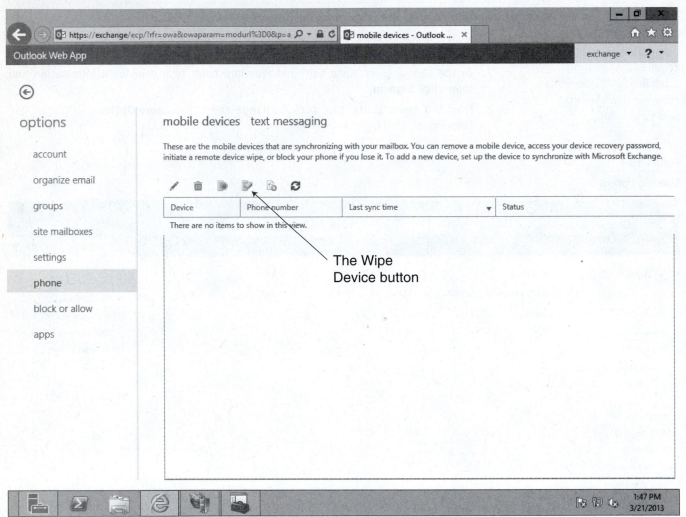

The Wipe
Device button

Securing Your Communications Using SSL

Secure Sockets Layer (SSL) is an encryption protocol that enables mobile devices to connect to Exchange ActiveSync over a secure encrypted link. It ensures that all data passed between the mobile devices and the server is private. A digital certificate is used to authenticate the server's identity to the mobile device.

When you set up Exchange Server 2013 to run the CAS role, a virtual directory is created for Exchange ActiveSync. The virtual directory is used by Internet Information Services (IIS) to enable access to Exchange ActiveSync and the Outlook Web App. To manage authentication and enable the server to authenticate itself to the mobile device, an SSL certificate must be configured for the Exchange ActiveSync virtual directory.

You can obtain your SSL certificate by purchasing it from a third-party *Certificate Authority (CA)*. A CA creates and manages the distribution and revocation of certificates. An alternative approach is to use *Active Directory Certificate Services (AD CS)* to install your own CA. AD CS provides the certificate infrastructure and is used to create certificate authorities that issue and manage certificates. Once you have obtained your certificate, you can configure SSL on your Exchange ActiveSync virtual directory.

 CONFIGURE SSL ON THE EXCHANGE ACTIVESYNC VIRTUAL DIRECTORY

GET READY. To configure SSL on the Exchange ActiveSync virtual directory, perform the following steps.

1. Log in with local Administrative privileges on the server hosting the Exchange ActiveSync virtual directory.
2. Server Manager opens automatically. If it does not open, click the **Server Manager** icon on the task bar.
3. Click **Tools** > **Internet Information Services (IIS) Manager**.
4. Expand *servername* > **Sites** > **Exchange Back End**.
5. Click **Microsoft-Server-ActiveSync** and then double click **SSL Settings**.
6. In the middle pane, under *SSL Settings*, confirm that *Require SSL* is selected.
8. Under *Client certificates*, select **Require**.
9. In the *Actions* pane, click **Apply** and then close the IIS Manager console.

MANAGING CLIENT AUTHENTICATION

When you install the CAS role on Exchange, you automatically install a default self-signed digital certificate. The certificate is used to authenticate that the computer is what it claims to be. The certificate also protects against someone tampering with data exchanged between the client and the server.

You typically use a self-signed certificate when you do not want to set up a *public key infrastructure (PKI)* to purchase a commercial certificate. A PKI includes the hardware, software, policies, and standards necessary to centrally administer the issuing, renewing, and revocation of certificates. The major disadvantage of self-signed digital certificates is you can exchange information only with those who know you personally. In other words, there is no third party to validate that your digital certificate is authentic.

To increase the level of security, consider configuring your server to use a trusted certificate from a recognized third-party CA or use a trusted Windows PKI CA.

You can set up your own PKI by configuring one or more CAs that can be used to create the digital certificates for computers and users in your organization. If the computers and users are part of an Active Directory environment, you can set it up so that all your computers have the company's CA chain installed. Users and computers can then automatically be assigned the appropriate digital certificates for signing documents and encrypting messages.

If you purchase a commercial certificate, the vendor's root certificate is automatically installed on your Windows computers by default. This enables your computers to automatically trust these CAs. You can also share the certificate with users who are not members of your organization.

Commercial organizations such as VeriSign and Thawte offer three types of commercial certificates:

- Class 1: These certificates are issued to individuals who have a valid e-mail address. They are designed to be used for digital signatures, access control, encryption, and noncommercial transactions in which proof of identity is not required.

- Class 2: These certificates are issued to individuals and devices. They are designed with the same features as Class 1, but for transactions in which identity is required and information in the validating database is sufficient. They are used for device authentication, messaging software, content integrity, and confidentiality encryption.
- Class 3: These certificates are used by individuals, organizations, servers, devices, and administrators for CAs. They are also used for root authorities. These certificates are designed for digital signatures, encryption, and access controls where proof of identity must be assured. They are appropriate for server authentication, messaging, software, integrity of content, and confidentiality encryption.

■ Supporting Broadband Connectivity

 THE BOTTOM LINE Over the last few years, each version of Windows released has supported mobile computers more and more. With Windows 8.1, Windows features mobility improvements and support for embedded wireless radio. In addition, Windows 8.1 supports broadband tethering and metered networks.

CERTIFICATION READY
Support broadband connectivity, including broadband tethering and metered networks
Objective 3.2

In Windows 8.1, *Internet Sharing* is usually referred to as *tethering*, where you can share the mobile broadband network (including Bluetooth, USB, and Wi-Fi) connection with other devices. When you share your mobile broadband network, you allow the computer or device becomes a *tethering access point*.

Internet Sharing can be turned on by using the Settings charm on the mobile broadband-capable device. Once Internet Sharing is turned on, any device that can connect to a Wi-Fi network can connect to it.

 CONNECT TO A WORK FOLDER

GET READY. To connect to a Work Folder, perform the following steps:

1. From the *Settings* charm, click **Change PC settings** and then click **Network**.
2. Under the *Mobile Broadband* heading, click the network name.
3. On the *Mobile Broadband* page, enable **Internet Sharing for the network**. If the mobile broadband network is disconnected, the device will automatically connect to the mobile broadband network before setting up the Wi-Fi network.
4. If you have created the necessary service metadata package, the PC triggers an event telling the Windows Store mobile broadband app to run an entitlement check. The PC waits for the mobile broadband app to respond before Internet Sharing is turned on.
5. After the mobile broadband network is turned on and any required entitlement checks have passed, the mobile broadband connection is shared by using a private Wi-Fi network that uses Wi-Fi Direct Autonomous Group Owner mode with a customized network name. This ensures that any Wi-Fi device can connect to the network.
6. After Internet Sharing is turned on, from the *Mobile Broadband* page, click **Edit** to change the network name and password. The Wi-Fi network will restart when the network name or password is changed.

The Wi-Fi network must use WPA2-PSK. By default, the network name is set to <Device Name><4 digits>, which is recognizable to the user by being short enough to fully fit in the Networks list and unique enough to distinguish among multiple devices. IN addition, the password is set to a default of 12 random digits. When you change the password, the password must be at least 8 characters in length. The icon for the mobile broadband network is automatically updated throughout Windows to help customers remember that the network is being shared by other people.

When Internet Sharing is turned on, the network on the client device is automatically set as a metered connection. Windows then provides settings to reduce unnecessary bandwidth consumption on the mobile broadband network. In addition, you can see how much data has been used by client devices using the mobile broadband app.

When Internet Sharing is turned on, the PC cannot go into Connected Standby or sleep to ensure that client devices do not lose their Internet connections. After the last client device has disconnected from the tethered network, Internet Sharing will wait for five minutes. If no other client devices connect, Internet Sharing is turned off and the PC returns to the normal power state.

You can connect to a tethered network using a Wi-Fi device in the same way you connect to any other Wi-Fi network. However, if a user connects to a tethered network with the same Microsoft account credentials on both devices running Windows 8.1, the following things happen:

- If Internet Sharing is not turned on when the Windows 8.1 device connects, the two devices create a Bluetooth connection and Internet Sharing is turned on.
- The connection is automatically configured (network name and SSID) by automatically retrieving the credentials from the tethered network.

Metered connections can result in high costs when it comes to transferring and synching your computers. Windows 8.1 provides a mechanism to help you configure your system to recognize them and reconfigures itself to reduce costs.

The days of unlimited broadband networks are quickly coming to a close as more broadband companies adopt metered plans similar to what they now have in place for your mobile devices. The premise behind metering is that a small percentage of users are consuming the majority of the bandwidth by streaming videos, playing online games, or downloading large files from torrents. To protect against exhausting the available bandwidth, Internet Service Providers (ISPs) are rolling out plans that feature data limits that once exceeded, will result in additional billing. These are known as *metered Internet connections*.

Windows 8.1 provides you with a way to reduce the amount of data you send and receive over a metered connection. When a connection is metered, Microsoft indicates you may see the following effects:

- Automatic sync of Offline Files may be disabled.
- Updating of the start screen may be stopped.
- Windows Store app downloads may be paused.
- Only Priority updates will be downloaded from Windows Update
- Tile Updates are limited to 50 MB per month.

➕ MORE INFORMATION

By default, Windows considers Wi-Fi networks to be non-metered while mobile broadband networks and Ethernet network connections are set to metered.

SET A WI-FI NETWORK CONNECTION TO METERED

GET READY. To set a Wi-Fi connection to metered, perform the following steps.

1. Log in with administrative credentials to your Windows 8.1 PC.

2. Move your mouse to the bottom right of your screen and click **Settings** from the *Charms* bar.

3. Click the **Internet Access** icon.

4. Right-click your wireless network connection and choose **Set as metered connection** (see Figure 10-9). At this point, Windows will keep track of the amount of data you are using.

Figure 10-9

Setting a metered connection

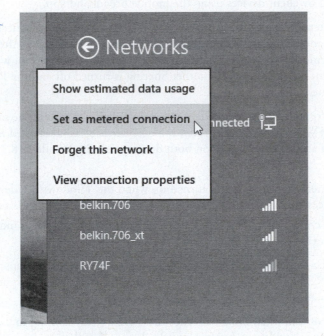

5. Right-click the wireless network connection and choose **Show estimated data usage** to monitor how much data you are using.

6. Open **Task Manager** and click the **App History** tab to view which applications are using the most data over the metered connection.

You can also lower your data usage costs by performing the following additional tasks on a metered connection:

1. Go to **Settings** and click **Change PC Settings**

2. On the *PC Settings* menu, click **Devices**.

3. Under *Download over metered connections*, drag the slider to **Off**. This will block the download of device drivers from Windows Update and device info while you are working over a metered connection.

4. Go back to the *PC Settings* menu and click **Sync your settings**.

5. Under *Sync settings over metered connections*, drag the slider to **Off**.

To return your setting to non-metered:

6. Go to **Settings**.

7. Click the **Network Icon**.

8. Right-click your metered connection and choose **Set as non-metered connection**.

■ Supporting Mobile Device Management by Using Windows Intune

THE BOTTOM LINE

While Lesson 12 provides more details about Windows Intune, this section focuses on using Windows Intune to provide comprehensive mobile device management for user's mobile devices. With Windows Intune, you can deploy polices to secure mobile devices, perform a hardware inventory, distribute applications, or wipe mobile devices.

CERTIFICATION READY
Support Mobile Device Management by using Windows Intune, including Windows RT, Windows Phone 8, iOS, and Android
Objective 3.2

With Windows Intune, you can manage mobile devices directly or through Exchange ActiveSync. Exchange devices can be managed using on-premises servers and hosted Microsoft Office 365 Exchange services in the cloud. If System Center 2012 R2 Configuration Manager is deployed in your environment, you can use the Windows Intune service to manage mobile devices while performing all management tasks in the System Center Configuration Manager console.

Windows Intune can manage Windows Phone 8/8.1 devices, iOS devices, and Android devices. To enroll Windows devices, you must deploy the Windows Phone 8 company portal app to the devices. The company portal app, which can be downloaded from Microsoft's Download Center, must be code-signed with a certificate that is trusted by Windows Phone 8/8.1 devices.

To enroll iOS devices, you need to obtain an Apple Push notification service certificate that enables Windows Intune to securely communicate with the Apple Push Notification service. To obtain an Apple Push Notification, you must download the Certificate Signing Request from Windows Intune and then request an Apple Push Notification service certificate from the Apple website.

To enroll Android devices, you must download the Android company portal app from Google Play. This application will let you enroll Android devices for direct management.

To enroll devices, you will need to perform the following steps:

1. Set the Mobile Device Management Authority for Windows Intune.
2. Set up direct management for mobile devices.
3. Provision users for device enrollment.
4. Enroll devices.

 SET THE MOBILE DEVICE MANAGEMENT AUTHORITY

GET READY. To set the Mobile Device Management Authority, perform the following steps:

1. Open the **Windows Intune administrator** console.
2. In the workspace shortcuts pane, click the **Administration** icon.
3. In the navigation pane, click **Mobile Device Management**. The *Mobile Device Management* page appears (see Figure 10-10).

Figure 10-10

Opening the Mobile Device
Management page

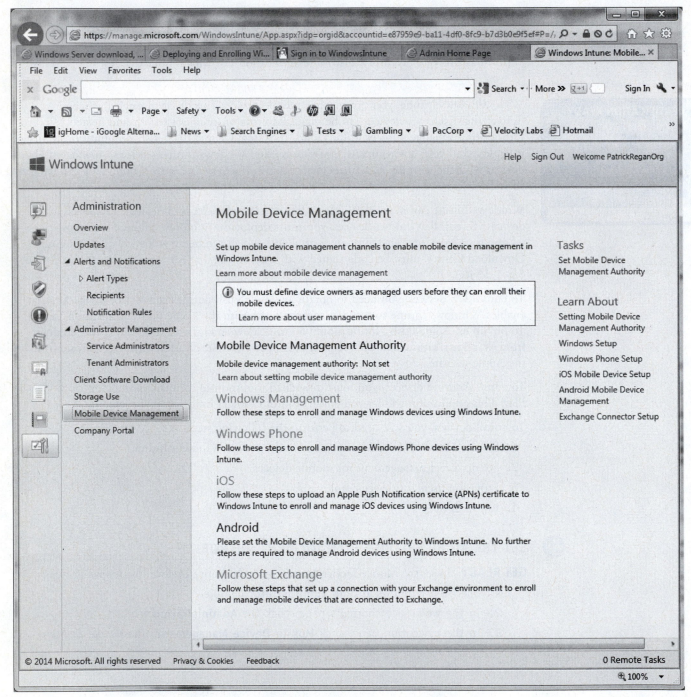

4. In the *Tasks* list on the right of the page, click **Set Mobile Device Management Authority**.

5. The *Set MDM Authority* dialog box appears. You cannot change this selection at a later time. Therefore, if you will use the Windows Intune console to manage mobile devices in the future, check the box and click **Yes** if you want to use Windows Intune to manage mobile devices.

 SET UP DIRECT MANAGEMENT FOR MOBILE DEVICES

GET READY. To set up direct management of Windows Phone 8/8.1 devices, perform the following steps:

1. Open the **Windows Intune administrator** console.

2. In the workspace shortcuts pane, click the **Administration** icon.

3. In the navigation pane, under *Mobile Device Management*, click **Windows Phone**. Figure 10-11 shows the *Windows Phone Mobile Device Management Setup* page.

Figure 10-11

Setting up Windows Phone Mobile Device Management

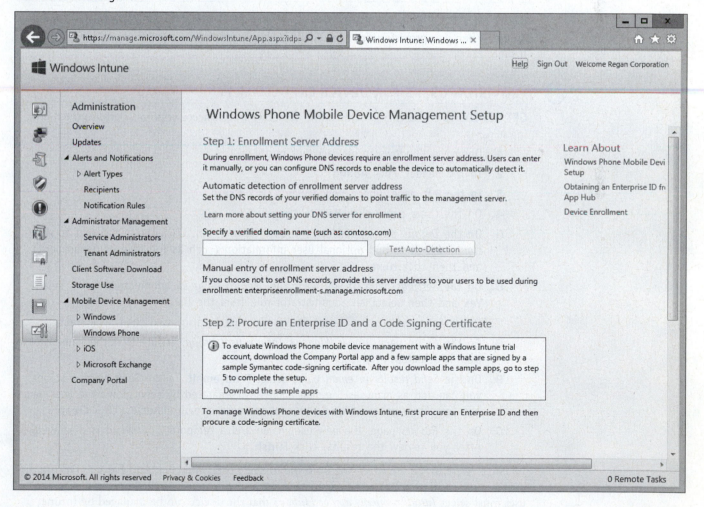

4. Under *Step 1: Enrollment Server Address*, type the name of the verified domain and then click **Test Auto-Detection**.

5. Scroll down to the *Step 5: Upload and Deploy the Company Portal* section and click **Upload Signed App File**. To open the Windows Intune Software Publisher Wizard. Click **Next**.

6. On the *Software setup* page for the *Specify the location of the software setup files* option, click the **Browse** button to browse to the signed Windows Phone 8 company portal app that you generated when you completed the prerequisites.

7. Under the *Code-signing certification* option, click the **Browse** button to browse to the code-signing certificate (.pfx) file. In the *Certificate password* text box, type a password for the certificate. Click **Next**.

8. On the *Software description* page, complete the fields (*Publisher, Name*, and *Description*). These fields will be seen by the users on their devices. You will also specify an URL for software information and specify a category. Click **Next**.

9. On the *Summary* page, click **Upload**.

10. When the software is uploaded, click **Close**. The company portal can now be automatically deployed to all users who enroll.

Before users are able to enroll their devices, users must be members of a Windows Intune user group. When you provision users, you define device owners as managed users in Windows Intune.

 PROVISION USERS FOR DEVICE ENROLLMENT

GET READY. To add users manually to the Windows Intune account portal, perform the following steps:

1. Open the Windows Intune account portal.

2. In the header, click **Admin**.

3. In the left pane, under *Management*, click **Users**.

4. On the *Users* page, click **New > User**.

5. On the *Details* page, complete the user information. Click the arrow next to *Additional details* to add optional user information (such as job title or department) and then click **Next**.

6. On the *Settings* page, if you want the user to have an administrator role, select **Yes** and then select an administrator role from the list.

7. Under *Set user location*, select the user's work location and then click **Next**.

8. On the *Group* page, under *Windows Intune user group*, ensure that the name of the user is selected.

9. On the *Send results in email* page, select **Send email**. In the *Send email* text box, you can add as many as 5 e-mail addresses, separated by semicolons; the user name and temporary password would be sent to these e-mail addresses. Click **Create**.

10. On the *Results* page, the new user name and a temporary password is displayed. After you review the results, click **Finish**.

To enroll Windows 8.1 devices, log in to the Intune portal and click Add Device. During this process, users will provide their credentials. After a certificate is installed on the device, the user must select *Install company app or Hub*, so that the device can be managed by Intune.

■ Resolving Mobility Issues

THE BOTTOM LINE

To successfully resolve mobility issues, you need to be familiar with the technology used and have a systematic approach to analyze and determine exactly what is wrong. It requires you to isolate the problem device(s), confirm basic connectivity, evaluate mobile device policies, and determine whether existing infrastructure devices (firewalls, routers) are potential sources of mobility problems.

The process for resolving mobility issues depends upon what method you use to deploy and secure them. Here are a few things to consider when resolving mobility issues:

- Isolate it to the client or the server. If a single mobile device is experiencing the problem, the problem points to the device. If multiple devices are having problems, the server is most likely the culprit.

- Review the version of ActiveSync and the model of the mobile device. The features available with ActiveSync differ from device to device because it is up to manufacturers to determine what features they want to support with the protocol. It can be changed from one version of the operating system to another.

- Confirm basic connectivity and review the settings on the mobile device to make sure the server name and account click are correct for the device.

- Log in to the EAC and select Mobile Mobile Device Access to see whether the mobile device shows up. If you do not see the device, there is a connectivity problem.

- Review device policies to see whether any of them are blocking the device. If they are, you can create an exemption for the device, assign a less-restrictive policy, or adjust the policy to no longer block the device. You can also tell the user that current security policies prohibit the use of the device.

- Review device error messages on the mobile device. These errors can provide insight about where the problem may be located (client, server, or connections between the two).

- Review authentication settings. If SSL is configured, review the certificate and make sure it has been approved by a trusted CA.

- Review your personal and perimeter firewall rules and settings to make sure the traffic is not being blocked.

➕ MORE INFORMATION

For additional troubleshooting tips when working with Microsoft Exchange ActiveSync, search Microsoft's website for "Troubleshooting Exchange ActiveSync."

There are a variety of ways mobile clients can connect to an Exchange Server. Problems with connectivity can be the firewall (blocked ports), a corrupted DNS server, certificate issues, or proxy misconfiguration. To help determine where the problem is, you can use the Microsoft Remote Connectivity Analyzer website. This is a public website, outside of your public firewall, that enables you to run simulated connections using a test account from your network. The test simulates the client access method you choose. Tools on this site break down the progress and identify exactly where the communication fails. You can also access links to additional resources to help you resolve the problem.

SKILL SUMMARY

IN THIS LESSON, YOU LEARNED:

- It is important to establish a BYOD policy for your organization to support your mobile users and protect your network from security risks. This process involves creating an acceptable use policy, gaining management support, and communicating the policy to your end users.

- Exchange ActiveSync is a client synchronization protocol based on XML that helps you connect mobile devices to Exchange mailboxes.

- Exchange ActiveSync features vary from device to device, depending on which features the manufacturer wants to support with the protocol.

- When setting up Exchange Server, ActiveSync is enabled by default. If you have a mailbox set up, you can automatically sync your mobile device with it.

- Remote wipe can be used when a mobile device is lost or stolen.

- You can configure policies that control the types of mobile devices that can connect to the network, the complexity of the passwords required, and the number of password attempts allowed.

- Configuring a new mobile device mailbox policy involves setting password parameters (complexity, minimum length, password lifetime, and password recycle counts), enabling encryption on the mobile devices, and determining the number of sign-in failures allowed.

- Employees who use mobile devices can perform a remote wipe of their device by logging in to OWA.

- You can use your Microsoft account, PC settings, and Sync Center to ensure a consistent experience for users who move between devices. Solutions include synchronizing your PC settings across your desktop, laptop, and smartphone using your Microsoft account; and also configuring Sync Center to maintain access to files and folders stored on a network file share when you are offline.

- Work Folders allow users to store and access work files on a sync share from multiple devices, including personal computers and devices (including bring-your-own devices).

- In Windows 8.1, Internet Sharing is usually referred to a tethering, where you can share the mobile broadband network (including Bluetooth, USB, and WiFi) connection with other devices. When you share your mobile broadband network, you allow the computer or device to become a tethering access point.

- With Windows Intune, you can manage mobile devices directly or through Exchange ActiveSync. Exchange devices can be managed using on-premises servers and hosted Microsoft Office 365 Exchange services in the cloud. Windows Intune can manage Windows Phone 8/8.1 devices, iOS devices, and Android devices.

- There are several ways to troubleshoot problems with mobile device connectivity. Some of the approaches include isolating client/server issues, reviewing versions of ActiveSync, confirming basic connectivity, using the EAC, reviewing device and firewall policies, reviewing error messages on the mobile device, and checking authentication settings.

Knowledge Assessment

Multiple Choice

Select the correct answer for each of the following questions.

1. Which of the following is *not* a question you would ask when developing a BYOD policy?
   a. Who are the owners of mobile devices?
   b. What services can mobile users access and use?
   c. What happens if a mobile device is stolen?
   d. What devices do an employee's family members use at home?

2. Which of the following is a client synchronization protocol based on XML that enables you to connect your mobile device to your Exchange mailbox?
   a. HTML
   b. HTTPS
   c. Exchange Server connector protocol
   d. Exchange ActiveSync

3. A Class 2 commercial certificate can be issued to which of the following?
   a. Individuals only
   b. Individuals and devices
   c. Individuals, organizations, servers, devices, and administrators
   d. Individuals, organizations, servers, and devices

4. Which of the following types of mobile device management works through the Exchange Server connector using the capabilities of ActiveSync and does not require a PKI?
   a. In-depth mobile device management
   b. Light mobile device management
   c. EAC device management
   d. Soft mobile device management

5. Which of the following information can be synched on an untrusted PC? (Choose all that apply)
   a. Lock screen and your account picture
   b. Local password, passwords used on websites via Internet Explorer
   c. Browser history, bookmarks, and favorites
   d. App settings

6. Which of the following are ways in which Sync Center syncs your mobile devices and offline files? (Choose all that apply)
   a. One-way
   b. Peer-to-peer
   c. Three-way
   d. Two-way

7. When scheduling for offline file sync, which of the following are examples of event triggers that can be configured? (Choose all that apply)
   a. Logging on to your computer
   b. Shutting down the computer
   c. Locking Windows
   d. Unlocking Windows

8. Which of the following actions creates a sync conflict? (Choose all that apply)
   a. You delete a file in a shared folder after another person makes a change to the same file while they are offline.
   b. You have a file stored locally and in a network folder, and both have changed since the last sync.

    c. You open a file while offline.

    d. You open a file from a network share while connected to the network.

9. Which of the following allows you to store and access work files from a sync share, which can then be accessed from multiple devices (including bring-your-own-devices)?

    a. Offline folders

    b. Folder redirection

    c. Work Folders

    d. Central Placement

10. Which of the following are methods to connect to a Work Folder? (Choose three answers)

    a. Group Policy

    b. URL entry

    c. Auto Discovery

    d. ActiveSync Policy

11. What of the following allows you to use your Windows 8.1 device as a tethering access point?

    a. Band Hopping

    b. Key Sharing

    c. File Sharing

    d. Internet Sharing

12. When setting up Windows 8.1 for metered connection, which of the following may happen?

    a. Automatic sync of Offline Files may be disabled

    b. Only Priority updates will be downloaded from Windows Update

    c. Updating of the start screen will not be disabled

    d. Windows Store app downloads may be paused.

Best Answer

Choose the letter that corresponds to the best answer. More than one answer choice may achieve the goal. Select the BEST answer.

1. Which of the following tools is used to manage your mobile device policy as well as deploy and inventory software installed on your mobile devices?

    a. Exchange Server with ActiveSync

    b. WSUS/Group Policy

    c. SCCM 2012 with Exchange Server connector

    d. Group Policy

2. Which of the following types of certificates provide the best way to identify users on your network while still enabling you to identify these same entities to others outside of your organization?

    a. Self-signed certificates

    b. Class 1 commercial certificates

    c. Class 2 commercial certificates

    d. Class 3 commercial certificates

3. Which of the following is the most important component for managing mobile device polices within your organization?

    a. BYOD (Acceptable Use Policy)

    b. SCCM 2012

    c. Exchange Server 2013 with ActiveSync

    d. IT support

4. Which of the following are Exchange ActiveSync policies that can be used to protect your remote device? (Select all that apply.)
   a. Require a password
   b. Require encryption on the device
   c. Enforce password lifetime
   d. Number of sign-in failures before device is wiped

5. Which of the following options provides the most efficient way for users to wipe their mobile devices when they know for sure they were stolen?
   a. Submit the request for their admin to wipe the device.
   b. Call their admin and ask him or her to wipe the device.
   c. Wait for the person who stole it to attempt to log in, which wipes the device based on existing mobile policies.
   d. Use the OWA web address to connect and wipe their mobile device.

6. Which of the following tools is best to use when you have bookmarked your favorite sites and want to make sure they are available across multiple PCs?
   a. Export your favorites to a network folder and use Sync Center to sync them across your PCs.
   b. Configure them to sync via PC Settings.
   c. Make them part of your roaming profile.
   d. Store your favorites in OneDrive.

Matching and Identification

1. Match the following terms with the related description or usage.
   _____ a) BYOD
   _____ b) Exchange ActiveSync
   _____ c) Exchange Server connector
   _____ d) In-depth mobile device management
   _____ e) Light mobile device management
      1. Requires a PKI; enables you to secure over-the-air enrollment; monitor and remediate out-of-compliant devices; inventory devices; and deploy applications.
      2. A client synchronization protocol based on XML.
      3. A mobile device management type that works through the Exchange Server connector and uses the capabilities of ActiveSync available on the Exchange Server.
      4. Establishes a connection with the Exchange Server and pulls the mobile device details into the SCCM database.
      5. Employees who bring their own devices to the workplace and expect to use and connect them to access corporate resources.

Build a List

1. Specify the correct order of the steps that must be completed to configure the Exchange ActiveSync virtual directory for SSL.
   _____ Confirm that *Require SSL* is selected.
   _____ Select **Require**.
   _____ Double-click **SSL Settings**.
   _____ Click the **Microsoft Server-ActiveSync** virtual directory.

2. Specify the correct order of the steps that must be completed to remotely wipe a mobile device.

_____ Click the **Wipe Device** button.

_____ From the menu at the top, click **Exchange** and then choose **Options**.

_____ Type your login information and then click **Sign-in**.

_____ From the menu on the left, click **Phone**.

_____ Open **Internet Explorer** and type your OWA web address.

3. Specify the correct order of the steps that must be completed to synchronize your PC settings.

_____ Click **Change PC Settings**.

_____ Log in with your Microsoft account and press the **Windows logo key + i**.

_____ Under *Settings to Sync*, drag the slider bar to the right to turn on sync for the item.

_____ Select **Sync Your Settings**.

_____ Set **Sync your settings on this PC** to **On**.

4. Specify the correct order of the steps that must be completed to set a Wi-Fi connection to metered on a Windows 8.1 computer.

_____ Select the **Internet Access** icon.

_____ Log in with administrative credentials.

_____ Right-click the wireless connection as choose **Set as Metered**.

_____ Select **Settings** from the *Charms* bar.

■ Business Case Scenarios

Scenario 10-1: Syncing Your Mobile Users

Many of your users are bringing their smartphones and tablets to work. Once at work, they ask that you provide the wireless access key to gain access. You want to allow your Exchange Admins to continue to manage mailbox issues while transitioning the management of mobile devices and their associated policies to another small group within your IT department. Is this possible? If so, how should you approach it?

Scenario 10-2: Configuring Digital Certificates/Authentication

You set up Exchange Server 2013 on your network, which created a virtual directory. You want to make sure it is as secure as possible, so you decide to use the self-signed digital certificate created during the installation process. You make sure this certificate is trusted by all your internal users and computers. If you know you need to share the certificate with users who are not members of your organization, what should you do?

Supporting Client Compliance

70-688 EXAM OBJECTIVE

Objective 3.3 – Supporting client compliance. This objective may include, but is not limited to: Manage updates by using Windows Update and Windows Intune, including non-Microsoft updates; manage client security by using Windows Defender, Windows Intune Endpoint Protection, or Microsoft System Center 2012 Endpoint Protection; manage Internet Explorer 11 security; support Group Policy application, including Resultant Set of Policy (RSoP), policy processing, and Group Policy caching.

LESSON HEADING	EXAM OBJECTIVE
Managing Endpoint Security	
Managing Updates Using Windows Update	Manage updates by using Windows Update and Windows Intune, including non-Microsoft updates
Managing Windows Server Update Services (WSUS) 4.0 Using Windows Server 2012 R2	Manage updates by using Windows Update and Windows Intune, including non-Microsoft updates
Determining a Deployment Strategy	
Reviewing the Update Services Console	
Understanding the WSUS Infrastructure	
Configuring Clients to Use WSUS	
Using Computer Groups with WSUS	
Selecting Server-Side Targeting Versus Client-Side Targeting	
Approving and Installing Updates on the Client Computers	
Managing Updates by Using Windows Update and Windows Intune	Manage updates by using Windows Update and Windows Intune, including non-Microsoft updates
Understanding the Automatic Update Approval Rule	
Approving Updates Manually	
Declining Updates	
Managing Client Security Using Windows Defender	Manage client security by using Windows Defender, Windows Intune Endpoint Protection, or Microsoft System Center 2012 Endpoint Protection
Exploring the Home tab	
Exploring the Update tab	

KEY TERMS

Action Center

ActiveX controls

ActiveX Filtering

add-ons

Application Reputation

Automatic Update Approval rules

autonomous (distribution) mode

client-side targeting

cookie

Default Domain
Controller Policy

Default Domain Policy

Dynamic security

downstream servers

Group Policy

group policy objects (GPOs)

inheritance

InPrivate Browsing

loopback processing

Microsoft Active Protection
Service (MAPS)

phishing

Pop-up Blocker

replica mode

Resultant Set of Policy (RSoP)

Secure Sockets Layer (SSL)

security zones

server-side targeting

SmartScreen Filter

synchronization

System Center Endpoint
Protection (SCEP) client

Tracking Protection

unblocking

upstream server

Windows Defender

Windows Server Update
Services (WSUS)

Windows Update

■ Managing Endpoint Security

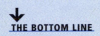

THE BOTTOM LINE

Managing the security of your clients and computers involves a multi-layered approach. To ensure your systems are protected, you need to make sure you have the latest service packs and patches for the operating system and the current updates for Microsoft and third-party applications to maintain stability. You can accomplish this using Windows Update on each Windows 8.1 computer or using Windows Server Update Services (WSUS) to manage and approve your updates from a central server.

To protect against malware, spyware, and viruses, you need real-time protection that can be provided by Windows Defender or through antimalware policies created and deployed to System Center Endpoint Protection (SCEP) clients.

Application Reputation provides protection from downloading malware through the use of SmartScreen, which is used in Internet Explorer and File Explorer. In this lesson, you learn more about how each of these works.

■ Managing Updates Using Windows Update

THE BOTTOM LINE

Windows Update provides your Windows 8.1 users with a way to keep their computers current by checking a designated server. The server provides software that patches security issues, installs updates that make Windows and your applications more stable, fixes issues with existing Windows programs, and provides new features. The server can be hosted by Microsoft or it can be set up and managed in your organization by running the Windows Server Update Services (WSUS).

CERTIFICATION READY
Manage updates by using Windows Update and Windows Intune, including non-Microsoft updates
Objective 3.3

On a Windows 8.1 computer, you can access the Windows Update feature though the Control Panel (*Control Panel > Windows Update*).

From the Windows Update window (see Figure 11-1), you can check for updates, change settings, view the updated history, see installed updates, and restore hidden updates.

> **+ MORE INFORMATION**
>
> At one point, Windows Update was the source for downloading the latest service pack and patches for Windows operating systems. Microsoft Update was used for other updates related to MS Office programs. Over the years, these have basically been merged under the Microsoft Update name.

Figure 11-1

Viewing Windows updates

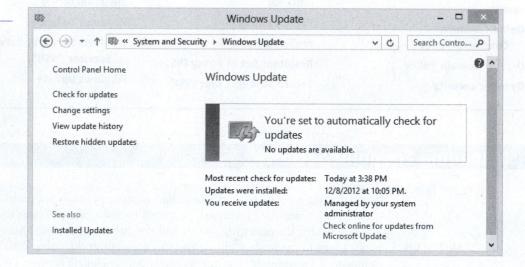

Windows updates are organized into the following categories:

- **Important updates:** These updates are designed to maintain computer security and reliability. Examples might include a patch for a security issue that allows an unauthenticated remote attacker to gain control of your system or update to your definition files used to detect viruses, spyware, and other unwanted software.

- **Recommended updates:** These updates are designed to keep your computer running smoothly.

- **Optional updates:** These are optional updates (such as installing a codec pack that enables you to view RAW camera files or troubleshooting an incorrect keyboard layout for computers) that run a multi-language version of Windows 8.1.

When you first install Windows 8.1, you have the option to choose how you want Windows Update to function. It's possible to make changes after Windows 8.1 is installed unless your Administrator has disabled this option via a Local Group policy or a Domain-based Group policy for your user and/or computer account.

Group Policy settings related to Windows Update can be found in the following locations:

- *Computer Configuration > Policies\Administrative Templates > Windows Components > Windows Update > Configure Automatic Updates*

- *User Configuration > Policies >Administrative Templates > Windows Components > Windows Update > Configure Automatic Updates*

REVIEW YOUR WINDOWS UPDATE SETTINGS

GET READY. To review your Windows Update settings on a Windows 8.1 computer, perform the following steps:

1. Log in with local Administrative privileges.

2. Press the **Windows logo key + I** and from the menu, choose **Control Panel**.

3. Click **System and Security > Windows Update**.

4. In the *left* pane, click the **Change settings** link.

5. Under *Important updates,* click the **drop-down arrow** to review the options for installing important updates.

6. Click **Cancel** to exit and leave your existing setting for Windows Update configured to *Install updates automatically (recommended)*.

The options for Windows Update include:

- **Install updates automatically:** Updates are automatically downloaded in the background and are automatically installed based on the maintenance window specified. Windows runs automatic maintenance daily at 3:00 AM (this is the default, but it can be changed) to perform tasks such as system diagnostics, security scanning, and software updates. Automatic maintenance occurs only if your computer is idle.

- **Download updates but let me choose whether to install them:** Updates are automatically downloaded in the background. You also have the option to receive updates the same way you receive your important updates.

- **Check for updates but let me choose whether to download and install them.** Windows checks for updates but lets you decide whether to download and install them.

- **Never check for updates (not recommended):** Windows does not check, download, or install important updates.

 **MORE INFORMATION**

Microsoft releases security and other patches for the software and operating systems on the second Tuesday of each month. This day, called Patch Tuesday, is used to roll out patches designed to fix recently discovered security holes.

From the Windows Update dialog box, you can also perform the following tasks by selecting the appropriate link from the panel on the left (see Figure 11-2):

Figure 11-2

Viewing the Windows Update links

- **Check for updates:** Selecting this link forces Windows to contact the Windows Update server at Microsoft. When it is completed, you can see how many updates are available along with tracking information about the most recent check for updates and when updates were installed last.

- **Change settings:** Selecting this link provides you with options to configure how Windows Update functions, including which updates to download, how often to check for updates, how often to download new updates, and if Microsoft non-Windows updates are included.

- **View update history:** This link provides you with a list of updates that are installed on your computer, their names, statuses (canceled or succeeded), their importance (important, recommended, or optional), and their installation dates. To remove an update, you can select the *Installed Updates* link at the top of the *History* page.

- **Restore hidden updates:** These are updates that you have informed Windows to not notify you about or install automatically.

- **Installed updates:** Provides information (name, program, version, publisher, and installation date) for all currently installed updates.

Managing Windows Server Update Services (WSUS) 4.0 Using Windows Server 2012 R2

 THE BOTTOM LINE

WSUS provides a centralized server that can be used to manage the deployment of updates from Microsoft. Instead of having each of your Windows 8.1 computers connect to Microsoft to check for updates, consider using *Windows Server Update Services (WSUS)*. WSUS enables you to centrally manage the deployment of updates released through Microsoft, track compliance, and provide basic reporting functions.

CERTIFICATION READY
Manage updates by using Windows Update and Windows Intune, including non-Microsoft updates
Objective 3.3

The main components of WSUS are:

- **Windows Server Update Services (WSUS):** This is installed on a Windows server behind your perimeter firewall. This service enables you to manage and distribute updates to WSUS clients. It can also update sources for other WSUS servers.

- **Microsoft Update:** This is the Microsoft website WSUS connects to for updates.

- **Update Services console:** This is the console that can be accessed to manage WSUS.

Setting up WSUS involves the following:

1. Determining a deployment strategy.
2. Installing the WSUS server role.
3. Specifying an update source for the WSUS server.
4. Synchronizing updates to the WSUS server.
5. Setting up client computers.
6. Approving and installing updates on the client computers.

Determining a Deployment Strategy

Determining the appropriate deployment strategy for WSUS ensures that you have the right servers installed in the appropriate locations based on how your organization is geographically dispersed. It also helps you recognize when and where to place WSUS to reduce needless traffic across your WAN links.

You can deploy a single WSUS server to connect to the Microsoft Update Servers and download updates. Figure 11-3 shows an example of a single WSUS deployment in which the clients are connecting to a single server running WSUS. The server connects and downloads updates directly from the Microsoft Update servers. The process of connecting and downloading updates is called **synchronization.** While a single server option works well in a small office environment, it does not scale very well for companies that have their employees located across branch offices.

Figure 11-3

Deploying a single WSUS server

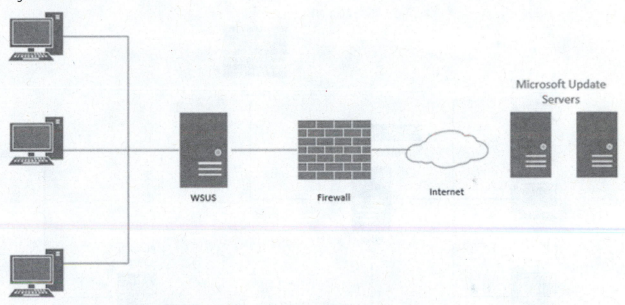

In situations where you need to service a large number of clients or where your computers are dispersed geographically, you should consider implementing more than one WSUS server. The additional WSUS servers can be configured to obtain their updates from the first WSUS server or they can get them directly from the Microsoft Update servers.

When multiple servers are used, the server that obtains updates from Microsoft is called the **upstream server.** The server(s) that obtain their updates from the upstream server are called **downstream servers.** If multiple WSUS servers are used, you need to make sure the server-to-server and server-to-client communications use the Secure Socket Layer (SSL).

Figure 11-4 shows how you might configure multiple WSUS servers when you have a branch office. In this example, the WSUS server at the branch office functions as the downstream server obtaining its updates from the WSUS server (upstream) at the main office either over a VPN or over an intranet connection. The WSUS server at the main office will download the updates from the Microsoft Update servers and distribute them to the downstream WSUS servers. Both the main office and branch office servers can then make the updates available to their clients on their own local network. This utilizes bandwidth more efficiently. In general, Microsoft recommends that you do not create a hierarchy that is more than three levels deep due to propagation issues.

Figure 11-4

Implementing multiple WSUS
servers

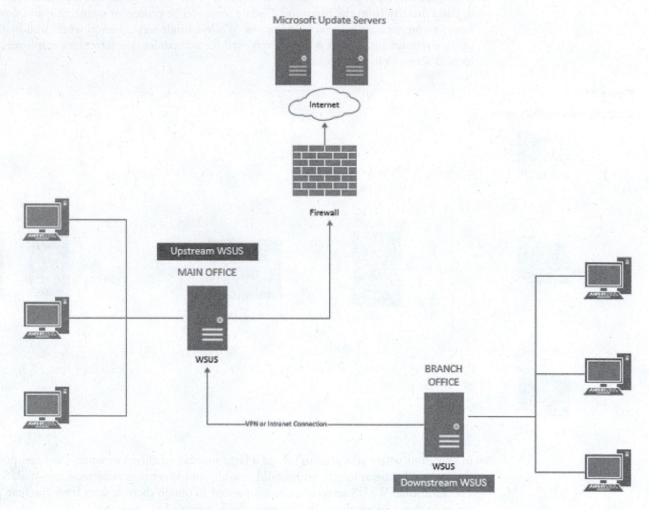

+ **MORE INFORMATION**

WSUS uses port 8530 for the HTTP protocol and port 8531 for HTTPS to obtain updates from the Microsoft Update
servers. In order to communicate with the Microsoft Update servers, make sure you do not block them at your
perimeter firewall.

INSTALL AN UPSTREAM WSUS SERVER

GET READY. To install an upstream WSUS server on a Windows Server 2012 R2 domain controller, log in with administrative privileges and then perform the following steps:

1. Click **Manage > Add Roles and Features** and then click **Next**.

2. Select **Role-based** or **Feature-based installation** and then click **Next**.

3. On the *Select destination server* page, make sure your domain controller is
   highlighted and then click **Next**.

4. On the *Select server* roles page, click **Windows Server Update Services**.

5. When you are prompted to install additional features required for WSUS, click **Add
   Features** and then click **Next**.

6. Click **Next** to continue.

7. On the *Select features* page, click **Next** to continue.

8. Read the information about WSUS and then click **Next**.

9. Under *Role services,* confirm **WID Database** and **WSUS Services** are checked and then click **Next**.

10. On the *Content location selection* page, make sure *Store updates in the following location* is checked, type **c:\WSUSupdates**, and then click **Next**.

    This drive location, which must have at least 6GB of free disk space, can be used to store updates for client computer to download quickly.

11. Read the information about the *Web Server Role (IIS)*, and then click **Next**.

12. On the *Select role services* page, click **Next** to accept the defaults.

13. Click **Install**.

14. On the *Installation progress* page, click **Close** and then wait for the installation to complete.

15. From the *Server Manager* console, click the yellow triangle and then click **Launch Post-Installation tasks**.

    When you see the message *Configuration completed for Windows Server Update Services at <servername>*, you can continue to the next step.

16. Click **Tools > Windows Server Update Services.** When the *Windows Server Update Services* appears, click **Next**.

    You might need to minimize *Server Manager* to see the *Windows Server Update Services Configuration Wizard*.

17. On the *Join the Microsoft Update Improvement Program* page, deselect the option **Yes, I would like to join the Microsoft Update Improvement Program** and then click **Next**.

18. On the *Choose Upstream Server,* click **Next** to choose to synchronize this server with Microsoft Update.

19. On the *Specify Proxy Server* page, click **Next**.

20. On the *Connect to Upstream Server* page, click **Start Connecting**.

21. After the server connects, click **Next** to proceed.

22. Click **Download updates only in these languages** and then choose **English**. Click **Next**.

23. Scroll down and deselect **Office**. Continue to scroll until you see *Windows*. Deselect everything except **Windows 8.1 Language Packs, Windows 8.1, and Windows Defender**. Click **Next** to continue.

    This reduces the space and time needed to download updates. If this were a real production server, you would download the application and operating system updates to match your needs.

24. On the *Choose Classifications* page, accept the defaults and then click **Next**.

    This ensures you obtain the Critical Updates, Definition Updates, and Security Updates.

25. On the *Set Sync Schedule* page, click **Next** to accept the default setting.

26. Click **Begin initial synchronization** and then click **Next**.

27. Click **Finish**.

    Your system synchronizes with the Microsoft Update Servers in the background.

28. On the *Update Services* page (see Figure 11-5), you can expand your server name and then click **Synchronizations to view the progress**.

Figure 11-5

Monitoring the progress of the
WSUS synchronization

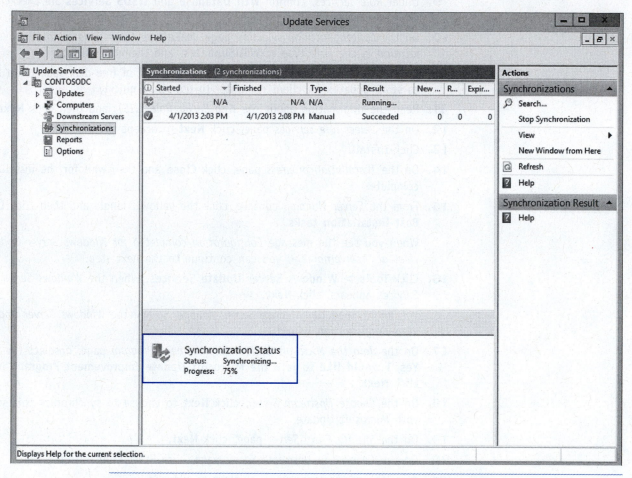

Now that you have your upstream server configured, you can set up a downstream WSUS
server on another computer in your domain. In the following exercise, you use a nondomain
controller (for example, the member server).

 INSTALL A DOWNSTREAM WSUS SERVER

GET READY. To install a downstream WSUS server on a Windows member server, log in with
administrative privileges and perform the following steps:

1. Click **Manage > Add Roles and Features** and then click **Next**.
2. Click **Role-based** or **Feature-based installation** and then click **Next**.
3. On *Select destination server* page, make sure your member server is highlighted and
   then click **Next**.
4. On the *Select server* roles page, select **Windows Server Update Services**.
5. When you are prompted to install additional features required for WSUS, click **Add
   Features** and then click **Next**.
6. Click **Next** to continue.
7. On the *Select features* page, click **Next** to continue.
8. Read information about WSUS and then click **Next**.

9. Under *Role services,* confirm **WID Database** and **WSUS Services** are checked and then click **Next**.

10. On the *Content location selection* page, make sure *Store updates in the following location* is checked, type **c:\WSUSupdates**, and then click **Next**.

    This drive location, which must have at least 6GB of free disk space can be used to store updates for client computer to download quickly.

11. Read the information about the *Web Server Role (IIS)* and then click **Next**.

12. On the *Select role services* page, click **Next** to accept the defaults.

13. Click **Install**.

14. On the *Installation progress* page, click **Close** and then wait for the installation to complete.

15. From the *Server Manager* console, click the yellow triangle and then click **Launch Post-Installation tasks**. When you see the message *Configuration completed for Windows Server Update Services at <servername>*, you can continue to the next step.

16. Click **Tools > Windows Server Update Services**. When the Windows Server Update Services appears, click **Next**.

    You might need to minimize the *Server Manager* to see the *Windows Server Update Services Configuration Wizard*.

17. On the *Choose Upstream Server* page, click **Synchronize from another Windows Server Update Services server**. In the *Server name* field, type the name of the server you set up WSUS on in the previous exercise and then click **Next**.

18. On the *Specify Proxy Server* page, click **Next**.

19. On the *Connect to Upstream Server* page, click **Start Connecting**.

20. After the server connects, click **Next** to proceed.

21. On the *Choose Languages* page, click **Next** to accept the default setting *Download updates only in these languages* and *English*.

22. On the *Set Sync Schedule* page, click **Next** to accept the default setting.

23. Select **Begin initial synchronization** and then click **Next**.

24. Click **Finish**. Your system synchronizes with the upstream server in the background.

25. On the *Update Services* page, you can expand your server name and then click **Synchronizations** to view the progress.

When the downstream WSUS server synchronizes with the upstream WSUS server, it downloads updates in the form of metadata and files. The update metadata can be found in the WSUS database. The update files are stored on either the WSUS server or on the Microsoft Update servers. The location is determined when you set up WSUS. In the earlier examples, we configured the WSUS server to store the updates in the *c:\WSUSUpdates* folder.

If the server is a downstream server, the products (Office, Developer Tools, Exchange, Skype, System Center, Windows, and so on) and classifications (critical updates, definition updates, drivers, security updates, and so on) included with the synchronization are set up on the upstream server.

The first time the downstream server synchronizes, it downloads all of the updates you specified. After the first synchronization has completed, the server downloads only updates made since the last synchronization.

Now that you have installed an upstream and a downstream WSUS server, you might wonder which components are installed with WSUS:

- **.NET Framework 4.5:** Provides core support for running ASP.NET 4.5 standalone applications and applications that are integrated with IIS.
- **Remote Server Administration Tools:** Includes snap-ins and command-line tools for remotely managing roles and features.
- **Web Server (IIS):** An ASP.NET web service application that requires IIS to deliver access to the services it provides.
- **Windows Internal Database (WID) used by WSUS:** A relational data store used only by Windows roles and features.
- **Windows Process Activation Service:** Generalizes the IIS process model and removes the dependency on HTTP.

Reviewing the Update Services Console

After completing the installation, you can access the Update Services console. In Server Manager, choose *Tools > Windows Server Update Services*.

Figure 11-6

Reviewing the folders in the Update Services console

The Update Services Console includes the following features (see Figure 11-6):

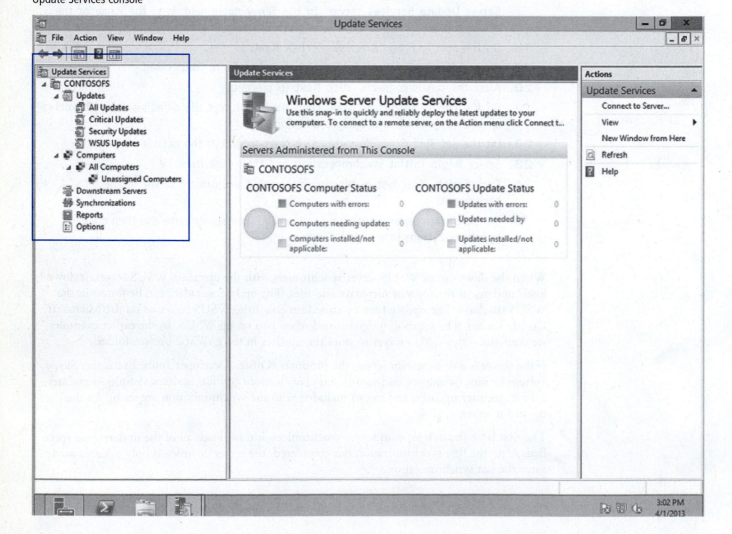

- **Updates:** Updates, used to repair and/or replace software, consist of metadata (properties of the actual updated data) that allows you to determine its uses and the update files that are required to install the update on a computer. These updates are categorized under the following nodes: All Updates, Critical Updates, Security Updates, and WSUS Updates.

- **Computers:** These groups are created by default during the WSUS installation. Groups enable you to target your updates to specific computers and to stagger your rollout of updates. You do not see any computers in the console until you have configured the clients to use WSUS.

  - **All Computers:** Includes all computers.

  - **Unassigned Computers:** If a computer is not assigned to a group, it is added to this node the first time it contacts the WSUS server.

- **Downstream servers:** This lists the downstream servers that obtain their update files, metadata, and approvals from this WSUS server instead of from Microsoft Update or Windows Update.

- **Synchronizations:** During synchronization, the WSUS server downloads updates in the form of metadata and files from an update source. This can be another WSUS server or from the Microsoft servers and Windows Update servers.

- **Reports:** These reports allow you to monitor updates, computers, and synchronization results. You can also roll up data form downstream servers.

- **Options:** This folder provides access to tools you can use to modify settings on the WSUS server. Using the tools provided, you can specify how you want to approve the installation of updates, change your synchronization schedule, clean up old computers, update files from the server, and choose how data is displayed in the Update Services console.

Understanding the WSUS Infrastructure

> When you have both upstream and a downstream WSUS servers run on your network, you might want to control how update approvals, settings, computers, and groups are managed. To do this, you must first understand the two modes WSUS can run in: replica and autonomous.

As you learned from setting up the upstream and downstream WSUS servers earlier, you have two options about where you obtained your updates. You can synchronize directly from the Microsoft Update servers or from another WSUS server on your network. The choice you did not have to make at the time was whether or not your downstream WSUS server was going to run in replica or autonomous mode. By default, your downstream WSUS server was automatically set to run in in autonomous (distribution) mode.

In *replica mode*, a WSUS server mirrors update approvals, settings, computers, and groups from the upstream server. In other words, the downstream server cannot be used to approve updates; they must be performed on the upstream server.

If you are operating the WSUS server in *autonomous (distribution) mode*, it enables you to configure separate update approval settings while still retrieving updates from the upstream WSUS server.

Now that you understand the difference between the two, there might come a time when you decide that you want to manage the approval of all updates from the upstream server. This is common in situations where you have a downstream WSUS server at a branch office that has no IT support staff. If that happens, you need to understand how to configure your downstream WSUS server to run in replica mode.

→ **CONFIGURE A DOWNSTREAM WSUS SERVER TO RUN IN REPLICA MODE**

GET READY. To assign your downstream WSUS server to run in Replica mode, log in to your member server with Administrative privileges and then perform the following steps:

1. The *Server Manager* console opens automatically. If it does not open, on the task bar, click the **Server Manager** icon.

2. Click **Tools > Windows Server Update Services**.

3. From the pane on the left, click **Options** and then choose **Update Source and Proxy Server**.

4. Click **This server is a replica of the upstream server** and then click **OK**.

5. From the left pane, expand **Updates** and then click the **All Updates** folder.

6. In the middle pane, change the status to **Any** and then click **Refresh** (see Figure 11-7).

Figure 11-7

Reviewing All Updates

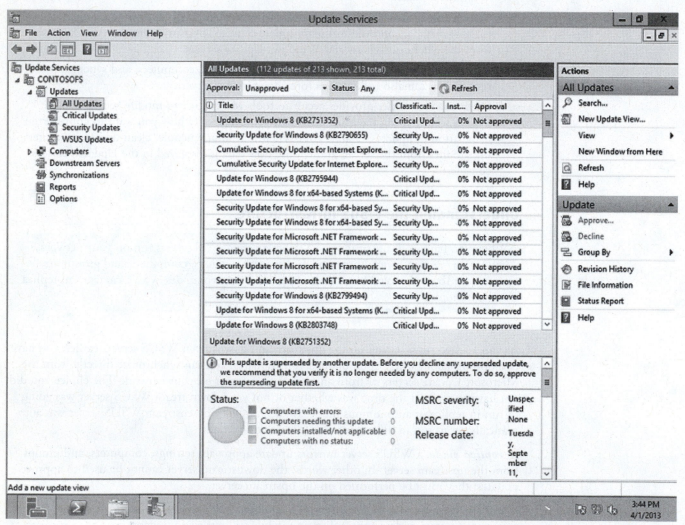

7. Right-click the first update in the list. In the menu that appears, notice that the option to *Approve* or *Decline* the update is disabled. The downstream server has been configured in replica mode earlier. Updates can be approved only on the upstream server.

8. Close the **Update Services** console.

Configuring Clients to Use WSUS

For clients to obtain their information from your WSUS servers, you need to first configure them. By default, your computers are configured to communicate directly with the Microsoft Update servers. With an Active Directory domain present, you can create a Group Policy Object to configure your clients.

 CREATE A GPO TO ENABLE AUTOUPDATE FOR CLIENT COMPUTERS

GET READY. To create a GPO to enable AutoUpdate for client computers in an Active Directory domain, log in in with Administrative credentials, and then on your domain controller, perform the following steps:

TAKE NOTE*

This can be performed on a Windows 8.1 client with Administrative tools or at the Domain Controller for the domain using the Group Policy Management console.

1. The *Server Manager* console opens automatically. If it does not open, on the task bar, click the **Server Manager** icon.
2. Click **Tools** > **Group Policy Management**.
3. Right-click the **Group Policy Objects** folder and choose **New**.
4. In the *Name* field, type **WSUS AutoUpdate** and then click **OK**.
5. Expand the **Group Policy Objects** folder, right-click **WSUS AutoUpdate**, and then choose **Edit**.
6. Expand the **Computer Configuration** > **Policies** > **Administrative Templates** > **Windows Components** > **Windows Update**.
7. In the *details* pane, double-click **Configure Automatic Updates**.
8. Under *Configure Automatic Updates*, click **Enabled** and under *Configure Automatic updating*, review the options.
9. Under *Configure automatic updating*, make sure **3-Auto download and notify for install** is visible. Read the information in the *help* panel to understand how this setting works. Click **OK** when finished.
10. Double-click **Specify intranet Microsoft update service location**.
11. Under *Specify intranet Microsoft update service location,* click **Enabled** and then type the URL of the upstream WSUS server you set up earlier. For example, if your domain controller's name is ContosoDC, type **http://ContosoDC:8530**. (8530 is the default port used by WSUS.)
12. For the *intranet statistics server*, type the same information.
13. Click **OK**.
14. Close the **Group Policy Management Editor**.
15. Right-click the domain container (contoso.com) and choose **Link an existing GPO**.
16. Choose **WSUS AutoUpdate** and then click **OK**.
17. Close the **Group Policy Management** console.

TAKE NOTE*

Perform these steps on a Windows 8.1 computer that is a member of the Active Directory domain.

18. Restart your Windows 8.1 computer and then log in with Administrative credentials to the domain.
19. In the Windows 8.1 *Start* screen, type **cmd**. In *Results,* right-click **Command Prompt** and then choose **Run as administrator**.
20. From the *Command Prompt window*, type **gpresult /r** and then press **Enter**. The *WSUS AutoUpdate GPO* should appear under the *Computer Settings* > *Applied Group Policy Objects* section of the report. If it does not, type **gpupdate /force** and they try **gpresult /r** again.
21. Type **wuauclt /detectnow** and then press **Enter**. This forces the Windows 8.1 computer to contact the WSUS server immediately.

22. Open the **Update Service** console on the domain controller running WSUS (**Server Manager > Tools > Windows Server Update Services**).

23. Expand the **Computers > All Computers** group. You can see the computer under the *Unassigned Computers* group.

Using Computer Groups with WSUS

After configuring your clients to use WSUS, organize them into computer groups. This enables you to target specific systems for updates. WSUS comes with two built-in groups: All Computers and Unassigned Computers. If you don't have a need to configure and manage your computers separately, you can stay with these groups. If you want to test the impact the updates will have on your computers and any line of business applications before rolling them out to your entire organization, then new groups should be complete.

Here are a few things to note about computer groups:

- If a computer is not assigned to a specific group, it appears in the Unassigned Computers group in the console.
- A computer can be a member of more than one group and groups can be built in a hierarchical structure.
- If you create a group hierarchy, an update rolled out to a parent group is also distributed to child groups.

 CREATE A GROUP IN WSUS

GET READY. To create a group on your domain controller running WSUS, log in with Administrative privileges, and then perform the following steps:

1. Open the **Update Services** console if you closed it earlier (**Server Manager > Tools > Windows Server Update Services**).

2. Expand the **Computers** node, right-click **All Computers**, and then choose **Add Computer Group**.

3. In the *Name* field, type **IT Staff** and then click **Add**.

4. Confirm the group appears under the **All Computers** node. Keep the *Update Services* console open to use in the next exercise.

Selecting Server-Side Targeting Versus Client-Side Targeting

Computers can be assigned to groups using either server-side targeting or client-side targeting. ***Server-side targeting*** involves moving clients to computer groups using the Update Services console. ***Client-side targeting*** involves using Group Policy for domain computers or Local Group Policy Editor for nondomain computers. When using client-side targeting, you configure the computers to add themselves automatically to the computer groups by specifying the group in the *Computer Configuration Policies\Administrative Tools\Windows Components\Windows Update\Enable client-side targeting* policy. Client-side targeting works well when you organize your computers into organizational units based on their configuration or function.

These settings are configured on the WSUS Server via *Update Services > Options > Computers*.

Selecting the *Use the Update Services* console is using server-side targeting; computers are automatically added to the Unassigned Computers group. The other option, *Use Group Policy or registry settings on computers*, configures the WSUS server to support client-side targeting.

USE SERVER-SIDE TARGETING TO MOVE A COMPUTER TO A GROUP

GET READY. To use server-side targeting, on your domain controller running WSUS, log in with Administrative privileges and then perform the following steps:

1. From the *Update Services* console, expand **Computers**.
2. In the *Unassigned Computers* group, right-click the **Windows 8.1 computer** and choose **Change Membership**.
3. Select **IT Staff** and then click **OK** to add the computer to the group.
4. Click the **IT Staff** group, and in the middle pane, confirm the computer appears. Keep the *Update Services* console open to use in the next exercise.

Approving and Installing Updates on the Client Computers

Updates downloaded to the upstream server will not be distributed to WSUS clients automatically. As the WSUS administrator, you have to approve them first. If you look under *Options > Automatic Approval*, you can see the following default WSUS settings:

- **Update Rules:** Under this tab, you can specify rules for automatically approving new updates when they are synchronized. The default rule approves security and critical updates for all computers.
- **Advanced tab:** The following options are configured by default under this tab: Automatically approve updates to the WSUS product, Automatically approve new revisions of updates that are already approved, and Automatically decline updates when a new revision causes them to expire.

As the administrator, you can change which updates are automatically detected, which ones are automatically approved, and which groups of computers are targeted to receive the updates.

APPROVE AND DEPLOY WSUS UPDATES

GET READY. To approve and deploy WSUS updates, on your domain controller running WSUS, log in with Administrative privileges, and then perform the following steps:

1. From the *Update Services* console, expand **Updates** and then click **All Updates**.
2. Set the *Status* to **Needed** (see Figure 11-8) and then click **Refresh**.

Figure 11-8

Setting the Status to Needed updates

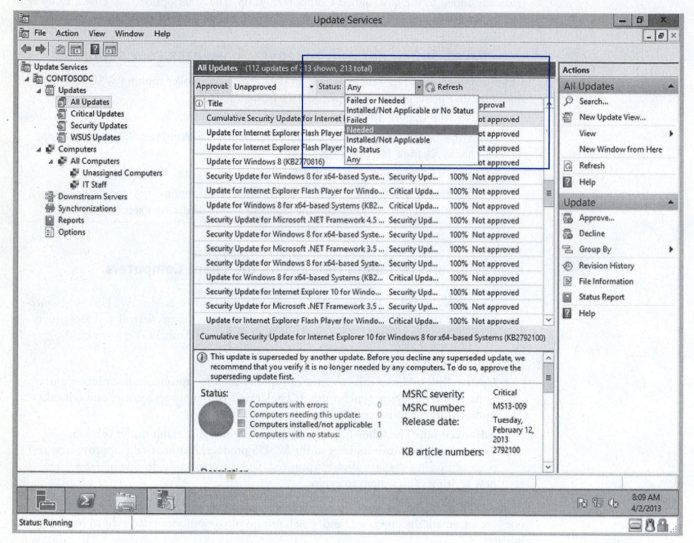

3. Right-click one of the updates and choose **Approve**.

4. In the *Approve* Updates box, click **IT Staff > Approved for Install**.

5. Click **OK**.

6. When the approval process completes, click **Close**.

Now, on the Windows 8.1 Client, perform the following steps:

1. Log on to a Windows 8.1 computer that is a member of the domain.

2. In the Windows 8.1 *Start* screen, type **cmd**. In *Results,* right-click **Command Prompt** and choose **Run as administrator**.

3. From the *Command Prompt* window, type **wuauclt /detectnow** and then press **Enter**. Close the **Command Prompt** window.

   This causes the client to detect available updates, automatically queue them for download via Background Intelligent Transfer Service (BITS), and then present a notification to install the updates on the client.

4. Right-click the notification icon and choose **Open Windows Update**.

5. Click **Install Updates**.

6. If you are prompted after the updates are completed, click **Restart now** to complete the installation of the update.

Managing Updates by Using Windows Update and Windows Intune

THE BOTTOM LINE

In Windows Intune, updates are managed via the Updates workspace (see Figure 11-9). When you are in the Update workspace, you can view any pending updates, approve or decline updates, configure the automatic approval settings, and set the deadline for update installation in automatic approval rules. From the workspace, you can approve not only Microsoft updates but non-Microsoft updates.

Figure 11-9

Managing update in the Updates workspace

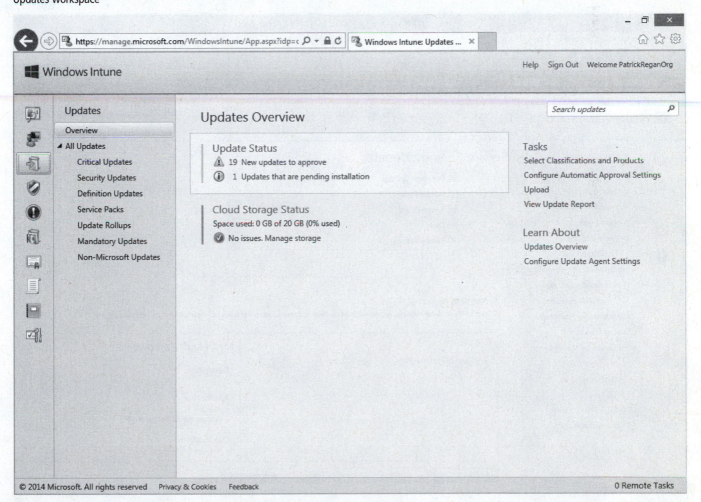

When working with updates, not all of them are applicable to your situation. To help stream-line the process of managing updates, Windows Intune distinguishes the updates according to their respective product categories and update classifications. Product categories are used to organize software by product name; update classifications are arranged according the specific type of update (service pack, critical update, or definition update). Windows Intune checks for updates only on the products and update classifications you select.

REVIEW PRODUCT CATEGORIES AND CLASSIFICATIONS

GET READY. To review products and classifications, perform the following steps:

1. Log in to the **Windows Intune Administrator** console at https://admin.manage. microsoft.com.

2. In the *left* pane, click **Administration**.

3. Click **Updates** (see Figure 11-10).

Figure 11-10

Reviewing product categories and update classifications

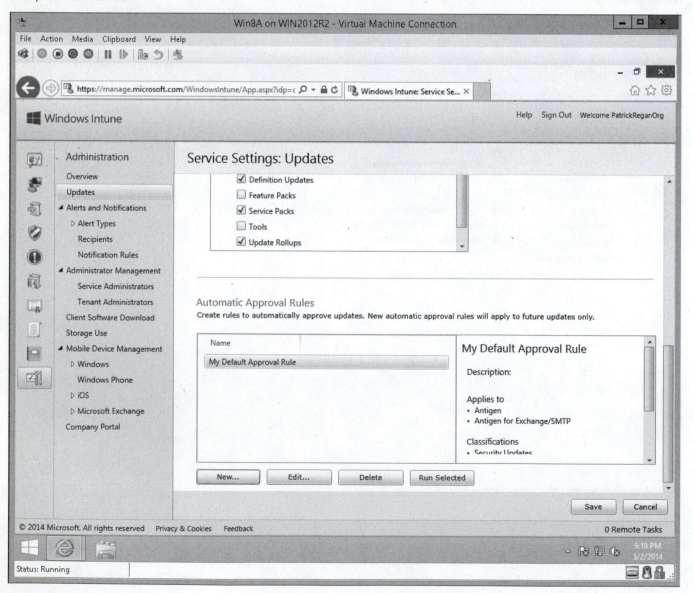

4. Review the product categories that you can filter on and then review the update classifications you can filter on.

5. Scroll down to the bottom until you see the *Automatic Approval Rules* section.

Understanding the Automatic Update Approval Rule

Creating ***Automatic Update Approval rules*** can help streamline the management of your computers. When you create a rule, Windows Intune automatically approves the installation of all critical and security updates as soon as Microsoft releases them. This ensures your clients are updated as soon as possible.

 CREATE AN AUTOMATIC UPDATE APPROVAL RULE

GET READY. To create an Automatic Update approval rule, perform the following steps:

1. If you still have your console open from the previous exercise, skip to Step 4; otherwise, log in to the **Windows Intune Administrator** console at: https://admin.manage.microsoft.com.

2. In the *left* pane, click **Administration**.

3. Click **Updates**.

4. Scroll down until you see *Select Automatic Approval Rules* and then click **New**.

5. In the *Name* field, type **My Default Approval Rule** and then click **Next**.

6. Select **All Categories** and then click **Next**.

7. Under *All Classifications,* select **Critical Updates and Security Updates** and then click **Next**.

8. Choose **My Test Group** and then click **Add**. Click **Next** to continue.

9. Review the information summary and then click **Finish**.

10. Confirm your new rule appears under the *Automatic Approval* rules section (see Figure 11-11).

Figure 11-11

Confirming your Automatic
Update approval rule

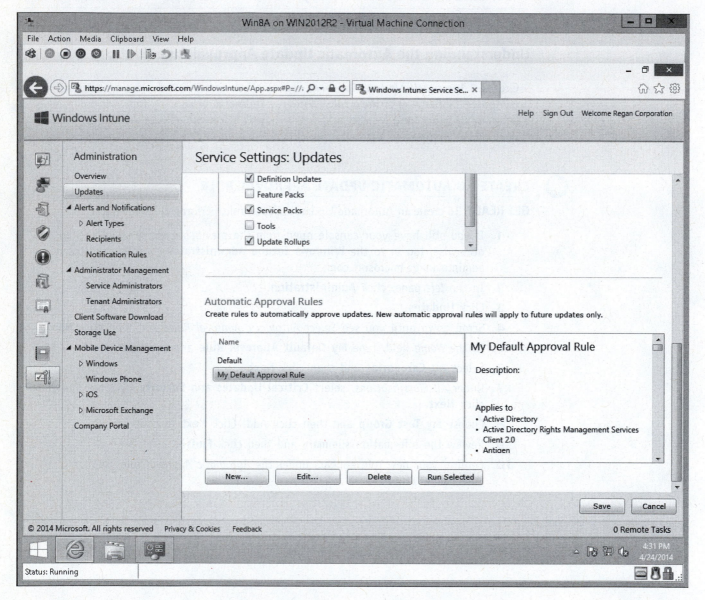

11. Click **Run Selected** and then click **Save**.

This forces the rule to evaluate updates on all computers that run Windows
Intune agents in the group you specified. After the review, the updates are made
available to the computers in the group when they next check in. By default,
the Windows Intune agent checks in every 8 hours for updates. When updates are
available, Windows Intune installs the updates. If you click Save, the rule applies
only to future updates as they are released.

> **+ MORE INFORMATION**
>
> The frequency an agent checks for updates is configured via the Policy workspace. The recommended setting is 8 hours, but you can set the frequency to occur between 8 hours and 22 hours.

12. In the *left* pane, click **Updates**.

13. View the status of the updates. Leave this open to use in the next exercise.

Approving Updates Manually

> You might want to review and manage some updates a little closely before approving and deploying them. In these situations, perform a manual update from the Update workspace.

In Windows Intune, you can manage updates from Microsoft Update and from third parties. Microsoft updates are included in the Windows Intune console; third-party updates require additional setup. When approving a Microsoft update, you can approve it for an individual group or for multiple groups. To approve an update for multiple groups, you take advantage of the parent and child group hierarchy. For example, you can approve the update for the All Computers group and its child groups receive the updates via inheritance.

> **+ MORE INFORMATION**
>
> To select multiple groups, you can use the Ctrl or Shift key when selecting the updates to approve.

➜ APPROVE AN UPDATE MANUALLY

GET READY. To approve an update manually, perform the following steps:

1. Log in to the **Windows Intune Administrator** console at https://admin.manage. microsoft.com.

2. In the *left* pane, click **Updates**.

3. Under *Update Status*, click **New updates to approve** (see Figure 11-12).

Figure 11-12

Viewing the updates to
approve

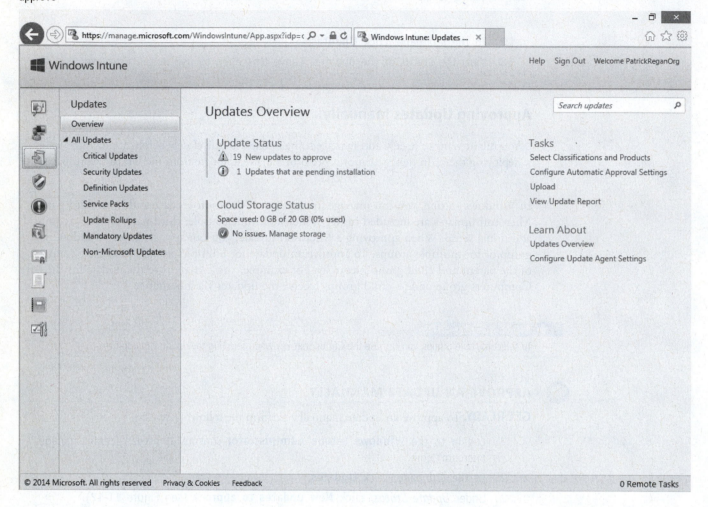

4. Click one of the updates and review additional information about it.

   Figure 11-13 shows the updates available for Windows 8.1 running the Windows Intune agent. By clicking on the name of the update, you can see how many computers need that specific update. By selecting the **Computers that need this update to be approved** link under *Current status*, you can see the name of the actual computer the update is applied to.

Figure 11-13

Reviewing updates that are available

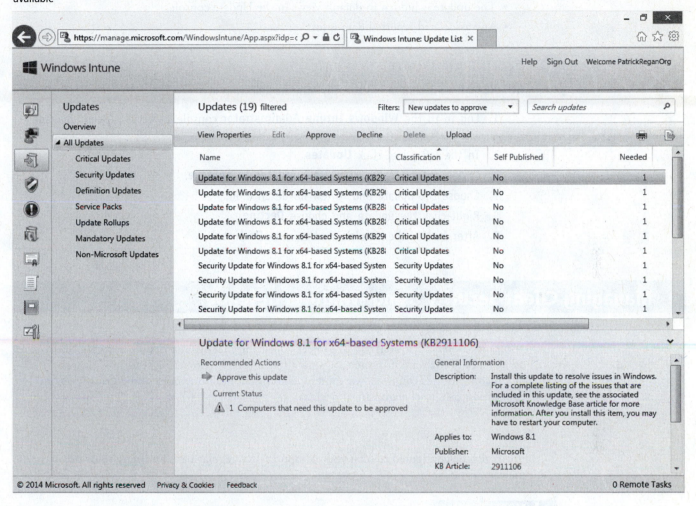

5. Choose one the updates and click **Approve**.
6. On the *Select the groups to which you want to deploy this update* page, choose **My Test Group** and then click **Add**.
7. Click **Next**.
8. Under *Approval*, click **Finish**. Review the message at the bottom of the page for additional information regarding the updates.
9. Click **Finish**.

Declining Updates

In the previous sections, you learned the process for approving updates either manually or automatically via the Automatic Approval rules. You can also decline updates.

When you decline an update:

- All approvals for the update are removed.
- The update is hidden in default views in the Update console.
- Any associated reported data is lost.

 DECLINE AN UPDATE

GET READY. To decline an update, perform the following steps:

1. Log in to the **Windows Intune Administrator** console at https://admin.manage.microsoft.com.
2. In the *left* pane, click **Updates**.
3. Under *Update Status,* click **New updates to approve**.
4. Choose the update and review its description.
5. Right-click the update and choose **Decline**.
6. After reading the warning prompt, click **Decline**.

■ Managing Client Security Using Windows Defender

Windows Defender is designed to protect your computer against viruses, spyware, and other types of malware. It protects against these threats by providing real-time protection in which it notifies you if malware attempts to install itself on your computer or when an application tries to change critical settings.

It can also be configured to scan your computer on a regular basis and remove or quarantine malware it finds.

+ MORE INFORMATION

Windows Defender automatically disables itself if you install another antivirus product.

CERTIFICATION READY
Manage client security by using Windows Defender, Windows Intune Endpoint Protection, or Microsoft System Center 2012 Endpoint Protection
Objective 3.3

At the heart of Windows Defender are its definition files, which are downloaded from Windows Update. The definition files, which contain information about potential threats, are used by Windows Defender to notify you of potential threats to your system.

To access Windows Defender from the Windows 8.1 menu, type *Windows Defender* and choose it from the *Results*. Figure 11-14 shows the Windows Defender Home tab.

Figure 11-14

Viewing the Windows Defender Home tab

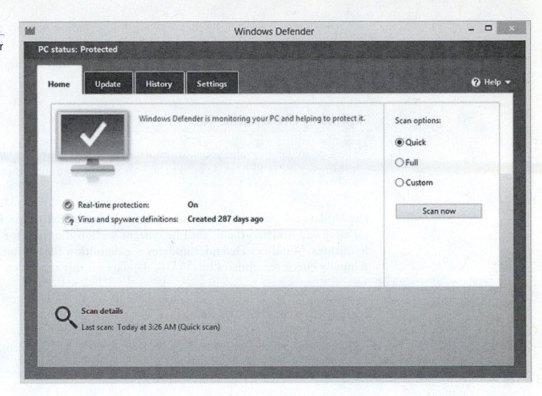

Exploring the Home tab

The home tab allows you to check the status of Windows Defender, including whether Windows Defender is up to date and whether Windows Defender is protecting your system. It also gives you the option to initiate a scan.

When looking at the Home tab, you should always look for a green message indicating *Your PC is being monitored and protected* and you should also make sure your system is up to date. Other components include:

- **Real-time protection:** Real-time protection uses signature detection methodology and heuristics to monitor and catch malware behavior. Signature detection uses a vendor's definition files to detect malicious programs. If the program contains code that matches the signature, the program most likely contains the virus. This works well when the threat has already been identified, but what happens in between the time the virus is released and the definition file is made available? That's where heuristics can help. It is used to monitor for suspicious activity by a program. Suspicious activity includes a program trying to copy itself into another program, a program trying to write to the disk directly, or a program trying to manipulate critical system files required by the operating system. These are indicators of possible malware activity that heuristics can detect.

- **Virus and spyware definitions:** When a new virus is discovered, Microsoft creates a new virus signature/definition update. Each definition file contains a piece of the actual virus code that is used to detect a specific virus or malware. During scans, the content on the computer is compared to information in the definition files. Because new viruses are created every day and existing viruses are modified regularly, it's important to keep your definitions updated.

- **Scan options (Quick, Full, and Custom):** A Quick scan checks the areas that malicious software, including viruses, spyware, and unwanted software are most likely to infect.

A Full scan checks all the files on your disk including running programs. A Custom scan is designed to check only locations and files you specify.

- **Scan Details:** This area of the Home tab provides information on when the last scan was performed on the computer.

Exploring the Update Tab

> The Update tab provides you with information about your virus and spyware definitions. It is important to keep these current to ensure your computer is protected at all times.

The Update tab provides information about when the definition files were created, the last time you updated them, and the current version numbers for the virus and spyware definitions. Windows Defender updates the definition files automatically, but you can manually check for updates by clicking Update on this tab.

Exploring the History Tab

> The History tab provides information about items that have been detected in the past and the actions that were taken with them.

The categories of items are as follows:

- **Quarantined Items:** These items were not allowed to run but were not removed from your computer.
- **Allowed Items:** These items were allowed to run on your computer.
- **All Detected Items:** These items provide a list of all items detected on your computer.

 REMOVE A QUARANTINED ITEM

GET READY. To remove an item that has been quarantined, perform the following steps:

1. Open **Windows Defender**.
2. Click the **History** tab.
3. Click **Quarantined Items** (see Figure 11-15).

Figure 11-15

Removing a quarantined item

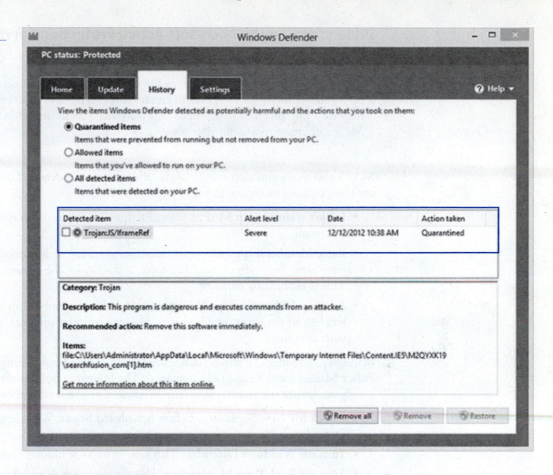

4. Click **View Details**.
5. Select the detected item and then read the description.
6. Click **Remove**.

Exploring the Settings Tab

The Settings tab is where you can fine-tune how Windows Defender works.

In the Settings tab, you can:

- Enable or disable real-time protection.
- Select the files and locations you want to exclude from the scanning process.
- Select the file types you want to exclude from the scan.
- Select the processes you want to exclude.
- Configure Advanced settings that include enabling scans of archive files (cab/zip), scanning removable drives, creating system restore points, allowing users to view full history results, and establishing how long you want to hold quarantine files before they are removed. By default, Windows Defender scans archive files and removes quarantined files after three months.
- Turn on Windows Defender.

Understanding the Microsoft Active Protection Service (MAPS)

On the Settings tab, you can also determine whether you want to participate in the *Microsoft Active Protection Service (MAPS)*. MAPS is an online community that can help you decide how to respond to certain threat types and it serves as a resource to help stop the spread of new viruses and malware. The information that you send helps Microsoft create new definition files.

MAPS also sends you alerts when unclassified software is detected on your computer. There are three options to choose from:

- **I don't want to join MAPS:** Selecting this option means no information is sent to Microsoft.
- **Basic Membership:** This option sends information to Microsoft about where the software came from, the actions you took, and whether the actions you took were successful. This is enabled by default.
- **Advanced Membership:** This option sends Basic membership information such as the location of the software, file names, how the software operates, and how it has impacted your computer.

Windows Defender can also be configured via the Local Group Policy Editor or Group Policy Management Editor (AD domains). The following policies are located in the *Computer Configuration\Administrative Templates\Windows Components\Windows Defender* node:

- **Check for New Signatures before Scheduled Scans:** When enabled, Windows Defender checks for new signatures before running the scan.
- **Turn off Windows Defender:** This setting turns Windows Defender on or off.
- **Turn off Real-Time Monitoring:** This setting controls whether Windows Defender monitors your system in real-time and alerts you malware for potentially unwanted software attempts to install or run on the computer.
- **Turn off Routinely Taking Action:** This setting determines whether Windows Defender automatically takes action on malware that it identifies.
- **Configure Microsoft Active Protection Service Reporting:** This setting determines the type of membership you use with MAPS. Options include *No Membership*, *Basic Membership*, or *Advanced Membership*.

 SCHEDULE A WINDOWS DEFENDER SCAN

GET READY. To schedule a Windows Defender scan, log in with Administrative privileges and then perform the following steps:

1. Press the **Windows logo key + r** and in the *Run* dialog box, type **taskschd.msc**.
2. In the left pane, expand **Task Scheduler Library > Microsoft > Windows > Windows Defender**.
3. Double-click **Windows Defender Scheduled Scan**.
4. Click the **Triggers** tab and then click **New**.
5. In the *Begin the task* field, choose **On a schedule**.
6. Under *Settings*, select **One time** and in the *Start* field, change the time to 5 minutes from your current time.
7. Make sure the **Enabled** check box is checked and then click **OK**.
8. To close the *Windows Defender Scheduled Scan Properties* dialog box, click **OK**.
9. Open **Windows Defender** to see the status of the scan on the Home tab. Click **Cancel scan**.

Managing Client Security Using SCCM 2012 Endpoint Protection Client

THE BOTTOM LINE

The System Center Endpoint Protection (SCEP) client, integrated with System Center Configuration Manager 2012 (SCCM), provides a central point of management for deploying and managing malware threats.

System Center Endpoint Protection (SCEP) client, a product in the Microsoft System Center 2012 suite, is designed to protect clients and servers from malware threats. Although many of the products were offered as standalone versions in previous releases, SCEP is now integrated with the System Center Configuration Manager. SCCM provides a central console for managing application delivery, device management, and security. By integrating SCEP with the Configuration Manager, you now have the ability to take advantage of its remediation and compliance capabilities, as well as the protection features provided by Endpoint Protection.

Using Endpoint Protection with Configuration Manager, you can manage your antimalware policies and Windows Firewall security for client computers and servers and monitor compliance and security across your entire organization. This provides the following capabilities and benefits:

- You can target antimalware policies and Windows Firewall settings to selected computers.
- You can use Configuration Manager Software updates to obtain the latest definition files and keep your client computers current.
- You can send e-mail notifications, use in-console monitoring, and view reports when malware is detected on client computers.
- You can monitor the status of computers (total active clients protected by Endpoint Protection), which clients are at risk, and malware remediation status (failed remediation, full scans required, client settings modified by malware, malware remediated in the last 24 hours, status of deployed antimalware policies, the definition status on computers, and so on).

In addition to installing the Configuration Manager client, SCEP installs its own client that is used to detect and resolve malware and spyware. The client also detects and addresses root kits that are used to gain administrative access to the computer and perform automatic definition and malware engine updates.

> **CERTIFICATION READY**
> Manage client security by using Windows Defender, Windows Intune Endpoint Protection, or Microsoft System Center 2012 Endpoint Protection
> Objective 3.3

+ MORE INFORMATION

The Endpoint Protection Client can also be installed on Hyper-V servers and guest machines.

 PERFORM A MANUAL INSTALL OF THE SCEP CLIENT

GET READY. To perform a manual installation of the SCEP client, log in to your Windows 8.1 computer with administrative privileges and then perform the following steps:

TAKE NOTE *

This requires an installation of System Center Configuration Manager 2012 to gain access to the shared folder.

1. Connect to the **SCCM 2012 Server** at **\\servername\SMS_sitecode\client**.
2. Double-click the **scepinstall** file.
3. When the *System Center 2012 Endpoint Protection Installation Wizard* starts, click **Next**.

4. On the *Licensing* screen, click **I accept**.

5. Select **I do not want to join the program at this time** and then click **Next**.

6. Enable the option **if no firewall is turned on, turn on the Windows Firewall (recommended)** and then click **Next.**

7. Click **Install**.

8. Click **Finish**. SCEM installs the latest virus and spyware definitions from Microsoft and then performs a quick scan (see Figure 11-16).

Figure 11-16

Performing Quick scan with the System Center Endpoint Client

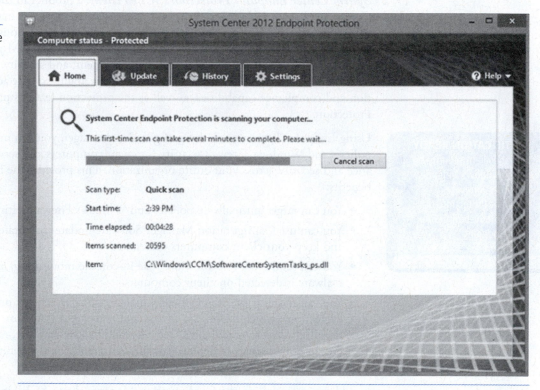

To manage malware, you create antimalware policies that contain settings used for Endpoint Protection Client configurations. You then deploy these policies to your computers and monitor them from the *Configuration Manager\System Center 2012 Endpoint Protection Status* node.

CREATE AN ANTIMALWARE POLICY

GET READY. To create an antimalware policy, log in in to your server running SCCM 2012 and then perform the following steps:

 TAKE NOTE This requires an installation of System Center Configuration Manager 2012.

1. Open the **Configuration Manager** console, right-click **Antimalware Policies**, and then choose **Create Antimalware Policy** (see Figure 11-17).

Figure 11-17

Creating an antimalware policy

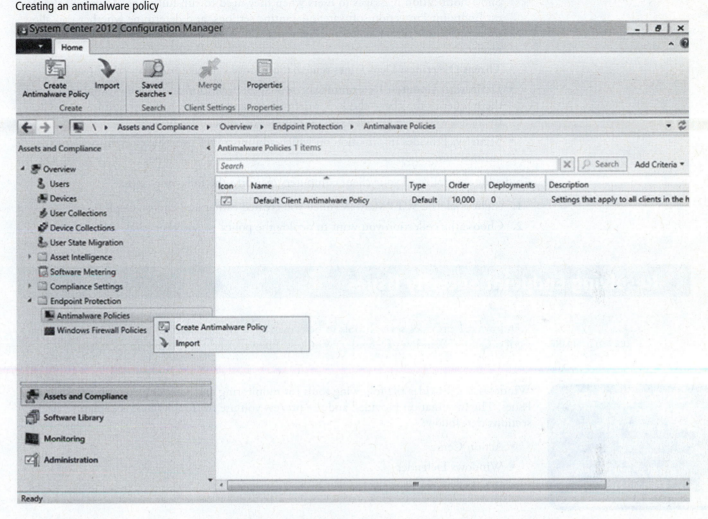

2. In the *Name* field, type a name and description for the policy. For example, type **SCEPMalwarePolicy**.

3. Click each link in the *left* pane to configure the policy according to your requirements.

The following provides information about each of the settings for the antimalware policy:

- **Scheduled scans:** Determines the scan type (quick/full) to use and whether or not to enable randomized scans to prevent computers from sending their antimalware scan results to the Configuration Manager database.

- **Scan settings:** Determines whether to scan mapped drives on the client when running a full scan.

- **Default actions:** Determines how to respond when malware is detected on the client. Options include using the action recommended in the definition file, quarantining the malware, and removing it or allowing it.

- **Real-time protection:** Configures real-time protection, determine whether you want to scan system files, download files and attachments, and allow users on client computers to configure real-time protection settings on their client.

- **Exclusion settings:** Determines which files and folders you want to exclude from the Endpoint Protection scans.

- **Advanced:** Enables you to create a system restore point before computers are cleaned. Show notification messages to users when they need to run full scans, download the latest Endpoint Protection software, quarantine settings, and determine whether you allow users to exclude files, folders, and file types, and whether they can view the full history results.
- **Threat Overrides:** Determines remediation actions to take based on the threat ID.
- **Definition Updates:** Determines the source for definition and engine scanning updates, the frequency the client checks for definitions, and whether to force definition updates to clients who have missed a certain number of consecutive updates.
- **Security:** Provides information on which administrative users have permission for the antimalware policy.

To deploy the policy to your client computers, perform the following steps:

1. Right-click the SCEPMalwarePolicy you created earlier and choose Deploy.
2. Choose the collection you want to deploy the policy to and then click OK.

■ Resolving Endpoint Security Issues

THE BOTTOM LINE

Windows 8.1 provides several tools to help manage endpoint security issues. These include Action Center, Windows Defender, Windows Firewall, and third-party applications.

> **CERTIFICATION READY**
> Manage client security by using Windows Defender, Windows Intune Endpoint Protection, or Microsoft System Center 2012 Endpoint Protection
> Objective 3.3

Windows 8.1 provides the following tools for monitoring and resolving endpoint security issues. The information provided and the process you use to troubleshoot is explained in the sections that follow:

- Action Center
- Windows Defender
- Windows Firewall

Resolving Endpoint Security Issues Using Action Center

> *Action Center* provides a central location for viewing notifications regarding problems with your hardware and software. It also provides information related to security and maintenance of the computer. When a problem does occur, you receive a notification in the task bar.

When there is a problem with your computer, you will see either a red x on the Action Center icon or a yellow message. The red x (see Figure 11-18) indicates a problem that needs to be addressed soon, whereas a yellow message indicates a task that you should consider addressing. Right-click the icon, and then select *Open Action Center* to view more information about the problem.

Figure 11-18

Viewing the Action Center red flag notice

Action Center is organized into two areas when it comes to reporting problems: The Security category and the Maintenance category (see Figure 11-19).

Figure 11-19

Reviewing the Security category and the Maintenance category

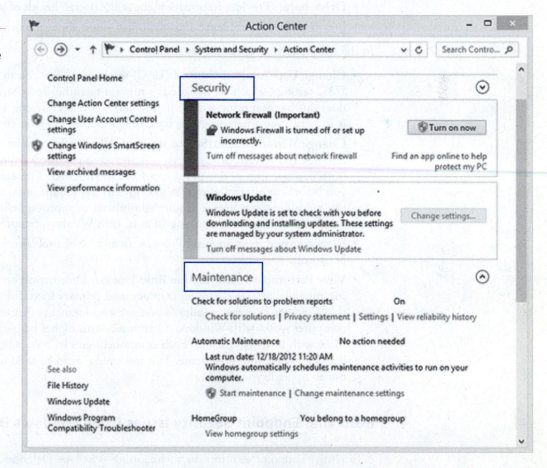

Under the Security section, you can view information about the status of Windows Firewall, Windows Update, and Windows Defender. If these security features are not controlled by a Group Policy, you can configure them via the interface. Red indicates a warning message that should be addressed now, whereas Orange indicates something that you should consider addressing to improve the overall performance and stability of your system.

In Figure 11-19, a critical message indicates the Windows Firewall is turned off or set up incorrectly. Selecting *Turn on now* removes this message from the console, assuming the firewall was accidently turned off. In the case of the Windows Update message, there are additional updates available. Because Windows Update is controlled by the system administrator (via Group Policy), the option to change settings has been disabled on this computer.

The Maintenance section provides you with the following options:

- **Check for solutions to problem reports:** Provides solutions to any problem reports you've sent to Microsoft. These reports typically contain the name and version of an app that is not working and the date and time the problem occurred. They also include diagnostic information to help determine the cause of the problem.
- **Start automatic maintenance and change settings:** Schedules automatic maintenance to run daily at 3:00 AM to perform tasks such as software updates, security scanning, and system diagnostics.
- **View HomeGroup settings:** Allows you to change your network location, leave the HomeGroup, and make changes to advanced sharing settings.
- **Manage File History:** Allows you to change settings, restore personal files, and initiate a copy of files.
- **Drive status:** Provides information about the overall health of your drives.
- **Device software problems:** Provides information about the overall health of your devices.

In the left pane, you can configure additional settings.

- **Change User Account Control (UAC) settings:** Allows you to make changes to the UAC settings, which are designed to prevent unauthorized changes to your computer. It does this by prompting you for permission before performing a task. The default setting is to notify you when programs try to make changes to your computer.
- **Change Windows SmartScreen settings:** Allows you to make changes to the Windows SmartScreen feature. SmartScreen is designed to provide warnings before you run unrecognized apps or download files from the Internet. The default setting is to warn you before running an unrecognized app but not require administrative approval. You can modify settings here to require administrative approval before running an unrecognized app or not doing anything (that is, turn Windows SmartScreen off).
- **View archived message link:** Provides an archive of problems you have reported to Microsoft.
- **View Performance information link:** Provides information on how your processor, memory, graphics, gaming graphics, and primary hard disk perform based on the Windows Experience index. These are measurements that tell you how well your computer works with Windows. Computers with higher base scores perform better than those with lower base scores. Each component gets its own subscore; the total base score is based off the lowest subscore. This information can be used to determine whether or not to upgrade your hardware.

Resolving Endpoint Security Issues Using Windows Defender

To resolve endpoint security issues while using Windows Defender, it's important to understand what each alert level means and what to do about each.

Alert levels are as follows:

- **Severe or High:** These alerts should be addressed quickly because they can result in the loss of personal information or damage your computer.
- **Medium:** These alerts can affect privacy or make changes to your computer that can impact its use in a negative way.
- **Low:** These alerts might indicate something is attempting to collection information about you or change how your computer works. In most cases, this is something that you have agreed to when you installed the program.

Windows Defender automatically prevents software that results in Severe or High alerts from running, and it places these things into the Quarantine Items category. For Medium and Low alerts, you need to do a little more research. If you don't trust the publisher of the software, you can either block it from running or uninstall it. In each case, Windows Defender provides information about the detected item, provides you with a description of the program, and provides you with the recommended action to perform. For example, in the case of a Trojan virus, you see it is tagged with a severe alert level. Windows Defender also informs you the program is dangerous and executes commands from an attacker. The recommended action is to remove this software immediately.

Resolving Endpoint Security Issues Using Windows Firewall

Issues with Windows Firewall typically revolve around allowing apps to communicate through the firewall. To resolve problems, open the Windows Firewall (*Control Panel > System and Security > Windows Firewall*) and check its current settings.

As shown in Figure 11-20, Windows Firewall is designed to block all connections to apps that are not on the list of allowed apps and notifies you when it blocks a new app.

Figure 11-20

Viewing Windows Firewall settings

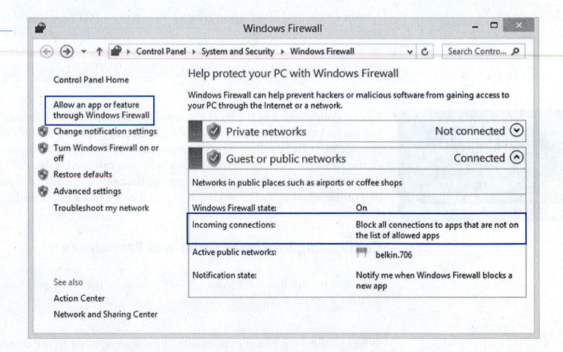

In the left pane, you can click *Allow an app or feature through the Windows Firewall*. In the dialog box that appears, you can add, change, or remove allowed apps and ports by selecting the *Change settings* button. In general, it is more of a risk to add an app to the list of allowed apps than it is to open a port. Ports stay open until you close them; apps use the communication link only when they need it.

The process of adding an app or opening a port is called **unblocking**. This enables the app to communicate through the firewall.

In situations where an Administrator has configured the Windows Firewall with Advanced features, you need to review the Inbound, Outbound, and Connection Security rules to determine whether there are conditions set to allow the traffic that you want to pass. In some situations, you may have a rule that allows your computer to interact with another one only if it is using IPsec to encrypt and authenticate the session. In these situations, you need to review the Connection Security rules to see whether there are further constraints that might help you resolve the problem.

Resolving Endpoint Security Issues with Third-Party Software

> If you use third-party software (firewalls, anti-virus, malware, and so on), you need to consult the appropriate product documentation to determine your options.

Windows Defender is designed to disable itself when it detects another anti-virus or malware program running. If you use other third-party apps, consider how these interact with each other, ensure you have the latest updates and patches, and ensure you have the latest versions of the software.

■ Supporting Group Policy Applications

THE BOTTOM LINE

> *Group Policy* is defined using *group policy objects (GPOs)*, which are the collection of configuration instructions that the computer processes. To assign a GPO, it is linked to an Active Directory container (site, domain, or organizational unit). However, you can take steps to control which GPO affects a computer or user.

CERTIFICATION READY
Support Group Policy application, including Resultant Set of Policy (RSoP), policy processing, and Group Policy caching
Objective 3.3

Group Policy is one of the most powerful features of Active Directory; it controls the working environment for user accounts and computer accounts. Group Policy provides centralized management and configuration of operating systems, applications, and user settings in an Active Directory environment. For example, you can use Group Policy to specify how often a user must change his password, to set the background image on a person's computer, or to determine whether spell checking is required before a user can send an e-mail.

Configuring Processor Order and Precedence

> To understand how GPOs are applied, you must first look at the order in which group policies are applied.

When configuring group policies, the settings are applied to the computer or the user. Computer configuration settings are processed when a computer starts, and user configuration settings are processed when a user logs on. Group policies are processed in the following order:

1. When a computer first starts up, it establishes a secure link between the computer and a domain controller.
2. The computer obtains a list of GPOs that are applicable to the computer.
3. Computer configuration settings are applied synchronously (one by one) during computer startup before the Logon dialog box is presented to the user. If any startup scripts are configured through GPOs, the scripts are processed synchronously and have a default timeout of 600 seconds (10 minutes) to complete. Because the user has not logged on yet, the process is hidden.

4. When the computer configuration settings have been applied and the startup scripts have been applied, users use the Ctrl+Alt+Del option to log on.

5. A user is authenticated and the user profile is loaded.

6. The computer obtains a list of GPOs that are applicable to the user. Again, GPO processing is hidden from the user.

7. After the user policies run, any logon scripts defined by GPOs run, which are executed asynchronously (multiple scripts to be processed at the same time).

8. The login script defined for the user in Active Directory user properties is executed.

9. The user's desktop is displayed.

UNDERSTANDING GROUP POLICY INHERITANCE

A computer and user can be affected by multiple GPOs. GPOs are processed in the following order:

1. Local policy
2. Site
3. Domain
4. OU

Although the domain and OU are used to deploy GPOs based on the location of the user and computers within Active Directory hierarchy, the Site is used to define GPOs based on physical location.

By default, a Group Policy uses *inheritance*, in which settings are inherited from the container above. In other words, Group Policy settings flow downward, into the lower containers and objects. Generally speaking, the settings are cumulative unless there is a conflict with a setting defined in a previous GPO. By default, if there is a conflict between settings, the domain controller that is processed later overwrites the setting that was established previously.

If a site, domain, or OU have multiple GPOs, the group policies are processed in order as stated by its precedence. A GPO with higher precedence (lower number) prevails over a GPO with lower precedence (higher number).

When Active Directory is installed, two domain GPOs are created by default:

- *Default Domain Policy:* Linked to the domain. It affects all users and computers in the domain, including domain controllers. It specifies the password, account lockout, and Kerberos policies. These policies can be configured only at the domain level. To configure other settings at the domain level, you should create additional GPOs linked to the domain.

- *Default Domain Controller Policy:* Linked to the Domain Controllers organization unit, which then affects the domain controllers. It contains the default user rights assignments. You should also use it for auditing policies. It has a security filter to include only Authenticated Users.

As an example, the contoso.com domain has the Sales OU, which contains the West OU (see Figure 11-21). You create GPO1 and GPO2 GPOs and link them to the domain. You create GPOSales1 and GPOSales2 and link them to the Sales OU. You create WESTGPO1 and WESTGPO2 and link them to the WEST OU. The policies are processed in the following order:

1. Local policy
2. GPO2
3. GPO1
4. Default Domain Policy

5. GPOSales2

6. GPOSales1

7. WESTGPO2

8. WESTGPO1

Figure 11-21

Displaying GPOs for a domain

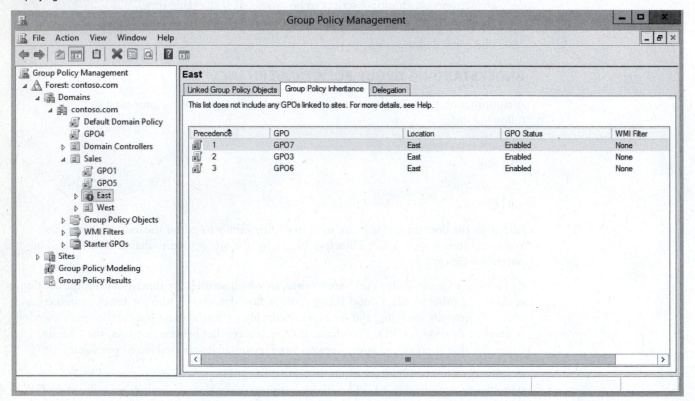

If all the GPOs configure the same setting, the setting defined with the GPO with the highest precedence (lowest number) will be used. Of course, if you configure settings defined in the password, account lockout, or Kerberos policy, only the domain level policy (such as the Default Domain Policy) would be used because these can be set only at the domain level. If you need to change the precedence, use the following procedure.

 CHANGE THE PRECEDENCE OF A GPO

GET READY. To change the precedence of a GPO for a container, perform the following steps:

1. Open **Server Manager**.

2. Click **Tools > Group Policy Management**. The *Group Policy Management console* opens.

3. Navigate to and click the container (site, domain, or OU) that has GPOs that you want to modify.

4. Click the **Linked Group Policy Objects** tab.

5. Click the GPO that you want to modify. Then use the arrow icons (**Up**, **Down**, **Move To Top**, and **Move To Bottom**) to move the GPO up or down on the list.

6. Close the *Group Policy Management console*.

MANAGING GROUP POLICY LINKS

To disable a GPO for a container, right-click the GPO for the container and choose Link Enabled. A checkmark shows that the link is enabled; if there is no checkmark, the link is disabled. Disabling the link for a container affects only the container and does not affect other containers to which a GPO is linked.

After a GPO is created, you can manage how the GPO is used by performing the following actions:

- To view the containers that a GPO is linked to, click the GPO in Group Policy Management and view the Scope tab.
- To delete a link to a container for a GPO without deleting the GPO, right-click the GPO for a container and choose Delete. When you are prompted to confirm that you want to delete the link, click *OK*.
- Alternatively, you can disable the link or delete a link for a container by right-clicking the container in the Scope tab and choosing Link Enabled or Delete Link(s), respectively.

You can disable the user configuration settings, the computer configuration settings, or both settings by right-clicking the GPO under the Group Policy Objects and choosing GPO Status. You can then choose the appropriate option. However, note that when you change the GPO status, it affects all containers to which the GPO is linked.

Using Filtering with Group Policy

As previously explained, Group Policy flows downward, from the upper containers to the lower objects. However, you might want to define a GPO and not want the GPO settings to be overwritten by other GPOs. Or you might not want the GPO to flow downward, to lower containers.

The exceptions to the processing of group policies can be modified with the following options:

- Block policy inheritance
- Enforce option

CONFIGURING BLOCKING OF INHERITANCE

By default, Group Policy flows downward, to the lower containers and objects. You can prevent the inheritance of policy settings by blocking all Group Policy settings from the GPOs linked to parent containers in the Group Policy hierarchy. GPOs linked directly to the container and GPOs linked to lower containers are unaffected.

 BLOCK THE INHERITANCE OF GPOs

GET READY. To block the inheritance of GPOs, perform the following steps:

1. Open **Server Manager**.
2. Click **Tools > Group Policy Management**. The *Group Policy Management console* opens.
3. Navigate to and click the container (site, domain or OU) that you want to stop inheritance from above.
4. Right-click the container and choose **Block Inheritance**.

   An exclamation point inside a blue circle appears for the container, and the checkmark indicates inheritance is blocked in the context menu.

5. Close the *Group Policy Management console*.

You should use block inheritance sparingly. Instead, you can use security group filtering to control what group policies.

CONFIGURING ENFORCED POLICIES

As an example, you might want to apply a GPO yet you do not want that GPO to be over-ridden by a GPO that is executed later. By enforcing a GPO link, the GPO takes the highest precedence, which will prevail over any conflicting policy settings in other GPOs. In addition, an enforced link applies to child containers even when those containers are set to Block Inheritance.

 ENFORCE A GPO

GET READY. To enforce a GPO, perform the following steps:

1. Open **Server Manager**.
2. Click **Tools > Group Policy Management**. The *Group Policy Management console* opens.
3. Navigate to and click the GPO in the desired container.
4. Right-click the GPO and choose **Enforced**.
5. When you right-click a lower container, you will see that the enforced GPO has a high precedence (low number).
6. Close the **Group Policy Management** console.

Configuring Loopback Processing

As you recall, GPO computer configuration settings are applied when a computer starts up and GPO user configuration settings are applied when a user logs on. Group Policy *loopback processing* is used to assign user policies to computer objects. Therefore, no matter who logs on to a computer, the user policies are applied to the computer.

As the name implies, loopback processing allows the Group Policy processing order to circle back and reapply the computer policies after all user policies and logon scripts run. It is intended to keep the configuration of the computer the same regardless of who logs on.

The loopback policy is enabled using the Group Policy Management Editor by modifying the settings in *Computer Configuration\Administrative Templates\System\Group Policy\Configure user Group Policy Loopback processing mode*. After you enable the setting, you can choose between the following two loopback processing modes:

- **Replace mode:** The user settings defined in the computer's GPO replaces the user settings normally applied to the user. The Replace mode is useful in a situation such as a kiosk, classroom, or public library, where users should receive a standard configuration.

- **Merge mode:** The user settings defined in the computer's GPOs and user settings normally applied to the user are combined. If the settings conflict, the user settings in the computer's GPO take precedence over the user's normal settings. This mode is useful to apply additional settings to users' typical configurations, such as mapping additional printers, replacing the wallpaper on a computer, or disabling certain applications or devices in a conference room or reception area.

For computers that are shared by more than one user (such as a kiosk, classroom, or public library), you can use the Replace option to reduce the need to undo actions that are applied by the settings for the user logging on.

Configuring Group Policy Caching

Starting with Windows 8.1 and Windows Server 2012 R2, you can cache GPOs to improve performance when processing synchronous policy settings.

When a system gets new Group Policy settings, it writes that policy to a local store (c:\windows\system32\GroupPolicy\Datastore). If Group Policy is running in synchronous mode, it reads the most recently downloaded version of the GPO from the local store when the system is rebooted. As a result, the GPOs are processed faster and the boot time is shorter, particularly if the system is off the premises or you have a slow connection.

To configure and manage Group Policy caching settings, open a GPO and navigate to the *Computer Configuration\Policies\Administrative Templates\System\Group Policy* node and then enable and configure the *Configure Group Policy Caching* settings.

Troubleshooting GPOs

The ***Resultant Set of Policy (RSoP)*** identifies the actual policies that are applied to a computer and the user that logs into that computer.

Windows Server 2012 R2 provides the following tools for performing RSoP analysis:

- The Group Policy Results Wizard
- The GPResult.exe command
- The Group Policy Modeling Wizard

To help you analyze the cumulative effect of GPOs and policy settings on a user or computer in your organization, you can run the Group Policy Results Wizard. To run the Group Policy Results Wizard, the following must be true:

- The target computer must be online.
- You must have administrative credentials on the target computer.
- The target computer must run Windows XP or newer.
- WMI must be running on the target computer and ports 135 and 445 must be available to access WMI on the target computer.

 RUN THE GROUP POLICY RESULTS WIZARD

GET READY. To run the Group Policy Results Wizard, perform the following steps:

1. Open **Server Manager**.
2. Click **Tools > Group Policy Management**. The *Group Policy Management console* opens.
3. Navigate to and right-click the **Group Policy Results** and choose **Group Results Group Policy Results Wizard**.
4. When the *Group Policy Results Wizard* starts, click **Next**.
5. On the *Computer Selection* page, click **Another Computer** and then type the name of the computer in the text box. Click **Next**.
6. On the *User Selection* page, click the user that you want to check and then click **Next**.
7. On the *Summary of Selections* page, click **Next**.
8. On the *Completing the Group Policy Results Wizard*, click **Finish**.

9. Under the *Group Policy Results* node, click the desired user on computer.

10. Click the **Details** tab.

As shown in Figure 11-22, the settings are applied and the GPO where the settings come from. It also displays the applied GPOs and the list of the Denied GPOs.

Figure 11-22

Viewing the Details tab for Group Policy Results

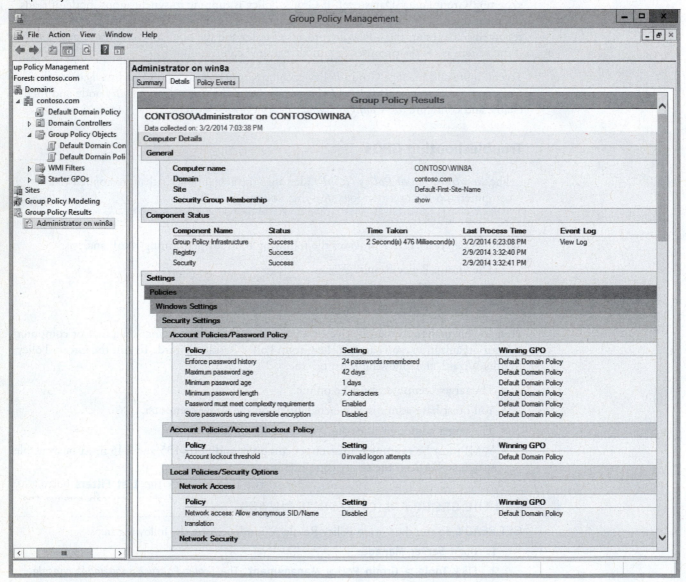

11. Close the **Group Policy Management** console.

After you generate an RSoP report with the Group Policy Results Wizard, you can right-click the report to rerun the query, print the report, or save the report as either an XML file or an HTML. If you click Action menu and choose Advanced View, the Resultant Set of Policy snap-in opens, which you can use to view all applied settings, including IPsec, wireless, and disk quota policies.

The command version of the Group Policy Results Wizard is the GPResult.exe command. To view the Group Policy Results, execute the following command:

```
gpresult /s computername /user username /r
```

Moving computers from one OU to another OU, changing a GPO, or adding or removing an OU can result in unexpected changes. Before you make any of these changes, you should evaluate the potential impact by using the RSoP for the user and computer to make sure you understand what GPO settings are applied and where they are applied. Then use the Group Policy Modeling Wizard to perform a What-if Analysis based on the desired change. To perform Group Policy modeling, right-click the Group Policy Modeling node in the Group Policy Management console tree, choose Group Policy Modeling Wizard, and then perform the steps in the wizard.

 RUN THE GROUP POLICY MODELING WIZARD

GET READY. To run the Group Policy Modeling Wizard, perform the following steps:

1. Open **Server Manager**.

2. Click **Tools > Group Policy Management**. The *Group Policy Management console* appears.

3. Navigate to and right-click **Group Policy Modeling** and then choose **Group Policy Modeling Wizard**.

4. When the *Group Policy Modeling Wizard* starts, click **Next**.

5. On the *Domain Controller Selection* page, click **Next**.

6. On the *User and Computer Selection* page, in the *User information* section, click **Browse**. In the *Choose User Container* dialog box, navigate to the OU where you want to place the user and then click **OK**.

7. In the *Computer information* section, click **Browse**. In the *Choose Computer Container* dialog box, navigate to the OU where you want to place the computer and then click **OK**. Click **Next**.

8. On the *Advanced Simulation Options* page, if desired, select **Slow network connection** and/or **Loopback processing**. You can also specify the site from the pull-down menu. Click **Next**.

9. On the *User Security Groups* page, the current groups for the user is displayed. You can click the **Add** button to include additional groups and/or you can click a group and then click the **Remove** button to remove the group. Click **Next**.

10. On the *Computer Security Groups* page, the current groups for the computer is displayed. You can click the **Add** button to add additional groups and/or click a group and then click the **Remove** button to remove the group. Click **Next**.

11. On the *WMI Filters for Users* page, you can click **All linked filters** (the default setting) or you can click **Only these filters**, then click the **List Filters** button to display the WMI filters that are linked to the GPO, and then you can remove the WMI link. Click **Next**.

12. On the *Summary of Selections* page, click **Next**.

13. When the wizard completes, click **Finish**.

14. Click the **Details** tab to view the GPOs and GPO settings that are applied.

15. Close the **Group Policy Management** console.

Managing Internet Explorer 11 Security

THE BOTTOM LINE

Internet Explorer offers a number of features to protect your security and privacy while you browse the web, including phishing filters, Protected Mode, Pop-up Blocker, Add-on Manager, download files or software notification, and the use of digital signatures and 128-bit secure (SSL) connections when using secure websites.

CERTIFICATION READY
Manage Internet Explorer 11 security
Objective 3.3

Using the Internet, you can use your web browser to access information from throughout the world. Unfortunately, that also means your computer or private information can be accessed by others.

Managing Cookies and Privacy Settings

Your web browser can reveal plenty of information about your personality and interests. Therefore, you need to take steps to ensure that this information cannot be read or used without your knowledge.

A *cookie* is text stored by a user's web browser. It can be used for a wide range of functions, including identifying you as a user, authenticating you as a user, and storing your site preferences and shopping cart contents. Cookies can provide a website with a lot of helpful information that can make your browsing experience easier and faster, but they also can be used by spyware programs and websites to track your online behavior. Unfortunately, some websites will not operate without cookies.

 DELETE COOKIES AND TEMPORARY INTERNET FILES

GET READY. To delete cookies and temporary Internet files, perform the following steps:

1. Open **Internet Explorer**.
2. Click the **Tools** button and then click **Internet Options**.
3. On the *General* tab, under *Browsing history*, click **Delete**.
   The Delete Browsing History dialog box appears (see Figure 11-23).

Figure 11-23

Deleting cookies and temporary files

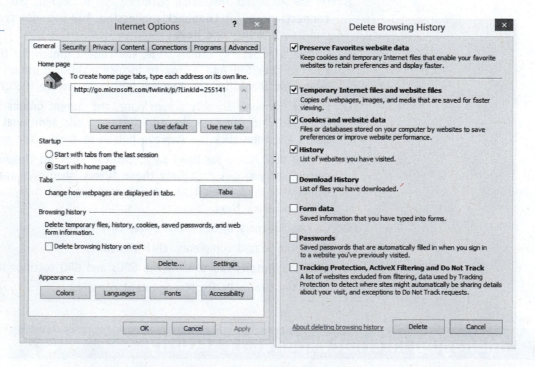

4. Ensure that the **Cookies** check box and the **Temporary Internet files and website files** check box are selected. Click **Delete**.

Being aware of how your private information is used when browsing the web is important to helping prevent targeted advertising, fraud, and identity theft.

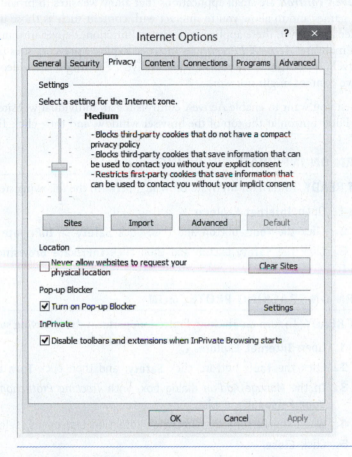

CHANGE PRIVACY SETTINGS

GET READY. To change privacy settings, perform the following steps:

1. Open **Internet Explorer**.
2. Click the **Tools** button and then click **Internet Options**.
3. Click the **Privacy** tab (see Figure 11-24).

Figure 11-24

Configuring your privacy settings

To configure your privacy settings, adjust the tab slider to a new position on the privacy scale. The default level is Medium; it is recommended to configure Medium or higher. If you click the Advanced button, you can override certain settings and if you click the Edit button, you can allow or block cookies from individual websites.

To prevent Internet Explorer from storing data about your browsing session, Internet Explorer 11 includes *InPrivate Browsing*. This helps prevent anyone who might be using your computer from seeing where you visited and what you looked at on the web.

When you start InPrivate Browsing, Internet Explorer opens a new window. The protection that InPrivate Browsing provides is only in effect during the time that you use that window. You can open as many tabs as you want in that window, and they will all be protected by InPrivate Browsing. However, if you open another browser window, that window will not be protected by InPrivate Browsing unless you configure that window to also use InPrivate Browsing. To end your InPrivate Browsing session, close the browser window.

Some websites can be used to gather information about which pages you visit on the Internet. *Tracking Protection* blocks this content from websites that appear on Tracking Protection Lists. A Personalized Tracking Protection List included with Internet Explorer is generated automatically based on sites you visit. You can also download Tracking Protection Lists and then Internet Explorer will periodically check for updates to the lists.

Pop-up windows are very common. While some pop-up windows are useful website controls, most are simply annoying advertisements—with a few attempting to load spyware or other malicious programs. To help protect your computer, Internet Explorer's *Pop-up Blocker* can suppress some or all pop-ups.

ActiveX controls are small applications that allow websites to provide content such as videos and games and to allow you to interact with content such as those used in toolbars and stock tickers. However, these applications can malfunction, deliver unwanted content, or can contain malware. *ActiveX Filtering* in Internet Explorer prevents sites from installing and using ActiveX applications. Of course, when ActiveX Filtering is on, videos, games, and other interactive content might not work.

When you want to enable ActiveX controls for an individual website, visit the website, click the Filter button at the top of the browser window, and then click Turn off ActiveX Filtering.

TURN ON INPRIVATE BROWSING

GET READY. To turn on InPrivate Browsing, perform the following steps:

1. Open **Internet Explorer**.
2. Click the **Tools** button and then click **Safety > InPrivate Browsing**.
3. Click the **Safety** button and then click **InPrivate Browsing**.

TURN ON TRACKING PROTECTION

GET READY. To turn on Tracking Protection, perform the following steps:

1. Open **Internet Explorer**.
2. Click the **Tools** button, click **Safety**, and then click **Turn on Tracking Protection**.
3. In the *Manage Add-on* dialog box, with *Tracking Protection* selected, double-click **Your Personalized List**.
4. When the Personalized Tracking Protection List opens, select Automatically block.
5. Click **Close**.

CONFIGURE THE POP-UP BLOCKER

GET READY. To configure the Pop-Up Blocker, perform the following steps:

1. Open **Internet Explorer**.
2. Click the **Tools** button and then click **Internet Options**.
3. Click the **Privacy** tab.
4. Click **Settings**. The *Pop-Up Blocker Settings* dialog box appears.
5. To allow pop-ups from a specific website, in the *Address of website to allow* text box, type the URL of the site and then click **Add**.

   Repeat the process to add additional sites to the *Allowed sites* list.
6. Adjust the *Blocking level* dropdown list to one of the following settings:

   - **High**: Blocks all pop-ups
   - **Medium**: Blocks most automatic pop-ups
   - **Low**: Allows pop-ups from secure sites

7. Click **Close** to close the *Pop-Up Blocker Settings* dialog box.

8. Click **OK** to close the *Internet Properties* dialog box.

 CONFIGURE ACTIVEX FILTERING

GET READY. To configure ActiveX Filtering, perform the following steps:

1. Open **Internet Explorer**.

2. Click the **Tools** button and then click **Safety > ActiveX Filtering**. There should now be a check mark next to ActiveX Filtering.

Configuring Security Zones

> To help manage Internet Explorer security when visiting sites, Internet Explorer divides your network connection into *security zones* based on four content types. For each zone, a security level is assigned.

The security for each security zones is assigned based on dangers associated with zone. For example, it is assumed that connecting to a server within your own corporation would be safer than connecting to a server on the Internet.

The four default content types are:

- **Internet Zone:** Anything that is not assigned to any other zone and anything that is not on your computer or your organization's network (intranet). The default security level of the Internet zone is Medium.

- **Local Intranet Zone:** Computers that are part of the organization's network (intranet) that do not require a proxy server, as defined by the system administrator. These include sites specified on the Connection's tab, network, paths (such as \\computername\foldername), and local intranet sites (such as http://internal). You can add sites to this zone. The default security level for the Local internet zone is Medium=Low, which means Internet Explorer will allow all cookies from websites in this zone to be saved on your computer and read by the website that created them. Lastly, if the website requires NTLM or integrated authentication, it will automatically use your username and password.

- **Trusted Sites Zone:** Contains trusted sites which you believe you can download or run files from without damaging your computer or you believe you can download data or that you don't consider to be a security risk. You can assign sites to this zone. The default security level for the Trusted sites zone is Low, which means Internet Explorer will allow all cookies from websites in this zone to be saved on your computer and read by the website that created them.

- **Restricted Sites Zone:** Contains sites that you do not trust; downloading or running files might damage your computer. You can assign sites to this zone. The default security level for the Restricted sites zone is High, which means Internet Explorer will block all cookies from websites in this zone.

To determine which zones the current web page falls into, look at the right side of the Internet Explorer status bar.

 MODIFY THE SECURITY LEVEL FOR A WEB CONTENT ZONE

GET READY. To modify the security level for a web content zone, perform the following steps:

1. Open **Internet Explorer**.

2. Click the **Tools** button and then click **Internet Options**.

3. In the *Internet Options* dialog box, on the *Security* tab, click the zone on which you want to set the security level. Figure 11-25 shows the *Security* tab and the *Custom level* dialog box.

Figure 11-25

Configuring the Security Content Zones

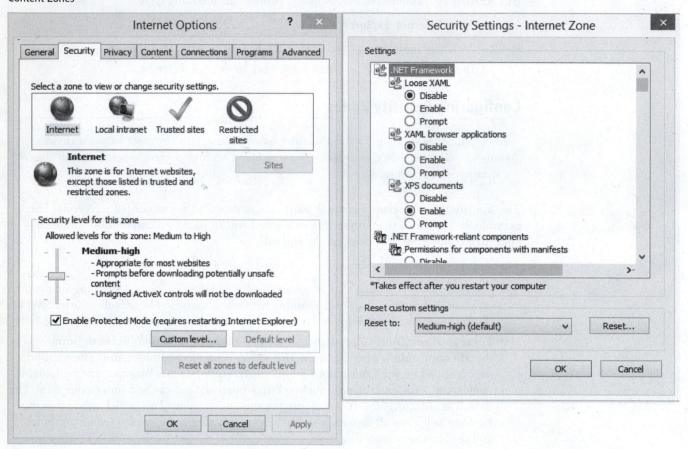

4. Drag the slider to set the security level to High, Medium, or Low.

   Internet Explorer describes each option to help you decide which level to choose. You are prompted to confirm any reduction in security level. You can also click the custom Level button for more detailed control.

5. Click **OK** to close the *Internet Options* dialog box.

For each web content zone, there is a default security level. The security levels available in Internet Explorer are:

- **High**: Excludes any content that can damage your computer.

- **Medium**: Warns you before running potentially damaging content.

- **Low**: Does not warn you before running potentially damaging content.

- **Custom**: Creates a security setting of your own design.

The easiest way to modify the security settings that Internet Explorer imposes on a specific website is to manually add the site to a different security zone. The typical procedure is to add a site to the Trusted Sites zone, to increase its privileges, or add it to the Restricted Sites zone to reduce its privileges.

ADD A SITE TO A SECURITY ZONE

GET READY. To add a site to a security zone, perform the following steps:

1. Open **Internet Explorer**.
2. Click the **Tools** button and then click **Internet Options**.
3. Click the **Security** tab.
4. Select the zone—either **Trusted sites** or **Restricted sites**—to which you want to add a site.
5. Click **Sites**. The *Trusted sites* or *Restricted sites* dialog box appears.
6. In the *Add this website to the zone* text box, type the URL of the website you want to add to the zone and then click **Add**. The URL appears in the Websites list.
7. Click **Close** to close the *Trusted sites* or *Restricted sites* dialog box.
8. Click **OK** to close the *Internet Properties* sheet.

 MODIFY SECURITY ZONE SETTINGS

GET READY. To modify security zone settings, perform the following steps:

1. Open **Internet Explorer**.
2. Click the **Tools** button and then click **Internet Options**.
3. Click the **Security** tab.
4. Select the zone for which you want to modify the security settings.
5. In the *Security level for this zone* box, adjust the slider to increase or decrease the security level for the zone. Moving the slider up increases the protection for the zone and moving the slider down decreases it.
6. Select or clear the **Enable protected mode** checkbox, if desired,
7. To exercise more precise control over the zone's security settings, click **Custom level**. The Security Settings dialog box for the zone appears.
8. Select radio buttons for the individual settings in each security category. The radio buttons typically make it possible to enable a setting, disable it, or prompt the user before enabling it.
9. Click **OK** to close the *Security Settings* dialog box.
10. Click **OK** to close the *Internet Properties* sheet.

Using Dynamic Security and Protected Mode

Internet Explorer offers multiple security features to defend against malware and data theft, including Dynamic Security and Protected Mode. ***Dynamic security*** is a set of tools and technology that protects your computer as you browse the Internet with Internet Explorer. It includes ActiveX opt-in, Security Status Bar, Phishing Filter, Address Bar Protection, and Protected Mode.

The Security Status Bar keeps you notified of the website security and privacy settings by using color-coded notifications next to the address bar. Some of these features include:

- The address bar turns green to indicate websites bearing new High Assurance certificates, indicating the site owner has completed extensive identity verification checks.
- Phishing Filter notifications, certificate names, and the gold padlock icon are now also adjacent to the address bar for better visibility.

- Certificate and privacy detail information can easily be displayed with a single click on the Security Status Bar.
- The Address Bar is displayed to the user for every window, whether it's a pop-up or whether it's a standard window, which helps to block malicious sites from emulating trusted sites.
- To help protect you against phishing sites, Internet Explorer warns you when you're visiting potential or known fraudulent sites and blocks the site if appropriate. The opt-in filter is updated several times per hour with the latest security information from Microsoft and several industry partners.
- International Domain Name Anti-Spoofing notifies you when visually similar characters in the URL are not expressed in the same language.

If Internet Explorer is still using its original settings, you'll see the Information bar in the following circumstances:

- When a website tries to install an ActiveX control on your computer or run an ActiveX control in an unsafe manner.
- When a website tries to open a pop-up window.
- When a website tries to download a file to your computer.
- When a website tries to run active content on your computer.
- When your security settings are below recommended levels.
- When you access an intranet webpage, but have not turned on intranet address checking.
- When you started Internet Explorer with add-ons disabled.
- When you need to install an updated ActiveX control or add-on program.
- When the website address can be displayed with native language letters or symbols but you don't have the language installed.

To help protect your computer, Internet Explorer protected mode means that it runs as a low integrity procedure, which means that Internet Explorer writes to only low-integrity disk locations such as the Temporary Internet Files folder and the standard IE storage areas, including the History, Cookies, and Favorites folders. As a result, protected mode is a feature that makes it more difficult for malicious software to be installed on your computer.

TAKE NOTE * Protected mode is not a complete defense against malware. Therefore, it is recommended to use an up-to-date antivirus package with anti-spyware capability and to keep your system up-to-date with Windows and Internet Explorer security updates and patches.

 ENABLE PROTECTED MODE

GET READY. Before Protected mode can be enabled, you must ensure that UAC is enabled. To enable Protected mode, perform the following steps:

1. Open **Internet Explorer**.
2. Click **Tools > Internet Options**.
3. Click the **Security** tab.
4. Click **Enable Protected Mode**.

Configuring SmartScreen Filter and Phishing

> *Phishing* is a technique based on social engineering. With phishing, users are enticed to go (usually through e-mail or other websites) to illegitimate websites that look similar to legitimate websites in an effort to persuade users to supply personal information, such as passwords and account numbers.

To help protect against phishing, Internet Explorer 8 includes *SmartScreen Filter*, which examines traffic for evidence of phishing activity and displays a warning to the user if it finds any. It also sends the address back to the Microsoft SmartScreen service to be compared against lists of known phishing and malware sites. If SmartScreen Filter discovers that a website you're visiting is on the list of known malware or phishing sites, Internet Explorer will display a blocking web page and the Address bar will be shown in red. From the blocking page, you can choose to bypass the blocked website and go to your home page instead or you can continue to the blocked website, though this is not recommended. If you continue to the blocked website, the Address bar will continue to appear in red.

To protect your privacy, information that is submitted to the SmartScreen web service is transmitted in encrypted format over HTTPS. This information is not stored with your IP address or other personally identifiable information and will not be used to identify, contact, or provide advertising to you.

You can set up the browser by using express settings or by configuring settings individually. The express settings option enables the SmartScreen Filter, but you can disable it at any time by clicking the Safety button on the toolbar and selecting SmartScreen Filter > Turn off SmartScreen Filter (which displays the Microsoft SmartScreen Filter dialog box).

Even without SmartScreen Filter turned on, you can remain safe from phishing attempts as long as you obey the following unofficial rules of web surfing:

- Don't trust hyperlinks.
- Never supply a password or any other confidential information to a website unless you type the URL yourself and you are sure that it is correct.

Managing Add-Ons

> To make Internet Explorer more flexible, Internet Explorer allows you to add *add-ons* to your browser, such as extra toolbars, animated mouse pointers, stock tickers, and pop-up blockers. Add-ons are downloaded from the Internet and installed as an executable program.

The four basic types of add-ons supported by IE are as follows:

- **Toolbars and Extensions:** Enable the browser to open and manipulate websites or file types that IE does not support natively. Some applications add their own toolbars to IE, enabling you to work with their documents within an IE session.
- **Search Providers:** Enable the user to perform searches directly from the IE interface using search engines on the Internet or the local network.
- **Accelerators:** Enable users to send text or other media they select in an IE browser window to another application, such as an e-mail client or an Internet resource (such as a blog).
- **Tracking Protection:** Enables you to import and export XML files containing InPrivate filters.

VIEW YOUR CURRENT ADD-ONS

GET READY. To view your current add-ons, perform the following steps:

1. Open **Internet Explorer.**
2. Click the **Tools** button and then click **Manage Add-ons** (see Figure 11-26).

Figure 11-26

Managing add-ons

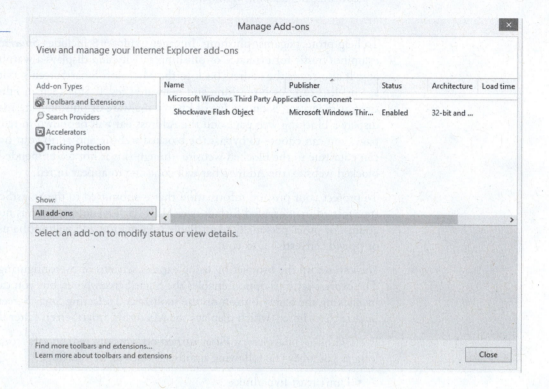

3. Under *Add-on Types*, click **Toolbars and Extensions.**
4. Under *Show*, you can select one of the following views of your add-ons:

   To display a complete list of the add-ons that reside on your computer, click **All add-ons.**

   To display only those add-ons that were needed for the current webpage or a recently viewed webpage, click **Currently loaded add-ons.**

   To display add-ons that were pre-approved by Microsoft, your computer manufacturer, or a service provider, click **Run without permission.**

   To display only 32-bit ActiveX controls, click **Downloaded controls.**
5. Click **Close.**

 DELETE ACTIVEX CONTROLS

GET READY. To delete ActiveX controls you have installed, perform the following steps:

1. Open **Internet Explorer.**
2. Click the **Tools** button and then click **Manage Add-ons.**
3. Under *Show*, click **Downloaded controls** to display all ActiveX controls.
4. Click the ActiveX control you want to delete and then click **More information.**
5. In the *More Information* dialog box, click **Remove.** If you are prompted for an administrator password or confirmation, type the password or provide confirmation.

→ **DISABLE ADD-ONS**

GET READY. To permanently disable add-ons, perform the following steps:

1. Open **Internet Explorer**.
2. Click the **Tools** button and then click **Manage Add-ons**.
3. Under *Show*, click **All add-ons**.
4. Click the add-on you want to disable and then click **Disable**.

Configuring Secure Sockets Layer (SSL) and Certificates

You might need to transmit private data over the Internet, such as credit card numbers, social security numbers, and so on. You should use http over SSL (https) to encrypt the data sent over the Internet. By convention, URLs that require an SSL connection start with https: (instead of http:).

Secure Sockets Layer (SSL) uses a cryptographic system that uses two keys (one key to encrypt the data and another key to decrypt the data). The public key is known to everyone and a private or secret key is known only to the recipient of the message. The public key is published in a digital certificate, which also confirms the identity of the web server.

When you connect to a site that is secured using SSL, a gold lock appears in the address bar along with the name of the organization to which the CA issued the certificate. Clicking the lock icon displays more information about the site (see Figure 11-27), including the identity of the CA that issued the certificate. For even more information, you can click the View Certificate link to open the Certificate dialog box.

Figure 11-27

Viewing certificate information

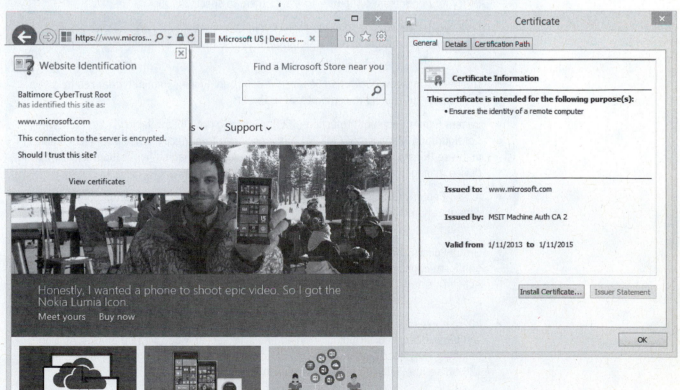

When visiting certain websites, Internet Explorer might find problems with the digital certificate, such as that the certificate has expired, it is corrupted, it has been revoked, or it does not match the name of the website. When this happens, IE will block access to the site and display a warning stating that there is a problem with the certificate. You then have a chance to close the browser window or ignore the warning and continue on to the site. Of course, if you chose to ignore the warning, make sure you trust the website and you believe that you are communicating with the correct server.

SKILL SUMMARY

IN THIS LESSON YOU LEARNED:

- Managing the security of your computers involves a multi-layered approach. This requires the latest service packs and patches that protect against malware, spyware, and viruses.

- Windows Update provides you with a way to keep you computers current by downloading and installing updates from the Windows Update site. Alternatively, you can centralize the administration, approval, and deployment of updates by using Windows Server Update Services (WSUS).

- Servers that obtain updates from Microsoft are called upstream servers and those that receive their updates from an upstream server are called downstream servers.

- WSUS supports both replica mode and autonomous mode configurations. Replica mode mirrors update approvals, settings, computers, and groups from the upstream server, whereas autonomous mode allows you to configure separate update approval settings.

- Server-side targeting involves moving clients to computer groups using the Update Service console; client-side targeting utilizes Group Policy for domain computers and Local Group Policy for nondomain computers to assign them to specific groups.

- Windows Defender is designed to protect your computer against viruses, spyware, and other types of malware in real-time through the use of virus signature updates and definition updates.

- The Microsoft Active Protection Service (MAPS) is an online community that can help you decide how to respond to certain types of threats.

- System Center Endpoint Protection (SCEP) client is a product available via System Center Configuration Manager (SCCM) 2012. It is designed to protect clients and servers against malware threats. SCCM provides a central console for managing application delivery, device management, and security across your organization.

- Action Center provides a central location for viewing notifications regarding problems with your hardware and software and information related to the security and maintenance of your PC.

- Group Policy is based on group policy objects (GPOs), which are a collection of configuration instructions that the computer processes. To assign a group policy, it is linked to an Active Directory container (site, domain, or organizational unit). However, you can take steps to control which group policy affects a computer or user.

- Internet Explorer offers a number of features to protect your security and privacy while you browse the web, including phishing filters, Protected Mode, Pop-up Blocker, Add-on Manager, download files or software notification, and the use of digital signatures and 128-bit secure (SSL) connections when using secure websites.

■ Knowledge Assessment

Multiple Choice

Select the correct answer for each of the following questions.

1. Which of the following features can protect your PC against malware? (Choose all that apply)
   a. Windows Defender
   b. SCEP client
   c. File History
   d. SmartScreen

2. When Microsoft releases a new code pack that enables you to view RAW camera files, which of the following update categories does this update fall under?
   a. Recommended updates
   b. Important updates
   c. Optional updates
   d. Suggested updates

3. Which of the following locations is where you can configure how Windows Update functions?
   a. Control Panel > System > Windows Update
   b. Control Panel > System and Security > Windows Update
   c. Control Panel > System > Security > Windows Update
   b. Control Panel > Network and Internet > Windows Update

4. Which of the following statements is true of a replica mode WSUS server? (Choose all that apply)
   a. It mirrors update approvals, settings, computers, and groups from the upstream server.
   b. It mirrors update approvals, settings, computers, and groups from the downstream server.
   c. It can be used to approve updates.
   d. It cannot be used to approve updates.

5. Which of the following statements best describes server-side targeting? (Choose all that apply)
   a. Server-side targeting uses the Update Services console to move computers into computer groups.
   b. Server-side targeting uses Local Group Policy editor to create a group policy designating the computer group to add the computer to.
   c. Server-side targeting uses Group Policy Management console to create a group policy designating the computer group to add the computer to.
   d. Server-side targeting results in computers initially being added to the Unassigned Computers group.

6. Which of the following commands, when run on a Windows 8.1 client, detects available updates from the WSUS server, queues them, and then presents a notification to install the updates.
   a. `wuauclt /detect`
   b. `wuauclt /detectnow`
   c. `wuauclt /force`
   d. `wuauclt /renew`

7. Which of the following scan options are available in Windows Defender? (Choose all that apply)
   a. Quick
   b. Full
   c. Optional
   d. Custom

8. Which of the following tabs is the location of the quarantined items Windows Defender finds?
   a. Home tab
   b. History tab
   c. Update tab
   d. Settings tab

9. Which of the following terms best describes the name of the SCEP client install file?
   a. scepinstall.exe
   b. scep.exe
   c. SCEPclient.exe
   d. clientEP.exe

10. Which of the following features is an early warning system that alerts you before running unrecognized applications or downloading files from the Internet?
    a. Application Reputation
    b. Action Center
    c. SCEP Center
    d. Windows Defender

11. Which of the following are default group policies that are already created in Active Directory? (Choose two answers)
    a. Default Domain Controller Policy
    b. Default Computer profile
    c. Default User Profile
    d. Default Domain Policy

12. GPOs are assigned to users by which of the following actions?
    a. By being linked to a container in Active Directory
    b. By being assigned to a security group
    c. By being assigned to the user
    d. By being assigned to a computer

13. When you assign a GPO at the domain, which of the following actions ensures that it is not overridden by another GPO?
    a. Using a block policy inheritance.
    b. Using the Enforce option.
    c. Using loopback.
    d. Using the No override option.

14. Which of the following is *not* a basic type of add-on?
    a. Toolbar and Extensions
    b. Search Providers
    c. Privacy Plug-in
    d. Accelerators

15. When an ActiveX component needs to be approved, a(n) _____ bar will appear.
    a. orange
    b. red
    c. yellow
    d. blue

16. Which of the following content zones automatically uses your username and password to access websites that are assigned to the zone?
    a. Internet Zones
    b. Local Intranet Zone
    c. Trusted Sites Zone
    d. Restricted Sites Zone

17. Which of the following technologies is used to protect against phishing?
    a. InPrivate Browsing
    b. InPrivate Filtering
    c. SmartScreen
    d. SSL

18. When using SSL, the public key is found in a _____.
    a. digital certificate
    b. cookie
    c. smartfilter
    d. accelerator

19. What happens when you have two GPOs assigned to the same OU?
    a. The GPO that was created first has higher precedence.
    b. The GPO that was created last has higher precedence.
    c. The GPO with the lowest priority number assigned has higher precedence.
    d. The GPO with the highest priority number assigned has higher precedence.

20. Which of the following tools is used to determine which GPO is assigning a particular GPO setting?
    a. Group Policy Results Wizard
    b. Group Policy Modeling Wizard
    c. Gpupdate.exe
    d. Group Policy Editor

21. Which of the following statements is true of using Automatic Update Approval rules? (Choose all that apply)
    a. They streamline only critical updates.
    b. They streamline critical and security updates to as soon as they are released by Microsoft.
    c. They cannot be used in Windows Intune on Windows 7 computers.
    d. They are created in the Administrator workspace in the Windows Intune Admin console.

Best Answer

Choose the letter that corresponds to the best answer. More than one answer choice may achieve the goal. Select the BEST answer.

1. To ensure computers in three branch offices (with no IT support onsite) receive Windows Updates on a regular basis along with those in a main office, which WSUS configuration provides the best solution with the least amount of administrative for the approval and distribution of updates and the least amount of traffic over the WAN link?
    a. Single WSUS server at main office. Branch office PCs configured to use this server.
    b. WSUS server at main office and downstream WSUS servers at each branch office running in autonomous mode. PCs configured to use the local WSUS server.
    c. WSUS server at main office and downstream WSUS servers at each branch office running in replica mode. PCs configured to use the local WSUS server.
    d. WSUS server at main office and downstream WSUS servers at two branch offices running in replica mode and one running in autonomous mode.

2. Which solution is best for protecting 100 PCs in a network against malware and ensuring they run the latest definition files while also monitoring them for compliance?
   a. Configure Automatic Updates.
   b. Install Windows Defender.
   c. Install SCEP client.
   d. Install SCEP client, enable Endpoint protection via SCCM 2012, and create and deploy an antimalware policy.

3. Which of the following should you implement to provide the highest level of protection for your clients and servers?
   a. Windows Firewall
   b. Windows Firewall + Windows Defender
   c. Windows Firewall + Windows Defender + SCEP
   d. Windows Firewall + Windows Defender + SCEP + Antimalware policy

4. Which Windows Update option ensures your system receives and uses the most current updates?
   a. Install updates but let me choose whether to install them.
   b. Download updates but let me choose whether to install them.
   c. Check for updates but let me choose whether to download and install them.
   d. Centrally approve and deploy updates using WSUS.

5. Which MAPS option provides you with the best option for responding to and stopping the spread of new viruses and malware?
   a. Basic membership
   b. Advanced membership
   c. Not joining MAPS
   d. Configuring Advanced Membership on one PC and not joining MAPS on the rest of your computers.

Matching and Identification

1. Match the following terms with the related description or usage.
   _____ a) Application Reputation
   _____ b) Action Center
   _____ c) Autonomous mode
   _____ d) Client-side targeting
   _____ e) Downstream server
   _____ f) MAPS
   _____ g) Replica mode
   _____ h) Server-side targeting
   _____ i) Synchronization
   _____ j) Upstream server
       1. Uses group policies to configure computers to add themselves automatically to computer groups in the Update Services console.
       2. Provides a central location for viewing notifications regarding problems with your hardware and software. It also provides information related to the security and maintenance of your computer.
       3. WSUS servers that obtain their updates from a WSUS server that has been configured to obtain its updates directly from Microsoft.
       4. Involves moving clients to computer groups using the Update Services console.
       5. The process of connecting and downloading updates.

6. This WSUS server mode enables you to configure separate update approval settings while still retrieving updates from the upstream WSUS server.
7. An online community that can help you decide how to respond to certain types of threats.
8. A mode in which the WSUS server mirrors update approvals, settings, computers, and groups from the upstream server.
9. A WSUS server that obtains its updates directly from Microsoft.
10. The early warning system that alerts you before running unrecognized applications or downloading files from the Internet during the time between a release of a virus and definitions to protect against it.

Build a List

1. Specify the correct order of the steps that must be completed to set up a WSUS Server.
   _____ Specify an update source for the WSUS server.
   _____ Synchronize updates to the WSU server.
   _____ Determine a deployment strategy.
   _____ Install the WSUS server role.
   _____ Set up client computers.
   _____ Approve and install updates on client computers.

2. Specify the correct order of the steps that must be completed to create a computer group in WSUS from the Update Services console.
   _____ Expand the **Computers** node, right-click **All Computers**, and choose **Add Computer Group**.
   _____ Confirm the group appears under the *All Computer* node.
   _____ Open the **Update services** console.
   _____ Type a name and then click **Add**.
   _____ Log in with Administrative privileges.

3. Specify the correct order of the steps that must be completed to removing a quarantined item in Windows Defender.
   _____ Click **Quarantined Items**.
   _____ Open **Windows Defender**.
   _____ Select the detected item and read the description.
   _____ Click **View Details**.
   _____ Click the **History** tab.
   _____ Click **Remove**.

4. Specify the order in which group policies are processed.
   _____ Establishes a secure link between the computer and the domain controller.
   _____ Applies user configuration from GPOs.
   _____ Applies computer configuration from GPOs.
   _____ Displays Login dialog box.
   _____ Obtains a list of user-based GPOs from the client computer.
   _____ Obtains a list of computer-based GPOs for the client computer.
   _____ User logs into system.
   _____ Displays User Desktop.

Choose an Option

1. Which tab should you select to view items quarantined by Windows Defender?

Figure 11-28

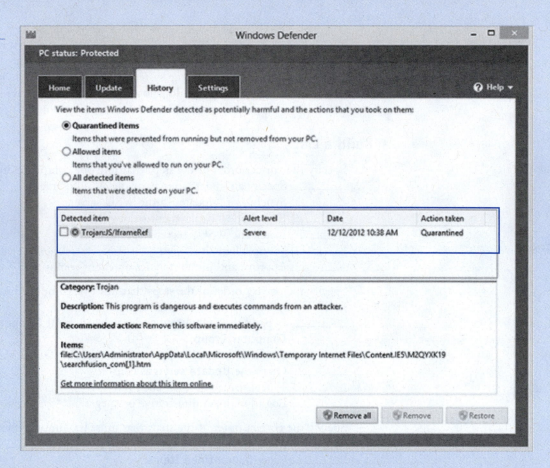

■ Business Case Scenarios

Scenario 11-1: Windows Defender Quarantine

After working on a Windows 8.1 computer running Windows Defender, it maintains quarantined files from the past several months. Is it possible to configure the computer to remove quarantined files on a weekly basis? If so, explain the steps involved.

Scenario 11-2: WSUS

WSUS server is set up at a branch office that gets its updates from a WSUS server at the main office. The option to approve updates is not available on the branch office server, yet it receives updates from the WSUS server at the main office on a regular basis. What is the problem?

Managing Clients by Using Windows Intune

70-688 EXAM OBJECTIVE

Objective 3.4 – Manage Clients by using Windows Intune. This objective may include but is not limited to: Manage user and computer groups; configure monitoring and alerts; manage policies; manage remote computers.

LESSON HEADING	EXAM OBJECTIVE
Introducing Windows Intune	
Exploring Windows Intune Configuration Requirements	
Deploying the Windows Intune Client	
Reviewing Windows Intune Administrator Roles	
Managing User and Computer Groups	Manage user and computer groups
Configuring the Company Portal	
Exploring the Company Portal from the User's Perspective	
Customizing the Company Portal	
Configuring Monitoring and Alerts	Configure monitoring and alerts
Reviewing Standard Reports in Windows Intune	
Configuring Alert Types	
Selecting Recipients	
Managing Remote Computers	Manage remote computers
Reviewing Software Assets	
Reviewing Hardware Assets	
Managing Windows Intune Policies	Manage policies

KEY TERMS

criteria membership

direct membership

recipients

Windows Intune Groups

Windows Intune Company Portal

Windows Intune Cloud + On-Premise Configuration

Windows Intune Stand-Alone Cloud Configuration

Windows Intune + System

Center Configuration Manager

Windows Intune Tenant Administrator

Windows Intune Service Administrator

■ Introducing Windows Intune

THE BOTTOM LINE

Windows Intune is a cloud-based management solution that allows you to manage your computers when they are not inside your corporate network. Windows Intune helps you manage your computers and mobile devices through a web console. It provides the tools, reports, and licenses to ensure your computers are always current and protected. For mobile devices, it also allows you to manage your remote workforce by working through Exchange ActiveSync or directly through Windows Intune.

Windows Intune can be operated in cloud-only mode or in a new unified configuration option that integrates the cloud-based environment with Microsoft System Center 2012 Configuration Manager Service Pack 1.

Windows Intune utilizes a subscription model in which you are charged on a per-user basis.

Here are some of the things you can do with this cloud-based management solution:

- Manage your mobile devices and computers through a web-based console anywhere at any time through Exchange ActiveSync and System Center 2012 Configuration Manager.
- Manage your Windows Intune subscription, add new users and security groups, set up and manage service settings, and access service status via a Windows Intune Account portal.
- Assess the overall health of devices across your organization using the Windows Intune Administration console.
- Organize users and devices into groups (geographically, by department, and by hardware characteristics).
- Manage updates for computers in your organization.
- Enhance security of your managed devices by providing real-time protection, by keeping virus definitions current, and by automatically running scheduled scans.
- Access the overall health of your managed devices through the use of alerts.
- Deploy policies to secure data on mobile devices to determine which mobile devices can connect, enroll, rename, and un-enroll devices.
- Wipe mobile devices in case they are stolen.
- Deploy software and detect and manage software installed on computers.
- Manage licenses purchased through Microsoft volume Licensing agreements.
- Run reports on software, hardware, and software licenses to help confirm current needs and to plan for the future.
- Provide a cloud-based, self-service portal where users can enroll and manage their devices, search for and install software applications, and request help.

■ Exploring Windows Intune Configuration Requirements

THE BOTTOM LINE

Windows Intune deploys a client agent on each device that you want to manage. The Windows Intune agent communicates back to the Windows Intune administration console, allowing you to inventory software and hardware assets in your organization.

Windows Intune can be deployed with the following configurations:

- *Windows Intune Stand-Alone Cloud Configuration:* With this configuration, you have to administer your computers and devices (Windows 8, Windows RT, Windows Phone 8, and Apple iOS) through the Administrator console. Although this configuration allows you to create and manage policies, inventory your devices, and upload and publish software, it does not support the discovery of mobile devices.

- *Windows Intune Cloud + On-Premise Configuration:* This configuration integrates Windows Intune with your existing Active Directory and Exchange environment. With this configuration, you can discover mobile devices using Exchange ActiveSync, synchronize your user accounts with your Active Directory, and manage your mobile devices through Windows Intune.

- *Windows Intune + System Center Configuration Manager:* This configuration allows you to manage your computers and mobile devices from the System Center Configuration Manager 2012 console.

Deploying the Windows Intune Client

You can install the Windows Intune client on computers running Windows XP Professional (SP3), Windows Vista (Enterprise, Ultimate, or Business Edition), Windows 7 (Enterprise, Ultimate, or Professional), and Windows 8 (Professional and Enterprise). You can deploy the Windows Intune client on both physical computers and virtual machines.

Before installing the Windows Intune client, you need to consider how you want to handle malware. If you have existing software that protects against these types of threats, Windows Intune Endpoint Protection detects the software and does not install the Endpoint component.

The following options are available for deploying the client:

- **Administrator Deployment:** Using this option, you basically download the client software and manually install it on the target computers. You can automate the process by using Group Policy if you need to install it on a large number of computers.

- **User-Initiated Enrollment for Computers:** Using this option, users can self-enroll their computers through the Windows Intune company portal.

- **Install the client software as part of an image:** Using this option, you can deploy the Windows Intune client as part of a system image deployment. The computer is automatically enrolled when the image is installed.

 PERFORM AN ADMINISTRATOR DEPLOYMENT OF THE WINDOWS INTUNE CLIENT

GET READY. You need to agree to and set up a Windows Intune account to complete this exercise. To complete an administrative deployment of the Windows Intune client on a Windows 8 computer, perform the following steps.

1. Log in to the Windows 8 computer on which you want to install the Windows Intune Client software.

2. Open Internet Explorer, type **https://admin.manage.microsoft.com** into the address field, and then press **Enter**.

3. If the message *This application requires Microsoft Silverlight* appears, click **Get Microsoft Silverlight**, and then select **Run**.

4. To accept the licensing agreement, click **Install now**.

5. On the *Enable Microsoft Update* page, click **Next**.

6. In the Windows Intune console's *left* pane, click **Administration**.

7. Click **Client Software Download**.

8. On the *Client Software Download* page, click **Download Client Software** (see Figure 12-1).

Figure 12-1

Downloading Windows Intune client software

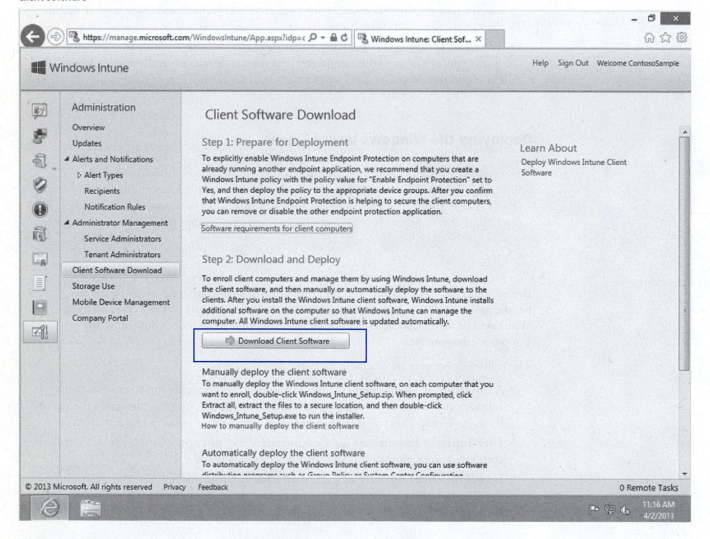

9. From the Windows Internet Explorer box, click **Save as**.

10. In the *Save As* box, click **Desktop** and then click **Save**. This places a file named *Windows_Intune_Setup.zip* on your desktop.

11. Minimize the Windows Intune console, right-click the **Windows_Intune_Setup.zip** file, and then click **Extract All**.

12. In the *Select a Destination and Extract Files box,* click **Extract**. After the extraction has completed, you should see two files: *Windows_Intune_Setup.exe* and *WindowsIntune.accountcert*. These files must be kept together at all times. The WindowsIntune.accountcert is used by the setup program.

13. Double-click **Windows_Intune_Setup.exe**.

14. When the *Windows Intune Setup Wizard* opens, click **Next**.

15. Click **Finish**. Windows Intune continues to update and install software on the computer. You can use the computer while the process continues in the background.

16. Maximize the Windows Intune console and then click in the left pane. When the pane slides out, click **Groups > All Devices**.

When the installation is done, you should see the computer name listed (see Figure 12-2). Leave the Windows Intune Administrator console open to use in the next exercise.

Figure 12-2

Viewing the computer as it appears in the Windows Intune Administration console

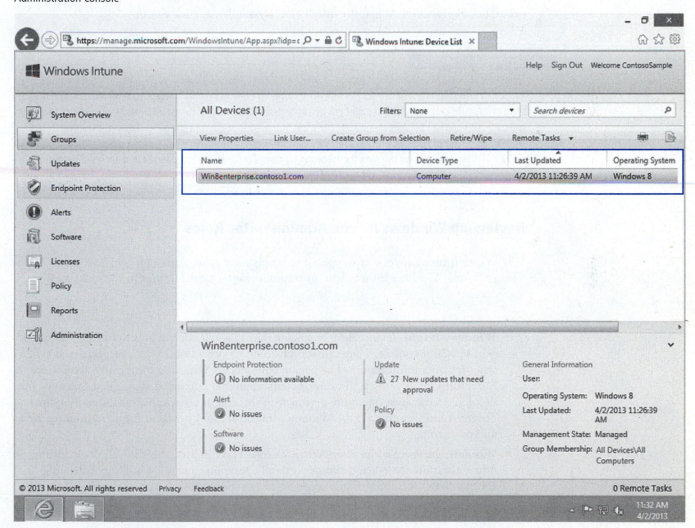

➕ **MORE INFORMATION**

After the installation has completed, the protection and update agents continue to perform additional setup and configuration steps. This includes downloading the required malware definitions and any other agent updates. The computer should appear in the Windows Intune Administration console in a few minutes, but it can take up to 30 minutes to complete the inventory and status updates process.

In the previous exercise, you performed an Administrative deployment, and the Windows 8 computer was enrolled as part of the installation. If you wanted to allow your users to self-enroll their computers, they would need to be an administrator on the local computer, connect to the Windows Intune portal using an Internet Explorer browser, and use a Microsoft Online ID. To learn more about how self-enroll works, visit Microsoft and search *Windows Intune User-Initiated Enrollment for Computers*. When performing this process, following are the general steps:

1. Click *All My Devices*.
2. Click *Enroll your computer*.
3. Click *Download Software*.
4. Click *Run*.
5. Click *Next to*. To start the Windows Intune Setup Wizard, click *Next*.
6. Click *Finish when*. When the installation is completed, click *Finish*.

➕ MORE INFORMATION

To install the Windows Intune Client as part of an image, search Microsoft's website for *Windows Intune Installing the Client Software as Part of an Image.* When working with images, you will most likely deploy them to multiple computers, which might not be connected to the Internet. For an installation of the client to complete, you need an Internet connection; therefore, you need to make sure the computer with the image is not enrolled before it has been fully deployed to the client. To accomplish this, you can perform a delayed installation of the Windows Intune client by using the following command command-line argument to launch the install: `Windows_Intune_Setup.exe /PrepareEnroll`.

Reviewing Windows Intune Administrator Roles

Windows Intune supports two types of Administrator roles. Although both can gain access to the Windows Intune Administration console, they do differ in the tasks they can execute:

- *Windows Intune Tenant Administrator* role: Has full control and rights regarding the Administrator console. They can add or delete service administrator accounts and assign other tenant administrators. The person who sets up Windows Intune and accepts the Microsoft Online Subscription Agreement when it is purchased is assigned this role. You should create at least one more person with this role as a backup. You assign Window Tenant Administrators via the Windows Intune account portal at https://admin.manage.microsoft.com.

- *Windows Intune Service Administrator* role: Has full access to the Windows Intune Administration console and can perform all operations including adding or deleting another Services Administrator account. They cannot modify data in the console but instead can only view the data it contains and run reports. Windows Intune Service Administrators are assigned via the Windows Intune Administrator console at https://admin.manage.microsoft.com.

Managing User and Computer Groups

THE BOTTOM LINE

To make the process of deploying Windows Intune policies, software packages, and software updates more efficient, consider using Windows Intune Groups. ***Windows Intune Groups***, which are used to quickly organize and manage your computers and users, are created and managed in the Groups workspace. These groups apply only to Windows Intune and are completely separate from Active Directory groups, although you can use AD security groups as part of a query to select members when creating a group. After your groups are set up, you can deploy Windows Intune policies, software packages, and software updates to them.

CERTIFICATION READY
Manage user and computer groups
Objective 4.4

You can create groups that include users and you can create groups that include devices. What you cannot do is include users and devices in the same group. Most administrators create groups that are organized in one or more of the following ways:

- Geographical organization: Portland, Seattle, Los Angeles
- Departmental organization: Executives, Human Resources, Marketing
- Physical organization: Desktops, Laptops

In the Groups workspace you see the default groups created for devices and for users when Windows Intune is initially setup. For example, you will find the Windows 8 computer you installed the Windows Intune Client software on earlier, under the *All Computers* group.

After a closer look, you should see there is a hierarchy for the groups. For example, the All Direct Managed Devices and the All Exchange ActiveSync Managed Devices are child groups under the parent All Mobile Devices. You can deploy software updates, policies, and software applications to multiple groups or to a parent group while excluding one or more child groups. You can also add and exclude specific group members.

+ MORE INFORMATION

To protect your production environment, consider creating a test computer group that can be used to roll out and trial new updates. Once in place, you can select the members from within the Windows Intune console. This should be reflective of the different operating systems you want to test on. Even though computers are added to the new group, they still retain their membership in any other groups. This allows you to still assign updates to them without impacting other computers in those groups.

When setting up a group in Windows Intune, you have the option to manually or dynamically add users or devices to a group. You can also take a mixed approach and use both methods when creating a group.

- ***Direct membership:*** The process of manually adding users or devices from within the Windows Intune console. You manually include and exclude specific members from the group.
- ***Criteria membership:*** This involves defining certain types of criteria that Windows Intune runs a query against to find users or devices. When it finds users or computers that match the criteria, it dynamically adds them as members to the group. The group automatically updates with members as changes occur.
- ***Mixed:*** A group that consists of members added manually and dynamically.

When adding devices to a group using membership criteria, you have the following options to include or exclude members from the parent group (see Figure 12-3):

- Computers from organizational units you specify
- Computers from domains you specify

Figure 12-3

Defining membership criteria

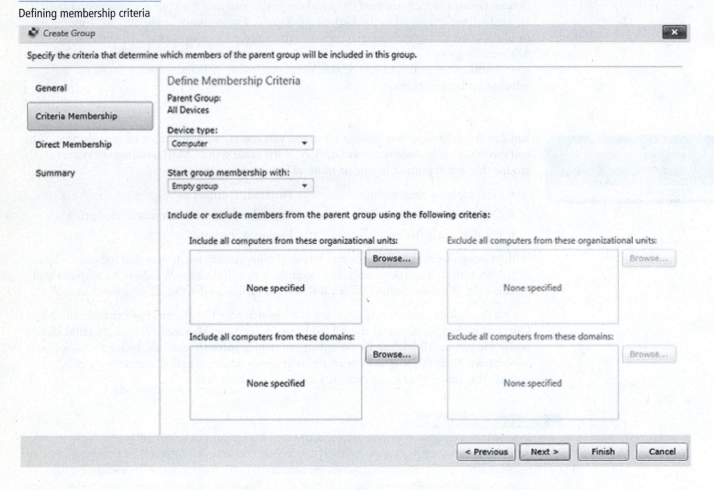

When defining direct membership, you have the option to include or exclude specific members form groups you specify.

Group membership is recursive. This means that if you use a dynamic membership query and set the criteria that a user is a member of an AD DS security group named marketing to be included in the group, you can pick up additional indirect users in the query. For example, if Mary is a member of the Marketing Interns security group and the Marketing Interns security group is a member of the Marketing security group, then she is included in your query and added to the Marketing group.

CREATE A DEVICE GROUP USING DIRECT MEMBERSHIP

GET READY. To create a device group using Direct-based membership, from the Windows Intune Administrator console, perform the following steps:

1. Log in to the **Windows Intune Administrator** console at https://admin.manage. microsoft.com.
2. In the *left* pane, select the **Groups**.

3. Under the *Tasks* menu, click the **Create Group**.

4. In the *Group name* field, type **My Test Group**.

5. In the *Description* field, type **Computers used to test deployments of new updates**.

6. Under *Select a parent group,* click **All Devices**.

7. Click **Next**.

8. On the *Define Membership Criteria* page, click **Next**.

9. On the *Define Direct Membership* screen, click **Browse**. Be careful to select the *Browse* button that is just to the right of the *Include specific members* field. If you select the one on the far right, you will exclude specific members.

10. Choose the Windows 8 computer you installed the Windows Intune client software on in the earlier exercise, and then click **Add**. Your Windows 8 computer should appear in the *Include specific members* column. Click **OK** to continue.

11. On the *Define Direct Membership* page, click **Next**.

12. Review the *General Criteria Membership and Direct Membership summary* page, and then click **Finish**.

13. Under *Groups*, click **My Test Group**, and then click **Devices**. The computer should appear as a member of the group.

■ Configuring the Company Portal

THE BOTTOM LINE

The *Windows Intune Company Portal* provides self-service connection point for users to request help and select apps to install. It gives users access to perform self-service tasks, such as adding or removing their computers from Windows Intune, selecting applications to install (made available to them by the Administrator), and contacting the technical support administrator.

Exploring the Company Portal from the User's Perspective

When a user connects to the company portal, he has the option to install a Company Portal app on his computer from the Windows Store. This will create a tile on the user's Start menu (see Figure 12-4).

Figure 12-4

Viewing a company portal tile

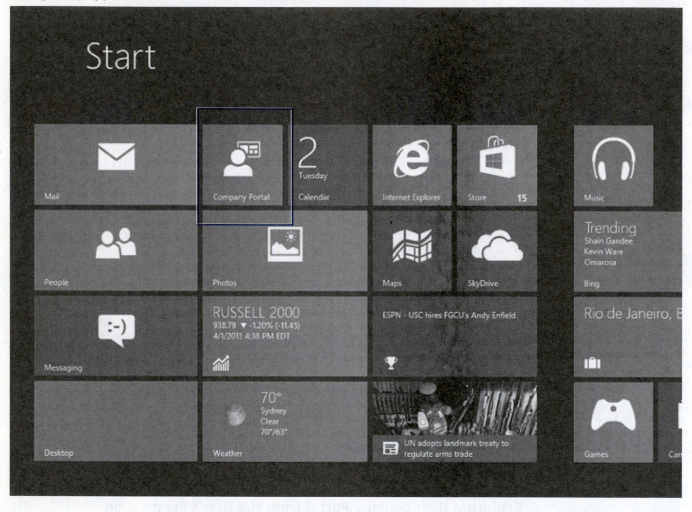

When the user clicks on the tile, he needs to log in using his assigned Windows Intune user name and password. After he is authenticated, the company portal page appears (see Figure 12-5).

Figure 12-5

Viewing a sample company
portal from the user's
perspective

Contoso

company apps

New Apps
The most recent apps to be published

All Apps

All
Categories

devices

Win8enterprise....

If the user clicks the Apps tile, he is prompted to visit the Windows Store to install the
Company Portal app. After completing the installation, a new Company Portal tile is
placed on the Windows 8 Start menu. The user can then access the portal through
this app.

Clicking on the *New Apps* icon enables users to view the most recently published apps made
available to them via Windows Intune. Selecting an app presents the user with a prompt
(see Figure 12-6) to confirm the computer and device they want to install the app on and
then perform the installation process.

Figure 12-6

Installing App Prompt

After it is installed, the app appears as a tile on the company portal page.

+ MORE INFORMATION

Applications can be installed on a remote as well as a local computer. To monitor progress, you can see the application install status on the Apps page of your company portal.

Customizing the Company Portal

You can modify the look and feel of the company portal (see Figure 12-7) through the Windows Intune Administrator console.

Figure 12-7

Configuring the company portal

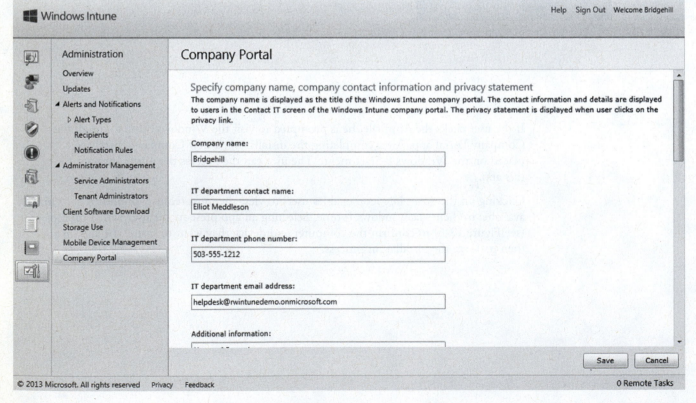

When customizing the portal, information that can be customized includes:

- **Company name:** Appears as the title of your company portal.
- **IT Department contact name:** Appears on the Contact IT tile.
- **IT department phone number:** Appears on the Contact IT tile.
- **IT department email address:** Appears on the Contact IT tile.
- **Additional Information** (such as hours of operation): Appears on the Contact IT tile.
- **Support website URL:** Specifies the website and website name that users can contact for support (name and URL). This can include your IT department phone number, email address, and any additional information you want to provide. Only the name, not the URL, is displayed on the Contact ID page
- **Theme color:** Customize the theme color and choose a background for the Company Portal app.

Configuring Monitoring and Alerts

THE BOTTOM LINE

Computers configured with the Windows Intune agent can be tracked both on and off the corporate network. As computers are configured with the Windows Intune agent, they start to report back to Windows Intune. Because Windows Intune is cloud-based, users do not have to be attached to your corporate network to receive updates, patches, or help removing malware.

CERTIFICATION READY
Configure monitoring
and alerts
Objective 4.4

Using Windows Intune, you can monitor your on-network and off-network machines through standard reports and you do so in real-time.

Reviewing Standard Reports in Windows Intune

Windows Intune offers several types of reports. Although Windows Intune provides a snapshot of your machines through its reporting feature (see Figure 12-8), you should also monitor them in real time.

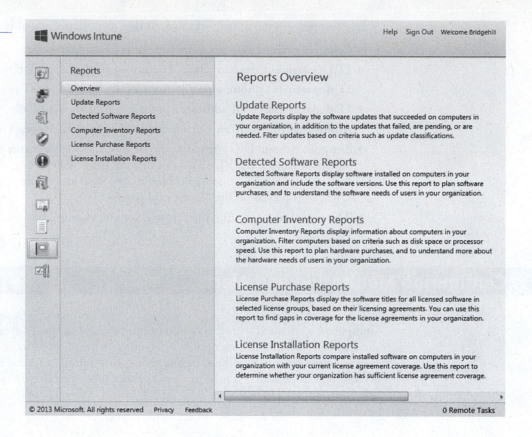

Following are the Windows Intune report types:

- **Update Reports:** Provide information about software updates that succeeded, failed, and are currently pending or those that are needed on computers in your organization.
- **Detected Software Reports:** Provide information about software installed on computers in your organization.
- **Computer Inventory Reports:** Provide information about hardware used in your organization.
- **License Purchase Reports:** Display licensed software titles across your organization.
- **License Installation Reports:** Compare installed software with your current licensing agreement.

You use Windows Intune Alerts and reports to:

- Identify computers that are not running Endpoint Protection Software.
- Identify computers running another malware protection product.
- Investigate and troubleshoot malware activity.
- Identify computers that need updates or computers where updates have failed to install

The Alerts workspace is designed to help you quickly assess the overall health of the computers in your organization The Alerts workspace enables you to perform the following functions:

- Configure alert types.
- Select recipients for email notifications.
- Associate recipients with notification rules.

Configuring Alert Types

> The Windows Intune Alerts workspace can be used to monitor and manage the overall health of your computers. By using the alerts, you can gain a better understanding of how your computers run and take the necessary steps quickly before a problem impacts your end user's productivity.

There are over 180 alert types available in Windows Intune. Based on your organization's needs, you can enable the alert types you think are important and disable those that are not appropriate for your network environment. You can also configure alert thresholds that are used to determine how often an alert is triggered before it is displayed.

Selecting an alert (see Figure 12-9) provides you with additional information in the bottom pane.

Figure 12-9

Viewing alert types

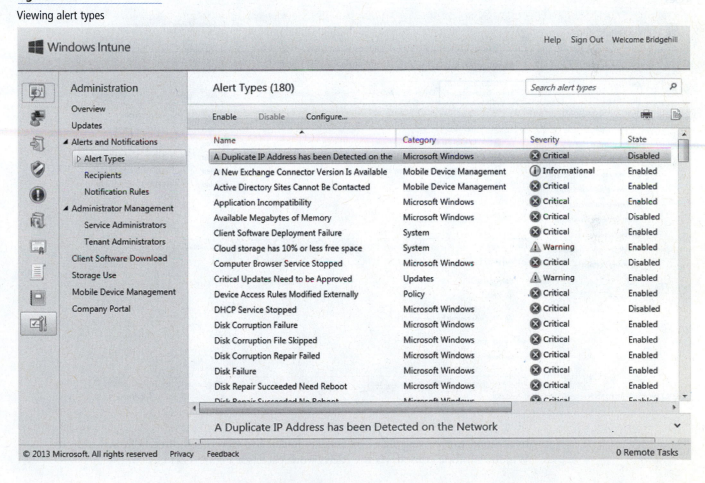

Selecting Recipients

> *Recipients* are individuals who you assign to receive email notifications when alerts occur. Recipients are assigned in the *Administration > Alerts and Notifications > Recipients* location of the Windows Intune Administrator console. To add a new recipient, just select *Add* and type the recipient's email address and specify the language to use for email notification. After you have a list of recipients in place, you need to select Notifications Rules.

Windows Intune has five notification rules that you can target to a recipient. They include:

- All Alerts
- Critical Alerts
- Informational Alerts
- Remote Assistance Requests
- Warning Alerts

To add a recipient to one of these alert types, from the menu, choose *Administration > Alerts and Notifications > Notifications Rules. Under Notification Rules,* click the alert type, and then click *Select Recipients* (see Figure 12-10). Select the box next to each recipient that you want to receive email notifications specified by the rule and click *OK*.

Figure 12-10

Selecting recipients for alert types

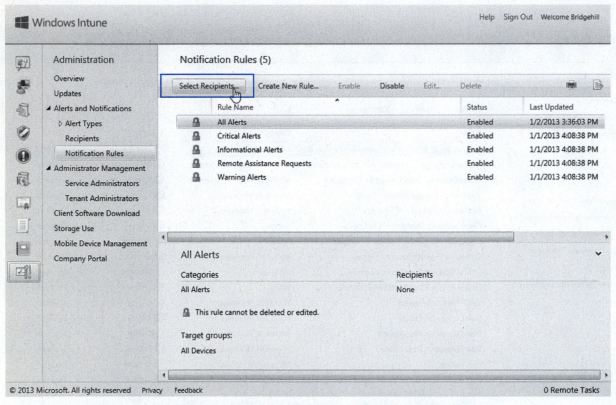

In addition to receiving alerts via email, you can also view alerts directly from within the Windows Intune console via the Alerts workspace (see Figure 12-11).

Figure 12-11

Monitoring alerts

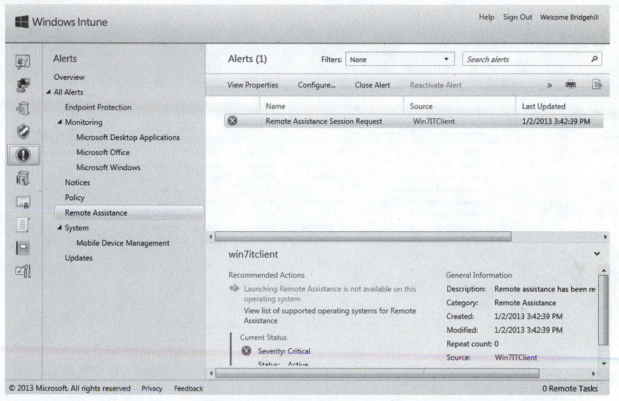

Managing Remote Computers

THE BOTTOM LINE

Understanding software and hardware assets can aid in the planning and deployment process of new software and hardware across your organization. Managing your assets means knowing what software and hardware your organization has.

CERTIFICATION READY
Manage remote computers
Objective 4.4

You can use software inventory to effectively manage the software and licenses used in your organization. This provides information such as the:

- Types of software installed on computers
- Number of copies installed
- Version of software installed
- Publisher
- Category of Software

Reviewing Software Assets

Figure 12-12 shows an example of software information collected from a single Windows 8 virtual machine that runs the Windows Intune agent. This was accessed in the Groups workspace for a Windows 8 computer. From here, you can view the information, print it out, or export it to a CSV or HTML file for further analysis.

Figure 12-12

Collecting software with the
Windows Intune agent

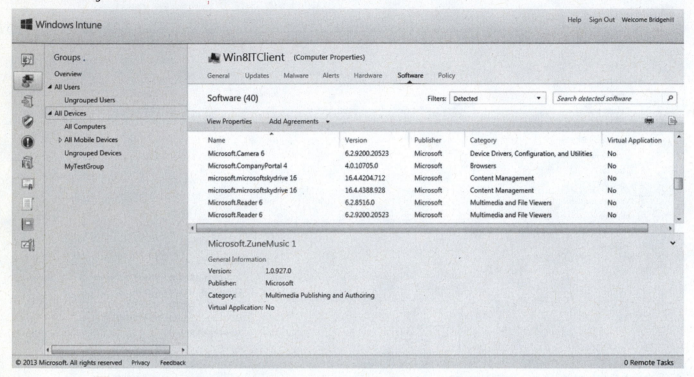

You can also run a Detected Software Report from the Reports workspace to view software
installed on computers across your organization. To further refine the report, you can select
only software that meets selected criteria (device group, publisher, and/or category). Categories
can include browsers, multimedia and file viewers, and operating system and components.

 CREATE A DETECTED SOFTWARE REPORT

GET READY. To create a detected software report, perform the following steps:

1. Log in to the **Windows Intune Administrator** console.
2. In the left pane, click **Reports > Detected Software Reports**.
3. Under *Select publishers*, click **Edit**.
4. Select **Include only the following**, choose **Microsoft**, and then click **OK**.
5. Under *Select categories*, click **Edit**.
6. Select **Include only the following**, choose **Browser** and **Operating System and Components**, and then click **OK**.
7. Click **View Report**.
8. Move your mouse over the icon in the upper right hand corner and click **Export**.
9. On the *Select the export format for your data* page, click the **down arrow** and choose **.html**. Click **Export**.
10. Choose Desktop as the location to save your file to, and then type **MyWin8Report**.
11. Click **Close**.
12. Open the file and view the report you created. Close it when you are done.

Reviewing Hardware Assets

In addition to tracking the software used on managed computers, Windows Intune also collects hardware information from the agent. This happens automatically or on a customizable schedule, and the process is entirely invisible to the end user.

There are several benefits to collecting an asset inventory in your organization. They include the ability to:

- Assess whether or not you are maintaining corporate hardware standards (such as processor and memory).
- Track asset depreciation.
- Locate and troubleshoot computers in large organizations.
- Provide information about what computers need an operating system upgrade.
- Provide information about which computers can support a software package.
- Identify computers with common hardware characteristics to aid in deployment of software.

The following information can be collected and reported on both mobile devices and managed computers:

- Operating systems
- Manufacturers
- Models
- Chassis types
- Available disk space
- Physical memory
- CPU speed

+ MORE INFORMATION

You can run a Computer Inventory Report from the Reports workspace to view hardware installed on computers across your organization. To further refine the report, you can select only computers and devices that meet selected criteria (operating system, model, chassis type, CPU speed, and so on).

In Figure 12-13, you can see an example of hardware information collected from a single Windows 8 virtual machine running the Windows Intune agent. This was accessed via Groups > All Devices > Hardware for a Windows 8 computer.

From here, you can view the information, print it, or export it to a CSV or HTML file for further analysis.

Figure 12-13

Collecting computer hardware
information

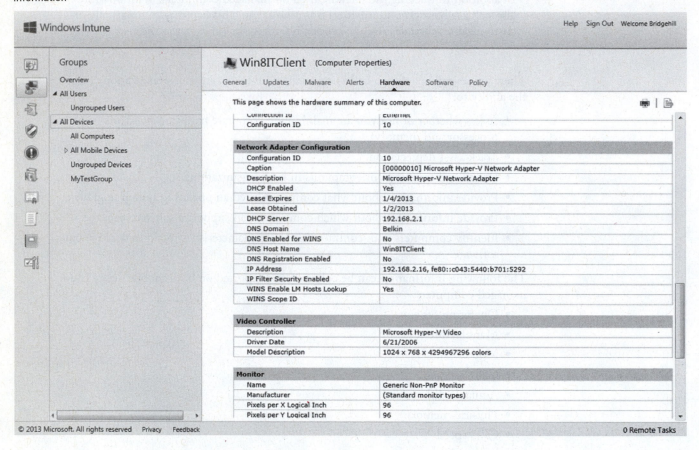

The information provided is broken into the following sections in the report:

- **System:** Name, Manufacturer, Model, Physical memory, Last User to log on
- **System Enclosure:** Chassis type, Serial Number SMBIOS Asset Tag
- **BIOS:** Name, Version, Manufacturer, Release Date
- **Processor:** Name, Architecture, Clock Speed
- **Physical Disk:** Name, Manufacturer Model, Caption, Partitions, Size, interface type
- **Logical Disks:** Name, Drive Type
- **Network Adapter:** Name, Manufacturer, Product Name, MAC Address, Speed, Connection Status
- **Network Adapter Configuration:** DHCP enabled, DHCP Server address, IP address, leaser information, IP address information, IPsec status
- **Video Controller:** Description, Drive Date, model
- **Monitor:** Name, Manufacturer, Pixels per inch, screen height/width
- **Printers:** Name, Share status, local/network, driver name
- **Physical Memory:** Capacity

CREATE A COMPUTER INVENTORY REPORT

GET READY. To create a computer inventory report, perform the following steps:

1. Log in to the **Windows Intune Administrator** console.
2. In the *left* pane, click **Reports** > **Computer Inventory Reports**.
3. Under *Select operating systems,* click **Edit.**
4. Select **Include only the following**, choose **Windows 8**, and then click **OK.**
5. Click **View Report.**
6. Move your mouse over the icon in the upper right hand corner, and then click **Export.**
7. On the *Select the export format for your data* page, click the **down arrow** and choose **.html.** Click **Export.**
8. Choose **Desktop** as the location to save your file to, and then type **MyWin8InvRpt.**
9. Click **Close.**
10. Open the file and view the report you created. Close it when you are done.

Managing Windows Intune Policies

 THE BOTTOM LINE
To help control the security settings on mobile devices, computer updates, Endpoint Protection, firewall settings, and the end-user experience, Windows Intune has policies. These policies apply to domain-joined computers in any domain and to non-domain joined computers.

CERTIFICATION READY
Manage policies
Objective 4.4

Since Group Policy can be used to set many of the same settings, when you deploy Windows Intune client software and establish Windows Intune policies, you need to ensure that the clients do not receive GPOs with similar and/or conflicting settings.

 SET THE DEFAULT WINDOWS INTUNE POLICIES

GET READY. To set up the default Windows Intune Policies, perform the following steps:

1. Open the **Windows Intune Administration** console.
2. In the workspace shortcuts pane, click the **Policy** icon.
3. Under Tasks, click **Add Policy.**
4. In the Create a New Policy dialog box (as shown in Figure 12-14), the following policy templates are displayed in the list of templates in the left pane:
   - Mobile Device Security Policy
   - Windows Firewall Settings
   - Windows Intune Agent Settings
   - Windows Intune Center Settings

Figure 12-14

Adding a Windows Intune policy

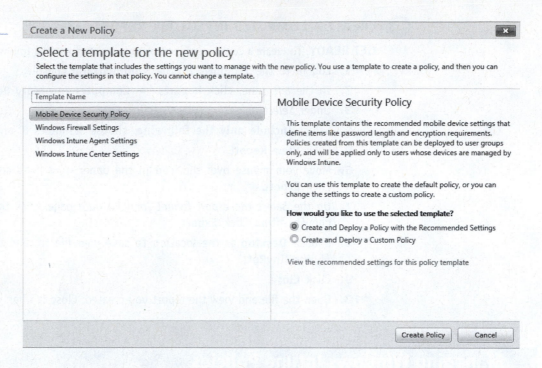

5. Select the policy template you wish to set up and click **Create and Deploy a Policy with the Recommended Settings**. To view the settings before you create the policy, click **View the recommended settings for this policy template** that will be used as the default for this policy.

6. After you configure the settings that you want to apply in your default policy, type a name and an optional description for the policy, and then click **Save Policy**.

7. When prompted to specify whether you want to deploy the policy now, click **Yes**.

8. In the Select the groups to which you want to deploy this policy dialog box, select the **All Devices** group or **All Users** group (depending on the policy you have selected) and click **OK**.

9. Repeat these steps as needed for your other default policy settings.

SKILL SUMMARY

IN THIS LESSON YOU LEARNED:

- Windows Intune is a cloud-based management solution that helps you manage your computers and mobile devices through a web console.

- Windows Intune can be deployed in a Windows Intune standalone configuration, a cloud+ on premises configuration, and integrated with System Center Configuration Manager.

- You can deploy the Windows Intune agent to both physical and virtual PCs.

- Windows Intune Tenant Administrator and the Windows Intune Service Administrator are the key administrative accounts in Windows Intune.

- Direct-based membership involves manually entering members of groups, whereas Criteria (dynamic query) members are automatically managed via membership in security groups you specify during setup of the group.

- Windows Intune is based on the concept of workspaces. The Update workspace is used to view, approve, decline, and configure automatic approval rules.

- Windows Intune provides a portal to allow users to perform self-service tasks, such as adding and removing computers Windows Intune manages, selecting applications to install, and requesting technical support.

- Windows Intune provides real-time information on hardware and software used across the organization and standard reports to help you forecast needs.

- To help control the security settings on mobile devices, computer updates, Endpoint Protection, firewall settings, and the end-user experience, Windows Intune has policies. These policies apply to domain-joined computers in any domain and to non-domain joined computers.

■ Knowledge Assessment

Multiple Choice

Select the correct answer for each of the following questions.

1. On which operating system can you install the Windows Intune? (Choose all that apply)
   a. Windows XP Professional (SP3)
   b. Windows Vista Business Edition
   c. Windows 8 Professional (physical computer)
   d. Windows 8 Consumer (virtual client)

2. Which command is used to perform a delayed installation of the Windows Intune client when working with images?
   a. `Windows_Intune_Setup.exe / DelayEnroll`
   b. `Windows_Intune_Setup.exe / DelayedEnroll`
   c. `Windows_Intune_Setup.exe / PrepareEnroll`
   d. `Windows_Intune_Setup.exe / PreparedEnroll`

3. Which administrator role in Windows Intune can create and delete *all* other types of accounts?
   a. Windows Intune Service administrator role
   b. Windows Intune User Management Administrator role
   c. Windows Intune Tenant Administrator
   d. Windows Intune SuperAdmin Role

4. Which of the following are true about Update groups? (Chose all that apply)
   a. They can be organized geographically.
   b. They are managed via the Updates workspace.
   c. They can mix both users and devices in the same group.
   d. They are managed as part of a group hierarchy structure.

5. Which type of group is created manually in the Windows Intune Administration console?
   a. dynamic query-based group
   b. direct-based group
   c. security group
   d. dynamic group

6. Which task cannot be performed when using the Windows Intune Company Portal?
   a. Adding a computer to Windows Intune
   b. Removing a computer from Windows Intune
   c. Contacting Technical Support
   d. Installing Windows applications made available to other users by the Windows Intune Administrator

7. Which Windows Intune report provides information about software updates that have failed?
   a. License Purchase Reports.
   b. Update Reports.
   c. Detected Software Reports.
   d. Software Update Reports.

8. How many alert types are available in Windows Intune?
   a. 20
   b. 60
   c. 100
   d. Over 180

9. Which of the following are Policies available in Windows Intune? (Choose all that apply)
   a. Mobile User Security Policy
   b. Mobile Device Security Policy
   c. Windows Intune Agent Settings
   d. Windows Firewall Settings

10. When establishing Policies in Windows Intune, what precaution should you take?
    a. Ensure that you do not use the similar or conflicting settings with a GPO.
    b. You should only need one master policy.
    c. If you have domain and non-domain devices, it is best to create domain and local policies instead of using Windows Intune policies.
    d. Before apply settings, run the Policy Simulator.

Best Answer

Choose the letter that corresponds to the best answer. More than one answer choice may achieve the goal. Select the BEST answer.

1. Which method is best for sharing hardware information with an employer who provides information on 20 computers and who wants to see which operating systems are currently installed and which require additional memory upgrades?
   a. Take a screen shot of each computer's hardware settings via the Groups workspace.
   b. Visit each computer and record the information manually.
   c. Export hardware information obtained on each computer from the Groups workspace to a CSV file and send it via email.
   d. Create a Computer Inventory report and set the criteria to only show computers running those operating systems with a selected amount of memory.

2. A Windows Server 2012 Active Directory-based network of 10 technically adept users uses which method to roll out the Windows Intune client that best fits its deployment needs?
   a. User-Initiated Enrollment of computers.
   b. Install the client as part of an image.
   c. Download and install the client on each user's computer.
   d. Download and install the client on each user's computer via Group Policy.

3. Users and devices are distributed across two states. They use both laptops and desktops. Which is the best approach to organize them using the Windows Intune group structure?
   a. Set up one group for Laptops and another for Desktops.
   b. Set up State 1 and State 2 groups, and then set up Laptops and Desktop groups as child groups under each.
   c. Set up State 1 and State 2 groups.
   d. Use the default settings for groups configured by Windows Intune when it is first installed.

4. Which Windows Intune report provides the most applicable information regarding the software installed on your users' devices of your company's license agreement?
   a. Update Reports
   b. Detected Software Reports
   c. License Purchase Reports
   d. License Installation Reports

Matching and Identification

1. In order of first to last, identify the ten steps to create a Computer Inventory report that includes the Windows 8 operating system as the criteria, and save it as an html file to your desktop.

   _____ Log in to the Windows Administrator console.
   _____ Select View Report.
   _____ Select the Reports icon.
   _____ Select Export by moving your mouse over the icon in the upper right hand corner.
   _____ In the Navigation pane, click Computer Inventory Reports.
   _____ Select .html as the export format and click Export.
   _____ Under Select Operating systems, select Edit.
   _____ Type a name for the report and save it to your desktop.
   _____ Select Include only the following and select the Windows 8 check box. Click OK.
   _____ Click Close.

2. In order of first to last, identify the ten basic steps to create an Automatic Update Approval rule for a specific user group named MyTestGroup.

   _____ Log in to the Windows Intune Administrator console
   _____ In the left pain, select Administration.
   _____ Select Updates.
   _____ Select All Categories, and then click Next. -
   _____ Select MyTestGroup, and then click Add. Click Next. -
   _____ Select Critical Updates and Security Updates, and then click Next.
   _____ Click New to create the rule.
   _____ Type a name and description for the rule.
   _____ Click Finish.
   _____ Confirm your new rule appears under the Automatic Approval rules section.

Choose an Option

1. Which icon do you select to access the Updates workspace to view a pending installation of a service pack?

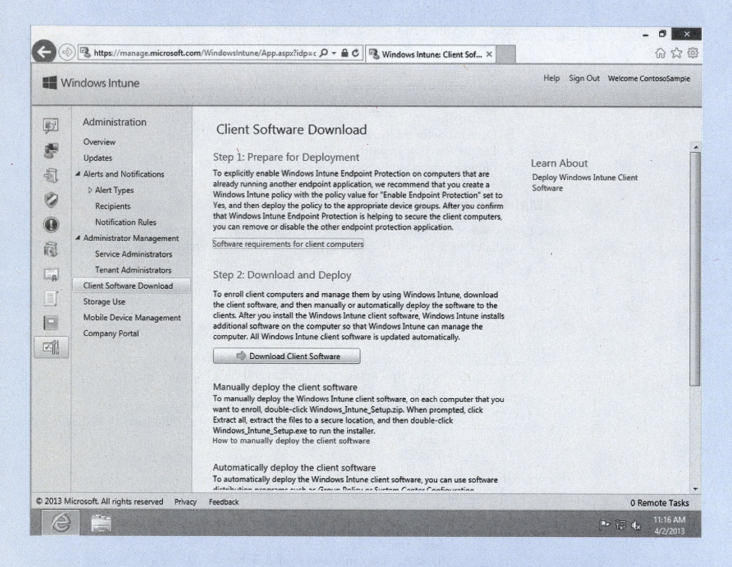

■ Business Case Scenarios

Scenario 12-1: Windows Intune Administration

If you cannot modify data after logging into the Windows Intune Administration Console, but you can view the data and run reports, what is the problem?

Appendix A
Exam 70-688 Supporting Windows 8.1

Exam Objective	Objective Number	Lesson Number
Support Operating System and Application Installation		
Support operating system installation	1.1	1
Support desktop apps	1.2	2
Support Windows Store and cloud apps	1.3	3
Support Resource Access		
Support network connectivity	2.1	4
Support remote access	2.2	5
Support authentication and authorization	2.3	6
Support data storage	2.4	7
Support data security	2.5	8
Support Windows Clients and Devices		
Support operating system and hardware	3.1	9
Support mobile devices	3.2	10
Support client compliance	3.3	11
Manage clients by using Windows Intune	3.4	12

Index

Note: Page numbers followed by 'f' and 't' indicates figure and table respectively.